Balzac

'Graham Robb, as chatty and urbane as his subject, confidently
negotiates the vast expanses of Balzac's life in an unusually witty
biography that reads somewhat like a detective story as Mr Robb
tracks down the connections between the life and work of the
great novelist of the nineteenth century.'
New York Times Books of the Year

'Robb's own energy and apparent exuberance enable him to capture
the essence of the novelist who was to be not only the founder of the
modern novel, but an inspiration to Dostoevsky, Flaubert, Henry
James, and such great names as these.'
Evening Standard

'Graham Robb has written a splendid biography. It honours its
subject by imitating some of the marvellous alloy of his example.
For instance, it is well researched and at pains to follow Balzac from
place to place and adventure to adventure. But there is a touch of
slang and dash about it too, a journalistic ruffle to the prose which
reads easily and sits well.'
Irish Times

'This well-written and entertaining account is alive with sharp
parallels and paradoxes alerting us to the immediacy and
contradictions of the subject.'
European

'Robb's biography is admirably precise, investigative, and sharply
detailed . . . The definitive character of the book encourages him
to probe several areas glossed over by earlier Balzacians.'
Spectator

'Graham Robb does a masterly job of synthesizing the most recent
scholarly research, providing an engaging, highly readable version of a

GRAHAM ROBB was born in Manchester in 1958. He was educated at Oxford and Vanderbilt University in the United States. He was awarded a British Academy Postdoctoral Fellowship and was a fellow of Exeter College, Oxford, from 1987 to 1990. He has published widely in nineteenth-century French literature and his highly acclaimed adaptation of Claude Pichois and Jean Ziegler's biography of Baudelaire appeared in 1989. His latest book is *La poésie de Baudelaire et la poésie française, 1838–1852.*

Balzac

A BIOGRAPHY

BY

GRAHAM ROBB

PAPERMAC

First published 1994 by Picador

This edition published 1995 by Papermac
an imprint of Macmillan General Books
25 Eccleston Place, London SW1W 9NF
and Basingstoke

Associated companies throughout the world

ISBN 0 333 63950 2

135798642

A CIP catalogue record for this book is available from
the British Library

Typeset by CentraCet Limited, Cambridge
Printed and bound in Great Britain by
Mackays of Chatham plc, Chatham, Kent

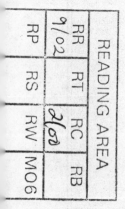

CONTENTS

[vii]

CONTENTS

[viii]

CONTENTS

LIST OF ILLUSTRATIONS

INTRODUCTION

WHATEVER Balzac's claims on our interest as one of the great European writers – the founder of the modern novel – he was also a lover, businessman, political campaigner, tourist, treasure-hunter, inventor, con-man and interior decorator who participated in the age he described with a fullness and energy that make him an excellent subject for biography. Beyond his study walls he was not, like most of us, a straw careering down life's stream; Balzac was a mechanical dredger that carved out its own river-bed as it went along, and the events of his life are, to an unusual degree, expressions of a personality.

Balzac is both the embodiment of his age and its most revealing exception. He arrived in Paris from the provinces at a time when class distinctions were beginning to dissolve, and completed his father's rise from peasant origins to become the friend of bankers, diplomats and politicians, the accomplice or enemy of almost every writer worth knowing, the lover of two duchesses and, eventually, the husband of a Polish countess whom he courted for sixteen years by correspondence. From the moment he decided, as it were, to become a genius, Balzac's life resembled an encyclopedia with a plot: his legal studies, his self-imposed seclusion in a garret from which he hoped to emerge a great philosopher and poet, his fascination with the secret, sordid life of the city, his first, pseudonymous novels – gory, sentimental and memorably bad – his disastrous business ventures that showed him every aspect of the book-trade he later depicted in *Illusions Perdues*. By the time Balzac achieved fame with *La Peau de Chagrin* in 1831 as a rosy-cheeked, chubby Romantic, his incongruities were already well established: a rationalist who tried to harness supernatural powers; a social observer who turned characters into real people and the real people he loved, seduced or exploited into characters; a brilliant businessman who was always on the edge of bankruptcy; an expert fantasizer who believed that the vital fluid known as will-power diminishes with every desire; a defender of the Family with at least one illegitimate child and a wide repertoire of sexual appetites; a man with a phenomenal capacity for self-deception who can be treated (according to Henry James) as 'a final authority on human nature'.[1] With time, Balzac's ironies have, if anything, increased: the realist who was really a visionary; the political thinker who stood for parliament and denounced the evils of democracy; the monarchist hailed by Marxists as a revolutionary and whose works, for that reason, have always filled out the shelves of bookshops in Communist countries; the last traditional story-teller and father of the modern novel whose tales have confused or inspired most modern schools of criticism.

All creators disappear in their creations; but there, too, they provide the keys to mysteries they may not have solved or even formulated themselves. Balzac's principal creation was *La Comédie Humaine*, comprising over a hundred novels, short stories, studies and several unfinished works. Intellectually as well as politically, the period covered by *La Comédie Humaine* is the great turning point of European history, an age of revolutions during which an industrial economy was imposed on what was still a feudal society. Balzac's epic of modern life is the last attempt by any writer to comprehend and educate a whole world in all its diversity, to offer a complete, unified, scientific picture of society and human experience, from the evocative trivia of day-to-day existence to the complex, organic machinery of power and bureaucracy. With Shakespeare and Dickens, Balzac is the most prolific creator of memorable characters in Western literature: there are over 2000 of them in *La Comédie Humaine* alone, joined to each other by an endless umbilical cord of family relations and coincidences (the genealogical table of Balzac's characters covers three walls of his house in Paris); although if one includes characters who were removed from later editions, those who are not named or whose existence is only implied, and a few animals with recognizable personalities, the total rises to well over 3500.

La Comédie Humaine is just the largest continent on the Balzacian planet. His other works consist of his early 'commercial' novels which he disowned and later republished under different titles; some even earlier attempts to find his feet in almost every imaginable genre; over thirty erotic tales in a form of medieval French devised by Balzac for his own use; a repertoire of comedies and dramas; two decades of literary and political journalism, including what amounts to an eye-witness account of France under Louis-Philippe; five volumes of omnivorous correspondence, bulging with another hundred tales of financial and emotional catastrophe and triumph, and which continue to expand as new letters come to light. Balzac's letters to his future wife, published separately, form an unusually detailed diary of a writer's life – or, more accurately, a gigantic novel with real protagonists which is approximately one-quarter the size of *La Comédie Humaine*. There are also notes, sketches, fragments, books signed by other people, self-advertisements, prefaces, manifestos, pamphlets, plans for legislation, anecdotes, aphorisms, and some of the most adventurous travel writing in the nineteenth century.

Balzac's enormous *œuvre* has provided the basic fuel for this biography. Everything has been read, in most cases at least twice. While this may conceivably have the disadvantage of imbuing the biographer with an incurably Balzacian view of reality and thus invalidate any claim he may have had to objectivity, Balzac can hardly be grasped if he and the world he created and inhabited have not been circumnavigated in at least one direction. Balzac recognized this himself when he wrote to Countess Maffei in 1837: 'I find people very impertinent when they say I am deep and then try to get to know me in five minutes. Between you and me, I am not deep, but very wide, and it takes time to walk around me.'[2] (It is true that he hoped the Countess would put his claim to the test.)

Since I started out on this walk seventeen years ago as an undergraduate, I hope to have covered enough ground to produce at least the illusion of three dimensions.

BALZAC'S LIFE in written form almost deserves a biography of its own. After the affectionate accounts by his sister and Théophile Gautier, Balzac became the common denominator of a set of anecdotes and was depicted either as a dangerously depraved *parvenu* with the body and brain of a peasant and the costume and pretensions of an aristocrat, or as a bumbling incompetent, an accidental genius, incapable of distinguishing fact from fantasy. In coping with fame, Balzac brought to life an image that still conspires against him – the coffee addict, chained to his desk from midnight till dawn, writing pornographic stories in his monk's robe; the unwanted child who blundered into life equipped with every emotional and intellectual disadvantage.

Faced with a compendium of myths, the majority of Balzac's early biographers appear to have asked themselves Wittgenstein's first recorded philosophical question – 'Why should one tell the truth if it's to one's advantage to tell a lie?' – and failed to come up with a convincing answer either way. Some of Balzac's most disreputable, opportunist characters lived on to wreak revenge on their creator in skimpy, exploitative biographies, where virtuous sentiments go hand in hand with plagiarism and where patterns of cause and effect are established with devastating confidence, while lip-service is paid to the unpredictability of life. With the substantial, scholarly biographies of André Billy (1944), Stefan Zweig (1946) and André Maurois (1965), Balzac's posthumous fortunes changed: a less moralistic attitude to his work produced a recognition that someone who turned himself so effectively into a contemporary myth could hardly have floated over half a century of French society on a cloud of unconsciousness. A more private and ambiguous Balzac began to emerge. Later biographers – Pierre Citron and Maurice Bardèche – have crept up on him by studying the obsessions that drive his novels, while the astonishing variety of critical approaches attracted by *La Comédie Humaine* has turned the biographer's peep-hole into a giant screen. It would be a shame, though, if biography had advanced only to a parting of the ways: in one direction, the enchanted forest of myth (and, of course, the sleeping novelist), in the other, the pebbly field of fact and detail in which Balzac is studied through the evidence of his spade. There is no reason to believe that any aspect of his work – including those traditionally thought to be the preserve of academe – should be inherently dull. Nor is it necessary to believe that divulging scholarly detail in an interesting fashion should contaminate and cheapen it. All that is lost is the spurious moral advantage of having overcome boredom in acquiring knowledge.

Having allowed myself to be convinced by Balzac that imagination is an ally of the truth, I have fallen quite happily into the trap of telling a story. Sometimes, teasing a thread out of so much material means making one's mind up about things when it would be far more pleasant to remain in doubt. However, I have always tried to present the evidence in such a way that the reader feels fully qualified to disagree – and if no one does, then I can hardly claim to have presented Balzac in all his inexplicable vitality. All the anecdotes used to illuminate the story can either be corroborated, or else they spring from Balzac's own inventions and conversations and form part of the Balzac legend.

This is the first full biography of Balzac in English since those of Mary Sandars (1904), Frederick Lawton (1910) and Francis Gribble (1930). In the meantime, there have been translations of the biographies by Zweig and Maurois. There was also an excellent short summary of Balzac's life written by one of his most scrupulous translators, Herbert J. Hunt (1957), as a companion to his study of *La Comédie Humaine*, and a beautifully illustrated account by V. S. Pritchett (1973) based on the biographies by Billy, Zweig and Maurois. Yet interest in Balzac – not only in the English-speaking world – has continued to increase. Since the biographical study of Balzac's works by Maurice Bardèche in 1980, thousands of books and articles have appeared, new facts have been unearthed, the twelve-volume Pléiade edition of *La Comédie Humaine* has been completed under the direction of Pierre-Georges Castex, Roger Pierrot has published an updated edition of the letters to Mme Hanska, and Balzac's juvenilia and the *Contes Drolatiques* launched a new edition of the *Oeuvres Diverses* in 1990. Anyone who travels through Balzac's real and fictional worlds owes such a large debt to those who built straight roads through them and made it possible to admire the scenery that it is easy to forget what heroic efforts Balzac inspired in his admirers. I have made use of all this material, and have also contributed new facts, anecdotes, interpretations, solutions to mysteries and, of course, questions. Nothing else could excuse the enormous conceit of telling the story of one of the world's greatest story-tellers.

TITLES ARE quoted in French in the text, with translations – or titles of the best-known English translations – supplied in the index. Most of Balzac's titles are simultaneously comprehensible and untranslatable, as a glance at the index will show.

All translations are my own. Many of the passages – and even titles – appear in English here for the first time.

Sources of all quotations are given in the notes, except where the original can easily be located, for example by the date of a letter.

Occasionally, in order to avoid cluttering up the text with note numbers, sources pertaining to the same subject have been grouped in a single note.

It is not necessary to know anything of Balzac's works in order to read this biography, though one of the reasons for writing it was to encourage a personal rediscovery of his stories. It is hoped that this will be construed as a service to the reader. Biography is often practised as a form of lion-taming without the risks. Perhaps more than any other writer, Balzac has been treated with a tone of condescension which is sometimes applied wholesale to the past and which makes one suspect the biographer of trying to revel in the ultimate advantage: life over death. In Balzac's case, one should not be so sure that this advantage exists. Oscar Wilde's premonition of his own downfall in that of a Balzac character should serve as a warning to anyone who decides now to descend into the great nineteenth-century epic with its hundred open doors and only one exit:

> A steady course of Balzac reduces our living friends to shadows, and our acquaintances to the shadows of shades. His characters have a kind of fervent fiery-coloured existence. They dominate us, and defy scepticism. One of the greatest tragedies of my life is the death of Lucien de Rubempré. It is a grief from which I have never been able completely to rid myself. It haunts me in my moments of pleasure. I remember it when I laugh. But Balzac is no more a realist than Holbein was. He created life, he did not copy it.

BY WRITING about Balzac as well as consorting with his characters, I have discovered that the side-effect mentioned by Oscar Wilde can be neutralized and even reversed. In all the recent talk about the art of biography – its status as disguised autobiography (while autobiography is the story of an invented character) – one important ulterior motive has been missed: the chance to put friends and institutions to the test. I have taken this opportunity with all the eagerness the subject seemed to merit.

Claude Pichois, who first showed me through the streets and salons of *La Cousine Bette* and helped me on several occasions to renew my *carte de séjour* for the nineteenth century, has read the typescript and made some vital suggestions and corrections. Thanks also to Peter

Straus and Starling Lawrence, who managed to make their observations incisive and encouraging at the same time. Stephen Roberts
pointed out various defects whilst appearing to do the opposite.
Geoffrey Neate's erudition and hospitality have been invaluable. I am
grateful to Jean Bruneau for his comments and assistance.

Special thanks to my agent, Gill Coleridge, who is responsible for
this book in ways both practical and intangible.

The following people answered questions and generally smoothed
the path of research. Jean-Paul Avice at the Bibliothèque Historique
de la Ville de Paris, Thierry Bodin, Alain Brunet (for practical help
with Chapter 13), Philip Collins, Ghislaine Courtet, Nicole Dinzart at
the Bibliothèque Municipale de Tours, Helen Dore, Pierre Enckell
(for words found only in Balzac), Jim Hiddleston, Gregory Hutchin-
son, Georg Kreisel, Anne Panchout, Helen and Raymond Poggenburg
(for books and lodging), Edward Preston, Everard Robinson (for an
equivalent of the Château de Saché), Claire Tomalin and Jean Ziegler.

I am greatly indebted to the collections and expertise of the
following libraries and institutions. In France: the Bibliothèque
Nationale, the Bibliothèque de l'Institut (Fonds Spoelberch de
Lovenjoul), the Maison de Balzac at Passy, the Château de Saché, the
Musée des Beaux-Arts de Tours, the Musée de Ville-d'Avray, the
Musée des Beaux-Arts de Besançon, Archives de la Ville d'Orléans,
Archives de la Ville de Villeurbanne. In Britain: the Taylor Institution
Library, the Bodleian Library, the National Portrait Gallery and the
Library Automation Service of Oxford University. In the United
States: the W. T. Bandy Center for Baudelaire Studies at Vanderbilt
University. Also the American and British Societies for Psychical
Research.

Balzac would have been dedicated to Margaret, but she made so
many improvements to it and was so irresistibly honest from the very
beginning that she was practically its co-author.

G. M. R.

PART ONE

CHAPTER ONE

Provincial Life

(1799–1814)

'NOTHING IS insignificant,' Balzac declares, characteristically – the mother's diet, the father's virility, and, most important of all, the 'posture' of the parents at the moment of conception.[1] Balzac inherited his passion for genetics from his father, who had 'strange ideas' for improving the human race. Unfortunately, his father never indicated how the great creator of characters was himself created. For us, the story of Balzac's life must begin with his birth at 11 a.m. on 20 May 1799 in the city of Tours.

Almost a century later, during his Balzacian pilgrimage to the Loire Valley, Henry James was shocked to find that the man who 'took in more of human life than anyone since Shakespeare' was born in a house 'in a row' – 'a house, moreover, which at the date of his birth must have been only about twenty years old'. 'If the tenement selected for this honour could not be ancient and embrowned, it should at least have been detached.'[2] It seems fitting, though, that a life devoted to exploring the private worlds of his contemporaries should have begun within hearing of the neighbours.

Balzac himself was always delighted with his initial coordinates. Born in 1799 with what he called a centenarian's constitution, he had the best possible chance of seeing three centuries. The year was also historically appropriate. Bonaparte was about to make himself First Consul. Balzac too would create an Empire, a fictional world so real that Oscar Wilde would be able to describe him only half-humorously as the inventor of the nineteenth century.

As for the house which disappointed Henry James, it was in the busy centre of Tours, in 'a street with a pavement on either side' – in fact, 'the only street in Tours', for the others are 'dark, winding, narrow and damp'. A street which lacked only one thing according to Balzac: a memorial to the region's most famous sons, Descartes and

Rabelais.[3] With its warm climate and easy abundance, Touraine had always provided a nutritious medium for geniuses. Returning in later years, Balzac would experience the delicious sensation of being buried up to the neck in a giant *pâté de foie gras*.[4] For him, his native land was a peculiar combination of Romantic exoticism and womb-like comfort, a land of lotus-eaters in the middle of France. Once you get there, he claims, you will remain – 'indolent, idle, and happy'. But Balzac was different. He would suffer the 'transplanting' which, he says, enables the Tourangeau to bear fruit.[5]

Finally, he was equipped with a name worthy of a genius. His father had been born a Balssa. It was and still is a common name in various forms in the mountains of the Auvergne – the name of a highland peasant; and so, as he rose through the ranks of society, he changed it to the name of an ancient noble family, eventually adding the supposedly aristocratic 'de'. With its sturdy symmetry and decisive consonants, the emphasis falling on the second syllable, 'Balzac' was not a label but a powerful talisman. According to the pronunciation of one of Balzac's characters, the Z 'goes off like a rocket'.[6]

THE SAME IMAGE could easily be applied to Balzac's father.[7] Bernard-François Balssa came from a hamlet near Albi in the South of France. He was born in 1746 into an uninterrupted line of peasants, the first of eleven children. Not content with helping his father in the fields, he asked the parish priest to teach him to read and write, and became a clerk in a lawyer's office. There, he discovered how French society worked and, before his twentieth birthday, set off for Paris to seek his fortune.

By the time he was thirty, Bernard-François had achieved what would normally have taken several generations. He served an apprenticeship as clerk to the Public Prosecutor, then became Secretary to the King's Council in 1776. His position won him some powerful friends. No doubt he was helped by the fact that he became a Freemason. During the Revolution, he steered a prudently erratic course. As a member of the Commune, he seems to have been infected with revolutionary fever. A police report reveals that Citizen Balzac was seen on the night of 6 August 1792 in possession of a sabre, 'intending to go and decapitate the King and Queen'. As usual, he was a step ahead of his contemporaries. But his enthusiasm spilled over political boundaries: under the Terror, he organized escapes for several of his former protectors. It was a risky business. An unknown benefactor, perhaps Danton, saved him from the consequences of Robespierre's inquiries by sending him north to take charge of food distribution in the Army. Bernard-François was still in provisions when he was transferred to Tours in 1795.

The move pleased him enormously. He revelled in the land of Rabelais, 'that illustrious teller of tall stories whose unshakeable good humour he admired'.[8] He even came to see Touraine as his true home. Protected by the local Prefect, General Pommereul (a fellow Free-mason), and revered as an eccentric, he was asked to become mayor of the city. He refused in order to devote his considerable energy to running the hospital which he took over in 1803 and where he fought disease and civil servants with equal courage.

The astonishing rise of Bernard-François is not easy to explain. Balzac the son typically put it down to an inexhaustible supply of that mysterious physical force, will-power. To prove his point, he used to tell a story about his father's early days in Paris:

> He was given room and board in the house of the Public Prosecutor. According to the custom of the time he took his meals with the other clerks at his employer's table. That day, they were having partridge. The Prosecutor's wife, who was eyeing up the new clerk, asked him, 'Monsieur Balzac, do you know how to carve?' 'Yes, Madame,' the young man replied, blushing to the roots of his hair. He plucked up his courage and grabbed the knife and fork. Being entirely ignorant of culinary anatomy, he divided the partridge into four, but with such vigour that he smashed the plate, ripped the tablecloth and carved right through to the wood of the table. Not very adroit, but tremendously impressive. The Prosecutor's wife smiled, and from that day on the young clerk was treated with great respect in the house.[9]

In 1797, Bernard-François finally decided to marry. Anne-Charlotte-Laure Sallambier was an attractive young woman from a very proper, very ambitious family of haberdashers in the Marais district of Paris. The marriage had been arranged by her father, a former colleague of Bernard-François. Laure was only eighteen years old, her husband was fifty. Even for the time it was an odd match; but both partners stood to gain. Bernard-François, intent on enjoying the rest of his life in peace, allowed his dependants 'the freedom he wanted for himself'.[10] For Laure, a husband with old-fashioned ideas about marital tolerance was a guarantee of independence.

If there were no other sources of information, Bernard-François might be thought to have been invented by his son. He had a quality normally found only in characters in comic novels: an indestructible belief that he exerted personal influence over the laws of nature. (His own daughter compares him to Uncle Toby in *Tristram Shandy*.) His great hobby was longevity. By conserving one's 'vital forces' – fresh air, comfortable clothes, chastity in moderation and a single pear for dinner – one could live to the age of 100. Confident of success, he invested most of his fortune in a *tontine*, an early form of life insurance. The proceeds went to the last surviving investor. It was an excellent way of ensuring that his family would look after him in old age. Balzac later concluded, with a nice example of lateral thinking, that the secret of long life is to have an absorbing hobby.

It was sixteen months before the first child arrived. Louis-Daniel was born on 20 May 1798. He lived for only thirty-three days.[11]

HONORÉ EMERGED exactly one year after Louis-Daniel on 20 May 1799. His father ignored what some might have seen as an ominous coincidence and named his son after St Honoré whose day had just been celebrated. Then, as if to emphasize the fact that he was untainted by religious superstition, he failed to have his son baptized.

Balzac's first mistress later described him almost flatteringly as 'an eagle hatched by geese'.[12] Balzac agreed. He may have pointed out in support of this view that, a few hours after birth, he was taken from home and put out to nurse. It was a sad example of poetic injustice: he was sent to the home of a man who sold poultry.

His sister Laure gives a typically charitable explanation of this in the short biography she published after her brother's death: 'My Mother had lost her first child by trying to feed him herself. When little Honoré came along, they chose a handsome nurse for him living on the edge of town in a nice, airy house surrounded by gardens.' Louis-Daniel's death certificate confirms that he had been nursed by his mother, though interestingly, he died, not at home, but at the poulterer's house a few streets away.[13]

Mme Balzac had obviously succumbed to her husband's theories and been persuaded to raise her first-born according to the precepts set down in Rousseau's *Émile*. On Honoré's birth certificate, the initials 'N.P.E.' – '*nourri par étrangère*' – prove that she was not prepared to repeat the experiment with her second child. Unfortunately for Honoré, his brother's death was not the only reason for what he came to see as his mother's desertion. In 1799, social life was reviving after the long years of revolution, and Honoré's young mother was keen to seize the opportunity. As Balzac points out, more fairly than many of his biographers, but still with a hint of bitterness, 'Women were fighting over the heroes of the Empire, and ninety-nine per cent of mothers put their babies out to nurse.'[14] His correspondence also implies that Louis-Daniel had something to do with this treatment: 'My Mother hated me even before I was born . . .'[15]

For Balzac's father, the nurse was a reasonable compromise: peasants led healthier lives than so-called civilized people; the air on the edge of town was cleaner; and not every alternative form of nursing was bad. As a baby, Bernard-François had been taught to suck milk from a goat. This, it was suggested by an anonymous biographer,[16] was why he behaved like one later on. Bernard-François saw it as one of the secrets of his iron constitution: had not the infant Zeus been suckled by the goat called Amalthea?

Myths of a humbler variety have grown up around Balzac's early years, partly because there are enough nurses in his fictional world to make almost any combination of events seem possible. Balzac's 'Realist' techniques obscure matters even more: those tales which have the 'unmistakable' ring of truth are often pure fantasy, while others enveloped in an aura of unreality may be transpositions of actual events. However, one persistent myth can be dispelled. Honoré was always thought to have spent his first years in the home of a policeman. He claims in a letter to his future wife that he was put out to nurse '*chez un gendarme*'.[17] As so often with Balzac, the more comforting version – the potentially unbridled prodigy attached to a pillar of the local community – turns out to be false. Balzac was using the word *gendarme* in its colloquial sense: a large, cantankerous woman.[18]

The bullish nurse may be one of the fictional monsters with which

Balzac surrounds his earlier self, the sad and loving hero, cast out into a harsh but engrossing world. Even so, at an objective distance, the distortion resolves itself into an unpleasant reality. Honoré's ejection from the nest proved to be more than just a medical precaution. He was left with his nurse long after he was weaned, and spent his first years across the river in the village of Saint-Cyr, looking down over the city. By the time he returned to his parents, he was four years old.

Unhappily, Balzac came to share his father's view that mother's milk is the only proper food for a child: anything else, he says, is likely to produce an unnatural, deformed creature:[19] perhaps the creature who sometimes appears in burlesque disguises in Balzac's novels. There are many strange evocations of maternal flesh in his work – all providing substantial food for psychoanalytical speculation. One scene has a hunchback fantasizing about cooking a large breast which he proposes to devour 'even without sauce'.[20] In *La Vieille Fille*, the earnest young hero drools over the great expanse of Mlle Cormon's bosom, sitting there like 'a plump partridge enticing the gourmet's knife'.[21] The disturbing combination of sexual yearning and sadism strongly suggests violent resentment at his mother, a sense of loss, and the will to reconquer what was lost. But the hunchback and the earnest young hero also have fictional lives of their own.

In September 1800, Honoré was joined by his sister Laure and perhaps in 1802 by the second daughter, Laurence. The following year, they were taken to visit Mme Balzac's mother in Paris. Shortly after the visit, Balzac's grandfather died of a heart attack. He was two years younger than Bernard-François, who probably made some apposite remarks about the noxious air of Paris and the need for fresh vegetables. Mme Sallambier came to live with her daughter in Tours, where she became a close but ineffective ally of the Balzac children.

HONORÉ AND LAURE were deemed presentable enough to return home in 1803. The Balzacs were about to move to a new house at number 29 in the same street.[22] Unlike the house Balzac was born in, which disappeared with much of the old city in the bombing raids of 1940, the second house still stands at 53 Rue Nationale. To the children, it was a great mansion, with its stables and outhouses, two kitchens, five cellars and a large salon looking on to the street from the first floor where Mme Balzac entertained her many visitors. Honoré was installed at the top of a wooden staircase on the third floor.

The nurse's home seemed a paradise in comparison. The children were submitted to regular inspections. Saying goodnight was a tense, solemn ceremony. Mme Balzac was a nervous mother; she prided herself, according to Laure, on being able to detect traces of misbehaviour on her children's faces. Perhaps these silent interrogations are the origin of Balzac's lifelong interest in physiognomy: not an academic interest, nor even a literary manual for character descriptions, but a means of survival.

Honoré's brief interlude at his parents' house is marked by two anecdotes which vividly convey the mental landscape of his childhood. The first is told by Balzac himself in *Le Lys dans la Vallée* – thus, an account written thirty years later and attributed to a fictional character. Whether this is more or less revealing than an 'objective' account is a matter of opinion. As far as biographical evidence is concerned, the problem is one of chronology rather than accuracy:

> I was an object of such indifference that the governess often forgot to put me to bed. One evening, curled up peacefully under a fig tree, I was gazing at a star with that passionate curiosity which takes hold of children and which my precocious sadness filled with a kind of affective intelligence . . . My Mother happened to notice that I was missing. Our governess – a terrible woman called Miss Caroline – hoping to avoid a reprimand, confirmed my Mother's unjustified fears by saying that I hated being in the house. She claimed that, without her close surveillance, I would already have run away from home. I was not stupid but cunning, according to her, and of all the children entrusted to her care she had never encountered such a wicked boy as I. She pretended to search for me and called out. I answered. She came up to the fig tree, knowing I was there. 'What were you doing?' she asked. 'Looking at a star.' 'You weren't looking at a star,' my Mother interjected from her balcony. 'What do boys of your age know about astronomy?'[23]

The conniving governess also appears in Laure's biography. Mlle Delahaye, she writes, specialized in inculcating respect, obedience and, above all, fear. It should be said that governesses occupied an awkward social limbo between the bourgeoisie and the servant class and were paid very little. If they had a fussy employer like Mme Balzac, intimidation probably seemed the safest tactic. As Balzac suggests, the root of his problems was his mother – anxious to impose her authority, prone to interpret intelligence as insubordination and, disastrously, wanting some suitable recompense for her trouble. 'There comes a time', says Balzac, 'when children judge their parents.'[24] For him, that time came early; and perhaps his mother realized she was being judged.

The story from *Le Lys dans la Vallée* shows how Balzac tends to dress his earlier self in the costumes of Romantic heroes. There are echoes in his memories of childhood of Rousseau's *Confessions* and particularly of stories describing passionate, even incestuous relationships between children – *Paul et Virginie* and Chateaubriand's *René*. But Honoré seems to have borne little resemblance to the melancholy waif he likes to evoke. Laure remembered him as 'a lovely child', and 'when we were taken out for walks together, people would notice him because of his happy disposition, his well-formed, smiling mouth, his big brown eyes, sparkling yet gentle, his high forehead and his thick black hair'. Laure ingeniously explains that Honoré's cheerful demeanour put him at a severe disadvantage: his happiness and blooming health preserved his mother from 'those latent anxieties' which express themselves in special treats and affectionate behaviour. Honoré's father was inclined to let nature take its course, but his mother was more in tune with the times: children for her were constitutionally in need of correction and little more than potential nuisances.

The oldest nuisance was provided with a small red violin. It gave Honoré his first chance to find an audience, in this case Laure: 'He used to scrape away at the strings for hours on end . . . and his radiant expression showed that he thought he was hearing melodies.' Laure would beg him to stop: 'Can't you hear how pretty it is?' he asked in astonishment. Honoré may have been inspired by the recent example of Paganini who, it was said, held audiences spellbound with his furious improvisations. Balzac's early discovery of this great enigma of Art – that Beauty is more often in the mind of the artist than in the eye of the beholder – would produce the 'philosophical studies', *Gambara* and *Le Chef-d'Oeuvre Inconnu*. In both tales, the dream of impossible perfection destroys the work itself. It was high time that Honoré descended to the rudiments.

Mme Balzac had been thinking of tutoring Honoré herself.

Luckily for him, she decided against it, sacrificing her maternal worries to her busy social life. Shortly before his fifth birthday, in April 1804, Honoré was sent as a day boy to the nearby Pension Le Guay.[25] In this cramped little school in the old heart of Tours, the sons of tradesmen and the bourgeoisie, rubbing shoulders since the Revolution, learned to read and write for 6 francs a month. It was a six-hour day. For most of it, the boys were read to by an old man called M. Docque whose hands shook and whose clothes had survived half a century's changing fashions. Occasionally, M. Benoist would take over and demonstrate joined-up 'English' handwriting and – Balzac's favourite – calligraphy.

Honoré was escorted to school every day by his father's servant. He was equipped with a small lunch basket, containing some cheese or dried fruit. When lunch-time came, the basket was a source of embarrassment (according to an account in which every verifiable detail has turned out to be autobiographically correct and which Balzac's sister treats as personal history). The other boys tucked into the pork dishes for which Tours is still famous: a sort of 'brown jam' spread on slices of bread (*rillettes*) or leftover pork pieces fried in fat, which looked like cooked truffles (*rillons*). There was nothing luxurious about these dishes, but Honoré had never tasted them at home and was taunted by his supposedly less fortunate classmates when they noticed his greedy eye.[26]

In *Le Lys dans la Vallée*, Balzac tells the sad story of his attempts to get back at the mockers and the persecution that ensued: stones wrapped in a handkerchief thrown at his back and the family servant forced to defend him. The picture of his early days is almost certainly painted black. Later reports of his behaviour at school suggest that he was a rebellious pupil, far from unpopular with boys of his age, enthusiastic and gullible enough to be made fun of, but not easily repressed. Besides which, the Pension Le Guay was his only real contact with the types and idioms of Tours which he always mentions with affectionate nostalgia. The incidents described in *Le Lys dans la Vallée* are an expression of a more private truth. The real villain in Honoré's eyes was his mother. In the novel, when the servant tells the narrator's mother of the bullying, her retort seems to come straight from one of Mme Balzac's scalding letters: 'That dratted child will cause us nothing but grief!'

Unfortunately, there are no school reports on Balzac before 1807. According to the narrator of *Le Lys dans la Vallée*, the teacher, seeing him always gloomy, despised and alone, confirmed his family's suspicion that he was a bad lot. But Le Guay himself informed his superiors in a terse report written in 1810 that there was nothing much to be said about boys between the ages of five and seven who are only just learning to read.[27] All we know for certain is that Balzac contracted smallpox during his three years at the Pension Le Guay. It was a mild dose, and, unlike the *rillettes* incident, left no permanent mark.

AT THE AGE of eight, Honoré was fitted out and sent away to the town of Vendôme, 35 miles north-east of Tours on the road to Paris. The ancient Collège de Vendôme was to be his home for the next six years.[28] During that time he would see his mother exactly twice – despite the fact that Vendôme enjoyed a more regular coach service than it does today.

The Collège de Vendôme was reputed to be one of the finest schools in France, receiving 'the flower and elite' of the great provincial cities, including Tours – hence, presumably, Mme Balzac's choice of school. Significantly or not, on the very day Honoré was despatched to Vendôme, she paid for half a year's pew-rent at Tours Cathedral.[29] It was the place to be seen, especially if one's husband had a reputation as a free-thinker.

A more distressing reason for choosing Vendôme – the *real* reason as far as Honoré was concerned – appears in the school prospectus: 'Parents are requested not to call their children home; even in the holidays.' In other words, once admitted, the child belonged to the school body and soul until his studies were completed – or, in Balzac's case, until he ceased to function as a normal human being. Parental visits were strongly discouraged and permitted only at Easter and on prize-giving days, one of which usually coincided with Easter.

This was the time-honoured system of the Oratorians, who had founded the school in 1623. The Oratory was often contrasted with its pedagogical rivals, the Jesuits. The Oratorian approach was more sensitive to historical change, not to say infected with rationalism and newfangled notions; but it was their unfailing flexibility that had enabled them to survive the Revolution. The buttons on the school uniform (a round cap and sky-blue collar) told the story: the *fleur-de-lys* had been replaced at a suitable moment with the words '*Arts et Sciences*'. A few years later, Napoleon was inserted in the Catechism as 'He whom God has summoned in difficult times' to 'defend the State with his powerful arm'. By the time Balzac arrived, secularization was well established: only seven of the sixteen teachers had ever been members of the Oratory, and those seven had been released from their vows. Still, Vendôme was a flourishing anachronism, proud of its claustral atmosphere and venerable eccentricities. Other schools under the Empire marched to the beat of a drum; Vendôme, harking back to earlier days, ordered its day by the bell.

The large, monastic school, which is still a *lycée*, occupied the centre of the town. Its ancient grey walls, which backed on to the diminutive River Loir (a tributary of the Sarthe), marked off a vast enclosure containing 'the buildings necessary in such establishments': a chapel, a theatre, a sanatorium, a bakery, gardens and fountains. There were 228 pupils, divided into four sections: *Minimes, Petits, Moyens* and *Grands*. Each section had its own dormitory and class-rooms. All the rooms gave on to a shared quadrangle which led to the refectory.

This was the historic institution from which Balzac would emerge in the spring of 1813, not clad in the bright wings of genius, but more a chrysalis than before – pale and scrawny, dazed with indiscriminate reading, unable to communicate and living with alarming ease in his private world, with no outward sign of any adult personality.

On arrival (22 June 1807), Honoré was inscribed in the register as number 460 and defined for the first time by his contemporaries thus: 'Aged eight years and five months; has had smallpox, without infirmities; sanguine temperament; easily excited and subject to fever-ishness'. 'Sanguine' had its older sense: light-hearted and changeable, with a ruddy complexion; or, as the headmaster's son later remembered, he was 'a fat little boy with chubby cheeks and a red face'.[30]

The first blush of over-excitement was brought on by the refectory, to which Balzac devotes a long, wistful passage of *Louis Lambert*. Talking at meal-times was tolerated, and so a sort of 'gastronomic commerce' had evolved: 'If one of the *Moyens*, sitting at the head of his table, wanted a portion of red beans instead of dessert (for we were given dessert), the following offer, *A dessert for some beans!*, would pass from mouth to mouth until some glutton accepted. . . . If several requests were identical, each one bore a number, and the cry would be, *First beans for first dessert!* There was never any mistake.' The noise generated by 200 boys negotiating their menus astonished visitors to the school. In the capitalist jungle of *La Comédie Humaine*, the Vendôme refectory comes close to being an image of the perfect society.

Other Vendôme specialities, designed to sweeten the bitterness of exile, were the allotments on which the boys could grow their own vegetables, and a thousand pigeons nesting in coops around the walls. There was also a small shop selling marbles, penknives, pencils, prayer-books (rarely sold), and, if the main ingredient was supplied by the consumer, pigeon pâté.[31]

The Fathers (as they were still called) endeavoured to remove 'those small embarrassments of fortune which are a very frequent subject of comparison amongst the boys'.[32] Once again, though, Balzac experienced the power of money in post-revolutionary France. He received only 3 francs pocket money a month. His father's apparent stinginess could be attributed to that other great mover of Balzac's world – single-mindedness. Poverty and spartan virtues, Bernard-François had discovered, were the surest path to happiness, and since it usually took most of a lifetime to reach that conclusion, his son would enjoy the inestimable advantage of being poor while he was still at school. Honoré may have questioned this philosophy when he noticed that his friends always had enough money to spend at the shop.

In spartan virtues, Vendôme left nothing to be desired. A contemporary picture of a mathematics lesson shows the master teaching with his hat on and his collar turned up, despite the presence in the room of a large stove.[33] Balzac often talks of the warm and gentle climate of home, 35 miles down the road, where the sun ripens the vineyards of Vouvray. In the monastic cold of Vendôme, he suffered more than most: 'His hands and feet were covered with chilblains every winter. Quite often, because of this inconvenience, he had to be spared the rod, which was still in use at that time, and his punishment would be commuted to a detention.'[34] Leather gloves were for sissies: anyone who dared to be seen wearing them would sooner or later find them irreparably shrivelled up on top of the stove.

The dormitories were no better – bug-infested, smelly, the floors coated with that mysterious 'collegial *humus*' spawned by 'the thousand occupations of every pupil' and other, more definable sources of 'atmospheric corruption': buckets of cold water used for washing in the morning, food smuggled out of the refectory, pigeons left mouldering in lockers.[35] Each dormitory was divided into cubicles, 6 feet square, with bars across the top and grated doors. They were locked with a great clattering every night. Writing in 1810, Joseph de Maistre mistakenly describes this ancient type of dormitory as a thing of the past – a regrettable loss, he asserts, since 'vice is so contagious'. In boarding schools especially, evil thoughts, actions and books spread like disease.[36]

Honoré was rarely in a position at first to worry about contamination. Most of his time was spent in 'prison'. This meant one of two things. Either the offender was locked up in his dormitory cubicle (schoolboy slang, hinting darkly at medieval torture, referred to these cubicles as 'wooden breeches'); or, weather permitting, he was marched off to the *alcove*, a small, draughty cupboard under the stairs in the *Minimes*' part of the school.

Balzac might be suspected of exaggerating the importance of captivity in his early years. Prison cells, after all, are the hatcheries of many a Romantic imagination: from 1800 on, poets tend to incubate in cupboards and toilets. The realities of life at Vendôme, however, required very little imaginative transformation. The damning reports Balzac gives of himself in *Le Lys dans la Vallée* and *Louis Lambert* were cheerfully confirmed years later by the school janitor: 'Remember M. Balzac? I should think I do! I had the honour of escorting him to the dungeon more than a hundred times!'[37]

These, it should be noted, were not paltry half-hour detentions. The headmaster's son, who was also a teacher, records that in his first two years at Vendôme Balzac spent no less than four days a week in the *alcove* – 'except when it was freezing'. The reason for this extraordinary treatment was the boy's 'invincible repugnance for any prescribed work': 'You could get nothing out of him whatsoever, whether class-work or set exercises.' Balzac's publishers would have sympathized. As he himself appears to confess, with redeeming superlatives, 'I became the least active, the most idle, the most contemplative of all the *Petits*, and as a result, I was punished more often than any other pupil.'[38]

How did Honoré fill those long hours in prison? Despite advocating divided dormitories, Joseph de Maistre warned that too much unsupervised confinement was a dangerous thing, since 'the worst company a young man can keep is himself'. Perhaps Balzac was beginning to acquire some of that pernicious 'boarding-school education' he so often refers to, after which a child may leave the school 'a virgin, but certainly not chaste'.[39] Honoré was better company for himself than most boys. Sitting in his 'wooden breeches', listening for the crunch of strategically placed nutshells under the master's approaching boot, he was actively ruminating, becoming an expert at re-creating in his mind's eye scenes he had read about in books, observing his own thoughts. Other boys had imaginary friends, Balzac had his memory: 'Whenever I like, I draw a veil over my eyes. Suddenly I go back into myself, and there I find a dark room in which all the accidents of Nature reproduce themselves in a form far purer than the form in which they first appeared to my outer senses.'[40]

For all its dust and decrepitude, Vendôme was also Balzac's first glimpse of society as a process of unnatural selection. One of his less gifted classmates passed judgment on the Oratorian system by going mad. The same fate befalls the narrator's friend in *Louis Lambert*, and it may count as Balzac's finest achievement at school (since his academic record is remarkably unimpressive) that he kept his sanity and managed not to become a vegetable – though there was soon to be some doubt about this.

Fortunately, his store of mental food was unusually large. Even before Vendôme he was reading for hours on end, adventure stories like *Robinson Crusoe* or *The Iliad*, stirring accounts of Napoleon's victories, and, of course, the Bible, which his father had been annotating with a view to writing a history of the Hebrews. Reading at Vendôme took the place of physical exercise, which in any case consisted only of the occasional forced march to the headmaster's country house and a compulsory picnic. Even break-time, for Balzac, was taken up with extra lessons in mathematics. This was an idea of his father's, who hoped to see Honoré compete for a place at the prestigious École Polytechnique.

These private lessons were held in the school library, which had been a repository for books confiscated from monasteries during the Revolution. Balzac's tutor, Father Lefebvre, judged by his superiors to have 'more imagination than discernment, and a taste for miracles and philosophical systems', buried himself in his own mysterious investigations while his charge was left to roam among the shelves and borrow whatever took his fancy. The prisoner of Vendôme was particularly taken with tales of the early Christian martyrs.

Not surprisingly, the *alcove* figures in Balzac's earliest known letter. It was written during his second year at the school:

Vendôme, 1 May [1809]

My dear Mama,

I think Papa was quite upset when he found out I had been in the alcove. Please console him with the news that I got a merit. I am not forgetting to rub my teeth with my handkerchief. I have started an exercise book in which I copy out my exercises neatly and I got some good marks, and in this way I hope to please you. I send you all my love, as well as to all the family and the gentlemen of my acquaintance. Here are the names of the pupils who got prizes and who come from Tours:

Boislecompte.

(He's the only one I can remember.)

BALZAC HONORÉ,
Your obedient and
affectionate son

Balzac wrote this letter on the day after prize-giving. It was the cruellest time of year. As usual, his parents had failed to turn up, sending instead some advice on hard work and dental hygiene. They missed seeing Honoré pick up a small bound copy of Voltaire's *Histoire de Charles XII*, inscribed to '*Honoratus Balzac*' in recognition of his merit in Latin prose.

This is the only letter to have survived from Balzac's schooldays; but it contains the first glimmer of his formidable powers of observation. The awkward expression immediately following 'all the family' sounds suspiciously like a euphemism, or revenge for neglect. Some of these 'gentlemen' were indeed almost members of the Balzac household. Little Henry, born six months after Honoré was sent to Vendôme – over five and a half years since the Balzacs' last child – was living proof that Mme Balzac had not yet said farewell to Youth and Pleasure. Worse than that, she turned out to have maternal instincts after all – but highly selective instincts: Henry was the illegitimate apple of her eye. There was gossip in Tours about her liaison with a local landowner called Jean de Margonne, who later left 200,000 francs to Henry in his will.[41] Balzac himself confirmed in 1848 that Jean de Margonne was Henry's father, and there are signs, as we shall see, that he had other evidence of his mother's dereliction of 'duty'.

One of Mme Balzac's lovers, and little Henry too, were to meet horrible deaths – one in *La Grande Bretèche*, the other in the optimistically entitled *Le Doigt de Dieu*.[42] Both stories were written in the early 1830s but perhaps conceived, in spirit, at Vendôme.

For Honoré, maternal solicitude took the form of literary criticism. His over-emotional letters were ridiculed for their turgid, self-pitying style, which may explain why this relatively sober specimen has survived. The handwriting, however, is an amazing mixture of neat, almost cramped letters lined up between a heading and a signature brandishing enormous, swirling capitals and many a superfluous flourish. Balzac's first letter gives a graphic image of an exuberant mind raised in solitary confinement.

THERE ARE signs that, from the age of ten, the most punished of the *Petits* was beginning to acquire some respectable mediocrity. He obtained another merit in Latin prose in 1812. In his school reports from 1809–11 (which are the only reports now extant) his 'conduct' is always 'good', his 'disposition' 'happy' or 'very happy', while his 'character' evolves from 'slow' to 'gentle' and finally to 'childish'. The value of these opinions is somewhat diminished by the fact that the reports on other boys are almost identical: the teachers clearly felt that all possible infant personalities could be adequately expressed with half a dozen adjectives.

A surer mark of progress is the fact that Balzac was making several friends: Louis-Lambert Tinant, who may have given his name to the novel based at Vendôme; Barchou de Penhoën who, like Balzac, spurned conventional hobbies and developed a precocious interest in metaphysics (he later became an authority on German philosophy); Bois-le-Comte, mentioned in Balzac's letter quoted earlier, who ended his career as French ambassador in Washington; Armand Dufaure, a future Government minister and colleague of de Tocqueville. It says a lot for Vendôme, or about the *milieux* from which it drew its pupils, that many of Balzac's friends and acquaintances became prominent in public life – politicians, lawyers, journalists, including some of the overseas contingent from the Antilles or New Orleans. Balzac came to know his fellow exiles during the week before prize-giving when the other boys were ostentatiously gorging themselves in town with their mothers and fathers.

More importantly from his parents' point of view, Honoré was at last spending some time in the classroom. As is often the case, the greatest pedagogical influence was unintended – Father Lefebvre engrossed in his miracles while Honoré ingested the library – but there were two remarkable teachers whose intrusions into his private world were a welcome change from prison and who provided him with an object for what seemed to be his unwanted affection.

Lazare-François Mareschal was a much-loved teacher, almost a father to the boys.[43] He was also Balzac's first literary adviser outside the family. On discovering that Honoré had been pursuing his own curriculum, filling his desk with reams of pretentious prose, but still failing to produce the set work, he told him a cautionary tale about a little bird falling out of its nest because it tries to fly before its wings are fully grown.

Mareschal spoke with the hypocrisy of experience. He himself was an inveterate writer of verse with an unschoolmasterly penchant for erotic poetry and twittering tributes to whatever regime happened to be in power. Lilies, Phrygian caps, imperial eagles flitted in and out of his eulogies with perfect timing. When Napoleon passed through Vendôme on the night of 14 August 1808, Mareschal rushed out two

Latin inscriptions in the Emperor's honour which were placed at the town gates. His pupils were given a chance to benefit from their teacher's hobby in the form of a highly unusual Latin Grammar. The sentences which the boys were invited to render into French reveal a desire to stimulate the puerile mind with something more inspiring than Gauls in ditches: 'I have seen Lesbia's sparrow', 'A girl was hiding behind the bushes', 'Venus, her feet naked, has fastened the girdle of her flowing robe', and one particularly unconventional offering which would have struck a chord with Honoré if he knew that he and his brother were not sons of the same father: 'O Gods, grant this woman the ability to give birth and not to sin.'

As one of Balzac's contemporaries put it, Mareschal's brother-in-law, Jean-Philibert Dessaignes, acted as ballast to Mareschal's flights of fancy.[44] Dessaignes was held in awe because he had all the appearance of a scientific genius: he re-created lightning in the school laboratory and was known to have conducted important experiments in magnetism and phosphorescence which were recognized by the Académie des Sciences. In fact, Dessaignes was an original thinker for his time and may well have awakened Balzac's interest in producing rational explanations for 'spiritual' phenomena. Thought, for Dessaignes, as it would be later for Balzac, was a tangible force, moving in a fluid or magnetic medium. 'Of course, in our eyes', wrote Balzac's contemporary, 'he was Europe's leading scientist.' Dessaignes had the charm of incomprehensibility; he used strange new words when he talked about his subject. At prize-giving in 1799, for instance, he had entertained the assembled pupils and parents with a discourse on how in days gone by eloquent writers untainted by civilization would take up their pens only 'when they experienced a certain electrical tremor in the precordial region which raised their organs to the pitch of their subject'. For anyone hoping to find the secret of writing masterpieces, this was an exciting view of inspiration: instead of waiting for the breath of God, perhaps the vital spark could be created artificially?

Though a somewhat distant figure, Dessaignes gave the cheering impression that the outside world (and perhaps the inner world too) was less static than the cloisters of Vendôme might suggest. Balzac himself must have felt a precordial *frisson*, since he drafted a 'treatise on will-power' – thought until recently to be a purely fictional title invented for *Louis Lambert*, but which must have existed previously in some form: it was mentioned by a schoolmate of Balzac's in an article published several months before *Louis Lambert* was written.[45]

The *Traité de la Volonté* had a short life: it was discovered by a teacher who sold the paper it was written on to a Vendôme grocer . . . Balzac's first known work was used to wrap up sweets.

BALZAC HAD more than just a treatise on will-power hidden in his desk. Linguistics was another brave new world, offering access to knowledge on a scale undreamt of by those who planned the curriculum. While the other boys toiled away at their exercises, Balzac was devouring dictionaries, discovering etymologies, developing that taste for omniscience which asserts itself in every part of *La Comédie Humaine*. But the vast sweep of *Louis Lambert*'s scientific and mystical readings reflects a later stage in Balzac's life. It would be some time before these early investigations bore fruit.

Of course, Honoré had ulterior motives, even at the age of ten. Some of the older boys belonged to the Vendôme 'Academy' – a junior version of the Académie Française which met twice a year in the presence of the rest of the school to recite and discuss its members' latest compositions. Balzac never succeeded in being elected to either. Still, the boys in his own year admired him for undertaking an epic poem, that most prestigious of literary genres, which even M. Mareschal had not attempted. The subject of the poem was the annihilation of the Inca Empire by the Spanish, a perfectly acceptable theme, so long as one understood that it referred, not to Napoleon, who was even now subduing the Iberian Peninsula, but to the excesses of the late monarchy. Only one exclamatory fragment was ever produced:

O Inca! ô roi infortuné et malheureux![46]

Hardly enough to make the mighty despair, but enough to earn Balzac a derisory nickname from the older boys: '*le Poète*'. Genius, says Baudelaire, 'has the privilege of enormity in every sense'.[47] Balzac manages here to cram into a single alexandrine – the twelve-syllable line of classical French verse – most of the basic errors pointed out by treatises on versification. The caesura falls cripplingly in the middle of a word – '*in | fortuné*' – one of the worst prosodic sins. One vowel adjoins another in no fewer than four places (which probably makes this a unique example in French literature of multiple hiatus). Best of all, the alexandrine is one syllable too long. Hindsight makes it possible to say that Balzac was bursting the seams of traditional genres. At the time, it only proved the headmaster's point.

Ironically, 'the Poet' had been inspired by Marmontel's celebrated historical romance, *Les Incas* (1777). But *Les Incas* belonged to an inferior class of literature: it was just a novel.

Honoré's blundering ingenuity extended with greater success to the world of objects. Cooped up in the dormitory or under the stairs, he discovered other ways in which to exercise his already characteristic ability to perform symbolic acts. He constructed clocks,[48] and, as the headmaster's son later remembered, 'was considered, at least at Vendôme, to be the inventor of the three-nib pen' – a revolution in writing lines and a fitting start for one of the century's most prolific novelists: one device to measure passing time and another with which to conquer it.

In the eyes of his teachers, however, six years after entering Vendôme, Balzac had done little more than acquire the basics: Latin, geography, history, physics and chemistry, fencing, music, and a sufficiently inadequate grasp of mathematics to make his later financial dealings one of his least realistic novels. Oratorian education, as applied to pupil number 460, was rapidly reaching a point of diminishing returns. And the boy appeared, if anything, to be regressing . . .

BALZAC DISAPPEARED from Vendôme in mysterious circumstances. His sister Laure gives the official family version:

> He was fourteen years old when the Headmaster, M. Mareschal, wrote to our Mother between Easter and prize-giving, asking her to come with all possible speed and fetch her son away. He was afflicted with a sort of *coma*[49] which was particularly worrying to his masters since they could find no cause for it. As far as they were concerned, my brother was a lazy pupil and so this cerebral illness could scarcely be attributed to any mental fatigue. Honoré had grown thin and puny. He was like those somnambulists who sleep with their eyes open. Most of the questions put to him he failed to understand, and

he did not know what to say when you asked him without warning, 'What are you thinking of? Where are you?'

This surprising condition, which he later understood, was the result of a sort of intellectual congestion (to use his words). Unbeknownst to his teachers he had devoured a considerable portion of the rich school library. Those serious books had developed his mind to the detriment of his body.[50]

As Laure points out, this is her brother's own diagnosis. 'Intellectual congestion' was a professional malady to which budding geniuses were prone – or so Balzac's novels tell us. Several of his heroes are at some point in their lives glutted with knowledge, victims of their enormous appetites. Romantic heroes of the time are rarely seen in this embarrassing condition, egg-bound or thinking beyond their means; but in *La Comédie Humaine* the silent philosopher appears time and again sunk in torpor, inwardly surveying the fantastic realm of ideas, outwardly giving every sign of being an idiot. Like waterfalls seen from a distance, says Balzac, their minds appear to be motionless.[51]

Patterns of cause and effect are difficult enough to establish in a living patient. Imaginary autopsies are even less reliable and it would be rash to associate this peculiar lethargy with Balzac's later, more recognizable illnesses. One might just as well accept the equally ambitious diagnosis which was usual in such cases. The headmaster talked of his pupil's '*taciturnité*' and '*grande insouciance*' – *insouciant* meaning, not carefree, but detached and indifferent. This, combined with an abnormally pale complexion (for a red-faced boy), weight loss, general listlessness and a recent history of prison all pointed to the same conclusion. A popular *Traité sur les Habitudes et Plaisirs Secrets* (1760) which was used in boarding schools well into this century claims that these are the classic signs of self-abuse. Similarly, in Balzac's *Le Médecin de Campagne*, the effeminate and bookish Adrien is removed from school for the same reason (a quick inspection of his knee convinces the doctor . . .), and, as for Balzac, the cure – which we *do* know about – is fresh air, exercise and company.[52]

There is of course a less abstruse reason for Balzac's hasty departure. Implicit trust in punitive school systems has tended to obscure the fact that Balzac had spent a dangerous amount of time in solitary confinement. He was surely right to think that his father was 'upset' when he learned that his son had been languishing in the *alcove*. Just as Honoré was leaving for Vendôme in 1807, his father was completing his first and most remarkable pamphlet: a dissertation 'on the means of preventing thefts and murders, and of restoring the men who commit them to a useful role in society'.

Like many a supposed crank, Balzac's father was unusually clear-sighted. Here, he put forward the seemingly hare-brained idea that prison did little to prevent crime and that rehabilitation was the path to follow. Bernard-François had seen several of his friends imprisoned under the Terror: when he saw the wretched product of six years' expensive education he must have recognized the symptoms. 'My Father was very anxious about his son's condition,' writes Laure, and Grandmother Sallambier apparently exclaimed: 'So this is how the school returns the pretty boys we send them!' Unless something were done quickly, little Honoré was well on his way to a life of crime and an early death.

Balzac's own feelings were certainly more complex. He had been happy in prison. He had discovered the excruciating timetable he adopted for most of his life: huge blocks of time devoted to a single, uninterrupted activity. As if in memory of Vendôme, Balzac wrote in a monk's robe. In his 'dark room', 'embarrassments of fortune' and his mother's unfairness ceased to exist. There, the mind could seek out those secret principles which, according to Dessaignes, governed the whole universe. In the gloom of the *alcove*, every aspect of life had an equal claim to reality; everything was interconnected.

The mind was not just a private playroom but an arsenal. Vendôme's dormitories are the birthplace of European Realism. And in Balzac's rival universe, Vendôme is also the school from which Vautrin the master-criminal emerges, seething with extraordinary powers and a passionate desire to dominate the society he understands and, therefore, despises.[53]

As with Vautrin, however, there is an element of self-destruction in Balzac's behaviour. His mother had convinced him of his own defects and of the impossibility of ever pleasing her. Later, suicide would seem to be the logical solution. At Vendôme, it was a kind of self-induced madness. In *La Rabouilleuse* (1840–2), the adolescent torpor of one of those unpromisingly inert geniuses, the painter Joseph Bridau, is ascribed not only to his intense concentration but also to a familiar situation in Balzac's novels: his mother saves all her love for his worthless brother. Neglected, Joseph neglects himself, taciturn, detached, his gigantic head suggesting, to the narrator, genius, to his parents, hydrocephalus.

The humiliated pupil, convinced that his mother had placed him in the orphan's role, is easily eclipsed by the Rabelaisian face of the famous novelist, rattling window-panes with his great guffaws, exploding with stories, treating Paris as his stage, irresistibly happy, with a child's ability to lose himself, concentrate and be distracted. But this is Balzac too – fragile, immature, painfully believing that genius is the only alternative to death, and that 'no decent education is complete without suffering'.[54]

ACCORDING TO a pleasant tradition, Honoré was nursed back to health by his loving family, provided with tutors who came to the house, and only entered the local Collège de Tours fourteen months after his premature return from Vendôme. In reality, he was given two months to become normal again and then put on the coach for Paris.

The black sheep had returned to a household which had more pressing concerns than 'intellectual congestion'. Bernard-François's protector, General Pommereul, had gone to Lille several years before, leaving his old friend without his masonic shield against two successive archbishops, both extremely meddlesome. They were probably tired of being addressed as 'Citizen Archbishop'. One of them had even been included, thanks to Pommereul, in a biographical dictionary of 'atheists'. With the blessing of the Church, the new Prefect was poking his official nose into Bernard-François's business, hinting, unjustly, at misappropriations in his running of the hospital and wondering why the Balzacs of Tours were so wealthy when their peasant relatives back in Albi were, quite properly, poor. In November 1814, Bernard-François would have himself transferred to Paris.

His wife was partly to blame for this official hostility. Public life in the provinces at a time of social upheaval was as perilous as a military campaign: 'If she is too well-dressed, a woman gives the impression of being frivolous and even irresponsible,' she advised Laure at the time of her marriage. 'People start saying that your husband is *too* successful in his dealings . . . If my Mother had warned me of this, I should never have had all the women of Tours on my back. Because of his age, your Father was tactful enough to say nothing. We were able to afford very elegant clothes for me.'[55]

Mme Balzac measured social success by the envy she inspired in other women and was an obvious target for malicious gossip. She was attractive even at the advanced age of thirty-five; she enjoyed an elderly husband who ignored her affairs in the name of domestic peace. (Balzac's novels are full of such enlightened husbands.) And things were not improved by the fact that, on selected occasions, the Balzacs were now in the habit of ennobling their name with a 'de'. It was a common conceit, but one which seemed more than usually pretentious in the Balzacs' case, hinting as it did at some connection with the ancient and noble Balzacs of Entragues, extinct though they were.

Honoré was introduced in this way to the delightfully petty world of provincial intrigue. Learning to survive, as his sister Laure suggests, by watching his mother's unpredictable changes of mood, he was becoming an expert in the art of observation. With Laure, whose company he enjoyed immensely, he practised his skill on the specimens of Tours society who came to visit and who reappear, transported to Angoulême, in the first part of *Illusions Perdues*:[56] would-be Parisians painfully laced up in cheap imitations of the current fashions, dignified people who have temper tantrums when they lose at cards, mothers hunting husbands for their repulsive daughters, men who memorize passages of Cicero or descriptions of the latest agricultural machinery for use in conversation – all of them more or less consciously obeying a complicated set of social rules. Balzac was soon to discover that the Germans had a name for this amusing activity – a word he was one of the first French writers to use in the modern sense: it was Anthropology.[57]

During the day, Honoré was pressed into service as his brother's playmate and, by all accounts, enjoyed himself. If Mme de Balzac caught him gazing dreamily at beautiful sunsets (as Laure remembered), lapsing once again into thoughtfulness, she sent him off to help little Henry fly his kite. But there would always be a nagging unhappiness. Names, for Balzac, have a mystical significance, and it would not have escaped his attention that Henry – endowed at birth with his brother's consonants and sporting a fashionable English *y* instead of the usual *i* – was supposed to be the new improved version of Honoré. His mother rarely bothered to conceal her preference, even in the will she drew up in 1832 during a cholera epidemic: the majority of her books were to go to her 'dear son Henry' (to judge by Henry's pathetic record at school this was wishful thinking), along with the big coffee-pot, while the books on 'metaphysics' and the little coffee-pot go to Literature's greatest coffee-drinker, soberly referred to as 'Honoré Balzac my elder son'.[58]

In the early tale, *Le Doigt de Dieu* (1831), the 'child of love' is pushed down a steep slope by the 'child of conjugal duty' and disappears, screaming, into the thick mud of the river as an unnamed narrator – suddenly appearing in the story – watches from behind a tree. This extraordinary, almost mythical scene conveys a strong impression of unconscious motive in the creation of characters and hints at sinister analogies between the art of the novelist and voodoo. The rest of the story makes it clear, however, that the pins were intended for his mother's effigy. Balzac never bore a lasting grudge against Henry, who, as if by divine decree, turned out to be everything his elder brother was accused of being: weak-willed, lazy, constitutionally immature, he ended his life as an unsuccessful surveyor in the Tropics. Balzac's attitude to Henry is more accurately expressed by the dedication 'To Henri de Balzac' of *Le Bal de Sceaux* – a cautionary tale which shows that spoilt youngest children always disappoint their parents and never in the end get what they thought they wanted.

IN LATE SPRING or early summer 1813, Honoré left for the capital. It was to be a tantalizing preview of Paris – one of the main protagonists in *La Comédie Humaine* – and is characteristic of Balzac's first engagement with a subject: imaginative rather than practical. He was installed in the Ganser–Beuzelin boarding-school, which was a sort of independent dormitory for the nearby Lycée Charlemagne in the heart of the Marais.[59]

The Marais, which has an important place in Balzac's early years, was not quite the Paris a young man dreamed of conquering. It was a shabby version of the provinces where grass grew between the paving-stones.[60] Except for the occasional carriage, the streets were silent. The Marais had been in comfortable decline since the end of the seven-teenth century when tradesmen first moved in among the mansions and palaces, built at a time when the Marais was the quartier of the aristocracy. When Balzac arrived it was teetering between bourgeois respectability and seediness. Its unusually disparate population included civil servants, shopkeepers, retired people, a few lingering aristocrats, the ubiquitous, all-seeing concierges and, according to Balzac, other curious species like police spies and fortune-tellers who were attracted by the quiet streets and cheap restaurants.

The boarding-school was typical of its surroundings. It infested the once magnificent Hôtel Salé (now the Musée Picasso), ransacked by the mob during the Revolution when it was the property of the Archbishop of Paris, then gradually eroded by two decades of boarders.[61] The school was one of the many evocative remnants of a more settled age which survive to this day in the Marais, charmingly dilapidated and, often surprisingly, inhabited.

As the crocodile of boys made its way through the damp streets before emerging 'as if from a cellar'[62] into the Rue Saint-Antoine opposite the Lycée Charlemagne, Balzac inspected the crevices and doorways, deciphering the 'hieroglyphics' of architectural oddities, investing all this *humus* on a grand scale with 'the enormous signifi-cance which objects acquire in the novels of Fenimore Cooper' – 'a tree trunk, a beaver's dam, a rock, a motionless canoe, a branch drooping down to the water'.[63]

Very little is known about this eight-month stay in Paris, but the fragmentary nature of the evidence probably corresponds to Balzac's experience: a glimpse of Napoleonic splendour during a march past in the Tuileries Gardens;[64] visits to an unidentified aunt in the equally provincial Île Saint-Louis – 'ancient as a cathedral, painted like a miniature, sumptuously dressed, she lived in her *hôtel* as if Louis XV had never died'.[65] Other parts of the city fixed themselves in his personal mythology: famous theatres and restaurants which he vowed to visit when he was older, and that place of perdition, about which some of the boys told stories in which they were the dubious heroes – the Palais-Royal where prostitutes and publishers lived in symbolic proximity.

[28]

Balzac was saved from 'perdition' for the time being by the distressing efficiency of the Ganser–Beuzelin institution which shunted its pupils to and from the Lycée and made sure they did their homework. He does appear however to have made some furtive voyages of discovery within the school: 'Remember those long conversations fomented by the Devil', he asks the readers of his *Physiologie du Mariage*, 'those nocturnal recreations, that itching to reveal our discoveries to one another? Never were La Pérouse, Cook or Captain Parry so ardent in their pursuit of the poles as schoolboys sailing on that sea of iniquity.'[66]

IT WAS A good time to catch the smell of imperial decadence. The allies had invaded in the East. Napoleon left for the frontier in the spring of 1814 with a small, untrained army. Paris was on the point of surrendering; the monarchy would soon be restored, to the relief of most of the population. But, reasoned Balzac's parents, schoolboys brought up in admiration of the Emperor were in a potentially dangerous situation.

Mme Balzac volunteered to salvage Honoré from the anticipated troubles – not before arranging a meeting in Paris with a Spanish count she had known as a refugee in Tours. The gorgeously named Ferdinand de Hérédia, Comte de Prado Castellane was a dainty little man whose fictional counterpart is described in one of Balzac's stories as having 'more brushes for his manicure than most women have for their *toilette*'.[67] He was about to have a disastrous effect on Balzac. The story of Mme Balzac's love affair can be reconstructed from letters sent to her by Hérédia, now held in the Lovenjoul Collection. One letter mentions a pantomime the two lovers attended together in Paris; it ran from 3 February to 13 March 1814, which confirms the version of events given in *Le Lys dans la Vallée*.[68] The next day, Mme Balzac collected her troublesome son from school. Whether or not Balzac knew what was going on, unpleasant memories and suspicions constantly surface in his work. Eighteen years later, Mme Balzac was able to read a horrendous story her son had set in Vendôme: a young wife's Spanish lover is bricked up alive in the bedroom wall and left to die. His name, barely disguised, is Férédia.[69]

The long journey back to Tours was memorably miserable. They spent the night at Orléans, Honoré hoping to act out the scene of the loving son flying to his mother's arms, Mme Balzac all too ready to accuse him of play-acting and then exasperated with his silence. The coach passed the road to Vendôme the following day and stopped to change horses at Blois where the Empress Marie-Louise was sent that month to sign the last imperial decrees.

Napoleon's Empire was in disarray and so was Balzac's life. He ran to the bridge over the Loire intending to jump in. The parapet was too high.[70]

This was the first of several reported suicide attempts, none of which were meant to succeed. This one may conceivably have been inspired by knowledge of his mother's romantic adventures, or simply by a feeling that he was not loved. His mother, as she later told him herself, thought that Honoré took after his father 'in character and mind',[71] and in his view, he and his father were both deprived of her affection. In a letter to his future wife in 1846, he would talk of his filial adoration turning gradually to fear, and his fear to indifference; but the tone of the letter suggests an intermediate stage: 'I never had a mother, and today *the enemy* has declared herself. I have never shown you this wound – it was too horrible, and *it has to be seen to be believed*.'[72]

THE LASTING significance of Balzac's first real experience of Paris lies in his return to what he came to consider as his true mother – the Loire Valley. Leaving the grime of Paris for Touraine in early spring was a revelation. These days imprinted themselves in Balzac's mind so deeply that they recur in his novels throughout his life. His walks in the countryside with its farms and châteaux 'like cut diamonds', its changing views – sand-flats, slopes planted with vineyards, the Cher and the Indre lined with poplars 'under a warm, hazy sky'[73] – corresponds in nearly all of Balzac's brilliant Touraine landscapes to a sexual awakening:

> Nature had adorned herself like a woman going to meet her lover;
> my soul had heard her voice for the first time, my eyes admired her,
> as fertile and as varied as I had imagined her in my dreams at
> school.[74]

The Loire itself, as Balzac describes it, closely resembles his ideal of feminine beauty – full, powerful, with broad curves, generous, mature and above all maternal: 'A young woman has a thousand distractions, but older women have none. Their love is the Loire at its estuary: immense, and swollen with all the disappointments and tribulations of life.'[75]

It is especially revealing that Balzac's future wife, scanning his novels for telltale signs of infidelity, managed the unusual feat of feeling jealous at his evocations of Nature in *Les Paysans* (she pruned them of their more erotic adjectives after his death): the soft, warm smells of the earth under the morning mist 'like a woman rising from her bed'; Nature, 'in the Spring, pert and provocative like a brunette, in the Autumn, mellow and melancholy like a blonde'.[76]

Whether or not Balzac found a human object for his love at the age of fifteen is unclear. His sister later reported in a letter to the wife of Victor Hugo that her brother ripened early and engaged in amorous adventures interesting enough for her to keep quiet about them[77] – perhaps with the young Englishwoman mentioned in *Louis Lambert*[78] (there was a large English community in Tours), or the mysterious girl in the red dress who appears more than once in otherwise muted descriptions of the Loire Valley.[79] In some respects the object is of little importance. Balzac's huge capacity for passionate feeling did not always allow him to distinguish between male and female or, for that matter, between animal, vegetable and mineral.

One of Balzac's favourite walks, ironically, was to the Château de Saché, where he was to write some of his finest novels: Saché was the property of a family friend, Jean de Margonne. Balzac always talked of him with affection, even after he found out that he was Henry's father.

APART FROM this entering into possession of his homeland, the short period preceding the family's move to Paris was marked by two rather comical events. Both incidents have the great interest of situating Balzac, with appropriate ambiguity, in the social hierarchy of Restoration France.

The first was a ball held by local dignitaries to celebrate the passage through Tours of the returning Duc d'Angoulême, nephew of Louis XVIII.[80] Now that Napoleon had abdicated, everyone was pretending

to have supported the monarchy all along. Honoré was sent as his
father's envoy and sat on his own, overwhelmed by the dazzling
dresses and the general odour of aristocracy. Until, that is, a woman
sat down next to him 'like a bird settling on to its nest':

> All at once I was struck by the sight of plump, white shoulders . . .
> shoulders tinged with pink, which seemed to blush as if naked for
> the first time . . . I stretched up, trembling, to see the bodice and was
> utterly entranced by a bosom, chastely covered in gauze, but whose
> pale-blue, perfectly rounded globes could be seen lying snugly in
> folds of lace.

His reaction (at least in the novel) was instantaneous: he lunged at the
exposed flesh like the worst sort of Romantic lover. Understandably,
the woman emitted a piercing shriek and gravitated away. Only then
did he realize how ridiculous he looked in his Sunday best – a puny
adolescent 'trussed up like an organ-grinder's monkey'.

This presageful incident is described in *Le Lys dans la Vallée*, no
doubt greatly embellished. Balzac tends to exaggerate his clumsiness
and in these portraits of himself as an adolescent there is little trace of
the laughter and exuberance his sister remembers. However, the ball
itself is a true memory and provides us with one of the first signs of
Balzac's fascination with the higher realms of society and of his efforts
to comprehend and assimilate them – both physically and in imaginative re-creation.[81] But the episode also betokens his exclusion from
these higher realms. For all his genealogical fantasies, Balzac's father
was born a peasant, and his well-known eccentricity tended to
undermine his wife's attempts to appear respectable. On the other
hand, as Honoré had discovered at the Pension Le Guay, he was not
entirely a member of the lower orders either. This social uncertainty,
which his contemporaries would often point out as something rather
suspicious, is one of the secret keystones of Balzac's vast reconstruction
of French society, and it expresses itself on several occasions in
unexpected ways.

Balzac's other significant brush with the monarchy came as a result
of the two prizes he won at the Collège de Tours, which he attended
as a day boy from July to September 1814. In ludicrous disproportion
to the achievement (particularly since he was repeating a year), he was
decorated with the newly established Order of the Lily.[82] The printed

certificate is inscribed, of course, to M. *de* Balzac. It informs him in a benignly threatening fashion that His Majesty Louis XVIII has 'every confidence in his loyalty and devotion to His Royal Person'.

The Order of the Lily was an embarrassing (and, in Balzac's case, futile) attempt by the new regime to apply the sponge of vanity to any residual Napoleonic fervour. In addition, Balzac's Lily was probably an indirect reward to Bernard-François for his patriotic pamphlets, conceived in a spirit of anticipatory conciliation and couched in such expediently ambiguous terms that they could be reprinted under different regimes. Most notable among these is a resonant tract of 1809 which proves that Bernard-François, no less a visionary than his son, was the first person to think of erecting a pyramid in front of the Louvre.[83] The implicit allusion – obvious at the time – was to Napoleon's conquest of Egypt, which explains why a later pamphlet, published under the Restoration, called instead for an equestrian statue of Henri IV.

All this artful wavering says as much about Bernard-François's equivocal status as it does about the need for civil servants to hold 'correct' views. Similar contradictions can be detected when Balzac tries to define his own historical place in society. His illustrious name was one of his proudest possessions, and yet, as he told a friend in 1835, 'Nobility today means an income of 500,000 francs or personal fame.'[84] Continuing his father's energetic climb up the social ladder, Balzac was to be an extraordinary example of the social mobility he so often condemns as the root of rampant individualism and of a new 'nobility' – a vulgar aristocracy based on money.

He would also follow in his father's footsteps by suggesting improvements to the city he was about to discover or rediscover at the end of 1814. But his own most colourful idea for a monument betrays a less patriotic desire to exploit both the splendours and the miseries of Paris. Balzac's monument would go in the other direction. His plan was to sink a spiral staircase in the middle of the Luxembourg Gardens by which tourists could descend to the catacombs which stretched for a great distance under the noble Faubourg Saint-Germain and the plebeian Faubourg Saint-Marceau.[85]

CHAPTER TWO

Parisian Life

(1815–1819)

B Y THE TIME the Balzacs returned to live in Paris in the winter
of 1814, Honoré had decided to become great and famous.
'He was beginning to say that people would talk about him
one day',[1] and this alone was enough to make him a topic of
conversation. He was laughed at by his family – somewhat hypocriti-
cally, since they tended to consider themselves unusually worthy of
other people's attention. Laure and Honoré's nickname for it was 'the
Celestial Family'. The oldest child was simply continuing a tradition.
According to Laure, he 'accepted all the teasing and laughed louder
than anyone else'. In Balzac's world, laughter is the sound of the
creative spirit. To his parents and even his sister, it was a sign of
childishness. Perhaps the two are not incompatible.

At this stage, and for the next few years, Balzac's 'vocation' was all
desire and no object. If asked what the source of his greatness was to
be, he could not have said. Maybe philosophy, or poetry and the
theatre, eventually leading to a career in politics; but these were only
the means to an end. He claimed in 1834 that he was 'intoxicated'
with his thirst for fame until the age of twenty-two: 'I wanted my
reputation to be a beacon that would attract an angel. There was
nothing attractive about *me*. I deemed myself a hopeless case.'[2]

The romantic notion of greatness born of some incurable
deficiency is common in Balzac's letters. It reflects his will to derive
new courage from the memory of obstacles overcome, to see even the
most common aspects of growing up as part of an extraordinary story,
and also, perhaps, to give a positive sense to years which might
otherwise appear to have been wasted: 'After a childhood like mine',
he wrote in 1842, 'you must either believe in a glorious evening or
throw yourself in the river.'[3] By declaring his intent at the age of
fifteen, however, he was also demonstrating his typically unromantic

grasp of method. Imbued with his father's quaintly Cartesian approach to life (putting the cart before the horse), he identified the first piece of equipment needed for the trip to glory as Genius. Balzac's earliest surviving notes, which have their place in this chapter, provide some useful instructions in the matter. For the time being, the method could best be described as a secular equivalent of Christ's injunction, Act as if you have faith,[4] and it was to prove remarkably effective.

Paris was the perfect setting for the attempt, a place where the bourgeoisie could now acquire high status and where appearances were not the opposite of reality but its precursors. When they begin to circulate in the great city, usually in the early years of the Second Restoration (after Waterloo), the ambitious young heroes of *La Comédie Humaine* quickly realize that they can best attain their goals by appearing to have achieved them already. Shiny leather boots, glamorous waistcoats, ties of the proper colour for the time of day, they discover, can open any door.[5] A more subtle and desperate device involves the use of a toothpick: a starving man who saunters along the boulevard picking at his teeth stands a better chance of being invited out for a meal than a man who begs for food. Balzac later found that financiers referred to this sort of display as 'creating confidence'.[6]

Balzac's own self-confidence illumines his tortuous progress through adolescence and early adulthood. With some writers, viewing the years of 'apprenticeship' in the light of their final apotheosis is a romantic conceit, a homage to the legend in which the biographer assumes the role of ventriloquist. With Balzac, hindsight shows us the adolescent as he foresaw himself, the product of his own Herculean labours, defiant, on some future eminence, laughing at his enemies.

Even now, he was qualifying for life as a public figure. He was already accustomed to criticism, perhaps even jealousy. 'You can't possibly know what you mean when you say that, Honoré', his mother liked to inform him when he said something clever.[7] He also possessed that enviable talent that might come in useful in politics and would certainly be indispensable in literature: an ability to believe firmly in implausible things. Laure had great fun with her brother's imagination. One day, she entrusted him with what she claimed was the precious seed of a cactus plant from the Holy Land. Honoré placed it in a pot, nurtured it, and watched it grow into a pumpkin.

Some of these anecdotes sound like attempts to reclaim Balzac for the family, and it may be worth noting that when she wrote the biography of her brother, Laure had already written several stories for children. The chocolate-box images suggest the coexistence of a different Honoré – one who was already giving his mother good reasons to be worried. Despite her increasing fascination with the writings of mystics like Swedenborg and Saint-Martin, Mme Balzac did not consider credulity to be an asset. Her husband would not live for ever (whatever *he* might think) and Honoré would become the head of the family. Ambition was not enough. If the man with the toothpick actually believed he had eaten a meal, his chances of survival were slim.

For the next few years, Bernard-François remained in charge of the company which handled supplies for the First Military Division in Paris. He had a handsome salary of 7500 francs. Honoré was free for a time to concentrate on the essentials.

The family had taken an apartment at 40 Rue du Temple, a busy street on the western edge of the Marais, which Balzac already knew from his previous stay. In *La Comédie Humaine*, he remembers it as the site of a bizarre vestige of Paris's ancient drainage system: a huge, gaping mouth, five feet high and with a movable grill to catch the rubbish. One day in 1816, after a heavy rainstorm, a little girl who was taking some diamonds to an actress in the nearby Ambigu Theatre was swept up by the raging torrent 'and would have disappeared if a passer-by had not come to the rescue'.[8] In Balzac's vision of the Marais, archaeology and melodrama belong to the same domain. Streets, houses and even unimpressive objects like drains never merge altogether into the abstraction of an 'adult' view; they, too, have personalities and stories to tell. The building itself contained an interesting historical relic. Mlle de Rougemont was a dowager friend of Grandmother Sallambier. As a young woman, she had known Beaumarchais, the creator of Figaro. Balzac talked to her for hours, effortlessly remembering anecdotes and details, gestures and conversations unknown to Beaumarchais's biographers: hence the impression he often creates in his novels of having witnessed scenes which took place before his birth.[9] The house, like so many of these six-storey buildings, was a microcosm of French society. One door led to the secret world of recent history and Balzac's future career, but another led to corridors more predictable and dull. Number 40 was also the home of Victor Passez, an old friend of Bernard-François and the family's solicitor.

In the New Year (1815), Honoré was attached to yet another strand of his father's web of connections. He became a pupil of the Lepître boarding-school. It was only four streets from home, yet Honoré was admitted as a boarder. Like the Ganser–Beuzelin institution, the Pension Lepître sent its boys to the Collège (formerly the Lycée) Charlemagne. Why Honoré was not immediately returned to his first school, whose directors were also friends of the family, is not clear. Probably his father thought it prudent to trumpet his loyalty to the new regime by patronizing a prominent Royalist.

A fat little man with a club-foot, a crutch and the appalling handicap, for a teacher, of a name which means 'the Clown', Lepître had been chosen by Marie-Antoinette (and heavily bribed) to help free the royal family in 1792. The conspiracy failed, thanks to Lepître, who accidentally changed the course of history by stupidly requesting that the Dauphin be supplied with a copy of *Télémaque*, Fénelon's manual for future monarchs . . .[10] When Balzac arrived at the school, Lepître was in the habit of boasting that he shared the disabilities of the new king: obesity and a club-foot. Balzac might have pointed out, as he does so often in his novels, that Louis XVIII's other well-known handicap was impotence.

Unfortunately for Lepître and his hero, Napoleon returned from Elba. In March, he was in Paris; in June, at Waterloo. As the victorious allies advanced on the capital, the fires of Napoleonic passion were still smouldering. A contingent of pupils from the Pension Lepître, stirred up by no less a person than Mme Lepître, set off to mount the barricades at Vincennes, Honoré almost certainly among them. Lepître hobbled behind, down the Faubourg Saint-Antoine, shouting threats.

Shortly afterwards, on 29 September, Balzac left the school. He was given a perfunctory certificate attesting his good conduct. It was a mere formality. As Lepître reported to the Ministry of Education, in his usual tone of obsequious arrogance, the Bonapartists had been sent packing, along with the mutinous Mme Lepître.

Balzac's Bonapartist tendencies are a surprise to anyone who enters *La Comédie Humaine* through the grand portal of the 1842 Preface, with its famous defence of monarchical principles; but the contradiction is superficial. The question of inheritance and the preservation of a few powerful families would be more important to Balzac than the pedigree of the ruling dynasty. The main difference lies in his attachment to the image of Napoleon. Napoleon had risen from obscurity like Balzac's father. Unlike his father, he managed to impose his authority and provided the young nation, which had been orphaned by the Revolution, with firm foundations. Now, in 1815, he suffered the fate of all visionaries: 'Curses rained down on him at the moment of his defeat.'[11] In some ways, Napoleon was Balzac's ideal father. *He* would not have given Mme Balzac a free hand in the house, nor allowed her to capitalize on that 'diminution of paternal power' which began with the decapitation of Louis XVI. 'That power which once endured until the death of the Father was the only human tribunal in which domestic crimes were judged.'[12]

It seems appropriate, therefore, that the only page of schoolwork which Balzac or his sister filed away contains a piece on Brutus, founder of the Roman republic. Inspired perhaps by David's painting, Balzac describes in stirring prose reminiscent of a Corneille tragedy the ranting of Brutus's wife: a staunch republican and iron-fisted father, Brutus has had his sons put to death for plotting the restoration of the monarchy.[13]

Honoré certainly profited from his father's multifarious interests, which at this time included all things Chinese. 'At the age of fifteen, I knew everything it was possible to know, in theory, about China.'[14] He was also aware that while his father gazed on the Celestial Empire, pointedly admiring its pious respect for fathers, he was failing miserably in his paternal duty. There is something of this dual assessment in *L'Interdiction*, where the Marquis d'Espard is prosecuted by his wife for neglecting their children's education and for turning them into experts on the various Chinese dialects.[15] Bernard-François also looms large in the early novel *Jean-Louis* as the blithering philosopher who continually questions the existence of unquestionable things. He publishes pamphlets on a vast range of subjects, including 'an eminently useful work' – perhaps a veiled comment on Bernard-François's career – which lists '172 Honest Ways in Which to Acquire Other People's Property'. A strangely serious passage of *Jean-Louis* interrupts the evocation of what is supposed to be a harmless, likeable lunatic:

It is a most unfortunate thing, but Philosophy makes people selfish and hard-hearted. The scholar, given up entirely to his books, has no tears for the misfortunes of others. . . . In his world, Reality does not exist; and this man in search of Truth, who is willing to sacrifice everything in order to obtain it, lives constantly surrounded by chimeras.

Balzac's grandmother shared her grandson's sensible view, judging Bernard-François to be 'the weakest man I ever knew – to say the least'.

BALZAC'S SUBVERSIVE activities during his nine-month stay at the Pension Lepître (January–September 1815) were not confined to politics. The historian Jules Michelet was a contemporary of Balzac's at the school. In an autobiographical *Mémorial* written in 1820, 'not to be read by my children before their twentieth birthday', he dwelt on his lonely years in the boarding-house and recalled particularly the prevailing taste among the boarders for 'pretty young boys'.[16] Some of Balzac's early adult relationships and risky descriptions of 'those passions which arise only towards the end of adolescence'[17] suggest that he was not unaffected by the trend. Sexual desire also found more conventional outlets, thanks partly to the school concierge who, in the venerable tradition of his profession, turned a blind eye on nocturnal expeditions. Michelet, for example, mentions two classmates who 'could claim to have been the pillars of the most respectable brothels in Paris'.

Respectable brothels were beyond Balzac's means, but it is likely that he was finally able to satisfy his curiosity about the Palais-Royal and the seedy Wooden Galleries which surrounded it. 'That sinister accumulation of refuse' 'reminiscent of a gypsy encampment', he calls it in *Illusions Perdues*.[18] In these 'arsenals of corruption and immorality', which a contemporary guide recommends to intrepid tourists,[19] almost every known trade was represented. Until the 1830 Revolution, even the Stock Exchange was there, inviting sarcastic comparisons. As evening fell, this 'terrible bazaar' lit up in all its glory. Prostitutes arrived from the adjacent streets, drawing such huge crowds that 'you had to crawl along at a snail's pace'. Nobody minded: it was a good excuse to gape at the women with their outlandish hairstyles and low-cut dresses – 'all that shameful poetry which now belongs to history':

> The dazzling flesh of shoulders and breasts glittered amid the almost uniformly dark colours of the men's clothing and produced the most magnificent contrasts. . . . Respectable citizens and persons of the greatest consequence rubbed shoulders with men who looked like gallows-birds. Those monstrous conglomerations of humanity had such an intoxicating influence that even the most insensitive people were affected. . . . When those ignoble wooden shacks were demolished, there was widespread and unanimous regret.

Back at school, the concierge took full advantage of his mostly captive market. He smuggled in forbidden books and that substance that was to become the corrosive fuel of Balzac's fictional world: coffee. Colonial produce was expensive and, therefore, a status symbol as much as a treat. Balzac, artificially impoverished as he had been at Vendôme, obtained his coffee on credit – a highly significant event: it was his first debt. Mme Balzac was horribly unimpressed by this sign of approaching manhood. She flew into a predictable rage, doubting the educational value of coffee, declaring that Honoré was consuming his sisters' dowries, and concluded that 'Marat was an angel compared to me.'[20]

Honoré may have agreed with Marat that blind obedience always presupposes extreme ignorance; but his rebellious behaviour – republicanism, promiscuity and coffee-drinking – is also indicative of his lifelong search for security. Debts, for many writers of the period, were a fashionable sign of independence. For Balzac, they became a discipline, a chain to fix him to his desk. His prodigious consumption of coffee and his endlessly recurring debts are surprising symptoms of a dependent personality. Balzac's greatest and most tenacious creditor for many years would be his mother.

The story of Balzac's first debt comes from *Le Lys dans la Vallée*; but a similar memory resurfaces in his correspondence in 1843, with similar ambiguities:

> One should not allow oneself to be governed by such concerns, and in any case I have the probity of a woman and a schoolboy. Owing money is so deeply humiliating to me that the source of my courage

lies in that very humiliation: it makes me blush as if I were fifteen years old. Once I have paid off my last creditor, I shall never again be in debt![21]

After leaving Lepître's unwholesome establishment, Balzac returned for the last stage of his official education to Ganser and Beuzelin. In an article published in 1842, he hailed the two directors as models for the restructuring of the French education system.[22] They seem to have done little for Balzac's school record. His sister claims that, in the absence of a decent library, Honoré became a keen linguist.[23] No doubt this was one of his aspirations, but there is no trace of any uncommon achievement in Latin or French. In fact, in his mother's view, he was outstanding only in the other direction. A lapse in Latin translation prompted one of her apocalyptic letters, almost worthy of the wife of Brutus:

> I am unable, my dear Honoré, to find words strong enough to express the grief you have caused me. You really make me very unhappy. When I do everything I can for my children I should expect them to make me happy. That kind and worthy M. Gancer [*sic*] has informed me that you came 32nd in Latin Unseen!!! . . . So now I am deprived of the great pleasure I had promised myself for tomorrow. . . . What emptiness in my heart! How long that day will seem!

The 'great pleasure' was to have been a family get-together on Charlemagne Day (a national holiday for good pupils) – lunch, dinner, and 'one of our nice instructive little chats'. And to think, she went on, that 'Charlemagne was such a thoughtful man, so fond of hard work!' It was difficult indeed to imagine the founder of the Holy Roman Empire coming 32nd in Latin Unseen; but Mme Balzac must have known that her son was an admirer of Charlemagne as he was of Napoleon. Later, she would have discovered that he was also an admirer of the enterprising spirit of Genghis Khan and Attila the Hun – both of them unsung administrators and tributes to the power of hard work and ambition.[24]

In September 1816, Balzac came to the end of what is inappropriately referred to as his education. He had attended two of the finest schools in France – Vendôme and Charlemagne – and emerged with all the appearance of an autodidact. Even novels written thirty years later, with their long lists of prestigious names and erudite allusions, betray a hotchpotch of readings, partially assimilated and valued for their aura rather than their substance. Balzac's manner of accumulating knowledge and his motives for doing so were clearly at odds with institutions which instructed, crib-sheet in hand.

Balzac passed through the system with that significant mediocrity so often recorded at this point in the lives of original thinkers. At the time, of course, there was no guarantee that this was anything other than a disappointing start in life; and perhaps Balzac really was a slow beginner. But it is no coincidence that, like the classical education system, critics adhering to classical principles would pass negative judgment on Balzac's work. Like Honoré on the day he left school, his novels lack the smug sufficiency of the perfectly finished product. Grouped in *La Comédie Humaine* – which is itself unfinished – they retain and radiate the will-power and the potent sense of loss that produced them.

MME BALZAC was dangerously bored. She was thirty-eight years old and her social life now centred on her family and their shopkeeper friends in the Marais. She undertook to plug the gaps in Honoré's knowledge and to provide him with 'lessons on all the sciences that had been neglected at school.'[25] These sciences probably included magnetism, the study of the mysterious fluid discovered or made up by Mesmer. Magnetism seemed to provide the missing link between the physical and spiritual worlds. Mme Balzac used it to cure her aches and pains.[26] Then there was phrenology, Gall's science, on which the family doctor, Nacquart, was an expert. Both were fascinating combinations of neurology and fairground magic and were to find their most successful applications to date in Balzac's novels.

The idea behind this educational fervour was that Honoré should not have a minute to himself. Accordingly, he was now released from bondage into servitude and sent to the chambers of his father's friend, Guillonnet-Merville, as a junior clerk.[27] As retirement drew near, Bernard-François may have foreseen financial difficulties, and what could be more useful than having a lawyer in the family? The immediate advantage was that Honoré would be fed and supervised.

He enrolled at the same time as a law student at the École de Droit. 'Doing law', throughout the nineteenth century, is more often than not a synonym for doing nothing. Not so in Balzac's case. The walk from the practice in the Marais to the École de Droit in the Latin Quarter was precisely timed so that he could be asked to account for any deviation.[28] The student himself submitted willingly at first; Balzac liked to see himself in the role of family provider. Besides which, law was the first solid rung on several different ladders. Balzac's career had apparently begun.

The junior clerk set off every morning in the dark at five o'clock. He worked with his fellow clerks in a large, dusty, overheated room, smelling of food and paper, littered with yellow posters announcing auctions and seizures of property. The windows were so grimy that the lamps burned until ten in the morning.

Balzac returns many times to this room in his fiction. It reappears in *La Comédie Humaine* as a kind of bathyscaphe that was lowered each day into the murkiest waters of the social seas. Through the portholes, lugubrious creatures could be seen swimming unhappily in their native element, undescribed except in dull, forensic documents:

> I have seen a father perish in a garret, penniless and destitute, abandoned by two daughters who owed him their incomes of 40,000 francs! I have seen wills thrown on the fire, mothers stripping their children of their inheritance, husbands stealing from their wives, wives using the love they inspired to kill off their husbands, turning them into fools or lunatics so as to live in peace with a lover. I have seen women implanting in their legitimate child such tastes as would lead it to death and thus enrich the child of love.... Those abominations which novelists think of as their inventions always fall short of the truth.[29]

The man talking here is Derville, Balzac's honest lawyer, modelled on Guillonnet-Merville. These 'abominations', many of which seem to be a nightmare version of life at home, give some idea of what was going through Balzac's mind as he copied documents at the head clerk's dictation. In lectures at the École de Droit, the terminology was explained: solemn words which stood for monstrous truths. 'Adultery' conjured up a grim procession of 'Tears, Shame, Loathing, Terror, clandestine Crimes, bloody Wars and headless Families'.

Marriage itself was a Dark Continent. 'Later', Balzac writes in *Physiologie du Mariage*, 'as he came to the most civilized shores of Society, the author realized that the severity of marital laws was tempered almost everywhere by Adultery. He found that the number of illicit unions was vastly superior to the number of happy marriages. . . . But, like a stone cast into the middle of a lake, this observation was lost in the abyss of the author's tumultuous thoughts.'[30]

The second part of Balzac's training took place in the building where his parents had their apartment: Balzac entered the chambers of the family's friend and solicitor Victor Passez in April 1818. Passez is probably the lawyer Balzac describes as an insect in reverse: the bright young butterfly transmuted by his deadening work into 'a larva enfolded in its shroud'.[31] There, he had the opportunity to study bankruptcies and sales. He was sent to deposit money or to obtain signatures on marriage contracts. The real job, says Balzac, was to remain a pillar of virtue in the midst of corruption. His legal education was almost complete: after learning how to draw up contracts, he learned how to get round them. Best of all, he had seen the inside of more homes than many people saw in a lifetime. As Balzac declares in his portrait of 'Le Notaire', after such training, 'it is difficult for a young man to be pure: he will have seen the oily wheels of every fortune, the hideous wrangling of heirs over corpses not yet cold, the human heart grappling with the Penal Code'.[32]

The knowledge Balzac gained was not quite as useful as his father might have hoped. Lawyers seemed to exist to serve the practice, not their clients. Litigants arriving at the chambers of Guillonnet-Merville were greeted symbolically as they crossed the courtyard with pellets of bread shot from the upper windows by the clerks. When they entered the room, looking around for the chair which was carefully not provided, they became the butt of practical jokes and rude insinuations. A few years later, Balzac pretended to give the general public the benefit of his experience in a small handbook for 'Honest People' on 'the art of not being fooled by rogues'. He warns the hapless reader that there is no defence against the legal profession, though he does recommend an investment of 300 francs in wine and truffles (for the clerks). 'No wonder so many people prefer to remain poor.'[33]

When calculating the profit and loss of this portion of Balzac's life, it is usual to imagine the figures of his fiction rising, in skeletal form, from the files. Balzac later thanked Guillonnet-Merville, more abstractly, for teaching him 'enough procedure to conduct the affairs of my little world',[34] and his sister reports a lawyer using *César Birotteau* as a reference work. In some respects, Balzac's imagination had as much need of direct experience as a banker needed banknotes. In his two and a half years as a clerk, he acquired much more than a handful of anecdotes and a set of rules. He knew now of the inexhaustible store of secrets continually amassed by a hypocritical society. He also made a discovery for which there seemed no serious application at the time: that within the language one knew, there was a virtual infinity of other tongues. Legalese coexisted hilariously with the jargon of the clerks: an idiom that went back to the Middle Ages and yet was very modern, with its puns, catch-phrases, distorted proverbs, private allusions and incongruous comparisons.

Despite or because of the atmosphere of corruption, Balzac was happy in his surroundings. The clerks were a lively bunch and included several budding writers. Balzac had come in the wake of a young man who was now making a name for himself as a playwright: Eugène Scribe.[35] The messenger boy, Jules Janin, was the future 'Prince of Critics' who condemned the cynical view of society presented in *Illusions Perdues*.[36] Thanks to two other clerks, both acquaintances of Balzac in the chambers of Maître Passez, he springs to life now in the eyes of his contemporaries on the edge of adulthood:

> In those days he was slender rather than bulky, and thin rather than fat in the face. He had a florid complexion and bright, shining eyes. The way he held himself and the way he walked showed a certain self-satisfaction and bore those marks of vigour and health one commonly finds on provincial faces.[37]

Another contemporary, who had known Balzac at Vendôme, adds the following details: 'thick, black hair in an untidy mess, a bony face, large mouth and, even then, broken teeth'. 'In no way was he a ladies' man.'[38]

Both critics were writing after Balzac's death; but even without his reputation, he seems to have elicited strong reactions. He appeared stupid and clumsy, offensively or amusingly sure of himself, both approachable and private. Almost everyone who met him remembers his dark 'magnetic' eyes as if they belonged to a different body. Most of these early descriptions are coloured either by envy or mere astonishment that Honoré Balzac should have become a great writer:

> The head clerk was a rather jovial fellow who liked his little joke. . . .
> 'D'you know what we found in Balzac's desk?' he said to me one day, roaring with laughter. 'A copy of Montaigne! Balzac reading Montaigne! Ha! ha! ha!' A few months later, I heard that Balzac had left the profession, and the head clerk told me, with another fit of Homeric hilarity, 'Would you believe it? . . . Balzac's writing in the newspapers! . . . He came and showed us some tawdry little theatrical review which had an article by him . . . It was really awful, really silly! . . .' I confess I was quite inclined to believe him.[39]

Honoré had closer relations with older people. Guillonnet-Merville was a 'likeable, witty man'[40] who preferred to conduct business over food and drinks. He remained in touch with his 'dear and glorious pupil' and invited him every year to an anniversary dinner, sometimes enticing him with the promise of 'an affectionate young lady who has come especially'.[41] Balzac dedicated *Un Épisode sous la Terreur* to his former employer. Part of his problem in finding friends of his own age was that he was pursuing an ideal of friendship: 'Since my youngest days, at school, I have been searching, not for friends, but for a friend. I share the opinion of La Fontaine and have yet to find that which my demanding and romantic imagination depicts in such a brilliant light.'[42]

Here, seven years on, Balzac was convincing the Duchesse d'Abrantès of his guileless devotion. But at the time there was another reason for his lack of close friends: his incessant teasing, perhaps better described as an affectionate tampering with the lives of other people. One of the clerks, Édouard Monnais, reports evenings spent drinking punch and playing dance music in the chambers of Maître Passez. When the cards came out, so did Balzac's favourite pun: 'Where's your *monnaie*, Monnais?', and so on *ad nauseam*. (When he became a music critic, Monnais changed his name to 'Paul Smith'.) Balzac's father came in for the same treatment. Honoré liked to send him into a frenzy by pretending to believe that the figures on Chinese vases and screens were actually supposed to be entirely realistic: they lacked perspective because of the peculiar structure of the oriental eyeball.[43]

This delight in manipulating others for sheer pleasure – or to make them more interesting than they were – is easily missed in the adult writer. Balzac was a natural actor and a great applauder of his own performances, and such narcissistic behaviour could be very offensive to other egos.

When women were at stake, Balzac planned his behaviour more carefully. At a party in the home of Maître Passez, he explained to his friend from Vendôme that he could compel an attractive young woman to cross the room and kiss him by projecting magnetic beams in her direction. Failure made little impression on him: 'Before long', he boasted, 'I shall possess the secret of that mysterious power. I shall force all men to obey me and all women to adore me.' On another occasion, Monnais was passing the house in the Rue du Temple when, looking up, he caught sight of Balzac through the bars of the window, arranging his tie by candle-light: 'I can still see the self-satisfied smile on his face; and if I wanted to paint an allegory of Confidence and Alacrity, I should seek no other model.' Since returning to Paris, Balzac had been taking lessons from a dancing master at the Opéra. At the balls on the outskirts of the city where his sisters were paraded in front of prospective suitors, he tried out his skill. After an embarrassing fall, he noticed the women laughing at him and 'vowed to dominate society by some other means than drawing-room graces and accomplishments'.[44]

FROM 1816 TO 1818, Balzac was an assiduous student, but not at the École de Droit. The Sorbonne offered a more attractive programme. Three young professors, all in their twenties, were drawing huge crowds to their lectures.[45] Guizot, the future Prime Minister, was Professor of Modern History. Villemain arrived from the Collège Charlemagne in 1816 to present a wonderfully appetizing view of literature. The old moral judgments gave way to a combination of historical fact and personal sensibility. Works of literature could be studied, not for their cargo of imperishable truths, but as an expression of society. Romanticism had entered academe and, most exotic of all, so had works from other European countries: Goethe, Byron, Walter Scott, and that playwright who until then had been considered too vulgar to be placed on any syllabus – William Shakespeare.

The most influential of the three was Victor Cousin. Amazingly, he taught philosophy without requiring his pupils to reach his own conclusions. He introduced Kant to the French and a generation of Romantic writers to the pleasures of reading without understanding. Cousin's attempt to distil a lasting theory from all previous systems had something of the wishful fundamentalism of Structuralism; but Cousin was opposed to 'geometrical' thought. He dared to make the vague, subjective science of psychology the basis of philosophy, and to identify 'the disinterested emotion of Beauty' as the aim of the Arts – or, as he put it famously, 'Art for Art's sake'.

Balzac caricatured Cousin in 1832 as the man who tried to prove to everyone's satisfaction that Plato was Plato.[46] This was at a time when he believed that writers should propound 'fixed opinions', not send their audience lurching off on oceans of doubt and speculation. In 1818, however, Balzac's antennae were trained on anything which promised intellectual adventure. After lectures, he ran to the library or wandered through the Latin Quarter, looking for rare and curious books, then rushed home 'with his head on fire' to tell his sisters what he had learned. He wanted to roll all his ideas together into an explanation of Everything. At the Natural History Museum, he listened to Cuvier, 'the greatest poet of our century', the man who excavated antediluvian civilizations from the quarries of Montmartre, 'reconstructing worlds from whitened bones, rebuilding cities from teeth, like Cadmus, repopulating a thousand forests with all the wonders of zoology'.[47]

Balzac was inspired to pursue his career as a philosopher. In 1818, he began work on a 'Discourse on the Immortality of the Soul'. His legal training had made him suspicious of systems, and yet here he was searching for his own coherent system of thought. He sounds, significantly, like his atheist father. Immortality, he concludes almost before beginning, is a dangerous fantasy, a product of arrogance and superstition. Man is a single substance, and an 'immaterial substance' is a contradiction in terms. Of all the explanations offered for existence, Balzac favours the Epicurean idea that the world was created when God was drunk.[48] This, of course, was the sceptic's professional joke; but it is interesting to see Balzac blaming creation on a divine failure to use contraception.

The 'anxiety of influence' is not much in evidence in Balzac's jottings, which include an unfinished essay on the nature of poetic genius. Rather, he seems to be cheered on by his predecessors, most of whom he came across in primers and anthologies: Pythagoras, Plato, and the materialist philosophers of the eighteenth century. If anything, Balzac was *under*whelmed by the intellectual achievements of humanity. Confident in the size of his appetite, he drew up a list of the entire range of human inquiry for future reference – 164 items in all, including necromancy, gyromancy, demonography, gastronomy, cosmography, zoology, meteorology, uranography, astronomy, dioptrics, acoustics, pneumatology, psychology, surgery, medicine, pathology, cervology and so on, through megalanthropogeny, differential calculus and cereal-growing, to presbyterianism, numismatology and, finally, diplomacy.[49]

The philosophical substance of Balzac's first literary work, parts of which did not emerge until the 1990 edition of the *Oeuvres Diverses*, is invaluable in tracing the development of his thought. Here, on these large, pale-blue sheets of paper are the first signs of a desire to reconcile positivism and mysticism, and thus, perhaps, to reconcile the opposing views of his father and mother. Both promise immediate access to the Truth. Or, as Raphaël reflects in *La Peau de Chagrin* when remembering his adolescent studies, 'I thought I could clamber up to heaven without a ladder.'[50] With a tone of authority and ponderous excitement, leaving large left-hand margins as if for the teacher's comments, Balzac actually reaches some highly original conclusions. The mystery of genius, for example, might yet be solved, he claims, a hundred years before Saussure, by a study of the principles of language.

The greatest value of these notes is almost incidental. Already, the story of humanity's belief in immortality interests him as much as abstract intricacies. It is significant too that he preserved these juvenile pages and notes scribbled on tiny scraps of paper. To him, they were the first chapter of a remarkable life, early evidence of the birth of genius, a contribution, in short, to 'megalanthropogeny'. For the title of his discourse also refers to the 'immortality' of the writer.

The law clerk's outburst of philosophical writing does indeed mark a great discovery. Returning to prime causes was a way of starting afresh. This time, he would construct his life on his own terms: 'Time had not yet begun its march; Death was not yet born; the Sun appeared for the first time.' Balzac goes on in this section of his discourse to make an intriguing and important pronouncement. He highlights literary expression as the means of discovering and consolidating an identity:

> Many people write so that others will read their thoughts; but the man who wishes to hold fast to that which is solid will write in order to make his reader think. That is my aim.
>
> I may at least be granted the courage of having started with the most disheartening of subjects.[51]

EVEN AT THIS point in his life it is difficult to see where Balzac found enough time. His own view, often expressed in his unhappiest letters, was that he was borrowing years from the future, like the hero of *La Peau de Chagrin*: 'There are still some people who persist in seeing *La Peau de Chagrin* as *a novel*,' he writes in 1838.[52] Apart from his work as a clerk, he was effectively taking two degrees and embarking on a new career. There was only one long interlude, and perhaps it was this that saved him from overheating: summer holidays with an old friend of his father, Villers-La Faye, who was seventy years old – the right age for Honoré.

Villers-La Faye was the mayor of L'Isle-Adam, north-west of Paris on the River Oise in a valley surrounded by forests. The apprentice philosopher and the former priest with Voltairean views enjoyed each other's company. Honoré went dancing and boar-hunting. His host invited pretty girls to the house and, on the local doctor's recommendation, procured him some ass's milk. Perhaps this was a sign of poor health: it was usually prescribed for tuberculosis. Villers-La Faye wanted to help his young friend in his 'great labours'. Balzac described this valley as his 'inspirational paradise'.[53]

Together, they visited the neighbouring estate where a misanthropic millionaire, who used to turn up at the Opéra with gold-dust instead of powder on his wig, had re-created his favourite Italian scenes with a complete lack of taste. The present occupant lived in this Romantic Disneyland with an orang-utan. Balzac saw it trying to play the violin: 'He looked questioningly at the silent wood with an aimless wisdom which had something miraculous and incomplete about it.'

Balzac sympathized. 'The instrument becomes a soul for the artist and a source of melody only after long periods of study.'[54]

CHANCE, 'the greatest novelist',[55] now took a hand. Honoré was about to benefit from a conjunction of three unfortunate events. Bernard-François reached retirement age in April 1819, but was never granted his full pension. Papers went missing, bureaucrats procrastinated and Bernard-François launched a barrage of letters at the Ministry. Was this the reward for his highly acclaimed history of rabies (*Histoire de la Rage*), in which, prophetic as ever, he made out the case for dog licences? He reminded the Minister of his 'extraordinary zeal' in composing an unpublished history of Military Supplies for which he received 'praise so flattering that I dare not think myself worthy of it'. All in vain. The Balzacs, until then quite comfortably off, would have to tighten their belts, particularly since Bernard-François had invested large sums in his employer's bank: it was declared insolvent in 1817. The family prepared for a move to the depressingly small town of Villeparisis, 15 miles to the north-east of Paris, where one of Mme Balzac's cousins had just bought a house.

At the same time, a peculiar incident occurred – something so out of the ordinary that it has frequently been dismissed as irrelevant. One of Honoré's paternal uncles, Louis Balssa, was convicted of strangling a peasant woman who was six months pregnant. On 16 August 1819, in a public square in Albi, he was beheaded. The proceedings had dragged on for a whole year, but the family in Paris, with all its influential connections, did nothing. A guillotined brother could be dreadfully compromising for Bernard-François, who was anxious not to throw any spokes into the wheels of bureaucracy. Louis Balssa had been convicted on the 'evidence' of contradictory rumours, the gossip of his fellow prisoners and, more than anything else, his 'very bad reputation'. Before being led out to the guillotine, he again protested his innocence, claiming that the son of a wealthy family – the same that had given Bernard-François his first job – had paid him 200 francs to say that he was the father of the unborn child. Strangely, his allegation was never investigated. Years later, according to local rumours recorded in 1934, the man accused by Louis Balssa confessed to the murder on his deathbed.[56]

No direct allusion to the trial is made in any of the family's letters, at least not in those that have survived; but we know that Bernard-François was informed of the proceedings by one of his nephews who travelled up from Albi. Did Honoré know too? There is an extraordinary spate of decapitations in his early novels, and perhaps equally revealing is his famous attempt to save Sébastien Peytel from execution in 1839. For Honoré, this would have provided fresh, sinister evidence that respectability in his own family was no more than a thick veneer.

Gossiping neighbours may, then, have hastened their departure for Villeparisis. In the seemingly quiet residential areas of Paris, Balzac estimates the speed of interesting rumour at about 9 m.p.h. When the Duc de Berry was assassinated on the steps of the Opéra in 1820, the news spread to the heart of the Île Saint-Louis in ten minutes.[57]

All eyes now turned on Honoré. There were responsibilities to be faced. Having saved up all his examinations for the end of his course, he passed his first law baccalauréat at the start of 1819. Then, at the worst possible moment, on 1 July, the École de Droit was closed. One of the lecturers had sparked off a controversy over the question of whether émigrés returning to France with the Bourbons should recover their confiscated property. Troops with opinions of their own were sent in, riots ensued and the Government suspended all lectures.[58] Balzac gratefully accepted the excuse. He told Maître Passez that he would not be returning to his desk.

The family seized the opportunity to act out another melodrama. This time, the text was that the ungrateful child had been selfish enough to invent a vocation for himself: he wanted to be a writer! And that was not all: he had had the astonishing good luck to be offered a full-time job by Passez, with the chance to take over the practice after a short apprenticeship. In the circumstances, Honoré's decision was obviously a worrying development; and yet his parents were prepared to fund the experiment, quite generously too.

The inconsistency says much about life in the Balzac household. Seen at a distance of 170 years, people might appear as they would in a hall of mirrors – faintly ludicrous and, whatever their faults, endearing. Drawn into the daylight, the Balzacs retain their distortions. Their taste for play-acting, encouraged by Honoré's enthusiasm and perhaps by boredom, helps to explain why his dunderheaded scheme was funded when he had shown no sign of unusual ability.

Writers were always poor; patrons had vanished with the Revolution. Still, adventures like these, however inconvenient or irritating the consequences, were more entertaining than whist and backgammon.

Family friends were pulled into the pantomime and invited to give their opinion, though the Balzacs kept quiet about the unrefusable offer from Maître Passez. According to one, Honoré's main asset was his elegant handwriting: he would make an excellent bookkeeper.[59] Others blamed the father for being too weak, and Bernard-François agreed: 'It's because nobody would listen to me,' he told his elder daughter that year. 'They softened him up with idle pleasures when he should have been treading the path of toil and hardship that leads to success.' Instead of thrusting on to become head clerk, he continued, Honoré fancied that his time was better spent learning the titles of plays and the names of actors and actresses. 'Not that I condemn that sort of knowledge; but when it gets in the way of the work that really matters . . .'.[60]

It was a dangerous gamble. Honoré was given two years to succeed, or – far more likely and even desirable – to fail. He was installed in August 1819 in a mean little room near the Bibliothèque de l'Arsenal on the eastern edge of the Marais. The Balzacs left for Villeparisis, exhorting Honoré to keep his head down and telling everyone else that he had gone to visit relatives in Albi. Perhaps they were afraid of being thought irresponsible, or perhaps it was simply an amusing conspiracy. In accordance with the game, Honoré would be instructed, via his sisters, to write letters with false addresses, full of made-up news about the Balssas in Albi – though not, of course, about the guillotined uncle.

They were betting that poverty and loneliness would bring him to his senses. Honoré said farewell to the family and returned, excited and determined, to the prison-house of his boyhood.

CHAPTER THREE

Dreams

(1819–1820)

T HERE ARE photographs which claim to show from the outside the attic-room in which Balzac embarked on his new career.[1] Unfortunately, the numbering of the Rue Lesdiguières changed long ago, and the original number 9 was demolished during the construction of the tiny Boulevard Henri IV which joins the Île Saint-Louis to the Place de la Bastille. The narrow side-street which is really Balzac's second birth-place gives no sign of having occupied a moment in literary history. Still mostly residential and with a few self-effacing shops, it seems indifferent even to its name: Lesdiguières or Lesdiguière, with or without a 'de', depending on the direction from which one enters the street.

The room itself is described in some of Balzac's novels: fragments, so he claimed, of autobiography. 'Nothing could be more horrid than that garret with its dirty yellow walls, smelling of poverty.' It was small and had a low ceiling; but Balzac was always able to find wider perspectives: 'Study lends a kind of magic to our surroundings. The flimsy desk at which I wrote . . . the queer designs on the wallpaper, my furniture, everything came to life, every object became my humble friend – silent accomplices in the moulding of my future.'[2]

As I sat at my window, breathing in the air, I allowed my eyes to wander over a landscape of brown, grey or red roofs with slates or tiles covered with green or yellow mosses. The view seemed to me at first monotonous, but I soon discovered peculiar beauties in it. . . . Sometimes the pale glow of the street-lamps cast yellowish reflections up through the fog, showing the roofs in faint outline along the streets, packed together like the waves of a great motionless sea. The fleeting, poetic effects of daylight, the mournful mists, the sudden shimmering of the sun, the silence and magic of night, the mysteries of dawn, the smoke rising from every chimney, each detail of that strange world became familiar to me and entertained me. I loved my prison, for I had chosen it myself.[3]

Balzac had also decided what his prison would look like before he ever saw it. Garrets were well established in the 1820s as the natural breeding ground of poets. France had its own clutch of Chattertons who had either perished in picturesque misery or, like Gilbert, written tearful odes just in time for their funerals. Balzac in turn was supposedly playing the romantic game of Death or Glory, a game in which he was 'both the gambler and the stake'.[4] Friends visiting him in his poetic retreat were suitably impressed by a tallow candle stuck in an empty bottle, a rickety table, a chair losing its straw, a makeshift bed half-concealed by two nasty little curtains, and evidence of a saintly diet: bread, nuts, fruit, and water, not bought but lugged home from the local fountain.[5]

By the time Balzac dictated to a critic the introduction to his *Études Philosophiques* in 1834, his little room had become the centre-piece of a gloriously untruthful painting of himself:

It was during those days of indigence inflicted on him by the will of his Father, who was opposed at that time to the poet's vocation – days to which we owe the splendid story told by Raphaël in *La Peau de Chagrin* – that M. de Balzac, taking refuge in an attic near the Bibliothèque de l'Arsenal, in 1818, 1819 and 1820, laboured unceasingly to compare, analyse and epitomize the studies which the philosophers and physicians of Antiquity, the Middle Ages and the previous two centuries have made of the human mind.[6]

Last and probably least, after the evocative pictures and descriptions, there is what Balzac would have hated to see described as 'the reality'. François Vidocq, a reformed criminal who became head of the Sûreté and ran his own detective business, one day informed the novelist that reality could sometimes be more dramatic than anything found in novels.

BALZAC: Ah! my dear Vidocq. So you believe in reality? How charming! I never should have thought you so naive. Reality! You must tell me all about it. You've actually been to that wonderful land. Come off it! *We're* the people who make reality.[7]

It must hardly be worth mentioning, therefore, that Balzac's ivory tower was not an attic at all. It was a room on the respectable third floor; and if near-starvation kept his mind 'in a state of singular lucidity',[8] it was either by choice or because he had forgotten to go out for supplies. Neither was the prisoner of the Rue Lesdiguières entirely alone. The Balzacs' old housekeeper carried letters to and from Villeparisis, staggering up the stairs with baskets of laundry or potatoes and fruit from the garden. There were visits too from Théodore Dablin, the only family friend who knew that Honoré was not recovering from an illness in Albi but lying low in the city.[9] Dablin, a retired ironmonger, was a nuts-and-bolts sort of man; it was he who had recommended a career in bookkeeping. Balzac respected honest opinions, and when it came to his writing (or what Dablin sarcastically called his 'children'), he was mature enough to hear unpleasant truths. There are several letters in which he urges the 'perfidious' Dablin to come and criticise his work: 'You are under the impression that I live a long way from you, but that's a philosophical error. If you read Newton, you'd realize that I'm but a step away.'[10] From time to time, family members also dropped in: the Balzacs had kept a pied-à-terre in the Rue du Temple as an escape-valve. When the bickering reached a climax they could sweep off to Paris for a few days and sulk at an impressive distance.

It would be a travesty of poetic justice if the room in the Rue Lesdiguières did not appear in so many different guises, because its occupant was also a product of his own imagination. Balzac had several different faces, and the curiously incompatible portraits which exist of him seem to confirm the fact that his characters were not just the result of observation but parts of his own personality. This is the period during which he became, at least for a time, a dramatist, a novelist, a satirist, a sociologist, a man of leisure in the day and a galley-slave at night, a recluse and a *flâneur*, and even, according to one of his letters, a werewolf. Balzac was discovering that an image was one of the tools of his trade, as essential as a goose quill or a bottle of ink. His first act of freedom was, as usual, appropriate. His mother had given him a mirror and was outraged to learn that he had bought himself another one – a square mirror with a gilt frame. What could Honoré possibly want with two mirrors?

An answer lies, perhaps, in the unpublished text entitled *Théorie du Conte*. Balzac depicts himself, in something resembling a biographer's nightmare, opening the door into the writer's secret retreat:

> Yesterday, when I returned home, I saw a countless number of copies of my own person, all jammed up against one another like herrings in a barrel. They sent my face reverberating off towards some magical horizon, just as the light of a lamp placed in the middle of a drawing-room is repeated to infinity between two facing mirrors.[11]

Even without visitors, Balzac was rarely alone. There is even proof – scientific proof – that the room stuffed full of Balzacs was more than a novelist's fantasy:

> One day, I went along with Mme de Girardin to the Rue du Bac to see Dupotet the hypnotizer. Out of curiosity he gave my hand to his best somnambulist. She, having placed my hand on her stomach, dropped it with a start. 'What sort of mind is that?!' she said. '*It's a world*. It *scares* me.'[12]

Literary criticism by divination is rarely practised nowadays, but its general conclusions appear to be as reliable as those reached by more conventional forms of analysis.

These competing voices reach a discordant climax in Balzac's early letters and notes. Voices in search of a novel which bear witness to his indecision, or, more precisely, to a series of decisions, each one wholeheartedly embraced. At the Bibliothèque de l'Arsenal, he continued, if not to sum up every intellectual achievement since Antiquity, at least to argue imaginatively with philosophers of the past. He undertook a translation of Spinoza's impenetrable *Ethics* (an obscure but significant moment in the history of philosophy in France), and tried to re-create the intellectual arena of 200 years before. Balzac places Descartes in the ring with his principal commentators and steps in to throw some punches of his own: '*Je pense, donc je suis*, you say, but in my opinion you could also say, *Je suis, donc je pense*. . . . You doubt material existence and should therefore also doubt your doubting.'[13] Despite the characteristic objection to Descartes's agonizing over imponderables, these philosophical essays are not quite as instructive as they seem. They represent only one aspect of Balzac at the age of twenty. Descartes and Spinoza shared the room with more trivial and troublesome voices. 'You wanted to hear how I'm settling in, dear sister. . . . Well, I've engaged a servant! – A servant, dear brother? What *are* you thinking of? – He's called Myself. . . . He starts to sweep the room, but he's not very good at it. – Don't make so much dust! – But Sir, I can't see any dust. – Hold your tongue and get on with it, you sophist.'[14] Imaginative creation was already, paradoxically, a form of procrastination.

In view of this constant fermentation of myth and reality, it scarcely matters, then, that the 'aerial tomb'[15] from which Balzac's characters first emerged no longer exists. For, as he says, autobiographically, of Gambara the brilliant composer, 'without being drunk, he was in that state when all one's intellectual powers are overexcited, when the walls of a room begin to glow, when garrets lose their roofs and the soul flies about in the world of spirits'.[16]

AFTER A WEEK of settling in – painting the walls white, making a screen out of blue paper, hanging his mirrors – 'the bachelor on the third floor'[17] sat down to work. He very soon postponed his philosophical investigations, probably with some relief at his own decision. Veering to the other extreme, he hatched the plot of a comic opera entitled *Le Corsaire*. It was based on the latest Romantic import: Byron's tale of Conrad the pirate. The *pièce de résistance* was to have been the song of the jolly rovers gloating about their life of freedom on the dark blue sea. Unfortunately, Balzac's *Corsaire* ran into an insuperable difficulty: 'Where the devil am I going to find a composer?'[18]

Reflecting that Posterity would be more likely anyway to open its doors to a work properly dressed in rhyming alexandrines, he decided to compose a five-act tragedy in verse: *Cromwell*. This was a huge undertaking, especially for someone who was suffering horribly from toothache: 'A tragedy is normally supposed to contain *2000* lines. That means having between 8 and 10,000 thoughts, without counting all the other thoughts needed for the ideas, the plan, the characters, the situations, the customs of the time,' etc.[19] Perhaps the ironmonger was right to see Balzac as a natural accountant. Devising 2000 lines which satisfy all the rules of French versification, particularly when the writer was not a natural poet, has something of the mechanical activity which Balzac claims all great writers need. Bayle counted roof-tiles; Spinoza polished lenses; Balzac, later, methodically read every entry in Michaud's biographical dictionary.[20] The incidental benefits derived from writing *Cromwell* would be less apparent.

The subject Balzac had chosen was a fashionable one, and he was not alone in choosing it. The young Mérimée was about to attempt a *Cromwell* in prose. Five years later, Hugo's imperious manifesto of the Romantic movement would appear as a preface to his own *Cromwell*. In 1819, Balzac was following in the footsteps of one of his favourite lecturers, Villemain, who had just published an erudite *Histoire de Cromwell*. It was modern history in disguise: Cromwell was Napoleon and Charles I, Louis XVI. Balzac, too, hoped, with astonishing optimism, that his work would become 'the breviary of kings and nations'.[21]

Any monarch using *Cromwell* for such a purpose would be courting disaster. Balzac's ideal state seems to be a benevolent constitutional monarchy; but the message is garbled by the characters themselves. Trapped under the ice of classical conventions, they nevertheless have a disturbing tendency (as do many of Balzac's characters) to wriggle free of their author's meticulous plans. Charles dies a noble victim of the machiavellian Cromwell, who, for all his evil scheming, is supposed to represent the inalienable right of freedom. At the end of the play, Cromwell 'lingeringly savours the blood of his prey', while Queen Henrietta wisely returns to her native France, expressing the wish that 'execrable Albion' might be swallowed up by the sea.

Cromwell tends now to groan under the weight of Balzac's mature work, but the play is still quite readable on its own terms. Several years before French Romantic drama finally stumbled into its infancy, Balzac's *Cromwell* shows symptoms of what was to come: a historical subject and a melodramatic setting among the tombs of Westminster Abbey. The woodenness of the characters says more about French classical theatre, 200 years old and showing its age, still corseted in 'Aristotelian' rules. For the same reason, it would be unfair to accuse Balzac, as many have done, of filching lines from other playwrights. The term 'plagiarism' is practically meaningless in a literary form which, like popular music today, was largely a matter of rearranging existing phrases. With his practical, beginner's approach to inspiration and his talent for mimicry, Balzac recognized the genre for what it was. Stark originality was not a virtue and any good lines were fair game. The manuscript includes a memo headed 'Imitations for *Cromwell*',[22] and at one point Balzac notes drily in the margin: 'This is a verse which I took without scruple from Racine, who took it from Corneille, who took it from Rotrou, who probably borrowed it from someone else.'[23]

As winter approached, Balzac was spending most of his weekly allowance on firewood so he could work through the night. By candle-light, he struggled with his alexandrines, stuffing his thoughts into twelve-syllable segments, driven on by his dreams: 'Nothing, nothing but love and glory can fill the vast space that is in my heart.' 'If I'm not a genius, I'm done for,' he told Laure. 'I shall have to spend my whole life as a mediocrity, stuck with my desires.' 'If by chance there's any Genius for sale in Villeparisis, buy me as much as you can. . . . I'm in desperate need of it.'[24]

Six months later, in the spring of 1820, *Cromwell* was finished – all 1906 lines of it. Balzac took it to Villeparisis and read it out in front of the family and a group of friends. After what must have been almost two hours if he read the whole play, there was an embarrassed silence. The verdict was a unanimous yawn.

Mme Balzac wanted an expert opinion on what she saw as her investment. So much laudable hard work must have produced something of value. Laure was about to marry a young canal engineer called Eugène Surville.[25] Surville asked his old tutor from the École Polytechnique, Andrieux, to read the manuscript, which had been copied out by Mme Balzac. A few days later, Laure and her mother paid him a visit. In a touching act of criminal devotion, Laure stole the scrap of paper on which Andrieux had made his notes, and thus preserved the first authoritative judgment of Balzac's work: 'The author should do *anything he likes, but not literature*.'[26]

Balzac, as Laure puts it sardonically, did not go out and hang himself. Like his father, he had a frightening capacity for believing that his original premise had been correct. When Bernard-François heard of a man who had indulged himself in every conceivable manner and yet lived beyond 100, he concluded: 'Well, he obviously shortened his life, didn't he?'[27] Similarly, Honoré deduced that he was simply not meant to be a tragedian. It appeared that this was also the considered view of Andrieux. When Mme Balzac returned the stolen notes, he told her that, with a guiding hand, her son might well become a writer, but never a dramatist.[28] Balzac's contemporaries would have several opportunities to offer him the same piece of advice.

Two years later, Balzac himself admitted that *Cromwell* was 'worthless' and could not even claim to be an 'embryo'.[29] Yet however much one might agree with its progenitor's opinion, the miracle is that *Cromwell does* exist. Balzac was tackling something so contrary to his genius that the will to succeed is more impressive than the play itself. Reading *Cromwell* and comparing it with Balzac's later works gives the impression of a salmon struggling against the current, not losing but gaining strength, hoping to reach the quiet waters upstream where it will eventually spawn. In 1820, to everyone but the author, it seemed as though this particular fish had been swimming up the wrong stream.

IN THE MEANTIME, Balzac had made some interesting discoveries almost by accident. It was impossible to spend time with philosophers and tragedians without being beaten into submission by tedious difficulties or unattainable excellence. He soothed his mind by reading novels which he picked up at the Palais-Royal or rented at *cabinets de lecture*. Novels, of course, were a waste of time – books written mainly by women and read by servants. To an educated person, there was something inherently immoral about a genre which allowed the author to say anything and at any length. Novels, Flaubert's *Dictionnaire des Idées Reçues* decrees, 'pervert the masses'; or, as Balzac's father liked to say half a century before, 'Novels are to Europeans what opium is to the Chinese.'[30]

There are several scenes in *La Comédie Humaine* in which Balzac shows what happens to ordinary people when they take a dose of this literary opium. The solicitor's wife in *Modeste Mignon*, for instance, samples what she takes to be an English novel, *Childe Harold's Pilgrimage*:

Perhaps it had something to do with the translation, but it gave me quite a turn. My eyelids began to flutter. I couldn't go on. There are some impossible comparisons: rocks swooning, the lava of war! . . . It's like an Englishman on holiday: you have to expect some strange behaviour, but there are limits! . . . And there are too many virgins! . . . It's exasperating!³¹

Remembering his own beginnings which, even in a happy mood, he thought of as a wasteful apprenticeship, Balzac liked to distance himself from what he saw as exploitative writers. But passages like these suggest his first excitement at the possibility of affecting people directly and dramatically, of infiltrating the reader's bloodstream like a drug and bringing hordes of admiring women to his door. One day these dreams would be realized. In the 1820s, it was not the sort of writing that normally brought distinction. In France at least, what we think of as the nineteenth-century novel did not exist. The Empire variety, as one of Balzac's characters puts it, was a crude combination of plot summary and speech for the prosecution:³² one thing after another and a moral at the end. Tastes, however, were becoming more refined. Sophisticated foreign novels were in demand. As usual, chauvinism managed to coexist with mass importing from the enemy nation of what some regarded as commercial rubbish: grim and gory tales of the supernatural, the Gothic novels of Ann Radcliffe and Walpole, Maturin's Melmoth (who resurfaces later in Balzac's modern Paris), and Matthew 'Monk' Lewis's cowl-and-dagger tale of lust and megalomania. Ruined castles, dungeons, ghouls, bad weather and, of course, virgins had never been so popular.

The early 1820s also saw the first outbreak of *walterscottomanie*.³³ Translations began to appear in Paris: *L'Antiquaire, Ivanhoë, La Fiancée de Lammermoor, Les Aventures de Nigel*. Tartan became fashionable for women. There were Walter Scott plays and paintings, furnishings and fancy-dress balls. Edinburgh became a place of literary pilgrimage. One reviewer was even moved to cry. '*Vivent l'Angleterre et les Anglais* [sic]!' Not only had Walter Scott crossed the Channel, which, like the Rhine, was still a great cultural barrier, he had also bridged the gap between the salons on the first floor and the servants' rooms on the sixth.

Balzac read the novels and was spellbound. This was not the constant nagging of moral points or the endless stream of impossibilities, but the mysterious entanglements of Nature and mood. Characters, by no means all aristocratic, expressed themselves exotically in something resembling normal speech. The reader was transported like a tourist to places where the past had never been laid to rest but where it coloured and inspired the present, where the smallest artefact was an emblem or a key to another world. The mixture of 'authentic' detail and romantic adventure was a powerful potion whose effects survived the reading of the novels.

These first sightings of a new literary continent were a great encouragement and consolation to Balzac in his room. Here was proof that there need be no official segregation of noble sentiments on the one hand and trivial perceptions on the other. Even perched in the philosophical crow's-nest, surveying the great unanswerable questions, his mind was turning to less abstract dramas. Balzac's notes on the atheist philosopher Baron d'Holbach end with a phrase of enormous accidental significance – a phrase which throws a bridge between these two parts of Balzac's life and between two literary forms: 'In *Sténie*, when I have Job deny the existence of God, he uses other arguments. True, he makes some logical errors, but he does so wittingly and in order to seduce his mistress.'[34] Philosophy in action: eternal truths soon lost their interest, but sin was always original.

The other attraction of the novel for the author of *Cromwell* was that it did not have to rhyme. It was almost as easy as writing letters, especially when the letter-writer himself was already a half-fictional creature, not wasting time in Paris but visiting relatives in Albi. Best of all, the novel had popular appeal. With the spread of literacy it, too, might lead to glory, albeit via the back-streets. The idea of extracting profit from idle amusement was like an offer from the Devil. Balzac's gradual discovery of his product and its market does indeed have something magical, even immoral, about it. His later obsession with 'purity' and the loss of literary virginity sounds suspiciously like a judgment on his own decision to take what seemed at first the smoothest path.

Balzac's earliest novels date from this period of voluntary imprisonment: *Sténie*, *Falthurne* and *Corsino*. None were ever finished, and perhaps none *could* be finished. Each one goes off in a different direction, and together they form a highly personal anthology of contemporary fashions in the French novel. But they also lead back to the fantastic room milling with Balzacs. Discovering the Novel, Balzac was discovering himself.

The earliest is probably *Sténie*, begun towards the end of 1819 and abandoned in 1822. Appropriately subtitled *Les Erreurs Philoso-phiques*, it begins with the following declaration: 'Do not expect to find in my letters the method, eloquence and audacious philosophy for which you gave me so much false praise in the meetings of our little academy where we debated so passionately the great questions concerning human happiness.' It is most unlike Balzac to start with an excuse, but this was unfamiliar territory. The subject, however, was not.

Sténie is an epistolary novel – the variety which had the most respectable antecedents. It tells the sad story of a young man's love for his 'sister' – the girl who was raised by the same nurse on the outskirts of Tours. They meet again in adolescence when Job saves Sténie from drowning in the Loire, always richly symbolic in Balzac. They fall in love, but, true to her Romantic roots, Sténie is engaged to another man – a tediously reasonable fellow called M. Plancksey. What follows is a tragic tale of duty and passion, with echoes of Rousseau, amplified by the unmistakable accents of Bernard-François and perhaps by the contrary views of Balzac's mother, for whom Man was born depraved but is everywhere too much at liberty. Technically, it was an ambitious novel, its form precluding any direct intervention from the novelist, but for all its clumsiness, it still manages to carry the reader along on a wave of sexual frustration. Balzac was feeding on his own life. Some of the autobiographical elements are a predictable product of experi-ence or lack of it. The Balzac household is much in evidence, for example in the idea that love and marriage are mutually exclusive. Other personal echoes are more surprising, particularly Job's almost incestuous love for Sténie – a common enough theme in Romantic fiction, but it may be no coincidence that Balzac began his first novel at exactly the time when his 'dear, kind, lovable and loving little sister'[35] Laure was being courted by her future husband.

Shortly after Laure's marriage in May 1820, Balzac created a splendidly improbable and sexually ambiguous character in his second attempt at a novel, eventually entitled *Falthurne*. Again, there are hints that this literary form of relaxation could also become a kind of intelligent mirror. Falthurne is the first of many seductively androgyn-ous creatures in Balzac's work. Like the junior clerk with his magnetic eye-beams, Falthurne has inherited the ancient wisdom of the East. For the purposes of the story, ancient oriental wisdom means those naturally occurring powers which, it seems, anyone can harness, at their own peril: walking through walls, seeing into the future, being preternaturally beautiful and, like a good novelist, controlling people's emotions. The scene is set, rather skimpily, in Naples in the tenth century; the background, borrowed from Gibbon's *Decline and Fall*, is the Norman invasion of Italy, and the ostensible subject is the hostility of the Church to the transcendent wisdom of Falthurne.

The real subject is Balzac. Here, as in *Sténie*, one feels that writing itself expresses urges not easily put into print. Unlike Dickens with his bluntly significant names, Balzac tends to brand his imaginary flock with more subtle, cryptic designs. By his own account, names have a spell-like quality. 'Falthurne', we are told, is an amalgam of two Greek words ($\phi\alpha\lambda o\varsigma$ and $\tau v\rho\alpha\nu\nu o\varsigma$) which together mean something like 'tyranny of light'.[36] Balzac later assured Mme Hanska, with surprising seriousness, that this was indeed the correct and intended etymology. She, being familiar with Balzac's sexual appetites, had obviously reflected on the possible root of the first syllable – *phal(lus)* – or certainly would have done when she saw Balzac spell the first word, perhaps by mistake: $\phi\alpha\lambda\lambda v\varsigma$. Did Balzac not tell her that sometimes he had to work himself up to write a novel by 'masturbating his brain'?[37] Time and again, his unsqueamish comments on the act of creation hint strongly that, no matter how brilliant or successful, writing could only be a partial satisfaction.

Falthurne is a thick, murky broth concocted by too many cooks. An Italian manuscript written by a certain Abbé Savonati is unearthed by a soldier in Napoleon's army. He leaves it with his uncle, a primary-school teacher called M. Matricante who, undaunted by his ignorance of Italian, translates it. M. Matricante grumbles and winces at the Abbé's esoteric mumbo-jumbo, apologizes for improbabilities (there are many), adds a few Romantic images of his own, complains about the niggardly pension which drove him into print in the first place, and, as if in passing, makes some highly perceptive remarks:

> What leads me to accredit the truth of what great Savonati has conveyed to us is the way in which he conscientiously tells us everything. In novels written nowadays, writers pay little heed to their heroes' stomachs. They send them off on errands, embroil them in adventures which leave them as breathless as the reader, and yet they are never hungry. In this respect, they bear little resemblance to

the author. In my opinion, this, more than anything else, serves to discredit this type of work. Does anybody eat in *René*? . . . Whatever period you depict, you will find that people had dinner.[38]

Like so many serious artistic innovations, the Realist novel first emerges with a self-conscious smile on its face.

Balzac was still imitating rather than innovating, laughing at his own attempts to be a modish writer. As the blundering footnotes of *Falthurne* suggest, he was even sneering at the hackneyed device of the discovered manuscript which allowed him to laugh at himself. . . . Confusion worse confounded? To judge by the more florid purple passages, Balzac was wise to restrain himself. His natural tendency was to exaggerate and embellish, and most of his work at this time combines portentous statements about existence with a rather watery kind of wit. M. Matricante's ridiculous interventions show that Balzac was fully aware of his limits or, worse, his absence of limits.

Since none of the letters written by Balzac in 1820 have survived (who would have bothered to keep them?), these fragments are of special interest. They present a bewildering, contradictory image of the writer as sorcerer's apprentice: ebullience alternating with embarrassment, determination with doubt, grandiloquence with discretion, self-indulgence with self-denial. Most of all, a composite quality associated with creatures such as werewolves and vampires: a monstrous egotism (to which Balzac disarmingly confesses) and a desire to inhabit other bodies. The manuscripts from the Rue Lesdiguières lead through a lurid gallery of self-portraits, some highly flattering, others repulsive apparitions glimpsed in the looking-glass. The colossal conceit of inventing Falthurne, for example, is mocked by a burlesque monk called Bongarus. The monk's physiognomy betrays the characteristic 'stupidity of genius': like Balzac, he is expelled from his monastic school; Bongarus is far too clever for his teachers. Though Balzac was growing thin in his garret, he also seems to have a physical premonition of himself. A large stomach, a triple chin, a square head, thick hair plastered down and one redeeming feature (in this alone, Bongarus differs from the future Balzac) – 'magnificent teeth'.

The most striking of these antithetical images provides the basis of the last novel conceived in the Rue Lesdiguières: *Corsino*. Here again, Balzac seems to be preparing to do battle with himself.

Corsino has noticed a curious discrepancy in the world: Nature is serene and simple, but Society is full of spurious complications. Complications which, for example, allow university professors to earn a living by explaining them to other people. Corsino decides to combine the amorality of Nature with the convenience of Society and lives in a delightful state of utter selfishness in the north of Scotland. A Marquis de Sade of the Highlands.

Corsino has a friend with an anagram for a name: Néhoro. Néhoro/Honoré is knowledgeable, wise, pure of heart, generous, loving and horrendously ugly. The manuscript ends after fifteen pages and we never find out whether the two friends destroy each other or reach a happy compromise. No doubt the dénouement would have involved Maria, the local angel of mercy who lives like a peasant and looks like a queen. Balzac, suddenly failing to keep a straight face, notes that this exquisite girl 'would be a lucky find for any novelist who had to tell this story'.

In 'real life' Balzac was hoping for just such a lucky find. Now that Laure was married, he had lost his 'muse', and without a muse, the reason for writing in the first place was no longer quite so obvious. Each time his immediate female audience disappears, a worrying gap opens up; the original aim seems to vanish. These are the only times when Balzac comes close to having writer's block. Behind his gleeful contemplation of these divergent paths and personae was a disturbing question. Can the emptiness be filled with the creatures that emptiness itself produced? Or are there hidden dangers? Balzac often laments the fact that he was detained too long in childhood by his writing. For an exceptional writer, he was in very close coincidence with the fiction of his age. The Romantic hero, too, often takes the form of that curious and unhappy creature: an ugly Narcissus. But sometimes the pool into which he stares acquires an unexpected depth and beauty, and even comes to life itself.

In the opening pages of *Sténie*, Balzac returns to Tours, in fact to the very street in which he was born, the 'unchanging street with changing names'. (The Rue de l'Armée d'Italie had now been rechristened the Rue Royale.) The familiar view unravels, as if unhappiness remembered could be forgotten: 'The city is round, and its western edge has the finest view in the world, equal to that of Naples.' Now, however, it contains previews of future retreats and

pleasures, the humble pastimes of the property-owner and the vora-
cious lover:

> As you follow the hill, gradually the cottages with their smoking
> chimneys grow more sparse and in the curves and angles of the
> hillside, country houses catch your eye, replacing the thought of
> poverty with an image of wealth and its delights. . . . Finally, like a
> ghost, the pointed tower of Roche-Corbon rises above the enchant-
> ing landscape around Vouvray. . . . And then one's gaze is lost in the
> bluish distance which leaves you wanting still more. Nature, in these
> parts, resembles those flirtatious women who conceal their treasures
> so that imagination will increase them.[39]

BEFORE LEAVING the Rue Lesdiguières, one other Balzac remains
to be mentioned, perhaps the most secret of them all. 'The open-air
Balzac', Henry James wrote in 1875, 'has been little commemorated.'[40]
Even now, the standard image is the darkened room, the monk's robe,
the writing hand, the inexhaustible pot of coffee; Balzac in a picture,
like his characters, indissociable from the furniture. But in the evenings, when he could venture out without fear of being recognized,
he had begun to indulge in a peculiar hobby:

> I was living then in a little street which you probably do not
> know: the Rue de Lesdiguières. . . . Only one passion could ever
> drag me from my studious routine; and even that was a form of
> study. I used to go out in order to observe life in the *faubourg*, its
> people and their character. Being as poorly dressed as the workers
> and paying no heed to decorum, I aroused no suspicions. I was able
> to mingle with them as they stood in groups, haggling and quarrel-
> ling with one another as they left their work. Observation had
> already become for me an intuitive activity; it allowed me to
> penetrate the soul without disregarding the body; or rather, it
> comprehended outward detail so well that in the same instant it
> passed beyond. It imbued me with the power to live the life of the
> individual I was observing, to substitute myself for him, like the
> dervish in the Arabian Nights who takes over the body and soul of
> those over whom he utters certain words.
>
> When, between eleven o'clock and midnight, I came across a
> worker and his wife returning together from the Ambigu-Comique,

I would amuse myself by following them from the Boulevard du Pont-aux-Choux as far as the Boulevard Beaumarchais. . . . In listening to these people I could espouse their lives. I felt their rags upon my back; I walked with my feet in their tattered shoes; their desires, their wants – everything passed into my soul, or my soul passed into theirs. It was the dream of a waking man.[41]

This 'optical gastronomy',[42] as Balzac calls it elsewhere, seems so natural and everyday to its possessor that we tend when we read about it to equate it with something quite unremarkable in ourselves, making allowances for the storyteller's patter. Yet this was more than just informed reverie or a cunning meditation. Balzac's 'dream' was a kind of hallucination which feeds not on fantasy but on truth, a detailed vision which could be summoned up and modified at will, and which explains, better than any chronological list of visits and investigations, why his subjective history of nineteenth-century France exudes completeness and infallibility.

This new-found faculty was heightened by the need to remain incognito. During his furtive walks in the streets or when watching a play at the Comédie Française from a screened box, he was forced to examine every face. His parents' snobbish deceit is partly responsible for the fact that some of Balzac's tales foreshadow the modern detective novel. The solitary philosopher or – an apt expression – the private eye gathers the strands of a mystery by means of his superior logic, remaining anonymous in a city where 'things are numbered, houses guarded, streets kept under surveillance'.[43] Spies, for Balzac, count among the closest analogues of the literary genius.[44]

The fact that the 'open-air Balzac' remained hidden from view for so long says much about the age he lived in. A bourgeois writer tracking passers-by at dusk could be up to no good. Balzac himself considered his imaginings for a time as something faintly reprehensible or even dangerous: 'Is it second sight, or one of those gifts which, if abused, would lead to madness?' 'A lunatic is often a man who dresses up his thoughts and turns them into beings which he can see and talk to.'[45] Balzac constantly resorts to these wilful hallucinations, not only for 'material' but also as an escape from unhappiness and worry. His insistence on prime causes and fundamental beliefs comes to seem a necessary support. However much they contradict the apparent laws of his fictional world, these tenets are also the walls which mark off the limits of an Empire.

There is also a more plainly social reason for the relative neglect of the prowling novelist. Walking in the streets for pleasure was still a novelty; and it was only pleasant if the walker kept to the new boulevards with their stone pavements and gas-lighting. Balzac's quartier, on the other hand, was wedged in the seamy perimeter of the city at the tail-end of the boulevards – not the best place for an evening stroll.[46] Most of Paris was still almost medievally filthy. As Rastignac discovers in *Le Père Goriot*, it was impossible to save on cab-money and still arrive for dinner with shiny shoes and clean tails. The streets had changed little since an English traveller, Arthur Young, visited the city in 1787 and found it 'the most ineligible and inconvenient for the residence of a person of small fortune of any that I have seen':

> Walking, which in London is so pleasant and so clean, that ladies do it every day, is here a toil and a fatigue to a man, and an impossibility to a well-dressed woman. The coaches are numerous, and what are much worse, there are an infinity of one-horse cabriolets, which are driven by young men of fashion and their imitators, alike fools, with such rapidity as to be real nuisances, and render the streets exceedingly dangerous, without an incessant caution. I saw a poor child run over and probably killed, and have been myself many times blackened with the mud of the kennels. This beggarly practice, of driving a one-horse booby hutch about the streets of a great capital, flows either from poverty or wretched and despicable economy.[47]

It is worth remembering that this mud, which nineteenth-century writers repeatedly talk of gilding or transmuting into gold, was mud of a particularly unpleasant and varied constitution. Balzac was seen more than once sporting it on his clothes in respectable establishments. Rubbing shoulders with the city and writing about it was a rare combination.

Balzac's descent into the street is a great moment in literature. He seems to have suspected its importance as early as 1822, long before the first novels which would eventually take their place in *La Comédie Humaine*. In a strange little story, also abandoned, he retraced one of his foraging expeditions in 1819–20. The title of the story is *Une Heure de ma Vie* and it begins with a typically materialist view of mental processes: 'One day, I needed to replenish my brain which was suffering from a heavy loss of thought.' The narrator takes his depleted mind to the Palais-Royal, the perfect place to look for 'pompous' ideas for his tragedy. After a few minutes of cerebral window-shopping, he suddenly finds himself, like Byron on the Bridge of Sighs, standing in a symbolic position. On the one hand, the Comédie Française, the young tragedian's Mecca; on the other, 'a spectacle which often presents itself to the Parisian eye and in front of which one normally passes with indifference': a beggar whose rags inspire the observer with a thousand conjectures. At this point, *Cromwell* fades into the background.

By the time he wrote this story early in 1822, Balzac had already come to a literary conclusion: History had always been a panorama of all the doings of those enormous human flocks called nations; but so far, only the shepherds and sheepdogs had come under scrutiny: 'there is still a great deal to be done.' With a sort of matter-of-fact originality, which Balzac himself could not have fully recognized in 1822, he sees that uncommon views call for unconventional frames. With its echoes of Laurence Sterne and its prefiguration of the Realist novel, *Une Heure de ma Vie* shows how Balzac's habit of inflating microcosms, of extracting a story from a tiny starting-point, sets the novel on a path which leads to Proust and Joyce. It is significant, though, that the story was never published. Balzac wanted to achieve his aims before he died; and to someone who had yet to find himself, that meant imitating first and innovating later. Yet for all his hard work and his habit of writing with one eye on the prize, like many writers in a period of change, he was ripening in idleness.

Many of Balzac's walks took him out beyond the edge of the city, towards the factories in the east, 'the *faubourg*, the open road, the majesty of nothingness': 'one of the most magnificent parts of Paris, with its stunning view'.[48] Here, the new Père Lachaise cemetery, which opened its gates in 1804, had become a fashionable place for an evening constitutional among the tombs before returning in a carriage to the city. Balzac went there to do research for *Cromwell*, because, as he told Laure, 'Of all the emotions of the soul, Grief is the most difficult to depict.'[49] His research trips bore little fruit. When Charles I is led off to the scaffold, Henrietta's monologue ends with what can only be described as a cheap trick: 'Great God! Extreme misfortune! . . .

Unhappy woman! Be silent! . . . Your cries are in vain!' But Balzac felt at home among the dead, in this 'microcosmic' Paris with its streets and house-numbers, and its decor of pyramids and obelisks, Grecian temples, Moorish genies and Gothic ruins. It was like a library of books containing only first and last lines. One day, he found the tomb of an army major who was known to the family: 'The inscription read, "Here lies M. Mallet . . . passed away 5 August 1819. . . . This monument erected by his *inconsolable* widow." Think about that! If you ask me, he must have written it himself.'[50]

At Père Lachaise, Balzac dreamed of posterity. The writer, he thought, must become dead to the world for many years before emerging, as he had planned to do, from his 'aerial tomb' with a masterpiece in hand. Significantly, this necropolis looming over the living city forms the backdrop of the theatrical end of *Le Père Goriot*. Rastignac buries the father who has been shamelessly abandoned by his daughters – one of whom, Mme de Nucingen, has become Rastignac's mistress and his passport to high society. Then, left alone in the failing light, the twenty-one-year-old hero merges with his creator:

> He walked up towards the highest part of the cemetery, and saw Paris spread out below him along the two banks of the winding Seine. Lights were beginning to shine. His eyes fastened themselves almost greedily upon the space that lay between the column of the Place Vendôme and the dome of the Invalides.[51] There lay that glittering world he had hoped to conquer. He stared at that humming hive as if sucking out its honey in advance, and pronounced these impressive words: 'It's you or me, now!'
>
> And by way of throwing down the gauntlet to Society, Rastignac went to dine with Mme de Nucingen.

CHAPTER FOUR

Gutter Poetry

(1821–1822)

WHEN THE LEASE on his room expired at the end of 1820, so did Balzac's hopes of an easy victory. Unlike Rastignac, he had no invitations from beautiful women married to fabulously rich bankers, and there was no arch-criminal to mastermind his conquest of Society. He had several reams of paper comprising a finished tragedy which nobody liked and some unfinished novels which no one had read. In September, Balzac had been exempted from military service when he drew a high enough number in the lottery. The exemption certificate gives his height as 5 feet 2 inches (well below the average) and his profession, belatedly, as 'law student'. It was about as accurate as giving his profession as 'writer'. The only dinner invitation came from home: his father saw him wasting away to nothing, expending all his precious life-force in orgies of thinking. Laure was about to leave with her husband for Bayeux, and Honoré would take her place at Villeparisis. Hopefully, he would be able to contribute his share to the family finances. He was to stay in Villeparisis, on and off, for the next two years.

Yet, like Rastignac in the inauspicious Pension Vauquer, Balzac was on the verge of meeting two fairy godmothers who would set him on the road to Glory. One, a real 'angel',[1] would provide him with a thread to enter the labyrinth with new confidence; the other, who concerns us more particularly in this chapter, was a less heavenly sort of angel who offered him an axe with which to hack his way straight through to the centre. In the space of a few months, Balzac would learn the trick of converting his dreams into money – but at what cost to himself and his writing?

This is a curious period, almost an anomaly in Balzac's life. Every life, especially that of a writer, suggests the ideal course it might have taken; but these years seem to create a gulf too wide to have been

[73]

bridged by the same person. Large parts of it have therefore been swept under the carpet by many of Balzac's biographers, impatient to reach the 'true' Balzac or perhaps concerned not to tarnish the idol. Balzac himself rarely mentions his apprenticeship as a money-making author, except as a continuation of his struggle up from obscurity, or, obliquely, as part of the sentimental education of Lucien de Rubempré, the central character of *Illusions Perdues*. But since the origins of genius interest him in his novels as much as those of complete idiocy, neither did he forget the struggle. It was the foundation of his own genius, the misery which preceded and explained the splendour. In 1836, in order to repay some urgent debts, he republished most of his early pseudonymous novels. One of the friends who helped to trim and polish them for publication prefaced *La Dernière Fée* with a short biography of their author, now, it was claimed in a manner designed to produce disbelief, dead and buried.[2] The fictitious biography of 'Horace de Saint-Aubin' (the pseudonym under which five of the novels appeared) is an engaging story in its own right; it was inspired or even written in part by Balzac himself. In one episode, Horace, still desperately squeezing his mind for a masterpiece, meets the illustrious Honoré de Balzac, then working on his first *Scènes de la Vie Privée*. Horace is overwhelmed by Balzac's superior ability and eventually gives up literature altogether. *Vie et Malheurs de Horace de Saint-Aubin* is a disguised confession, but a confession none the less. Here where the story seems at its most fantastic, it is also closest to the truth.

Lumps remain under the carpet. Balzac emerged from adolescence into a self-satisfied immaturity, as if ready for a normal professional life – the sort of person who might well benefit from a few years of subservience. Legend demanded that the writer issue forth from his garret, like Lucien's incorruptible counterpart, D'Arthez, to surprise the world with his sudden genius. Balzac lapsed into the bosom of his family, with apparent gratification. His letters show few signs of the originality which his early fragments seemed to promise. One is inevitably reminded of Baudelaire's exasperation and envy when briefly entrusted with some of Balzac's juvenile scribblings:

> Nobody could ever possibly imagine how clumsy, silly and STUPID that great man was in his youth. And yet he managed to acquire, to

get for himself, so to speak, not only grandiose ideas, but also a vast amount of wit. But then he NEVER stopped working.[3]

The job of the hagiographer is to inspire affection for the subject; that of the biographer is to account for the astonishment of Balzac's most sympathetic acquaintances when they heard that silly old Honoré was the author of those wonderful tales which began to appear at the end of the 1820s. Like Lucien de Rubempré, who looks, at first with horror, on the commercial face of literature and sees the soul-destroying spectacle of 'poetry in the gutter',[4] it is as if Balzac, after rising or descending from his 'aerial tomb', had still to suffer a kind of death. His childhood had not yet finished with him. The years that follow would lead him eventually to a form of suicide and to the sort of despair that only the most painful self-awareness could produce. Without this, Baudelaire's question could never be answered, and Balzac himself would be little more than the common denominator of a set of anecdotes or a trite reproduction to adorn or disfigure his Complete Works, and not, as Baudelaire later declared him to be, his own most heroic creation.

VILLEPARISIS: the name itself was like an ugly diminutive of Paris. With its 500 Villeparisians, its dusty main street and its six coaching inns, it was the sort of place that only horses were glad to see when they stopped for a rest on the road to Meaux. The Balzacs occupied a rough-cast, rustic-looking house which backed on to the fields and woods along the Canal de l'Ourcq. Across the road was a count living in a paltry château, and at the end of the village a married couple called de Berny who used Villeparisis as their summer resort. The big events were the weekly washing, the sanding of the courtyard ('a sensational piece of news'[5]), village fêtes and the interminable soap opera of adultery and its human consequences which Balzac would transform into great drama in his *Scènes de la Vie de Province*, modelling himself, as some critics complained, on village gossips: 'The almost cloistered existence of the inhabitants of a small town forms in them the invincible habit of analysing and explicating the actions of others'; the smallest deviation from the norm and 'everyone thinks they have stumbled on a secret'.[6] The discovery of adult life in the provinces would be completed by a long visit to Laure and her husband in Bayeux from the end of May to the beginning of August 1822.

For Balzac, the indignity of returning home was alleviated by the chance to observe the clockwork life of this little world and most of all by the amazing sight of the Balzac household – a sight that was to furnish the opening chapters of the first truly Balzacian novel, *Wann-Chlore*, begun in 1822 but not published until 1824. Three adults besieged by their manias and in the grip of hypochondria were a fascinating subject for an informed observer. Granny Sallambier found her failing organs an endless source of interest and was continually catapulted by her 'nerves' from Villeparisis to Paris and back again; she finally fidgeted herself to death in 1823. Not to be upstaged, her daughter frequently took to her bed, issuing instructions so vague that she could always claim to have been disobeyed and performing invisible acts of kindness so she could complain of ingratitude. According to Bernard-François, she had perfected the art of collapsing backwards into an armchair. Balzac portrayed her in *Wann-Chlore*. Like Mme Balzac, Mme d'Arneuse blames her husband for forcing the family into 'exile': 'I have always *execrated* the countryside, you know. Someone of my standing and habits should be living in Paris; but I shall probably never see it again.' Writing *Wann-Chlore* would be a liberating experience for Balzac. The family enjoyed reading the novel and thought it one of his best. It seemed that unflattering portraits were seldom recognized by the models. Vanity was the best insurance against libel suits. Balzac repeated the experiment many times throughout his life, reciting character sketches to the people who inspired them: 'We looked on with great anxiety, thinking it impossible that they should fail to recognize themselves, but then they would say, "How true to life! I didn't realize you knew Mr Thing. It's a perfect likeness!"'[7]

The obvious discrepancy between the Balzacs and the family lampooned in *Wann-Chlore* is the fact that the father has passed away; but this is a trifling difference. Like Grévin in *Le Député d'Arcis*, Bernard-François was 'training to be a corpse'.[8] He occupied his retirement with the maintenance of his body, taking medicinal pills, drinking the sap of trees, and surveying the domestic pageant with appalling equanimity. He was going to crawl unburdened to the grave no matter what.

Wann-Chlore also contains a portrait of Balzac by himself – a fairly flattering portrait which hints that his reinsertion into domestic life, for all his past unhappiness, was quite smooth. He had had his fling and was now becoming one of the family, all the more a member for having once been excluded:

> His face bore the mark of suffering ... but it soon became apparent that he had endured no lasting injury in his fall and that his soul might yet come into bloom. The first thing one noticed about him was his inexhaustible kindness which, however, did not exclude a certain subtlety. He was witty, but he was candid. Being somewhat unbridled in his manners and expressions, he inevitably offended some by the readiness with which he yielded to every impulse of his wanton mind. Though he spoke correctly and even eloquently, he none the less indulged in witticisms which contrasted sharply with his usual manner of expressing himself but which suited perfectly the man as a whole. Still, he was capable of conforming to propriety and could sometimes be rather dignified. . . . He was short but very well proportioned. His complexion, his vivacity and everything else betrayed those defects one associates with nervous temperaments: an intellectual intensity and warmth of feeling which leave no room for Reason's icy counsel. As fancy took him, he was excessively gay or plunged in melancholy; but this unevenness of character was superficial; for generosity, enthusiasm and the noble self-confidence of Youth always re-emerged.

The deliberately polished air of this sketch belies its content. All its qualifying clauses, its modifications and provisos, seem to strain to hold extremes of temperament together: a desire to copy and conform perpetually frustrated. Balzac had such a clear idea of who and what he wanted to be that he could scarcely have been himself. 'I'm simplicity itself, and proud of it.'[9] His letters to Laure in 1821 and 1822 add rough lines and smudges to the picture. They are filled with the yearnings of 'little Honoré' (he often talks about himself in the third person), craving fame and a lucrative marriage. He vows, only half in jest, to write Romantic odes after learning that Lamartine had been pursued across the Alps by a doting Englishwoman: '*Je ai 15,000 livres sterling de revenu, foulez vous meu épousair*? . . . And he did!' Novels were a stop-gap solution: 'Dirtying paper: that's the only means I have – ignominious as it is – of becoming independent.' 'Since yesterday, I have given up hoping for dowagers and shall settle for thirty-year-old widows.' The sight of Bernard-François, 'the Pyramid of Egypt, immovable even as the planet falls apart around him', was like a goad: 'An old man is someone who has had their dinner and watches other people come to eat theirs. But *my* plate is empty, it has no gilt edges, the tablecloth is dingy and the food is tasteless. I'm hungry, and there's nothing to satisfy my appetite.' Taken out of context, as they often are, some of Balzac's exclamations have the poignant tone of the Romantic hero, his genius stifled by petty circumstances: 'I have yet to enjoy the flowers of life, though I have reached the only time of year in which they bloom.' In context, they have a more grating, even petulant sound, and it is revealing that in the first edition of Balzac's correspondence the text of some of these letters was altered: 'Will my single, immense desire – to be famous and to be loved – ever be satisfied?' Balzac actually wrote, without pausing to punctuate, 'I only have two passions love and glory and nothing has been satisfied yet and never will be.'[10]

Family life had one horrible lesson in store for the 'candid' young man with his 'inexhaustible kindness'. It was learned at the expense of 'Milady Plumppudding', the family name for Laurence. In contrast to Laure, she was overweight, hopelessly immature and scatterbrained, and Mme Balzac had no difficulty persuading her of her inadequacy. It was time she married. An attractive fellow of thirty-three, rejoicing in the name of Amand-Désiré Michaut de Saint-Pierre de Montzaigle, presented himself.[11] Dazzled by the multiple 'de' and warned, by Montzaigle himself, of imminent competition for his estimable hand, the Balzacs convinced themselves it was a perfect match. Laurence was sacrificed to their vanity. Two sets of wedding invitations were printed: one, for friends of the family, gives the bride's name as 'Laurence Balzac', the other inserts the usurped particle.[12] Mme Balzac was thrilled: 'He has been and still is so widely known in society that there will probably be many sour faces when they hear that Laurence Balzac is marrying M. de Saint-Pierre de Montzaigle.' Montzaigle's fame had even reached the files of Police Headquarters: a Government spy had reported him making rude remarks about the King in public places. The resulting inquiry revealed nothing more subversive than gambling, whoring and billiards. These activities, in fact, could be construed as advantages! Bernard-François sagely observed that the bridegroom had indulged himself so fully in his youth that 'the only thing he has left to do is become a good husband'; and since he was a champion billiards player, there was little danger of his losing any money. Balzac alone saw him, too late, as a shallow, arrogant, selfish man, immune to experience but astute enough to lavish all his charms on his future mother-in-law. Curiously, in the letter in which he tells his elder sister about Montzaigle, Balzac mentions *Clarissa Harlowe*. Perhaps he remembered that Samuel Richardson's aim was to refute 'that dangerous but too commonly received notion, that a reformed rake makes the best husband'. The lesson was lost on Balzac; he was amused by the latest domestic drama. Laurence woke up after the wedding to find herself married to a monster. Balzac briefly alludes to her misery in a letter sent to Laure in February 1822; but then he uses it as an opportunity to air his latest philosophy of life: 'Shouldn't we just laugh at misfortune and good fortune alike when they reach extremes and never take anything seriously, like Democritus? Isn't that the true philosophy? . . . Grief drains you, but gaiety restores you and gives you energy.' Unlike Balzac, Democritus started laughing only when he left the house.

A few months later, Laurence was spending her evenings alone in her husband's big drawing-room, reading Montesquieu's *Esprit des Lois* by the light of a single candle (a sad attempt to find amusing topics of conversation), while Montzaigle strutted off to his cafés and casinos. She wrote pathetic letters home asking for money; Montzaigle saw his wife as a letter of credit from the in-laws. The Balzacs withdrew into their collective shell, bemoaning their daughter's ineptitude. In 1825, after the birth of her second child, at the age of twenty-three, she died, probably of tuberculosis, though the cause of death might just as well have been given as grief and exhaustion. The inventory drawn up after her death shows that almost everything had gone to the pawnshop – everything except a wardrobe filled with Montzaigle's elegant clothes. One year later, the perfect husband married a seventeen-year-old.

Remorse is not a motive one readily associates with Balzac; yet when he passionately condemns the institution of marriage as 'legal

prostitution' and denounces the piffling 'education' meted out to
women, it is difficult not to remember his facile hedonism at the time
of Laurence's marriage. Especially when the character who condemns
it most effectively bears the name 'Aiglemont' – almost a mirror image
of 'Montzaigle', without the precious 'z'.[13] If Balzac had not sensed
the family within himself, his bitter incriminations of his mother,
whom he accused of murdering Laurence,[14] might not have been so
virulent. Even at the age of twenty-two, he feared contamination:

> I must tell you, in complete confidence, that poor Mama is turning
> into Granny, only worse. I was hoping that the period she has
> reached in her life might affect her whole constitution and change
> her personality, but it is not to be. Oh, Laure, watch out for yourself,
> and let's both watch out for each other. The whole family has a
> nervous disposition. When you are young you can fool yourself, but
> that sickness creeps up on you little by little.[15]

In 1844, Balzac told Mme Hanska that he had long been observing
'the eerie transformation of my sister into my mother'.[16] By then, he
had his own fictitious families and could afford to be pessimistic about
heredity. In 1821, with fashionable ideas about the nature of genius,
he was still capable of finding hopeful signs for his own future in his
parents' eccentricity: 'There are no two families in the world like ours,
and I do believe that each of us is unique in our own way.'[17]

The weight of experience is most obvious, not in the scattered
remarks of letters written under the influence of passing events, but in
the contrast between the triviality of Balzac's juvenile descriptions of
life in the provinces and his later *Scènes de la Vie Privée*, like *Eugénie
Grandet*, where 'observation' acquires a visionary quality, each phrase
pregnant with other stories, some of which will never be told: 'There
are in some provincial towns houses whose appearance weighs as
heavily on the mind as the gloomiest cloister, the most mournful ruin
or the dreariest stretch of barren land. . . . Life stirs so little in them
that a stranger would think them uninhabited – but then suddenly he
meets the cold and dismal gaze of a motionless figure whose almost
monastic face leans over the window-sill at the sound of a stranger's
footstep.'

*

IRONICALLY, when Laurence fell in love with another man after becoming engaged to Montzaigle, it was because of money that Balzac had steered her away from him. He was a twenty-eight-year-old writer whom Balzac had met in Paris early in 1821. 'So you hadn't heard that poor Laurence had a crush on Auguste de l'Égreville? Don't say anything that might make her think I gave the game away, but I had the hardest time convincing her that writers make terrible husbands, financially speaking of course.'[18] Balzac subsequently spent many years trying to persuade Mme Hanska that the opposite was true.

Auguste Lepoitevin – or, when circumstances demanded, Le Poitevin de l'Égreville – is the man who claimed to have 'created' Balzac.[19] He was tall and handsome, held himself like a soldier but had an insubordinate gleam in his eye: Balzac's first fairy godmother. During a visit to his parents' pied-à-terre in Paris, a friend from the École de Droit had told him of a man who knew how to make money writing novels. Balzac invited this magical person to the cheapest restaurant in Paris: it was Flicoteaux, on the Place de la Sorbonne, the 'temple of hunger and destitution' described in *Illusions Perdues*, where the menu never changed, though the ingredients seemed to vary, and a well-known sign promised 'All the Bread You Can Eat'.[20] At the end of an 'execrable' meal, as he folded his napkin, Lepoitevin muttered with a fine sense of the occasion, 'To be continued.'[21] The young man was more appetizing than the meal. Fortunately Lepoitevin shared Balzac's opinion of himself: 'He's a fine boy [Balzac wrote about himself again in the third person], he's got a brain, and best of all he's a chatterbox. If all that talk were set in type, it would come to thirty printed pages.'[22] Lepoitevin saw the sign: 'All the Novels You Can Publish'. An agreement was reached. Balzac was to concoct some stories which Lepoitevin would tidy up and sell to publishers. Over the next five years, nine novels appeared pseudonymously; three of them were written in collaboration with Lepoitevin, the other six by Balzac on his own. In 1822, no fewer than five novels shot off the presses. Balzac finally had a regular job, and even, like Rastignac, a persuasive and experienced criminal (or almost) to help him up the ladder.

Years later, still stuck in the slimepit of satirical journalism, Lepoitevin reminisced about his great discovery. The following account was given in 1841 to a young socialist writer who turned up at Lepoitevin's *Figaro* (an ancestor of the modern newspaper) to ask for a job:

> You're lucky to have found me, you are. Everyone I've put to work has ended up successful. I'm the only one who's come to nothing and I'm older than they are. I created them all! Take little old Balzac – he's one of mine! He and I made loads of plans together! I wrote a fair few novels with him – his worst novels, I'll grant him that. He was so young and sweet and naive and happy and easy to work with in those days. He was like a little cannonball, broad-shouldered the way you are, his head on his stomach and his stomach on his legs! Hard-working and modest! Now he's got a terrific reputation – incredible, I can't understand it! I knew him when he was just starting out! He took himself seriously, the snob, and now he won't even spare a glance for his old mate. Oh, I could tell you stories about him, I could – and what stories![23]

Lepoitevin thus has the distinction of being the only person who ever described the young Balzac as modest, and it says much about his own consuming personality. When he talked, it was like listening to a novel: not a word of truth but highly entertaining. Unusually for him, Balzac invited him home. Lepoitevin found a kindred spirit in Bernard-François; they shared a taste for tall stories. Why, he was asked, had he not been a soldier when Napoleon was conquering Europe? Actually, he claimed, he was chosen to join a crack regiment, 'a special force which Napoleon would have sent to India to do away with the English if the Russian campaign had not been such a disaster'.[24] In the dark world Balzac was entering, Lepoitevin on several occasions would try to assemble a special force of his own, using the new, less expensive power of newspapers.

This dubious *deus ex machina*, descending on to the stage just as Balzac comes of age, has always been a villain in the eyes of Balzac's most partisan admirers, perhaps because, to anyone attracted by his later political views, individual effort, however undistinguished, is preferable to the achievements of a collective. Lepoitevin may have 'corrupted' Balzac and egged him on to literary idiocies; or he may have shown him the magic formulae that first allowed him to captivate readers. Whatever effect he had, he clearly occupies a larger place in his life than the more respectful or distant figures whose presumed influence is discussed at great length.

Lepoitevin's father had been an actor in the rowdy Boulevard theatres. Auguste grew up thinking of literature as his bread and butter. Noting the surge in demand for novels, he enlisted the help of some friends and proved that this new commodity could be mass-produced. Later, he applied the same pragmatic principles to journalism, practising blackmail via the gossip columns and exerting more or less random political influence via the actresses he won over with favourable reviews. Balzac's supposedly savage caricatures of the gutter press owe much to the lessons of his collaborator, naively unscrupulous, hungry for fame but too sentimental when it came to the crunch or too intent on outright victory to take advantage of the openings he created for himself. Lepoitevin would have been dismayed to see how little information we now have on him. He is best known as the editor, in the 1840s, of the luridly named 'news' paper, *Le Corsaire-Satan*, a paper which Balzac once defined as 'a literary sewage-pipe transporting the most revolting calumnies'.[25] The producers of the sewage were a team of mostly unpaid writers whom Lepoitevin called his 'little cretins'. Some of these cretins – Baudelaire, Champfleury, Henry Murger – became distinguished novelists and poets. Like Balzac, many of them were reluctant to admit that they owed their first moments of glory to this literary 'vampire' who, almost like Oscar Wilde, put his genius into his life and other people's talent into his work.

Lepoitevin's claim to have created Balzac is a nice embellishment; but it serves as a reminder that he was one of the most efficient 'midwives' of nineteenth-century French literature. And it reminds us too that *La Comédie Humaine* is not an immaculate conception but the long-overdue result of an excruciating and unsightly affair. Balzac had first to be exploited before he could exploit himself. This, at least, is what Lepoitevin must have told him. A degree of unease may nevertheless be in order. Balzac's so-called *romans de jeunesse* (stretching the limits of what might be called 'youth') are not outstanding works of fiction. If he had died at the age of twenty-eight, few would have mourned the loss of a genius; his memorable name would appear in lists as a mere example; at best, a thesis-writer would have described him as 'unjustly neglected' and pointed to a few exceptional passages or skilful imitations of Walter Scott. Balzac himself saw these novels as a separate *œuvre*: illegitimate children, the embarrassing result of awkward experiments. What he refers to as his 'first work' is actually a novel, *Le Dernier Chouan*, published eight years later in 1829. Scholars with an interest in the matter can detect germs of brilliance in the most unpromising performances; unfortunately, such germs have sometimes been detected in novels now known to be by Lepoitevin alone. Whether or not this mercenary period in Balzac's life is regrettable is another matter. There is after all no reason why commercial criteria should not have helped him to become one of the world's most popular novelists; and there is even a pleasing irony in the fact that market forces helped produce a series of novels which Marx and Engels, after Victor Hugo, hailed as a brilliant unintentional diatribe against capitalism.

Balzac's parents were unsure about his lucky break. Bernard-François deemed this pandering to public tastes a dishonourable and inconvenient line of work. How could you tell your readers the truth and what they wanted to hear at the same time? Fashions changed; his son would spend his life running after bandwagons. Balzac was prepared to make the sacrifice. Great days were dawning for writers, he said; censorship laws had been abolished (though not for long) and newspapers would soon control the world: 'Anyone who is in any way connected with the Press will be an important person.' 'All you need is talent, Father.'[26] His methods had evolved but his aims were intact. Two years before, *Cromwell* was written as a voucher to be redeemed at some future date in Parliament: 'Writers are the people most readily sought out during political crises because . . . they know the human heart.'[27] Balzac's correspondence shows that he was a keen follower of elections and political events; he himself would stand as a candidate. Nevertheless, barring a crisis caused by supernatural powers, it seemed unlikely that the Government would seek the advice of a popular novelist. The family, whose verdicts still mattered to Balzac, even feared public disgrace if the Villeparisians found out they had been harbouring a pornographer in their midst. In the end they agreed but insisted on a *nom de plume*. Balzac submitted willingly. It was a wise decision; he often had reason to be glad that the name of Balzac was kept for better things.

The pseudonym he chose bears witness to his faith in anagrams no matter what the result: Balzac's first three novels are signed by an entity calling itself Lord R'Hoone. Anything with an apostrophe looked English and therefore promised something fashionable. It was also faintly reminiscent of Thomas Moore's hugely successful 'oriental' tales, *Lalla Rookh*, which Balzac read and imitated in the second version of *Falthurne*. Lepoitevin, who wrote under the name Viellerglé (an anagram of l'Égreville), approved. Only an ignoramus would think that a man called R'Hoone had actually existed; everyone else would assume that the author had reasons to hide behind a mask and would buy the book to find out what they were. In addition, the unnamed novelist could, if necessary, rope himself in as a character in his own right. This, in fact, is how Lord R'Hoone's maiden novel begins, and Balzac even intended devoting a whole book to *La Famille R'Hoone*, perhaps a forerunner of *Wann-Chlore*. Finally, as if by chance, this splendidly silly name possessed the mysterious appropriateness of Balzac's onomastic creations: an occult sign, a *rune*, the writer's shameful secret.

Having been warned by the family doctor, Nacquart, that he was about to find him a *real* job, Lord R'Hoone worked flat out. In July 1821, *L'Héritière de Birague* was finished. Eighty-two thousand words supposedly extracted from the manuscripts of Don Rago, ex-Benedictine prior (alter ego of Étienne Arago, brother of the famous astronomer and friend of Lepoitevin). The manuscripts were 'published by his two nephews', Viellerglé and Lord R'Hoone. A 'Preliminary Novel, otherwise known as a Preface' explains 'candidly' – 'since we are and always have been extraordinarily modest people' – that these manuscripts are all the two disgruntled nephews inherited from their malicious uncle. Making the best of a bad job, they offer the manuscript to a publisher. The novel itself is a dark and stormy tale of a sweet young thing forced to marry a scoundrel because the scoundrel has wooed the mother-in-law with a combination of gallantry and blackmail. It takes place, of course, in an ancient castle, but the voice of fresh experience is rarely silent for long: 'A woman of forty years', writes the son of Mme Balzac, 'is never praised with impunity.'

The spurious nephews had an amazingly happy ending; it was to be the first of several. In October 1821, Lepoitevin sold *L'Héritière* to a publisher called Hubert for 800 francs. If Balzac had taken up the offer from the family solicitor, he would have been earning about 100 francs a month. A meal at Flicoteaux's cost 1 fr. 10. At a steady rate of six novels a year, once he had a good head of steam, Lord R'Hoone would be rich, 'the man of the moment, the most prolific novelist (and the nicest), and ladies will love him like the apple of their eye and all the rest; and then that little squirt Honoré will bowl up in a horse and carriage, his head held high, a haughty expression on his face, and a bulging purse'.[28]

Hubert was a good publisher with whom to lose one's literary virginity. He specialized in the 'Gothic' and his catalogue included French translations of the works of Maturin, the Irish priest whose *Melmoth the Wanderer* was a European bestseller. Suitably enough, Hubert's shop was in the Wooden Galleries at the Palais-Royal. Balzac must have passed his window many times and seen the titles which were now advertised on the inside cover of his own book – all servings of the same gory dish, each dressed a little differently. This was generic literature, the author's name was mentioned only if he was famous:

Emma or The Wedding Night
Juliette or The Misfortunes of a Life of Guilt
Duels, Suicides and Love Affairs in the Bois de Boulogne, with two
    attractive engravings
Crime and Fatalism
Nocturnal Nuptials or The Subterranean Passages of the Château
    d'Orfeuil
The Tower of Bog or The Strict Father

It has been suggested that Balzac's 'pre-Balzacian' novels are parodies of the genres in vogue, and thus implicit criticisms of pulp fiction; and yet this too is an element of imitation. Parody and intrusive authors were part of the ploy. Monsters were deflated by humour then reinflated by fear and suspense. Walter Scott himself uses drinking scenes and sarcastic narrators to bring light relief from the serious action. When Lord R'Hoone complains of the frustration caused him by his own lascivious evocations of young ladies or when, for once, he decides to dispense with the rosy-fingered dawn, he is treading prudently in the footsteps of his predecessors. For all the praise now lavished on the work which Balzac himself refused to recognize, any reader expecting to find any obvious originality would be disappointed. The ingenious rehabilitation of the *romans de jeunesse* is due in part to a desire to salvage something of worth from what amounts to several days of often tedious reading. However, aesthetic value is not the be-all and end-all of every book. If these pseudonymous novels are read for their representative qualities, they suddenly become interesting. After a thousand pages, when the appetite for bludgeoning villains and helpless maidens begins to sicken, they can still be admired as detailed, practical manuals on How To Write Popular Romantic Fiction. Balzac had learned the tricks of his trade with astonishing speed. Tricks, none the less, which might easily be summarized, if only to highlight the contrast with his later work:

THE PLOT

All plots end in marriage and/or death. There are only so many possibilities. Borrow the plot of a successful play or another novel. Balzac once stated that the quickest way to earn money was to use the plots of Corneille's plays.[29] Loose ends are not a problem: they can be tied up in a flurry of conclusions as the story hurtles to a close.

THE CHARACTERS

Comic characters have funny names and verbal ticks. Most of Balzac's early comic creations are shadows of his father: the lunatic philosopher in *Jean-Louis* or Dr Trousse (= 'Dr Instrument Case') in *Clotilde* whose trademark is obsessive use of the first-person pronoun and a bizarre theory, central to Balzac's work, which recurs in a more thoughtful form in *La Peau de Chagrin*: 'I, for example, owe my good health to the fact that I never think.' (Such phrases are like anticipatory parodies of himself.) A villain is sufficiently defined by his or her unspeakable deeds: once Enguerry-the-Miscreant has beheaded a son in front of his parents and then plunged the parents into boiling oil, there is little point sketching in the nuances of his personality. There should always be a mystery character whose identity is not revealed until the end. A mystery character, being mysterious, does not have to be developed. In the third novel published by Hubert, *Clotilde de Lusignan ou Le Beau Juif*, the Black Knight turns out to be Gaston II, Count of Provence, who turns out to be the Handsome Jew of the title. Clotilde survives the test of her loyalty by trying to stab herself at the altar rather than marry the villain: love (this is the message) conquers even anti-semitism and the author makes a considerable saving on the number of principal characters.

PLASTERING OVER THE CRACKS

Haste breeds inconsistencies. The novelist will blame the manuscript he claims to be publishing. It may have lacunae (Balzac uses this excuse repeatedly in *Clotilde*). Or the 'author' of the manuscript may have been incompetent. This can be pointed out in a footnote. Footnotes create an air of authenticity and, more importantly, obviate the need to redraft clumsy passages.

MAINTAINING INTEREST

When describing medieval France, it is useful to refer to contrasting or unchanged aspects of modern life. Public transport and the state of the roads are favourites with Balzac. Every few chapters, a smattering of severed limbs should be introduced or a maiden should be undressed (by her nurse). Cruelty and lust cover a multitude of sins.

MAXIMIZING PROFITS

Time and money can be saved by filling up the pages with short paragraphs, minuscule chapters and long epigraphs. This was known as 'whitening' the text. All but the most distinguished novels were published in four duodecimo volumes, totalling about 1000 pages. Straight prose may use up only half the space that dialogue takes up. Misunderstandings are particularly valuable to the novelist: they complicate the plot, delay the dénouement and greatly prolong any conversation.

MARKETING

In the book itself, appeal to the female reader's generosity. In his fifth novel, *Le Vicaire des Ardennes*, Balzac urges the public to buy the book because his travel expenses were never reimbursed by the publisher. In

Clotilde, he promises to satisfy the reader's curiosity on certain points if popular demand takes the book to a fifth edition.

Chances of success were increased if the author organized the critical reception of the book himself. *L'Héritière de Birague* was reviewed in February 1822 by a certain Pigoreau; he praised its 'elegant style' and 'comic verve'. Pigoreau was not entirely disinterested; he was a bookseller who sold novels published by Hubert. By August that year, Pigoreau (or Balzac and Lepoitevin) had realized that a 'good' review was not necessarily the best sort of advertisement: *Clotilde* is recommended to readers 'in search of strong emotions'; but, adds the bogus pedant, 'it is thoroughly improper to revel, as the author does, in massacres and in the torments inflicted on unfortunate people'. 'Reviews' could also be inserted for a fee in most newspapers. Thus, an anonymous Balzac praises *Clotilde* in *Le Pilote* as the work of a promising young writer who, he lies, 'is known for several other works which were well received by the public'.

Finally, there is evidence of behaviour still more improper in the title-page originally planned for the fourth of these novels. It appeared at the end of 1822: '*The Centenarian or The Two Béringhenns*, by Lewis; published by M. Horace de Saint-Aubin'.[30] The attribution to Lewis has been described as 'strange', since Balzac was clearly copying, not Lewis's *The Monk*, but Maturin's *Melmoth* in this tale of a 400-year-old monster who renews his vital fluids by killing young women. 'Strange' maybe, but for other reasons. Why should Balzac want to ascribe his work to someone else? Because Lewis was a name which guaranteed sales, and Lewis had died in 1818, unlike Maturin, who was still alive and still writing novels. Balzac's later, avowed imitation of *Melmoth* (1835), is one of the weakest stories in *La Comédie Humaine*. Was this the revenge of the dead novelist?

After the first two novels, Balzac was writing on his own, using Lepoitevin as an agent. For a young man with Romantic ideals, this was unusually competent: professionalism of the highest degree and perhaps an early sign of a new form of writing, in which technique and even parody are as important as ideas and 'sincerity'. Sitting in Laure's old room at Villeparisis, or visiting Bayeux, with occasional trips to the Marais, and with a few days in Touraine for his health, Balzac had mastered the two most popular genres: the *roman noir* and the *roman gai*. His third novel, the second to be published, was a *roman gai*. *Jean-Louis ou La Fille Trouvée* is the French Restoration equivalent of a cheap comedy film, packed to the point of incoherence with convenient coincidences, abductions and other forms of rascally behaviour. The hero is a working-class boy with a quick sense of humour and a great physique. Women find him irresistible but Jean-Louis remains touchingly loyal to Fanchette. Since the scene is set in 1788, he makes colourful plebeian jokes about rotten aristocrats. Carry On Revolting, or Bing Crosby in a Phrygian cap. For all its blandness, it was rather daring in parts, to judge by a worried letter from Hubert asking Balzac to excise words like *Liberté*, *Peuple* and *Despotisme*: 'seditious fervour', the publisher called it.

Balzac's more serious ambitions, which did not include inciting revolt, were still just visible. *Clotilde*, for example, contains hints that these gaudy characters are meant to be *types*, summing up an era or an aspect of society. 'Scenes of human life' there are aplenty, Lord R'Hoone observes, 'but rarely are we offered scenes from the lives of those great masses called Nations'. These prophetic observations begin to sound like a pretext. His more urgent ambition was less abstract. 'My reputation is growing every day as one can see from the following survey':[31]

L'Héritière de Birague	Sold	800 francs
Jean-Louis	id.	1300 francs
Clotilde de Lusignan	id.	2000 francs

Two thousand francs for *Clotilde* was wishful thinking: most of the payment was conditional on enormous numbers of the novel being sold. Happily, Balzac had despatched the novel in two months. As his own frequent calculations will have shown, this was twenty pages a day. For a while it seemed that time was the only obstacle. The earliest surviving list of projects dates from 1822. It is headed 'ORDER OF THE DAY. Make 3000 francs or it's Dishonour, Destitution and Co.' Balzac's mental shopping list is divided into seven columns: six melodramas, two vaudevilles (*Les Deux Mahomets* and *Garrick*), one opera, seven novels, one comedy, three brochures (one entitled *La Politique Mise à Nu*). The tragedy column is empty.

While he was writing, there was little time to think. Balzac believed in his novels while they were still half-formed. Sheer energy and a clear view of the ideal carried him through; but once the ink was dry, he was left unsatisfied and passed judgment on his own work with a sense of shame. Two months after drawing up his triumphant survey, a little over a year after his meeting with Lepoitevin, he wrote again to Laure. She had not received her copy of *L'Héritière de Birague* because the scales had fallen from his eyes: 'It is absolute *pigswill*; I now know its true worth, though pride still whispers to me that it's as good as all the other stuff that's published.' As for *Jean-Louis*, there were 'a few good jokes', but the plot was 'detestable'. At least the housekeeper liked it. Balzac returned home one day to find her collapsed in laughter: 'Ah, Monsieur! What a funny book!' Her reaction was all the more gratifying since she was 'at death's door'. But was this the public Balzac hoped to reach? The bourgeois audience was less appreciative. Balzac had gone to visit Laure in Bayeux. On 5 August 1822, Mme Balzac wrote to her daughter, knowing that Honoré would see or be told about the letter.[32] She was furious: he had refused to follow her advice on the more gruesome episodes in *Clotilde*. The scene in which the Miscreant's heart is plucked out was 'utterly unrealistic and such a thing is impossible to do anyway'. 'Why did you not speak to me about it, Laure? I was waiting to hear your thoughts on the subject. What did you make of the *airy window*, the *slender beam of light*, the word *suave* bandied about all over the place, *silky movements* mentioned far too often ... and a thousand other things in dreadful taste and of the very worst kind and which we failed to notice because dear Honoré read his chapters to us with such fire and passion?' 'Honoré thinks himself a poet, but I have ever been of the opinion that he is not.' *Clotilde*, she went on, was proof of his childish arrogance and obstinacy; and he was far too quick to take offence! The flippant young men he had befriended were ruining him. She had shown the novel to all her closest friends and they all agreed.

Mme Balzac's savage letter might lead one to suspect that she had seen herself, unconsciously or not, in the evil, adulterous mother of Clotilde. The similarities are striking, especially in Mme Balzac's sinister closing remark: Laure was to share these strictures with her brother, 'but beware of discouragement. With the principles he has, it could be fatal.' Perhaps she was remembering the journey home from Paris in 1814. Laure wrote back almost at once: 'Honoré said nothing, except that it was all true; and then he looked very sad and upset and went to sit on the ottoman while I went through your letter with him.' Certainly, the novel was a disgrace, but why persistently ignore Honoré's virtues, his kindness, his jolly disposition? At least the path he was following was paved with good intentions. And anyway, she added, 'How many writers achieve perfection with their first work?'

Traces of Balzac's depression are apparent in the self-deprecating preface ('to be read if possible') to *Le Vicaire des Ardennes*. It is dated 30 September 1822, thus, shortly after Balzac's return from Bayeux. 'I am young, inexperienced, and know nothing of the French language.' This is certainly not just false modesty. Balzac liked to tell younger writers that it was only after twelve years of study and practice that he began to master French or even had an inkling of its possibilities – the suggestion being that the majority of writers never bothered to learn the French language ('not well known in France').[33] He also claims to be twenty years old, ugly enough to frighten his friends if they met him in the woods at night, a martyr to hypochondria (a sign of unused talents), and given to prowling about the Père Lachaise cemetery. Once again, the novel is presented as a manuscript. This time, however, there is an important difference: the manuscript was stolen from a dying man, the hero of the story. This, too, verges on the imaginative truth. Like Rimbaud, or, for that matter, Lord R'Hoone and Horace de Saint-Aubin, Balzac gave up writing more than once, though the interval between despair and new resolve is sometimes imperceptible. *Clotilde* was Lord R'Hoone's farewell performance. Balzac had begun on a series of false starts that would continue far beyond his adolescence. Some of his novels have as many as sixteen different beginnings; in this, his life is a mirror-image of his writing. The story of his rise to fame as it appears in biographical dictionaries is just a fair copy.

When he started work on *Le Vicaire des Ardennes*, Balzac was snatching victory from self-imposed defeat. He had a new publisher, a new pseudonym and a new subject, and his partnership with Lepoitevin was dissolving. The 'old' Balzac of *Clotilde* and *Jean-Louis* was relegated now to the role of wretched 'author', 'a poor Bachelor of the Arts just embarking on his first ventures in *Commercial Literature*' (an unpleasant and provocative expression at a time when the helplessly inspired writer was a cherished cliché). The lacklustre novelist with no original work of his own advertises a series of non-existent novels on

[92]

such tantalizing topics as treachery, necrophilia and other Romantic misdemeanours: *The Bolster or Secret Memoirs of a Household; The Dead Woman's Fiancé; The Bastard*; and – a concession to exoticism – *The Gondoliers of Venice.*

Balzac's sarcasm coincides not only with the emergence of a new style but also with the early months of his first love affair – an affair that lasted ten years. Both express a form of liberation from his upbringing, a redirecting of his obsession with his own family. Even the most flagrantly exploitative scenes of his early novels have a curious depth, perhaps due to the speed with which they were scribbled down. 'Poetry in the gutter', but also a poetry which only the gutter could reveal. This background of untidy struggles is essential for understanding the famously fluent writer known throughout France as 'the most fertile of our novelists'.[34] Balzac derided this pre-emptive epitaph which he himself dreamed up. Forced, as he saw it, to seek his fortune and independence by writing novels when, like any Tourangeau, he yearned for a life of idleness, he likened himself to a modern Prometheus walking around with a terrible pet gnawing at his heart. The same image appears, for the first time in Balzac's work, in the passage which his mother found so unrealistic:

> The madwoman, like the vulture hacking away at Prometheus, continues to wallow in the blood of her victim [whom she supposes to have murdered her son]. She glances round wildly at the horrified witnesses of the scene, and, plunging her bloodied hands into the Miscreant's body, rends his skin, gouges into his flesh and, pulling it apart, extracts his still-beating heart. She brandishes it with ingenuous glee, waving it about in a manner suggestive of desire for vengeance and maternal love. She jumps up and down, emitting little inarticulate squeals.

Compared to the gory doings of the Miscreant, this is almost a mercy-killing; nevertheless, the juxtaposition of maternal love and the excision of a heart is more unsettling than the routine carnage of earlier chapters. Psychoanalysis had yet to put a damper on fictional horrors; the constraints imposed by 'public morality' were only half as effective. The claustrophobic atmosphere of this horror story is also in some ways the atmosphere of home. Balzac, after all, was still surrounded by his family; they, not the general public, were his immediate audience. The passage was retained in spite of the family's advice, which on other occasions Balzac was willing to follow. Symbolically and in reality, he was doing violence to his own talent. Like the Miscreant and the other outcasts of his early novels, he had a sense of his own guilt. Moreover, the novels themselves and the sardonic prefaces and footnotes which accompany them seemed to justify, perversely and almost with pleasure, his mother's condemnation. But there was hope. When Balzac was composing this purple passage, he was about to escape from the nightmare. Shortly after, without there being, for the moment, any other outward sign of change, he gave his heart to someone else: the Balzacs' neighbour at Villeparisis, Laure de Berny. She was a woman he often referred to as his mother.

CHAPTER FIVE

Divine Intercourse

(1822–1824)

My dearest darling, descend like the heavenly dew! My breast awaits thee, thy garden is in bloom, my heart burns, my head is crowned with roses. The vine perfumes the air. The dove has entrusted its nest to the highest branches of the poplar. The rippling moonlight breaks on the ripples of the silvery lagoon. The only sound is that of the swan returning to its mate. Descend! Come, my love, or my tears will fall on the perfumed bed I have prepared with my own hands.[1]

S UCH WAS the power of love over Balzac that it loosened the ties of his Enlightenment upbringing to produce this extraordinary second version of *Falthurne*, a combination of Ossian and the Song of Songs, drenched with religious and sexual imagery: clouds shaped like pyramids, mysterious lights escaping from the pores of metaphysical beings, flowers exuding their strange, olfactory language. Balzac's sustained burst of Romanticism, though quite in keeping with the time, is surprising in view of his anti-religious background at home and at school. It also implicitly contradicts his liberal leanings in politics. The Romantic movement was still synonymous with the Catholic revival; the nostalgia of elegiac poets was also that of the dispossessed nobility or of those who identified with it. The more violent, satanic Romanticism of the disaffected young bourgeoisie would emerge only with the 1830 Revolution. A net cast almost anywhere in Balzac's unpublished notes brings to light some improbable fish. The only hint in *Falthurne II* of the future historian of *La Comédie Humaine* is perhaps the returning swan – a characteristic intrusion of real life. A wider knowledge of literary clichés would have told Balzac that swans in such contexts are supposed to remain silent until their dying breath.

Eight years later, Balzac was standing in line outside the Comédie

Française to witness the first night of Hugo's *Hernani*, the first official blow struck for the Romantic movement. From the roof of the theatre the defenders of classical drama pelted the rebels with floor-sweepings. Balzac, always a lightning-conductor for symbolic phenomena, was struck by a cabbage stalk.[2]

The 'delicate censor' (because she liked it) who inspired this long and uncharacteristic prose poem was Laure de Berny. She had such an influence on Balzac's life as his teacher, his literary and financial adviser and sponsor, his lover, his surrogate mother and, finally, his friend, that he later told Mme Hanska: 'From 1822 to 1832 my life was an exception. . . . Chance treats me like those fantastic desert animals who experience only a few rare moments of joy in their lives and who sometimes perish without having perpetuated their species.'[3] Biologically this was a huge exaggeration, but emotionally it was true. If Balzac described his first lover in the letters he began to write in March 1822 as a deity – 'the focus of my thoughts', 'more than a friend, more than a sister, almost a mother and even more than that a sort of visible divinity', 'a theme for my life' – this was not just the fashionable commandeering of religious symbols for private passions. The emergence of 'Horace de Saint-Aubin' (a name borrowed from Mme de Berny's circle of acquaintances) heralds a period of several 'conversions' in Balzac's life: an apparent religious conversion which spawned a deeply ambiguous *Traité de la Prière*; the revelation of new paths in literature in *Le Vicaire des Ardennes*; and, at last, a glimpse of redemption and fulfilment in the woman who bore that 'cherished name', Laure.

MME DE BERNY had everything Balzac thought he should look for in a lover. She was forty-five years old and thus, according to his oft-repeated views on older women, ready to sacrifice everything; she was passionate, perceptive, mocking and as seductive as anything that promised instant experience. She was also married to a cantankerous man much older than herself with whom she had long ago negotiated a sensible compromise: raising the children in exchange for her 'freedom'. M. de Berny had been a court counsellor. This too would prove useful.

Balzac first knew her as a mother, having offered his services as her children's tutor. He enjoyed visiting her house at the end of the street with its high grey-stone walls, its grand staircase and spacious drawing-room with French windows giving on to a peaceful garden.[4] The aristocratic air of the house – a contrast with the Balzacs' boorish homestead – was a reflection of her past. Mme de Berny was full of historical interest. Her mother had been one of Marie-Antoinette's chambermaids; her father, a German musician called Joseph Hinner, was the Queen's harpist. When she was christened, the King and Queen were her godparents; the Duc de Richelieu held her over the font. Ten years later, after her father's death, her mother married Jarjayes, the man whose plot to rescue the Queen was wrecked by Balzac's headmaster.[5]

At least in the early days, Mme de Berny's pedigree was a large part of her charm in Balzac's eyes. His mother, for the same reason, had already made envious overtures: it was so much more pleasant to be seen setting off for Paris in an elegant carriage than to take the public coach.[6] For Balzac, there were literary as well as social reasons to be attracted. Writing about history in the manner of Walter Scott was still a means to an end; making love to history, so to speak, promised more immediate rewards. And love affairs, unlike literature, provided something that writers rarely enjoyed: an exact measure of success. Balzac soon discovered too that there was a rich source of pride and self-confidence in the fact that he was following in the footsteps of a historical personage. His immediate predecessor as Laure de Berny's lover was M. de Berny's brother;[7] but before that, she had lived on and off for fifteen years with André Campi, a fierce Republican who had grown up in the same house as the Bonapartes in Ajaccio and had remained a close friend and accomplice of Napoleon's brother, Lucien. Some of the 'eyewitness' accounts from the world of imperial espionage in *Une Ténébreuse Affaire* are almost certainly those of André Campi, retold by Mme de Berny.

For us, the greatest value of this affair is the eyewitness account it provides of what would otherwise be a rather murky mind, far from the centre of the literary world, cloaked in pseudonyms and represented by a handful of novels that sound like Maturin or Walter Scott or the popular French novelists of the day, or the servant of them all, but not Balzac. This is particularly so since, for the following four years, only eighteen of Balzac's letters have survived. The letters to

Mme de Berny almost disappeared too. At her request, they were burned by her son after her death in 1836;[8] but the rough drafts of the letters composed in 1822 – sometimes several drafts for the same letter – were kept. Few writers ever made so little use of a litter-bin and the Lovenjoul Collection now bears witness to the amount of paper that would eventually be condensed into several thousand pages. Suddenly, in this impromptu epistolary novel, much of it sharing space with novels in progress, a rich personality appears – one is almost forced to say unexpectedly – far richer than the cynical wit implied by the works of Lord R'Hoone. For the first time, Balzac emerges in adult form, not, like most letter-writers, intermittently expressing aspects of a more or less continuous character, but a whole personality in pursuit of an aim, bringing its arsenal of emotions to bear on the desired object. His first letter was, romantically and implausibly, given the size of Villeparisis, anonymous:

You are unhappy, I know, but your soul has riches which you yourself do not suspect and which might still attach you to life.

When you appeared to me, you did so with that grace which surrounds any creature whose suffering comes from the heart. I love those who suffer, even without knowing them. Thus, for me, your melancholy was a charm, your misfortune a magnet, and from the moment you revealed the beauties of your mind, all my thoughts involuntarily attached themselves to the sweet memories I have of you.[9]

This 'young soul' was 'ordinarily filled with presumptuous sentiments', but had decided now to live without hope, though Balzac's opening remark about continuing attachments to life suggested anything but despair. One subtle contradiction follows another: he was 'excessively timid, madly in love and so chaste that he dare not say "I am in love"'. All he sought was her compassion and to offer up his 'unsullied and impeccable soul'. But then another contradiction: the reply was to be sent to 'Mr Manfredi', a Byronic name with an Italian ending. To a well-read woman, such a name would hint fairly strongly that the hopeless young soul might not be content with so little. Such sentimental hyperbole is by no means unusual in love-letters of the time – spiritual exaggerations were a normal part of middle-class courtship – but Balzac had had more practice than most and was now exploiting clichés far more adroitly and humorously than in his novels. He had found a new focus for his writing, a difficult audience that was infinitely more intelligent and demanding than the clientele of *cabinets de lecture*.

Most of the ploys which Balzac uses in these letters recur in stories in *La Comédie Humaine* and he usually explains them so fully and with such obvious delight that it is hard to believe they could fail. The second letter, for instance, like many of the others, was 'the last'. This time, the tactic was (as he put it himself) 'humility' and disarming honesty. Proof of the former consisted in sending Mme de Berny verses by another poet, André Chénier. In fact, the poem is by Balzac, its meaning apparent to anyone with a basic grasp of erotic euphemism: a 'naive' butterfly is stung by a bee and 'dies' among the petals of a disdainful red rose. The honesty – a stroke of genius – came in the following phrase: 'This young scatterbrain peered for an instant into the well and thought he spied the head of the goddess who was hiding there; but perhaps it was just his own head that he saw.' This touching self-awareness was a tactical retreat inviting the adversary to rush into the gap.

Mme de Berny, one gathers, stood her ground. She had children and a husband, and in any case she was too old. She had even had a son who, had he not died in 1814, would have been the same age as Balzac. This, of course, was one more argument in favour, and the novelist's repertoire was far from exhausted. After attributing his own verses to Chénier, he sent her a long definition of what it meant to be in love: 'To love is to lose all trace of individuality, to live the life of another.' In the circumstances, it was an ironic remark. If Mme de Berny had read the recent translation of *Melmoth the Wanderer*, she might have noticed some curious similarities.... Another device which allowed Balzac to combine wooing with novel-writing practice was to put words into the loved one's mouth: 'My God! If I were a woman and forty-five years old and still pretty, I should behave very differently, I can tell you. I should first have tried to fathom the character of the man who worshipped me.' The result of such an attempt would, naturally, be love, and, he went on to save her the trouble of concluding, 'I should have yielded to love and endeavoured to rediscover in that emotion the delights of youth, its innocent illusions, its naivety and all its charming privileges.' Still she resisted.

He appealed to logical argument. If her principles were 'philosophic' she should realize that life could be enjoyed to the full without fear of damnation; if Christian, she should say to herself, 'Hurting someone is a crime, a crime I am committing. . . Is it my fault if Society is built on unnatural foundations?' 'There are means', she was supposed to reflect, 'of not hurting anyone'. Balzac was increasingly impatient for consummation. By April 1822, he was resorting to outright requests and by April, too, he was completely in love and perhaps on the point of losing hope for real: 'I need a heart into which I can pour out this excess of sensibility, this flame by which I shall eventually be consumed. Is it possible to achieve intimacy without becoming irrevocably tied?' He included a tempting offer to look after the children and to act as their adviser, for, as he pointed out with charming indiscretion and as a reminder of how little she had to lose, 'Some fathers, because of their age or character, are ill-suited to the task.'

Thanks to Mme de Berny's resistance, two important aspects of Balzac's own character emerge very clearly from these letters. One is the destructive power of sexual frustration: a common and expedient theme in letters to Mme Hanska when she was hundreds of miles away from the Capital of Sin in the Ukraine. Balzac talks to her of being 'frozen' or 'stultified' by unsatisfied desire. It was one of the few things which stemmed the tide of his writing; but it is also one of the great themes of his work – the creative instinct calling for more than one outlet. Balzac had no need of psycholinguistics to tell him that the will to write and the will to reproduce had more than a metaphorical connection.

The other, perhaps related aspect is a quality which is almost never associated with Balzac, though he mentions it again and again as one of the great neglected subjects of literature: timidity. As Mme de Berny had discovered when, with an insolence to which her standing entitled her, she warned Mme Balzac about her son's lamentable lack of restraint, timidity did not always express itself in trembling silence. Erratic behaviour was also a symptom of this terrible affliction. Terrible because it forced even the most honest people, like Cousin Pons, to harbour secrets, 'to make of their hearts a sanctuary' – 'a phenomenon which many superficial people translate with the word *egotism*'.[10] When Balzac bemoaned the quirk of fate which 'dealt me a triple dose of timidity' and followed the assertion with a passionate two-page letter, this was not a lie. Words were not always adequate to express the truth. His heart, as he often told Mme Hanska, remained a secret to almost everyone he knew; it was the innermost compartment of a Chinese box.[11] Faced with the enormous volume of his work, 'lost for words' is not a phrase that leaps to mind; yet difficulty in expressing oneself is a powerful motive for writing. A famous note in Balzac's album has, in its seeming absurdity, a disquieting air of accuracy: 'My life is one long silence.'[12] And it is surely significant that Balzac is the only prominent writer of the Romantic period in France who never wrote or thought of writing his autobiography.

The epistolary novel of 1822 was a glorious triumph for timidity. In May, they met at nightfall in Mme de Berny's garden and exchanged an unforgettable kiss. Balzac renamed the bench they sat on an 'altar'. Mme de Berny had finally listened to reason. 'A writer once said', she wrote in her only known letter from this period, 'that happiness is not something that can be *found*; it simply grows of its own will; but I would say instead, my divine cherub, that you constantly create it; it emanates from you like scent from a flower – to plagiarize T[homas] M[oore].' 'Your talents are enormous, but your darling senses and understands them all. Oh! why are there not one thousand souls within me that I might give you all I should like to give and as I should like to give it ... for nothing that belongs to me is mine!'

Because of his rapid 'victory' Balzac is either praised or upbraided for the literary ruses of his correspondence; but there is little reason to suppose that modern readers of his letters are any more perceptive than the woman who received them – a woman who could have claimed more fairly than Lepoitevin to have created Balzac. She, for Balzac, was the woman who taught him 'good taste'; she 'enlarged [my] skull between caresses and raised the curtain which hides the world's stage'.[13] The 'eagle hatched by geese' or, as Mme de Berny put it appropriately in a Romantic commonplace, the flower put forth by a dung-heap, had been badly brought up. He engaged in social intercourse as an actor harangued an audience; and his manners at table or in the drawing-room were abysmal. But like Balzac's friends from the École de Droit and, later, in the editorial rooms of newspapers, she found his performances wonderfully memorable and entertaining. He always seemed to be happy and it was difficult not to be happy when listening to him. Mme de Berny saw the writer beneath the pseudonym. Had she lived in the twentieth century she would have led a very different life. Even before she fell in love with him, Balzac seemed to offer the equivalent of a challenging new career.

Perhaps, then, the real reason for his success as a writer of love-letters was not any particular ruse but the mere exercise of ingenuity. Under Mme de Berny's guidance he began to make notes on the 'science' of surviving marriage and committing adultery (slyly presented a few years later in *Physiologie du Mariage* as a set of instructions for preventing it). Some of these notes contain helpful hints for would-be seducers – the fruit of the letters written in 1822 and one of the reasons why *Physiologie du Mariage* was placed on the Catholic Index of proscribed books: 'The chief merit in women's eyes is to love them. If you cannot win their hearts, win their minds; get vanity on your side. And if you cannot get them to love you, contrive to make them fonder of themselves. Do not allow them to remain indifferent; they seek emotions against which nothing can prevail.' The main thing was to keep writing and, if you failed, it would only serve to show that you had been labouring under a misapprehension, for 'a woman who is no longer deceived by a love-letter is a monster'.[14]

IT WAS AT this point that Mme Balzac shunted her son off to Bayeux, hoping to nip the romance in the bud. However, after his return he started visiting '*that house*' twice a day: 'I wish we were 100 miles from Villeparisis. . . . He does not realize that they are simply trying to make a fool of him.'[15] In November 1822 the whole family moved back to the Marais for a time. The lovers continued to meet in the capital and in 1824 Mme de Berny would help Balzac to furnish his own apartment in the Rue de Tournon on the Left Bank. 'I fear', Mme Balzac wrote on that ominous occasion, 'that this retreat is merely a pretext for indulging without any restraint in a passion which will be his downfall. He fled from home with that woman and she was away in Paris for three whole days.'[16]

Balzac's romantic success was reflected in new optimism, and at the start of the year he was looking forward to independence. He told his sister he was going to work 'like the horse of Henri IV before it was cast in bronze and this year I hope to earn the 20,000 francs which will form the basis of my fortune'. He signed a covenant with his father, promising to pay him 1200 francs a year for room and board. Lighting, heating and laundry were not included:[17] a lodger whose life revolved around publishers' deadlines and a lover could be very expensive to keep.

Paris, as usual, supplied the start of another adventure. One day Balzac was stopped in the street by a publisher called Pollet.[18] His *Librairie Théâtrale et Romantique** was fast becoming a Parisian institution. Most of the plays performed in the capital were on his list. Scribe, the playwright from the chambers of Guillonnet-Merville, had already signed up. Pollet must have been alerted to this rising star by Lepoitevin since he had a contract ready in his pocket for Balzac's next two novels, *Le Centenaire* and *Le Vicaire des Ardennes*, both to be published under the pseudonym 'Horace de Saint-Aubin'. Balzac was easily seduced. Pollet paid less than Hubert but offered the sop of a cash advance, which was especially attractive at a time when currency was in short supply.

In life, hopes of fame and fortune; in literature, ambitions of a metaphysical variety. A 'phantasmagoria' which would now be classified as science fiction, *Le Centenaire* appeared in November 1822. It earned Balzac several enthusiastic or mildly hysterical reviews. Even the derogatory reviews contained enticing criticisms: they bemoaned the sort of literature that led to a general loosening of corsets. The *Journal des Théâtres* had visions of 'the most intrepid female novel-readers swooning' at this product of the vogue for 'the extraordinary, the bizarre and the incomprehensible . . .': 'in a word, *Romanticism!*' In the *Annales Françaises des Arts*, an authoritative critic sounding suspiciously like Balzac used *Le Centenaire* as a pretext for defending the modern novel – something entirely new, he claimed. The storage capacity of literature had been greatly increased: 'A frame which can accommodate the effects of passion, moral observations, the depiction of manners, scenes of domestic life, etc., etc.; and this genre which is the one and only real achievement of modern literature is anathematized by all and sundry.' The Centenarian himself believes that if ripe young maidens continue to present themselves at the right moment, then he will live for ever and, as a logical consequence, become

---

* *Romantique* was still used as the adjectival form of *roman* (novel).

omniscient, the walking 'archives of Nature and the Human Race'. Balzac shared his hero's dream. He wanted, as he would throughout his life, to be more than just an omniscient *narrator*: as a prelude to his review of the novel he gave a potted history of narrative forms from Homer to Walter Scott. The history ends with a certain 'Horace de Saint-Aubin'.

Le Vicaire des Ardennes was published almost at the same time. It too was a success, but of a very different kind. In some ways, this novel, which few were able to read, was the real basis of Balzac's fortune, though several years would pass before its promise was realized. In the meantime, Balzac had to be content with a *succès de scandale*. Accidental incest had been a popular and acceptable subject since Chateaubriand's *René*, but not when it was aggravated by the fact that the central protagonist was a priest. Balzac was exploiting two markets at the same time: the romantic fairy-tale and the pleasantly unedifying 'philosophical' story. Yet he also managed to fulfil some of the grand hopes for the modern novel expressed in his anonymous review of *Le Centenaire*. To the reader who has entered the back-streets of Balzac's juvenilia having first explored the boulevards and squares of *La Comédie Humaine*, it is here that the sound of the author's voice is first heard again. And not only his voice. Several seemingly peripheral aspects of his peculiar methods make their first appearance with *Le Vicaire*: his nail-biting tactics for meeting dead-lines, his talent for advertising, and the first exchange in a long and hilariously inconsequential conversation with that troublesome contingent of his audience, officialdom.

Taking advantage of his long stay in Bayeux, Balzac had assigned to his sister Laure and her husband the job of providing a plot and as many chapters as they could manage. They were far too slow. After returning to Paris he wrote in a panic to ask for the manuscript, claiming that Lepoitevin was also going to write a *Vicaire*: 'He hasn't started yet, but he might easily catch me up. He's got the speed to do it.' 'I doubt very much you'll be able to do two chapters a day each and get *Le Vicaire* to me by 15 September; and even then that would leave me only two weeks in which to redraft it.' Creation *ex nihilo* always seemed an awesome impossibility. God, he liked to say, only kept it up for six days. Once the text existed in some form the work was easy. Ninety per cent of Balzac's labour consisted not in writing but in rewriting and even his masterpiece *La Cousine Bette* began life as a short story written by his sister for a children's magazine. It was expedient in any case, since the unwritten book had already been sold to Pollet, to use whatever cheap labour was available, just as painters of large canvases enlisted the help of students to fill in the background. The contracts Balzac signed in the throes of enthusiasm were more tyrannical than any classical muse, but they prevented indecision and excessive reflection from ruining the work – or so Balzac maintains. Even now he was urging himself on with emergencies deliberately manufactured and acquiring those perilous habits which are part of what his contemporaries were too amazed or irritated to call his 'technique': 'Whichever parts of it are finished must go straight to the printers. So I shall write it while they are printing it.'

Whether or not necessity was the mother of invention, *Le Vicaire*, for a few memorable pages, introduced an entirely new tone into the French novel. It quickly becomes embroiled like its predecessors in a meandering plot into which a black-faced pirate called Argow improbably intrudes; but as the villagers of Aulnay stand around waiting for their new curate to arrive, they threaten for a moment to steal the show from the heroes and villains, coming alive in all their fascinating trivia – perhaps the result of following the little dramas acted out in the tedium of Bayeux. Historical details are no longer merely picturesque; they describe individuals, just as the characters all tell a story much larger than themselves. The general is evoked through the particular, not wedged artificially into the plot. In future, all reality would be grist to the mill. Science, too, was plundered for new insights and techniques. Balzac had purchased a 'superb' copy of Lavater's *Art of Knowing Men by Their Physiognomy* and had it bound: it was like a dictionary of the human face. Sure enough, in *Le Vicaire*, the colour of an eye, the shape of a face, the curl of a lip take on enormous scientific or artistic significance.

These innovations were honoured with an official mark of disapproval. *Le Vicaire des Ardennes* was the cause of Balzac's first skirmish with that many-headed, brainless monster – the same monster which knew all about Montzaigle and which worried for months on end about Bernard-François's entitlement to his pension. In 1822, bureaucracy for Balzac took the form of the Censor: an impressive title which usually concealed an anonymous clerk sifting through the ever-increasing numbers of novels for evidence of 'immorality' or, more to the point, anti-Government feeling. The Church was re-establishing itself in the State. Balzac's novel coincided with the promulgation of laws making 'outrage on religion' and questioning the divine right of kings serious crimes. A note appeared on the desk of the Inspector of Printing and Publishing. *Le Vicaire des Ardennes*, he was informed, was a pernicious work liable to arouse scorn for the State religion and its ministers. (The old priest Gausse's protruding shirt-tails were probably more inflammatory than the incest.) The most damning part of the report has to do with the mitigating circumstances: 'The absence of any talent and the absurdities one finds in this book would seem, however, to diminish the force of its attack on all that is most respectable and holy.' Prosecution was nevertheless recommended.[19]

Balzac was one of the first writers to make bureaucracy the subject of serious fiction, notably in *Les Employés* and the *Aventures Administratives d'une Idée Heureuse*, where he takes an un-Kafkaesque delight in its lumbering procedures. As he shows in these bureaucratic dramas which are still enlightening today, the monster was not so much malevolent as driven to almost random interference by its futile over-activity. Priests emotionally entangled with lusting parishioners were a staple of cheap fiction. Balzac read just such a tale, published in 1820 by a Mme S. P——. He even borrowed the plot. *Le Prêtre* (by Sophie Pannier) escaped prosecution for six years, whereas Balzac's barely reached the bookshops; and yet her most sordid imaginings – kissing in the confession-box, for example – are noticeably absent from Balzac's *Vicaire*. It was a serious treatment of a frivolous theme, and perhaps this, combined with the author's sarcasm, attacking not religion but novelistic clichés, helped to arouse the Censor.

On 26 November 1822, the Inspector of Printing and Publishing wrote to the Minister of the Interior who wrote to the Chief of Police who reported back to the Minister. The novel had been confiscated; the manuscript was removed from the author's home, despite the remonstrations of Mme de Balzac who tried to blame the publisher, and all the *cabinets de lecture* in the vicinity of the Palais-Royal had been scoured for stray copies. Someone had done a thorough job. The Chief of Police now applied to the Head of the Bureau of Printing and Publishing who asked his spies for a report on the author. The administrative sledgehammer was about to descend. It fell on the wrong nut. A 'Report on M. Balzac' was issued on 8 January 1823. He was, it said, a seventy-eight-year-old man with four children of whom the eldest had completed his studies; his views on religion and the monarchy were irreproachable and, most commendable of all, he had friends in high places. At this point, the matter was dropped and Balzac/Saint-Aubin survived to write a sequel to the story which had been the object of so much flattering attention.

Bernard-François had obviously answered the door to the spies and passed himself off as the delinquent novelist. The niggling of civil servants was of little concern to a man who, in his latest letter to Honoré, had expatiated on the subject of the chaos which had been reigning now

> for almost 2300 years, ever since it was discovered that we all possess an imperishable soul to comfort us by equating us thus with the innumerable masses moving without change in the incomprehensible space of the universe. A fine sight it is too, but what a racket those souls create, especially since there is neither up nor down, and maybe one day they will all rise up and come and sting us all over like the invisible harvest mite, and then women will be forced to remove their skirts if they do not wish to stand around scratching themselves in front of all of Israel.[20]

In league with his father, Balzac had successfully manipulated the bureaucratic chaos which masqueraded as order. This too might count as an important artistic achievement. The whimsical preface in which he talked of standing before the 'criminal court' of public opinion had been a virtual invitation to prosecute; and just in case a sleepy official missed the hint, a 'Note from the Publisher' on the last page boasted of an imaginary court case pending against the author. As soon as a verdict is reached, said Saint-Aubin, his next novel will be put on sale; 'and this new novel will be called *Le Criminel*'. *Annette et le Criminel* appeared as promised the following December, brazenly sub-titled 'Sequel to *Le Vicaire des Ardennes*'. Balzac referred to the confiscation and, adding insult to injury, pointed out that it was unusual to find a sequel to a novel in which, by the end of the story, almost all the characters were dead.

These sarcastic notes, for all their well-deserved gloating, come to seem more and more like an impatience with the limits of popular fiction. Each time, this impatience expressed itself as an intrusion of daily life – and the gap between the two was beginning to disappear.

LIFE AND fiction were especially close, uncomfortably so, in journalism, which began to take up more of Balzac's time after he met another entrepreneur of the Lepoitevin school: Horace Raisson. Delacroix, who painted Raisson's portrait, found this 'pen-pusher', whom he had known at school, an interesting subject: he was a liar, incorrigibly smug, pretended to be gormless, but 'he is and always will be the worst charlatan I know'.²¹ Raisson belonged to a new breed, the 'literary broker', forerunner of the literary agent. Despite their reputation, literary brokers were the right arm of many writers at a time when publishers were also booksellers and sometimes printers too. One of the many handbooks which Balzac and Raisson concocted in the 1820s (they include the handbook for 'Honest People') describes the work of a *courtier littéraire*: 'There is no point in his knowing how to write, but he must know how to talk, and talk at great length, talk volumes, in a word, in order to attract the buyer.' Balzac learned the lessons so well that he was able later in his career to drive at least one publisher into bankruptcy.

Raisson also had a useful father who, until 1822, had occupied a strategic position in the heart of the Ministry of Police.²² Like so many other people, it seems – even Mme de Berny's husband – Raisson *père* had been a colleague of Bernard-François, and one inevitably wonders whether Raisson was in any way connected with the decision not to prosecute Saint-Aubin. Whatever strange coincidences occur in Balzac's novels, and whatever secret societies he dreams up, they barely do justice to the human web which makes early nineteenth-century Paris seem like a middle-class village conducting its own affairs in the heart of a proletarian city.

In the company of Raisson and Lepoitevin, Balzac explored the depths of journalism and by some accounts quickly reached the bottom of his profession. He contributed articles, which included reviews of his own novels, to two ephemeral newspapers with liberal tendencies – liberal, that is, both politically and morally. One incident has proved particularly hard to explain away. The feudal right of primogeniture (the *droit d'aînesse*) had recently re-emerged as the question by which one's political allegiance was judged. It stipulated that a family's wealth should pass intact to the eldest son, thus preserving what Balzac calls 'permanent landed superiorities'. The whole *Comédie Humaine* could be read, superficially, as a defence of this conservative law, the principal means of averting democratic chaos and the splintering of the State into countless money-grubbing individuals. In the 1820s, however, Balzac was siding with the Liberals. Just like the journalists in *Illusions Perdues* whose best ideas come to them shortly before they sink under the table at midnight:

'Listen, lads,' said Finot [a composite of Lepoitevin, Raisson and others like them], 'the Liberals have got to stir things up because for the time being they have nothing bad to say about the Government; and you know how awkward that is for the Opposition. Does anyone want to write a pamphlet calling for the reintroduction of the *droit d'aînesse* so there will be an outcry against the secret designs of the Court? I'll make it worth your while.'

'I'll do it,' said Hector Merlin. 'It's what I believe anyway.'

'Your party would say you're compromising them,' Finot retorted. 'Félicien, why don't you do it? Dauriat will publish it and no one will be the wiser.'

'How much?' asked Vernou.

'Six hundred francs! You can sign it "Count C . . ."'

'It's a deal,' said Vernou.

'So you're going to elevate *canards* to the level of politics?'

'. . . All we're doing is attributing certain intentions to the Government so as to unleash public opinion against it.'[23]

The conversation in the restaurant where Balzac demonstrates the indirect influence of champagne on politics is a slice of his own life, prepared for public consumption fifteen years later. Early in 1824 a long, meticulously argued pamphlet on the *droit d'aînesse* was published by a M. D——, known to his liberal friends as Honoré Balzac. Its effectiveness can be gauged by the fact that it inspired a passionate counter-attack by a true liberal, who was convinced that M. D—— was a member of the Government and was incensed by its bare-faced hypocrisy.[24]

A liberal Balzac proposing a reactionary measure is a phenomenon which, as the saying goes, has exercised the ingenuity of critics. If true, that is, if Balzac's conversion to the other camp was still many years off, this is indeed an unusual sight: a writer renowned for his rigid convictions vigorously promoting a belief that was not his own. The *literary* answer is that Balzac was practising conformity to a given genre. Here, he was writing in the role of *agent provocateur* and doing so with great skill: when Laure told her husband that she suspected Honoré of writing the pamphlet, Surville refused to believe it. In his opinion, it must have been 'by a man between thirty and thirty-five who knows a lot about business'.[25] In some forms of literature the taboo against propounding views one does not hold is weak. Some professions freely allow and encourage it, and Balzac, like Walter Scott, had known 'the ambidexter ingenuity of the law'.[26] It would be impossible in any case to calculate the degree of Balzac's sincerity. The pompous tone of the tract could equally be irony or an attempt to sound like a real reactionary. Neither side would be able to tell. To many ears, however, the fact that Balzac chooses as his example a father with four children, together with the epigraph on the title-page, might sound an ironic, autobiographical note: 'Be lord over thy brethren, and let thy mother's sons bow down to thee.'[27] In fact, the epigraph was practically an invitation to launch a counter-attack. Those impressive words, conveniently accompanied by chapter and verse, are pronounced by Isaac when Jacob sidles into the tent with his goatskin hands to steal his brother's blessing.

There is little to suggest, then, that Balzac was leaning prematurely to the Right or even, for that matter, that his ruse was any more dishonest than the Socratic ploy of giving clear expression to one's opponent's views. The most upsetting lesson of the episode might be that it hints that Balzac's political conversion did not occur in a flash of light and that intellectual change is rarely recorded like the sound of a voice in the tremor of a brush-stroke. Perhaps, though, this was the seed of later reflections. After all, it is not unheard-of that being forced, even by money, to think hard about a subject previously ignored or judged in haste should lead to a change of mind.

Two months later, Balzac was cashing in on his historical research a second time. In all likelihood commissioned by a legitimist and another red rag to any true liberal, his anonymous *Histoire Impartiale des Jésuites*[28] was certainly impartial, the author's efficacy being unimpeded by personal conviction. He borrowed from other works including one by the Jesuit Cerutti which was itself a fine example of plagiarism. 'This is the cry of Truth and Innocence,' declares the epigraph, also taken from Cerutti – he of whom Balzac says, with a merry cynicism reminiscent of his fictional journalists, 'We shall not undertake herein to perform the task of which Cerutti has acquitted himself with such success and such care.'

In these pamphlets or *exercices de style*, as in some of Balzac's early novels, one senses his excitement at seeing dry research and everyday experience turning, as if by mystical transmutation, into money. Apart from what it would allow him to do later, money was a form of recognition, especially for someone who had suffered embarrassment at school through lack of it. But there was something else too. There was the thrill of espousing an opposite point of view and rendering it with all the finesse of a con-man or a novelist. One of Balzac's favourite alter egos is Gaudissart, the commercial traveller from Touraine who can sell any product from hair-restorer to insurance and do so anywhere except, like Christ, in his (and the author's) native region. The tracts on primogeniture and the Jesuits, in spite of the epigraph from Cerutti and in spite of Balzac's subsequent curse on the tribe of journalists, proved that 'Truth', or the ability to convey something resembling it, had very little to do with Innocence.[29]

Some people outside the family watched Balzac's progress with dismay. For one of his friends the confiscation of *Le Vicaire* was a blessing in disguise, a sign that he was frittering away his talents. The Censor, in his opinion, was the unwitting agent of divine intervention and Balzac should heed the warning before it was too late to turn back. Jean Thomassy had studied law in Paris, though Balzac probably met him when Hubert published his book, *De la Sensation qu'a faite en France la Mort de Buonaparte*. Balzac found in him a loyal friend who relished his last remaining contact with the literary world he left, too sensibly, for the boredom of provincial administration.

Thomassy is thought to have been responsible for setting Balzac on the path that led to monarchism and Catholicism. Balzac's public conversion to the 'Throne and Altar' camp would occur several years later, coinciding with his accession to a higher social sphere. Still, if any individual converted Balzac it would have been Thomassy, to judge by the unreasonable faith which Balzac later placed in his stylistic advice. Thomassy knew Balzac well enough to find his soft spot. With the cheering or depressing thought that human interest is indispensable to even the most elevated undertaking, he assured his friend that given an influx of 'moral and religious ideas', 'your talent will increase'; but he should first stop writing novels: 'They may serve as relaxation but should not form the single occupation of a young man who gives such high hopes to those who know him.'[30] It was a sad case of unenlightened self-interest: a glutton at life's banquet, Balzac was eating dessert before his dinner.

There were, however, encouraging signs. His wayward friend had started to elaborate a treatise on prayer. Such a work, Thomassy advised him, called for more than a good imagination. 'You need to have religious habits, and it is also necessary to have had prolonged intercourse with the deity.' Balzac, whose fondness for the mystic's confusion of the physical and the spiritual is one of the constant delights of his work, could not have agreed more. Since finding a new centre of attraction for his spiritual life in Laure de Berny, he was familiar with this source of inspiration, and it may have been after reflecting on Thomassy's recommendations that he rewrote the opening paragraph of his otherwise sober *Traité*. They were the words of an inspired disciple:

> Since I have acceded to a sphere of luminous delight and continual ecstasy by a channel which any man may take, I thought it charitable to tell other people how sweet was my initiation, how easy my progress on this path once the first obstacles were overcome, what luscious fruits refreshed my parched mouth, on what soft pastures I reposed, with what gentleness the Voice caressed my ear, with what nourishing perfumes my soul was gladdened.

Balzac was not an orthodox Catholic. As far as the Church itself was concerned he was converted probably early on to a pragmatic, positivist view. His famous assertion that Christianity should be enshrined in law as 'a complete system of repression of the depraved tendencies in Man' exactly follows the line taken by the pliant ex-priests at Vendôme. Whatever transcendent realities it corresponded to, Christianity provided Society with an efficient moral code. His occasional blunders when describing religious ceremonies suggest that he did little to plug the gaps in his religious education: breviaries and missals, chalices and ciboria are all jumbled up in his church scenes. For Balzac, spiritual power came from within and could manifest itself in tangible ways unrecognized by any institution. For an analytical mind convinced that all knowledge was there for the taking, mysticism was a logical conclusion.

If Balzac underwent a conversion at the age of twenty-five, it lay, as the ecstatic *Traité de la Prière* shows half-seriously, in the fulfilment of a long-frustrated need. Salvation through sexual intercourse is one of the themes of his life and work. Sometimes it takes a humorous form, as in the *Conte Drolatique* in which an eighty-two-year-old fornicator is saved from the scaffold by offering proof of his virility *in extremis*.[31] At other times, the tendency to see sexual relations, and even pregnancy, as the proof of affection which stands for all others, could be disastrous. The episode with the Duchesse de Castries in 1832 would be a terrible illustration of this. But even with Laure de Berny fulfilment was never complete.

At the end of 1823, the reading committee of the Gaîté Theatre was given the chance to consider one side of this dilemma. Balzac submitted a melodrama which was judged pretentious and badly put together but by no means beyond repair.[32] In fact, the theatre would have been pleased to accept the play had Balzac not rendered himself guilty of 'grave improprieties'. The 'dangerous' subject he chose, remarkable for the time, was the unrequited love of a black servant for his employer's wife. Racism was an uncommon theme, but Balzac, for so long the foreign body in his mother's family, made no emotional distinction between ostracism and sexual frustration. Both states led the victim to vengeance and destruction.

The other possible solution was expressed more mawkishly, as befits wishful thinking, in another Saint-Aubin: *La Dernière Fée ou La Nouvelle Lampe Merveilleuse* (i.e. *Aladdin 2*). Abel, the son of a brilliant chemist, has grown up as a child of Nature, believing in fairies. One day he meets one – a fairy with a girdle of pearls around her 'svelte and voluptuous waist'. The Pearl Fairy turns out to be the Duchess of Sommerset (*sic*), 'one of the prettiest women in England', and Abel, according to an old document found in a corner, is actually Count Osterwald: echoes of the little boy from Tours simultaneously ascending to the aristocracy and finding true love. 'And to this day, the purest bliss has crowned each day of Abel's life, and no doubt this undiluted happiness will endure.' This time, there was no sarcastic preface; but then Balzac's dream seemed to be coming true. Mme de Berny had waved the modern magic wand, a private income. 'Alas!' Balzac remembered in 1849, 'I thought *La Dernière Fée* was the best book in the world. A woman helped me to print the 500 copies which then spent three years languishing in a bookshop!'[33]

There were few signs indeed that 'religious' devotion was improving Balzac's work as Thomassy expected. By his own account, in 'sacrificing' himself to Mme de Berny he was handing over responsibility for his life, his reason for living and even his finances, just like a convert: 'Happy to live from now on in your heart . . . I shall nourish myself with memories, illusions and dreams, and my life will be entirely imaginative as it already was in part.' There was no accompanying attempt to change his life. Balzac later talks of the vain desire 'to solve my life by emotional pleasure'.[34] He even confided in Mme Hanska that though she saved him from himself, Mme de Berny 'tarnished the seven or eight years she gave me'.[35] This disconcerting reappraisal of their relationship was partly for the benefit of his distant lover and, one suspects, was suggested to him by the rhyme *Berny – terni* (tarnished). But was Balzac still dissembling when he told Mme Hanska that on their first momentous meeting in Neuchâtel in 1833, he suddenly realized that he had never truly been in love and that 'Mme de Berny was only my immense filial affection, frustrated by one mother and smiled on by another'?[36] Timidity and uncertainty, social as well as sexual, clearly made it easier, for example, to be a propagandist of other people's views and, later, to create hundreds of characters, each one convincing and complete. Such talents come at a price. This 'wonderful gift' which also allowed him, like a spirit, to 'traverse the intervening space' between him and Mme de Berny, was about to embroil him in such confusion that it is easy to believe him when he says his life did not begin until 1833.

Balzac's confusion was in some ways analogous to the problems faced by Sarrasine, the sculptor in one of his earliest short stories who falls in love with a beautiful soprano – a soprano who turns out to be a eunuch. In retrospect, Sarrasine appears to have been concerned to safeguard his sexual identity. Balzac, too, in his letters to Mme de Berny, addresses her not only as his mother but also as his friend (in the masculine), hinting at an attempt to fit even the most unconventional aspects of himself into the ideal new role. In a revealing episode, Sarrasine is expelled from a Jesuit school (like Balzac, during Easter) for sculpting a figure which Jung might have described as a composite symbol of the self, or which might also be seen, in view of the redemptive power Balzac ascribes to sex, as a shocking retranslation of *Christus erectus*.

CHAPTER SIX

The Price
of Free Enterprise

(1824–1828)

G LORY, says the anonymous biographer of Horace de Saint-
Aubin, is like a greasy pole: one after another, hopeful people
clamber up, only to slither down in a disgusting mess, until
one day all the grease has come off on other people's clothes and some
smug, undeserving contestant shins all the way to the top and takes all
the credit.[1] At the age of twenty-five – an age, he says, at which a man
has become the person he will remain for the rest of his life[2] – Balzac,
like his pseudonym Saint-Aubin, was back at the bottom of the pole,
covered in disgrace. His career as a novelist had come to an end. The
constantly accelerating procession of gambles and catastrophes that
followed was a protracted farewell to what Balzac himself marked off
as the final years of the first part of his life, or as another life altogether:
life as a manufacturer and a businessman, life, above all, as an incurable
optimist getting deeper and deeper into debt. His social ascent
continued – he was about to become entangled with an impecunious
duchess – but the producer of popular fiction, though still alive, almost
disappeared from view. Different personae came to the front of the
stage, most of them brilliantly unrepresentative of their profession:
the publisher, the printer, the compiler of coffee-table books and
manuals on trivial subjects – and then, as if returning to the very
rudiments of writing, the founder of the metal type used to print
books. As for the finished product, all the bits and pieces which can
be traced back to this period show Balzac surrounded by fragments of
a great work, but more like the owner of a curiosity-shop than an
architect. Balzac's historical research and mock-statistical studies of
modern life can be seen as the laying of literary foundations; but their
first obvious function was their contribution to one overriding goal:

paying debts. Without the increasingly uncalculated risks which culminated in the disaster of 1828, Balzac would not have spent the rest of his life trying to balance the books, by writing novels. This, as much as any cultural achievement like the invention of the modern novel or the portrayal of a civilization, was true heroism: 'I am more a great financier than I am a great writer, for I have settled my accounts with my pen.'[3]

Balzac's paradoxical pride in manipulating the forces he denounced in his novels is one of the persistent themes of his daily life. His short but amicable encounter with a young Baudelaire in the 1840s (they greeted each other by laughing uncontrollably in the street)[4] may well have something to do with the fact that Baudelaire had published a humorous article which others read as an insult but which Balzac must have recognized as a friendly homage: 'How to Pay Your Debts When You're a Genius'. 'I wanted to show', Baudelaire explained with a sense of his subject's congruity, 'that the great poet knows how to deal with a bill of exchange as easily as he unravels the plot of the most intricate and mysterious of novels.'[5] In 1838, a visitor noticed on the shelves which held the bound copies of Balzac's novels, standing next to the *Contes Drolatiques*, a sinister-looking volume bound in black. 'Take a look,' said Balzac. 'It's an unpublished work of some considerable value.' The title was *Comptes Mélancoliques*. It was a compendium of his debts.[6]

1824 was the first of those setbacks that Balzac liked to see as a personal Beresina or Waterloo. Perhaps because his liberal friends felt he was taking his royalist role too seriously, or because he made a better mercenary than they, *Annette et le Criminel* was efficiently demolished in the *Feuilleton Littéraire*. The fact that the same newspaper had just published Balzac's glowing résumé of his own novel was irrelevant. The editors decided to tell the true story on 12 May 1824. It was a savage review, obviously written by someone who knew Balzac well, and was probably the origin of his phobic reactions to printed criticism, even if the reviewer was a well-meaning accomplice. His 'mystical platitudes' were cruelly compared to the witty sermon on conscience of one of his favourite authors, Laurence Sterne. The characters were stilted, his writing sloppy and the whole book fantastic: only wet-nurses and infants would believe that a virginal heroine could fall for a hardened criminal, a forty-year-old

'Hercules with frizzy hair'. The attack was snidely presented as compassionate advice and, like most damaging criticism, contained some grains of truth. Saint-Aubin was basking in religious sentimentality, not because he was a supporter of the Church but because he was surreptitiously taking a collection for his own cause. Evidence of this was found in a hypocritical obsession with hangmen and prison cells: gallows humour without the punch-line – all very well for the notoriously morbid English reader, but the French would never stand for such displays of bad taste.

Balzac was enough of a connoisseur of modern literature to know that *Annette*, like *Wann-Chlore* – which he had recently retrieved from his files – was a highly original combination of Romantic melodrama and bourgeois realism. In fact, a note scribbled on the back of an invitation to a memorial service for Granny Sallambier suggests that the author hoped his novels would form the first wing of a greater edifice: '3 vols on the private life of the French'.[7] The sharpest sting lay not in the criticism itself – after all, it was the first duty of genius to be misunderstood[8] – but in the barely disguised intentions of the reviewer. It was a blatant attempt to destroy whatever reputation Saint-Aubin had built up over the last three years by making him a target for political and nationalistic prejudice. But then Balzac himself, like Lucien de Rubempré, had engineered his own downfall by antagonizing colleagues. He, too, had practised the simple art of wrecking a book and making it look like a conscientious review: 'That horrible pleasure, sombre and solitary, savoured without witnesses, is like a duel with an absent person, killed at a distance with the shaft of a pen, as if the journalist possessed that fantastic power of wish-fulfilment which the owners of talismans have in Arabian tales.'[9]

Worse was to follow. Shortly after Balzac moved into his fifth-floor apartment on the corner of the Rue de Tournon and the Rue Saint-Sulpice, a new edition of *La Dernière Fée* came out. It now had a more believable conclusion, borrowed from the last volume of the still unpublished *Wann-Chlore*: self-plagiarism had already become one of the time-saving tricks which make Balzac's work a bibliographer's dream. This time, even those who had supported *Annette* were silent. The *Diable Boiteux*, despite being one of the many journalistic pies in which Raisson had a finger, printed a nasty little review, summing up the reader's reaction to this 'fairly pleasant' novel with the words, 'So what?'

Wann-Chlore was to be Saint-Aubin's last throw of the dice. Ironically, it was greeted by two very commendatory reviews from a man called Henri (actually, Hyacinthe) de Latouche who in many ways was to be Balzac's literary saviour. Paul Lacroix reports, implausibly, that the anonymous *Wann-Chlore* impressed the literary avant-garde so much that it was attributed to a leader of the Romantic movement; but by the time the novel appeared in September 1825, Balzac had already changed his profession. And long before that, he wrote a strangely miserable 'postface' for *Wann-Chlore*, signed, unaristocratically, 'H. S. Aubin'.[10] It didn't matter what anyone said about the author, he wrote, because soon he would be an author no more: 'I believe I may claim to have ended my career as a novelist even more successfully than I had hoped.' Success in this case meant nothing more than a few Christian sentiments awakened in the hearts of some unknown readers; for this was his farewell novel. Whether he took the criticism to heart or simply drew conclusions from the fact that none of these novels was a commercial success, Balzac was clearly speaking now, not as Saint-Aubin, but as himself. In 1827, he received a letter from Loève-Veimars, the French translator of Hoffmann, who had evidently asked to see some of Saint-Aubin's work: 'Your letter', Balzac replied, 'is extremely flattering to me and I thank you most sincerely for your kind intentions; but some time ago now I condemned myself to oblivion after the public proved to me with some brutality that I was a mediocrity. I therefore took the public's side in the matter and dismissed the man of letters, replacing him with the man of metal letters.'

The betrayal of Balzac by his fellow journalists and the fall from grace of Saint-Aubin appear to have determined his course of action for the next four years and in some respects for the rest of his life. Bad reviews may be thought to be a normal part of the writer's life as injuries are of an athlete's; but it would be unreasonable to expect even the most professional to take their wounds with a pinch of salt.

The demolition of Saint-Aubin helps to explain why Balzac so often presents himself as a modern Diogenes, carrying his lantern through the streets of Paris in search of a friend. Such behaviour was perhaps unlikely to attract potential allies. Balzac made huge demands on those who fell into orbit around him, his first loyalty being always to his vocation and to the woman he worshipped at the time. As at school, he was more devoted to an ideal of friendship (and to ideals of most other sentiments) than to any imperfect example of it. So, even after the bitter experience of 1824, he continued to seek out the company of republicans. Three years later, according to Étienne Arago, Balzac heard of a secret society called the Vente Bleue, named after the organization which had planned Napoleon's downfall. The modern Vente Bleue was a group of young men religiously dedicated to the socialist principles of Saint-Simon. 'Ah!' sighed Balzac, drawn by the promise of camaraderie and occult power. 'How I should love to belong to the Vente Bleue!' After being admitted, he found it impossible to take all the rules and regulations seriously. He was accused once again of being an *agent provocateur* and was asked to leave the group.[11]

From time to time in the years to come Balzac would invite his younger friends to join a mysterious gang, an instant old boys' network whose members would infiltrate the newspapers, vote each other into the Académie Française, award themselves strings of medals and end their lives as peers, ministers and millionaires. One such association, the Société du Cheval Rouge (from the name of the grubby restaurant near the Jardin des Plantes where Balzac held the first secret meeting) actually existed; but its sole activities, apart from periodically gorging itself at the restaurant, consisted in publishing newspaper articles in praise of Balzac. The coveted posts promised to the junior members never materialized. The friends, it turned out, were supposed to be the machines in a privately owned factory.[12]

These seemingly preposterous schemes were really just a logical extension of the nepotism which characterized literary Paris; but on each occasion, Balzac found himself in a Garden of Gethsemane of his own making (and on most occasions applied a similarly messianic image to himself). Meticulous sabotage seems to haunt all his grand designs. The Cheval Rouge, for example, was nearly a non-starter because Balzac could think of no writers worthy of membership. There was an underlying motive, however. By constantly renewing his disillusionment Balzac maintained an image of himself as the lone genius pitted against his contemporaries – 'the great gambler without cards, Napoleon without troops, the investor without capital'.[13] In 1824, he had yet to discover the logic behind his own behaviour, just as he had failed to identify those aspects of his novels which might be profitably exploited. Once it was discovered, there would be nothing to stop him conquering society and enlisting the help of the profession which he felt had tried to crush him.

The crisis of 1824 had another more dramatic and immediate result. Étienne Arago was crossing a bridge over the Seine one evening when he saw a motionless figure leaning over the parapet. It was Balzac. 'I'm watching the Seine and thinking about crawling under its humid sheets.' Arago saved the day by inviting him to dinner.[14] It may have been this that prompted Balzac many years later to remark of the gluttonous Cousin Pons: 'No one ever has the courage to bid their last farewell to a habit. Many people on the point of committing suicide have been stopped on the threshold of Death by the thought of the café where they go to play dominoes every night.'[15]

The incident on the bridge, like the pathetic attempt at Blois ten years before, can only be understood in a wider context; and as with most accounts of Balzac's behaviour, if cheerfulness fails to break in at any point, the account can hardly be trusted. Suicide appears to have occurred to him at something like five-yearly intervals. This alone is more revealing than any motives which might be attached to a particular attempt. More than an adolescent infatuation, suicide was 'an old mistress' and, like the talismanic presents from Mme de Berny whose loss – a cuff-link dropped on the Place Saint-Sulpice – betokened disaster,[16] each 'suicide attempt' became the souvenir of a period in his life or of a state of mind. As late as 1845, he was experimenting with hashish, in those days heavily tinged with opium, to see if it would provide a pleasant means of killing himself if Mme Hanska abandoned him.[17] (It would.) 'The much-frequented waters of suicide' is a phrase he uses, with alarming flippancy, when telling her of a seemingly distant time when, drowning in debts, he stood, as Lucien de Rubempré does,[18] at the iron gate leading into the Tuileries Gardens, planning his own death. On that occasion, which turns out to have been only a few days before he wrote to Mme Hanska about it, Balzac was 'rescued' by the former head clerk from the law practice who, having 'a sacred respect for genius (that expression always makes me laugh)', arranged a loan at 5 per cent plus a mortgage on his complete works.[19] The most 'Balzacian' parts of Paris are not just his rooms and residences, but also the places where, like Lucien de Rubempré at the Conciergerie, he looked at the world for the 'last time': the bridge on the Seine, the gate on the Rue de Rivoli, and, perhaps after the *Cromwell* fiasco, the moat where the Bastille had stood, 'in the days when there was no water in it'.[20]

In 1824, to judge by his sudden intense activity, Balzac chose what he called 'suicide by hard labour'.[21] The situation called for drastic measures. First, his friends had betrayed him, and now his ideal was in danger of disintegrating. The dream of achieving fame and fortune with the same double-edged sword would survive for the next few years in some fruitless attempts to become a verse poet; two poems published in the *Annales Romantiques* of 1827, which Balzac printed.[22] Even after publishing eight novels, each one better than the last, Balzac still had great respect for the reigning hierarchy of genres. 'It may be rubbish,' he said of a turgid drama by the academician Jacques Ancelot, 'but it *is* in verse.'[23] Fortunately, in Balzac's mind, there was nothing degrading about supporting one's dreams in other ways. Rousseau earned a living by copying out music. Balzac later claimed that his ability to make money with novels was just a happy coincidence: he also happened to be good at making paper flowers and would gladly pay his debts by doing that if it left him time for writing.[24]

There was another, more pressing reason to find a new source of income. He was practically a kept man, deeply in debt to the woman he loved. In *Melmoth Réconcilié*, he describes the impotent rage of a man who loves a perfect woman. Knowing himself to be inferior to his idol,

> he feels capable of holding up a stage-coach to lay his hands on some money if he hasn't enough for the gifts he wishes to lavish on her. Such is man, sometimes rendering himself guilty of a crime in order to appear great and noble in front of a woman or a particular audience. A lover is like a gambler who would consider himself dishonoured if he did not pay back what he owed to the *garçon* of the casino, and who commits atrocious crimes, robbing his wife and children, stealing and killing so as to turn up with his pockets full of money and his honour intact in the eyes of those who frequent the fatal establishment.[25]

The options, then, were clear: crime or gambling. The first was a temptation which presented itself to Balzac in an unusually pure form. Once or twice in *La Comédie Humaine*, he poses the problem in a little fantasy that was to make a deep impression on Dostoevsky and, indirectly, on Rastignac's literary relation, Raskolnikov. What if, simply by wishing, and without anyone ever finding out, you could cause the death of a Chinaman on the other side of the world and, by so doing, become fabulously rich? Maybe conscience would force you to resist; but what if the Chinaman were old, sick and obnoxious, and you were infatuated with a rich and beautiful woman you wanted to marry?[26] It was a thought that Balzac had already aired in *Annette et le Criminel*: 'Wouldn't you even now be in *your* hotel and *your* carriage, saying "*my* horses, *my* estate, *my* money", and not scrupling to use the phrase, "A decent fellow like myself!"?' The fact that Balzac applies a similar analogy to book-reviewing suggests that crime, in practical terms, meant journalism and associated activities. In fact, he kept up his lucrative partnership with Raisson,[27] though there is only circumstantial evidence of foul play, hidden away in the suggestive coincidences of detailed chronologies. On 3 February 1825, he is known to have borrowed from the Bibliothèque Royale (later, the Nationale) a book on Mary Stuart by the sixteenth-century historian, Adam Blackwood. Three years later, Raisson published his 'own' *Marie Stuart*, most of which is plagiarized.[28] (The book was printed by Balzac.) Then there is the question of the various apocryphal 'memoirs'. The publisher Baudouin had acquired a small manuscript by Napoleon's Lord Chamberlain. Balzac secretly added the results of his own investigations and pumped it up into four volumes which were subsequently used by Tolstoy in his research for *War and Peace*.[29] A few years later, in league with another writer, L'Héritier de l'Ain, who specialized in having other people's memories, he manufactured the *Mémoires* of Sanson, chief executioner during the Revolution.[30] Crime paid, but it was hard work: there were other *Mémoires de Sanson* on the market and speed was essential. He also had a hand in some other novels of dubious parentage. Among them is the first volume of a long-winded story published by Lepoitevin early in 1827: *Le Corrupteur*,[31] in which a young seminarist called Ernest is perverted by a criminal who has escaped from the hulks at Yarmouth. Like Vautrin, and like Balzac himself in moments of crisis, Édouard Fulbert believes that obeying the laws of Nature – meaning the survival of the least scrupulous – 'is not only a pleasure and a necessity, but also a duty'.

All these bibliographical oddities represent only part-time work. Balzac's main course of action was the traditional alternative to suicide: gambling, first with time, then with money. Few letters survive from 1825, but towards the end of the year, signs of a huge undertaking begin to emerge from the family's correspondence.[32] In November his father talks of labours which even Hercules would have declined. Balzac had just been on a trip to Touraine with his mother and Henry, who was now seventeen years old and as useless as ever. They stayed with Jean de Margonne in his little château in the remote village of Saché. Balzac was to escape there many times in order to 'replenish' his brain. But, as Mme de Balzac noted, 'suffering all the torments of an unhappy mother', he was too exhausted to convalesce. Back in Paris, *Wann-Chlore*, though published without the author's name, was ignored by nearly all the papers, even by Lepoitevin's gossipy *Lorgnette*. In desperation, the publisher replaced the title-page on the remaining copies with a new one which admitted that the author was Horace de Saint-Aubin. Still the press was silent, with the notable exception of Latouche. At the start of 1826, after Balzac's brief visit to Villeparisis, Bernard-François was worried: Honoré had some of the symptoms of tuberculosis; he was developing nervous tics. For four days, he wrote nothing, and, 'without having made any useful progress whatsoever in society', he was already worn out and decrepit.

Balzac's Herculean labours were a characteristic digging out of enormous foundations for a building which might never exist – the literary equivalent of the gigantic fortifications and harbour wall being constructed at Cherbourg. Balzac had seen the works in 1822 during his stay in Bayeux and wrote to Mme de Berny, full of admiration for modern engineering and the spirit of enterprise: 'After being there, no more obstacles seem to exist, because another scale of comparison for the impossible has been constructed.' As Balzac explained in his later study of Catherine de Medici – a splendid patchwork remnant of the original plan – he had 'patiently and minutely' examined the principal periods of French history.[33] His aim was to produce what he refers to, in 1825, as a *Histoire de France Pittoresque*[34] – not the endless parade of battles and speeches, but social history, a re-creation of 'the spirit of the age', 'mores in action'. Balzac had already made a start on his impossibly thorough *Histoire* with *L'Excommunié*, which he never finished.[35] The story was based in Touraine at the end of the fourteenth century. His intention to depict the spirit of the age through the details of everyday life coexisted happily, too happily, with the desire to entertain: 'Everything was confusion and pillage in those days. Murder, incest, arson, crimes of every sort were common. Serfs were killed like flies. . . . Immorality was so prevalent that the *pâtisseries* themselves were given obscene names and shapes.' There was obviously something about everyday life that made it extremely funny or grotesquely melodramatic when it was written about in a serious fashion – especially life in the Middle Ages. The pornographic *Contes Drolatiques*, with their Rabelaisian romps and archaic language, are evidence of the difficulties Balzac encountered before he realized it was possible to be a historian of modern life. For a writer living in emotional exile in the prudish nineteenth century, it was all too easy to be nostalgic about a period when everything was confusion, pillage and corruption.

Balzac was to spend large parts of the next three years incubating this project in the Bibliothèque Royale. Working there, he claimed – with an image that says much about his approach to knowledge – was like doing battle with a hydra: for every head chopped off, two more sprouted in its place. As his father insisted, he was gambling with time: he would soon be thirty. But Balzac became addicted to the constant renewal of hope. Like gamblers, he believed in systems. 'I only play socially', he assured Mme Hanska when she passed on reports from her interfering cousin Rosalie that he had been spotted sneaking into gambling dens, 'but I've never lost'.[36] The national lottery was just 'the opium of poverty',[37] but the roulette wheel was magic. Rastignac wins huge sums apparently by sheer will-power;[38] and one has the distinct impression that, in *La Rabouilleuse*, Philippe Bridau loses money, not because of the laws of probability, but simply because of his own stupidity and greed.

Wishful thinking had already led Balzac to the top of a slippery slope which seemed at times less daunting than the long uphill climb of French history. Early that year his search for a publisher for *Wann-Chlore* had brought him into contact with Urbain Canel. Canel had the wonderful weakness, in a publisher, of accepting only those books he liked himself. According to Philarète Chasles, a friend of Raisson and one of the future founders of comparative literature, Balzac was attracted partly by Canel's wife, 'Miss Anna': he liked to run his fingers through her beautiful body-length hair.[39] But he was also enticed by a revolutionary idea which Canel had the good sense to sell to Balzac. The plan was to offer the public the complete works of the great French classical authors 'in a single, easily transportable volume and at a price to suit every pocket'. A businessman friend of the Balzacs, Dassonvillez, considered it a good investment; he provided some of the capital, and promissory notes to Canel were signed by the ever-willing Mme de Berny. Balzac's enthusiasm, and fear that someone else might steal the idea, propelled him to Alençon in Normandy where he urged an engraver to supply the 'beautiful vignettes' for the books: 'Perseverance and courage, and glory and profit will be yours.'[40] He also dashed off prefaces on Molière and La Fontaine for the first two volumes, dwelling rather ominously on the latter's poetic ability to forget about his financial worries by drifting off into cloud-cuckoo-land.

Disaster arrived soon after. Booksellers were unwilling to stock the editions of an unknown publisher; the engravings – reproductions of drawings by Girodet's pupil, Achille Devéria – were skewed and clumsy; the printing was microscopic, and once all the instalments had appeared the price turned out to be an exorbitant 20 francs (approximately £60 today). The *Racine* and *Corneille* were shelved. Balzac's first spin of the wheel had produced a deficit of over 14,000 francs.

If the first venture failed, the answer was clear: take a bigger risk. It seemed obvious that in the world of unbridled capitalism, one simply had to stand in the right place to catch the money as it flew around unchecked. Whatever happened, as Balzac had just learned to his cost, the printer's bill was paid. Conclusion: become a printer.[41] The family had recently inherited some money and been able to buy the house at Villeparisis. Dassonvillez, hoping to recover his initial investment, eventually agreed in June 1826 to underwrite Balzac's debt to Canel. By this time, Balzac had persuaded his father to guarantee any future debts with the capital which was originally supposed to have provided him with a small emergency income. A printing works came on the market for 8000 francs. A printer's licence cost 22,000 francs. Mme de Berny's husband nudged some elbows at the Ministry, certifying that the would-be printer, though totally inexperienced, knew a lot about literature and was a trustworthy young man. Presumably this was taken to be a qualification. The official request to determine 'the morality and political leanings' of the applicant must also have been intercepted by M. de Berny: Balzac was said to belong to an estimable family in very easy circumstances; his conduct was 'regular'.[42] And so, on 4 June 1826, nearly seven years after embarking on a literary career in the Rue Lesdiguières, Balzac set up shop as a printer in the narrow Rue des Marais-Saint-Germain, taking in tow a typesetter called Barbier he thought worthy of a helping hand. He had about thirty workers on the payroll, a total debt of 70,000 francs, and a firm conviction that printing would do for him what it had done for Samuel Richardson: enable him to spend the rest of his life as a hard-working man of leisure. The printing works was Balzac's home for the next two years.

IT MIGHT BE as well to consider for a moment the person who was poised at the top of this slippery slope. For Balzac's failure as an entrepreneur coincided with success in another field. One might even be said to explain the other. There are two written portraits and a deceptively transparent drawing which offer a kind of *pre-mortem* of Balzac's rapid rise and meteoric fall as a businessman.

MOI ('Myself'), later renamed Scribonius and then Raphaël, is a minor character in *Les Martyrs Ignorés* (1837):

> Lives on the fifth floor. From Easter to Christmas, wears a pair of nankeen trousers with straps; in winter, thick woollen trousers. Blue waistcoat with not-very-gold buttons, calico shirt, black tie, shoes with laces, a hat made shiny by the rain and an olive-coloured overcoat. Dines in the Rue de Tournon at 21 sous in Mère Gérard's ground-floor restaurant, two steps down from street-level. . . . Craves knowledge and wolfs it down without digesting properly. . . . For the time being, has 600 francs a year but intends to become a millionaire. Gullible, easily taken in, always fearlessly setting off in pursuit of another lie. Vanquished on the battlefield, victorious in the tent.[43]

This is Balzac in 1825, seen through the wise but unrepentant eye of the bankrupt businessman. From 1829 on, each of his novels tells the story of a debt; every 'history of composition' in editions of his work is strewn with impressive sums of money and details of interest payments. Yet the determinedly flattering self-portrait in *Les Martyrs Ignorés* suggests that Balzac had suspicions about himself on the eve of his great initiative. In her last known letter to her brother, Laurence had warned him that he lacked the shopkeeper's mentality: his partners would dangle carrots in front of his face and his imagination would go galloping off. 'Everyone says that commerce is the only way to make a fortune but no one knows how many people meet their ruin in it.' He could hardly have been offended by his sister's prognosis since he offered the Duchesse d'Abrantès the following breathtaking description of himself three months later in July 1825. The idea was to convince her that whatever conclusions she reached concerning his personality would be wrong:

> I have the most peculiar character I know. . . . My 5 feet 2 inches contain every possible incoherence and contrast, and any who think me vain, profligate, pig-headed, frivolous, muddle-headed, foppish, negligent, lazy, dilatory, thoughtless, inconstant, over-talkative, tactless, ill-mannered, impolite, grumpy and moody, will be just as correct as any who say I'm thrifty, modest, brave, tenacious, energetic, untidy [a fashionable virtue, to be contrasted with 'foppish'], hard-working, consistent, taciturn, shrewd, courteous and always happy. Whoever says I'm a coward will be no further from the truth than anyone who says I'm extremely courageous, or, for that matter, learned or ignorant, highly talented or inept. Nothing about me surprises me any more. I'm beginning to think that I'm just an instrument on which circumstances play their tune.

Balzac's self-conscious naivety reveals itself as a mixture of romanticized portrait and caricature in the sepia drawing by Devéria, given to Mme de Berny in 1825 with the momentous words *et nunc et semper*. (In this case, it would be correct to say that Balzac was being true to his contradictions.) It is interesting to compare the Devéria drawing with the 1837 Salon portrait by Louis Boulanger. Balzac had a copy wrapped up and sent to Mme Hanska's château at Wierzchownia in the Ukraine, but he warned her in advance that Boulanger had seen 'only the writer and not the benevolence of the imbecile who will always be taken for a ride': 'All my misfortunes come from having offered assistance to weaklings who were stuck in the rut of adversity.

It was through trying to be of service to a printing worker in 1827 that I found myself, in 1829, crushed by 150,000 francs of debt and cast into an attic with nothing to eat.'[44] Devéria, on the other hand, captured Balzac before the public face had set. There is even an almost logical progression, in the many portraits of Balzac, in the gradual disappearance of what he calls the 'imbecile'. In Devéria's drawing, Balzac has something of the holy fool; the right side of the face especially has the moon-like features of a simpleton, with only the sensual lips and hypnotic eye hinting at depth or perhaps reminding the observer of Balzac's belief that genius often wears a mask of stupidity. Balzac would have pointed out the incipient double chin and prominent forehead as certain signs of tenacity and a powerful intellect. He would have drawn attention to the physiognomic fact that a nose slightly divided at its tip is the mark of an ability to sniff out secrets like a bloodhound.[45] But these features, too, are given a different sense by the contrasting shirt, floppy and wrinkled, and the chaotic hair which is reminiscent of a style made famous in modern times by Bob Dylan. Devéria, in fact, depicts Balzac as an 1820s matinée idol: the open collar, the feminine expression, the wholesale rejuvenation – this is supposed to be Balzac at the age of twenty-five or twenty-six – are all signs of what Balzac himself calls in 1830 the 'mania for youth' and the proliferation of spurious *enfants sublimes*, 'embryos who turn out posthumous works'.[46]

The face in Devéria's drawing is not the face of a successful businessman; but it was the face – despite the over-ambitious inscription – of a successful lover who was now branching out into new affairs. Balzac's confidence survived the failure of the pocket editions partly because he had climbed to an even higher sphere.

For this, he had his family to thank. Sister Laure and her husband had moved to Versailles, and the family followed soon after. Their original intention had been to remain in Villeparisis, but they were driven out in 1826 by the shocking behaviour of Bernard-François. He had exposed the family to what his wife described as blackmail. As a young man of sixty-two, while still in Tours, he had produced a passionate treatise on 'the scandalous disorders caused by young girls being betrayed and abandoned in utter destitution'. He and General Pommereul had set up an asylum for unmarried mothers, recognizing that 'Nature's battering-ram can demolish any social fortification, and that it is possible to lose one's honour without losing one's virtue'. Dogs, as he pointed out in his *Histoire de la Rage*, set humans a very bad example, which they invariably followed. Now, at the age of seventy-nine, he illustrated the problem by making a local girl pregnant while his wife was away in Touraine. Significantly, Balzac praised Molière that year in his preface for condemning 'the shameful passions of old men'. *La Cousine Bette*, written sixteen years after his father's death, implies a change of heart: at the age of seventy-five, Baron Hulot runs off at the end of the novel with the kitchen maid when aesthetic logic demands that he die a cathartic death.

By now, Mme de Balzac was an old hand at covering up scandals. She arranged with Laure to have an anonymous letter delivered to the aged parent, who might otherwise have been lured back to Villeparisis to face his expensive responsibilities.[47] The ploy worked, and to this day no definite trace has been found of Balzac's illegitimate sibling or of any descendants.

The family's move to Versailles makes it possible to complete the picture of Balzac at the start of his business career. Laure had been friendly with a daughter of the Duchesse d'Abrantès at school and was well acquainted with the family. Losing very little time, Balzac had himself introduced and launched his second love affair. This time, ambition was uppermost, and Balzac prudently maintained a critical distance: like Balzac's mother, sister and lover, the Duchess was called Laure; her other Christian names were Adélaïde and Constance. Balzac chose to call her Marie, a name he later bestowed on several other friends.

To someone who had hopes of writing a history of France, the Duchess was worth a thousand visits to the library.[48] She had been married to one of Napoleon's most intrepid generals, Junot, who distinguished himself at Toulon and then at Nazareth where, it is said, his 500 foot-soldiers routed 6000 Turkish horsemen.[49] In war, he was brilliant – violent, brutish, unencumbered by excess intelligence and slightly mad. His diplomatic career was dismal. The so-called 'Tempest' performed the relatively undemanding duties of Ambassador to Portugal in the period preceding his conquest of the same country. Later he was 'exiled' to the Illyrian provinces where his lunacy came into full bloom – two battalions of Croatian troops despatched to rid Dubrovnik of a nightingale – and shortly afterwards he threw himself out of a window at his father's house. Battles aside, his entire career was masterminded by his wife. She – as Balzac knew before he met her – had been a friend and even, so she hinted, a lover of Bonaparte long before the Empire, and was one of the few people who had ever dared contradict him. Napoleon honoured her with the nickname '*la petite peste*'. Now that the imperial tide had gone out, she was left behind like a cantankerous crustacean, reduced to living in a house in Versailles with her unpaid servants, whom she trained in the art of repelling creditors, treating the local shops as her personal pantry. She kept up her contacts in the anachronistic world of the Empire aristocracy, smoked opium cigarettes, watched her children go to the dogs, and lived on in a kind of internal exile pretending to be a monarchist. Thanks to her, Balzac would soon gain admittance to some of the most prestigious salons in France.

The Duchess had decided to supplement her non-existent income by writing her memoirs. Balzac, who also hoped that literature would pay his debts, was going to help her write them.[50] Not surprisingly, many historical scenes in his novels come from conversations with the Duchess, and perhaps it was because she was able to read Balzac's versions of her stories that her memory appears to have improved with age. At least one of her thirty-eight volumes of memoirs, still an important source on Spain and Portugal in the early 1800s, betrays her regal tendency to consider 'want' as a synonym of 'own'. She helped herself to large portions of other books on the subject and covered her tracks by inserting derogatory remarks about their authors.[51]

In temperament, the Duchess was a real aristocrat, and it was clear that Balzac could only become her lover if he knew his place. His was 'a distinguished mind', she conceded; not great, but certainly superior to the fashionable crowd. Balzac was later complimented in a curiously worded phrase in her book on Spain and Portugal for his rare talent as a conversationalist: 'I am not blinded by my friendship for him and see in him the wittiest man of our time.' 'To our shame, foreigners have a far higher regard for him as a writer than we do in France.'[52] In 1825, there were still some awkward obstacles to be overcome. Balzac had written in haste from an inn accusing her, as lovers were supposed to, of being indifferent and unfeeling. The Duchess decided to take him seriously, and Balzac was forced now to explain at great length that what he meant was that sensibility might be stifled by virtue, though of course it existed none the less. He added, hopefully, though too hastily, that women are never so powerful as when they humble themselves before men.

For all his social blunders, Balzac's letters to the Duchesse d'Abrantès are highly novelistic. The pining adolescent who begged for Mme de Berny's favours had to gird his loins for a tougher battle. In some, he sounds exactly like his fictional Napoleonic soldiers. History showed that the Duchess was sexually attracted to sturdy men who laughed in the face of certain death; and so Balzac told her of his 'energy', of 'that terrible ability to stiffen oneself against the tempest and to face adversity with a calm, unruffled brow': 'Subordination is intolerable to me. I have turned down every kind of post for that very reason. When it comes to subordination, I'm a real savage.' In the end, the Duchess was won over, not just by Balzac's usefulness to her or by his witty conversation, nor even by his military spirit, but by her discovery that he was caught up in love's 'flowery chains', attached to a woman seven years older than herself. Pretending to be ill, she managed to summon him back from Touraine. A few months later, the haughty tone of her letter reveals increasing intimacy, making allowances for social difference: 'But I must see you. However strange that may seem, *it is so.*' Mme de Berny had moved to the Rue d'Enfer on the Left Bank to be closer to her darling 'Didi', and was visiting him almost every day. She tried to make him see he was being manipulated by a selfish woman, that he was deluding himself if he thought that two lovers could be kept in separate compartments of his heart. She may even have forced a separation until the autumn of 1829. But Balzac was determined (to use the language of his *Physiologie du Mariage*) that the value of his share in the Duchess's life would go up: 'In order to gain the right to make a floor for oneself out of all the heads pressed together in a salon, it is necessary to become the lover of one of these high-ranking women.'[53]

SUCCESS WITH the Duchess augured well for the printing business but actually imposed an additional burden. Balzac was starting two new lives, and both would lead quickly to financial disaster. The 'horrible little street' in which he set up shop is now the Rue Visconti near the Odéon. 'Rebellious to all those embellishments effected by present-day aldermen', the Rue des Marais-Saint-Germain was cold and damp, and when Balzac described it in 1841 it was still without gas-lighting.[54] The house at number 17 has survived and still belongs to a publishing house. In 1826, it was a brand-new building with an expressionless façade, four storeys at the back, two at the front, with a large workshop on the ground floor taken over by the noisy printing-presses and piles of pages waiting to be bound. A dark corridor led to a sunless office where Balzac sat behind a grille receiving visitors and, he hoped, their remittances. A wooden staircase with an iron banister spiralled up to his small, high-ceilinged apartment, its walls covered quite modishly with blue percaline. Looking out on to the street, Balzac dreamed up reassuring historical omens for himself. Racine had lived for a few years at number 24. Balzac decided that this 'precious monument', which the Government should preserve and lease without charge to the greatest living poet, was in reality the house next door to his own, and that Racine had spent his entire life there. In those days, patrons were easier to find. How times had changed! 'It may be', Balzac writes in the unfinished story, *Valentine et Valentin* (not admitting, as usual, to any autobiographical interest), 'that this dwelling was not without natural beauty. Indeed, it was not until 1825 that, in the extensive gardens separating the houses, constructions destined for industry were erected.'[55]

The first fruits of Balzac's industry set the tone – or absence of it – for the next two years. On 29 July 1826, a leaflet advertising the *Long-Life Anti-Catarrhal Pills* of a druggist named Cure rattled auspiciously off the presses. It was closely followed by a book once thought to have been by Balzac: the *Petit Dictionnaire Critique et Anecdotique des Enseignes de Paris*, by an Idle Pedestrian.[56] Shop-signs would become Balzac's favourite source of characters' names,[57] but for now, the dictionary had a different significance. It is typical of several half-serious, pseudo-scholarly booklets printed by Balzac, some of which he may have helped to write. The art of extrapolating general principles from the minutiae of social intercourse found an expanding market at a time when clothes and manners were more than ever a sign of one's station in life: *The Art of Tying One's Tie* (sixteen lessons, plus a *Complete History of the Tie*); *The Art of Settling One's Debts and Satisfying One's Creditors Without Spending Any Money*; *The Art of*

Never Dining At Home; *The Art of Receiving Gifts Without Reciprocating*. Balzac's professional promiscuity was such that the list of books turned out by the Imprimerie H. Balzac says almost nothing about his personal tastes – except, of course, that everything was of interest. Nothing was turned down: poems, plays, popular remedies, directories of butchers, coal-merchants and wig-makers, politicians' memoirs, a foreigner's guide to Paris, a textbook by the mathematics teacher at Vendôme, almanacs, prophecies, manuals on fencing with sabres, entertaining guests, nursing babies, selecting servants, etc. Royalists and Liberals were equally welcome. Tracts by Freemasons were printed with the same characters used to denounce their 'odious' plots. Balzac appears to have supported every shade of political opinion at the same time, and this willingness to satisfy all customers may actually have frightened many away. In *Illusions Perdues*, the business of Balzac's fictional printer, David Séchard, suffers from the same enthusiastic neutrality: 'It was a time when in the provinces tradesmen had to profess a political opinion in order to attract customers.' Balzac adds that 'in the great melting-pot of Paris', no such affiliations were expected.[58] The records of other printers of the time suggest he was wrong.

In the end, the greatest profits would be literary and artistic. The Romantic painters, Paul Delaroche and Eugène Lami, moved in next door to Balzac's apartment in 1827,[59] and the business brought him into contact with some of the most fashionable young writers of the day. Victor Hugo himself, who was soon to start work on a novel about Notre-Dame, invited Balzac to his home to discuss a business proposition. Alfred de Vigny also came to the Rue des Marais when Balzac, no doubt reflecting on the setbacks he had suffered, was printing the third edition of Vigny's *Cinq-Mars ou Une Conjuration sous Louis XIII*. Perhaps the finest of all French historical novels, including those of Dumas, it was based on a period which Balzac himself had studied. It even begins with a lyrical overture on the calm beauties of Touraine, very similar to Balzac's own dreamy evocations in the unpublished, now yellowing manuscript of *Sténie*. Vigny could not have suspected his printer of being a potential rival: 'He was a very thin, very dirty, very garrulous young chap, who got muddled up in everything he said and salivated when he spoke because his excessively moist mouth had lost all its upper teeth.'[60] The 'young man' was only two years younger than Vigny; but Vigny was an aristocrat, a soldier, and a literary success. He, not Balzac, was being hailed now as 'the French Walter Scott'; he had even been introduced to the great man himself during Scott's visit to Paris in 1826. But in Balzac's eyes, Vigny was guilty of what might now be termed New Historicism: he had failed 'to restore their true sense to events', 'twisting history like an old cloth used to cover up a young statue', sneering at the truth 'so as to convince us that artists live on lies'.[61]

Vigny's unpleasant caricature comes from a letter written to his young cousin in Touraine shortly after Balzac's death. It was intended to highlight the great man's heroism in overcoming his natural defects and the contrast with the later red-faced, barrel-chested Balzac, his mouth miraculously arrayed with 'the neatest set of pearls imaginable'. Read in the context of the late 1820s, it accidentally says much about Balzac's charm. The unforgettable individual behind the grille looked nothing at all like a socialite, and yet he was. In the evening, the chattering printer emerged from the dirt and noise of the printing works to pursue his other new career as the protégé of the Duchesse d'Abrantès. Business went on after dark. In the snobbish, theatrical world of the literary salon, the same blustering young man was a mesmerizing performer, already in danger of becoming a kind of court jester. The art critic, Delécluze, saw him irrupt for the first time into the august salon of Mme Récamier where Chateaubriand was usually on display. It was, he supposed, like witnessing a reincarnation of Rabelais:

> Everyone fell silent and stared at the newcomer. He was not very tall and had broad shoulders. His features were rather common but revealed an extraordinarily lively mind. In his blazing eyes and in the sharp outline of his lips you could see the energy of thought and the fire of passion. . . .
>
> Balzac's naive euphoria, after he was introduced to the mistress of the house, can only be compared to that of a child. He was forced to summon up whatever reason he had left to prevent himself from flying into the arms of those who were present. He was so inordinately delighted that he would have made himself ridiculous had his joy not been expressed with such candour and sincerity.[62]

Surviving in this world, where 'a rip is a misfortune, a stain a sin',[63] required almost as much capital as printing books. Much of the money Balzac earned was immediately converted into clothes. The business was beginning to thrive in 1827, but the debts were thriving too, and Dassonvillez was proving over-cautious. Balzac and Barbier had been forced to sell the premises and machinery to this so-called friend of the family and were renting them back at over 500 francs a year. Balzac's social life went on regardless, almost as if he were reluctant to be free of debt. 'Debt', he wrote ambiguously in 1838, 'is a countess who is a little too fond of me.'[64] Debts, as well as lovers, focused the mind and channelled one's energies; but they very quickly became a habit. In keeping with the view that innumeracy is a Romantic virtue, it is often wrongly assumed that Balzac was an incompetent speculator, and the tendency to reorganize his affairs in retrospect used to be very strong among Balzac scholars, who have understandably included several businessmen. Nevertheless, it is hard to avoid the impression that, like a gambler, he was acting in his own worst interests. Curiously, Balzac's faith in the power of will coexists with a belief in predestination, and when he wrote these prophetic words in *La Femme de Trente Ans*, he was surely thinking of himself: 'There are thoughts which we obey without knowing what they are. . . . By going to see the Marchioness, he was following one of those pre-existing texts of which the experience and knowledge we acquire in later life are but the visible developments.' A Freudian idea in pre-Freudian terms.[65]

Dramatic proof of the risks Balzac was taking can be found in his private papers. Laundry lists have been greatly discredited as sources of biographical data; but any *a priori* exclusion of evidence should be highly suspect, especially when the subject is a writer for whom everything is interrelated. Balzac himself reminds anxious husbands that laundry lists are the most reliable chroniclers of love affairs.[66] Discussions with an unnamed lady – probably the Duchess – and a simple calculation (also a jibe at the new science of statistics) reveal that a woman engaged in a love affair will spend 150 francs a year more on clothes than in 'peacetime'. Naturally, there are minor variations to be taken into account. 'Some men', the lady informs him, 'wear one's clothes out more quickly than others.'

Balzac's own laundry lists are unusually revealing. Here, for example, is the list for 17 January 1827:[67]

4 cotton shirts (of which 2 fine)
3 cambric cravats (of which 2 fine)
4 cambric handkerchiefs
1 pair underdrawers
2 pairs socks
1 smoking-cap
3 waistcoats
1 undershirt
3 flannels
7 detachable collars
1 shaving-cloth
1 towel

Despite what Vigny's description might suggest, Balzac's apparent attention to cleanliness was actually quite extravagant for someone in his circumstances. It is true that, at a time when frequent bathing (say, once a month) was thought to lead to an unhealthy softening-up of skin and moral fibre, and eventually to impotence and general debility,[68] laundering clothes was the principal means of keeping up a clean appearance. But the vast social geography of smells in La Comédie Humaine and Balzac's aversion to the increasingly pervasive stench of tobacco smoke imply that his nose was more than usually sensitive, and that the dirt picked out by Vigny's critical eye was purely industrial.

The cost of these essential raw materials appears in the many bills from Balzac's favourite tailor, Buisson: each order averages about 200 francs, over one-third of the annual rent paid to Dassonvillez. Buisson is well known to readers of La Comédie Humaine as one of the outfitters of Rastignac, De Marsay and other spectacular dandies: flattering references in novels like Eugénie Grandet may serve to reinforce the illusion of reality by having real people mingle with invented personalities, but they also represent a novel way of paying bills 'without spending any money'. When Count Félix de Vandenesse in Autre Étude de Femme slips in a mention of Buisson – the tailor who dresses us all – Balzac was hiring out his character like an actor in a modern commercial.[69] In 1827, he had to count on future success: 'Talent, Sir', says the life-insurance salesman Gaudissart, 'is a bill of exchange which Nature gives to men of genius, and which matures only after a very long time. . . .'[70] The nankeen trousers sported by MOI at the Rue de Tournon (only for common people[71]) were supplemented by black dress-trousers in cashmere or tweed, a black frock-coat of fine Louviers cloth, and, once every two months, a new white quilted waistcoat of chamois leather. These frequent purchases reflect the inconvenience of having to wear white in order to be fashionable; they also indicate that Balzac's frame was beginning to expand. A waistcoat of the wrong size was unwearable, and when Balzac went to thank Latouche for his review of *Wann-Chlore*, his trouser-legs were curling up at the bottom, tugging against the thick straps which pulled them down.[72] Then there were all the indispensable super-fluities of the dandy: gold cuff-links, a cane, and the 1820s equivalent of a miniaturized personal organizer: 'a watch as flat as a 100-sou piece'.[73]

Balzac was going to be one of the best-dressed bankrupts in Paris. As the business sank in debt he gave all the outward signs of being happily afloat. In September 1827, he purchased a type-foundry. The same logic that had launched the printing works dictated a bold advance back up the chain of production. In December, the new company announced the purchase of a revolutionary printing technique called Fontéréotypie. The attempt to gain control of every stage of production is typical of Balzac. Ever since his early philosophical studies, he had been a rational fundamentalist: once the principle was found, the rest would follow. In business, this meant taking care of the pounds and assuming that the pennies would look after themselves. Barbier smelled ruin and bailed out. Three months later, in April 1828, the business collapsed.

The liquidation of Balzac, Barbier and Co. took many months. Eventually, most of the creditors would be satisfied – Balzac's partner and his predecessors, who had never been paid in full, suppliers of paper and machinery, typesetters, founders, mechanics, locksmiths and plasterers. Technically speaking, Balzac avoided the stigma of 'bank-ruptcy'. It was far worse than that. He was now in debt to his own mother to the tune of about 50,000 francs. Mme de Berny was owed a similar amount. Fortunately, Balzac's infidelity seems to have brought out what her rather cloying love-letters reveal as a taste for self-sacrifice. She took over the company and entrusted it to her son, Alexandre. Perhaps Balzac had been right all along. Under Alexandre de Berny's management, it became one of the busiest and wealthiest printing firms in Paris.

IN 1838, MME HANSKA, mulling over the pros and cons of marrying a man who had such faith in free enterprise, asked why it was that the characters in his books were so much more astute in financial affairs than the person who created them.[74] Certainly, a contemporary reader using *La Comédie Humaine* as an investment guide would probably have made a handsome profit. Balzac steered his banker, Baron Nucingen, and the moneylender Magus to undreamt-of wealth by having them invest, for example, in the Orléans Railway while he lost his own money on the Northern Railway.[75] He, too, marvelled at his inability to capitalize on his famous powers of observation,[76] but found no satisfactory answer: maybe, he guessed, it was over-confidence or the card-player's perverse desire to see whether chance would work as well as calculation.

Laurence had been right to warn her brother about his gullibility. Balzac took promissory notes signed by bankrupt booksellers or, on one occasion, accepted a shopful of unsaleable books as payment, even travelling to Reims to arrange the deal; and he gave ridiculously large discounts. But this is hardly an answer to Mme Hanska's question. Balzac's ideas, in fact, were excellent and should have succeeded. If imagination counted, his would be one of the great names in the history of French publishing. These ideas include a forerunner of modern book-clubs, with market research, jobs for women and salary-based pensions.[77] Over a century before the founders of the Pléiade series thought of it, Balzac was hoping to experiment with the use of Bible paper.[78] He also toyed with the idea of a children's encyclopedia.[79] And his best, most characteristic scheme – the last, symbolic word on Balzac's business mind – came with the 1837 edition of his *Oeuvres Complètes*. Potential subscribers to the edition were to send in their personal details; they would then be divided into eight age-groups and offered the incentive of life insurance: fifty beautiful volumes and the chance to retire with a 30,000-franc income.[80] There is a splendid contradiction in the thought of a subscriber to Balzac's *Oeuvres Complètes* reading about the economic ravages of misers, usurers and financiers, secure in the knowledge that the author has safeguarded his family's future. The plan never came to fruition: 'There are still', he wrote with typical understatement, 'a few administrative details to be settled'.

Balzac's failure was in large part the result of bad luck. 1826 saw the start of a recession that was to last beyond the 1830 Revolution. By the end of the 1820s, in Paris alone, more than 2500 people were declared bankrupt every year.[81] In addition, the lack of protective legislation and the scarcity of low-denomination banknotes made Paris a moneylender's paradise: debts, divided up and sold to third or fourth parties, accumulated disproportionate charges and multiplied like locusts. Political institutions characterized by their unrevised conservatism and nepotism, and the legal and economic system as a whole, were ill prepared for the first stages of industrialization.

For Balzac, the principal cause of his ruin was his mother.[82] True, she had lent him large sums of money, but it was never quite enough. . . . Even the faithful Laure – perhaps convinced of this by Honoré – claims that Mme de Balzac could easily have seen her son through the crisis:[83] Alexandre de Berny's success proves at least that the potential was there. But there was even more potential for disaster in Balzac himself. The significant fact here is that he wanted his mother to remain in the role of evil stepmother; his failure would form part of his difficult destiny – an attitude which can be construed either as a psychological problem or as an attempt to make daily life as interesting and dramatic as possible. In one of the passages which make up what might be called the autobiography of Balzac's unconscious, Raphaël de Valentin in *La Peau de Chagrin* pays off some of his debts by selling the island in the Loire on which his mother is buried.[84] Money would have meant independence from his mother; yet Balzac continued to create situations that tied him to her financially. Deliberate, conscious sabotage is certainly out of the question; nevertheless, he had a distinct tendency to produce emergencies which might have unlocked an enormous treasure-chest but which were just as likely to lead to failure – dilemmas, above all, which sooner or later called for heroic action. Otherwise, business would be little more than the acquisition of wealth. As he told the son of General Pommereul that year, practically inviting the obvious objection: 'What I myself feared – when I started up and courageously supported an establishment whose proportions verged on the colossal – has finally occurred.'[85]

Much later, in *La Comédie Humaine*, Balzac would reap the rewards of his catastrophe. It was because he himself had grappled with Capitalism as a creature of flesh and bone that he was able to show in characters like the perfumer César Birotteau that individuals could never be disentangled from historical and economic forces; and yet, through personal heroism, they could rise above them. The printing business was the first, poignant demonstration of Balzac's inspiring ability to make a drama out of a crisis.

Now, in the summer of 1828, like Birotteau and Raphaël de Valentin, Balzac was a hunted man, lying low in a city full of creditors.

> Those bank officials, those embodiments of the commercial conscience, clad in grey and wearing that silver badge which is their master's livery, had once been objects of indifference to me when I saw them pass in the streets of Paris; but now I hated them even before they hove into sight. . . . I WAS IN DEBT! To be in debt means that you no longer belong to yourself. Other men could call me to account for my life. Why had I been eating puddings *à la chipolata*? Why did I have ice in my drink? Why was I sleeping, walking, going about thinking and amusing myself instead of paying them back? . . . Remorse is easier to bear: it does not cast you into the street or into debtors' prison . . . it merely leads you to the scaffold where the executioner confers on it a kind of nobility. At the moment the axe falls, everyone believes you to be innocent, whereas society allows not a single virtue to the penniless rake.[86]

Few of these creditors would have approved of Balzac's plan of action. He bought the rights to the French translation of *Melmoth* (which he never used), ordered a pair of black dress-trousers from Buisson and yet another white quilted waistcoat, and then, with the help of his friend Latouche, found a cosy little villa hidden away near the Paris Observatory on the edge of the city next to a convent. The villa was rented in the name of M. Surville. Balzac had an idea for a historical novel. 'Pure chance' had provided him with a subject; and chance, too, it seemed, had sent him back to literature. In his new study, on top of the filing cabinet, he set up a plaster statuette of Napoleon and attached a small piece of paper to it. His next enterprise would be slightly more ambitious: 'What he was unable to finish with the sword, I shall accomplish with the pen.'[87] The man who proposed to reconquer Europe 'with the agile wing of the crow or the goose' signed himself 'HONORÉ DE BALZAC'.

PART TWO

PART TWO

CHAPTER SEVEN

The Last of the Chouans

(1828–1830)

T OWARDS THE beginning of autumn in the year 1828, shortly after dawn, a young man with a large, bulbous nose, a thick moustache and long hair brushed back behind his ears arrived in the courtyard of the Messageries Royales in the centre of Paris. Looking like a beggar after a visit to the laundry, with a dilapidated hat and an old, ill-fitting coat, Balzac was dressed for a long and uncomfortable journey. He was carrying such a small amount of luggage that he must either have been warned of the inadequacies of public transport in the region to which he was travelling or was expecting an unusual degree of hospitality on arrival.[1] Balzac had booked a seat in the diligence bound for Brittany, after inviting himself to the home in Fougères of Gilbert de Pommereul, the son of his father's old ally. The journey to Fougères took four days, but discomfort was of little concern to the traveller. All I need, he wrote, is a camp-bed, a mattress, a table (preferably quadrupedal), a chair and a roof; for Balzac had a mission. His historical research had turned up some curious anecdotes about the uprisings in the West between 1793 and 1800 when Royalist-backed guerrillas held out against the new Republic. He had already sketched a few dramatic scenes of the civil war which he had been intending to publish, as if still reluctant to expose himself entirely to the public gaze, under a pseudonym. As so often, when pulling together the threads of a new novel, Balzac attached them to a piece of his father's weave. By a stroke of good fortune, General Pommereul had taken part in Bonaparte's campaigns in Brittany against the Chouan guerrillas – so-called, perhaps, because they imitated the cry of the owl (*chuin* in the local patois) to warn each other of danger or to launch attacks on the Republican legions. It was the perfect subject, both for the debtor and for the would-be historian: a Fenimore Cooper adventure transposed to one of the wilder, more Romantic parts of France, with whole populations of eye-witnesses still alive to tell of the atrocities which had never been recorded by an impartial observer. With the Government on the brink of collapse, there might also be some interesting historical lessons to be extrapolated for modern times from the struggle of Republic and monarchy. Having spent the last few months hiding from creditors, picking through the wreckage of his latest disaster and determined now more than ever to conquer the city he was leaving behind, Balzac had a special empathy with guerrillas fighting a hopeless cause.

Debts, as much as the need to document himself, were driving Balzac to the frontiers of France. His friend Latouche, who by now occupied a large place in Balzac's affections, suspected his unprotectable protégé of taking a holiday: 'Expenses, nights spent on the leather of a coach-seat, headaches and an aching bum; what a bloody waste of time! ... What do I care if potatoes are cheaper in Brittany, or for that matter chickens and horses? It's my brain, not my stomach that keeps me alive.'[2] With his usual amiable belligerence, Latouche accused Balzac of playing outlaws like a latter-day Chouan instead of finishing the novel in Paris, and he was certainly right to suspect his friend of being inefficient. Contrary to the dogma of the Realist school and contrary to what many of Balzac's contemporaries pretended to know, such fact-finding journeys are exceptional in his career as a novelist. Balzac rarely made special research trips to the towns he intended to portray in his novels. His real itineraries can be traced on a large map of Europe; his mental journeys would form an impossibly detailed atlas. Despite illustrative quotations in guidebooks and a 'House of Eugénie Grandet' which was being shown to tourists almost as soon as the novel was out, Balzac visited Saumur only once, very briefly, at least ten years before the story was conceived.[3] Similarly, though he was praised in 1834 by a Belgian critic for his evocation of Douai in *La Recherche de l'Absolu*, he had never set foot in the town, and the Flemish house at the centre of the tale can still be seen, not in Douai, but in the Rue Briçonnet in the heart of Old Tours.[4] Even in *Le Dernier Chouan*, in the days before Balzac was completely let loose on his own imagination, the castle at Fougères is raised above its actual level, local characters are conflated and embellished, events and places reshuffled, famous views reversed or even borrowed from books.

Going west in 1828, Balzac was making a symbolic journey, back to the obscure, untidy roots of contemporary France. Travelling to Brittany, for any Parisian, was a journey back in time. The last stage was completed in an antiquated carriage called a *turgotine*; it reappears in Chapter 5 of Balzac's novel – a triangle on its point with two enormous wheels and only a leather curtain to shield two cramped passengers from the wind and the rain.[5] As it swayed and clattered through the towns and villages on the borders of Brittany – Mayenne, Ernée, the Pellerine Mountain, La Templerie, from where the forests of Fougères and the medieval town itself first come into view – signs of a still recent war began to appear. Crosses marked the site of battles and massacres. Balzac took notes and imagined the scene thirty years before. '"This is where General Lescure, the Saint of Poitou, was slain! Will you not avenge him?" Hearing these magic words, the Chouans surged forward with terrible force and the Republican soldiers had great difficulty maintaining their fragile formation.'[6] Though he was still harbouring a grandiose plan to devote one book to each period of French history, Balzac sensed that his true subject lay not in the colourful pageants of the distant past but in what seemed the thin confusion of the present; not blocks of time solidified by tradition, but time in motion. He was finally coming close to the formula he had been seeking since the Rue Lesdiguières. In the space of a few years, Balzac became a writer with a reputation which began to penetrate even the well-guarded cultural frontiers of France. But for him this was not at first an emergence into the light but a retreat into himself: 'For three years I worked without respite, from 1828 to 1831, and drew an iron circle around myself.'[7] Within this circle, Balzac would make several other apparently recreational journeys: to Mme de Berny's property, La Bouleaunière, near Nemours, to Tours, to Saché, and down the Loire on a boat to the Atlantic coast (not stopping at Saumur).

These journeys were symbolic, too, because the discovery of contemporary history took Balzac back to his childhood. The sub-title he eventually chose for the second edition of his novel on the Chouans was *La Bretagne en 1799*: the dawn of the century and the author's date of birth. And on each trip, he reverted, deliberately, to the primitive state in which the geniuses of his early works are formed: 'Oh! to lead the life of a Mohican, running over rocks, swimming in the sea, breathing in the air, the sun! I have seen what it is to be a savage! I have an admirable understanding of pirates, adventurers, lives spent in opposition.'[8]

Unlike his Chouans, Balzac was on the verge of a tremendous recovery, about to start production on what Henry James referred to as 'one of the most inscrutable, one of the unfathomable, final facts in the history of art':[9] a whole *œuvre* in a hundred instalments in the space of twenty years.

WHEN HE stepped down from the coach in the courtyard of the Hôtel Saint-Jacques at seven in the morning, Balzac made a lasting impression on General Pommereul's wife.[10] It was quite normal to wear old clothes for a long journey, but not *that* old. So much for Paris fashions. The Pommereuls' first act of hospitality was to march their guest off to the Fougères hatter, who was hard put to find a hat large enough. Mme Pommereul was transfixed by Balzac's giant head. 'When he took off his hat, everything else disappeared': he had 'a broad forehead which, even in the daytime, seemed to reflect the light of a lamp', 'an enormous mouth, always laughing in spite of its dreadful teeth', and 'brown eyes filled with gold which were as precisely eloquent as his words'. Other accounts, but no paintings, confirm the fact that, like the eyes of the miser Grandet, Balzac's eyes were flecked with gold. He studied them in the mirror and invited visitors to inspect them for themselves, showing himself off like the most curious piece in a collection. Julien Lemer remembered such a viewing in 1839: '"You're examining my physiognomy, aren't you, young man? Quite right – we must be observant in our profession.". . . He went and sat in an armchair placed in front of a window and said to us, "Come and see the specks of gold in my eyes. You must have heard of them. . . . The sun should be highlighting them quite nicely now." I moved in closer and, sure enough, I could see, in the sunlight, a very bright speck of golden yellow standing out almost in relief on the black background of his pupils.'[11]

Observing that Balzac's body had been prevented from attaining its natural proportions, obviously not for want of an appetite, the General's wife stuffed 'the poor boy' with food. 'He was so trusting, so kind, so naive and so candid that it was impossible not to love him. And the most extraordinary thing about him was his perpetual good humour. In spite of the misfortunes he had recently suffered, he had barely been with us a quarter of an hour when he had the General and me laughing until the tears ran down our cheeks.' In the morning, Balzac went charging off with his notebook, walking up to farmhouses and cottages, chatting with the peasants, playing with children, drinking cider and tasting the local specialities – buttered *craquelin* (a biscuit made of unrisen dough)[12] and *galette de sarrasin* (black buckwheat cake), 'the national dish, whose miserable delights can be appreciated only by the Bretons'.[13] He scribbled down anecdotes and regionalisms, and turned out to be an excellent investigative reporter. Wounds from the civil war were festering even in 1828; families had been split by conflicting loyalties; people still living were known to have butchered their compatriots or gone on pillaging raids. But Balzac extracted stories from the locals with the same ease with which he drew them from himself. In the evening, he returned triumphantly plastered with mud, exhausted and ready for dinner. He offered to pay for his board and lodging but had come without money. Instead, he told the tales which would appear two years later as the *Scènes de la Vie Privée* – incredible tales of families the General knew. 'When he had finished, we'd shake ourselves as if waking from a dream. "Is all that true, Balzac?" his host would ask. Balzac looked at the General for a moment, his eyes sparkling with irony and intelligence, and then with that laugh of his which set the windowpanes rattling, "Not a word of truth! Pure Balzac! Ha! Not bad, eh, General?"' After dinner, Balzac interviewed the musty remnants of the Fougères nobility who came to play cards, many of them amusingly illiterate after years of exile but convinced of their divine right. On other evenings, he wandered around the ruins of the castle, leaning over the parapet with his long hair waving in the breeze, looking quite the part, to the delight of the local bourgeois who noted a gratifying correspondence between Romantic vignettes and the reality: 'That's M. Balzac, the writer from Paris.'

After about six weeks, Balzac returned to Paris and, goaded on by Latouche, finished the novel six months after leaving for Fougères. Urbain Canel published it in March 1829 as *Le Dernier Chouan ou la Bretagne en 1800*. It was signed 'M. Honoré Balzac'.

Most of the reviews were disappointing, but there were encouraging inconsistencies and misunderstandings which reflected Balzac's originality. For the touchy *Journal des Cancans*, his descriptive passages were 'hideously truthful'; but *Trilby ou l'Album des Salons* found his writing obscure and shamelessly Romantic. Some complained that the story was too long and involved and many modern readers might agree. *Le Dernier Chouan* is both a love story and a history of the rebellion, and in its entanglements and digressions, with its tireless author dragging the reader through the thickets of description and anecdote, it comes to resemble the forests from which the Chouans burst forth with their picks and axes. In the Furne edition of his *Oeuvres Complètes* in 1845, Balzac felt it necessary to assure his faithful readers that the style of the first edition, 'somewhat convoluted and bristling with mistakes', had been tidied up. Criticism, as well as the cash payments made by magazines, may have diverted Balzac temporarily towards the more tractable terrain of the short story, and for most of his life it was the writer of short stories who was generally preferred to the novelist. Nevertheless, as Marxist critics pointed out almost a century later, *Le Dernier Chouan* was a huge achievement. Until a late review in the *Revue Encyclopédique* in 1830, nobody noticed that Balzac had created a new type of historical novel in which, instead of galvanizing the corpses of famous men and women, the novelist revealed historical trends by using representative characters or 'types'. And this is why, in spite of Balzac's sympathy for those characters whose ideas place them in opposition to the social order, the Chouans lose the struggle without much glory, stuck in an ideological rut, unable to adapt to the changing times, full of local colour, no doubt, but coloured, too, by blood which was uselessly spilled.[14]

BALZAC'S 'first'[15] novel, *Le Dernier Chouan*, is, of course, of great biographical interest, but not just as the first stone in the edifice. It was the result of an uneasy collaboration with Latouche, his closest friend and bitterest enemy: one year of passionate intimacy followed by a lifetime of hate. Latouche had acted as Balzac's agent and editor, and tried to prevent his friend from stopping at every step to examine 'the shiny little pebbles on the path'. As soon as the novel appeared, he expressed his admiration in *Le Figaro* for the uncanny realism of Balzac's figures. True, he had a financial stake in its success, but he was also able to appreciate the difficulties of bringing history to life. Latouche was about to publish his own historical novel, *Fragoletta ou Naples et Paris en 1799*, the story of a hermaphrodite who in some ways resembles the Amazonian spy in Balzac's *Chouan*.

It was unfortunate for their friendship that work brought them so close together. Like anyone with good ideas who forgets to point out how good they are and seems unlikely to realize their full potential, Balzac attracted advice in great quantities. He felt the need to protect himself from the persuasive, paternal criticisms of the older man; yet the attraction was mutual. Sainte-Beuve gives some idea of what Balzac meant when he called Latouche 'seductive' (after their falling out): 'He was not handsome, and yet people were drawn to him.' 'His hands were small and delicate, and he liked to show them off. His wit, grace and air of distinction made up for his physical defects.' 'The sound of his voice was flattering and ingratiating; it had something of the siren's song in it. It was difficult to break off a conversation with him. His words were caressing, too caressing, in fact, voluptuous even, though the perfidious man always liked to throw some sharp words at you in the end which soured the sweetness of his cajoling.'[16] Any sexual overtones in Sainte-Beuve's two-faced portrait of Latouche are intentional, and it is partly because of this that Balzac's agreeably ambiguous friend is worth rediscovering.

Two incidents in particular cast light on the man who almost became the male companion Balzac dreamed of finding. In 1826, Latouche had published a novel, anonymously, and passed it off as the latest literary indiscretion of the Duchesse de Duras. The Duchess was known to have written a story about a young man who showed an inexplicable reluctance to marry the woman he loved. Latouche claimed to provide the reason: Olivier was impotent. The choice of a sticky subject does not on its own explain why he refused to acknowledge his own work and why he appeared to value it mainly as a practical joke. The authorial reticence of Latouche is all the more surprising since *Olivier* is one of the finest long short stories of the early, 'pre-Balzacian' nineteenth century. Its tense, precise style, its muted ironies and use of an unmentionable affliction to make the reader the imaginative accomplice of the narrator appealed to Stendhal: *Olivier* inspired him to write his first novel, *Armance*. It may be, however, that the critical self-awareness which gives the story its deceptively prosaic tone prevented its author from recognizing and rejoicing in his own originality. It did not prevent him from noticing other writers' talent. Latouche owed his reputation to the poems of André Chénier which he had discovered and edited in 1819. Balzac was his second great discovery, and his own insecurity made him all the more eager to bring out the masterpiece he saw in Balzac's overcrowded mind. Inevitably, in his efforts to cure Balzac of his garrulity, he spent less and less time sugaring the pill and, after investing a great deal of time, money and thought in him, became jeal. us of other influences. 'I think I must still like you', he wrote when Balzac had failed to keep several appointments, 'because I'm still insulting you; but don't count on it.'

The second revealing incident is Balzac's move to the Rue Cassini, near the Observatory at the far end of the Luxembourg Gardens. He was helped to move in by Latouche, who had an unusual hobby – hanging wallpaper. Wallpaper was just becoming available to bourgeois households and, as Edgar Allan Poe puts it in his *Philosophy of Furniture*, was called upon to 'perform the office of the heraldic display in monarchical countries'. Balzac wanted an apartment fit for a literary king. In choosing the paper, cutting it to size and fitting it to all the difficult angles, Latouche's genius blossomed as it rarely did in his work. When he was unable to be there with his ladder and paste, he used his literary skills to describe in great detail exactly how his friends should hang the paper he had chosen for them.[17] For Latouche, Balzac's novel was like an extension of the home they planned to share. Without being a perfectionist, knowing, in fact, that Balzac's endless search for the perfect phrase could destroy the harmony of the original conception, he hated to see anyone fall needlessly short of their best. The final choice of decoration was left to the owner; Latouche was simply the cutter and paster. This unusual influence might be traced to the wallpaper which occupies an important place in the Pension Vauquer in *Le Père Goriot*.[18] Interior decorating was an excellent preparation for detecting clues about individuals in mass-produced objects.

Two or three years later, George Sand was invited to Balzac's hideaway in the Rue Cassini. The hand of Latouche was still in evidence in the incongruously feminine decor. Balzac had turned his rooms into 'an ensemble of ladies' boudoirs': the walls were 'hung

with silk and lined with lace'.[19] The bedroom, according to another
visitor, was like a bridal chamber, pink, white and perfumed; the
gallery on the first floor which joined the two pavilions of the house
was in white and blue stripes with a light-blue divan, and the whole
place was full of rare flowers in porcelain vases. Feminine objects lay
about – a glove, a slipper, an embroidered heart pierced by an arrow
– gifts from female admirers.[20] Balzac prided himself on being able to
live in what looked like luxury when anyone else would have been in a
hovel. Rooms filled up with bargains just as Balzac's sentences
expanded and exploded with afterthoughts and subordinate clauses.
Latouche saw it as another sign of his prolixity: 'Selling oneself to the
upholsterer for the next two years is the act of a lunatic!'

Because Balzac's letters were destroyed in a fire and because
Latouche wrote most of his in a state of irritation, the correspondence
gives an unbalanced view of their friendship. They appear to be
permanently at loggerheads, and their friendship is memorable not for
their fruitful collaboration but for the acrimony of later remarks:
Balzac's dismissal of Latouche as an 'envious, hateful, malicious man,
a mine of venom', 'the nastiest of all our contemporaries';[21] his savage,
critical shredding of Latouche's novel, *Léo*, in 1840; Latouche's
opinion that Balzac had 'observed the world through the little window
in the WC, and his vision has never recovered'.[22] The ostensible cause
of their break-up was Balzac's grudging and equivocal reception of
Fragoletta in May and June 1829. Irritatingly, he suggested that
Latouche was guilty of excessive brevity.[23] Latouche understandably
accused Balzac of ingratitude, of getting back at him for his incisive
criticisms of *Le Dernier Chouan* with peremptory comments which
profited no one. Attempts by Latouche to patch up the quarrel failed
and the friendship foundered in bickering about the money Latouche
had invested in Balzac's novel.

Normally, the blame is put on Latouche. In her autobiography,
George Sand brands him a neurotic, melancholy, disappointed man,
highly intelligent, especially when finding fault – with his own work
as much as with that of other writers – constantly rehearsing masterpieces but incapable of reproducing his brilliant conversation on the
page. However, Balzac was also to blame and the idea of guilt is not
particularly helpful. The violence of their attacks on each other shows
how strong the original fire must have been to have sputtered on long

after the friends broke up. Considering the fact that they had planned to live together, debts and textual criticism seem unusually trivial excuses to end a friendship. All the more reason to ask why they were drawn to each other in the first place.

Latouche provides us with the first clear signs of Balzac's versatile sexuality. The subject is such fertile ground for speculation that some preliminary remarks are called for.[24] On the one hand, a few drops of truth can be whipped up into a splendid, vaporous concoction with no nutritive value. On the other hand, the feminine aspects of Balzac have traditionally been ignored. W. B. Yeats counted him among those rare authors who combine intellect with the life that lies hidden in their blood and nerves – the bull and the nightingale.[25] Since Rodin's aggressive statue, with its defiant bulk and protuberances, the bull has been dominant.

It seems prudent, therefore, to say the 'last word' first, before wading into the mire of innuendo and conjecture. In the end, doubts should remain, and any precise conclusion would be an admission of defeat. Balzac's tendencies might best be described not as homosexual, heterosexual or both, but simply as sexual. He himself claimed to be able to judge novels by the following criterion: some novels are male, others are female and some puny specimens have no sex at all.[26] Presumably, his own novels belong to a fourth, pansexual category. The swell of undifferentiated desire which made him lunge at the plump flesh of the lady at the ball in 1814 led him to produce the truly mouth-watering descriptions of Lucien de Rubempré which entranced Oscar Wilde and inspired the creation of Dorian Gray. The short period of cohabitation with Latouche heralds the discovery, in Balzac's stories, not just of one form of sexual attraction but of sexuality in all its uncharted variety.

The principal reason why sexual 'deviance' in the early nineteenth century lends itself so poorly to analysis is that homosexuality itself had virtually no official existence. This is one of the great underground rivers of the nineteenth-century literary metropolis, and without Balzac a study of it during this period would mostly be the history of an absence. Occasionally, it seeps through the paving-stones, but one would usually expect to sight it only after much planning and preparation: a thorough knowledge of classical allusions, anecdotal history and contemporary slang. The taboo, it should be said, applied mainly to male homosexuality. Lesbians were still inhabitants of the island of Lesbos, and Sappho herself is usually deemed to have jumped off a cliff because she was abandoned by a man. However, the 'dissolute mores' of the Lesbians are often mysteriously referred to, even in William Duckett's exquisite *Dictionnaire de Conversation*, 'for the Use of Ladies and Young Persons, or the Necessary Complement to Every Good Education'.[27] Lesbians in the modern sense[28] frequently crop up in the company of prostitutes – both types of woman being sterile, according to a convenient prejudice. Moreover, one 'perversion' seems less unmentionable when combined with another. As Balzac's monomaniacs show, a vice in isolation takes on a life of its own and threatens to escape from the web of causes and effects which make society seem governable. Male homosexuality was touched on in stories of hermaphrodites, notably in Latouche's *Fragoletta* (1829), Gautier's *Mademoiselle de Maupin* and, obliquely, in Balzac's own *Séraphîta* (both 1835), but the hermaphrodite had honourable antecedents in Plato's *Symposium* and the ambiguous character nearly always starts out as a woman.

Balzac's introduction of male homosexual heroes into serious literature was not only an act of courage at a time when moral condemnation was the favourite weapon of hostile journalists, but also, less obviously, a remarkable *tour de force*. Literature abounded in misers, hypochondriacs, jealous lovers, parents betrayed by selfish children; but for Vautrin, Lucien de Rubempré and Eugène de Rastignac, Balzac had practically no models – at least no literary models. Hence his character sketches have a curious, composite quality which places them in an ill-defined area between gossip and superstition, physiology and mythology:

Lucien stood in that graceful pose which sculptors use for the Indian Bacchus. His face had the distinguished lines of classical beauty: a Grecian brow and nose, the soft whiteness of a woman's skin, eyes so blue they appeared to be black, eyes full of love . . . with long, brown lashes and eyebrows such as a Chinese artist might have drawn. . . . The smile of sad angels hovered over lips whose coral hues were heightened by beautiful teeth. He had the hands of a well-born person, elegant hands which women longed to kiss and whose every gesture men felt compelled to obey. Lucien was slender and of medium height. Looking at his feet, any man would have been

[155]

tempted to take him for a girl in disguise, especially since, like most men with subtle, not to say cunning minds, his hips were shaped like those of a woman. This is nearly always a reliable clue to character and was so in Lucien's case. Many times, his restless turn of mind led him, when he analysed the present state of society, to that depravity which is typical of diplomats, who believe that any means, however shameful, are justified by success.[29]

This astonishing description of Lucien occurs in the middle of that commonplace scene of Romantic fiction: two lovers under a leafy bower on a spring afternoon. Except that both characters are men: David Séchard and Lucien de Rubempré, in *Illusions Perdues*. Of course, the friendship is Platonic, but, on a deeper level, sexual:

One of the two friends loved the other to the point of idolatry, and that was David. And so Lucien commanded like a woman who knows she is loved, and David took pleasure in obeying. The physical beauty of his friend carried with it a superiority which he accepted, finding himself clumsy and common.

Whether or not biographical data brings us any closer to the 'truth' of a text, Balzac's life gives this scene a special nuance. David and Lucien are engrossed in a volume of André Chénier. In the year in which the scene is set, this is necessarily the volume edited by Latouche. In fiction, the bitterness dissolves. Without mentioning him by name, Balzac pays his ex-friend a charming compliment: 'David, too moved to continue reading, allowed Lucien to take the volume from him. "A poet rediscovered by a poet!" he said as his eye fell on the signature of the preface.'[30]

The tantalizing ambiguities of Balzac's descriptions, their aura of unspecified danger, come not only from taboos and censorship, but also from the fact that the carpet of artistic tradition wears thin in these places. These characters insinuate themselves into the reader's mind on a level so close to private or even unconscious thought that one is hardly surprised to learn that, for Oscar Wilde, 'One of the greatest tragedies of my life is the death of Lucien de Rubempré. It is a grief from which I have never been able completely to rid myself. It haunts me in my moments of pleasure. I remember it when I laugh.'[31]

Surprisingly, it is far from obvious to many 'professional' readers of *Le Père Goriot* or *Illusions Perdues* that the ambitious young Eugène de Rastignac or his more effeminate and fluctuating counterpart, Lucien de Rubempré, were ever intended to be seen in this light. One of Balzac's most attentive readers, Marcel Proust, has been accused of trying to conscript him for the cause, as if literature were ultimately a matter of sexual loyalties. Anglo-Saxon critics are particularly guilty of throwing a veil over some of Balzac's most subtle creations. Once unfairly attacked in his lifetime, the writer will forever be unfairly defended, even to his detriment, and even when the court has long since been empty. Balzac has suffered more than any other novelist from this kind of critical defence. And perhaps, before we pass judgment on the hypocritical century in which he lived, it should be said that, even now, one of the unwritten tenets of many academic critics is that the reader's naturally prurient mind should not be provided with too rich a feast.

Why, then, did Balzac choose this subject? One reason is that he had undertaken to uncover every aspect of society, particularly those clandestine activities which, by being suppressed or ignored, were able to exert a powerful, pernicious influence. But what of Balzac himself? Suspicions were aroused in his contemporaries partly because of his relations with known homosexuals like the Marquis de Custine and Hippolyte Auger, the dilettante socialist who helped Latouche to decorate Balzac's apartment in 1829. The more salacious gossip concerns Balzac's later relationships, as we shall see, all of them with men much younger than himself and all coming after his father's death. From 1831 to 1836, Balzac 'adopted' several attractive, incompetent young men, literary slaves he hoped to form, as Vautrin forms Rastignac and Lucien. But this was a period when Balzac was in full possession of his own talent – the novelist as God, carrying his experiments over into real life.

Latouche was different. He was Balzac's senior by fourteen years. The prurient ear of the Goncourt brothers registered a story that Mme de Berny grew jealous of Latouche.[32] Indeed, if she ever saw Latouche's letters to Balzac, she would not have been reassured. He wrote, for example, before Balzac returned from Fougères, in a phrase both crude and enigmatic: 'You who tell me to go and fuck off, apparently because friendship is female [i.e. changeable][33] and because you're trying to influence me by exploiting the feelings I have for you, come back and get fucked here in Paris – as quickly as you can.'

Latouche's letters are full of sexual innuendoes, some more subtle than others. Balzac himself hints that his former friend had a guilty secret, telling Mme Hanska that he may be odious but at least 'he hides his private life'. Even towards the end of his life, embittered and poor, Latouche never sold the story of Balzac's sins and errors. But when he calls his friend a 'pretty boy', he may simply be teasing. There are far stronger remarks in letters from Eugène Sue, who likes to sign off with breezy references to their respective sexual organs: 'Come and invite me to lunch', he writes, 'or to dinner, to supper or to bed. . . . Whatever you want . . . I admire your prepuce and am yours, Eugène S.'[34]

Breaking taboos was almost *de rigueur* for a member of the literary avant-garde. In Bohemian circles, it was fashionable to imitate aspects of women's behaviour and dress.[35] Adopting a female persona was part of the act and, at least with Latouche, any physical relationship is highly unlikely. Still, this intimate teasing has much to do with the sudden end of their friendship. Balzac had never shared a house with a close friend and found himself in deep emotional waters. Taboos, after all, are not just inconvenient rules but a form of self-censorship as well. When preparing the manuscript of *Le Père Goriot* for publication five years later, Balzac added a little scene which acts as an almost imperceptible reminder that the biggest surprises in life come from within. Jacques Collin (alias Vautrin) has just been arrested by the head of the Sûreté, shopped to the police by Mlle Michonneau. The horrible spinster has been informed that the escaped convict is 'not the sort of man who likes women' and has watched his seduction of Rastignac with interest:

> 'Monsieur is siding with Collin,' she replied, scrutinizing the student with an expression of venomous curiosity. 'And it's not difficult to understand why.'
>
> Hearing this, Eugène sprang forward as if to pounce on the old maid and strangle her. Her treacherous meaning was written on her face and in that instant it cast a terrible light in his soul.[36]

Whether or not this 'terrible light' fell on Balzac's conscious or unconscious mind when he engineered, so it seemed, the end of his friendship with Latouche, it began to illuminate some unexplored passageways in his writing. *Sarrasine*, for example, investigates homosexual desire, and Balzac's letters begin to refer quite frequently to the 'female' aspects of his own character. The most interesting text, however, concerns neither a man nor a woman.

At the end of 1829, just as Balzac was breaking up with Latouche, Henri Martin was entertaining Parisians with displays of the new art of lion-taming. One year later, Balzac's *Une Passion dans le Désert* appeared in the *Revue de Paris* and caused a sensation. It suggested that Martin's success was not entirely the innocent result of training. A soldier, lost in the Sahara, wakes up to find himself next to a sleeping panther. An unconventional though heterosexual love affair begins:

> It was a female. The fur on the belly and thighs was dazzlingly white. Several small patches, like velvet, formed attractive little bracelets around the paws. The muscular tail was also white but had black rings at its tip. The upper part of the coat was yellow like unpolished gold, but very soft and smooth, and it bore those characteristic marks reminiscent of finely drawn roses which serve to distinguish panthers from other members of the *felis* family. . . . When the sun rose, the panther suddenly opened her eyes and violently stretched out her paws as if to get rid of a cramp. Then she yawned, revealing the terrifying apparatus of her teeth. . . . 'Just like a flirtatious woman!' thought the Frenchman, as he watched her roll about, making delightful, coquettish movements.[37]

Even in bestiality, there is a thin line between physical and Platonic love. Balzac's novels offer no more concrete evidence than his life, but they do provide some beautiful illustrations of his growing skill at exploiting, for literary ends, every part of his – and his readers' – personality.

BALZAC'S REBIRTH as a writer coincided not only with the end of his friendship but also, more importantly, with the death of his father. On 19 June 1829, Bernard-François finally failed in his attempt to live for ever. He died shortly before his eighty-third birthday, old enough to claim a measure of success at a time when only 0.6 per cent of the

Paris population lived into their eighties.[38] In fact, he died prematurely, hurried into the grave by a coach accident.[39] Balzac identified more insidious causes: his father's consumption of pharmaceutical pills, which proved that the quest for immortality was a destructive passion. And there was also his senile virility of which at least one woman in Villeparisis had been given proof three years before when the Balzacs were forced to leave for Versailles.

Grief at losing the only person in the world who resembled himself was contaminated by emotions of a less edifying order. With a new sense of responsibility came a new sense of constraints: Bernard-François may have been more of a grandfather than a father, but he was the head of the household – a role Balzac was unable financially to assume. Although he inherited all his father's money, it passed immediately to his mother, but without eradicating the humiliating debt. It was all very well Bernard-François warning his son before he died that his mother would be his 'most dangerous, most cunning enemy in life',[40] but what had he done to protect him? Picking a quarrel with 'the Pyramid of Egypt' had always been difficult, and the sense of anger and frustration remained. Worse still, these feelings were intensified by guilt. Balzac heard of his father's death while he was away from Paris,[41] probably staying with Mme de Berny at La Bouleaunière in the lap of emotional luxury.[42] His name does not appear on the death certificate – Henry signed for his brother – and it is unlikely that he was able to return in time for the funeral which took place two days later at Saint-Merri in Paris. In the coming years, Balzac refers several times to young revellers who are disturbed in the midst of a good orgy by news of their father's death.[43]

> Already the flowers had been crumpled, eyes were glazing over, and everyone was intoxicated to the tips of their toes. In this momentary silence, a door opened and, as at Belshazzar's Feast, God made his presence known in the guise of an old, tottering, white-haired servant. He entered the room with a mournful air and threw a withering glance at the garlands, the vermeil chalices and pyramids of fruit. . . . Finally, he cast a shroud over all this folly by pronouncing these sombre words in a hollow-sounding voice: 'Monsieur, your Father is dying.'
> Don Juan rose and waved his hand toward his guests in a

manner which seemed to signify, 'Please excuse me; this is not the sort of thing that happens every day.'

Are not young people often surprised by the death of their father in the midst of life's splendours or in the madness of an orgy? Death is as sudden in its whims as a courtesan in her disdain; but Death is more faithful, for she has never deceived anybody.[44]

Through the mist of conflicting emotions the ghost of Bernard-François rises in grotesque forms in three short stories written in 1829 and 1830. These stories commemorate a period of difficult mourning and self-examination in Balzac's life. They are also the earliest short stories to be included in *La Comédie Humaine*, and the fact that Bernard-François just missed seeing his son become famous and successful under his own name gives the paternal presence a peculiarly ironic quality. The father's death preceding the son's long-delayed breakthrough by a few months is perhaps more than just a poignant coincidence.

Balzac's exasperation, with a hint of gloating, is apparent in *L'Élixir de Longue Vie*, published by the *Revue de Paris* in October 1830. Don Juan's dying father has asked his son to revive him after death by bathing his corpse in the magic potion. Keeping watch over his father's body, the son moistens one eye. It opens, and is, as one might expect, horribly eloquent, 'thinking, accusing, condemning, threatening, judging, speaking, shouting and biting'. Taking a towel, Don Juan squashes the eye and keeps the rest of the precious elixir for himself.

Two months later, *La Caricature* published *La Danse des Pierres*. The dance takes place in Saint-Gatien Cathedral in Tours, a source of potent childhood memories. 'It was there that, tired of life, I found myself shortly after the Revolution of 1830', 'reflecting on my doubtful future and disappointed hopes'. Wandering through the ecclesiastical 'forest of pillars', the narrator has a hallucination: the whole edifice begins to shake, the organ sounds and the colossal Christ nailed to the altar smiles at him with a 'malicious benevolence' which strikes fear into his heart. As usual, Balzac covered any autobiographical tracks by relocating the dance in Ostend in the definitive version and by pointing out the value of both stories as allegories of modern society: the deposition of Charles X and the weakening of the Church's foundations. But the 'malicious benevolence' of the Tourangeau Christ irresistibly evokes that other pillar of society, the oxymoronic Bernard-François, the apotheosis of an atheist, sneering on the altar as he sneered at the Church in Balzac's childhood.[45]

Finally, most gruesome of all, the story *El Verdugo* – the closest in date to Bernard-François's death – contains another eerie concurrence of fiction and its real trappings. A heroic son, Juanito – thirty years old, like Balzac – is forced, in order to safeguard the honour of his family, to decapitate his old father. Even the most literal-minded Freudian critic might find Balzac's lurid anecdote too neat a symbol, were it not for the fact that *El Verdugo* is the first work signed 'H. *de* Balzac'.[46] The disappearance of the father coincides with the adoption of the nobiliary particle. A symbolic inheritance. Financially and emotionally cut off from the family, it was as a writer that Balzac would assume his responsibilities and, at long last, gain his independence.

All these allusions to parricide can be adequately and prosaically explained. *El Verdugo* probably originated in the bottomless memory of the Duchesse d'Abrantès; *L'Élixir de Longue Vie* was a distillation of stories by Richard Steele and Hoffmann;[47] and the hallucination in Saint-Gatien Cathedral can be ascribed to the craze for 'fantastic' stories and traced back to Jean-Paul Richter's terrifying *Dream* of the death of God the Father, made famous in France by Mme de Staël's translation. Nevertheless, the choice of tales and the recurrence of themes in such a short period are certainly significant.

The immediate effect of Bernard-François's death was to send Balzac back to his *Physiologie du Mariage*, which he had printed in 1826 but never published. Friends had warned him of the scandal which would inevitably be whipped up by the work of a comic scientist who dealt with humdrum taboos like impotence, sexual needs and the menopause. Laure remembered her brother's irritation when they told him he was being presumptuous in trying to apply his comic talent to serious subjects. Touchingly, Balzac had this unpublished version bound with his father's *Histoire de la Rage*: marriage, too, was a kind of lunacy, a social disease perpetuated by prejudice. By joining his father in the same binding, Balzac acknowledged that this product of more enlightened days was in effect a collaboration. He even offered his father a curtain-call in the version which eventually appeared, signed 'by a Young Bachelor', at the end of 1829. Balzac's feelings towards his father are embodied in all their complexity in the cynical figure of the Marquis de T——. Bequeathing the author 'virile ideas' instead of hard cash, the Marquis instructs him that love should be abolished: love is a 'social luxury' which serves only to pollute society with infants. To the 'young bachelor', this mechanistic philosophy seems depressingly defeatist, little more than cowardly compromise and the pursuit of smugness. 'If conjugal peace leads to such disenchanting conclusions', he writes, 'I know of many a husband who would much prefer war'. Then, standing metaphorically over the grave, he bids farewell to the 'old carcass' of his father, that 'walking personification of marriage'.[48]

Balzac's interest in the Chouan uprisings, his ambiguous relations with Latouche, his shocking tales and, finally, his rejection of family life as personified by his father are all signs of the fact that his integration into society, like Rastignac's triumphant descent from the Père Lachaise cemetery, coincided with a loosening of the hand of convention. His upbringing – and perhaps even his unconscious mind – could now be turned to profit.

FOR THE REST of 1829, though scarcely able to afford necessities – 'postage and bus-tickets are terrible expenses for me and I stay at home so as not to wear out my clothes' – unable even to buy an extra copy of his own novel, Balzac gradually equipped his 'pretty monk's cell'.[49] It was already filling up with the books, all bound in red, which he had been collecting since his student days and which forced him out of the Rue Cassini eight years later. He had also acquired a maid called Flore who satisfied the dual criterion of blind devotion and undistracting ugliness.

Here on the rural edge of the city, 'between a Carmelite convent and the square where executions now take place',[50] Balzac locked himself away, concentrating his mind in isolation, four candles burning, shutters closed, curtains drawn, for days on end. He left the house only to stay with the Duchesse d'Abrantès at the Château de Maffliers near Chantilly. In November, he was working all day on *Physiologie du Mariage* and then, from nine o'clock until two in the morning, on the

Scènes de la Vie Privée. With their explorations of domestic mysteries and miseries and their dark, Rembrandtesque interiors, these six short stories retain something of their native milieu. Occasionally, the page sends up an obscure reflection of the writer at work. His silent activity is mirrored in characters who are sometimes quite unlike himself in other respects: 'At every hour of the day, passers-by could see this young working girl sitting in an old red velvet armchair, her head bent over an embroidery frame, passionately engrossed in her work.'[51] Or, in *Les Proscrits*: 'Returning to his abode, the stranger locked himself into his room, lit his inspiring lamp, and entrusted himself to the terrible demon of work, asking the silence for words and the night for ideas.'[52]

In a sense, Balzac was steeling himself against the impact of imminent success. The following months, during which he absconded from Paris just as a revolution was about to turn France in a new direction, are like a watershed in his life from which two larger rivers flow. Deep in his work, with almost masochistic determination, Balzac maintained the profitable feeling of a useless struggle. He wrote in January 1830: 'The days melt in my hands like ice in the sun. I'm not living, I'm wearing myself out in a horrible fashion – but whether I die of work or something else, it's all the same.' He increased the chances of the first disaster occurring by combining story-writing with plans to write for the stage. The author of *Cromwell* knew himself well enough by now not to learn from personal experience: failure was ultimately an encouragement. Among the plans were a *Don Juan* in collaboration with Eugène Sue and a whole series of dramas, to be sold to the public at 1 franc each, with a neighbouring journalist called Victor Ratier. Ratier saw for himself how Balzac worked, consuming huge amounts of time in one sitting, 'dining invariably on a consommé, a steak and a salad, with a glass of water, followed by a whole string of cups of coffee served with admirable patience by Flore'.[53] The dramas failed to materialize; instead, Balzac presented Ratier with the manuscript of a short novel, making him one of the first in a long line of people to receive such gifts. Soon he would be famous and the manuscript could be sold for a small fortune. This, too, had been produced in the same exhausting manner. To win a bet, Balzac had himself locked in a room with paper, pen and ink and emerged twelve hours later with the completed manuscript. With him, says Ratier, 'it wasn't presumptuousness. On the outside, he gave every sign of being overbearing and yet he was really the most modest man I ever knew. No one was quicker to recognize his own faults or more sincere in doing so. No one ever judged themselves more severely.'

The other river ran from the watershed in the opposite direction. In public, Balzac gave little sign of having recently been submerged in silence and night. When he entered a room, he immediately filled it up; in speaking, he appeared to transcend the normal distinction between standing and sitting.[54] 'There seemed to be a gap between himself and the floor. Sometimes he would bend down as if to snatch up a sheaf of ideas, then stand on tiptoe to watch his thoughts shoot up into the infinite.'[55] Writers who depict Balzac at this stage in his life often hesitate significantly in their choice of adjectives. Well-dressed but always untidy; short and thick-set, he occupied the vertical space of a tall person; not fat, but never impressing anyone as thin. Long before he put on weight, he possessed a kind of subjective rotundity – 'a supple envelope, by no means a burden to be carried about', weight that acted as an impetus not an anchor.

Balzac was difficult to classify not only because of his appearance. Emerging from obscurity at the age of thirty, and now inexplicably producing about 10 per cent of the titles in the *Comédie Humaine* to be, he presented himself in several salons as an entertaining *viveur*, conducting an involuntary publicity campaign for his own products. He told stories to the assembled guests – not an unusual activity at the time, but few people were able to make them up on the spot as Balzac did, egged on with suggestions from his audience; and no one but Balzac would interrupt themselves to admire the purple passages. Occasionally, the publicity campaign was more deliberate. Having spotted an advertisement for his *Physiologie* in the *Mercure de France*, which promised a full review in a coming issue, Balzac rushed round to the home of Lacroix, who wrote for the *Mercure*, to make absolutely certain he knew it was a masterpiece. Just in case he didn't, Balzac wrote the review himself.[56] It appeared in the issue for 23 January 1830: 'A lively, colourful, picturesque style, witticisms and sarcasms, pleasant anecdotes more pleasant yet in the telling complete our sincere praise of this curious work in which the thought is bolder than the expression and which, after Brillat-Savarin's *Physiologie du Goût*, will seem tasty to everyone.' Balzac's ploy might be discounted as arrogance, but then why should literary sensibility cease to function close to home? His enthusiastic review, which gives off the warmth of energetic conversation, should also count, objectively, as proof of the author's good taste.

When success came, it was suitably double-edged. With *Physiologie du Mariage* and the tales which had begun to appear in magazines, Balzac became a prominent member of the social and literary world of Paris. Yet the recognition he used to long for in such crudely material terms in the Rue Lesdiguières came as a result of writing which expressed an opposition to this society – a provocative voice crying out, very agreeably and very sociably, in the wilderness. For a long time, Balzac would be referred to as 'the author of *Physiologie du Mariage*' – 'that brutal book', wrote Jules Janin, 'which no one had yet dared write'.[57] It was an open secret that the world-weary 'young bachelor' was Balzac. He was accepted as a funny writer. But it was generally recognized, too, that he had made a serious attempt to counteract the deleterious effects of an outmoded institution and that he had done so to great effect. One reviewer recommended that newly-weds read it together in the aftermath of their honeymoon. Jules Janin sent a note to say that Balzac's horror stories of marital disharmony had consoled him for his temporary impotence. An old school-friend wrote from Martinique in 1833 hinting that Balzac's book had persuaded him to postpone his marriage.[58] Nevertheless, Balzac's success was proportionate to the scandal. A young baroness from Nohant called Aurore Dupin, who arrived in Paris in 1831, dressed as a man and began a brief collaboration with Jules Sandeau – hence her *nom de plume*, George Sand – reported to a friend that the demand for novelty was inducing writers to choose revolting subjects: 'Balzac has reached the heights of fame by depicting the love of a soldier for a tigress and the love of an artist for a *castrato*' (*Sarrasine*).[59] The *Physiologie* itself was a firework thrown at the feet of a staid society that was soon to recover quite easily from the July Revolution. It was a rearguard action disguised as an entertainment. Perhaps most subversive of all, Balzac had discovered his true audience in that repressed majority which he explicitly discouraged from reading the *Physiologie*: women.

Women were advised not to read the book, however, not because the author feared his own corrupting influence but because, 'without realizing it, they have already read it'.[60] Letters from Balzac's female admirers – too numerous for them all to be included in his published correspondence and, by one account, totalling more than 10,000[61] – began to arrive at the Rue Cassini in 1831. The daughter of a Lyon bookseller, after 'recognizing' the heroine of *Le Bal de Sceaux*, wrote to thank Balzac for enabling her to discover herself. She added, in a phrase which must have pleased him, since he had said it himself many times, 'You can see that these feelings exist in all classes, for I am not noble, nor even rich. . . . For me, true nobility is genius.'[62]

The bookseller's daughter put her finger on the real cause of these ambivalent attitudes to the new Balzac. He was unmistakably bourgeois, not to say plebeian; yet he consorted with duchesses and called himself *de* Balzac. Clearly, this was a man who did not know his place. An observer of salon life called Fontaney gave a characteristic description of Balzac when he saw him in the salon of the painter, Baron Gérard, in 1831. Fontaney is so preoccupied with social categories as to be practically unintelligible to the modern reader:

> M. de Balzac was there, and I was finally able to see this new star who owes his literary fame to *La Physiologie du Mariage*. A big chap with bright eyes, a white waistcoat, he holds himself like a herbalist, dresses like a butcher, looks like a gilder – the whole effect is impressive.
>
> He is the commercial writer *par excellence*. 'The *Revue de Paris*', he said airily, 'is the best journal in Europe – it pays the biggest fees.' How disgraceful![63]

Balzac was becoming a scapegoat for other people's unspoken social ambitions. Even today it is possible to find critics who sneer at Balzac for his clumsy attempts to rise above his station. Certainly there is some snobbishness in his continual pronouncements about the innate superiority of certain aristocrats, the obvious relish with which he reels off the names, pedigrees and blazons of his dukes and duchesses, counts and countesses, as if practising an elaborate bow; or the characters' unremitting need to remind themselves to behave with the effortless sophistication and impertinence required by their caste. Precisely why this fascination with aristocratic auras is felt to be ridiculous or offensive is something of a mystery. Balzac approaches the bourgeoisie in the same generalizing spirit. It probably has something to do with certain memorable comments made by Sainte-

Beuve, Proust and Henry James, none of whom are remarkable for their indifference to class or to their own rank in the social regiment. Perhaps also there is some residual feeling that the higher orders are entitled to a greater immunity from categorization than the dull masses which, it might be assumed, were never the object of the author's social aspirations. Moreover, if one takes as exemplars of the nobility the duchesses known to Balzac, the actors of *La Comédie Humaine* are consistently more human (or more effectively artificial) than the real thing. Balzac remained highly critical of the Faubourg Saint-Germain as a whole – too self-centred to look after its own interests, unaware of its political destiny – and for sheer undiscriminating snobbery, it would be hard to beat the pettiness and malice of journalists who reported the slightest faux-pas made by the novelist in the salons of Paris. The real problem was that other people were unsure of his place.

Still, the question remains: why did Balzac adopt the 'de', and why did he make such a show of his entirely improbable descent from the Balzac d'Entragues? Books, furniture, ornaments, china, watches, writing-paper and seals, even the door-panels, cushions and driver's seat of the coach he later acquired were emblazoned with the Entragues coat-of-arms. Balzac was moved to break his autobiographical silence in the preface to *Le Lys dans la Vallée* in 1836: 'I am not a gentleman in the historical and nobiliary sense of the word, which is so profoundly meaningful for families which belong to the conquering race [the Franks]. I say this countering pride with pride, for my father gloried in belonging to the conquered race [the Gauls].'[64] There was, he claimed, a prehistoric connection between this ancient family, which held out against the invaders in the wilds of the Auvergne, and the Balzacs of Entragues – a line that was now extinct. The fact that he did occasionally claim to belong to this upstart nobility of the Middle Ages, still recognized in modern times as the real nobility, is largely irrelevant or, rather, emblematic of something else. Turning arrogance into modesty, he justified his own intermittent hypocrisy by asserting that 'one should act in accordance with one's position'. For this very reason, Balzac had waited for success before adopting the 'de'. The particle, in any case, was no more indicative of aristocratic origins than a hyphenated surname in England, but like a new set of clothes, it allowed its possessor to circulate more freely in society.

Above all, it could stand for something far more important than an accident of birth. 'The aristocracy and authority of talent are more substantial than the aristocracy of names and material power,' he wrote in 1830.[65] Artists were continually showered with worthless medals and ribbons, but never had the Government been so stingy in its funding of the arts. This was a society which pretended that money was the great leveller – potentially, always potentially – and yet, in the end, rewarding avarice and mediocrity, it effectively preserved the old distinctions. The nobiliary particle, therefore, was not a self-written invitation to high society, but a symbol and, as it had been for Voltaire, both an aesthetic improvement to the writer's name and an act of defiance. Balzac was fascinated by the miniature human comedy of the Faubourg Saint-Germain with its giant repertoire of unwritten rules, but he lacked the principal qualification of the snob. Like his father, he was unashamed of his origins and sometimes made the point by turning up at expensive restaurants dressed like a worker or by taking his housekeeper to the Opéra.[66]

THE CLEAREST indications of Balzac's oppositional nobility can be found in his new journalistic career.[67] Sick of poverty and the constant threat of debtors' prison, he began to write for several newspapers which, in their different ways, represent the dawn of modern journalism. They also place Balzac's social rise in its cultural context. The dominant figures in the new press were similar, socially, to Balzac, drawing moral strength from their humble beginnings, grinding axes to great effect. The lithographer Charles Philipon had divided his time between Gros's studio in Paris and his father's wallpaper business in Lyon before co-founding *La Silhouette* in October 1829. For the first time in France, caricatures, notably those of Balzac's friend, Henri Monnier, were given equal prominence with the text, and even the 'View of Touraine' published by Balzac in this forerunner of the illustrated satirical magazine has a strongly pictorial quality – a textual imitation of the cinematic panoramas set up by Daguerre.

Balzac had also befriended Émile de Girardin and was frequenting the literary salon of his fiancée Delphine Gay. Girardin was another journalist trying to fight his way out of a social no man's land. His father, the Comte de Girardin, had refused to recognize his illegitimate son, who suffered all the setbacks of a bastard. His success as a newspaperman was directly related to his desire for revenge. In his case, the term 'press baron' is particularly appropriate. With Balzac, Hippolyte Auger and two other peripatetic writers – one of whom legitimized Émile by marrying his ageing stepmother – he founded the *Feuilleton des Journaux Politiques*. Normally, it consisted of brief reviews of all the latest books. Balzac, as usual, expanded his allotted space and contributed two courageous articles on Hugo's Romantic drama, *Hernani*. Social antagonism expressed itself as an impatience with trendiness and received ideas. The hype surrounding the first night was so successful that, even now, *Hernani* is firmly entrenched in university syllabuses as the most important Romantic drama, to the detriment of other plays, including those of Balzac; and yet, as Balzac insisted with only mild unfairness, all the impedimenta of classical drama were still there, all its painful improbabilities, actors temporarily going deaf, blind, ignorant or forgetful for the sake of the plot.

The same campaigning spirit and refusal to rely on official opinion were also apparent in the aptly named *Voleur*. Founded by Girardin, *Le Voleur* stole most of its material from other papers; it even borrowed parts of Balzac's *Physiologie du Mariage*. As Girardin put it with cynical honesty, *Le Voleur* preferred the scissors to the pen. Theft was common practice; admitting to it was not. 'This is the age of commercial transactions. Religion and Liberty go up and down in value, and every conscience has a fixed price.' The flippant attitude of *Le Voleur* concealed a serious critique of bourgeois values. Like Girardin, Balzac attacked the gerontocracy which was delivering the country into the hands of bureaucrats and financiers. The vehicle for his 'Satirical Complaints on the Moral State of Modern Society', however, was not *Le Voleur* but a fashion magazine also founded by Girardin: *La Mode*. Here again, Balzac gave the appearance of following market forces whilst injecting new ideas into the popular press. *La Mode* was the first serious women's magazine in France. Fashion was treated not simply as the uniform of class and conformity but as a mark of women's taste, intelligence and initiative. Balzac was at home in every context. He showed that fashion was an infallible sign of the times. Political and cultural stagnation was visible in the street: 'We all go about dressed in black like people who are in mourning for something.' His metaphorical mind was incapable of perceiving a fact in isolation; pulling at the smallest impression invariably brought up the whole root-system. Balzac's reflections on fashion would culminate in his *Traité de la Vie Élégante*, published in *La Mode*. This 'science of manners' disguised as a book on etiquette has the potency, in the context of the 1830s, of Roland Barthes's *Mythologies*. It shares with that collection of essays a quality common to most intellectual innovations: the revelation that something previously felt to be of limited interest could provide the basis of a great deal of informed discussion. It was also another diatribe against a ruthlessly materialistic society. Clothes, Balzac's narrator specifies, after supposedly interviewing no less an authority than Beau Brummell in exile in Boulogne, are designed to indicate to passers-by the rung one has reached on the social ladder: 'It is infinitely agreeable for a man or a woman to say to themselves as they contemplate their fellow citizens from a carriage: "I am above them. I splatter them with mud. I protect them. I govern them. And everyone can clearly see that I govern, protect and splatter them."'[68]

Balzac's 1830 articles are guerrilla journalism at its best. The constant underlying or overt theme of these articles is the devaluation of intellectual endeavour by the Bourgeois Monarchy, which, as Balzac saw, would only be reinforced, not created *ab initio* by the July Revolution. The change of regime would only confirm the political triumph of self-interest.[69] It was still commercial writing, as people like Fontaney never failed to remind him, and Balzac was still consuming large amounts of time and talent without appearing to produce very much of lasting worth. In the eye of the subscriber, all this was disposable literature. But there were consolations: society's exploitation of the writer could be matched with an organized exploitation of the market. *Le Dernier Chouan* and *Physiologie du Mariage* had failed even to pay the rent, whereas Balzac's newspaper articles, between the end of 1829 and the publication of *La Peau de Chagrin* in August 1831, brought him about 5000 francs. More importantly, his imagination, by some wonderful convenience, thrived on the need to entertain the unimaginative reader. Setting off for Fougères in 1828 with no money, confused ideas and a chaotic writing style, Balzac had learned to value and gain control of his own talent.

*

ANYONE WHO attempts to wind up the thread of one life into a well-rounded story is subject at times to an uncomfortable feeling that reality had unravelled itself in a very inconvenient fashion. The fact is that the self-appointed 'secretary'[70] of French society was not on hand when the July Revolution broke out.

The monarchy of Charles X had effectively restored the old privileges of clergy and nobility, and now confirmed the general suspicions of constitutional injustice by ignoring its electoral defeat in June and July 1830. Unofficial newspapers were banned, the newly elected Chamber was dissolved, and a large percentage of the electorate was disenfranchised. Riots ensued. After three days of street fighting, Charles X sailed for England and the Opposition placed its constitutional monarch on the throne: Louis-Philippe, representative, not of the *ancien régime* but of the modern bourgeoisie. The July Monarchy and Balzac's nineteenth century had begun.

Having travelled to the scenes of the Chouan uprisings two years before with his stenographer's notebook, Balzac somehow contrived to miss one of the great milestones in the long half-century his novels cover. From May until September 1830 he was enjoying the fruits of Touraine at a house called La Grenadière on the right bank of the Loire overlooking Tours.

The house, which was normally rented by the owner to English tourists or to the songwriter, Béranger, is the silent heroine of the tale, *La Grenadière* (1832). Turning off the main road from Paris to Nantes, a stony path led up the hillside between the terraced orchards to a small garden and a house painted yellow and green, with two large windows at the front and three attic-rooms. Through the trellises and fruit trees, there was a magnificent view of Tours and the Loire as far as Amboise: 'Everything is in motion around the possessor of this plot, standing motionless among his bright flowers and appetizing fruits.' Mme de Berny stayed with Balzac, and in June they sailed down the Loire to Nantes, visiting Le Croisic and Guérande at the furthest tip of the estuary. She left soon after and wrote from home to say that she had burnt his letters and kept the ashes: a morbid image of a love affair that was now turning into friendship. At fifty-three, she was almost an old woman, and in spite of himself, Balzac was growing tired of her relentless devotion, her endless extraction of eternal vows – at least according to a letter sent to Mme Hanska in

1848.[71] There is indeed an embarrassing similarity between Mme de Berny's letter in the summer of 1830 and the mawkish sentimentality Balzac so despised in the popular Romantics. But Balzac was suffering from general exhaustion and felt the need to return to the scenes and behaviour of his childhood. Here, he found his most satisfying political stance. Literature, he told Ratier, was no more than cheap prostitution, without adventure or personal risk: 'Oh, when one looks at these great skies of a beautiful night, one is ready to unbutton oneself in order to piss on the head of all the royalties of the earth.' One might say that a similar symbolic position was occupied by the house itself, a situation which recurs in Balzac's choice of buildings: apart from the city and dominating it, expressing the mixture of antagonism and attraction he felt towards Tours and his 'dear old hell', Paris.[72]

Balzac's perfectly ill-timed convalescence serves as a reminder that the writer himself usually hopes to catch history in the act with a sideways glance, beginning his stories, not with the guns and trumpets of calamitous events, but with a scene, a gesture or some seemingly trivial phenomenon of the sort which could be turned into a newspaper article or, with luck, a new science. Around 10 September, he took the coach back to Paris, leaving Tours at five in the evening and arriving at four the following afternoon. His father was dead, but he had new friends and social events to enjoy, and the polluted air of Paris was so bracing, 'for so vital a fluid abounds in crowded places that it has been noticed in Rome that malaria is unknown in the loathsome Ghetto crawling with Jews'.[73] In his *Théorie de la Démarche*, Balzac gives a glimpse of himself on this new day, rejoicing in the city which he used to contemplate from the heights of Père Lachaise:

> In 1830, I returned from that delicious Touraine, where women never age as quickly as in other regions. I found myself standing in the middle of the great courtyard of the Messageries Royales in the Rue Notre-Dame des Victoires, waiting for a carriage and not realizing that I was about to be confronted with the choice of writing inanities or making immortal discoveries. . . . I was idly observing the various scenes being acted out in the courtyard when a traveller suddenly dropped to the ground from the back of a coach like a frog leaping into the water. But as he leapt, the man was forced, in order to avoid falling, to stretch his hands out against the office wall that was next to the coach and to lean against it lightly. Seeing this, I

asked myself why. Of course, an expert would have replied, 'Because he was about to lose his centre of gravity.' But why do people share with carriages the privilege of losing their centre of gravity? 'Here', I said to myself, 'is a phenomenon which no one ever considers.'. . .

And then, from that starting point, a thousand questions arose, asked, in the shadowy depths of my mind, by a quite fantastic being – my new-born *Théorie de la Démarche*. Sure enough, a thousand tiny phenomena of our daily existence converged all at once on my original thought and rose up *en masse* in my memory like a swarm of flies hovering up at the sound of a footstep from the fruit they were sucking at the edge of a path. . . .

Do we have the power to exercise control over this constant phenomenon to which we never give a thought? Is it possible to economize and save up the invisible fluid which, unbeknownst to ourselves, we have at our disposal? . . .

What tears I cried over the chaotic state of my learning, from which I had extracted but a few miserable tales when I might have drawn from it a whole physiology of the human race![74]

It was time to put this invisible fluid to a better use.

Balzac's father, Bernard-François, *né* Balssa, by Marie-Eléonore Godefroid. (Bulloz; Institut de France)

Laure Sallambier, Balzac's mother, shortly before her marriage. Anonymous portrait, c.1797. (Musées de la Ville de Paris © SPADEM 1993.)

Balzac's sister Laure. Anonymous drawing, c.1808. (Musées de la Ville de Paris ©
SPADEM 1993.)

The Collège de Vendôme. Engraving by A. Queyroy, showing the part of the school in which Balzac served his detentions.

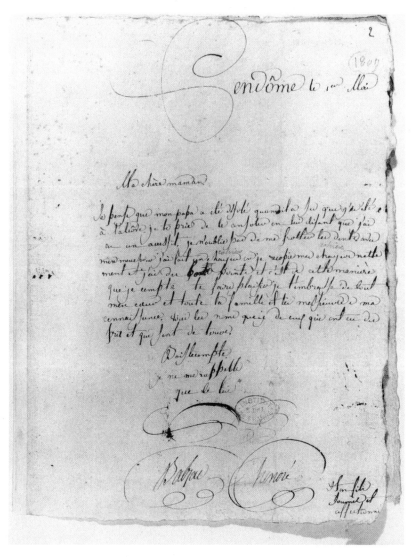

Balzac's earliest surviving letter, from the Collège de Vendôme, 1 May 1809: 'I think Papa was quite upset when he found out I had been in the alcove.' (Bulloz; Institut de France)

Above: Sepia drawing of Balzac in the mid-1820s, attributed to Achille Devéria. Inscribed by Balzac to Mme de Berny, *'et nunc et semper'*. 'A young soul, still naive – despite having foolishly drunk from the cup of Science' (letter to Mme de Berny, 23 March 1822). (Bulloz; Institut de France)

Facing page: The Place de la Bastille and Paris from the East. The Rue Lesdiguières, where Balzac had his 'garret', is among the houses in the centre. Engraving by Bertrand from Balzac's 'Histoire et Physiologie des Boulevards de Paris' in *Le Diable à Paris* (1846).

Laure de Berny, by H. N. Van Gorp, c.1810. 'From 1823 to 1833 an angel sustained me in this horrible struggle . . . She was a mother, a girlfriend, a family, a brother, an adviser; she formed the writer and consoled the young man . . . though she was under the authority of a husband, she managed to lend me 45,000 francs, of which I paid back the last 6000 in 1836, with 5% interest, of course' (letter to Eveline Hanska, 19 July 1837). (Roger-Viollet)

The Duchesse d'Abrantès, dedicatee of *La Femme Abandonnée*, by Gavarni, 1833.
(Musées de la Ville de Paris © SPADEM 1993.)

1, Rue Cassini, Balzac's home from 1828 to 1836, lithograph by Champin from a drawing by Auguste Régnier. No. 5 in the series, *Habitations des Personnages les Plus Illustres de France*. The house was demolished in 1897. (Roger-Viollet)

La Grenadière, by Daubigny. The house near Tours where Balzac spent the summer of 1830. The figure in the foreground is the songwriter, Béranger. 'Nowhere in the world will you find a dwelling so modest and so grand . . . a miniature Touraine in the heart of Touraine where all the flowers, fruits and beauties of that region are fully represented . . . La Grenadière will never be for sale' (*La Grenadière*, 1832). Balzac later hoped to buy it as 'a studious retreat'. (Roger–Viollet)

The Château de Saché, where Balzac wrote or conceived some of his finest novels. The owner, Jean de Margonne, was the father of Balzac's brother Henry. Anonymous drawing. (Musées de la Ville de Paris © SPADEM 1993.)

Zulma Carraud and her son Ivan, by Édouard Viénot, 1827. (Musées de la Ville de Paris © SPADEM 1993.)

The Marquise (later, Duchesse) Henriette de Castries, by Candide Blaize. (Roger-Viollet)

CONTES BRUNS.

PAR UNE

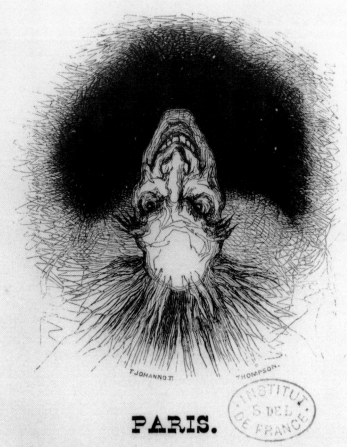

PARIS.

URBAIN CANEL, ADOLPHE GUYOT,
RUE DU BAC, N° 104.   PLACE DU LOUVRE, N° 18.

M. DCCCXXXII.

Title page of the anonymous *Contes Bruns* (1832), by Balzac, Philarète Chasles and Charles Rabou. Vignette by Tony Johannot, attributing the tales to '*une tête à l'envers*' ('a deranged mind'). (Bulloz; Institut de France)

Balzac at thirty-seven in his monk's robe, by Louis Boulanger. 'Boulanger has managed to capture the persistence that forms the basis of my character – my intrepid faith in the future' (letter to Eveline, 1 October 1836). (Musée des Beaux-Arts de Tours; P. Boyer.)

CHAPTER EIGHT

Absolute Power

(1830–1832)

TOURAINE had worked its magical effect. Balzac arrived back in Paris in the autumn of 1830 like a wound-up spring, ready to shoot off towards several new horizons – literary, political and social. But Paris, as he already knew, could absorb the energy of even the most vigorous human projectile:

> You know what Paris is like – a mound of sand, like those which the Loire rolls along: once you've put your foot in it, you're stuck. One day it's a business deal, the next a delicious soirée where you hear La Malibran singing, in the morning a bachelors' lunch, in the evening an urgent piece of work, and the gaping abyss swallows up your life which, if spent in solitude, would be rich and glorious.[1]

Not, he hastened to add, that he was as debauched as all that: 'I have been doing a horrendous amount of work. My orgies take the form of books.'

Managing sometimes on only two hours of sleep a night, he was beginning to concentrate his activities in an attempt to bridge the 'gaping abyss'. Those 'miserable tales' he had been publishing had become in his mind the springboard for a great masterpiece – a 'philosophical' novel which, with Victor Hugo's *Notre-Dame de Paris*, would be the literary event of 1831: *La Peau de Chagrin*.[2] The articles he had been feeding for over a year to the newspapers were finally building up into something more likely to stick in the public's memory: the *Lettres sur Paris* would establish him as the mouthpiece of the legitimists and lay the foundations of his own political career. As for his social life, it was becoming a game of hide-and-seek. His letters are full of denials and heroic complaints that he never enjoyed the excesses he depicted in his stories. Such was the power of imagination: a constant source of scenes for the writer and a perpetual disappointment to the reader. 'Many women who read the *Physiologie du Mariage* will not be happy to learn that the author is young, as orderly as an old office clerk, sober as an invalid on a diet, a water-drinker and a hard worker.'

This denial, in the preface to *La Peau de Chagrin*, was deliberately unconvincing enough to reinforce the image the novel created of a dissolute Bohemian with esoteric leanings for whom 'debauchery is to the body what mystical pleasures are to the soul'.[3] Balzac always had great fun with fame; it allowed him to savour that pleasure unavailable to obscure writers – travelling incognito – and to behave in public like the character of a novel; but he would also have cause to regret the increasingly autonomous existence of his 'image', as when a journal in 1839 published a drawing of a grubby individual sprawled on a bedroom chair in a monk's habit with a prostitute on one side (supposed to be his future wife), champagne bottles on the other and, most unrealistic of all, a pipe in his hand.[4] On that occasion, Balzac sued the newspaper,[5] but in a sense he was being ungrateful. The relative gullibility of the reading public in the new world of mass-communication enabled him to advance into the limelight while wrapping his true self in cloaks and costumes. Paradoxically, the proliferation of spurious Balzacs seems to strengthen his single-mindedness. His three-pronged attack on the literary, political and social world of the July Monarchy masks the deep coherence of his activities from 1830 on, and also the heroic contradiction at the heart of them. A contradiction hinted at by the fact that Balzac's symbol of self-restraint – the monastic robes he wore when writing – figures largely in the lists of his debts.

The pattern of Balzac's life is laid out, as if in a premonitory dream, in *La Peau de Chagrin*. Praised, decried, dramatized, parodied, stolen by Belgian publishers,[6] and recognized by both critics and public as a myth for modern times, it tells the tragic story of a young man, Raphaël de Valentin, who, having decided to throw himself into the Seine, wanders into an old curiosity-shop on the Quai Voltaire. The shopkeeper shows him an old ass's skin with Sanskrit letters encrusted in the tissue. By the light of a lamp, the hero reads this indelible inscription:

[176]

IF THOU POSSESS ME, THOU SHALT POSSESS ALL THINGS.
BUT THY LIFE SHALL BELONG TO ME. SO HATH GOD
WILLED IT. EXPRESS A DESIRE AND THY DESIRE
SHALL BE FULFILLED. BUT LET THY WISHES
BE MEASURED BY THY LIFE. HERE IT LIES.
WITH EVERY WISH I SHALL DIMINISH
JUST AS THY DAYS SHALL BE
DECREASED. DOST THOU
DESIRE ME? THEN
TAKE AND GOD
WILL HEAR.
AMEN.

Raphaël's wishes come true, whether by chance or by magic, and he becomes fabulously rich – hence the quaint title of the first American translation (1843): *Luck and Leather. A Parisian Romance.* But as the skin shrinks, his health declines and he condemns himself to live, impossibly, without desires. When he passes through his bedroom door in the morning, a special mechanism opens every door in the apartment so that he can walk unimpeded from one end to the other. Eventually, he dies in his native Auvergne, realizing, like his creator, that 'the mere possession of power, however great, does not provide the knowledge of how to use it'.

Combining the essence of his domestic scenes and fantastic tales, and believing that his own exceptional life was in some way typical, Balzac wanted his novel to provide the mathematical formula for human existence. The equation is given in two forms – one incomprehensible, the other horribly simple. First, the epigraph from Laurence Sterne:

In *Tristram Shandy*, this (in a slightly different form) is the accidental hieroglyphic traced by Corporal Trim's walking-stick when he tries to describe the freedom enjoyed by happy bachelors.[7] In *La Peau de*

Chagrin, it represents 'Life, with its bizarre undulations, its meandering course, its *serpentine* motion'. 'And the same significance', we are told, 'is concealed in the slightest incidents of this tale.'[8]

The epigraph, if we could but understand it, is the blueprint of every biography, past and future, the DNA of every human life. Unfortunately, we can't – though we can always say with Balzac that 'the things I find most charming in a tale are precisely those things I understand the least'.[9] Yet, with Balzac's characteristic mixture of fashionable flippancy and megalomaniac philosophizing, its meaning can be said to lie in its incomprehensibility. The epigraph reflects a shift in Balzac's philosophy, an awareness that pure materialism is a recipe for madness. Everything in the novel is subjected to modern rational analysis. An idea is said to be generated by an emanation of carbonic acid in a glass of champagne; a tiny variation in phosphorus levels produces a saint or a criminal, a genius or a cretin; and these days, says the hero, a new Messiah would find his every miracle forensically examined by the Académie des Sciences.[10] This chronic relativism is part of the allegory of post-revolutionary France which Balzac pointed out in his novel: civilization, creating new desires and unreasonable expectations, is a form of mass suicide. But the ass's skin, which survives the acids and compressors of the country's leading scientists, is also an allegory of the author, seeking the ingredients of his philosophy, after the death of his father, not just in mechanical philosophies, but in the mystics and psychic scientists his mother consulted.

The other formula of human existence sums up Balzac's ideal *modus vivendi* in a sentence. 'The exercise of *Will* consumes us, *Power* destroys us, but *Knowledge* leaves our feeble constitution in a constant state of calm.'[11] At birth, each of us has a finite store of vital fluid; with every desire that is conceived, the store decreases. The secret of life, as the old shopkeeper explains to Raphaël, is to hoard one's energy, to invest one's life, not in the senses, which grow dull, nor in the heart, which can be broken, but in the mind:

> My orgies have been the contemplation of oceans, peoples, forests, mountains. . . . I have an imaginary harem in which I possess all the women I have never had. . . . How can one prefer the disasters of your frustrated desires to the sublime faculty of summoning the universe to appear before the mind's eye, the immense delight of

moving without the trammels of Time or the chains of Space, of embracing all things, seeing all things, leaning over the ramparts of the world to interrogate the other spheres, to listen to God![12]

La Peau de Chagrin is an astonishing exercise in psychic autobiography. The theory that life is corroded by the very instincts it implies recurs throughout Balzac's life, even in the slightest details of his daily existence. Gavarni and Paul Lacroix both reported independently to the Goncourt brothers that Balzac's sexual activities were orchestrated with a particular theory in mind. Sex was a necessary expense of energy, but, like any other expense, it should not always be allowed to reach its natural conclusion: 'Sperm for him was an emission of pure cerebral substance, a sort of filtering out and loss, through the penis, of a work of art. And after some misdemeanour or other, when he had neglected to apply his theory, he turned up at the home of Latouche, crying, "I lost a book this morning!"'[13] (Balzac had apparently revised his estimate by the time he told Alexandre Dumas *fils* that 'a night of love' cost 'half a volume', though he added that 'no woman alive is worth two volumes a year'.[14])

How could Balzac be so sure that his theory was correct? Because, as his doctor warned him, he neglected to follow it himself.[15] The power of Balzac's theory of energy lies in the fact that it runs counter to his own natural impulses. He even on occasion elaborated counter-theories – for example, that 'too much sleep clogs up the mind and makes it sluggish'.[16] The monk's robe and the endless cups of coffee, which Balzac had now begun to use heavily as a mental stimulant, are symbols of this contradiction: abstinence and excess combined.

THE WRITING and promotion of the novel itself were illustrations of how to make an efficient use of vital fluid. The ass's skin was first unveiled in one of Balzac's articles in *La Caricature* at the end of 1830. *La Peau de Chagrin*, dreams the author, has been purchased by a wealthy patron of the arts for 1000 *écus* (5000 francs), with the proviso that only twenty copies be printed: an early example of the 'limited edition' trick. Other self-advertisements followed. The real contract was signed on 17 January 1831 with Urbain Canel and Charles Gosselin: 750 copies and the author was to receive 1125 francs and deliver the manuscript by 15 February. Shortly after the deadline, Balzac was instructing the impatient Gosselin in the hardships of literary creation: 'I can assure you that I have been working all night for nothing, writing sentences which are unusable.' 'I still hope to have the pleasure of seeing the book appear on 20 May.'[17] Five days before the new deadline, from Mme de Berny's home at La Bouleaunière, he sent about half the total manuscript to Gosselin, a man he described as 'a walking joint of beef on whom God has lavished all the thoughts an imbecile can have'.[18] Gosselin was informed that he would receive by the same post a pâté. Balzac's present must have stuck in his throat, since he would just have been reading the section of the novel 'leaked' to the *Revue des Deux Mondes* on 'How to Kill One's Uncle' and collect an inheritance. The preferred method is to have your already bloated uncle eat a *pâté de foie gras*.[19]

The novel finally went on sale, two days after Balzac finished writing it, on 1 August 1831. It was swept in on such a wave of publicity that it sold out before it reached the bookshops: extracts in the papers, a reading in the salon of Mme Récamier, articles from Balzac's network of 'Balzacking' friends (as one of them said) in the provinces, and a pleasant review in *La Caricature* by Count Alexandre de B——. The book is recommended for the simple reason that 'we like and admire M. de Balzac. Not the most subtle recommendation, perhaps', Balzac's pseudonym goes on, 'but at least this is a frank confession – a rare thing these days in journalism'. . . .[20]

Balzac may also have helped to write the review in *L'Artiste* signed 'J.-J. Salve' (Jules Janin) in which the novel is memorably defined as 'a highwayman-waiting-to-jump-out-at-you-from-behind-a-tree kind of book'.[21] (In *Illusions Perdues*, Balzac turns this review into the famous article with which Lucien de Rubempré 'revolutionizes' journalism.) A few critics had reservations. The ever-ambiguous Sainte-Beuve called it *'fetid* and *putrid*, witty, corrupt, inebriated, sparkling and marvellous'.[22] One critic delved into the past to reveal that Balzac had committed the heinous crime of writing novels for money. Others simply failed to understand: Balzac had written the book as a joke; the author was one of those new Romantics who thought ugliness was the true aim of Art; Balzac was trying to cause riots, etc., etc. However, one of the gods of Romanticism, unbeknownst to Balzac, read the novel in two evening sittings, shortly before his death, and pronounced it a perfect demonstration of the 'incurable corruption of the French nation'.[23] Often cited as a criticism, Goethe's comments were a precise recognition of Balzac's historical achievement – all the more remarkable for the fact that, in the novel, one of Raphaël's friends complains that his German mistress weeps buckets whenever she reads Goethe's sentimental twaddle.[24] Goethe himself had regretted the morbid influence of *Werther* and was probably appeased by Balzac's comparison of the old shopkeeper to Mephistopheles: 'The novel oscillates energetically and tastefully between the impossible and the intolerable.' 'He knows how to use the miraculous as a means of depicting in a very logical fashion the most curious events and states of mind.' It was Romanticism applied to the critical depiction of modern life, made into something more rewarding than an entertainment of the emotions.

The reading public loved it. A second edition was rushed out in September with twelve other tales. The *Romans et Contes Philosophiques*, with a Balzac-inspired preface by Philarète Chasles, were another foundation-stone in the future *Comédie Humaine*. At the Gaîté Theatre, a parody of the novel was performed (defeating the object with a happy ending),[25] and the following year, a young poet called Théophile Gautier – notorious for having attended the first night of *Hernani* in a pink waistcoat – devoted one of his 'Young Romantic' tales, *Les Jeunes France*, to a buffoonish recreation of Balzac's orgy scene: 'This is the point at which I'm supposed to pour wine down my waistcoat.... It says so in black and white on page 171 of *La Peau de Chagrin*.... And this is where I have to toss a 100-sou coin in the air to see whether or not there's a God.' The moral is that modern novels are difficult and dangerous to put into practice, especially if one's mistress refuses to play the part of the 'ravishing courtesan' on whose bosom the hero rests his booted feet.[26] Perhaps it was Gautier's deliberate grasping of the wrong end of the allegorical stick that prompted Balzac, when he first met Gautier in 1836, to preach 'a strange kind of discipline':

> We were to shut ourselves away for two or three years, drink nothing but water, eat only boiled lupins, like the painter Protogenes,[27] go to bed at six in the evening, get up at midnight and work until dawn, then spend the day revising, developing, pruning, perfecting and polishing our nocturnal labours ... and above all live in a state of

absolute chastity. . . . According to him, chastity increased the power of the mind a hundredfold and endowed those who practised it with unknown faculties. . . . The only concession he made – reluctantly – was to allow us to see a loved one for half an hour every year. Letters were permitted: they were good for one's style.[28]

As Balzac's doctor suspected, this strenuous discipline was only half the story. His orgies may have taken the form of books, as he claimed, but they also took the form of orgies, and if every dissolute detail of *La Peau de Chagrin* was suffused with an urgent moral sense, it was because Balzac's theory of will was the result of bitter – and not-so-bitter – experience.

Like Raphaël, Balzac had attended a gargantuan feast given by a banker, the Marquis de Las Marismas, who was launching an evening paper and realized that wine and women were the best way to assemble a decent team of journalists.[29] A more tawdry affair was recounted by Balzac's old partner in literary crime, Horace Raisson.[30] Balzac had asked to be present at a dinner so that he could take notes. Unfortunately, 'he was indisposed five or six times before the second course' – an unbelievable anecdote which serves to show, however, that when Balzac complained about his envious colleagues he was thinking of actual personal attacks. Far more gratifying were the claims of seven different women that they were the true model for the beautiful, cold-hearted courtesan, Foedora, watched by the hero from behind a curtain as she undresses in her bedroom.[31] According to a review of the novel, which Balzac had an opportunity to correct before it was published,[32] the scene had actually taken place: setting an excellent example to future novelists in the Realist tradition, Balzac had concealed himself in the room of the *demi-mondaine*, Olympe Pélissier.[33] He was obviously delighted with what he saw since he had a brief affair with the woman he called 'the most beautiful courtesan in Paris'.[34] Actually, Foedora has orange-coloured eyes and brown hair, whereas Olympe had black hair and dark eyes, and she was far more receptive to sexual advances. In any case, it is hard to imagine Balzac standing still behind a curtain for several hours. But it is easy to imagine reviewers assuming that the minute details and reflections recorded in the novel could only have come from personal experiment.

When Balzac met Olympe – shortly before she took up with the composer, Rossini – she and Eugène Sue were smashing up their shared apartment.[35] Balzac patched up her quarrel with Sue and became such a good friend that he felt able to propose to her, telling Mme de Berny that Olympe had proposed to him. Before accusing him of failing to stick to chastity and a diet of boiled lupins, it should be said that this, too, was a form of research. His portrayal of courtesans, like Esther in *Splendeurs et Misères des Courtisanes* or Josépha in *La Cousine Bette*, bears the mark of familiarity (not just the sort referred to by Gautier), and he avoids the sleazy clichés of other writers because of a curious sympathy: the lonely struggle of the artist – in dress, cosmetics, conversation and sex – rising from the lower orders and, in the end, if she survives, exacting a toll from the society which exploited her.

Eugène Sue himself was another link between reality and the novel, another example of this humorous or tragic discrepancy between theory and practice. It was thanks to him that Balzac became a regular in the 'Infernal Box' at the Opéra, where dandies gathered to talk in loud voices and criticize the performers during the perform-ance.[36] In the interval, they paraded in the foyer, a sort of 'magic lantern in which the principal personages of the day pose in the flesh'. There, wrote a friend of Balzac, the curious can find out whether or not Honoré de Balzac is really 'the pale and wispy knight of gentle, pensive mien' you imagined when you read his stories.[37]

With Balzac, most dreams and fantasies sooner or later come true. It was said that the members of the Loge Infernale had opera-glasses so powerful that they were intimately acquainted with all the faults and perfections of every ballerina. This sounds like just another piece of gossip until one notices in a letter to Mme Hanska that Balzac had some 'divine' opera-glasses made for him at the Paris Observatory.[38] 'All my pleasures are innocent,' he said; but surely this was another example of wasting vital fluid? In *La Peau de Chagrin*, having made a vow that no woman will arouse him and force him to formulate a desire, Raphaël sits in a box at the Opéra, with a sea of beautiful women spread out beneath him, armed with 'a special monocle of which the microscopic lens, skilfully inserted, destroyed the harmony of the loveliest features and gave them a hideous appearance'.[39]

Eugène Sue was at this time Balzac's main initiator, one of the models for the prize dandy of *La Comédie Humaine*: Henri de Marsay.

[183]

Through him, Balzac glimpsed the wilder side of social life, though, here, he was sometimes more a voyeur than a participant. Before he became famous for the interminable serial novels with a 'socialist' message which prompted comparisons with Dickens, Eugène Sue was one of the dandies who liked to be seen lounging in oriental settings wearing a dressing-gown and smoking a hookah. Long before the Betty Ford clinic, it was fashionable to be seen recovering from a dangerous addiction – the more exotic the better. Sue's choice was opium, and he seems to have shared his stylish hobby with an unsuspecting Balzac. In his hallucinatory 'Voyage de Paris à Java', published in the *Revue de Paris* in November 1832, and, later, in the *Traité des Excitants Modernes* in 1839, Balzac described the effects of his first cigar. Sue had decided to conquer Balzac's 'virginity' as a smoker. 'He forced me to smoke two cigars', and the tobacco had an effect which soon became apparent:

> I found the stairs to be made of a soft substance. . . . I took my place in the balcony. . . . My soul was drunk. What I heard of Rossini's *La Gazza ladra* was the equivalent of those fantastic sounds which fall from the heavens into the ear of a woman in a mystical trance. The music came to me through shining clouds, stripped of all the imperfections that human works contain and filled with that divine quality that the artist's emotion imparts to it. The orchestra seemed a vast instrument in which some incomprehensible, mechanical work was going on, since all I could make out were the necks of the double-basses, the darting of the bows, the golden curves of the trombones, the clarinets, the finger-holes, but no musicians. Just one or two powdered wigs, motionless, and two swollen faces, twisted into a disturbing grimace.
>
> 'This gentleman smells of wine,' whispered a woman whose hat kept brushing my cheek. . . .
>
> 'No, Madame, it is the smell of music.'[40]

Balzac's social orgies were more than just off-duty activities, and they prove that *La Peau de Chagrin* is not the tissue of fantasies it first appears. On the one hand, his association with the elegant fringe of Paris society indicated an impatience with the sedate, parochial literary salons, like that of his friend Charles Nodier at the Bibliothèque de l'Arsenal, where you had to be sure, Balzac wrote, to admire in the correct fashion (position yourself behind a taller person so that you have to stand on tiptoe) and use the correct words of praise: 'pyramidal', 'Moorish', and so on. 'In discussion, use the word *actualité*, then stoke the fire and say no more. Next day, everyone will be using the word *actualité* without worrying in the slightest about what it means.'[41] On the other hand, there was something of professional expediency in Balzac's socializing. Spending money was the best way of paying off debts. Raphaël's worldly-wise friend tells him that dissipation is like 'a political system': 'The lifestyle of a man who squanders his fortune can be a form of speculation; his capital is invested in friends, pleasures, protectors, knowledge.'[42] Balzac himself often expressed the same view – which he implicitly condemns in the novel. He was forced, he said, to submerge himself in the salon life of Paris, because the more people he knew, the bigger his reputation and the more money he could make. Profligacy started at home, and so he expanded his premises by renting another part of the house in the Rue Cassini in September 1831. He needed stables and a shed for his new carriage. He acquired a pair of horses which he christened Smogler and Briton. He also acquired two servants, Leclercq and Paradis (who presumably satisfied his master's mania for excruciating puns), and a cook called Rose, a real *cordon bleu* who had the frustrating task of cooking for a man who went out to banquets and dined at home on an egg.[43]

Finally, even in his attempts to relax, Balzac contrived to wear himself out. These are the last years of his life for which details of his day-to-day activities are lacking, but in those short periods in which reliable dated evidence of his comings and goings is particularly rich, he suddenly seems almost ubiquitous, and the least suspicious historian is led to consult the timetables of coach companies before recording Balzac's travels as literal truth.[44] On the evening of 7 September 1831, Antoine Fontaney saw him in the salon of Baron Gérard. Shortly afterwards, he turns up at Saché, 13 miles from Tours on difficult roads, Tours itself being twenty-three hours from Paris. On 13 September, Fontaney reports another sighting of 'the magnificent M. de Balzac', back in Paris in the salon of Mme Ancelot. On 20 September, he was at Baron Gérard's again; but then on the 23rd, we know that Laure sent some money to her brother at Nemours, 50 miles from Paris. Train travel was still in its infancy, but Balzac rushed about as if the TGV already existed, and it is one of the great mysteries of his work why none of his characters is ever seen taking the train.

La Peau de Chagrin, in short, is one of the finest novels ever produced by exhaustion. 'Have you measured your ass's skin', asked a friend, 'since you renovated your apartment and since your terribly modern carriage began to bring you home at two o'clock in the morning?' Balzac, like Raphaël, had paid for his knowledge. But in the details of his crowded life and in his constant willingness to be impressed, one senses a great power of abstraction and concentration. Balzac was able, or forced by his character, to keep his mind on distant targets. To prevent his energy draining away, he had a talisman of his own – his good humour which enabled him to thrive in the tiny, vicious world of literary Paris. To many, it seemed naivety, but the man who sent a symbolically lethal pâté to his publisher was able to transform even his hate into memorable episodes. All his insults are amusing. As much as Flaubert, Balzac was a connoisseur of stupidity, and now that his work was acquiring such a broad sweep of reference, everything was material for his books: 'I have some twenty-four hours of superficial anger during which I could kill him', he said of Amédée Pichot, who had failed to treat him with the respect that Balzac had come to demand of his editors, 'but afterwards, I think of my work and behave towards my books like those pashas who have so many children that they forget which mother they came from.'[45] Even his disagreements with the new director of the *Revue de Paris* produced an etymological pirouette for one of the *Contes Drolatiques*:

> The said Provost was Picot or Picault by name, whence came *picottin*, *picoter* and *picorer* [to peck or to pilfer]. Some said Pitot or Pitault, from which we get *pitance* [pittance]; others, as in the southern dialect, said Pichot, whence comes nothing worth a hoot.[46]

The reason Balzac's progress is dramatic and not just the bland pursuit of a career is that his distant targets continued to retreat as he advanced. *La Peau de Chagrin* is a symbol, but also a reality which Balzac's readers can hold in their hands: at the end of *La Comédie Humaine*, half an inch of paper contains all the plans and fragments which Balzac was never able to complete. This thin segment of his published work represents a disproportionate number of hopes and wishes, shrunk, like the skin, to the size of a willow-leaf.[47]

ONE OF THE plans which haunted Balzac all his life was the series of Rabelaisian tales known as the *Contes Drolatiques*, allegedly 'collected in the monasteries of Touraine' for the delectation of Rabelais fans. Balzac liked to think of these tales, which are part original, part pastiche, as his chief claim on posterity,[48] though this surprising estimate was really the result of a fear that they would be forgotten – as they have been, periodically. In a more objective mood, he called them 'arabesques' or graffiti, lovingly scrawled on the face of *La Comédie Humaine*.[49] There were supposed to be 100 of them, but in the end only thirty were published, in three sets of ten. Only with Balzac could thirty tales be called a fragment. To English readers, they are known as the *Droll Stories*, sometimes found lurking on the shelves of second-hand bookshops, with large-breasted women on the cover: 'the lustiest, most uproarious tales ever told', says one, 'completely unabridged and unexpurgated' translation[50] – a somewhat superfluous phrase in the circumstances since the mildest expurgation would leave a pamphlet too thin to be sold as a book. All the tales are written in Balzac's own medieval French, complete with archaic spellings and syntax, bursting into unintelligibility with those wonderful onomato-poeic words which the Académie Française had long since banished from the dictionary.

The subjects, too, were a form of protest at the new bourgeois society which had no regard for the truly important aspects of human existence: necrophilia, nymphomania, adultery and the essential bodily functions. The *Contes Drolatiques* are an orgy in the writer's playroom; words dance about like musical notes in *Fantasia*. The first collection was published in what seemed bad taste during the cholera epidemic of spring 1832. Actually it was rather appropriate since Paris was temporarily plunged into the Dark Ages, with a curfew, corpses carried through the streets at midnight, and the rag-pickers revolting when their rubbish heaps were swept away.

The opening tale had appeared in *La Caricature* in 1830 and reappeared the following year in the *Revue de Paris*. *La Belle Impéria* set the tone of the whole collection with the story of 'a cute little

Tourangeau priest' and his evening with the famous courtesan Impéria, who specialized in bishops and cardinals. It had the desired effect: an aphrodisiac in a time of miserable chastity.[51] The editor of the *Revue de Paris*, Louis Véron, wrote in alarm to warn Balzac that, 'in spite of the July Revolution, our subscribers are as prudish as ever, and to be perfectly honest, your writing is giving them erections ... Try to do something chaste if you can, if only to show them how versatile you are.'[52] The subscribers to *La Caricature* already had ample proof of Balzac's versatility. *La Belle Impéria* had been followed by a little anecdote called 'La Colique' which became *Les Joyeulsetez du Roy Loys le Unziesme*. Louis XI, we are told, liked to have his little joke. Some important Tourangeau bourgeois are invited to a feast where they stuff themselves 'like saveloys, from the gullet to the bung-hole of their bellies'. Unfortunately, the toilet is occupied by a life-size model of their host, and they are eventually obliged, after straining to contain themselves in the royal presence, to relieve themselves copiously in the main promenade of Tours. Balzac ends with the sort of message his father would have approved of and with a sense of civic responsibility: 'And since that day the bourgeois of Tours have never failed to defecate on the Mail du Chardonneret, in the knowledge that men of the Court had been there before them.'

Swinburne was very fond of Balzac's scatological tales,[53] and there is something appealing about his insistence on the theme of bowel evacuation. The *Contes Drolatiques* are a sign of the great unclogging of the writer's mind, the rediscovery of the literary heritage of his native Touraine, and his ability to extract a whole series of tales from one idea.

Once a new idea was found, Balzac treated it like a valuable treasure, or, as he puts it in the *Contes Drolatiques*, like the humble egg from which a brilliant cook concocts a hundred different dishes.[54] Sometimes, however, ideas turned out to be distractions and diversions. Other novelists, he complained, found a formula and stuck to it for the rest of their lives; but Balzac frequently tried to make sense of reality in ways that were entirely foreign to him. The most spectacular example of this dates from this period: a novel referred to in various letters, manuscripts and contracts as *La Bataille*.

From early 1830 until five years before his death, Balzac dreamed of describing a Napoleonic battle in a work 'in which one hears the roar of the cannon on the first page and on the last the shout of victory':[55] chaos contained by an account of the political causes and consequences. He talked with soldiers and visited battle sites. The idea was realized, not by Balzac, but by Stendhal in his worm's-eye view of Waterloo in *La Chartreuse de Parme* – and, much later, by Hugo in *Les Misérables*. For Balzac, almost alone among critics, Stendhal's was a magnificent achievement and he hailed it by describing how he would have done it himself. Only Stendhal's fragmentary, photographic point of view, however, could capture the mayhem of a real battle. Balzac, on the other hand, with his all-devouring, unitary approach, grasping the loom before the thread, was unable to close one eye and present reality in the abbreviated, abstract form that has become so commonplace in the twentieth century, pressing the reader's eye, as he says, to the general's telescope.[56] But it is one of the great delights of his work – and occasionally a source of impatience for the reader – that he was forever testing the limits of his art. *La Bataille*, or what remains of the planned 300-page novel, is like a tiny ruin on the outposts of the old empire of legends and epics. Here is the entire text as it survives (the fragment dates from the autumn of 1832):

THE BATTLE

Chapter First
Gross-Aspern

On the sixteenth of May in the year 1809 towards the
middle of the day [end of fragment][57]

Where Balzac did succeed quite brilliantly in a seemingly hopeless endeavour was in writing the history of the new regime as it happened. His *Lettres sur Paris*, purportedly issued to friends in the provinces (the replies are also by Balzac), began to appear in *Le Voleur* shortly after his return to Paris. From 26 September 1830, they were published every ten days until April 1831, by which time Balzac had decided that writing history was not enough: he was going to stand for Parliament and join in the battle himself.

Eventually, the *Lettres sur Paris* raise the banner of Balzac's new political credo: the need for a hereditary Chamber like the House of Lords to keep the King and People from each other's throats; a reinforcing of frontiers – Algeria, the Alps, the Rhine, and the annexation of that small department known as Belgium – so that France can fulfil its destiny as peace-keeper of Europe; encouragement for industry, especially for canal-builders (a favour to Balzac's brother-in-law); a less impervious society allowing talent to rise to the top; but also a dominant, dogmatic party, of whatever persuasion, in the elected Chamber.

The guiding principle is that the July Revolution had been hijacked by unimaginative cowards. The Government consisted of 221 human crutches propping up a politics of compromise, a pusillanimous *juste-milieu*, humming and hawing while men like Grandet the miser and Gobseck the usurer carved up the country's wealth between them. In December 1830, Balzac was calling for a temporary tyrant dedicated to democracy – someone just like himself: 'What we need is a young and vigorous man who belongs neither to the Directoire nor to the Empire, but who is 1830 incarnate, with its insights, its profound learning, its moral and political science, its enlightened patriotism; a man who does not allow sentiment to interfere with politics nor politics with his feelings.'[58] A Machiavelli of the middle-ground.

Balzac's new reactionary views emerge, however, only after a prolonged absence of quotable conclusions. This is Balzac at his least visible. The novelist is so well supplied with opinions on every subject, and so ready to share them with us, even at the expense of the plot, that it comes as a shock to see him flitting from one opinion to the other. Just as his battle scenes are drawn from pictures and prints, his history of the present was drawn from newspaper reports, and after scouring the early articles for signs of a firm political standpoint, it is rather unsettling to hear him warn a friend in November 1830 that 'the worker' (i.e. the journalist) should not be confused with 'the man': 'If you thought it was me, you were wrong; this is how the men you want to see running the country talk. There are expressions and ideas in these *Lettres* which come from the most influential people.'

Balzac's refusal to attach prefabricated meanings to the flimsy structure of daily events makes the *Lettres sur Paris* a very rare piece of political journalism for the time – a drama–documentary in which, if nothing much is going on, nothing much happens. It is, after all, the history of a 'Mediocracy': 'I thought, on my return to Paris, after listening to travellers' tales and reading the papers, that I should find the streets and boulevards half destroyed, the houses crammed with wounded; but, be reassured, my friend, the Royal Guard lost barely 1000 men and the people of Paris have but 800 heroes to mourn. . . . The streets look as they always did.' Balzac's generosity carried over into his intellectual life: searching for first principles and final truths, he still had the courage of his lack of convictions and an uncommon ability to believe in what was bad for him.

Balzac finally settled with a thump on the political Right. He wrote in the spring of 1831 to friends at Cambrai and Tours, asking for their support at the next elections. He also wrote to General Pommereul at the royalist outpost he had already represented in fiction: Fougères. Copies of an *Investigation* into Government policies were sent to be distributed in the respective constituencies. It was signed 'M. de Balzac, électeur éligible'. 'You know my principles,' he confidently informed the General, 'and in the new order of things, you would be a real father to me if you could see your way to promote my cause among the voters of your region.'

There were just two small problems – mere technicalities to Balzac but, to most of his biographers, convenient reasons not to take his political campaign seriously. First, General Pommereul could hardly have known what Balzac's principles were since, until recently, they were a mystery to the candidate himself. He was a politician without a manifesto, a one-man opposition. Recommending that the masses be ruled with a rod of iron made him sound like a legitimist; wanting to give them the means of rising above their station was the fantasy of a liberal. Because of the second problem, it was all academic anyway: not being a landowner, Balzac paid no direct taxes and was therefore not eligible to stand for Parliament. As usual, he was including the future in his calculations: a healthy fortune and a set of clear principles were just around the corner.

The elections passed in July. Balzac was taken up with the publicity campaign for *La Peau de Chagrin*. Success might have distracted him from his new vocation, but it didn't. He set his sights on a by-election to be held in Chinon in the summer of 1832. 'M. de Balzac's candidacy is truly *drolatique*,' sneered the *Figaro*, for once with some justification.

'This is the first time anyone has been seen caressing the voters with an ass's skin.' Nevertheless, the Chinon campaign was actually, in Balzac's mind, a straight-faced attempt to win a seat. In the salon of Olympe Pélissier he had met the Duc de Fitz-James, a daring, dashing orator who had the wit to find the *Contes Drolatiques* funny – and potentially compromising for a parliamentary candidate. Fitz-James was the head of the legitimists, or rather of the active wing of the party which refused to sit out the July Monarchy in sulking abstention. Presenting himself as 'a simple soldier' in 'the sacred cause', Balzac began to refine his views – for example, conscription should be confined to the lower orders – and published an oratorical appeal for an authoritarian government in the form of a short story called *Le Départ*: the last legitimate King of France, Charles X, is seen sailing away into a metaphorical sunset taking with him all hope of peace, justice and 'logic'.

Consorting with legitimists and contributing to their journals – *Le Rénovateur* and *L'Émeraude* – Balzac was marching on to thin ice. The Duc de Fitz-James and another of Balzac's royalist correspondents were arrested in 1832 on suspicion of conspiracy. Balzac's only brush with authority was an order to do his National Guard duty on the night of 17 April. Later, he would prefer a couple of days in prison to standing around in the cold; but this time, he bought a 6-franc sabre and dutifully turned up. Nothing should stand in the way of his candidacy. Backed by the party, he made a serious, practically suicidal attempt to achieve his taxable quota. First, he looked for a piece of property in Touraine, in the environs of Vouvray (his favourite wine). Then, incredibly, ignoring his own vivid warnings in *Physiologie du Mariage*, he started to look for a wife.[59] Marriage to a rich woman – preferably a young widow – would bring him the wealth he needed. He even courted the niece of the Duc de Fitz-James, the Marquise de Castries, from whom he had received an anonymous letter, in September 1831, complaining about his portrayal of women. A complete disregard for spelling indicated an aristocrat. Balzac replied at once with veiled offers of marriage. The ice was about to break. The Marquise, Balzac later said, destroyed his life of hard work and gave him nothing in return, refusing to satisfy the desires she so cruelly stirred up in him.[60] But disaster was still a few months away. For the time being, the important point is that Balzac had already drawn the main lines of his new political philosophy when he went into orbit around the Marquise de Castries. The idea that his candidacy was just a lover's ploy is therefore highly suspect, though the Marquise may have persuaded him to pretend that his own brand of legitimism was the official party-line.

In the end, Balzac did not stand for election in Chinon. The legitimists were either in disarray or in jail, and according to Balzac's host at Saché, Jean de Margonne, the local voters were apathetic, there was no hope of winning and Balzac would only be placing himself in danger. Worse still, no rich bride had fallen into his lap. Exactly why he failed to make himself eligible either matrimonially or politically is unclear; but a letter to Zulma Carraud (the wife of an army captain and friend of Laure whom Balzac first met at a prize-giving at Vendôme[61]) suggests one possible cause: 'If I found a wife and a fortune, I should have no trouble resigning myself to domestic bliss; but where am I going to find such things? What family would put their trust in a literary fortune?'

Balzac went on to hint that his own rigid criteria had saved him from domesticity: 'I should hate to owe my future to a woman I did not love or to one who had seduced me. Necessarily, therefore, I shall continue to live alone.' He was consoling himself. Zulma Carraud gave a more intimate interpretation of events and hinted at the passionate reticence underlying their own, long friendship: 'Humdrum happiness retreated at your advances; you frightened it away. There is such a brightness in your eyes that not everyone can bear it. They fear it because they cannot understand it or because they have dark corners which they hope to keep hidden. And then the idea of your superiority is not conducive to intimacy.' Since Zulma was forever warning him about success inflating his ego, she might also have been thinking of Balzac's own idea of his superiority.

Despite these setbacks, Balzac was still planning to go and woo the voters of Chinon at the end of May 1832 when an almost fatal accident occurred. Stepping down from his tilbury, he slipped and banged his head 'on the heroic paving-stones of July'. For twenty minutes he lay on the road, unable to collect his thoughts, 'and now it feels as if some wheel of my cerebral mechanism has slipped out of place'. 'I escaped death as if by a miracle.'

Even while telling friends of his fall, Balzac was talking of his 'irresistible' political vocation; but the accident forced him to stay in bed for several days. He was carried to his sister's house, bled copiously by the doctor, put on a special diet and ordered to stop reading, writing and thinking. Instead, he observed. From his bedroom window, on 5 June, he watched the funeral procession of General Lamarque pass down the Boulevard du Temple. As Laure told Mme Pommereul, he looked at the faces and saw a revolution in them. Physiognomic expertise or inside information? The funeral became the pretext for an insurrection in which the legitimists took part. Eight hundred insurgents were killed or wounded: the triumph of the bourgeoisie was virtually complete. At the time, it seemed to be the last convulsion of the July Revolution and the end of Balzac's political campaign. The next day, he left for the quiet woods of Saché. His mind was behaving in a strange manner; the wrong words kept coming to his lips. Not for the last time, he detected signs of madness in his 'cerebral mechanism'.

Balzac had reached an age when pure accidents were unthinkable. This particular slip took on the importance that a trivial occurrence might acquire in one of his novels. His description of the fall in political terms – 'the heroic paving-stones of July' – is significant, as is his premonition, from his sickbed, of the final insurrection. The Revolution had died and a new revolution was beginning in Balzac's life.

As a rational mystic, Balzac was especially fond of the idea of Leibniz that everything affects everything else.[62] In his *Théorie de la Démarche* in 1830, he had given his own illustration of the idea, placing it, as if with psychic foresight, after the description of the man who falls from the coach: 'A pistol bullet thrown into the water on the shores of the Mediterranean generates a movement that can be detected on the coast of China.' Nowadays the idea is more familiar as the beating of a butterfly wing in the Amazon affecting the weather on the other side of the world. Balzac would have been an ardent popularizer of Chaos Theory. His accident was a perfect example of sensitive dependence on initial conditions: a small event with apparently chaotic, unpredictable results, but which gives rise to patterns which are perceptible over long periods, patterns known as strange attractors. The term Balzac applies to the same phenomenon in human life is 'destiny'.

This rarefied level of analysis, which, in the philosophy Balzac was now expounding, is termed '*Spécialité*' (intuition seconded by science) lies outside the realm of conventional biography. None the less, there is a 'strange attractor' in the events leading up to Balzac's fall and his departure for Saché in June 1832. The fall itself may have been the result of 'chance' – which, for Balzac, is the word used when the chain of cause and effect is unknown – but the impact it had on his life raises serious questions about his motivation.

IT SEEMS ALMOST impolite to ask why Balzac should have wanted to dedicate himself so wholeheartedly to his country's interests, but it is impossible not to be struck by the fact that his independence as a writer coincided with his subservience to a political movement and even with a determined effort to break into the prison of marriage. From his earliest days, Balzac had nourished hopes of parliamentary glory. In this, he was in tune with the times: Vigny, Lamartine, Mérimée and Hugo all had political careers. But now the desire to make history as well as to write it signalled a need to find a fixed point in his hectic life by fitting himself into a hierarchy. Balzac's politics were a kind of mental hygiene rather than a set of convictions. Like Raphaël in *La Peau de Chagrin* and his allegorical equivalent – France after 1830 – Balzac was a one-man country in need of 'a *strong* and hierarchical government'. Just as the human mind, left to its own devices, quickly reached a state of anarchy, the 'feeble constitution' of France also needed a strong support. The 'new order of things' he referred to in his letter to Pommereul when he told him how he could become a 'real father' to him, was also the new order created in his life by the death of Bernard-François, perhaps even by the new possibility of freeing himself from debts to his mother.

Paradoxically, his public adoption of an extreme party line can be traced to the chronic objectivity and scrupulous wavering of the *Lettres sur Paris*. In an article published in *La Silhouette* in March 1830, Balzac had formulated an insight into himself that few of his other works would ever suggest:

> The artist is not privy to his own intellect. He operates under the influence of certain circumstances whose precise combination is a mystery. He does not belong to himself. . . .

A man who is accustomed to make of his soul a mirror in which
the whole universe finds its reflection . . . necessarily lacks that variety
of logic or stubbornness to which we have given the name 'character'.
There is something of the whore in him; he gets excited like a child
at anything that strikes his mind. There is nothing he cannot
imagine; he experiences everything.[63]

The idea that the writer's intentions are not necessarily a reliable
guide to the meaning of his work is normally attributed to Friedrich
Engels. Writing to Margaret Harkness in 1888, Engels remarked that
Balzac's acute perception of historical trends led him, in spite of
himself, to highlight the contradictions and injustices of society and
thus to promote the proletarian revolution he actively tried to prevent.
Engels shared the idea with Karl Marx, who had planned a full-length
study of the novelist.[64] In this view of things, Balzac, playing with
great confidence on the right wing, had swung his mighty boot at the
ball of History and put it in his own net. The remark was intended as
a compliment. Engels claimed to have learned more from Balzac 'than
from all the professional historians, economists and statisticians put
together', and it is curious to note that in 1831 *La Peau de Chagrin*,
with its right-wing warnings to the nation, was best appreciated by
socialist critics. It should be clear by now, though, that this presupposes a somewhat simplistic view of the novelist. (Engels, for example,
does not appear to have applied the same principle to his own writing.)
The supreme irony that he and Marx detected in Balzac's work was
already a painful truth to its creator.

This awkward self-awareness explains why Balzac began to have
what seem to be uncannily accurate premonitions of his own life and
work. The coherence of his seemingly contradictory activities runs so
deep that he was able now to predict his entire career, taking in at a
glance all his future work. Writing to Zulma Carraud in November
1830, he set out 'the system of government to which my whole life
will refer. This is a declaration of principles as unchanging as can be –
in a word, my political conscience, my plan, my philosophy, for which
I can claim the respect I accord to other opinions.' Long before
conceiving the idea of *La Comédie Humaine*, he was able to tell Baron
Gérard, when sending him *La Peau de Chagrin* with the *Romans et
Contes Philosophiques* (to be used for lighting his cigars), that 'the

general system of my work is beginning to unmask itself'. And by 1836, Balzac would have a detailed horoscope of his whole life: 'According to my own calculations, I shall publish my true masterpiece ten years from now [a reference to *La Cousine Bette*, begun in 1846?]. . . . It is written. I can show you the chronological table of my publications up to 1850'[65] – another premonition, it seems, since the table ends in the year of Balzac's death.

Politics, then, was not so much an alternative to literature as another aspect of the same desperate remedy:

My worship of women and my need for love have never been completely satisfied. In despair of ever being loved and understood by the woman of my dreams, and having found that ideal woman in one form only – in heart, not in body – I shall cast myself again into the tempestuous realm of political passions and the stormy, mind-deadening atmosphere of literary fame. I may fail in both endeavours, but be convinced of one thing: my desire to live the life of my century instead of spending my days in blissful obscurity is the precise result of the fact that common contentment has eluded me. When one has one's whole fortune to make, it might as well be great and illustrious, for, if I must suffer, I would rather do so in high than low estate. I prefer the daggers of fortune to mere pinpricks.[66]

Balzac was assuring his friend Zulma, who was a democrat, that he was not the average stick-in-the-mud legitimist, but a full-blooded Romantic, impelled by the thought of a paradise he had never had to lose. Of course, raging storms were not the best environment in which to acquire the quiet wisdom that the hero of *La Peau de Chagrin* so disastrously fails to achieve. Like Raphaël, Balzac was escaping into battle, and there was a persistent fear in this pattern of lunging attack and sudden change of course. Just when his early novels were maturing, he started out afresh as a businessman; after *Le Dernier Chouan*, he turned to journalism; even after the success of *La Peau de Chagrin*, he continued to channel most of his energy into politics, newspaper articles and short stories – almost forty of them published up to the end of 1832, when only two full-length novels had appeared under the name Balzac.

Not all these decisions and revisions can be explained by

depression or lack of money. For all his Byronic boasting, Balzac faced a practical difficulty which few writers ever enjoy. The problem with having so many ideas was that so many had to be sacrificed. Balzac treats happiness as something that can be regained or replaced with something else; but what of all the literary works that might never be pulled out of limbo? Balzac's correspondence is littered with these foetuses, like *La Bataille* or the seventy unpublished or unwritten *Contes Drolatiques*. For every work created, several works were lost, and regret at this is far more common in his letters than rejoicing in the finished product. As he complained to Mme Hanska in 1838: 'I often finish off a cottage by the light of one of my houses as it burns to the ground.'[67]

The alternative to this endless dissipation and mental gluttony was to commit himself entirely to a woman or a work of art. Here, too, there was fear – the fear of messing up his life again, the fear of a miser forced to gamble all his money.

In August 1831, Balzac had published an unforgettable parable which complements *La Peau de Chagrin* by showing the other horn of the dilemma. In *Le Chef-d'Oeuvre Inconnu*, the great artist, Frenhofer, has been slaving away for ten years on a painting so beautiful and so unutterably perfect that he loves it as his mistress. Frenhofer's pupil, Porbus, and a young artist called Nicolas Poussin are finally allowed to view the miraculous painting:

'Can you see anything?' Poussin asked Porbus.

'No. Can you?'

'Nothing.'

The two painters left the old man to his ecstatic contemplation and looked to see whether perhaps the light falling directly on the canvas was not neutralizing all its effects. Then they examined the painting from the right, from the left, standing in front of it, squatting down and standing up again.

'Yes, yes, it's a canvas all right,' said Frenhofer, failing to understand the reason for their scrupulous inspection. 'See? There's the frame and there's the easel, and here are my oils and brushes.' And he snatched up a paintbrush and handed it to them with a naive gesture.

'The old soldier's having us on,' said Poussin as he stared again at the spurious painting. 'All I can see are blocks of different colour in a confused mass bound by a multitude of weird lines which form a wall of paint.'

[Frenhofer overhears their conversation.] He looked for a moment at his painting and staggered back.

'Nothing! Nothing to show for ten years of work!'

This marvellous story struck a chord with Picasso, who produced an illustrated edition of it and later moved into the former Hôtel d'Hercule at 7 Rue des Grands-Augustins in which, he claimed, Balzac had located Frenhofer's studio;[68] it was there that he painted *Guernica* in 1937. Cézanne, too, according to Émile Bernard, saw himself in the mad artist. When asked one evening about Frenhofer and *Le Chef-d'Oeuvre Inconnu*, 'he got up from the table and, standing in front of me, repeatedly struck his chest with his index finger, thereby confessing, but without uttering a word, that *he* was the character from the story. He was so moved that tears came to his eyes.' Cézanne felt that Balzac had 'understood' him much better than Zola, whose Claude Lantier, in *L'Oeuvre*, he supposed to be an image of himself: one was 'impotent by genius', the other 'impotent by birth'.[69]

The irony which Balzac had the courage to perceive and act on so early in his short career is that the impossible desire for perfection destroys the work of art. *Le Chef-d'Oeuvre Inconnu* shows that in his imaginary world the disciplined artist enjoys absolute power, but how can the vision be communicated? How can the artist who is not content with merely *copying* reality rely on his own judgment? As time races on, the gap widens between the dream and the embodiment of the dream.

The enormous, all-containing *Comédie Humaine* would be a partial solution to the problem, though it too would remain a fragment; but an answer already lay in Balzac himself, in his conviction that he was equal to the vision. This painful hope is shown in a startling example of Balzac's habit of interfering with the logic of his own fables. In plot summaries, these little deconstructive rebellions of the story-teller tend to be lost. Frenhofer goes mad, as the story demands, and all his paintings are destroyed in a fire. But – as if Balzac had been unable to resist implanting hope in the story for himself and other artists – a dazzling fragment of the original vision was glimpsed on the canvas before it was incinerated. Not the most beautiful part of the body, but the most perfect example of it ever seen:

As they moved in closer, they noticed in a corner of the canvas a naked foot poking out of that chaos of colours, hues and uncertain shades. Out of that shapeless mist, an exquisite, living foot! They stood petrified with admiration at that fragment which had survived an incredible, slow process of destruction. The foot emerged from the painting like the torso of some marble Venus rising from the rubble of a city destroyed by fire.

'There's a woman under there!' cried Porbus as he pointed out to Poussin the layers of colour that the old artist had successively built up one upon the other under the delusion that he was perfecting his masterpiece.

CHAPTER NINE

Madness

(1832)

WHILE THE Government troops were quelling the riot in Paris, Balzac left for Touraine, hoping that his rebellious mind would settle down in Saché. His mental health had become an object of concern and morbid amusement to other people, and he wanted to give 'a glorious rebuttal' to the gossips who said he was sliding into madness. The rebuttal was to take the form of a novel eventually entitled *Louis Lambert*: it tells the story of a genius who transcends the normal plane of reality and goes spectacularly insane. It was typical of Balzac to douse a fire with petrol. Ignoring his own precept that to serve up one's life to the public was proof of a weak imagination and worse than prostitution,[1] he poured his own minutely remembered childhood into the novel: the Collège de Vendôme, its quirky assortment of teachers, its monastic regime, its pigeons, its smell, his fellow sufferers. The narrator, who identifies himself as the author of *La Peau de Chagrin*,[2] is supposed to be the best friend of the ill-fated boy genius, Lambert. Balzac must have believed he was dispelling the rumours. In the manuscript, he refers to his own undignified departure from Vendôme: 'My parents, alarmed at my mental state . . . removed me from the school and sent me to Paris.'[3] The allusion to his mysterious breakdown was wisely modified;[4] and yet the novel itself, ending as it does with the orphic utterances of a man in a cataleptic trance – the 'Thoughts' of Louis Lambert – was unlikely to be read as the work of an entirely rational being. No great critical acumen was required to see the narrator and the lunatic as two parts of the same personality. Once again, Balzac's writing was working out its own plans in defiance of the author.

Louis Lambert does give reason to wonder about Balzac's mental state. The novel is not just a philosophical treatise on the Swedenborgian idea of internal and external beings – the coexistence of the angel and the brute, revealed by certain psychic phenomena like telepathy and telekinesis. In line with *La Peau de Chagrin* and *Le Chef-d'Oeuvre Inconnu*, it develops the notion that 'Thought destroys the Thinker' – the tragic, self-defeating truth that Mme de Berny significantly missed when she told her wayward lover that the public would praise the novel only if they failed to understand it. By giving what seems to be an eye-witness account of life in the spiritual sphere, Balzac, in her view, was pretending to be God: 'You appear to have undertaken an *impossible* work.' 'If an author comes along and informs me that he has attained the goal of his spiritual aspirations, no matter how great he may be, I see in him only the braggart, his vanity shocks me, and the bigger he tries to make himself, the smaller he becomes in my mind.'[5]

The truth was that, in his own mind, Balzac had outgrown her, and in more than one sense, he was entering new domains. There is first-hand evidence that he was suffering from some type of clinical madness, and also from a less easily defined insanity which manifested itself in a dramatic chase: his breathless pursuit of the perfect woman across France (in body) and Europe and Asia (in spirit). One was the material woman: the Marquise de Castries. The other, Eveline Hanska, who also entered Balzac's life as an anonymous correspondent, was largely, before their meeting in Neuchâtel in 1833, a product of his imagination. Both women stand at a turning point that leads to the first great novels of Balzac's maturity. Already, the stories of this period hint at a psychological ultimatum: in some, life is a destructive force that must be constantly held in check; in others, seemingly *un*autobiographical studies of French society, Balzac returns to the calm and luxuriant regions of his own childhood – *Le Curé de Tours, La Grenadière*, the *Contes Drolatiques* and *La Femme de Trente Ans*. Once mental salvation was in sight, Balzac would commemorate his victory with another Tourangeau novel, the masterpiece that brings both currents of his writing together: *Eugénie Grandet*. The struggle that took place between his own past and present selves can best be described, with hindsight, as a second puberty.

THE FIRST SIGN of a change in Balzac's relations with women came with his departure from Paris. He left his mother in charge of his overstaffed house in the Rue Cassini and his complicated dealings with publishers and editors. To pay his debts (for clothes, carpets, book-binding and – a new passion – porcelain⁶), she was to sell the horses and sack the servants. Ever hopeful, he instructed her to keep the saddlery and make sure that Paradis and Leclercq left behind the smart blue livery he had designed for them. At all costs, she should avoid a court case: he was surrounded by enemies who would seize upon the slightest opportunity to make him look ridiculous. For that reason, his latest contracts stipulated that any journal publishing his stories should reject all negative reviews of his work.

It seems surprising that Balzac, who was so wary of other enemies, should hand the reins to his mother; but Mme de Balzac made an efficient agent, especially considering the huge number of errands he gave her. The real surprise is the almost embarrassing gratitude that oozes from his letters: 'I did not want another day to pass without letting you know how much I love you and what affection you arouse in me. Of course, these feelings are not simply a result of my poor Mother's inexhaustible generosity; but as you know, a single drop of water can make the cup run over.'⁷ Brother Henry probably had something to do with this resurgence of affection: the family had heard from Mauritius that the little waster had landed on his feet and married his landlady, who was a rich widow. He seemed to be set up for life. Honoré felt a pang of jealousy: 'I envy him the good fortune of being the first to make you happy,' he told his mother and went on – less convincingly – 'It made me bitterly regret the path I have taken and the fact that I am not even fulfilling my obligations towards you.'⁸

In the circumstances, it was a good idea to be seen to be loving, and the flowery compliments and grovelling say more about his mother's 'expectations' than they do about her son's emotional loyalties; for this is also the period in which most of his tales of fratricide and adulterous mothers were written. Without knowing it, Mme de Balzac had a dual existence: punished in fiction, appeased in reality. At best, Balzac's filial sentiments were ambiguous. This clinging to his mother was supposed to be part of a plan to free himself, and every now and then the vengeful voice of the work breaks through in the correspondence: 'If only I were the only one to suffer; but for four years now [since the collapse of the printing business], Mme de Berny alone has prevented me twenty times from going into exile.'⁹ And

[203]

there were other items of personal news that his mother would probably rather not have heard: 'My chastity is bothering me somewhat and causing me to lose sleep.'[10] Balzac had placed his mother in an unpleasant situation: there was something both cruel and pathetic in exposing her to all his financial secrets. As he reminded her – though never directly – it was *her* money she was taking care of and *her* money he was spending. She could see for herself that he was earning enough to balance the books. Why, then, did he always contrive to keep his head below water? More precisely, why, by threatening to bankrupt the whole family, had the son who felt his mother never loved him made her entirely dependent on him?

In his letters, Balzac presented a different view of the problem. His debts were a gigantic hole into which he had to tip the rubble of his writing, and his mother's nagging advice, though generally quite sensible from an accountant's point of view, was preventing him from filling the hole: 'You ask me to write in detail . . . but, my poor Mother, you obviously still have no idea how I live!' 'This morning I was about to start work full of courage when your letter came and *disorganized* me completely. How on earth am I supposed to have artistic thoughts when I am suddenly presented with your depiction of my predicament?'[11]

When Balzac sent this letter from Saché, there were already several other reasons for his being 'disorganized'. His attempt to spend 'a couple of weeks in a quiet corner' got off to a bad start. Coach travel always acted as a powerful stimulant, but the journey south had been unusually long and difficult. After the rioting sparked off by the funeral of General Lamarque, anyone leaving Paris was under suspicion. At every major town the *gendarmes* came out to meet the coach, checking passports and looking for escaping conspirators. Balzac had been thinking for some time of writing the *Histoire des Treize* – one of his first 'detective' stories. It would begin to appear in 1833, but it gives an excellent idea of Balzac's frame of mind in 1832: 'Thirteen men all struck with the same idea and endowed with sufficient energy to remain faithful to a single purpose.' 'Men of courage and imagination, bored with the humdrum life they were leading and drawn to Oriental pleasures by urges so long repressed that they reasserted themselves with a furious intensity.' 'Pirates in yellow gloves and riding in carriages . . . a new Society of Jesus on the side of the Devil . . . with a foot in every salon, a hand in every safe, an elbow on every street and a head on every pillow.'[12] The Duchesse de Berry, mother of the legitimist heir to the throne, was so thrilled when she read the first instalment in prison that she couldn't sleep. Her doctor wrote on her behalf to ask Balzac what happened next. 'The second part', he replied, delighted to have a fan in high places, 'is a little more profound than the first.'[13] In fact, the sequel, *La Duchesse de Langeais*, was a tale of personal vengeance that is also the story of the next few months. Yearning for 'Oriental pleasures', convinced of the hostility of his contemporaries, and considering occult power as the means to every end, Balzac was unlikely to find much peace of mind simply by leaving the city.

The Society of the Thirteen was just a fantasy – though it did become a reality for some readers.[14] Balzac was not arrested and finally arrived at the little grey château in the village of Saché, worn out, worried about his mind, and with several novels to write, including *La Bataille*. Henry had all the luck. Honoré would spend the next few months waiting for his own rich widow to turn up – the young Baroness Deurbroucq, a friend of Balzac's hosts, the Margonnes; but all he received was a polite thank-you letter for copies of his books.[15]

Saché today is instantly recognizable from Balzac's most famous descriptions of it, especially if one arrives from Azay-le-Rideau early in the morning and, as Balzac liked to, on foot:

> I climbed to a ridge and for the first time admired the Château d'Azay . . . and then, in a hollow, I saw the romantic walls of Saché, that melancholy abode, full of harmonies too solemn for superficial people but dear to poets whose soul is in mourning. Thus it was that, in the years to come, I grew to love its silence, its great wizened trees, and that mysterious aura that pervades its solitary vale![16]

Sitting at his desk in the small bedroom on the top floor of the château,[17] looking out at the ancient oaks which block part of the view of the Indre Valley but create the feeling of a secret place, unremarkable but memorable, living in a slower time, Balzac would write some of his finest novels – *Le Père Goriot*, *Le Lys dans la Vallée* – working at top speed. But his footsteps can be retraced only so far: the stone staircase which climbs from the main entrance, the salon, furnished as it was in Balzac's day. Some corridors can only be explored through the printed page, and not just because Balzac habitually broadens and embroiders the actual view in his writing. Saché is almost too pleasantly picturesque, too full of the insignia of Balzac's fame to convey the disillusion that is one half of the Romantic quest.

At Saché in mid-1832, it was a rainy summer, and Balzac found himself completely uninspired. The first problem was that he had become a tourist attraction. For Mme de Margonne – 'intolerant, bigoted, hunchbacked and humourless',[18] the very opposite of her jovial husband – Honoré was a novel entertainment to offer guests: 'There's no peace living in a château,' he told his friend Zulma. 'People come to visit and you have to dress at a particular time. Provincial people find it very odd that anyone should want to miss dinner in order to pursue an idea. Several good ones have already been throttled by their blasted bell!'[19] Even without distractions, ideas were in short supply. Balzac's special blend of coffee required a visit to several Parisian grocers and half a day's shopping.[20] The local variety was insipid: 'no great inspirations to be had with this coffee', he complained. The little boy from Tours had become a Parisian gentleman. In *Eugénie Grandet*, Cousin Charles arrives from the big city at his uncle's house in Saumur – the deepest depths of the provinces. 'What's that?' he asks, pointing to an oblong pot of glazed brown earthenware. '"It's boiling coffee," said Nanon. "Oh! my dear Aunt, I shall at least be able to leave some beneficial memento of my stay here. You're so backward! I shall teach you how to make decent coffee in a Chaptal coffee-pot."'[21]

The second obstacle to work was to prove a little more resistant to stimulants and may even have been aggravated by them. It can be glimpsed in a little-known description of Saché which dates from this period. In his 'Voyage de Paris à Java', Balzac presents a vision of the place which few visitors are likely to relive:

> I was stopped all at once in my tracks, as I drew level with the old Château de Valesne [another property of the Margonnes], by the ghost of the Ganges rising up before me! . . . The waters of the Indre had become those of the great Indian river. I mistook an old willow tree for a crocodile and the walls of Saché for the slender and elegant constructions of Asia. . . . There were seeds of insanity in this mental distortion of the beautiful objects of my native region. Something had to be done about it.[22]

Balzac's diagnosis was, roughly speaking, correct. When he talked about the verbal hallucinations he was experiencing, he was not just indulging in 'artistic' fantasies, as has been thought, but describing one of the symptoms of a series of related linguistic disorders for which a name had only just been found and which was not to be properly investigated until the 1860s: aphasia.[23] Perhaps he was still suffering the effects of his fall – certain types of aphasia are commonly caused by a stroke or a head injury – or perhaps the fall had merely revived a problem which first manifested itself in the mysterious 'coma' at Vendôme. The verbal and visual hallucinations were almost certainly tied to a congenital weakness, since the problem recurs throughout his life. In 1846, it would take the form of anomia or amnesic aphasia – a reduction in the ability to recall the names of objects for use in speech: 'In conversation, I find myself groping for nouns and forgetting the names of things.'[24] In 1832, Balzac's symptoms seem to indicate paraphasia – the mispronunciation of words or the use of inappropriate terms. The fact that Balzac was prone to a linguistic disorder might be thought a cruel irony – certainly for someone whose favourite sport was talking – but for the novelist it was also an exciting discovery. Some of the queer expressions produced by Louis Lambert are reminiscent of statements made by paraphasics, and it is fascinating to see Balzac putting his own mental illness to use in a work of fiction. Like his creator, Louis Lambert is simultaneously doctor and patient, investigating the links between thought and speech, analysing his bizarre utterances, not as mistakes, but as revealing formulae. This explains why Balzac's theories on mental illness are only partly derived from the work of the alienists he knew:[25] if La Peau de Chagrin was the result of mental and physical exhaustion, Louis Lambert drew some of its 'mysterious authority'[26] from nothing more transcendent than a bang on the head.

Naturally enough, when it appeared in October that year, Balzac's Notice Biographique sur Louis Lambert did nothing to stop the gossip. Apparently there was something entirely credible about the idea of a lunatic Balzac. The 'legend' was coming dangerously close to the truth and perhaps even beginning to modify it. There is a story that the explorer and 'scientific gossip' Alexander von Humboldt asked a psychiatrist friend to introduce him to a madman. The doctor gave a dinner to which he invited one of his patients. He also invited Balzac.

Strangely attired and with his hair in disarray, he babbled continuously with his mouth full. The inevitable confusion resulted.[27]

Humboldt was a regular in the salon of Baron Gérard and appears, ironically, in one of Balzac's stories in conversation with Louis Lambert as 'a Prussian scholar, renowned for the inexhaustible fluency of his speech'.[28] To judge by Balzac's story, he and Humboldt talked about the inadequacy of psychiatric terminology and the concept of 'madness'. But when Balzac was on one of his hobby-horses, he may well have conveyed the impression that he spoke from inner experience and even encouraged his listeners, like a good story-teller, to confuse the man with the work. 'Such a singular contrast of profound philosophy . . . combined with the variety and prodigality of an Eastern story-teller, expressed in a copious and brilliant language, frequently degenerating into violence or rising into the ostentation of positive insanity, I have never met with,' wrote an English visitor to the Rue Cassini. 'His excess of vanity prevented me from drawing any distinct principle from him. He declaimed for an hour on the extent of his labours.'[29] For this reason, it would be wrong to exclude some of the more ridiculous stories told about the hare-brained novelist simply for the sake of anecdotal accuracy. Léon Gozlan remembers Balzac turning up one night at the home of a friend and asking him to join an expedition to the East. He had come into possession of the Prophet's ring, stolen by the English a century before; the Grand Mogul was offering mountains of gold and diamonds for its return. The friend refused to believe him, Balzac ranted and raved about his lack of faith and eventually fell asleep on the carpet.[30] Another Balzac trivialist scoffs at him for thinking that a laundress passing one night in a Versailles street was a secret agent sent by Russian nihilists to spy on him. Balzac hid behind a tree, quaking with fear.[31]

The real value of these anecdotes is accidental. Far from showing what a fool he was to believe his own fantasies (though he often did), they show Balzac weaving a few scraps of truth into a web of mystery: he was in fact a friend of the orientalist, Hammer-Purgstall,[32] who had supposedly given him the Ring, and it was quite possible, at a time when Balzac was said to be writing a book in defence of Russia, that the enemies of the Czar would take an interest in his activities.[33] In most of these stories Balzac should have the last laugh. The implication is that he was easily taken in and yet his sceptical listeners were gullible enough to believe that the teller himself believed the story.

As in his work, Balzac was exploiting expectations. Madness in the early 1830s had a high market value. It was the heyday of the 'mad genius', and Balzac adopted the cliché as part of what he later called his 'Balzac costume'.[34] However, even for his friends, it was becoming increasingly difficult to distinguish the man from the maniac, and it may be that Balzac himself occasionally failed to make the distinction. In February that year, he published a collection of spine-chilling tales, threaded together as a conversation in a high-society salon. The *Conversation Entre Onze Heures et Minuit* was written for a volume entitled *Contes Bruns*, to which Philarète Chasles and Charles Rabou also contributed. The anonymous tales were collectively ascribed to a picture of a maniacally grinning head, printed upside-down – a *tête à l'envers* or 'a deranged mind'. To the irritation of the other contributors, Balzac behaved like a megalomaniac, elbowing his fellow writers out of the way, criticizing them in advance, as Rabou complained, by wondering in his *Conversation* whether a 'textual copy' of reality might not be as beautiful as the usual 'idealization' of modern life. Most annoying of all, he gave his own address, which by now was well known to the public, thereby signing himself for all three as the *tête à l'envers*.[35]

Any literary tourist who saw the engraving of Balzac's house by Régnier and went to view the mad novelist for himself would probably not have been disappointed. George Sand remembered Balzac seeing his guests on their way after a 'peculiar' meal consisting of boiled beef, melon and champagne *frappé*:

> He went to put on a lovely brand-new dressing-gown which he showed off with all the glee of a little girl, and he was going to go out with it on, a candle-holder in his hand, in order to accompany us as far as the gates of the Luxembourg Gardens. It was late, the *quartier* was deserted, and I pointed out to him that he would get himself killed when he returned on his own. 'Not at all,' he retorted. 'If I meet any robbers, they will either think I'm a lunatic and be afraid, or take me for a prince and leave me alone.'[36]

In the literary world, a lunatic *was* a kind of prince. Balzac's doctor, Nacquart, many of whose diagnoses imply that he felt that flattery was the best medicine for his patient, had told him that 'madness is always lurking at the gates of those great minds which function to excess'.[37] The very fact that Balzac reported this to his sister is a sign of his growing tendency to glory in his fame. He continually refers to himself as an '*artiste*' (a fashionable new word for a writer) and even exults in his professional egotism. Auguste Borget, a young painter to whom Balzac was introduced by Zulma Carraud, was shocked to hear Balzac tell him that year: 'I am no longer a brother; neither am I a son or a friend. I am a brain. . . . Other lives must contribute to mine.'[38] In the crisis to come, Balzac's mental disorder went hand in hand with a kind of *folie de grandeur*, exacerbated by a contrasting reality: an inability to satisfy his sexual and emotional needs and a feeling of helplessness in the face of his own exorbitant ambitions.

During his month at Saché, Balzac began to live in his own illusions. Just as he had promised a white Arab pony to Latouche – and always believed he had actually received it – and just as he later gave his publisher a magnificent carpet as a thank-you present, and left him to pay for it,[39] Balzac was convincing himself now that he had already completed novels which were little more than a title and a misty idea. As his first, bemused English biographer puts it, 'He speaks of works yet in his brain as actual possessions: romances, still to be written, have, in his imagination, the value of debentures in a first-class railway.'[40] Balzac's correspondence retraces in great detail the itinerary of these non-existent novels. Several of his publishers were victims of these delusions which began as a form of self-discipline. In 1833, Louis Mame took the coach to Nemours in order to collect what Balzac called the manuscript of his long-overdue novel, *Le Médecin de Campagne*. On arrival, all he found were chapter summaries and an unapologetic author.[41] In organizing his work, Balzac was turning his vivid imagination against himself, resting on imaginary laurels as he never did on real achievements. On 23 September 1832, he was congratulating himself on finishing *La Bataille*: 'It's a really fine book, but it cost me a great deal of trouble and hard work.' Eight days later, he was discussing the terms of a contract for a second edition of the book and deciding what to do with the money. Finally, on 10 October, he confessed to Zulma: 'You win! Not a single line is written.' By incurring debts and signing contracts for imaginary works,

Balzac appeared to fit his own definition of madness: 'A lunatic is a man who sees an abyss and falls into it.'[42]

Balzac's mythomania was also receiving some outside encouragement. He was being presented now with countless new images of himself, many of which were extremely agreeable. People had begun to behave in strange ways, dropping things in his presence or going suddenly speechless.[43] Ever since he had established in *La Femme de Trente Ans* that true feminine beauty begins only with middle age, 'beautiful unknown women' had been turning up at his door.[44] Three or four perfumed letters came every day, some of them from abroad – 'it has all become rather tiresome' – and they reached him with the flimsiest of addresses: 'M. de Balzac, Man of Letters, Paris'.[45]

On 16 July, Balzac left Saché and walked to Tours, where he caught the coach for Angoulême. He was to spend a month with his friends, Zulma Carraud and her husband, and completed many of the stories he had hoped to work on at Saché, writing *La Grenadière* in a single day during a game of billiards.[46] Most of the time, he stayed in the house, for, as he told his mother on 20 July, his fame had preceded him: 'A young man *fell ill* when he heard I was staying here.' The sick young man was later known to Balzac as the journalist, Albéric Second. In his memoirs, he remembers that Balzac went to have his hair cut in town. The ladies of Angoulême who had been hoping to catch sight of him besieged the barber's shop, 'arguing over the precious locks that had fallen from the cherished head as if they were holy relics'.[47] Such was Balzac's popularity that despite his well-known aristocratic sympathies the local Cercle Constitutionnel promised him their votes if he wanted to represent them in Parliament: 'Is it true?' he wondered. 'Are they trying to trick me? – I don't know; but if it is true, it makes me all the more hopeful.'[48]

Later, Balzac would learn to exploit his legend as he had used his mental illness in *Louis Lambert*. By 1845, he was able to draw a lesson, ostensibly from the mental disasters of other writers: 'Vanity is killing Villemain, as it killed Lassailly and Gérard de Nerval, and it's eating away at Lamartine and Thiers. Hugo has the head of a madman, and his brother, the great unknown poet, died insane. It's all very worrying. There is nothing more dangerous than allowing oneself to be worshipped. We should bless our critics.'[49] In 1832, things were getting out of hand. News reached the Carrauds from Gravelines in the north of France that Balzac had been locked up in Charenton lunatic asylum – a rumour which originated in Paris with the Duchesse d'Abrantès – and he had only himself to blame when, in December, the *Revue de Paris* hinted that the last instalment of Balzac's *Les Marana* had been delayed because the author had gone mad.[50] Balzac was furious, but then his failure to deliver the third instalment was more than usually galling for both the publisher and the subscribers since, in keeping with a habit which often surprises the reader who pauses to measure the thickness of pages read, Balzac had stated at the end of the last section that the preceding 'purely introductory tale' (more than half the total) was not in fact the main subject of the story.[51]

Perhaps there was some truth in the editor's association of authorial high-handedness with insanity. When Balzac stated that he existed now only as an all-absorbing brain, it was meant in part as a warning to Borget, who rashly offered to serve as Balzac's secretary. But it was also a reference to the self-destructive spirit of his work, when, as Balzac thought, devotion to his reputation was not tamed and channelled by a woman.

BALZAC'S STAY at Angoulême was marred by an incident which proved to be the prelude to his most disastrous attack of mythomania. Zulma was married to an army officer fifteen years older than herself. Major Carraud's sullen resistance to the new regime had led to his being removed from Paris and sent to a place where he could do no harm: an unintentionally sarcastic bureaucrat made him Inspector of the Gunpowder Factory at Angoulême. Like so many of the Empire heroes in *La Comédie Humaine*, the Major had grown cranky and obstreperous, wallowing in self-pity, dwelling on his eight years' imprisonment in Italy and the ingratitude of his superiors. Balzac was about to start work on *Les Marana*. He borrowed some aspects of Zulma's life for his Spanish heroine, Juana, who is forced to marry a French officer in order to save her 'honour'. She finds herself stuck with a spineless mediocrity, humiliated by her own superiority, her acts of kindness go unrewarded, her little acts of revenge unnoticed.

George Sand, of all people, cites as an eccentric notion Balzac's view that the famous murderess, Mme Lafarge, could plead extenuating circumstances because the victim was her husband.[52] Zulma's life in Angoulême might have suggested the idea. In *Les Marana*, Juana stabs her husband to death to save *his* honour. Balzac offered Zulma a less drastic solution by asking her to go to bed with him. Wisely, she refused, wondering, like most of Balzac's female friends at one time or another, why he enjoyed such a reputation as an expert on feminine psychology. With a family to care for, she told him in a letter, she hadn't the time to transform herself into the sylph-like creature Balzac desired: fashionable elegance and generosity of heart are incompatible, she informed him, and she was 'ugly, short and had a limp'. Besides which, she hated dishonesty and wanted to maintain the critical distance that was the basis of their friendship. Balzac's craving was purely physical, 'and I am too proud to be chosen under the influence of such a need'. She was sure he would be able to satisfy his desires elsewhere – if only he wouldn't always confuse his needs with his pride. . . .[53]

Zulma was referring to the Marquise de Castries, who had invited Balzac to join her and her uncle, the Duc de Fitz-James, in Aix-les-Bains where they were taking the waters. From Savoy, they would travel on together through Switzerland into Italy. When Balzac accepted the invitation, he set in motion a series of events some of which are quite minutely prefigured in *La Peau de Chagrin*. The story of Raphaël de Valentin contains some startling premonitions which have been concealed by the more general, mythic resemblance with Balzac's life as a whole. For the next few months, it was as if he were reliving the events of a life already mapped out in fiction. The commonplace that his writing is based on experience holds true, except that, in this case, the experience came after the writing.

Claire-Clémence-Henriette-Claudine de Maillé de La Tour-Landry, Marquise (later Duchesse) de Castries, was his latest infatuation – the latest and last of the older women Balzac expected to play the joint role of mother and lover.[54] Since receiving her anonymous letter in 1831, he had been engaged in what seemed to be a romantic correspondence and by the time he left Zulma's home for Aix-les-Bains, he had already symbolically transferred his affection from Mme de Berny to the Marquise by sending her the ecstatic 'Fragment' that Louis Lambert sends to his darling Pauline. The tone of the fictional letter distinctly echoes the letters from Mme de Berny, and the proximity in the correspondence of Mme de Berny's protestations of love and Balzac's equally adoring replies to the Marquise seems a sad injustice. When Mme de Berny corrected the proofs of *Louis Lambert* that summer, perhaps she guessed that she was reading passages inspired by the letters Balzac had received from the Marquise. She was no longer begging him to sacrifice his other women. 'What I do want is their secrets and their letters.'[55]

If Balzac had complied with her request, she might have discovered some similarities between herself and the Marquise. At thirty-six, Henriette de Castries was well past her prime in the conventional view. In her case – and in Balzac's eyes – the poignancy of incipient old age was enhanced by the fact that she had been ostracized by the Faubourg Saint-Germain, ostensibly because of her scandalous affair with the son of the Austrian statesman, Metternich – probably also because she was too witty and intelligent. In the salons of the Faubourg – a nineteenth-century Beverly Hills, where 'dogs, monkeys and horses'[56] were treated better than servants – 'thinking is kept to a minimum'.[57]

When Balzac was recruited to her alternative salon of artists and writers (some of whom, like Balzac, had risen to the bait of an anonymous letter[58]), she was a tragic figure. Her lover had died of tuberculosis and she herself had been partially crippled in a riding accident. Balzac was delighted to be admitted to her *hôtel* with its old-fashioned furniture, its eighteenth-century screens and neoclassical decor. The Marquise was a representative of a period, the Directoire (1795–9), of which Balzac so far had had little experience: 'that sick, disabled woman, stretched out on her chaise-longue, languidly but without affectation, her noble, chivalrous face, a profile more Roman than Greek, and red hair on a very high, very pale brow'.[59] This is how Philarète Chasles described her. Balzac's description (pre-fiasco) is infused with the observer's desire: beautiful, extremely fragile, 'a heart that was in some way proud of its grief', eyelids chastely lowered, 'and if she looked about her, she did so sadly, as if keeping the fire of her eyes for secret contemplations'; 'her sensitivity was evident in the miraculous delicacy of her skin – a sign that rarely deceives'; 'her neck was perhaps a little too long' but it gave her head 'vague affinities with the magnetic convolutions of the serpent'; 'though her corsage was modest, it did not entirely conceal the elegance of her form'. 'Thus, all

superior men were mysteriously drawn to this soft and silent woman.'[60]
As a social historian, Balzac should have known that the Marquise's
magnetic influence and flirtatious behaviour were part of her education. He did, however, seem to be aware, despite what his subsequent actions suggest, that his vision of the Marquise was that of a
novelist, pursuing the still shadowy idea of a character in his mind:

> I have to go clambering up to Aix in the Duchy of Savoy [he wrote
> to Zulma], running after someone who quite possibly is trying to
> make a fool of me. She's one of those aristocratic women you
> probably detest, one of those angelic beauties one likes to imagine
> with a good heart – the Duchess *par excellence*, very disdainful,
> loving, sharp, witty, coquettish – like nothing I've ever seen before!
> One of those phenomena of which few examples now remain. And
> she says she loves me and wants to keep me locked away in a
> Venetian palace . . . (I keep no secrets from you!), and wishes me to
> write only for her in future. One of those women you absolutely
> have to worship on your knees when that is their wish, and whom it
> is such a pleasure to conquer.[61]

Once idealized in this way, the Marquise could only be either very
good or very bad. In fact, the novel had already been written. This
was the first premonition from *La Peau de Chagrin*. Balzac was
returning to the early pages of the story: 'An aristocratic woman', says
Raphaël, 'when she places a barrier between herself and the world,
flatters every sort of vanity in me – vanity that is one half of love.'[62]
Unlike the letter, the novel contained a moral. It was a moral that
Balzac chose to ignore.

On 21 or 22 August 1832, after a last flurry of messages for his
mother, Balzac left Angoulême at midday and set off across France
from west to east, an awkward journey requiring several changes of
coach. At Limoges, he had a lightning tour of the town and then
boarded the diligence for Clermont.[63] The weather was perfect.
Leaving behind the meadows of Limousin, Balzac inspected the
scenery 'under all the requisite conditions',[64] recording it so vividly
that he was able to give an accurate description of it over eight years
later in *Le Curé de Village*: 'Five leagues after Limoges . . . the
landscape takes on a sad and melancholy air. Wide moors and steppes
without grass or herds of horses stretch away to the mountains of

Corrèze on the horizon. . . . In the mind of the thinker and the poet who pass through it, this dreary region conjures up visions of the Infinite – a terrible thought for certain souls.'[65] For the present, Balzac had more urgent matters on his mind. At Clermont, he changed for Lyon. And then, out of the blue, after a brief halt at Thiers, another warning. . . . Just as he was climbing back into the coach, the horses galloped away, he slipped, grabbed the strap and his 80 kilos crashed against the door; his leg was gashed open down to the bone. There was no time to waste: the driver laid him out on the seat and he survived without treatment until the coach reached Lyon two days later. There, he saw a doctor, corrected the proofs of *Louis Lambert* and set off for Aix-les-Bains, arriving somewhat embarrassingly by public transport, six or seven days after leaving Angoulême.

Aix was still a quiet backwater, but during the season its population doubled and plush carriages with coats-of-arms on the door shared the streets with farmers' carts.[66] The Marquise suspected that her battle-scarred visitor had depleted his resources by coming to see her. His dinners were paid for and she had reserved a pleasant room for him at the hotel (only 2 francs a day), with gorgeous views of the valley and the mountains to the west of the Lac du Bourget, the setting for Lamartine's famous elegy, 'Le Lac'. He had all day to himself and then joined Mme de Castries's party for dinner in the aristocratic Club. There, he met Baron James de Rothschild, who promised him the use of his personal mail service. The Marquise was charming and Balzac prepared for what he fervently hoped would be his reward.

The Club at Aix was the second premonition; Raphaël de Valentin had been there before him. By coincidence, it was to the very same place that the hero of *La Peau de Chagrin* had been sent by his doctors to convalesce.[67] And the similarities were more than topographical. At Aix-les-Bains, another doctor tells Raphaël that with the 'keen, pure air' of the high altitude and with his being 'over-oxygenated by the ardent temperament of men who are destined for great passions, he was further stimulating a combustion that was already too rapid'. Was it the same doctor who examined Balzac's wound when it reopened after he climbed to the summit of the Dent-du-Chat? Maybe it was worth shedding a little blood for the description of the view which Balzac added to the forthcoming edition of *La Peau de Chagrin* – a description in which passion and its antidote are curiously combined: 'The view from the mountains changes the conditions of optics and perspective. A 100-foot fir-tree seems no taller than a reed, wide valleys appear as narrow as mountain tracks.' 'There you can find a balm for all the vexations of life. . . . It is a place which deepens and purifies passion. A kiss is somehow magnified. Only when surrounded by that beautiful scenery was he able to bear his burden; there he could remain idle, meditative and free from desire.'[68]

Reliving his last novel, Balzac was also living his next one in advance. On an excursion to the Grande Chartreuse monastery on 19 September, he was struck by an inscription on a monk's cell and stood under an archway for ten minutes: '*fuge, late, tace*' ('flee, hide, and be silent'). Perhaps he had missed his vocation. He had the idea of writing *Le Médecin de Campagne*, in which a man called Benassis, after being spurned by the woman he loves, devotes the rest of his life to the godforsaken peasants of a remote village in the region of Grenoble. 'I worked for three days and three nights and have now completed a volume entitled *Le Médecin de Campagne*', he told his mother shortly before starting work on it.

Balzac's ascetic urge came after weeks of trying to 'conquer' the Marquise. All this time, he had been arming for battle. Reinforcements were ordered from Paris: white ties and shirts, new boots, gloves, pomade for his hair and a bottle of Eau de Portugal. In case that wasn't enough, his mother was to take two pieces of flannel which had been worn on the stomach to his favourite hypnotizer, keeping them wrapped up in the paper so as not to contaminate the bodily 'effluvia', and make a careful note of the doctor's prescriptions. The particular mention of a foot suggests that Balzac was hoping to cure Mme de Castries of her disability and earn some tangible proof of her gratitude.

A relationship that remains Platonic for too long becomes a financial disaster, Balzac likes to say, notably – of course – in *La Peau de Chagrin*.[69] More serious yet than his rate of spending money was the rate of his erotic 'combustion'. It seems that a premature attempt to seduce the Marquise had failed by the time the party arrived at Geneva on 14 October. He was directed to a cheap room in the most expensive hotel, but refused to be discouraged; they were on their way to Italy, and Italy was the land of unbridled passion. Before leaving Geneva, he hit on the idea of a romantic pilgrimage. He and the

Marquise drove out to the Villa Diodati where one of the great encounters of literature had occurred: it was there that Byron met the Shelleys in 1816. Balzac convinced himself that the correct conjunction was at hand; like Raphaël, he would be 'Byron or nothing'.[70] In the historic villa above the shores of Lake Geneva, he launched his final attack.

THAT NIGHT, or soon after, the Geneva police registered the departure 'for Paris' of M. de Balzac. His final lunge had met with a look of disbelief and, no doubt, a tart allusion to his social status. To the Marquise, Balzac was an amusing friend who made the long stay in the spa town more bearable, and though she did have a malicious sense of humour, she seems to have been genuinely upset and shocked at his complete failure to understand the situation. He had treated her as if the man she had loved and whom she loved even in death – young Metternich – was just one in a line of several lovers.

Balzac was utterly humiliated. In his view, the Marquise had given him a glimpse of 'paradise' and slammed the door in his face. The series of events prefigured by his own novel was complete, or almost. In his writing – but not in his conscious mind – he had worked out, down to the smallest contingency, what should inevitably happen to a man like himself. He was 'destroyed', like Raphaël, by a cold-hearted woman who toyed with his emotions. Now, at last, the character in the novel had incarnated herself: 'I have indeed encountered a Foedora,' he wrote the following January, 'though I shall never describe her in my novels; but when I met her, *La Peau de Chagrin* had already been out for some time.'[71]

Balzac did describe the woman. He was so frustrated and enraged that the fiasco fuelled three separate stories written in the next few months in virtual hiding at La Bouleaunière with Mme de Berny. It was a desperate attempt to 'transfer the life of [his] heart to his brain', to extinguish 'this burning which is spreading and which may devour me': 'An incredible coldness has gradually overtaken what I thought was passion in a woman who first approached me in a noble spirit. I am terrified of knowing the cause and I do not want to draw the logical conclusions that my observational science forces me to reach. I close my eyes like a little child.'[72] In the *Conte Drolatique*, 'Dezesperance d'amour' ('true in every detail'[73]), the frustrated lover of a flirtatious woman slices off her left cheek as a punishment for her cruelty when she finally relents – which makes her love him all the more. In *La Duchesse de Langeais* (its original, unsubtle title was *Ne Touchez Pas la Hache* – 'Don't Touch the Axe!'[74]), the innocent hero, Montriveau, is seduced by a bored society coquette who uses religion as 'a cold shower' when the heat of passion becomes too intense and then throws him away 'like a squeezed lemon'. Afterwards she comes to fear the anger of 'this man with the neck of a bull' – always a mark of the author's presence: for Balzac, born a Taurus, a short neck was a sign of greatness, 'perhaps because Nature wishes the hearts of such men to be close to their brains'.[75] A sign, too, he claimed, with more gloomy precognition, of a person prone to apoplexy. True to his neck, Montriveau captures the Duchess with the aid of the secret Society of the Thirteen and threatens to brand her with an iron. His real vengeance comes when she falls in love with him – too late – and retires to a convent.

The third story tells a similar tale. The unpublished 'Confession' which became *Le Médecin de Campagne* was written almost immediately after the event and comes closest to revealing what actually happened. Even here, however, Balzac remained hidden, maybe even from himself: 'How did this frightful catastrophe occur? In the simplest manner. One day I was everything to her, the next I was nothing! . . . During the night, a woman had passed away: it was the woman I loved. How did it happen? I do not know. . . . In accordance with that execrable custom of society women, she offered me her "friendship"; but to accept her friendship would have been to absolve her of her crime. I wanted nothing of it.'[76]

The teller of these stories, like Balzac himself, is more interested in revenge than his unrequited love. His pride now seemed little more than unjustified vanity. Balzac's nose had led him astray. There is a significant discrepancy between Balzac's version of events and his actual movements: after leaving Geneva, he was still planning to join the Marquise in Italy and one suspects that the final blow was not so much the fiasco itself as the rumours which began to spread of the novelist's humiliation. His later relations with Mme de Castries, even after he sent her the proofs of *Ne Touchez Pas la Hache*, asking for her corrections, were, if not exactly friendly, at least enlivened by a faintly sexual antagonism.

The fiasco was far more than the end of an unhappy and expensive love affair. Something common to all three stories is the social rank of the lady. In his last two novels, Balzac had been flirting with autobiography, as if using story-telling as a form of self-analysis; finally, in Geneva, he was brought face to face with himself and saw some unpleasant truths. For one thing, he was still his father's son, the upstart bourgeois taking revenge on aristocrats for his undeserved obscurity. For the man with a sense of destiny, people could be used as post-horses, driven hard and left to die at every stage.[77] But for all the skilful scheming of the last ten years, Balzac had just been trampled underfoot.

His humiliation also took him back still further to the roots of his vocation. The Marquise was the last of Balzac's older women and, on one level, offered new proof that his mother never loved him: it was a long-delayed awakening from childhood. By now, of course, he was a different person, but in his novels he had been living in the past. Superficially, there was his personal pride, manifesting itself in gloves and pomade, but more importantly there was his pride as a novelist. In this respect, this was his worst failure, and Balzac's destructive rage is directly analogous to the fury of Frenhofer when he sees that all his work has been in vain. He, too, was undeniably mad, at least if this other definition of madness in Balzac's scrapbook was accurate: 'A lunatic is often a man who clothes his thoughts, turns them into living beings, sees them and speaks to them.'[78]

Failure was doubly exasperating because, as his most widely read novel showed, he was somehow aware of the traps he set for himself and yet was unable to profit from his own foresight. When Balzac revised *La Peau de Chagrin* the following year for its third edition, he must have marvelled at his own futile prescience. On closer reading, the story contains yet another little detail that could have reminded its author why the Marquise might have been reluctant, after her accident, to engage in passionate affairs. In a mock-philosophical discussion with Foedora, Raphaël had wondered aloud why she refused to bestow her favours on anyone: 'Do you perhaps have imperfections which render you virtuous in spite of yourself?'[79] Or, as he had already noted in his scrapbook: 'There are some women who are forced by hidden defects to remain virtuous.'[80]

BALZAC'S RECOVERY from temporary insanity was typical in two ways. First, two articles which appeared in the *Revue de Paris* in October and November 1832 show that, in the end, his mind was as much a source of curiosity as it was of suffering. The 'Lettre à Charles Nodier', written with a borrowed pen in an *auberge* at Annecy during his stay at Aix, is intended as a spur to investigations of bizarre psychological phenomena. God is incomprehensible, but there are mysterious regions of the mind which should be scientifically studied: for example, healing at a distance – an ability Balzac was beginning to discover in himself.[81]

The second article was the 'Voyage de Paris à Java', large parts of which are pure fantasy, especially a delirious passage on the writhing bodies of native dancing-girls which so shocked the printers that it had to be removed. It was all untrue anyway, as Balzac admitted in the article: a friend of the Carrauds who had actually been to Java assured him that the women were ugly.[82] But this is what makes the article so compelling: a hybrid of natural history and hallucination, built on the tension of dream and reality and the overriding urge to include everything, even those 'scattered memories whose intimate eloquence has no equivalent in human language'. 'He's mad', the reader is expected to conclude. 'Don't believe him: he thrives on illusions! . . . He hasn't been to Java any more than you or I.' People reached this conclusion of their own accord: the Prince de Metternich was of the opinion that Balzac's work was a sort of homeopathic treatment for lunatics, a vaccination for the brain[83] – and when Balzac met him in Vienna in 1835, he told him he was quite right. Madness could be conquered if it was transformed into knowledge by the written word. Unlike some of the modern schools of criticism which have fed on his work, Balzac never suspected imagination of being an obstacle to the truth: 'Let's get back to reality', he is reported to have said to a friend (Jules Sandeau) who had just attended his sister's funeral. 'Who is Eugénie Grandet going to marry?'[84]

Balzac's return to reality at the end of 1832 was the start of another dream and it consisted of another real-life novel. In his usual way, he had already written the first words before the last one was over. The heroine in this novel would be a good angel and it would have a happy ending. The dénouement would occur, again, at the Villa Diodati: Balzac was determined to use it as a scene. In life, as in his novels, he could preserve the illusion of reality in the face of the most obvious contrivances. This time, however, he would not be in the role of the child; he would be the father of a new generation.

CHAPTER TEN

The Ideal Woman

(1832–1834)

THE PROBLEM facing Balzac at the end of 1832 was apparently insoluble and his method of solving it impeccable: how to make dream and reality coincide and find the perfect relationship with the perfect woman. The key to the problem was a simple truth which only superficial people would think of as the moral of a fairy-tale: 'You are always what you wish to be'[1] – and if your dreams fail to materialize, the fault lies, not with circumstances, but with the formulation of your desire.

By now, Balzac was an expert in the art of wanting things. Reality was there to be absorbed and transformed rather than simply observed. Just as his characters were acquiring all the attributes of real people (soon they would begin to recur in different stories as if they actually existed), so Balzac was learning to re-create himself in new relationships. If his fictional world was 'to compete with the Record Office',[2] he too could rewrite his official certificates. Remembering his first meeting with Mme Hanska, he liked to say that he was 'born in September 1833',[3] and it is certainly true that the first letters to Mme Hanska show a new Balzac bursting into life. But would a novelist so hungry to take on other natures be content with just one alter ego and a single form of perfection?

The person Balzac decided to place in the role of Ideal Woman – and who eventually became his wife five months before his death – first appeared in his life with the alluring vagueness of a character in search of an author. On 28 February 1832, she had an anonymous letter posted to him from Odessa. Signing herself '*L'Étrangère*', she gave no return address. The letter has been lost, which is all the more unfortunate since it is easily the most important letter Balzac ever received. Some idea of its contents can be gleaned, however, from Balzac's replies. 'The Stranger' expressed regret at what she thought was the cynicism and atheism of *La Peau de Chagrin*: women were portrayed as evil monsters. She urged him to return to the more elevated ideas of the *Scènes de la Vie Privée* with their angelic victims. Balzac was always affected by any suggestion that his works were irreligious and was sufficiently impressed by the letter to take the unusual and expensive step of inserting a reply in the classified ads of the *Gazette de France*, which he hoped would be read in Russia. On 4 April, the paper carried the following lines, hidden away among advertisements from publishers and piano-teachers:

M. de B. has received the letter that was sent to him on 28 February. He regrets that the means of replying has been withheld, and though his wishes are not of a nature that permits them to be published here, he hopes at least that his silence will be understood.

This intriguing message which said so little and so much was the start of a correspondence that continued almost until the end of Balzac's life. It forms one of the most detailed diaries of an author's life ever written, and for anyone who tries to unravel a 'real' Balzac from all the characters of *La Comédie Humaine* and the personae of the letters, its survival seems to be an extraordinary stroke of good luck: what secrets might have disappeared in conversation had Balzac not conducted the greatest love affair of his life at a distance? But this should also make us wary: the letters to Mme Hanska are one novel among many, a novel with its own logic, its own ideal dénouement, its own inconsistencies and purple passages, and, of course, its own Balzac. Significantly, the earliest letters predate the fiasco with the Marquise de Castries. By launching a new affair before the other was over, Balzac was insuring himself against defeat with an emotional economy that is an exact parallel of his overlapping novels, each one feeding on the other, intellectually and financially; or, as the ex-businessman put it at about this time in his scrapbook, 'All my other passions were just a deposit for this one.'[4]

Another unsigned letter arrived from abroad that spring, and by May 1832, the mysterious Stranger had become 'the object of [his] sweetest dreams'. Balzac's 'unsullied' imagination was hard at work, fleshing out the figure that still had no name. Several times now he had caught himself 'galloping through space and flying to that unknown land in which you, a stranger, live, the only member of your race. I have imagined you as one of the invariably unhappy remnants of a people who were broken up and dispersed throughout this earth, perhaps exiled from heaven, but each with a language and feelings peculiar to that race and unlike those of other men.' Balzac was showing the mystery woman the part he expected her to play. His own role was clear: a man aged by experience whose heart had remained young, a writer condemned to hard labour by his desire 'to represent all of Literature by the sum total of my works' – 'and now', he went on, without any obvious attempt at irony, 'I am obliged to tackle every subject so as not to be accused of impotence'.[5]

Balzac's first letters to the unknown woman were the longest he had ever written. Each one contained a potted history of his mind, each one an outline for the autobiography he never wrote: his extreme sensitivity, his loneliness as a child, the evil circumstances that threw him into so many different professions, his powers of observation quickened by shyness and suffering. Balzac was spreading out his past life like a carpet in front of a potential buyer. To make his point as memorable as possible, he resorted to the famous image from Gray's 'Elegy written in a Country Church-Yard': the flower that is 'born to blush unseen, / And waste its sweetness on the desert air'. Gray's little flower is a hardy perennial of Romantic fiction. In *Northanger Abbey*, Jane Austen includes it among the soothing quotations that every heroine should know by heart. Balzac stamped it with his own inimitable mark: 'It may happen that you will never receive another letter from me; and the friendship you have brought into being may resemble a flower which perishes unknown in the depths of a forest, blasted by a thunderbolt!'

Balzac summons up such a tone of confidence and sincerity that it is as if they were already deeply in love, and it is here that one of the paradoxes of his writing comes sharply into focus. In his novels, such high-flown romantic language nearly always has an ironic undertone; in his letters, no such reticence stands in the way. The letters were a declaration of love and a dramatic sign of Balzac's faith in self-fulfilling prophecies. The correspondence would become a conspiracy, both writers setting the scene and establishing their respective characters with an urgency not always evident in Balzac's expositions. So much space lay between them that there was no point in being brief or holding back, especially when 'civilization itself is under threat' (a legitimist sentiment that might appeal to a rich lady living in Czarist Russia). To Balzac's delight, the woman replied in a similar vein. His soul, she supposed, must be centuries old, and his 'exterior must give little idea of his ardent imagination': 'You must be aroused, the sacred flame of genius must be kindled within you and then you appear what you are, and you are what I sense you to be: a man with superior knowledge of the human heart.' With her to protect him from pitfalls and temptations, his work would be more than sublime, it would be divine! Balzac had a strong impression of being fully understood.

By the spring of 1833, five or six letters had been exchanged, and when Balzac returned to Paris after Mme de Berny had nursed his wounded pride back to health, he had enough elements for what he admitted was an entrancing, even a destructive, fantasy: 'You have awakened several different forms of curiosity in me, and you are guilty of a charming coquettishness which I cannot find it in myself to condemn. You do not realize how dangerous it is for a lively imagination and a misunderstood heart, a heart that is full of rejected love, when it glimpses the vaporous form of a young and beautiful woman.' All he knew, or thought he knew about her (since his letters were being collected somewhere in Paris by an unknown messenger) was that she was young, solitary and living in the wilds of the Ukraine. She was a feudal princess surrounded by serfs, he decided, with a penchant for mysticism, above all unspoiled by 'our Parisian society which so violently excites the passions and where everything is at once so great and so petty'. He knew also that she was Polish – hence the reference to the exiled race: the Polish insurrection had been crushed by the Czar in 1831, and when refugees began arriving in Paris, Poland became the great political cause of the Romantics, the successor to Byron's Greece.

Gradually, over the next few months, Balzac discovered the truth and was thrilled to see that reality was equal to the dream. Eveline Hanska, the fourth of seven children, came from a historic Polish family, the Rzewuskis, many of them brilliant warriors, statesmen, adventurers and lunatics.[6] One of her ancestors bricked his mother up in a tower to obtain his inheritance; her father's cousin had become a Bedouin chief and led a revolt of the Cossacks against the Czar. Balzac's vision of her as 'the daughter of a land enslaved' was flatteringly inaccurate: Eveline's immediate family had thrown in their lot with Russia and avoided persecution. Her father had become a senator of the Empire. He was living in a medieval castle at Pohrebyszcze in the Ukraine when Eveline was born on 25 December – or, in the Gregorian calendar, on 6 January – sometime between 1801 and 1806. Her exact age has always been a mystery and she did nothing to clear it up. Balzac chose 1806 as her date of birth and he was probably right. In 1819, for the sake of the family fortune, she was made to marry a count, a dull and melancholy man more than twenty years her senior.[7] Wenceslas Hanski* was a creature long since extinct in France: he held sway over 3035 serfs (counting only males) on a 21,000-acre estate at Wierzchownia in the province of Kiev.[8] As Balzac later observed, the estate was bigger than a French *département* and the château itself 'a Louvre', filled with oriental carpets, Italian Renaissance masterpieces, huge mirrors and bearskin rugs in front of enormous fires. There were 300 servants and craftsmen, a small orchestra, a hunt, famous wine-cellars, a hospital and – its saving grace for Eveline – a well-stocked library. By comparison, the Marquise de Castries was a pauper. In front of the mansion was an avenue, a river and some houses; everything else was corn as far as the eye could see. Beyond the estate the roads were poor, the district was isolated and when there were no visitors or trips to Kiev and Odessa, it was miserable. There, Eveline spent the best part of her youth. She had a four-year-old daughter called Anna. Her first four children had died.

Receiving a letter from the man who wrote *La Peau de Chagrin* must have been one of the most exciting things that had happened to her, and perhaps, when she wrote to Balzac, she was thinking enviously of Caroline, her eldest sister. Caroline had left her ageing husband and had affairs with Mickiewicz, the Polish poet, and Pushkin; she was considered politically suspect. Eveline was a more dutiful daughter, but she too had dreams of being the guiding spirit of a man of destiny. It was practically the only career that was open to her. Balzac would be her distant soul-mate; he would also be a wonderful source of first-hand information on the glittering world of the literary capital. Until then she had had to rely on the gossip of her compatriots and relatives in Paris. One of them must have told her

---

* Hanski is the masculine form of the name.

about that unprepossessing 'exterior' that gave little idea of the novelist's 'ardent imagination'.

In retrospect, Balzac seems to have been part of Eveline's long-term plans – but only in retrospect. Some Balzac scholars, both male and female, have been over-protective of their hero, demanding unmotivated passion from his lovers and excusing his own infidelities in the name of artistic need. Eveline's 'crime' is that she was unfaithful to him after his death. In fact, without conflating different periods, there is little basis for judgment. All but two of her letters to Balzac have disappeared: after some of them were stolen by his blackmailing housekeeper in 1847, Balzac burned all the letters he had received.[9] What remains suggests a mixture of timidity and effusiveness: 'a heart that is forced to lock up everything in itself'; a well-read woman who was known for her intelligent conversation; great seriousness, even humourlessness, when it came to her own affairs; someone who had the obstinacy of a younger sister, a desire to devote herself to a cause, the fear of seeing her life pass by 'in a painful dream', and the fascination with the occult that was endemic in her family.

When Balzac saw his vision come to life in such a brilliant fashion, he began to imagine himself in letters to the Countess as one of her serfs, a peasant attached to his glebe, a *moujik* forbidden from ever setting eyes on the princess he serves. (She had told him they would never meet.) In these early letters we come closer than at any other point in the correspondence to catching Balzac in the act of invention, stirring his characters into life, teasing out a story from a handful of facts. George Sand envied him his ability, when conducting research for a novel, to take exactly what he needed and no more – even without a general notion of the end-product; he was innately efficient.[10] The initial idea was like a miniature universe which he inflated from the inside, expanding it until it seemed incapable of containing any more examples of his knowledge, but then somehow setting it all in motion. Even the most complex characters were purely functional at first; they were invented to serve the needs of the plot – administrative assistants who turned out to have interesting personalities. This is what Balzac was doing in his letters. By placing Eveline in the snowy steppes of Russia, he was fitting her into an imaginary domain that had been waiting for characters – a domain that had occasionally materialized in his work, in the 'Voyage de Paris à Java' or in the Asiatic vision of Saché. Beyond Western Europe, Balzac's geography was like an ancient map; Russia to him was part of the mysterious Orient.[11] Eveline would have been slightly ruffled to find herself pushed so far to the East: in her mind she was a misplaced European. By a curious coincidence, she asked if Balzac had ever known the model for Foedora in *La Peau de Chagrin*.[12] Balzac told her about the Marquise de Castries, but did not mention a poem he had planned to write, long ago, in the summer of 1823. The poem was set in the Russian Embassy in Paris where a young man called Georges falls in love with a Russian princess called Foedora: 'Before long they will be married', says the poet, and, despite Foedora's fondness for 'the bright gaiety of France', 'Georges wishes to return with her to the depths of the Russian forests'.[13] Another dream from the past was coming true.

Meanwhile, Eveline was setting out in the other direction. Early in 1833, she and her husband left with their travelling court of servants for Vienna where Wenceslas had grown up. The Government was stingy with its passports and M. Hanski received his on condition that none of his party set foot in France, 'that land of Jacobins'. That summer they travelled from Vienna to Switzerland, first to Neuchâtel, the home of their daughter's governess, Henriette Borel. A meeting was planned. Far from worrying about possible disappointments, Balzac continued to foster the image of himself as a virginal soul struggling to survive in the 'mud' of Paris. The image was tarnished somewhat a few months later when Eveline dipped into the *Contes Drolatiques*. Balzac panicked: 'Oh, my angel! One must have a heart as pure as yours to read *Le Péché Véniel* and enjoy it for what it is.' (What it is is a detailed account of what happens to an innocent young bride when she marries a lecherous ex-Crusader.) 'It is a gem of naivety,' he added hopefully.

Eveline realized that there was more to Balzac than he hoped would meet the eye, and her curiosity quickly became an engrossing challenge. She asked to see a picture of her immaterial lover, but Balzac had so far refused to have his person treated as a piece of public property. That year, he informed the editor of a St Petersburg magazine that his face was not available for consumption and that the art of lithography had been turned into 'a sort of apotheosis with a market value, prized by a civilization that has done away with any idea of a future life'.[14] To Baron Gérard, who asked to paint his portrait, he gave a different reason, saying, as he told Eveline, that he was not 'a pretty enough fish to be done in oil'.[15] As a favour to her, he agreed to be included in a collection of drawings by Auguste Régnier to form an album entitled *Habitations des Personnages les Plus Illustres de France Depuis 1790 Jusqu'à Nos Jours*. The drawing shows a very rural Rue Cassini, with the garden that had become one of Balzac's hobbies. At a window on the first floor, a male figure in a dressing-gown, too thin to be an accurate representation of the occupant, is reading a letter or a manuscript. A goat is tethered in the garden. When 'chained' to his desk by work, and when the image of Prometheus or a galley-slave seemed inappropriate, Balzac liked to compare himself to it: 'When will the capricious hand of fortune untie me? I do not know.'[16] Eveline found the goat image distasteful.

It was fitting that Balzac's face should remain invisible for the time being. The correspondence with Eveline is like an experimental novel in which the female protagonist is always trying to pull in extraneous realities but which the hero is determined to keep on course, whatever tricks he has to use. As in a work of art, the end justified the means. His friendship may have been 'strong and sincere', as he claimed, but there was the sincerity of the novelist – whose 'spirit' was forever making the journey to Russia, spending huge amounts of mental 'postage, by the fireside' – and the constantly beleaguered goodwill of the letter-writer, whose body was not always the servant of his spirit. In the autumn of 1832 Eveline was unpleasantly surprised to receive a letter written in an entirely different hand. Balzac had asked Zulma Carraud to help him out and, together, they had concocted a reply. The offending letter has never been found and was presumably destroyed by Eveline. In fiction, Balzac was a brilliant unraveller of plots. In reality, he was a little more clumsy; but even then the devices that allowed him to tie up loose ends became the pretext for another story. 'You asked me rather distrustingly about my two different scripts; but I have as many different styles of handwriting as there are days in the year – without being in the least bit fickle. My inconsistency comes from my having a mind which can imagine everything and yet remain pure, like the looking-glass which is tainted by none of the objects it reflects.' This was partly true: Balzac's handwriting does sometimes change from one sentence to the next, and some of his experiments in calligraphy show that he would have made an excellent forger. Moreover, as the letters show, the forger improved in relation to the detective's skill.

THE LETTERS from the mysterious princess gave Balzac a new reason to throw himself into his work. With every month he began a new countdown to 'freedom'. Soon, all his debts would be paid and he could travel to Switzerland. He woke at one in the morning, worked until eight, took a nap for an hour and a half, then drank a cup of coffee and worked again until four in the afternoon. During dinner, he received visitors, which is probably why there are so many descriptions of Balzac eating, or rather shovelling food into his mouth and spraying it about the table. He ate from his knife like a peasant. Immediately after dinner, he went to bed on a full stomach. Dreams provided him with useful material and he found that problems with characters or plot often solved themselves while he slept.[17]

Balzac had a knack for finding ironic images of himself in history and mythology: the walking Prometheus or the lupin-eating Protogenes are typical examples. In January, as he prepared for a long bout of writing, he compared himself to Empedocles, who, it is said, cast himself into the crater of Etna in order to start a rumour that he was divine.[18] In a more optimistic mood, Balzac turned up at a masked ball held by Alexandre Dumas in April 1833 dressed as Phoebus.[19] He had decided to dazzle the literary world with a new novel called *Le Médecin de Campagne*. He worked on it for the best part of a year, from September 1832 to September 1833. The original version, conceived in a flash at the Grande Chartreuse and composed in the heat of frustrated passion, was modified and expanded and, like many of Balzac's revised texts, scrubbed clean of its most blatantly autobiographical elements. Once again, he was going to surpass himself; he was tired of being thought an immoral writer. *Le Médecin de Campagne*, like its predecessor *The Vicar of Wakefield*, would have 'the simple beauty of the Gospels', it would be read by concierge and *grande dame* alike, and, like the Gospels, it would have an enormous readership. He wanted it to sell 'like prayer-books',[20] and in order to achieve his goal, he brought to bear his whole arsenal of publishing tricks. The first edition would be anonymous, carrying a picture of

Jesus stumbling under the Cross instead of the author's name (though there was a quotation from a certain 'De Balzac'), and then the second edition, hot on its heels, would be given an extra boost when the author's name appeared on the title-page.

Sure enough, Balzac's plan received a mark of divine approval. Just as he was telling Mme Hanska that he was writing an updated version of *The Imitation of Christ*, she, in her role as his 'good conscience', was posting a copy of the book to him. When it arrived, Balzac saw a mysterious sign: 'How is it that you thought of sending it to me just as I had the idea of dramatizing contemplative poetry? The holy book was flying through space, accompanied by its sweet procession of thoughts, and reached me just as I was launching myself into the delicious realms of a religious idea and', he added, to stress how indispensable she had become to him, 'despairing of ever completing this magnificently charitable work.'

Like the letters to Mme Hanska, *Le Médecin de Campagne* is a disconcerting example of Balzac's dual sincerity, of his ability to bring together several motives in a single action. The story of a mountain village dragged out of the Dark Ages by a reforming doctor, purged of its population of cretins, trained to compete and amass wealth, and weaned on to a more sophisticated diet ('a butcher in a village is a sign of intelligence'[21]), was placed on the Academy's short list for the Prix Montyon. This was a prize awarded each year as a reward for virtuous fiction; the winner received a 'medal of encouragement' and a large sum of money. Balzac later denounced its implicit hypocrisy, its encouragement of vapid moralizing and self-centred philanthropy, though he also entered one of his novels for the prize in 1841, calculating that the prize-money would pay off one-third of his debt.[22] In 1833, he drafted a short prefatory note for *Le Médecin de Campagne*[23] in which he chided the late Baron Montyon for failing to grasp the obvious fact that virtue was its own reward: Montyon's ill-considered prize was the kiss of death for any self-respecting writer. Instead, there should be a prize for genius – which is probably why, in 1833, Balzac said he wanted to spend the prize-money on a statue of that least virtuous of writers, Rabelais, to be erected in the public square at Chinon.[24]

When the winner was announced, Balzac saw his *Médecin de Campagne* pipped at the post by *Le Petit Bossu* (*The Little Hunchback*), an impeccably virtuous novel by a Mlle Ulliac-Trémadeure who wrote stories for children.[25] One reason for the Academy's decision was political: Balzac was advocating policies that would nowadays sound like the manifesto of an ecology party on the far Right. The newspapers took a different view and greeted the novel with what Balzac was keen to see as 'torrents of insults' – actually just a trickle of disappointed reviewers who found it boring, dogmatic and over-stuffed. Even now, with its interpolated disquisitions on irrigation, agronomics, public health and town-planning, *Le Médecin de Campagne* is a delight mainly to those who like to see Balzac spreading himself out in his own novel. (Significantly, one of the longest digressions is centred on a meal.) For all his plans to corner the market in piety, Balzac had refused to capitalize on his readers' expectations; and this is why, like so many of his novels, *Le Médecin de Campagne* improves with familiarity. Most novelists of the time give the impression of having measured out a small quantity of ideas in advance, to be used in the confection of the story. Balzac continues to pour, regardless of the container, while still in the act of creation, and almost every paragraph contains the ingredients of several other novels. Read with Balzac's own criteria in mind, it was a success: 'You set out to write a tale', he told the poet Émile Deschamps after reading his latest short story, 'and ended up going further than you first intended, like all great minds who (if you'll excuse the analogy) always widen the hole through which they pass because of their enormous size.'

If *Le Médecin de Campagne* had won the Prix Montyon, it would have been a travesty of conventional justice. For Balzac now, 'virtue' was tied up with his reputation and fortune. It was a literary challenge, appealing to those few remaining souls who were too simple to find excitement in 'the poetry of evil'.[26] Eveline Hanska and Laure de Berny acted as guarantees of his moral intentions, and so, while the objective voice of social concern dominates in the novel, the correspon-dence gives a quite contrary view of the work in progress.

There is probably little point in separating out Balzac's motives. The cohabitation of the ideal and the practical is the chief reason why his friends found him so funny – or, if their own interests were involved, immoral. Just as the smallest incident could give rise to a story, so a grand idea could suddenly be reduced to a tiny, immodest motive. The novel was autobiographical at one remove. Balzac was using it to solve the problem faced by the country doctor: is it possible to enjoy the benefits of modern civilization without sacrificing the virtues of poverty and suffering? For Balzac, the answer was yes.

From here on, the line between his public and private life is not always easy to find. His perennial debts, increasing whether or not he had time to spend money, seem more and more like an excuse to give his whole life over to work. The editor Armand Dutacq reports that Balzac once sat down with him to solve the problem of perpetual motion, and thought he had succeeded, until he realized that the machine was 'two horses short'.[27] Something of this sort of approach is apparent in the slightly lopsided phrases of the letters to Eveline – phrases whose reason strikes one almost at the same time as their oddness: 'I have the same scorn for money that you yourself profess. But money is indispensable and that is why I am going to work all out on the great and extraordinary enterprise that will burst onto the scene in January.'

The great enterprise was the forerunner of *La Comédie Humaine*. Entitled *Études de Mœurs au XIXe siècle*, it would include nearly all of Balzac's novels and stories divided into four series: *Scenes of Private, Provincial, Parisian* and *Country Life*. The first allusions to this partly prefabricated monument date from the middle of 1833. Balzac begins then to refer to his *œuvre* in the singular – a seemingly small deviation from the norm which was felt, however, to be either ridiculously far-sighted or intolerably pretentious, as if he were trying to admire himself from beyond the grave.[28] *La Comédie Humaine* itself was still a few years off, but the great scheme was already casting its shadow over Balzac's daily life.

Mere dates, perhaps . . . In April 1833, for the first time in ages, he took a rest and did almost nothing. Since his near-fatal accident in 1832, he had been suffering occasional bouts of depression and inertia; he decided to spend the month at Zulma's house in Angoulême. The correspondence falls silent. 'My doctor ordered me to remain, like Nebuchadnezzar, as an animal. And I did.'[29] Then, in May, he thought of the *Études de Mœurs* and was able to return to work.

At least in its infancy it was more than just an aesthetic idea. There is a marvellous expediency in all of Balzac's plans and this is perhaps his closest resemblance with the country doctor. Why does Benassis decide to become a doctor rather than a priest or a politician? 'Because,

Monsieur, when a peasant is ill and lying helpless on his sick-bed or recovering from an illness, he is forced to listen to logical arguments. . . . It was this consideration that made me a doctor.'[30] Similarly, Balzac's great project made several virtues out of necessity. First, by transforming his published writings into building-blocks instead of milestones on the way to an ultimate masterpiece, it gave him the courage to continue what was started. Everything he did now would contribute to a greater whole, like investments in a savings scheme. Second, it provided him with ancillary tasks which could be performed without the aid of inspiration: correcting, revising, rearranging. Finally, it allowed him to repackage and resell his products. The revelation of his *œuvre* marks an important change in Balzac's life, as important as the discovery of the Eastern princess. He could live now with a clear view of perfection – perfection in the sense of an ideal, but also in the sense of completion, embodied both by Eveline and the work to be.

For this reason, the new novels Balzac was writing tend to disguise an important feature of his work: he was now spending a large percentage of his time revising earlier works – *Physiologie du Mariage*, *Le Dernier Chouan*, *La Peau de Chagrin* – and it is no longer possible to think of him simply disgorging stories on to the page. For the rest of his life, he continually reworked his own creations, living with his own past and making improvements to it. It was a chance to redeem his mistakes and to see his achievements in a more objective light: 'At the moment', he warned Eveline (and future readers of his correspondence), 'I am in the paroxysm of composition and shall only have good things to say about the novel. When it's done, you'll be hearing all the lamentations of the man who sees nothing but mistakes.' Here at last, the Christian contrition of *Le Médecin de Campagne* is matched by the tone of its author. 'You are my audience,' he told Zulma, 'you who have the courage to help me extirpate the weeds from my paddock, you who exhort me to improve myself.' Instead of the futile belligerence of his sessions with Latouche, there was a new eagerness to garner criticism, from wherever it came, and it was this that had helped to turn the painfully personal confession into a novel of self-improvement. He began to use the services of a proofreader who specialized in grammar. He came along, 'scalpel in hand', and found 'a thousand errors' in *Louis Lambert*: 'Alone in the evening I cried with despair and with that rage that takes hold of you when you recognize your faults after working so hard.' When he visited Laure, he took along the proofs of his latest novel. His two nieces, aged ten and twelve, cut them up and pasted them on to large sheets of paper, leaving plenty of room for Uncle Honoré's corrections. To help them with their French, he got them to mark what they thought were mistakes with a little cross and then he would explain the finer points of grammar. Sometimes they went too far: 'The nieces became purists and discussed the text like M. Chapsal . . . swelling with pride which the master saw fit to repress.'[31]

Sometimes, he invited criticism for other reasons. Running up to her apartment on the Quai Saint-Michel, he deposited piles of proofs with George Sand and read hers in exchange – not that she was ever known for grammatical accuracy. Her recollection of these sessions in a letter to Flaubert in 1866 is interesting because it sounds very much like a lesson learned from Balzac: 'Neither person changes as a result. Quite the contrary. Usually one becomes more firmly rooted in one's conviction. But in so doing one expands it, explains it more clearly and develops it to the full.'[32]

Le Médecin de Campagne is the first novel written under this new regime and its supposed defects are probably a direct result of it. Balzac was distracted by his preoccupations, eager to give his *œuvre* a strong moral structure. It is significant that the episode which became instantly famous is also the part in which a character most completely takes over from the author. The 'Life of Napoleon Told by a Soldier of the Imperial Guard to Peasants in a Barn' was published separately in June and promptly stolen by unscrupulous publishers. The anonymity ruse rebounded: 20,000 pirated copies were sold, according to Balzac. Criminals made good judges. *La Bataille* was never written, but the 'Life of Napoleon' – from Corsica to Saint Helena in 7000 words – is a little epic in itself, a miracle of concision in an ever-expanding universe.

The other, more visible change in Balzac's life, as he dug himself deeper into work, came in his professional affairs. He had begun to establish himself as a publisher's nightmare. Each publisher in turn – Charles Gosselin, Louis Mame and, soon, Edmond Werdet – found himself sucked into a story of Balzac's making, the conclusion of which was always supposed to be the victory of the novel itself.

Balzac refused to see these 'merciless' tradesmen as his equals: they were servants of his reputation. He thought, quite rightly, that he was promising them a share of immortality. Gosselin was the first to suspect he must have stumbled into a different reality and was either dealing with a crook or with what Baron Rothschild described from the financier's point of view as 'a very frivolous man'.[33] The frivolous man, it appeared, had had another reason for wanting *Le Médecin de Campagne* to be anonymous. It made it easier for him to wriggle out of a contract with Gosselin which specified that Balzac's next five volumes should be published by him. Ignoring the terms of the contract, Balzac sold *Le Médecin de Campagne* to Louis Mame, and when Mame wondered why he did not want his name to appear on the cover, explained: 'In all conscience, I cannot put my name to it seeing that I have signed an agreement with Gosselin; and in spite of all the slanderers I wish to remain a man of honour.'

This is a less celebrated aspect of Balzac's legal training: for him, contracts only became binding after a court case, but they were a useful form of persuasion. 'You, Monsieur', fumed Gosselin, 'have a legal code for your own personal use when you deal with publishers, and since I am familiar only with the normal one, I failed to notice yours. I am ashamed of my ignorance!' Gosselin agreed to several new deadlines, and when he complained, Balzac, full of patience and sweet reason, told him that, whatever the law might think, no one could write a book in such a short space of time. Books were not pieces of cloth. Some other course of action, 'more worthy of us both', should be found. If Gosselin grew too impatient – and he was not the most accommodating of publishers – Balzac kept to the moral high ground. He asked for no apology, 'and though I am very sensitive to any injury that is done me, I am sometimes able to forgive and forget'. He had an answer for everything. If the publisher refused to reprint his novels, he was chided for his small-mindedness. If he insisted on the terms of a contract, Balzac gently reminded him that 'for men of worth, mere money is not a sufficient reward for their labours'. Gosselin's letters understandably became more cold and official, and then Balzac pointed out, to his amazement, that 'for some time now the harmony which should exist between an author and his publisher has been lost. . . . It dawned on me that you had no wish to continue doing business with me.' Gosselin finally gave up, which is precisely what Balzac wanted.

There was an element in this of Balzac's fondness for winding people up to bring out the best or the worst in them. He was a keen observer, but he was also adept at producing the sort of behaviour that was worth observing. Advances and deadlines were also a risky way of keeping his nose to the grindstone; and even without that, his procedure is not quite as cavalier as it seems. There was an underlying motive which few publishers were likely to accept as an excuse but which was really quite a good reason to behave aggressively. Whatever his particular circumstances, Balzac was conscious of being a privileged member of a persecuted minority and instead of just complaining about it, he tried to improve things. The following year, he published a magisterial *Lettre Adressée aux Écrivains Français du XIXe Siècle*. A milestone in the history of French publishing, it formed the basis of future copyright law and was the first step towards the founding of the Société des Gens de Lettres. It also persuaded the public that Balzac was France's leading writer, or so he claimed himself, with an honesty not always associated with literary campaigners. In the *Lettre*, he asserts the moral right of authors to their own works, asking simply that the law protect the products of the mind as it would a bale of cotton. Belgian publishers were stealing novels as soon as they appeared in magazines, and the pirated copies, which were sold quite openly in France, often came out before the official first edition – the only one for which the author received royalties. Novels were adapted for the stage without the author's consent and huge profits could be made at his expense. Everyone in the book trade was the agent of a great injustice.

In Balzac's mind, therefore, no matter what he did when dealing with publishers or other 'parasites', right was on his side. Driving them to distraction was part of a noble campaign. Sometimes, he dreamed up interesting forms of revenge. In 1835, two plays based on *Le Père Goriot* were performed simultaneously in two Paris theatres. As usual, the author of the original book received nothing. Balzac decided to make an example of it and invited the cast of both plays to celebrate the first night, which had been a great success, at the Château de Madrid restaurant in the Bois de Boulogne. A carriage picked up the actors and actresses outside the theatres and left the playwrights and directors standing on the pavement.[34]

On other occasions, the conviction that injustice had been done brought out a violent side to Balzac's character which was not entirely sublimated in his work. The champion of law and order was quite capable of behaving like a hooligan, and this apparent anomaly has proved unsettling enough for some critics to ignore it or pretend that the evidence is inconclusive; however, the evidence is quite clear and someone who was so good at inventing criminal minds should certainly be granted responsibility for his criminal actions.

On 1 August, Mame took Balzac to court. He was still recovering from bankruptcy and had finally grown tired of waiting for the rest of *Le Médecin de Campagne*. Balzac was annoyed at Mame's refusal to publish it in one prayer-book-sized volume. Naturally, Balzac lost and was ordered to deliver the manuscript as agreed. He decided to appeal, but in the meantime, as the *commissaire de police* reported, he went down into Paris at dawn to his old printing-shop where the book was being set in type. At 6 a.m. he was let into the building by his old partner Barbier and then spent the whole day carefully messing up the formes which were waiting to be printed; the whole book would have to be reset. 'Branding has been abolished for criminals,' he wrote, somewhat ironically in the circumstances, 'but the pen will scar that human scorpion with an indelible mark of infamy.'

Eleven hours of painstaking destruction could hardly be called an unpremeditated act. Nor could Balzac's smashing of a bookshop window in the Palais-Royal when he spotted a pirated edition of one of his novels.[35] On each occasion, he was happy to pay for the damage: he was defending his 'children' and making his point with the same energy in destruction that he showed in creation. Nevertheless, not all his violent acts can be attached to altruistic motives. There is no mistaking the thrill of imaginative vandalism in his account of the sadistic pranks played by 'the Knights of Idleness' on the inhabitants of Issoudun in *La Rabouilleuse*; nor, a few years later, in his repeated demolition of his neighbour's garden wall at dead of night.[36] Even in his writing – the puns and alliterations of the *Contes Drolatiques*, a chapter in *Physiologie du Mariage* that consists entirely of random sequences of letters – creation and destruction were never far apart.

ON THE EVENING of 22 September 1833, three weeks after *Le Médecin de Campagne* went on sale, Balzac left Paris. He told Zulma that he was going to Besançon to find the special paper he needed for his book club. The other story he used was that he was going to Rome, and it was true that he was setting out on a kind of pilgrimage.

Without stopping to sleep, he stayed with the mail-coach and reached the 'sombre' and 'prudish' town of Besançon[37] on the morning of the 24th. He was welcomed by a young journalist, Charles de Bernard, who had been writing admiring reviews of Balzac's novels in the local press and who could claim to be his first literary disciple: Bernard's novels were considered for much of the nineteenth century to be a 'safe' alternative to Balzac.[38] The master was in a hurry. He toured the town with Bernard, failed to find the paper he needed, and left the same evening. Crossing the Juras, he descended into Neuchâtel the following day through the wild scenery of the Val de Travers, feeling more than ever like 'the hero of a love story'. He took a room at the Hôtel du Faucon, slept in a bed for the first time in four days and awoke feeling more refreshed than he did when he left Paris.

The Hanski party had rented a large town-house called the Maison Andrié. Its garden lay at the foot of the fashionable promenade that led up the promontory known locally as the *Crêt*. From the top there was a view of the lake. Balzac sent a note announcing his arrival: 'I shall go to the promenade and remain there from one until four; I shall be looking at the lake which I have not seen before.' He was frantic with impatience. As he left the hotel, a beautiful woman passed by in the street: 'How strange if it were her,' he thought. (It was, he later discovered.) Then he walked to the Maison Andrié, crept silently into the courtyard, 'whose smallest pebble is engraved on my memory, its long planks and sheds', and looking up, saw a face at a window. 'I could no longer feel my body,' he told her later, 'and when I spoke to you I was in a daze.'[39]

That afternoon they met above the lake. Eveline recognized him at once. He was short but larger than life, charming but always on the verge of vulgarity – obviously the author of his novels, and yet. . . . 'Balzac is very like you,' she told her brother in what is probably her most revealing letter.

> He is gay and cheerful and lovable just like you. There is even
> an external resemblance and both of you look like Napoleon. . . .
> Balzac is a real child; if he likes you, he tells you so with the candid
> openness of that age when one has yet to learn that words are for

disguising one's thoughts. . . . When one sees him, it is hard to imagine how so much knowledge and superiority could go hand in hand with so much freshness, grace and childlike naivety in heart and mind.[40]

To Balzac, she was even more beautiful than he had dared imagine. 'We're twenty-seven years old,' he confided in Laure,

we're ravishingly beautiful, we have the most beautiful black hair in the world and that soft, wonderfully delicate skin of dark-haired women. We have an adorable little hand, the heart of a twenty-seven-year-old, naive – a real Mme de Lignolle [the virginal heroine of a libertine novel whose husband is impotent[41]] – and reckless enough to throw her arms around me in front of everybody, not to mention colossal wealth. But what's that compared to a masterpiece of beauty?

It is interesting to note that each was delighted with the other's 'naivety'. They were obviously a perfect match.

With their exiles and tourists, the cities of Switzerland were the switchboards of international gossip. The 'dreadful Marquise de Castries' heard of Balzac's good fortune and was jealous, or so he gloated in his letter to Laure.[42] Unfortunately, he was happy only in mind. He was so charming that he also won over Wenceslas: 'A dratted husband didn't leave us for a single second in five days. . . . Neuchâtel is a little town in which an illustrious woman from abroad cannot move without being seen. I felt I was in a box at the theatre. Restraint is not my *forte*.' Relief came during an excursion to Rousseau's retreat on the island on the Lac de Bienne. Wenceslas was sent to organize lunch and there by an oak tree they stole a kiss and made feverish plans: Balzac would cross the uncharted plains of the Crimea and the Ukraine; she would contract an illness that could only be cured in Paris. They were both simultaneously disappointed and elated. The Hanskis were leaving to spend the winter in Geneva; but they promised to meet again before the end of the year.

On 1 October, Balzac woke at 5 a.m., walked up to the *Crêt* and looked down on the sleeping Maison Andrié for half an hour. There was no sign of life. That morning he left Neuchâtel on top of 'a sort of chicken-coop', wedged between five Swiss peasants 'like a beast being taken to market', but still managing to admire the scenery. At Besançon, he spent the day with Charles de Bernard and the town librarian (a friend of Charles Nodier), who heard that the famous novelist had gone to Switzerland to chivvy some debtors who were behind with their payments. . . . The trip had clearly done him good: 'His overall appearance is rather modish yet tasteful. He talks well – unpretentiously and incoherently.' 'The subject on which he talks best and with the greatest pleasure is himself. . . . He wants to be crowned the King of Literature, and will be in six years' time. Then his role as a writer will be over and he will go into politics, etc., etc.' As for Nodier, 'he will disappear without trace because he has failed to organize his works into a whole'.[43]

Back in Paris, Balzac entered one of the busiest periods of his life. Everything was going well. An honest, intelligent publisher his own age, Louise Béchet, agreed to bring out the *Études de Mœurs* in twelve volumes. Shortly after, she handed Balzac over to her employee, Edmond Werdet, the most willing and obsequious victim a writer could ever hope to meet. Balzac resumed work on a short novel called *Eugénie Grandet*. It was to be the greatest critical success of his career – so successful that he almost regretted writing it: reviewers were always asking why all his novels couldn't be as simple, chaste and classically restrained.[44] Balzac drew Eveline's attention to the love story: the devotion of Eugénie to her Cousin Charles. Defying her miserly father, she presents the wastrel with her little treasure of gold coins, just as Eveline had secretly given money to Balzac for his debts. But Balzac could transport the same emotional experience into very different bodies. By his own admission, Balzac is also Grandet himself, gloating over his treasures, valuing them in proportion to the cunning used to acquire them and the damage done to his rivals. Grandet is not simply an object of moral condemnation nor even just an example of destructive economic practices; he embodies a vital force, an *idée fixe*, and this is where Balzac rises above the sentimental novelists of his day. The stroke of genius at the end is that Eugénie does not die a martyr's death but lives on to become the daughter of her father's obsession: 'The pale cold glint of gold was destined to suffuse that saintly life and lead a woman who was all feeling to look upon any show of affection with distrust.'[45] In *Illusions Perdues*, a grief-stricken

Lucien de Rubempré writes bawdy songs over the corpse of his mistress; Balzac wrote a tragedy in the midst of great happiness.

The most spectacular result of the flood of creativity that followed Neuchâtel is the story of a travelling salesman, 'the illustrious Gaudissart', who sounds and looks like a cartoon Balzac and whose statue now stands in the centre of Vouvray: 'saturated with the vices of Paris, he can affect the *bonhomie* of the provinces'. An excellent mimic, as fluent as a hot-water tap, with a pear-shaped stomach and a face like a pumpkin, little legs but surprisingly agile, Gaudissart travels to Touraine to sell life insurance. A local wag in Vouvray directs him to the home of a well-known madman. What follows is a *tour de force* in which each man has what he thinks is a rational conversation, but on entirely different topics: a strong echo here of Balzac's correspondence with his publishers.

The story of this hero of modern times had an unusual origin which makes the author seem even closer to his character. Mme Béchet's printer had chosen too small a fount, which meant that one of the volumes that were to make up the *Scènes de la Vie de Province* was eighty pages short. To fill the gap, Balzac improvised the story of Gaudissart in a night. Of course, it had been gestating in his brain and writing it down was only the physical part of the job. But still, if he worked, as usual, from 1 a.m. to 8 a.m., and since *L'Illustre Gaudissart* contains about 14,000 words, then he averaged 33.3 words a minute, which is about the same rate as a slow typist. Writing at this speed, he wore out more than just a few pens. On 23 November, he recorded the fact that the thing which kept him company at night – his chair – had fallen apart, thus providing us with the clearest indication of what he actually looked like when writing: 'That's the second chair I've had shot out from under me since launching the present battle.' Proof, perhaps, of Balzac's theory that mental energy transfers itself to the material plane.

Despite the 'battle', he was still finding time to write long letters to Eveline. All of them are written in a tiny hand, because large packages were likely to be held up at customs; and all of them extend to the limits of every page. (Whenever she left a blank space at the end of a letter, he wondered if she still loved him.) Writing these passionate, witty letters was an exhausting break from writing novels.

It was, he said later, like a French colonel writing home during the Retreat from Moscow.[46] But then Eveline had a gift for eliciting urgent replies. She teased him about his reticence during their excursion to the Lac de Bienne and wondered why she had not been asked for a lock of her hair. Because, said Balzac, he wanted enough to make a chain for her miniature portrait but did not wish to 'plunder that dear head I worship'; he was like Buridan's hungry ass, starving to death between two equidistant haystacks. As with Mme de Berny, however, he felt quite capable of devouring both at the same time – the ideal and the physical: 'How I adore your thick accent, your generous, voluptuous mouth, if you'll permit the expression, my angel of love. I am working night and day so I can go and spend a fortnight with you in December. I shall cross the Juras when they are covered in snow, but I shall be thinking of the snowy-white shoulders of my darling.' Balzac was beside himself with anticipated happiness. His love was like a plant, 'spreading out its palms and branches' in his soul; he was a bird, 'building its nest one twig at a time, playing with a wisp of straw before bringing it back to the nest'. In fact, other plants had already begun to poke through the soil and he was already lining other nests.

JUST BEFORE Christmas 1833, Balzac set off for Geneva with the manuscript of *Eugénie Grandet* in his bag. Just over a year had passed since he left the city in disgrace and humiliation. Now, he was referring to his second meeting with Eveline as the 'dénouement'. The rewriting of the Marquise de Castries disaster novel was almost complete.

He had been intending to revel in revenge by staying in the same cheap hotel room he had occupied in October 1832. Compromising with convenience, he settled in the Auberge de l'Arc which was close to the Hanskis' house in the Pré-Lévêque quarter. There were dinners, excursions, gifts – a ring for Balzac, a coffee-maker and *cotignac* (quince paste) for Mme Hanska – and secret trysts at Balzac's *auberge*. Balzac later remembered their 'terror' at being found out. One particularly momentous meeting, the precise details of which escape us, occurred on 26 January 1834. On that 'Unforgettable Day', he received some incontrovertible proof that he was loved – among other things, it seems, an early offer of marriage. (Wenceslas Hanski was not in good health.) And, of course, they visited the Villa Diodati and spent a day 'which erased the thousand griefs I felt there a year before'.[47]

A few weeks later, Balzac was correcting the proofs of *Ne Touchez Pas la Hache*, the story inspired by the Marquise de Castries. On the last page, he inscribed the magic date: '*Genève, au Pré-Lévêque, 26 janvier 1834*'. It marked a victory over the past and, he hoped, the beginning of a new era.

CHAPTER ELEVEN

Family Planning

(1834–1836)

FTER FORTY-SEVEN days of bliss, Balzac returned to Paris in
early February 1834, crossing the Jura Mountains on foot and
plunging into a morass of domestic complications to which
the expression 'a bachelor's life' hardly does justice. The letter in which
he enthused to Laure about his beautiful Countess contained the
following bombshell – dropped in passing, without so much as a new
sentence:

> . . . another secret I have to tell you is that I'm a *father* and am now
> responsible for the sweetest person, the most innocent creature that
> ever fell like a flower from heaven. She comes to see me in secret,
> without asking me to write or take care of her, and says, 'Love me
> for a year and I shall love you all my life!'[1]

The identity of the mother of Balzac's child remained a mystery
for many years. Luckily, in his desire to mark the event, he left clues.
The second edition of *Eugénie Grandet* was dedicated to a certain
'Maria' whose name had already appeared in the epilogue of the first
edition and whose 'portrait', said the author, 'is the finest ornament of
this work'. In addition, the manuscript reveals that a reference to
Maria's 'motherhood' was removed before publication. The Balzac
scholar, Spoelberch de Lovenjoul, guessed that 'Maria' might be the
Marie Du Fresnay to whom Balzac bequeathed a statuette of Christ
on the Cross in 1847.[2] Several decades later, two other scholars
decided to find out if he was right.[3]

Family archives are not always thrown open to people bent on
uncovering an illegitimate line, especially if the cuckoo in the nest was
someone famous. However, the nephew of Balzac's child was happy
to confirm part of the hypothesis in 1946. Maria Du Fresnay, born in
1809, was the daughter of a minor novelist, Adèle Daminois. Among

her papers was a copy of the second edition of *Eugénie Grandet* in which the dedication to 'Maria' first appeared. Strangely, the page bearing the dedication came from an edition of the novel that was not published until 1870, twenty years after Balzac's death. An inspection of the binding showed that it had been sewn in with violet thread. Presumably what happened was this. When Maria received the book with a compromising inscription from Balzac, she tore the page out in case her husband found it. Then, some time after her husband died in 1866, she took the dedication from the later edition and restored her name to its rightful place. The fact that she did this almost forty years after offering herself to Balzac suggests that she kept her promise: 'Love me for a year and I shall love you all my life! . . .'

Balzac was delighted with the news – so delighted that he was calling himself a 'father' long before the child was born, in the same way that he pronounced novels 'finished' as soon as he thought of writing them: Marie-Caroline was only conceived in September 1833, before Balzac left for Neuchâtel, and was born in Sartrouville (where the château belonged to M. Du Fresnay) on 4 June 1834. The nephew remembered hearing from his Aunt Marie-Caroline that Balzac attended her first communion and often returned to see her, asking about her progress and playing with her. This tallies with two brief allusions in letters to Eveline much later in 1848, when old secrets could be told: 'I love Anna [Eveline's daughter] incomparably more than that little girl I see every ten years'; 'two messages invited me to *meet* Mlle Marie tomorrow at two o'clock in the Champs-Élysées so that I can see how beautiful she has become'.[4] The verb *rencontrer* is underlined, implying that, like so many secret lovers and fathers in *La Comédie Humaine*,[5] Balzac had to be content with a passing glimpse, a 'chance' encounter in a busy place. Curiously, only six months after Marie was born, in another premonitory scene, he showed Old Goriot tottering along to the Champs-Élysées on sunny days to watch his daughters pass by in their carriages.[6]

It is not absolutely certain that the child was Balzac's, but it is certain that he thought she was. A portrait of Marie-Caroline as a young woman offers no scientific proof of paternity, but one can certainly say that the imposing, generous face, large head, emphatic nose and dark, communicative eye is definitely not proof of the contrary. The mother herself was remembered by her grand-nephew as a large, unattractive, rather masculine woman with a pock-marked face; but Balzac saw her with the eye of a father, and though few novelists, as Swinburne said, are so cruel to their 'children', Balzac could also be more loving than any of their fellow characters, even in his microscopic portraits. 'I am not pretty enough for him,' thinks Eugénie when she falls in love with her handsome Cousin Charles:

> The poor girl did not do herself justice. . . . She had a very large head, the masculine yet delicately sculptured head of Phidias's Jupiter. . . An attack of smallpox, too mild to leave a mark, had slightly swollen the features of her oval face that was once so fresh and rosy. . . . Her nose was a little too prominent but in perfect harmony with a bright red mouth whose lips, with their thousand little lines, were full of love and kindness. The curve of her breast, though carefully concealed, caught the eye and stirred the imagination. No doubt she lacked the elegance imparted by fine clothes . . . but she possessed that beauty that is so easily missed and which only artists can appreciate.[7]

All this secret history was contained in the manuscript that Balzac took to Eveline in Geneva; but though she wondered about some of the women he portrayed, she seems not to have been jealous of Eugénie Grandet. Balzac could be as ingenious as any critic when discussing the models of his characters. At the end of the novel, he managed to dedicate it to both women at the same time, and the epilogue stands as a tribute to his efficiency in love affairs and his ability to love more than one woman as 'the only one'. He confessed that some aspects of the story may be exaggerated but begged the reader's indulgence for 'the patient monk in his cell, a humble worshipper of the *Rosa mundi*, of Mary, beautiful image of all her sex, the monk's bride, the second Eve of Christians'. Eveline was like Mary and Maria was like Eve, and both women would be flattered. 'Allow me to abbreviate your name,' he asked Eveline, 'that it might say more clearly that you are for me the only woman in the world.'

The day after hearing of Maria's pregnancy, he wrote to Eveline with 'some good news': on Tuesday, the *Études de Mœurs* would be bought by his new publisher. The future masterpiece had a home. And she shouldn't worry so about the small hiatus in his correspondence: he thought of her all the time and her suspicions were dishonourable. 'Love cannot survive without trust.'

In the circumstances, this was obviously quite true, if applied to Eveline. In the letter to Laure, he went on to list all the other women in his life who could not be told that he was a father: Zulma, the *Grande Madame* (Henriette de Castries), Mme de Berny, 'who guards me more jealously than a mother her baby's milk'. And then, muddying the water still more, he mentioned a mysterious creature who has never been identified and probably never will be: 'nor can I tell *her* who demands her daily ration of love and who, though she's as voluptuous as a thousand cats, is neither gracious nor a woman'.[8]

It is slightly unsettling to see Balzac's habit of enumeration applied in this way to real people: five women in a single paragraph. First, because it suggests a capacity for casual relationships more fleeting than many of those he has with his characters. Second, because the sudden increase in domestic detail hints that much more must remain hidden: what if Laure had obeyed her brother's instruction to burn the letter ('I have no wish to cause the slightest unhappiness by my indiscretions')? That year, Liszt told his lover, the Comtesse d'Agoult, of Balzac's belief that 'a man is not truly complete unless he has seven women': one for the home, one for the heart, one for the brain, one for the household, one for whims and follies, a woman to hate, and the woman one pursues but never catches.[9] The complexity of Balzac's life seems to have increased along with his capacity to cope with it, and it is quite possible that his opinion of what constituted a complete man simply reflected the current state of affairs.

The arrival of a child made no appreciable difference to Balzac's daily routines, but events conspired to strengthen his sense of fatherhood: the birth of Marie-Caroline in June, the memory of little Anna Hanska – most letters to her mother contained greetings from her 'horse' (meaning himself) – and then that spring, a visit to Issoudun, 140 miles south of Paris: 'a place that would have made Napoleon lethargic'.[10] Zulma's husband had retired from a life that was already a form of retirement and they had gone to live on her father's estate in Issoudun. A long, tree-lined avenue led from the town to a former convent called Frapesle set in 'English' gardens;[11] Balzac was given two rooms at the far end of the house. Zulma was pregnant with her second child, a boy lugubriously christened Yorick. She worried about the 'cretinization' that seemed to go with having babies, but Balzac found plenty to interest him and conceived the *Mémoires de Deux*

Jeunes Mariées, one of the last epistolary novels of French literature, eventually published in 1842 with an unprecedented wealth of detail on the realities of motherhood, from cracked nipples to post-natal depression, the pros and cons of nappies and the problems of communicating with a troublesome, semi-literate creature. A Rousseauist approach to the practical side combined with a realistic philosophy for the essentials which shows the appeal that little children had for Balzac: 'A child is a great politician one seeks to master, as one would a real politician – by exploiting its desires.'[12]

As for his real family, they were all 'off their heads', or so he told Eveline after wasting five and a half hours with them over dinner on his return. In practice, his notion of family responsibilities was entirely negative: like Bernard-François, he felt that a good father was one who was not a burden to his family. Now, however, the tables were turning. His mother never stopped worrying about money; she would have to be treated like a child, and he would have to have 'courage, ideas, energy and *thrift* for everyone'. (Thrift meant borrowing large sums from old family friends.) Then, in June 1834, little brother Henry turned up like a bad penny. It was not a wise move. The youngest child had nothing to show for his stint in the colonies but a pregnant wife, a stepson and almost no money. The following year, Honoré-Henry-Eugène was born. Balzac was happy that his line of the family would continue and bought his nephew an expensive cradle. Then he hatched a plan for Henry that was almost certain to fail and used his connections to put it into practice. His dependants would be shipped off to the Seychelles while Henry went about trading in the Indian Ocean. For Balzac, unattainable targets were a useful discipline, but Henry was immune to the lure of challenge: the first solution that occurred to him was suicide. Instead, he was persuaded by his brother to return to a life of hard work and poverty.

Henry's decline and fall provides a splendid example of Balzac's habit of taking one of his characters as the model for a real person. Shortly before urging Henry to head back East, he had been writing the closing scene of *Le Contrat de Mariage*. Ruined and humiliated by his wife and mother-in-law, Paul de Manerville sets sail for the Indies.[13] Too late, he opens the letter in which Henri de Marsay convinces him that 'Paris is still the land in which fortune flows most freely' – which is what Balzac himself believed. But by that time the ship is south of the Azores: 'What have I done to them?' he asks himself. 'This question', comments the narrator, 'is the question of an idiot, the sort of thing that occurs to a weak-minded person who, being blind to everything, foresees nothing.'[14] Henry was actually a competent town-planner; he helped redesign the capital of Réunion but fell victim to changes in the administration and ended his days as a surveyor in 1858. He died at the military hospital in Dzaoudzi on the Comoro Islands. His son – the last recognized descendant of Bernard-François – died on Réunion six years later, jobless and unmarried. Balzac had continued to offer sporadic support, but it is hard to avoid the conclusion that he helped his brother meet the sticky end that he, as a novelist, had decided he deserved.

Not all of Balzac's family feelings in the mid-1830s can be explained as a desire to exert influence. In his letters, there is less and less of the child and more of the man who regrets losing his sense of irresponsibility. His solitude in work was threatening to become real loneliness. Mme de Berny turned fifty-eight in May 1834. It was a sad spring. 'That light of my life', 'the heart that created me', 'my conscience and my strength' was failing. She was seriously ill, taking digitalis for her heart, exhausted from nursing her children, for whose sake she had left her husband. One daughter died in July, another had gone mad and been sent to an asylum, and 'her most beloved son', Armand, was on his death-bed. Her face, Balzac said, aged twenty years in a month. He was powerless: 'I tried magnetism on her, but my hand only increased the inflammation.'[15]

Le Lys dans la Vallée, one of the great neglected novels of Romantic literature, would be Balzac's farewell to the woman who was 'my whole family' – 'a life that is also one of my works'. His last stay at La Bouleaunière came in October 1835, when he read her the novel. It must have been a moving performance: *Le Lys dans la Vallée* ends with the death of Mme de Mortsauf, the spiritual mother of the young hero and a recognizable portrait of Mme de Berny. Before her death, pained by the hero's affair with an Englishwoman, Mme de Mortsauf refuses to see him. Balzac had turned Henry into a character; now he saw Mme de Berny imitating the character he had based on her. After October, Mme de Berny told him that they ought never to meet again. She died in July 1836 when Balzac was en route for Italy. A few months later he changed the ending of the novel exactly as she had asked him to do and softened the passage in which Mme de Mortsauf regrets at the last not having left her family for her lover. The scene of the novel is the Indre Valley close to Saché; it was there, in Balzac's mind, that Mme de Berny was buried.

In view of this continual farming out of family affections to other people, it would be easy to see Balzac's insistence on the crucial role of the Family in society as ironic, even hypocritical. But he had good reason to admire the idea of a family whilst rejecting it in practice. In childhood, he had learned to divide his feelings into different compartments, each one consistent with itself, like a novel. He was able then to be a son to several different mothers. These emotional compartments might be seen as the secret of his productivity – or as an object lesson in coping with rampant egotism. Memory is the mother of the Muses, but, says Balzac, forgetting is the secret of all great lives – forgetting like Mother Nature, 'which constantly renews the mysteries of her indefatigable procreation'.[16]

In his games of hide-and-seek, his experiments with fatherhood and his simultaneous lovers, even in the loss of Mme de Berny, one senses that Balzac had reached the open sea, with all sails out, a stiff breeze behind and a handy set of different flags to fly from the mast. A secret life, like adultery, was a powerful drug for the imagination, a great producer of plausible stories; and behind it all was a plan of action devised, perhaps instinctively, by someone who was used to seeing himself as one man against a multitude. The concentration of desiring energy, as every Balzac reader knows, increases its power a hundredfold. More than that, it allows the desirer to escape detection: 'In order to conceal one's thoughts, one must have only one. All complicated minds are easy to read, and that is why great men are always fooled by someone who is inferior to them.'[17] This concentration was not to be confused, however, with the single-mindedness of the peasant or the brute: 'Never will any mind have existed in so many different spheres,'[18] he boasted to Eveline, referring to the great novels of this period – *La Recherche de l'Absolu*, *Le Lys dans la Vallée*, *Le Père Goriot*, *Séraphîta*. 'I am forced to be ten men at the same time, with several spare brains, never sleeping, always being happily inspired and' – a seemingly impossible concomitant – 'refusing to be sidetracked.'[19]

*

As USUAL, Balzac looked to literature for an answer to his problems. With crises in his real and elective families, he set about exploiting the full potential of his fictional tribe. Recently, he had made a discovery so exhilarating that he ran all the way to Laure's house on the Right Bank and burst in shouting, 'Hats off! I am about to become a genius!'[20] He had suddenly realized that the same characters could be made to reappear in different novels and a self-sufficient universe created: the ultimate assertion of independence. A few writers before him had toyed with the idea of recurring characters, but no one had thought of applying it to their entire life's work. It was particularly exciting since, as Proust points out, the idea of recurring characters was indeed a discovery not an invention.[21] For six years, Balzac had been building a world that already had its own internal coherence and woke up to find himself the father of a gigantic family.[22]

Immediately, he set about making the necessary adjustments. Paul de Manerville first appeared as a minor character in *La Fille aux Yeux d'Or* before starring in *Le Contrat de Mariage*; but even before *Le Contrat de Mariage* was completed, Balzac made Paul's unfaithful wife, Natalie, the addressee of the letter which forms *Le Lys dans la Vallée*. Natalie's lover in turn crops up in *Le Contrat de Mariage*. As he revised them, earlier works were drawn into the system: *Le Bal de Sceaux* was written six years before the character was created, but when Balzac returned to it in 1842, Paul de Manerville was cited among the possible suitors for Émilie de Fontaine. Given the connection between Paul and brother Henry, it would be interesting to know what happens to him after he leaves for the Tropics in 1827; but, just as Henry effectively disappears, so does Paul de Manerville. Later allusions to him refer only to his life before 1827.

Once the ground was prepared, the roots and branches spread rapidly: twenty-three recurring characters in the first edition of *Le Père Goriot*, forty-eight in the later editions.[23] Family relations were established (the genealogy of Balzac's characters covers three walls of a room in his house at Passy). Year by year, his own universe took over from the real one. Events and characters from other stories were used increasingly as points of comparison as if they were historical fact. Real people were replaced by equally 'real' characters, especially in the final, large-scale correction of his complete works. Victor Hugo or Lamartine become Canalis, Delacroix becomes Joseph Bridau, and this wholesale conversion is one reason why Balzac's novels can still be read without constant reference to explanatory notes. It should be said, too, in light of Arthur Conan Doyle's assertion 'that he had never attempted to read Balzac, because he did not know where to begin',[24] that each novel can be read without any knowledge of the others, and they can be read in any order.

The main disadvantage of the system of recurring characters (though also a point of interest in itself) lies in the inconsistencies which Balzac never had time to iron out:[25] Rastignac undergoes a marked personality change between *La Peau de Chagrin* and *Le Père Goriot*; the Baron de Maulincour – related to Paul de Manerville by his grandmother – is poisoned by Ferragus in mid-1819 but admired that November by Rastignac in the company of some 'illustrious upstarts'; La Palférine is born three years after his father's death. Some characters change the colour of their eyes or hair, though, remarkably, Balzac's physiognomic science tends to remain consistent: Paul de Manerville is first depicted as a thrusting young dandy with black hair and blue eyes like Rastignac and De Marsay. In *La Comédie Humaine*, these are the attributes of characters who control their own destiny and, at the time, Paul seems bound for social success. In *Le Bal de Sceaux*, his hair is blond – a clear mistake by Balzac, but one which reflects the character's change in status: men with fair hair, like Lucien de Rubempré, tend to lack will-power and usually fall prey to domineering personalities. Paul's nefarious mother-in-law, for instance, has black hair and dark eyes.[26]

The tiny number of errors – visible only to readers armed with 100,000 filecards and proportionately insignificant compared to those of other novelists – prove that Balzac's characters were as real to him as if he were observing them in the outside world. In any case, the advantages are enormous. We get to know these characters in exactly the same way we become familiar with real people, little by little, by personal acquaintance or hearsay, learning of their childhood some-times many years after first meeting them (a process Proust termed 'retrospective illumination'[27]), discovering that we already know their friends or relatives, or finding out how they became so undeservedly rich. The illusion of three-dimensional reality proved to be so convinc-ing that while some readers are said to have doubted whether an individual called Balzac actually existed, others went to see the home of Ferragus in the Rue de Soly,[28] and an English lady (perhaps seeking a cure for mild psychosis) wrote to Paris for the address of that brilliant physician Horace Bianchon,[29] who appears, on and off duty, in thirty-one different stories.

By treating his characters as people who change and grow old, Balzac launched the novel into a new dimension – passing time, where life and death are real but where the novelist himself offers a kind of redemption: 'Shall I tell you something strange?' Goriot says to Rastignac in the novel which introduced the device of recurring characters to most readers. 'When I became a father, I understood God. He is everywhere in his entirety because creation came from him. That, Monsieur, is how I am with my daughters. Except that I love my daughters more than God loves the world, because the world is not as beautiful as God and my daughters are more beautiful than I.'[30]

It may actually be possible to identify the precise moment at which Balzac had his revelation. Laure claimed that the discovery coincided with the publication of *Le Médecin de Campagne*. This would place it at the end of 1833; but since *Goriot* is the first work in which the system plays a major role, it was always assumed that Laure's memory was at fault. However, hidden away in *Le Médecin de Campagne* is a crucial detail that may well have been the spark that sent Balzac rushing out into the street.

One inhabitant of the village reformed by Benassis is a man called Ginestoux. Ginestoux is the sole survivor of the fifty soldiers who formed the bridge over which the remnants of Napoleon's army crossed the Beresina during the Retreat from Moscow in 1812. Just before the novel came out, Balzac changed the character's name to Gondrin. Perhaps it was then that he remembered a story he had published in 1830 – *Adieu* – where a solitary survivor of the Beresina crossing was fleetingly mentioned, 'living, or rather suffering in a village in utter obscurity'.[31] Obviously, Gondrin and the previously unnamed character must be the same person. . . .

Gondrin could therefore claim to be the first of Balzac's 593 recurring characters. An obscure beginning, but not an unworthy one if the device that allowed Balzac to consolidate his own empire was inspired by an unsung hero of Napoleon's Russian campaign. And by a nice coincidence, there were actually *two* survivors of the Beresina crossing,[32] which means that Gondrin the pontoneer is also part of the bridge thrown between history and the world according to Balzac.

FIFTEEN MONTHS separated Balzac's stay in Geneva from his trip to see Eveline in Vienna at the end of her European tour in May 1835. Fifteen months during which he became a busy socialite and a prominent *habitué* of the Austrian Embassy in Paris. Eveline's cousin Marie Potocka had given him a letter of introduction to the Ambassadress, Thérèse Apponyi, and Balzac's future trips across Europe would be punctuated by visits to embassies and châteaux. For someone with connections, it was a much smaller continent than it is today, and the sheer convenience of knowing the right people makes Balzac's fascination with aristocrats seem a highly practical sort of obsession. In the same period, he started work on *La Recherche de l'Absolu*, in which a fanatical scientist twice sends the family fortune up in smoke in his search for the principle of matter; *Séraphîta*, the story of an angel, half-man, half-woman, passing through its final earthly transformation in the fjords of Norway; and then, on a visit to Saché in the autumn of 1834, his best-known, most widely translated novel, *Le Père Goriot* – the masterpiece of his early middle age as *La Cousine Bette* is the masterpiece of his premature old age.

When the first instalments appeared in the *Revue de Paris* at the end of 1834, *Goriot* had expanded from the story of a father whose obsessive love for his daughters survives their worst betrayals to include the corruption of young Eugène de Rastignac by one of literature's most memorable felons, Jacques Collin. In *Goriot*, Collin, an escaped convict, is living in Mme Vauquer's run-down *pension bourgeoise* ('for ladies, gentlemen and others') under the name Vautrin.

When a critic accused Balzac in 1846 of having dredged up Vautrin from the depths of his diseased imagination, Balzac assured him that the model existed, implying that he had been inspired by his meeting with the famous convict-turned-detective, François Vidocq.[33] As former head of the Sûreté, Vidocq might not have been terribly pleased. That April, Balzac and Alexandre Dumas attended a dinner held by the philanthropist Benjamin Appert.[34] The other guests were Lord Durham, Lord Privy Seal of England, Henri Sanson, the executioner of Marie-Antoinette whose 'memoirs' Balzac had written, and Vidocq himself. Balzac found Vidocq's company delightful and often refers to his amazing deductive powers. In particular, he recorded something Vidocq told him at the dinner: 'All the criminals he had arrested went from one to four weeks before recovering the ability to salivate.'[35] Which gives a certain authenticity to his psycho-physical portrait of Vautrin in *Le Père Goriot*: 'The very way in which he spat out a stream of saliva revealed an imperturbable sang-froid, suggestive of someone who might commit a crime in order to wriggle out of a tight spot.'[36]

In one important respect, however, Vidocq is quite unlike Vautrin. In his memoirs, Vidocq made it clear that he hated homosexuals. Vautrin, on the other hand, is drawn to Rastignac by sexual desire, coupled with a passion for imposing his will: with Vautrin's covert assistance, Rastignac is to scale the highest peaks of society and the criminal will enjoy his vicarious revenge.

It is interesting that this novel of sexual obsession, depravity and corruption should have become so firmly entrenched in syllabuses in the English-speaking world. It is also a great shame that so many readers owe their first (and often last) contact with French literature to the opening pages of *Le Père Goriot*. Anyone who was forced to decipher the long description of the Pension Vauquer word by word in a classroom might remember it as a small novel in itself: actually it lasts for about twenty-five pages in which Balzac not only sets the scene but also introduces all the characters. But to be told so soon that the novel may not be understood by anyone who lives beyond 'that illustrious vale of flaking plaster and gutters black with mud' (i.e. Paris) is not encouraging; and Balzac's encyclopedic vocabulary makes learning French in *Le Père Goriot* like learning to swim in treacle, especially since not all of Balzac's words can be found in dictionaries. Comparisons with *King Lear* gave the novel a kind of moral respectability. It was also felt to contain, in its introduction, the best example of Balzac's famous theory that people and the objects that surround them are organically interrelated:

> Mme Vauquer's ageing, puffy face, with a nose stuck in the middle like a parrot's beak, her dumpy little hands and body plump as a church rat's, her bulging, shapeless bust are in harmony with this room where squalor oozes from the walls and intrigue crouches in the corners. Mme Vauquer breathes its warm and fetid air without

being sickened by it. . . . Her whole person, in short, explains the boarding-house just as the boarding-house implies the existence of a person such as she.[37]

Show me the coat-hook, Balzac says elsewhere, and I will show you the boudoir.[38] Nowadays, the theory sounds more mystical than scientific, and even in Balzac's day, when the queerness and individuality of things were beginning to vanish, this type of depiction, later developed by Émile Zola to the point of paranoia, was felt to be one of the novelist's little idiosyncrasies. (The *Gazette des Femmes* parodied it by telling the story of a house whose walls were so thin and damp that it died of a chest complaint.[39])

The final irony is that the fame that placed the novel on so many reading-lists also gave rise to a number of excellent translations, which means that *Goriot* is one of the novels of *La Comédie Humaine* that can safely be read in English for what it is.

For us, it mirrors and to some extent explains the darker side of Balzac's adoption of the father's role. Just as he was dreaming up Vautrin's memorable seduction of Rastignac – an episode which, like so many of his most subtle scenes, he never mentions in his letters – Balzac was taking on a secretary: the twenty-three-year-old Jules Sandeau,[40] young, impressionable, attractive, and proof that Balzac's new inclination for younger people was not confined to women.

In a later incarnation, Vautrin seduces Lucien de Rubempré just as Lucien is about to kill himself. Similarly, Balzac caught Sandeau on the rebound from his lover, George Sand, who left him for the poet Alfred de Musset. The boy was in a pitiful state; he had taken an overdose of morphine but was saved by his weak stomach. When Balzac returned from Saché in October 1834, he moved him into the Rue Cassini. They would write comedies together and pay each other's debts. Sandeau was a doll with working parts: 'He will be housed like a prince; he can't believe his luck. I'm launching him in the masterpiece business with a thousand *écus* of debts and a bottle of ink as security. Poor child, he doesn't know what being in debt is! He's free and I'm enslaving him – it saddens me.'[41]

Sandeau turned out to be a bad mistake. In March 1836, he 'fled' from the Rue Cassini, unable to rattle off the books Balzac wanted him to write (though he subsequently became a quite prolific and popular novelist), leaving Balzac with still more debts. 'You can't possibly imagine such laziness and lack of urgency,' he complained to Eveline:

He has neither energy nor will. . . . No dedication in body or spirit. When I had spent on him what a great lord might spend on a whim and placed him in my lap and said, 'Jules, here is a play: please write it. And after that, another one, and then a vaudeville for the Théâtre du Gymnase', he told me it was impossible for him to be anyone's disciple. Since the implication was that I was trying to cash in on his gratitude, I didn't press the point.[42]

Sandeau had become a Balzac character without knowing it, almost a surrogate son who would be fun to train but ultimately disappointing. Laure remembered discussing her brother's characters with him – perhaps she knew that real lives were involved: 'Sometimes we would ask him to be lenient with a young man who was going to the bad. "Don't muddle me up with your sentimental scruples. Truth must come first. Those people are weak and incompetent; what must be must be. It's just too bad for them." In spite of all his bluster, their downfall did still cause him some grief!'[43]

Balzac's grief at losing Sandeau was tempered by the arrival at the end of 1835 of two new '*aides-de-camp*': Auguste de Belloy and Ferdinand de Grammont. Both men were in their mid-twenties, both were legitimists and therefore, Balzac supposed, less likely to agonize over the means employed to reach an end. Inevitably, they, too, proved to be 'weaklings' though not entirely useless. Belloy ('very jolly, badly behaved, horribly poor'[44]) provided Balzac with the plot and some of the text of the short story, *Gambara*, while Grammont devised and illustrated a magnificent series of coats-of-arms for all the families in *La Comédie Humaine*.[45] When the time came to revise his novels, Balzac inserted the appropriate heraldic descriptions – meaningless without a glossary but impressive all the same. The motto on his own coat-of-arms, filched from the Balzacs of Entragues, was one that might have wrenched a smile from the exhausted Sandeau: 'Day and Night'.

Even without Eveline's worry that Balzac 'had a crush' on Sandeau,[46] or the insinuations of the Duchesse d'Abrantès regarding his '*intimate friend*',[47] Balzac's recruitment of young helpers would give pause for thought. His correspondence in the mid-1830s constantly reminds one of the more sinister aspects of Vautrin as he leads Rastignac astray under Mme Vauquer's linden trees. Throughout this period, he refers to his 'androgynous genius', his 'woman's heart', his 'maternal' instincts; he wonders if Nature has not 'made a mistake'. When talking of his compliant character or his inability to resist temptation, he compares himself to a whore. He even adopted a false name – Widow Durand – and played games with his female persona: 'I shall flirt now only with men,'[48] he told Eveline in a dubious attempt to set her mind at rest when she picked up more gossip about his womanizing. When a young writer called Alfred Nettement asked him to contribute to a legitimist newspaper he was launching, Balzac replied in the bantering tone of Vautrin. The paper interested him: 'It is normal for women to take a strong interest in young things.'[49] His secretaries joined in the game and were obviously encouraged to do so. Sandeau addressed him as 'darling' ('chéri'),[50] as did a later secretary, Laurent-Jan, who signed off with the phrase, 'I press myself against your mighty breast'.[51] Grammont offered his services as a man 'who loves you now as no lover ever loved his mistress . . . as no angel ever loved God'.[52] The word 'angel' had homosexual connotations which Balzac had exploited in Vautrin's talk with Rastignac: 'If I were to give you just one more piece of advice, my angel, it would be this: don't stick to your opinions any more firmly than you would to your word.'[53] On the one hand, these allusions can be seen as a recognition that such master–pupil relationships often have a sexual component; in Balzac's case, they were also a product of that erotic energy that had once expressed itself in abject worship and was now barely distinguishable from a need to manipulate and mould.

He can hardly have been surprised, therefore, when friends started calling him 'Vautrin'.[54] They were thinking not only of Balzac the slave-driver but also of Balzac the man-about-town. In 1835, he employed a diminutive groom or 'tiger' to drive his coach and christened the boy Anchises[55] (perhaps because the mythical Anchises was a horse-thief in his youth). Anchises died soon afterwards as a result of an operation on an infected knee paid for by Balzac, who had left him out in a rainstorm. Nothing suspicious about that. Except that Balzac, as a mark of his grief, immortalized the groom in *La Maison Nucingen* as the little toy-boy of a Parisian dandy, with dark hints that the boy had been forced to leave England when his previous employer was accused of pederasty.[56] Unusual behaviour was in fashion. Balzac himself stirred up rumours so effectively that Gautier later talked of his fondness for 'vague pederasts',[57] and according to another friend, Philarète Chasles, he was said to share the taste of Emperor Tiberius for infants trained to cater to his sexual needs in the bath.[58] These rumours probably reflect a facet of Balzac's character rather than a personal habit; but they certainly reflect his portrayal of a society that was increasingly abandoned to market forces, where rich men have their carriages driven about by little cherubs 'with blond hair like a Rubens virgin'.[59] Balzac's admiration of decadent lifestyles was largely unaffected by his condemnation of the politics that allowed them to flourish.

In some ways, he had fewer scruples than Vautrin. His willingness to spend time and money and his tyrannical generosity are beyond doubt. Yet Vautrin's 'maternal' devotion to a young man's social ambitions contrasts with Balzac's dedication to his own cause. After signing the contract for the *Études de Mœurs*, he persuaded a twenty-seven-year-old novelist, Félix Davin, to write a massive introduction to his complete works – a guided tour among the galleries and domes of the unfinished cathedral. Davin knew he was employed as a hagiographer and did his best; but Balzac had to keep 'reprompting and recorrecting' him.[60] Eventually he snatched the pen and, as Davin's manuscript shows, added large slabs of unmitigated praise: 'The mind is amazed', breathed Balzac, 'by the concentration of so many qualities – for M. de Balzac excels in all things.' Davin's conclusion was subjected to the same treatment: 'And so may his onward march proceed, may he complete his work, never heeding the envious cries of critics whose measuring-stick can register only minute imperfections, not the beauties of the whole! May he forge ahead, for he knows his final destination!'[61] Some of this was false arrogance: in a world of inflated egos, only the most extreme form of self-absorption would be a memorable advertisement; and as Balzac knew from observing writers like Dumas and Hugo or the stars of Parisian salons, there was something irresistible about conspicuous egotism.

This ambiguous sponsoring of his young helpers can perhaps best be appreciated by considering the improvements he found time to make to his own image. He let it be known that his ambition was to possess 365 waistcoats;[62] he 'invested' in expensive trinkets, and had a magnificent walking-stick made for him with enormous tassels and 'an ebullition of turquoises' around a sculpted golden knob. The stick now occupies a cabinet in the Maison de Balzac like the totem of a forgotten religion – one of the most popular items with visitors and, like many famous monuments, surprisingly small. 'It has had more success in France than any of my works', Eveline was informed. His friend the painter, Auguste Borget, heard about it when passing through Italy;[63] it was said to have magical powers; without it, Balzac would be an ordinary mortal. Caricaturists were delighted. Extravagant walking-sticks came into fashion. 'They think I'm a frivolous man,' he complained and added – frivolously – 'I find it all highly amusing.'[64]

Balzac's walking-stick even inspired a novel by Delphine de Girardin, who had recently tried to patch up a quarrel between Balzac and her husband by proposing that they have an affair. *La Canne de M. de Balzac* is a silly romance in which Balzac's 'enormous cane' confers on the holder the power of invisibility.[65] (The notion of phallic symbols had yet to imprint itself on the popular imagination.) Balzac reported all this to Eveline: 'You must excuse me, but it seems the stick will be a matter of biographical interest.'[66] One is reminded of the feeble young man in Balzac's *Un Début dans la Vie* (1842), 'dazzled' by his fellow traveller's 'elegant cane with its golden knob'; but even geniuses who began their life in hardship, Balzac goes on to say, are prone to such puerile admiration.[67] Balzac was revelling in fame and the appearance of fortune in a very Vautrinesque fashion, exulting in stupidity and conducting a human experiment with those 'seven or eight hundred fools who make up society'.[68] The experiment was a great success. The widow of Benjamin Constant invited him to tea so she could admire his 'prestigious Talisman that fascinates every eye'.[69] It accompanied him to the Austrian Embassy where foreign diplomats stared at him 'like a beast from a distant land'.[70]

In one sense, the walking-stick actually did confer invisibility. Balzac's face and figure began to appear in the papers just as he began to withdraw from public life. These scraps of 'biographical interest' were sops thrown to journalists and scandal-mongers. Balzac saw himself as Alcibiades amputating his dog's tail lest the Athenians find something worse to say about him: 'They are making fun of my *abdomen*. Fine – that's all they have to laugh at.'[71]

1835 WAS A YEAR of 'blatant luxury and secret destitution' – a phrase that could easily be applied to France in 1835. Balzac had turned himself into a sign of the times. Like Vautrin, he presented himself as the product of a government that tried to make its citizens fit society instead of forming society for the people and thus allowed the rare exceptions to rise above it.[72] For all his apparent jollity, his social life – manufacturing anecdotes and writing his own biography – shows a deep-seated cynicism which is shared by his most lucid characters, whether good or evil. Unlike Dickens, Balzac is not a novelist who considers virtue or sentimentality a sufficient excuse for ignorance. Both the villainous Vautrin and the saintly Mme de Mortsauf provide their protégés with the same dispassionate view of society:[73] a set of laws, most of them unwritten. Learn what they are, turn them to your advantage and keep your true self hidden away where it can retain its purity. 'Enter that mass of people like a cannon-ball, or creep amongst them like a plague.'[74] Balzac's brutal training of his secretaries was a form of practical advice. With the pleasure of passing on experience and observing its sometimes disastrous effects on others, there was a paternal desire to gather a fresh family about him and to prepare his disciples for a world which divided humanity into 'the deceivers and the deceived'.[75] It was here that Balzac was at his most didactic and dictatorial. The moral influence exerted through friendship would always be more important to him than any literary imitations. Besides which, he knew that as a novelist he was inimitable.

1835 also brought a change that seems to remove the last shreds of safety-net between imagination and reality. By now, the conservation of that secret self was more than just a rearguard action. In letters to his various *confidantes* – none of whom had his entire confidence – his 'true self' had to be endlessly re-created. His life's work was all planned out; but what of the person who was to write it? And what of his original motives for writing? He was still unmarried, still in debt and still spending up to eighteen hours a day at his desk. Balzac usually seems too whole-hearted ever to be in two minds about anything, but sometimes he wondered what work was doing to his personality. He occasionally alludes to a peculiar feeling that his destiny was being worked out somewhere else, 'that something good or bad is happening to me, that it's about to happen and that I am not where I should be'. 'My friends have often seen me turn pale at the sound of a horse-whip singing out too loud; they would see me rush to the window and ask me what was wrong, and I would sit down again, trembling and depressed for several days.'[76]

That year, as if obeying an instinct of self-preservation, Balzac decided to create a concrete symbol of his inner sanctum. Mme Vauquer had her *pension*, Balzac would have his *boudoir*. In March, he vanished: 'I have taken an axe and severed all ties. Three days from now, I shall disappear into a cell that will be impenetrable even to my family.' He had rented a house at 13 Rue des Batailles in what was then a quiet suburb on a hillside west of Paris – Chaillot, an area of gardens and small vineyards. Balzac had the top floors and the attic; the apartment below was empty. The house was cramped and dilapidated, but as the visitor passed along a dismal corridor there suddenly appeared a view of the kind Balzac liked so much – the Seine, the Invalides, the Champ de Mars, all of Paris from Montmartre to the newly constructed Arc de Triomphe – 'a window dominating the city I want to dominate myself'. He stuck a 500-franc note on the wall and scribbled a note to the workmen: the money was theirs if they finished on time.[77] They were to install a soundproof *boudoir*, decorated in a style which suggested great luxury but which, on close inspection, was a tinselly, glittering illusion: against a curved wall at one end, a 50-foot Turkish divan, red and black wallpaper imitating silk with a Corinthian column design, candelabra on the walls, a chandelier on the ceiling, white marble ornaments, chairs covered in cashmere, a rug pretending to be Persian and, of course, a secret door. An estate agent might have sold it as a brothel.

Balzac described his *boudoir* in *La Fille aux Yeux d'Or* and the description was reproduced in a women's magazine as a source of handy hints on home decorating.[78] Balzac had become an arbiter of elegance. The same magazine passed on fashion tips culled from Balzac novels, and rich people all over Europe were furnishing their homes *à la Balzac*.[79] Understandably, when the *Journal des Dames et des Modes* quoted the description of the boudoir, it did not include the context:

the very feminine Henri de Marsay, possessor of 'a body that would not have disgraced a woman', is seduced by the daughter of a slave from Havana called Paquita Valdès. She makes love to him in the boudoir and, at the climactic moment, cries out the name of the woman she loves. Her female lover – who turns out to be De Marsay's half-sister – stabs her to death in a jealous rage, which enables De Marsay to observe the pleasing effect of red on white furnishings.[80]

In the story, Balzac attributes to the depraved Paquita the sacred words pronounced by Maria Du Fresnay: 'a single day with you . . . will be worth a whole lifetime'.[81] This seems an incongruous use of autobiographical material, but then the boudoir was a magical place: it acted as a portal allowing traffic to pass between Balzac's real and imaginary worlds. His publisher, Werdet, claims that Balzac used it to seduce a woman he met at a masked ball at the Opéra.[82] Eveline, on the other hand, was told that 'several men' had 'obtained the favours of respectable women' at the Opéra ball by pretending to be Balzac.[83] Gautier remembers being asked to stand in the room and shout at the top of his voice in order to test the soundproofing, for a reason which 'modern prudishness forbids me from stating'.[84] In Balzac's letters, the boudoir also brings up a figure from the past, strangely different from his recent portrayal of her. The Marquise de Castries, the woman who supposedly had 'destroyed' him, was invited to come and pose like a bird or a fairy on the divan in a tone that leads one to suppose she had finally relented.[85] And when he dedicated *Gambara* to his secretary, Auguste de Belloy, Balzac reminded him of the hours they had spent 'by the fireside in a mysterious and splendid retreat which no longer exists but which will live in our memory'.[86]

All this makes one wonder at Balzac's assertion that he was withdrawing into his boudoir because his much-talked-about social life was 'about to turn [him] into an ordinary man'.[87] Ostensibly, he was escaping from a growing pack of creditors, as well as from the sergeant-major who was supposed to make him do his National Guard duty – a dentist by trade: Balzac's least favourite profession.[88] But the boudoir was more than just a quiet place to work. Necessity became a pretext for more fantasies. Callers were required to memorize a series of passwords: 'Plums are now in season' placated the concierge; in the hall, 'I bring some Belgian lace', whispered to the servant, and finally, to the maid, 'Mme Bertrand is in good health'.[89] These games became more and more elaborate as the situation became more precarious, and these extreme precautions betray a growing discomfort with the world outside work, beyond 'the gates of ivory through which my soul escapes into the land of illusions'.[90] The practical purpose was lost: he could hardly have gone into hiding more ostentatiously.

While Balzac was living in his fantasy room, the creditors were closing in, but the fictitious 'Widow Durand' was hard to track down. In April and May 1835, he stayed at an unknown address in Meudon in the woods to the west of Paris where he finished *La Fille aux Yeux d'Or* and wrote a preface for the second edition of *Le Père Goriot*, defending it against critics who accused him of immorality. Then, on 9 May, he left for Vienna where he was to see Eveline for the last time until 1843. For most of the visit, he was writing and revising, emerging briefly, thanks to Eveline's connections, into the light of Viennese society.[91] He was introduced to Chancellor Metternich and lived up to his reputation, as a member of the local nobility reported: 'His conversation is not what one would call conversation . . . for he never pays the slightest attention to what one says to him.'[92] After visiting the site of the Battle of Wagram with the Austrian General, Prince Schwarzenberg (more research for *La Bataille*), he left Vienna on 4 June, passed through Munich on the 6th, sniffing at its frescoes, 'most of which are on a par with our café decorations in Paris', and returned to his hideaway on the 11th.

A YEAR AND A HALF before, on his return from Geneva, he discovered he was a father-to-be. A similar piece of news appears to have followed his return from Vienna. This time, the woman was not the sad provincial flower portrayed in *Eugénie Grandet*, but a beautiful, lively, prominent aristocrat. At the soirées of the Austrian Embassy in Paris, he had 'fallen under the spell' of an Englishwoman: Frances Sarah Lovell.[93] 'Sarah', as Balzac called her, was born in 1804 near Malmesbury in Wiltshire on an estate just large enough for the family to call themselves landed gentry. In Bath, she had married an Italian count, Emilio Guidoboni-Visconti. Like Wenceslas Hanski, he was a kind and unexciting man, an amateur apothecary who spent his time sticking coloured labels on to little bottles. Like most husbands whose wives were courted by Balzac, he was either impotent or seriously inattentive. He was also so friendly and tolerant with Balzac that one wonders whether he really had any cause for complaint.

Unfortunately Sarah and Eveline had several acquaintances in common in the diplomatic world and Eveline was quick to confront Balzac with the rumours. His anglophobia – as much a reaction to the unheroic, conciliatory foreign policy of Louis-Philippe as a firm prejudice – had a sudden resurgence, and dual-purpose phrases like this began to appear in his work: 'Englishwomen are either extremely beautiful or horrendously ugly.'[94]

With her tall, majestic figure, ash-blonde hair and (according to Balzac) un-English openness, Sarah fell clearly into the former category. Balzac was discreet enough to make it difficult to retrace the beginnings of their affair; but we do know from the invoice of a coach-hire firm that he twice travelled to Boulogne on the Channel coast.[95] First, on the night of 15 June 1835, he drove to Versailles, where the Countess had her summer home, then, the following day, to Boulogne. Sarah is thought to have returned to England at that time; Balzac might have seen her to the ferry. The second trip came in August; on that occasion, Balzac stayed in Boulogne for a week. Nine months later, a child was born – Lionel Richard. Lionel was the name of Sarah's other lover, the Comte de Bonneval: it was quite common to credit the real father in this way. In Versailles, however, rumour attributed the child to Balzac. Rumour would: even the son of the owner of the *tabac* in Saché was said to be Balzac's, though in that case Balzac would have to have visited the village in the summer of 1824.[96] No real evidence exists in either case, and the first indication in the correspondence that he and Sarah were lovers is Balzac's clumsy denial in a letter sent to Eveline in October 1836. Sarah herself, believing, apparently, that pregnancies were the result of an act of will, may not have known who the father was; but Balzac certainly had an opinion. When he dedicated *Béatrix* 'To Sarah' at the end of 1838,[97] he mentioned the 'motherly love' that shone in her eyes, and seven years later, a new edition of *Le Chef-d'Oeuvre Inconnu* was enigmatically dedicated 'To a Lord'.[98] It was unusual for Balzac not to reel off the full name and rank of an aristocratic dedicatee, but perhaps the title of the story itself was intended as a clue. The father of a thousand characters and at least one child was in the habit of comparing the production of babies to the conception and creation of a masterpiece[99]

– and, in both respects, this had been the most fertile period of his life.

Soon, according to his own theories, he would have to pay the price.

CHAPTER TWELVE

Illusions Lost and Found

(1836–1837)

BALZAC'S FINANCES were now in such a state that even the normally unexcitable authors who tell the story of his debts are moved to comment – a little later than might have been expected – 'Things were beginning to look serious.'[1] 'My second great defeat',[2] Balzac called it, remembering the collapse of his printing business in 1828. That was a minor setback in comparison. By putting 'defeat' in the singular, he was trying to give a heroic appearance to what was really a series of small disasters, piling up before he had time to write himself out of debt. In 1828, he was on the edge of a new career. Now, he was ageing rapidly. His hair was falling out or turning grey. The long Romantic locks swept back over his head and held in place with a dollop of pomade[3] gave way to a large toupee which sat up above his forehead.[4] Despite evidence to the contrary, he claimed his days of 'pleasing' women were over (admittedly in letters to Eveline).[5] Much of the time he was ill. He had bouts of arachnoiditis, an agonizing inflammation of the blood vessels which surround the brain. At the end of 1835, he felt a pain on the right side of his body. In mid-1836, while strolling in the grounds of Saché, he had what may have been a mild stroke: a *coup de sang*, in the vague terminology of the time, could be either a heart-attack or 'a momentary congestion of blood in the head'. 'Buzzing in the head' suggests the latter, but then three months later, when he complains of losing his balance, the former seems more likely, particularly since he reports having a 'seizure' the following December. There were also more trivial and persistent complaints. He began to sound like an old man: back-aches, chest-pains, inflammation of the bowel. Bronchitis had become a normal part of winter. He was reduced to a diet of milk. But more than the discomfort and the worry, it was the loneliness and the boredom that depressed him, the scintillating mind suddenly going dull: 'a kind of physical melancholy'[6] that contrasted horribly with his usual state. Eveline was given every chance to worry about him. He hoped to convince her that he was in no condition to be chasing after women and prepare her for a nasty shock when they met again: she would be kept up to date with 'the progressive destruction of the individual you met on the *Crêt* [in Neuchâtel] and whom I now resemble very little'.[7]

The jocular tone conceals a suspicion that the end had begun. He was measuring his life like a fuel-tank against the time needed to complete his portrayal of French society: 'I still have seven years work ahead of me if I count on producing three books a year like *Le Lys dans la Vallée*. By the time the main lines of my work are drawn and the frames filled in, I shall be forty-five. I shall no longer be young – at least not physically.' His health was so closely tied up with his work that, immediately after complaining of losing his balance, he added, 'Moreover, the trade in pirated copies is killing us.'

The real catastrophe for Balzac was that he could no longer rely on his pen to write him out of trouble. In 1836 and 1837, he wrote four novels (*L'Interdiction*, *La Vieille Fille*, *Les Employés* and *César Birotteau*), four short stories, the third set of *Contes Drolatiques*, part of *Les Martyrs Ignorés* and *L'Enfant Maudit*, a large portion of his rambling study of *Catherine de Médicis*, the end of *Le Lys dans la Vallée* and the beginnings of *Le Cabinet des Antiques* and *Illusions Perdues* – a mixture of the very modern and the medieval. He also threw himself back into journalism, drafted some plays and, for two months, worked from midnight to 6 a.m. One night, he dashed off 15,000 words, which represents a marked improvement on the thirty-three words a minute of *L'Illustre Gaudissart*. But then came the exhausting part: correcting proofs, purging his writing of errors – 'like mucking out the Augean stables'.[8] If one were to choose a symbol of Balzac's life in the stories of these years, it would be the splendidly silly contraption invented by the composer, Gambara. About the size of a grand piano with an extra keyboard and bits of wind and string instrument protruding, the panharmonicon is designed to do the job of an entire orchestra; 'but the imperfect state of this strange machine arrested the composer's developments and made his concept appear all the greater'.[9] Like Gambara with his proto-synthesizer, Balzac was destroying himself with impossible projects. The smallest interruption made the human 'steam-engine' lose pressure. He started eating less 'so as not to transmit the fatigue of digestion to the brain'. By July 1837, the situation was farcical: he was sporting a goatee beard like a young Romantic ('I who abhor all affectation') and was afraid of taking baths, in case his body, 'stretched to the highest degree', should suddenly relax. At times, the terrible truth was hard to avoid: 'The Goose that lays the golden eggs is sick.'[10]

In fact, the goose was simply overworked. Since 1833, Balzac's debt had been rising steadily. Recently, there had been the cost of setting up his boudoir, the trip to Vienna (5000 francs, but travelling and listening to music were now his only means of preventing himself from working), and endless baubles and trinkets, including a rhinoceros-horn walking-stick and – the next best thing to money – an expensive purse.[11] His mother complained that she fitted into his mental hierarchy somewhere after rings, walking-sticks and furniture; she observed pathetically that the numbers on the watch he had given her were too small for eyes that were always brimming with tears. Considering that the chronicle of her son's finances is like the diary of an obsessive gambler, her letters are remarkably calm. The big win was always just around the corner. 'Six months' hard work and I shall be free' (August 1834). 'Realistically, I need just one more year to pay off my debts' (December 1834 – accidentally dated 1835 by Balzac). 'At last I can see blue skies. Another five months and I shall be solvent' (October 1835). 'If I haven't found a solution a year from now, I might as well throw in the sponge' (June 1836). 'A newspaper has offered 20,000 francs if I can deliver *César Birotteau* by 10 December. . . . I must confess it would give me great pleasure to pay off in a matter of months the debts that have been weighing me down for nine years' (November 1837).

The *Histoire de la Grandeur et de la Décadence de César Birotteau* – the story of a perfumer and seller of hair-restorer who goes bankrupt – eradicated very few of Balzac's debts; but it did serve to show why the bucket which received his earnings never seemed to fill up. His method for achieving stylistic perfection forced him to pay for proof corrections out of the advances he received. One member of the younger generation who adopted him as a model – Édouard Ourliac – advertised *César Birotteau* by explaining to readers of the *Figaro* why the name 'Balzac' struck fear into every typesetter's heart. Each time they issued a set of proofs, they came back plastered with chaotic corrections; hundreds of lines whizzed off to the margins and burst into showers of words until the proofs were almost illegible.[12] Sometimes not a single word of the original remained, as Balzac boasted in the preface to *Le Lys dans la Vallée*: 'One day, I was pleasantly surprised to overhear someone shouting in the printing-shop of M. Éverat, *I've done my hour of Balzac; whose turn is it now?*'[13]

It was partly this unusual openness about writing habits that endeared him to younger writers. It also gave rise to a long debate about his diffuse and lumbering style: a mechanical digger to the little trowels of his contemporaries. *Le Charivari*, for example, announced that Balzac would soon be 'translating his complete works into French'.[14] The relatively uncluttered style of the letters to Eveline, which Balzac never re-read,[15] does suggest that some clarity was lost in the endless revisions; but perhaps it was not entirely a matter of personal taste. Critics of the time were principally concerned with style as a model; and if seen as something to be copied, any style as inimitable as Balzac's can certainly be described as 'bad'. His own opinion was that his 'horrible celebrity' among typesetters was a sign that he belonged to the classical tradition. Friends were invited to reach the same conclusion. Balzac bestowed bound copies of the proofs on them – the messier they were, the better the gift. By October 1837, he had 'a whole library' of them set aside for Eveline.

Balzac might still have kept afloat without the two ventures that were supposed to be his 'financial salvation'.[16] The first was the *Chronique de Paris*, a weekly magazine founded in 1834 by a business-man of Irish extraction called William Duckett. In a surge of optimism on Christmas Eve 1835, Balzac purchased six-eighths of the paper for 140 francs. It would have been an excellent deal if he had not agreed at the same time to underwrite all the costs. Young writers were recruited, among them Théophile Gautier and Balzac's admirer from Besançon, Charles de Bernard, who paid homage to his hero's 'rehabilitation' of thirty-year-old women by contributing a story entitled *La Femme de Quarante Ans*. Editorial dinners were held, a prospectus was drawn up and inserted in recent editions of Balzac's novels: the *Chronique de Paris*, said the prospectus, would 'distinguish itself as much by its urbanity as by its strict impartiality'. Balzac's private plans for the paper were like a parody of a 'real' one and a more accurate description of its contents. It would defend all the ideas he liked, support mediocrities who could not offend him and irritate ministers who refused to decorate him.[17] Most of all, the *Chronique* would be an outlet for his own novels; he was tired of being harried and exploited by editors and middle-men. Even now, he was taking the *Revue de Paris* to court for having sold the uncorrected proofs of *Le Lys dans la Vallée* to a St Petersburg magazine. The novel so admired by Mme de Berny would be paraded all over Europe in a state of undress. On 2 June, the *Chronique de Paris* published Balzac's long and bitter account of the trial in which he pilloried the editor, François Buloz, and anyone who took his side in the dispute. On 3 June, the court found in favour of Balzac, and for the benefit of future generations he republished his account as a long preface to the novel. An outpouring of hate became the prelude to a love story.

By then, the *Chronique* that was supposed to have saved him from crooks like Buloz was sinking. Incredibly, Balzac had decreed that it should come out twice a week. From February to July 1836, he managed to produce forty-one political editorials the main theme of which is that France should form a trading alliance with Russia against Britain. (A prudent policy in view of his future travel plans.) The other contributors lagged behind. In March, Balzac was enduring 'thirty-six-hour agonies twice a week with the *Chronique de Paris*, a paper staffed exclusively by invalids and the weight of which I bear alone for the excellent reason that part of my fortune is tied up in it'.[18] One calamity followed another. On 27 April, he was carted off in a van to the National Guard prison for seven days – the usual punishment for people who failed to turn up with a rifle to do sentry-duty for a night (a favourite subject with cartoonists).

> All my ideas have flown away. The prison is atrocious. . . . It's cold and there's no fire. The prisoners are people of the lowest order, gambling at the top of their voices. There isn't a moment's peace. They are all impoverished workers whose families would starve if they gave up two days' work. There is also the odd artist and writer who prefer a spell in prison to doing their guard duty.

Resourceful as ever, he managed to scrounge a table, two chairs and an empty dormitory; but then his old friend Eugène Sue turned up and prattled on for two days and nights – rich, secure and egotistical: 'It took just forty-eight hours to convince me that men without ambition love no one but themselves.'[19]

On leaving prison, Balzac suffered another setback. William Duckett had abandoned ship before the paper reached the rapids. In a final attempt to save it, Balzac redeemed his silverware from the person he refers to in his accounts as 'My Aunt' (the pawnbroker); he then laid on a dinner for a rich young man who hinted that he might buy some shares. The bill from the caterer lists such delicacies as sturgeon fillet, plovers *au gratin*, asparagus, and pineapple fritters. The food was eaten, speeches were made, but the only result was a promise from the young man that he would 'speak to Daddy about the proposal'.[20]

In July, the *Chronique* collapsed, mostly because of a lack of subscribers. But when Balzac had his attack in the grounds of Saché that June, he already knew the paper was doomed. It was there in the heart of the Loire Valley that he had the idea for *Illusions Perdues*, in which Lucien de Rubempré is sucked into the murky world of journalism, corrupted and finally spat out again to fall prey to Vautrin in a later novel. For Balzac, his paper was killed off by the advent of the first great daily newspapers, *Le Siècle* and *La Presse*; they were far cheaper and toed a more recognizable political line. What Balzac implausibly called his 'illusions' had been shattered once again. It was extremely inconvenient. The total loss was 46,000 francs. He shouldered the *Chronique*'s debts himself and guaranteed that all the shareholders would be reimbursed. It was an honourable defeat, but obviously not the act of a successful newspaper tycoon.

The second instrument of Balzac's salvation was to have been the publisher Edmond Werdet, the man Balzac wanted to have the exclusive rights to his novels but who turned out to be 'a rotten plank'.[21] The general idea was the same as for the *Chronique*: to gain complete control of his own products. If Werdet's memoirs are to be believed, Balzac used him as the counterweight on the pulley that was to hoist him to everlasting fame and fortune. This view has much to recommend it. Werdet certainly suffered the usual fate of Balzac's publishers on the way down; on one occasion, he hurried all the way to Nemours to collect a long-overdue manuscript, only to be told that Balzac had spent the weekend pruning fruit trees. However, Werdet's 400-page tale of woe has an almost happy moral to it, for it gradually becomes apparent that his humiliation was largely self-inflicted. By his own admission, he was 'on his knees' before Balzac's genius, in awe at his 'inconceivable arrogance', his seeming indifference to impending disaster, his erotic adventures with exotic women and, perhaps most amazing of all to someone who had slowly worked his way up the social ladder, his Bohemian habit of appearing in public in scruffy clothes or bursting in unannounced without removing his hat. Werdet's *Portrait Intime* of Balzac is like the confession of a jilted lover: 'I was unable to resist his wheedling. He could have robbed me of my last penny when he held me there with his dark and fiery, fascinating eye, full of magnetic fluid!' Werdet's pantry was regularly emptied by authors who invited themselves to dinner. Werdet moans about this in his memoirs, but it seems unlikely that he could have signed up so many names without being so openly infatuated with them. He was a foil for Balzac's public persona, providing him with his own special cutlery and a chair that was not only gilded like a throne but also several inches higher than the others. When the inferior guests crowned him with roses, Balzac gave no sign of taking it as a joke.[22] Some publishers might have considered themselves forewarned.

When Werdet's 'commercial boat' sprang a leak, Balzac urged him to learn from experience: 'What that tells you is that anyone who wants to be my publisher must have large amounts of capital.' All in vain: Balzac was still able to extract huge advances from him, though he was just as reckless in signing promissory notes for the benefit of Werdet. Not only did he pay him back – eventually – he helped him to run his life, as Eveline was told:

Werdet saw the mother of the woman he lives with burn to death on New Year's Day [1836]. He tried to put her out and burnt his hands. . . . He was stuck in bed for twenty days and I had to take care of business for him, because Werdet's business is *me*. I had to find 5000 francs for myself and 8000 for him. We shall have to suffer – both of us – for another ten months. The last four days have been frittered away on errands and transactions. All that wasted time![23]

Despite the heavy sales of Balzac's novels, some of which sold out on the day they appeared, Werdet had to declare himself bankrupt in May 1837. Balzac was forced to honour the notes he had signed – 13,000 francs, supplied by an advance from another publisher. He swore, again, never to be taken in. Guessing that Werdet would accuse him of exploitation, he soothed his disappointment by being unfair: 'I have sacrificed everything for that man and now he's trying to finish me off and refuses to act in our common interest.' 'I had him sized up in three months . . . but I was hoping he would follow my advice; but no, he has the body of a child and the brain of a cabbage, in addition to which he's as stubborn as a mule. And he has the fatal habit of saying *yes* and then doing the exact opposite or forgetting what he promised.'²⁴ After going bankrupt a second time in 1845 – still blaming Balzac's magnetic eye-beams – Werdet worked as a travelling salesman until he was crippled in an accident. He lost his sight, his wife and all his possessions, and eked out a miserable existence by slandering and idolizing his 'favourite author' – 'my sun, my lucky star, my intellectual Jupiter'.²⁵ Another wreck on Balzac's road to glory – but a suicidal wreck.

THE COLLAPSE of the *Chronique* and the ruin of Werdet turned Balzac into a hunted man and convinced him of the need for a holiday. Sarah Visconti came to the rescue. By mid-1836, Balzac's passion for her had blossomed into friendship: 'All it is, is that since Mme Visconti is very witty, very imaginative and full of fresh new ideas, M. de Balzac, being himself a superior man, enjoys her conversation, and since he has written a great deal and is writing even now, he often borrows those original thoughts she is always having.'²⁶ As luck would have it, Count Visconti's mother had just died and there were problems with the inheritance. Sarah very tactfully entrusted 'Bally' with the job of protecting the Count's interests in Italy. Balzac seized the chance. Equipped with a letter of credit from Baron Rothschild, he boarded a coach on the evening of 25 July and arrived five days later in Turin where he was to spend two weeks, fêted by Turin society and taken to all the best salons by the Countess Sanseverino, another friend from the Austrian Embassy.²⁷

As usual in times of crisis, Balzac's life resolved itself into a romantic novel. Jules Sandeau had introduced him to a young woman from Limoges called Caroline Marbouty.²⁸ After graduating from 'paternal domination to conjugal oppression' (her father was a magistrate and her husband a clerk of the court in Limoges), Caroline had come to seek her literary fortune in Paris where she contributed two short stories to Balzac's *Chronique*. Balzac called her 'a poor charming creature, condemned to live within the cold confines of a household'; she was 'a decent, virtuous woman'.[29] Not so virtuous, however, that she was not prepared to deposit her daughters in a boarding-school, dress up as a man and accompany Balzac to Italy, where she was mistaken for George Sand and had a very jolly time. In later works, she talks of her hopeless attempt to find happiness in a society where 'men put women in the most difficult position and then refuse to recognize them as their equals'.[30] Her feminist writings, even from a biographical point of view, are far more interesting than the much-quoted senile account of her travels with Balzac, dictated by his disembodied spirit when she was seventy-eight. The great connoisseur of women came close to being the ideal man, neither despot nor wimp – though not, of course, the ideal husband: he was so full of plans for other people's futures that 'you can only rely on him *in the present*'. 'Balzac', she told a close relative, 'is much preoccupied with *his ideas* and not very pleasant. But there is so much strength and intellectual power in him, so much superiority in all his being, that he seems attractive. Physically, he is not, though his head is beautifully expressive and strange.'[31] 'Will I be able to control myself? That is the question. For him, love is necessary as a form of physical exercise, and beyond that his whole life is given over to work. . . . I have turned my life inside out; it cannot be worse than it was.'[32] 'She entrusted herself to me for her escapade', Balzac told one of his hosts in Turin, 'since she knows I am so completely taken up with an all-consuming passion that I don't know whether women exist'.[33] After the trip, they rarely met again, but there was enough passion in their friendship for Balzac to prolong the return journey from Turin. Five days out; ten days back. They crossed the Simplon and dawdled expensively through Switzerland – Lake Geneva, Lausanne and (not forgetting Eveline) the sacred sites: the Auberge de l'Arc and the Villa Diodati. It was a strange sort of sentimental journey in which the novels of Balzac's life became entwined, and when he returned to 'life as a literary convict' he noticed 'a curious effect': 'Sometimes I wonder if it was all a dream and whether Turin really exists.'[34]

Balzac had been starved of a social life free from professional concerns, and it seems significant that he no longer wanted to travel alone. He was longing for 'distractions'. Italian society had delighted him – prestige without the affectations: a transvestite 'secretary' would never have been welcomed in the salons of Paris. Over the next few months, he modified his vision of Italy, especially after his second visit in 1837 when a pamphlet was circulated accusing the novelist – whose works had been available in Italian translation since 1830[35] – of portraying all Italians as traitors to the fatherland and adulterers.[36] The short story *Massimilla Doni* (1837) is a celebration of a world where 'every passion comes with its own excuse'[37] and where 'the morning is taken up with love, the evening with music and' – a courteous admission – 'the night with sleep'.[38]

It was February 1837 before Balzac was able to revisit what was now his favourite country. News of Mme de Berny's death was waiting for him when he returned. Mourning finally forced him to follow doctor's orders: 'I succumbed, and slept for fifteen to eighteen hours three days in a row.' It was the worst possible time to sleep. His 'floating debt' had reached 151,514 francs (about £455,000 today), of which only 40,000 francs was the 'safe' debt owed to family and friends. Rumours that he was about to be thrown into debtors' prison had 'paralysed' his credit; and, as he often remarks, there were no grants to be hoped for from a government that was 'afraid of being hoodwinked by men of intelligence – as if one could fake genius for very long'.[39]

Desperate measures were called for. In taking them, Balzac revolutionized French literature and greatly enlarged his readership; but he also created a new emergency that made his second trip to Italy less an excursion than a full-speed retreat. First, Émile de Girardin, whose daily newspaper, *La Presse*, had dealt the *coup de grâce* to the *Chronique de Paris*, asked Balzac for a novel. Girardin had realized that the sort of news people wanted to read was not news at all. If he could fill up one-third of the paper with a popular novel, circulation would increase. Perhaps he was thinking of Dickens's *The Pickwick Papers*, which began to appear in monthly instalments in April 1836, when Dickens was only twenty-four. Balzac offered Girardin *La Vieille Fille*, which thus became the first serial novel (or *roman feuilleton*) in France. It was published in twelve daily episodes starting on 23 October 1836.[40] In future, most of his novels would be sold twice – once to a newspaper, once to a publisher. A huge new market was being opened up by the very newspapers Balzac spent so much time despising. But there were problems which he never solved entirely and which to some extent justify his criticism of the press. Unlike Eugène Sue, who simply drivelled on from A to B without knowing what would happen at the end of the story, Balzac settled into his idea and expanded it until it formed a whole. How could he possibly turn out a fresh slice of plot every week? The other problem was that newspaper readers were not the same as novel readers. They wanted cliffhangers at the end of every episode, simplistic psychology, uncontroversial politics and details one's wife and children could read without embarrassment or harm. Balzac's tale of an elderly woman and her sexual needs did not fit the bill. Complaints flooded in to the newspaper, as Balzac in turn complained in a preface to *Les Employés* in 1838: 'Our readers, who happily read the atrocities of the *Gazette des Tribunaux* [which printed accounts of trials] and the despicable lies of the advertisements, raised a hue and cry over the excessively voluminous breasts of Mlle Cormon.'[41] It was a distressing affair. By dividing his novel into scenes of equal length, Balzac had done everything he could to cram it into the columns of *La Presse*, and his confidence was shaken, especially the following year when the forerunner of *Les Employés* appeared in the same newspaper and readers wrote to say it was boring and stupid: 'If that's so, then I really have blundered badly.'[42] Other papers attacked him (though they were actually attacking Girardin). Reviewers of *La Vieille Fille* pretended not to understand or to be shocked; they made fun of his peculiar blend of phrenology, physiognomy and characterology:[43] 'Thus', sneered the *Charivari*, 'M. de Balzac will tell you that if a man puts his left foot first, that means he has a special aptitude for languages of the North. If a woman habitually wears her hair in corkscrew curls, you can be certain that she is a dab hand at apricot jam.'[44]

Le Vieille Fille was in fact an unacknowledged success – but only for Girardin. In spite of the 'hue and cry', his paper's circulation increased enormously and made him seem a decent, moral fellow when he announced that Balzac's next offering – the story of a prostitute nicknamed 'the Torpedo' (the fish, not the missile) – would not be published.

The second emergency solution showed Balzac's faith in the magical quality of business deals and required much less work. He would liquidate his other literary assets. *La Recherche de l'Absolu* had been reviewed in the *Revue des Deux Mondes* by Sainte-Beuve. In an article full of half-compliments and scathing praise, he revealed to the *Revue*'s wide and important audience that Balzac had first sidled on to the literary scene under the cloak of Lord R'Hoone.[45] Balzac turned the revelation to his advantage and despite attempts to foil the deal by his old accomplice, Lepoitevin, redeemed the rights to his early 'pre-Balzacian' novels and sold them to the publisher Hippolyte Souverain. His 'secretaries' tidied up the messier tales, wrote two more, removed some excess severed limbs and personal allusions, changed the titles, and the novels were advertised, in a silly phrase which stuck to Balzac for the rest of his life, as the juvenilia of 'the most fertile of our modern novelists'.

If there was money in the past, there was also money in the future. In November came one of those moments of deceptive triumph Balzac depicts so well. He left for a long week in Saché 'to rest like a child on its mother's breast' (and to escape arrest), announcing that all his debts were paid, 'by which I mean the debts that were bothering me'. 'Today at two o'clock', he told the retired ironmonger who used to visit him in his garret in the Rue Lesdiguières, 'I signed a contract that puts an end to all my anguish and an agony that would have killed me had it gone on any longer. Now I shall only have to worry about you, my mother and Mme Delannoy [another family friend].'[46] The contract in question was for all his future works. All he had to do now was write them.

The pinhead on which Balzac was erecting yet another upside-down pyramid was a 50,000-franc advance. He was still deeply in debt, still unable to go to the Opéra for fear of being seen and still plagued with that imaginative optimism he so cheerfully explained in the preface to *Le Père Goriot*: 'For a long time now, the author's only intention in publishing books has been to obey that second destiny (so often opposed to our heavenly destiny) which social events forge for us and whose executors are known as *creditors* – a valuable breed, for their name signifies that they have faith in us.'[47]

The founder of the *Chronique de Paris*, William Duckett, whose costs Balzac had assumed, was sorely lacking in creditor's faith. He sold his debt to people who knew how to collect it. Balzac's nemesis now had several faces. He had his furniture moved from the Rue Cassini to the Rue des Batailles. When the bailiffs discovered his new retreat, he rented a room in the city at 22 Rue de Provence, broadcast his new address and never moved in. Auguste de Belloy offered him a bed which he may have slept in. On 8 February 1837, his beloved tilbury – lamps, embroidered cushions, coats-of-arms and all – was seized at the Rue Cassini.

For Balzac, 'losing illusions' was the same as finding out that optimism didn't work. Appropriately, therefore, the penultimate incident in his second great defeat was an abrupt return to that land where illusions were allowed to flourish. Though his old legal skills had proved effective, there were fortunately still problems with Count Visconti's succession. Sarah and Emilio asked for his help again. Théophile Gautier was invited along, but he was busy reviewing the Paris Salon; and so, on 14 February, Balzac set off alone for Italy. On the 18th, the sky above Milan lit up with a brilliant *aurora borealis*, and on the 19th, Balzac rolled into the city and took a room near La Scala in the best hotel in town, the Albergo della Bella Venezia.[48]

The Countess Sanseverino had supplied him with a letter of introduction for her brother, Prince Porcia, and his mistress, the Countess Bolognini-Vimercati. The man whose tilbury had just been seized in Paris was given the use of the Prince's private coach and his box at La Scala. The sculptor Alessandro Puttinati made a marble statuette of him – 'a work of affection', Balzac called it and showed his appreciation by paying for labour and materials.[49] Only his fellow writers were inhospitable: Balzac seemed to prefer the company of aristocrats. As Cesare Cantù recalled, he managed to be at his most irritating during a visit to the great Manzoni. Wearing a floppy hat and 'a sort of ribbon representing a tie', Balzac rattled on about himself, complaining that his venture in 'religious literature' (*Le Médecin de Campagne*) had not been as profitable as he hoped, and saying nothing of *I Promessi Sposi*, which he hadn't even read[50] – a good reason not to talk about it. For the rest of his holiday, he was showered with invitations and bombarded with newspaper reports which he probably had no time to read. When his watch was stolen in the street, there was a spate of sympathetic articles. Cesare Cantù observed that its speedy recovery proved that the police could be efficient after all. Another paper reported the emergence of a new style – the *'moda alla Balzac'* – and assumed it must refer to Balzac's unusual combination of white tie and black gloves. Perhaps a reflection of hasty packing.

The highlight of Milan was the salon of the twenty-three-year-old

Countess Maffei, who was to play an important role in the *Risorgi-mento* movement. In the face of financial disaster, Balzac enjoyed a sudden rejuvenation. He described the Countess in a letter to herself: she was like those statuettes he had been admiring, 'slender, svelte, sweet and pretty, slim, fragile, delicately worked, exquisitely formed and full of grace, pretty and with wonderful lines'. Count Maffei was sufficiently panicked to send emergency instructions to his wife:

All eyes are on that famous foreigner and everyone knows that he is spending large parts of the morning and evening in our home, neglecting families from whom he has none the less received countless invitations and marks of courtesy – which he has not received from us. . . . Since you have read his novels, you can judge for yourself how familiar he is with women and with that subtle art of seduction. . . . Do not suppose that the ugliness of his face will protect you from your inexperience or shield you from public opinion. Even deformity is masked by wit and the irresistible power of the man who knows how to open out at will every fold of the heart and mind. Remember, little Clara, that you are the darling of Milan.[51]

When Balzac travelled to Venice to obtain a signature on a document relating to Emilio's inheritance, it was to Clara that he wrote. His letters provide some valuable evidence of how he manufac-tured new illusions to replace the ones he lost. From his suite in the Albergo Reale – the suite that had been occupied in 1834 by George Sand and Musset – he had a view of San Giorgio Maggiore and its Campanile. The age of tourism had begun and in that most poetic of settings he found his imagination incapacitated by all 'those wretched English engravings' which had already shown him Venice in every conceivable light. 'My mind was like a *coquette* who has exhausted love in all its intellectual forms so that when she finds true love . . . she feels nothing.'

And the rain was casting a grey mantle over Venice which may be very poetic for that poor city which is crumbling on every side and sinking hourly into the grave, but it was not very agreeable for a Parisian who, for two-thirds of the year, enjoys a cloak of fog and a tunic of rain. One thing, though, delighted me: the silence of that moribund city. That alone would make me enjoy living in Venice, for it matches my secret inclinations which, despite appearances, tend to the melancholy.[52]

Five days later, the sun came out; he visited the whole city at speed, was stunned by its angels, the most beautiful being at 'Saint Pierre et Paul'[53] in the chapel of the Virgin. But the greatest attraction for the melancholy tourist was the gondola, 'a whole existence on its own': 'I confess I was heart-broken not to have the lady of my thoughts by my side, for it must be quite delightful to sit together in a gondola.' Balzac did not imagine the less flimsy Mme Hanska drifting along the canals of Venice. When he wrote to her, 'mingling past and future in the same sensation', he asked if she remembered seeing a little fifteenth-century house along the Grand Canal, after the Palazzo Fini, with two Gothic windows. There, they could make their home together; it would be cheaper than renting the Villa Diodati. Balzac had been finding Eveline's jealous suspicions more and more objectionable, and by a curious coincidence (or not), the little Gothic house on the Grand Canal was said to have been the home of Desdemona.[54] Perhaps Balzac knew. A year and a half later, Eveline learned that her lover was planning a five-act drama entitled *La Gina*: 'It's *Othello* in reverse,' he told her. 'La Gina will be a female Othello, and the scene is set in Venice.'[55]

BALZAC TOURED Italy for another month – far longer than he intended. He saw Florence, Livorno, Bologna, where he called on Rossini and Olympe Pélissier, and Genoa, where a dreadful 'mistake' occurred. He was placed in quarantine, which meant languishing 'in the most horrific *lazaretto*. I should have thought it unsuitable even for bandits.' While he was there, a Genoese merchant told him a secret that could make him a millionaire: it was to make 1838 one of his least productive years as a writer.

On 24 April 1837, Balzac finally left Milan, intent on squeezing the last drops of bliss from his Italian holiday before re-entering Hell. He retraced the journey in a letter to Eveline written from the Rue Cassini where '200 letters' were waiting for him, including three from her. The most revealing part of the letter is the date: 'Paris, 10 May'. Balzac had returned a week before.

I had a horribly beautiful journey and I am glad I did it. . . . I crossed the Saint Gotthard with 15 feet of snow on the paths I was forced to follow since even the tall posts that mark the road were buried and the bridges over the torrents were invisible, as were the torrents themselves. I almost perished several times, despite having eleven guides. I climbed the Saint Gotthard at one in the morning under a gorgeous moon and saw the sun rise over the snow – the experience of a lifetime. I descended so rapidly that in half an hour I went from 25 degrees below at the summit to so many degrees above in the Reuss Valley. And then the horrors of the Devil's Bridge. . . . I spent an enormous amount of time and money, but I had my money's worth. It's a superb journey and I shall have to do it again in summer in order to see those beautiful things in a new light.

Balzac perishing in the moonlit snow high in the Swiss Alps would have been one of the great Romantic deaths, and the thought had obviously occurred to him. As usual, he compared his exploit to a Napoleonic campaign – the Retreat from Moscow. Then, refreshed by his brush with death, he prepared to do battle with his creditors:

Now here I am back at work. I shall publish in rapid succession *César Birotteau*, *La Femme Supérieure* and *Gambara*; I shall finish *Illusions Perdues*, then *La Haute Banque* and *Les Artistes*. After that, we [that is, himself and Eveline's portrait] shall fly to the Ukraine where, perhaps, I shall be lucky enough to write a play that will end my financial torment. That is my plan of action, *cara contessina*.[56]

The immediate plan of action was less glorious. Balzac consulted his financial advisers. They all gave him the same advice: flee. He fled to the home of the ever-willing Viscontis, who owned a 'magnificent town-house' at 54 Avenue des Champs-Élysées – probably the Hôtel de Massa, which can now be seen 3 miles away at 38 Rue du Faubourg-Saint-Jacques, where it was transported stone by stone in 1928 to become the headquarters of the Société des Gens de Lettres.[57] Here, to Balzac's mortification, the newspapers took up the story.

Both the *Gazette des Tribunaux* and *Le Siècle* ran stories on a sordid case that was heard on 26 July 1837.[58] With a snide and gleeful tone that seems to justify all of Balzac's jibes at the aggressive philistinism of the July Monarchy, a lawyer called Favre recounted the efforts of

William Duckett to grasp that 'sylph-like' creature, 'the invisible, impalpable M. de Balzac (a ripple of laughter in the court)'. Having failed to capture 'the monster walking-stick whose repairs alone cost 18,000 francs', Duckett had obtained a court order which apparently allowed a bailiff to proceed to the Viscontis' house disguised as an employee of the mail-coach service. Balzac's signature was required for delivery of an Etruscan vase. The servant was persuaded to bring him to the door, where the man in disguise addressed him as 'colleague' because he had once co-written a melodrama. The parcel was unwrapped and proved to contain a sheaf of papers declaring that Balzac would be sent to prison unless he paid 3000 francs on the spot. The Viscontis lent him the money, and when *Le Siècle* printed the report on 28 July, Balzac wrote to its editor, Armand Dutacq, saying that, instead of ridiculing him, the paper should 'protest, along with all decent people, against civil imprisonment, which is practised now only for the benefit of vile usurers'. The letter was never published.

Balzac had been saved from debtors' prison; but it was after the event that he began to despair: 'I have hoped so many times that I am tired of hoping.'[59] Things had come to a head and still he had to work. He was like the dove sent out from the Ark, he told Eveline, except that the flood had not yet subsided.[60] In Paris, friends avoided him 'like the plague': 'Here I am all alone, but I prefer being alone in my isolation to that sugary sort of hatred which in Paris goes under the name of friendship.'[61] He thought of buying a cottage or a château on the banks of the Loire, but then, with a typical pirouette, enthused about the beauties of the modern city with its 'floor' of asphalt, its gas 'candelabra', its endless ribbon of glittering shop-fronts: 'In ten years we shall be clean and the mud of Paris will be struck from the dictionary.' 'I have abandoned the idea of returning to Touraine and shall remain a citizen of the intellectual metropolis.'[62] As a compromise, he settled on a site which lay between Sèvres and Ville-d'Avray,[63] just beyond the Porte de Saint-Cloud to the south-west of Paris, outside the jurisdiction of the National Guard yet close to the Paris–Versailles railway that was just then being constructed. He began to piece together a domain of his own by purchasing little plots of land to a total of 10,000 francs. His brother-in-law was to build him a house and a chalet for the Guidoboni-Viscontis who funded the project. 'The name of my poor hermitage is *Les Jardies*. That is the plot on which I shall settle like a caterpillar on its lettuce-leaf.'[64] A beautifully apt image: Balzac had found another way to devour his livelihood.

MENTALLY, Balzac survived the crises of 1837 by living two separate lives, each with its own settings and moods and with the Alps as a changing-screen. He also left two distinct images of himself – one on public display, the other enveloped in a little drama that has proved to be the most stubborn and tantalizing mystery of his life.

The public image was the portrait Balzac asked his mother to commission from Louis Boulanger as a corrective to a 'horrible lithograph' based on a caricatural statuette by Dantan;[65] it made him look like an indestructible Humpty-Dumpty with a stick. Boulanger's portrait of Balzac in his monk's habit was exhibited at the 1837 Salon and said by a women's magazine to depict 'a large individual wrapped to the chin in a flannel shirt like an umbrella in its sheath and looking at first like a canon from Tours – an unconscious memory of the scene in *Le Curé de Tours* in which Abbé Birotteau is locked out in the rain by his landlady. 'How different reality is from young ladies' dreams! Ah! the illusions that will be lost at the sight of that painting! The voices that will cry, "Give us back our Balzac!"'[66] Gautier, however – probably with Balzac's blessing – saw an almost mythological form that prefigures Rodin's statue: 'The full, voluptuous mouth, especially the lower lip, smiles a Rabelaisian smile in the shade of a moustache much lighter than the hair; the defiantly raised chin is joined to the neck by an ample, powerful fold of flesh that looks like the dewlap of a young bull.'[67]

Writing to Eveline, who was to receive the portrait, Balzac added a few brush-strokes of his own.[68] The eyes were nicely rendered and so was his doggedness; but Boulanger had painted out his white hair. There was too much pride and none of the underlying *finesse*; he looked like a roughneck soldier and a braggart. But Balzac's monastic robe had always acted as a paradoxical reminder of the proverb, '*L'habit ne fait pas le moine*'. He refers to the proverb himself[69] and it is this implied discrepancy that gives the portrait what Gautier called its 'bizarre harmony'.

The other image is a self-portrait painted in letters to a mysterious correspondent. Here, the crisis of Balzac's illusions makes his financial disaster seem a relatively trivial affair. His saint from the Ukraine had been showing an alarming tendency to step down from her pedestal and preach to the sinner. To Balzac's annoyance, she refused to behave like Mme de Berny. He pleaded with her for honest criticism of *La Vieille Fille* but never received it. All her comments were directed at him personally. She kept telling him he was 'frivolous': the critics had been saying much the same about his novels. Balzac retaliated, gently, but with the bitterness of disappointment: she still confused him with his work, she was uninformed and opinionated and worst of all judgmental. 'Allow me to tell you of a very bad feeling I have: I do not like my friends to *judge* me or to believe that my decisions are not necessary.'[70] A suspicion arose that he was on the verge of wanting to marry someone rather like his mother. He re-examined the face in the portrait that hung in front of him. She then received an astonishing physiognomic analysis of herself, straight from one of the novels. It says much about the nature of Balzac's love: 'Without your mouth, your forehead would be that of a hydrocephalic.' 'I found in your lips a few faint symptoms of cruel fury ... but repressed by kindness. Something violent at first, but then immediately reflection, kindness, sweetness and nobility return'; but 'if you were nothing but kindness you would be a sheep, which would be too dreary'.[71] The most telling details are those features which Balzac frequently interprets in his novels: a 'domed brow' signifies abundance of thought,[72] a fat chin implies a person who is demanding, even violent in love,[73] and 'a full figure is a sign of strength – but women built in that way are imperious, wilful, more sensual than loving ... inflexible and jealous'.[74]

Finding that Eveline was not up to her role, Balzac had begun to take his custom to another confessor – someone chosen for that purpose from the crowd of anonymous correspondents. Since he probably never knew her personally, it was easier to make her fit his needs, and so, from February 1836 to the middle of 1837, his 'true self' expressed its hopes and disappointments, not to Eveline, but to a woman he knew only as 'Louise'.[75]

The history of the twenty-three letters Balzac sent to the mystery woman is a tedious saga, full of obscure passages, futile controversies and wishful thinking masquerading as objective research. However, if the following theory is correct, it is a story worth telling, since it provides a splendid example of Balzac's fictions coming back to haunt him in real life; and even if the theory is incorrect, the letters are valuable for their sad, almost childlike tone – something quite new in Balzac's adult correspondence. 'Louise', in these letters, appears as the surrogate ghost of Mme de Berny, Balzac's late departed saint summoned back from the grave.

The story, very briefly, is this. Ten months after Balzac's death, on 28 June 1851, *La Mode* announced the publication of twenty-three intimate letters from him to 'one of the most elegant women in modern society'. Eveline applied for an injunction and *La Mode* was ordered to return the so-called 'Letters to Louise' to the vendor. They eventually resurfaced in the 1876 edition of Balzac's correspondence. Much later, a single letter from Louise herself came to light.

A scholar called Gustave Desnoiresterres was to have written an introduction to the letters when they appeared in *La Mode*. Thirty-six years later he was asked for any clue that might lead to an identification of Louise. Desnoiresterres, by then an old man, remembered only this:[76] 'The vendor was the husband of the lady herself, a certain Lefèvre'; and he added a seemingly irrelevant detail: 'It was said that Lefèvre had laid his hands on the papers of the vaudeville-writer, Théaulon, and in particular on a *Sardanapale* that was performed at the Odéon in about 1843.'[77] The Lefèvre in question can be identified as Louis Lefèvre, a very minor dramatist and, according to Desnoiresterres, 'a shrewd and enterprising fellow' who wanted to cash in on his wife's indiscretions.

The problem is that Lefèvre's wife was someone called Élisa Berger; none of her names was Louise. Either Desnoiresterres's memory failed him or Lefèvre had lied about the provenance of the letters. There followed a century of speculation, marked by one theory so difficult to prove that it took up an entire book.[78]

Prolonged ignorance gives a special value to the smallest fact. It occurred to the present theorizer (whose theory, it should be stressed, is not conclusive) that the reference to the vaudeville-writer Théaulon may not be just a random fact that floated to the surface of Desnoiresterres's decrepit memory, but a thread from the same piece of cloth, or at least a fruitful irrelevancy. Théaulon, it turns out, was an abnormally prolific playwright who collaborated with the 'shrewd and enterprising' Lefèvre. Among his hundreds of plays is one of the two

*Le Père Goriot*s that were adapted from Balzac's novel in 1835 – which means that Théaulon was one of the playwrights who was left on the pavement when Balzac whisked the actors and actresses off to the Château de Madrid.

A rather flimsy connection. Except that Théaulon's *Goriot* was performed at the Variétés Théâtre, where the role of Victorine Taillefer was taken by a young actress called Atala Beauchêne. Atala's presence at Balzac's celebration dinner is confirmed by one of the accounts;[79] and it is Atala who can now be considered as the most likely candidate for the role of 'Louise'.[80]

Born in Orléans in 1819, her real name was Louise-Agathe Beaudoin.[81] This is the first argument in favour. We know from her letter to Balzac that 'Louise' was one of her real names – but 'not the name I use in society'. 'I like it because it is my mother's name and I use it for you *alone*.' The mother's name is unfortunately still a mystery. The death certificate gives it as Thérèse, while the birth certificate calls her Françoise-Agathe. Her grandmother, on the other hand, was called Louise-Agathe and it is likely, as we shall see, that the letters to Balzac were collaborations between mother and daughter.

Mme Beaudoin was an ambitious woman, perhaps of necessity. Louise's birth certificate describes her as a servant (*domestique*) and mentions no father, which suggests that her employer had something to do with it. Some time later they moved to Paris, and at the age of eight Louise was thrust on to the stage by her mother who marketed her under the name '*la petite Atala*'. (It was not until 1846 that a law prevented children under fifteen from appearing on the stage.) By all accounts Atala was extremely fetching and, despite having a poor voice, became a successful actress in the boisterous Boulevard theatres: 'a svelte and ravishing virgin, casting love all around and arousing passions at will';[82] 'very young, short, with fine, delicate features and a slender form'.[83] This, however, was only her stage persona. The real Atala was not the wilting flower she usually played, according to a critic writing in 1832. She was a slim blonde who dressed expensively and gave extravagant supper-parties:

> She is better known in society than in the theatre. And when we say society we mean those gatherings where young men-about-town get together in order to squander their parents' money and lead what they call a short and merry life. There is not one of our good

restaurateurs, our jobmasters or our tilbury-drivers who is not well acquainted with the face of Mlle Atala Beauchêne.[84]

The same critic was told by Atala's admirably 'indulgent and obliging' mother that her lifestyle was funded by a rich lover. Balzac was often accused of exaggerating the 'depravity' of life behind the scenes. It is worth noting, therefore, that in 1832 Louise was only thirteen years old.

When Balzac began to receive letters from 'Louise' in early 1836, Atala and her mother moved in with the actor Frédérick Lemaître,[85] soon to be a friend of Balzac. (Coincidentally, Balzac later asked for Atala to be given a part in one of his plays.) Frédérick beat her and abused her, even during rehearsals, considering this an expression of love.

So, was Atala Beauchêne the mysterious Louise? Like 'Louise', Atala might reasonably have been described in 1851 as 'one of the most elegant women in modern society'. She had met Balzac in 1835, a few months before the correspondence began. We know also that Louise was not an unworldly woman. Thanking Balzac for the manuscripts he sent her, she begged him to look after himself 'in the name of that true and pure friendship that has chosen you and you *alone* among all the men I have known'. Atala, too, had several male friends. Her lovers were said to include Alfred Tattet, Roger de Beauvoir, the banker Aguado, Étienne Arago, director of the Vaudeville Theatre, and, later, the very sociable British Ambassador, Lord Normanby. All these men were known to Balzac.

This is important for the following reason: Louise sent two drawings to Balzac which he and his friends found excellent. When he told her this, she worried: 'As for my letters, they are most assuredly in my own hand and this is why I am fearful about those few lines I was childish enough to inscribe at the bottom of the sepia, for it is by my writing alone that I might be recognized by my friends.' The implication is that Louise moved in some of the same circles as Balzac, though without knowing him intimately: 'Indeed', Balzac wrote rather testily in April 1836,

I see you know almost nothing about me. You know nothing of *Le Lys dans la Vallée*, which is the object of an odious trial; you write to me in English; and it appears you are unfamiliar with a great many of my writings. If you knew that, like savages tracking friends or enemies, these little details can lead me to you, you would at least be touched by my restraint and would understand what I am seeking. I want to attach myself to something, to set foot on some dry land, however deserted you wish to make it; but do not let me fly about in an empty sky.

Since Balzac's sky was not entirely empty and since he was still receiving visitors, one of Atala's lovers might well have seen and recognized the handwriting on the sepia drawing.

Another important clue is provided by her writing-paper, which was stamped with the initials 'L.M.' and the coronet of a count. She claimed that neither initials nor coronet were hers: the paper was part of her disguise. Atala is said to have enjoyed the protection of a man described only as 'a liberal Count'. Perhaps it was the same man.[86]

The other letters add little to our knowledge of Louise. On several occasions, she sent Balzac flowers – a bunch of roses while he was in the National Guard prison. In August 1836, something 'painful' had happened to her. In mid-1837, after Balzac's return from Milan, the correspondence petered out. Balzac wished her happiness and returned to work; 'there, as in a fight, one is entirely taken up with the struggle; one suffers, but the heart falls silent'.

Before piecing the evidence together, it seems only fair to follow Atala, albeit very quickly, to her final curtain-call – in part because she represents a certain type of actress well known to readers of *La Comédie Humaine*. Despite the brutal treatment she received from Frédérick Lemaître, he turned her into a fine actress, so that, by 1846, she had grown, literally it seems, in stature: 'A tall stately woman, with fine eyes, and an agreeable voice', says an English guide to *The Theatres of Paris*, 'she treads the stage with remarkable ease and dignity; and possesses a sufficiently versatile talent to enable her to personate the *grande dame* and the *grisette* with equal success.'[87]

The rest of her career is in many ways typical of an actress's lot. Her greatest triumphs came with the Romantic dramas, *Kean* (always attributed to Alexandre Dumas but originally co-written by Théaulon) and Victor Hugo's *Ruy Blas*. Hugo himself praised her in a preface, saying that she played the Queen 'with rare and exquisite intelligence'; no nuance escaped her. By then, she was using her own name, Louise

Beaudoin. In 1839, she ran away from Frédérick. According to Frédérick's first serious biographer, Atala's mother wanted a more lucrative liaison for her daughter; she dictated a 'brutal' farewell letter and helped her to come to 'an arrangement' with the liberal Count.[88] After the 1848 Revolution, Atala visited Drury Lane with Dumas's company and acted in *Le Comte de Monte-Cristo*.[89] She was briefly in love with Dumas, like so many other actresses;[90] and like so many of her profession, she eventually disappears from view, 'an ageing actress' performing in provincial theatres. She retired to Lyon in 1885 and died a widow at Villeurbanne in 1894.

Assuming the identification is correct, what exactly happened? A faint and slightly disturbing picture of 'Louise' emerges which suggests that Balzac was perhaps right to want the mystery to persist. He may even have discovered something unpleasant about her: the short story, *Facino Cane*, was dedicated 'To Louise, in affectionate gratitude', but then, some time after November 1844, Balzac scratched out the dedication for no apparent reason. Before suggesting what that reason might be, there are two extra clues to be followed up. One is simply a curious fact: unlike all the other women who sent anonymous letters to Balzac, Louise knew practically nothing of his works. The other clue is provided by Balzac's own formidable powers of intuition.

We can deduce from her single surviving letter that Balzac suspected her of writing with the help of a female friend:

Why do you speak of a friend? I have not been hiding behind a friend. . . . You are right to trust me: never have you possessed a heart such as mine. . . . Alas! you do not know this heart that gives itself to you but cannot come to you. Yet you know that I am naturally virtuous, and honestly and genuinely respectable. It is true what you say at the end of your letter – that you still believe strongly in me in spite of everything, that I thank you for doing me justice, and that I love you sweetly and sincerely when you are that way.

There is, as Balzac points out, a certain inconsistency in her letter: a combination of experience and innocence, a clumsiness of expression that contrasts with the literary style and careful handwriting. If Louise is Atala Beauchêne, it may be that her ambitious mother, who pushed her on to the stage when she was still a child, acted as her chaperone when she took up with Frédérick Lemaître and dictated letters for her, had decided that the famous novelist who so generously invited her to an expensive restaurant might make a good 'protector'. Atala would be able to use her skill at impersonating a *'grande dame'*. As the little girl in the closing chapters of *La Cousine Bette* reminds us, this sort of mother–daughter partnership was not uncommon, and it may be no coincidence that, writing in 1846, Balzac named his character Atala – 'a female masterpiece in the mud of prostitution'.[91]

Another possibility is that Atala and her mother were hoping to obtain some valuable autographs – in 1851, *La Mode* was prepared to pay 3000 francs for the letters – or even to engage in that popular criminal activity of the time: blackmail. This would explain why she wrote love-letters to Balzac without knowing anything about his novels. It would also have confirmed Balzac's worst fears about actresses. In the second part of *Illusions Perdues*, they appear as part-time prostitutes, victims to be pitied but also dangerous objects of fantasy.[92] Balzac sounds here like one of his provincial bourgeois or like a conservative theologian, but his fictional actresses with their wretched lives are certainly closer to the truth than the fairy-like creatures of Gautier and Nerval.

None of this is definite proof, though it would be nice to think of Balzac corresponding and sharing fantasies with his own character: in *Le Père Goriot*, Victorine Taillefer is the innocent young girl who falls in love with Rastignac.

The final irony is that Balzac himself asked Louise not to reveal her identity. She was a frame for his illusions, another escape from the world of contracts and debts, above all – when Eveline refused to submit to the transformation – a phantasmic Mme de Berny re-created from the dubious letters of an unknown woman. But then Mme de Berny herself had been as much a symbol as a reality. Balzac's appetite for truth was competing with his need for fantasy, and it was not so much the financial defeat that depressed him, nor even his 'lost illusions' – the 'betrayals' of Sandeau and Werdet – as a diminishing ability to control and coordinate them. 'It seems to me that all my illusions form a whole,' he remarked in 1834;[93] and if all his illusions fitted together perfectly, wasn't that the same as reality? Money was just the token of that other, chaotic universe that always threatened to break in. 'And here I am in my study,' he told Louise, 'like a ship that is stranded in the ice.' 'You, Madame, should believe in a man's talent, but do not think the man equal to his talent. That only occurs in exceptional cases.' 'That is why I believe in nothing – though I am always ready to believe – and why I urge you to keep your illusions without going a step further.'[94]

PART THREE

CHAPTER THIRTEEN

Buried Treasure

(1838)

A FEW MONTHS after the last letter to Louise, Balzac rented a temporary apartment in Sèvres, persuading his brother-in-law to sign the lease. There, he hid from his creditors and contemplated his new property. It was the first he had ever owned and it stirred his imagination like a fresh ream of paper. The original idea had been to find some peace and quiet; he nearly succeeded too well. Ask anyone at the station for Les Jardies, he told friends, few of whom were able to find it at the first attempt. Not, as his young friend, the novelist and journalist Léon Gozlan would have it, because the real Les Jardies was somewhere else, but because sarcastic locals were in the habit of referring to the plot as 'M. de Balzac's vineyard'.[1]

When visitors finally arrived, they found a double gate at the foot of a steep mound just a few yards from the station. There was a bell and a black marble plaque bearing the words 'Les Jardies'. The gate opened on to a construction site. On top of the mound could be seen the skeleton of what Balzac hoped would be his home for the next ten years. There were also some glum-looking constructions stuck in a sea of mud – sheds and stables, the maisonette for the Viscontis and a cottage for an old couple, M. and Mme Brouette, who had served the Balzac family at Villeparisis. Balzac thus had a gardener whose name means 'wheelbarrow'. It all looked highly improbable. When Frédérick Lemaître was taken on a tour of the property he carried two stones with him which he placed at his feet to prevent him from sliding down the hill.[2] Balzac remained metaphorically unmoved. He saw quite a different scene: 'a pump to be swathed in clematis and other climbing plants, a pretty well . . . silence, and another 45,000 francs of debt!'[3] He decided to grow vegetables and convert the stables into a cow-shed so that he could supply the dairy needs of the surrounding countryside.[4] There would be a lake and an irrigation system.[5] He would produce his own wine and corner the market in pineapples by selling them at a quarter of the normal price. The idea came to him in the winter of 1837 when the ink was freezing in the inkwell. Gautier remembered hearing all about it: 'The 100,000 pineapples were already pushing up their jagged plumes of leaves above their great squared golden cones under enormous vaults of crystal; he could see them, he could smell their tropical aroma through his quivering nostrils; and when he leaned on the window-sill and watched the snow fall silently on the denuded slopes, the illusion hardly vanished at all.'[6] Nor did it become a reality. And yet, with the railway and the little country houses rich Parisians were beginning to build in Sèvres and Ville-d'Avray, Les Jardies should have been an excellent investment.[7]

The house itself ranks with Hugo's Hauteville House and Dumas's Monte-Cristo Castle as one of the great partnerships of mind and mortar in the nineteenth century. All that now remains of the property is the gardener's house, which has survived because Léon Gambetta died there in 1882. Balzac's dwelling had a shorter life. When he moved into it in July 1838, it was a skinny 'chalet' of three storeys, with two rooms on each floor and a covered gallery on the first. It had brick pilasters, green shutters and, in an annexe painted red, a makeshift staircase leading to a study on the top floor with 'the most beautiful view in the world': 'the hills where the woods of Versailles begin, and to the East, over Sèvres, a huge horizon beyond which lies Paris, whose smoky atmosphere blurs the ridges of the famous slopes of Meudon and Bellevue; and beyond that, the plains of Montrouge and the Orléans road that leads to Tours'. In one direction, horizons glimmering like the sea; in the other 'a Swiss valley, adorned with the most delightful factories'.[8] Cows, vineyards, the Loire Valley, a 'Florentine' villa, Swiss meadows ('without the inconvenience of the Alps'[9]): the view was refracted through the eyes of memory and desire, though there is still a nice panorama if one climbs to the top of the Avenue Gambetta and enters the Parc de Saint-Cloud, where Balzac liked to walk at night.

Inside the house, his love of gadgets expressed itself in a state-of-the-art bell-system with invisible wires (an invention borrowed from the playwright Scribe[10]); but the bells rang out in emptiness. The walls were bare except for Balzac's charcoal graffiti, which became a permanent feature:[11] 'Here an Aubusson tapestry.' 'Here some doors in the Trianon style.' 'Here a ceiling painted by Eugène Delacroix.' 'Here a mosaic parquet made of all the rare woods from the Islands.' There was also a charcoal Raphaël facing a charcoal Titian and a charcoal Rembrandt, none of which ever turned into the real thing: all *signifiers* and no *signifieds*. It was like an inhabitable book. Ornaments and decorations were to be made from Balzac's drawings – an expensive idea because he was a terrible artist – and the fireplace was to be in Carrara marble for which he wrote to a friend in Italy.[12] Everything in the house would tell a story. Even subsidence could be romanticized. According to Gérard de Nerval, Balzac had heard that penniless aristocrats in Venice were selling off the ancient pillars that had propped up their palaces for centuries.[13] The builders persuaded him to use rubble instead.

It was here that he started work on *Les Paysans*, which finally began to appear in 1844 but was never completed. As a working title he used the proverb, *Qui a terre a guerre* (to own land is to be at war).[14] In Balzac's case, war was a disagreement with his neighbour about the boundary wall; but that was to be the least of his troubles.

The story of Les Jardies has become so bogged down in gossip that it is easy to miss what it says about Balzac in 1838. Almost as soon as work began on the house, there were articles in the press. One story has been told more often than any other Balzac anecdote and still crops up from time to time. It was supposed to demonstrate his incorrigible naivety: Balzac built his house and forgot to include a staircase. In fact, it was common architectural practice to put the staircase in at the last moment – Balzac might have taken the Austrian Embassy as a model – and perhaps the real lesson to be drawn from Les Jardies is that, far from being too naive, he was too ingenious.

Friends might have recognized the danger signs: the flurry of plans for getting rich, the early symptoms of collector's mania and, most worrying of all, the owner's determined impersonation of a man at ease. The Duchesse d'Abrantès, who died that June, was encouraged in March 1838 to look forward to a breakfast of strawberries in Balzac's non-existent garden. He saw himself sitting in a little 'Eden' with mature vines that could be harvested 'within the year'. There would be fruit trees, poplars and magnolias. Like Mme Vauquer, he would have his avenue of linden trees.[15] A financial catastrophe it may have been, but Les Jardies is concrete evidence of Balzac's unerring sense of what was necessary for his work. This seems to be the only possible explanation of a peculiar phrase in a letter to Zulma Carraud dated 5 May 1839: 'My walls have fallen down at Les Jardies and it may be another year before I can enjoy the retreat that I have carved out of grief and penury; but the bother it has caused me has given me the energy I need to complete the task.'

Balzac's mud-heap, in other words, was really another spring-board. No sooner had he bought it than he was thinking of leaving France. Already, the 'defeat' of 1837 had inflated his ambitions. Bigger debts called for bigger solutions, and writing was once again a foot in fortune's door. On a visit to the Chambre des Députés, the 'stupidity of the orators and the idiocy of the debates' had convinced him that he should enter Parliament only at the highest level. By 'blasting open the gates of the French Academy', he would increase his chances of being made a peer and could then take his seat as a Minister.[16]

What actually happened was far more dramatic, and it shows that Balzac had not lost his taste for desperate gambles nor succumbed to anything as uninteresting as material greed. The first ominous signs of a great resolution emerge at the end of 1837: 'a serious and scientific affair'[17] was to take him south to Marseille and then across the Mediterranean to Sardinia. Almost like Rimbaud, he was on the verge of taking 'one of those sublime decisions which turn one's life inside out like a glove'.[18] 'I shall perhaps abandon literature in order to make my fortune.' As a dress-rehearsal for his expedition (still a closely guarded secret) he set off in the spring of 1838 to visit Zulma Carraud and then George Sand at her home in the Berry. It became apparent that his motives for leaving France were not purely financial:

After this life of solitude, how I long to take possession of Nature with a long and rapid dash across Europe. My soul is thirsting for immensity, for the infinite, for nature *en masse*, not divided into tiny parcels but seen in its great settings, moist with rain or bathed in sunlight, traversing great expanses and taking in whole countries instead of little villages.[19]

As Balzac rolled across the treeless plains of the Beauce, he thought of the Ukraine.[20] And here may be a good place to leave him briefly, as he contemplates a change of career, to catch up with the solitary Balzac, the inhabitant of the imaginary palace living in front of a sheet of paper from midnight to dawn – a Balzac we shall be able only to glimpse obliquely through a study door in his last ten years. A Balzac who can perhaps only be found in his novels.

TAKING FULL account of this other Balzac is of course impossible. His novels now extended far beyond his immediate preoccupations and experience, and the whole construction had enough centripetal force to pull in the social and geographical world of France from the Revolution to the July Monarchy. But the same battle between reality and self-deception was still going on in his writing, and Balzac's methods for accumulating knowledge provide keys to his personality which cannot be picked up so cheaply elsewhere. Watching him at work makes it easier to understand his behaviour in the next few years – his obsessions and his failures – and hopefully makes his plans seem less incredible than they are.

A peculiarity of Balzac's research techniques is that a minute item would suddenly engage all his effort while the mass of detail in the rest of the novel gave an impression of otherwise effortless omniscience. Sometimes, his flights of realism simply reflected the satisfaction of a personal need: the erudite passage on hair-restorer in *César Birotteau*, for example.[21] Sometimes, they indicated an attempt to plug a gap in human knowledge. Léon Gozlan was regaled with Balzac's story of how he swotted up on botany for *Le Lys dans la Vallée*. Since the Touraine landscape was to be one of the main characters, he needed to know 'the names of all those little grasses we trample underfoot in the country'. He interviewed his gardener. That was easy: lucerne, clover, sainfoin. . . . 'No! no!' Balzac interrupted. 'I'm asking what you call these thousands of little grasses here' – and he pulled up a fistful of grass. 'That, Monsieur? That's grass, that is.' Similar definitions were provided by a Tourangeau peasant and a professor of botany – 'and so, when I wrote *Le Lys dans la Vallée*, I was unable to give an exact description of those carpets of green I should have loved to depict, stalk by stalk, in the luminous and painstaking manner of the Flemish painters'.[22]

The lesson here is that gaps in human knowledge could be the

[301]

very opposite of an obstacle. In fact, the novelist who is so often blandly cited as the last bastion of an age that thought it could profitably label all the contents of the known universe, actually calls the whole naming process into question. Science, Balzac often remarks – perhaps reflecting on his early attempt to acquire all available wisdom – is a glorified form of cataloguing. When science failed to provide a name for every plant in *Le Lys dans la Vallée* (and there can be little doubt that he would have used the knowledge if he had it), he substituted his own floral idiom, and it is wonderful how more than adequate the substitute is. In the symbolic bouquets Félix takes to Mme de Mortsauf (as Balzac did to Mme de Berny), he smuggled the most intimate depictions of sexual desire past the censors – 'a double corn-poppy with its flower-heads on the point of opening', 'stems writhing like desires tangled deep in the soul'[23] – and in the process prevented the story from suffocating in a shower of botanical terms.

Balzac had revolutionized the novel by giving it a documentary, archival purpose; but one wonders how much the decision to be morally and historically useful was the unavoidable result of his personality. Realistic descriptions guaranteed the novel's lasting value, but they also served as funnels through which any eccentric lumps could be dissolved into the story. When writing *Séraphîta*, he introduced himself to the Swiss botanist, Pyrame de Candolle (an avid Balzac reader) and came away with notes on Norwegian flora,[24] in particular on a rare variety of saxifrage which blooms in the winter and shares with the androgynous Séraphîta an inability to reproduce itself.[25] The reason for this apparent excess of research becomes clear in the novel: a flower-collecting expedition high above the Norwegian fjords in the company of an angel on skis is so out of the ordinary that the attendant details require an extra boost of realism. If the flower was drawn from life, perhaps the angel was too?

It is often in the most 'visionary' passages of his work that Balzac seems closest to his daily self, using debts like tangible truths as a discipline to prevent him from revelling in fantasy – an ability (or an addiction) he was coming more and more to perceive, ironically, as a threat to his livelihood. In the novels, the problem was this: how could a person who was so much larger than life produce an accurate representation of it? One trace of the struggle can be found in the variants of *Eugénie Grandet*. Zulma Carraud congratulated Balzac on his precise evocation of life in the provinces; but then she singled out as unrealistic the most Balzacian character of all – Grandet. Balzac had made him far too rich. He insisted that he knew of such people in Tours, but when preparing the new edition of 1839 he bravely reduced Grandet's fortune from 21 million francs to a humdrum 11 million. Still the fight went on in his mind, and wish-fulfilment eventually regained most of the ground it had lost to credibility: in the final edition of 1843, Eugénie inherits 'not far off 19 million'.[26]

The thirst for knowledge and the need to preserve illusions in the face of it found their most dramatic expression in *La Recherche de l'Absolu*. Balzac consulted experts at the Académie des Sciences[27] and produced a 'mad' chemist who actually succeeds in manufacturing a diamond – unfortunately in his absence, so that the secret is lost. As Leslie Stephen sneered in 1874: 'Every accessory is provided to induce us, so long as we are under the spell, to regard the discovery of the philosopher's stone as a reasonable application of human energy.'[28] And it was a similarly implausible discovery that Balzac was about to consider a reasonable application of his own energy. Yet Balzac is one of the few writers we can happily believe when they call one of their characters a 'genius'. Research then was not a frantic snatching up of trivia but an attempt to stand shoulder to shoulder with that infinitely powerful inner being he first became aware of in the *alcove* at Vendôme. It has often been said that Balzac is cryptically present in the chemist's name, *BAL*tha*ZA*r Claës, but when we read of Mme Claës's courageous efforts to hold the family together, it is hard not to identify her with the author:

> 'Will you not tell me what you are seeking, Balthazar?'
>
> 'My poor child, you wouldn't understand a word.'
>
> 'Oh wouldn't I?. . . Ha! My dear, I have been studying chemistry now for nearly four months so that I can have a conversation with you. I have read Fourcroy, Lavoisier, Chaptal, Nollet, Rouelle, Berthollet, Gay-Lussac, Spallanzani, Leuwenhoëk, Galvani, Volta, in fact every book there is on the science you idolize. Come now, you can tell me your secrets.'[29]

For someone who knew very little of chemistry before starting the novel, Balzac did remarkably well. Some of the experiments he described or made up were not performed until a few years ago.[30] One particularly colourful exercise involves the use of solar energy.[31]

Balzac's house on a hill of mud and the expedition he was about to undertake are a logical extension of his novels. There is a great breath of optimism in his barnstorming research, an ability to savour ignorance like a healthy appetite. Like his father, he refused to be guided by established practice or to believe that it was possible to be constitutionally ignorant of anything. When the editor of the *Revue et Gazette Musicale* wrote to ask what had happened to his 'philosophical study' of music, *Gambara*, Balzac submitted one of his charming, disarming letters – a story-length account of his musical research that was published in the *Revue* by the grateful editor.[32] In it, he placed his investigations in a socio-political light, explaining that, before *Gambara*, he had been 'abnormally ignorant of musical technology'. His knowledge, he said, was purely emotional, the high point being Beethoven's Fifth Symphony – 'the only man who ever made me feel jealous'.[33] Instead of revelling in incompetence, he rejected the notion that the arts could be properly appreciated only by 'experts' and added, 'I shall always belong to that incorrigible and seditious party that stands for freedom of eye and ear in the republic of arts.' The revolutionary image was nicely chosen. He was still the ambitious bourgeois, enjoying a freedom of thought which had to be guarded like a fortress and which, when he put away the manuscript, was difficult to recapture. Then, the pen ran on to complain in letters about the endless struggle for survival, the 'enslavement' to writing and the impossibility of judging and rejoicing in the work he had just completed.

IT WAS IN 1838 that Balzac set about channelling some of his research energy into commerce and industry. There at least there was a reliable basis for judgment (money) and an end to all his problems. All, that is, except one: which plan to choose. The schemes he came up with can be divided into two categories, neither having much to do with literature: practical ideas which he never seriously thought of putting into practice, and impractical ones, which he did.

Among the first can be counted his ambitions for Les Jardies: the dairy, the wine, the pineapples and something that Victor Hugo had pointed out to him as a 'gold-mine': a feudal law, said Balzac, required all inhabitants of the *commune* to deposit their refuse at the foot of an ancient walnut-tree which happened to be on his property. A giant pile of manure would accumulate and Balzac would sell it to local farmers.[34] (Hugo later devoted a section of *Les Misérables* to 'the gold that is manure'.[35]) In Ville-d'Avray today, on the corner of the Avenue des Jardies, a Balzacian coincidence has placed a sign saying, '*Défense de déposer des ordures*'. Perhaps the manure scheme was the peasant in him coming out. And perhaps it was a gene from his mother's side that made him think of setting up shop on one of the main Boulevards as a purveyor of colonial produce: 'HONORÉ DE BALZAC, GROCER', it would say in letters of gold, and everyone would call in just to see him serving customers in an apron.[36] According to one version of the story, George Sand was to be the shop assistant, Gautier would roast the coffee and Nerval would weigh out the sugar.[37] Since the *grocer* was supposed to be the cultural antithesis of the *artist*, there was a sort of practical cynicism in the idea. 'One of the finest expressions of modern society' was how he defined the species in his contribution to *Pictures of the French* in 1840.[38] Balzac's fantasies are unusually instructive. The golden age of the shopkeeper was dawning and it is almost a shame that he never went ahead with the idea. He was that combination of gambler and public performer, with a sturdy indifference to the nature of the commodity, be it exotic fruit or fertilizer, that often makes for a successful businessman – and Balzac knew it: 'If, for the last ten years, I had been in the grocery business', he assured Eveline in 1843, 'I would now be a millionaire'.[39]

Another scheme associated with Les Jardies has a particularly modern ring to it and shows that Balzac's prophetic genius also operated outside his novels. The famous Paris–Versailles train turned out to be a desperately slow form of transport (Balzac had hoped it would whisk him into the city in ten minutes[40] – impossible even today), and the buses were not much better. He wrote to the director of the transport company protesting at the elimination of the 5.10 to Paris; he showed exactly how much money the company could make from people who wanted to dine or go to the theatre in town. The price of tickets should be allowed to fall below the psychological 1-franc barrier. Looking further ahead, he pointed out that 'the more departures and returns you have for Sèvres and Ville-d'Avray, the more people will go and live there'.[41] Like the characters who succeed in *La Comédie Humaine*, Balzac was aware – especially when making plans for other people – that business had to flow with the tide of history.

There were similar attempts to exploit improving communications in his plans for extending his influence abroad. On one occasion, he worked out how to monopolize the art world. A company would be set up to purchase all the masterpieces that came on the market. Balzac would then offer them to the nations of Europe and sell to the highest bidder. This, in fact, is what he later tried to do.[42] Now that such deals are commonplace, the hilarity of Balzac's early biographers seems misplaced. Grand designs and bags of money flit by in his correspondence so quickly that it is easy to treat them as fantasies; but he had a shrewd sense of what was possible and profitable. 'Tell M. Hanski that I think I have found a way of growing madder in Russia', he wrote in November 1837. 'That should wake him up.' Madder was grown for its root from which a red dye was extracted. The dye was often used for soldiers' uniforms, and one of the main industries of Kiev was the manufacture of woollen cloth for the Russian Army. By the time Balzac visited the Ukraine, the dye was being chemically produced. It was then that he devised a strategy for exploiting the vast timber reserves of the estate near Brody that belonged to Mme Hanska's son-in-law. The wood was to be sold to make sleepers for the French railways, in which Balzac had bought shares.[43]

Why, one might ask, did Balzac never become a millionaire? One reason was given by Balzac himself. When dining with George Sand, he announced (prematurely, no doubt) his discovery of the blue rose for which the horticultural societies of London and Belgium had offered a 500,000-franc reward. He would claim the reward and sell the seeds for 100 *sous* each. 'So why don't you start work on it at once?' she asked him. 'Ah!' he replied. 'Because I have so many other things to do!'[44]

The other reason is that the plans that most interested him were what lesser beings might have thought the stuff of fiction. Balzac had become fascinated with the idea of buried treasure – wealth in its purest and most sudden form. Digging for gold first struck him as the ideal solution to bankruptcy in 1829, when Mme de Berny persuaded him it was not.[45] Nine years later, he was telling Eveline that it was the best way to make a fortune without capital. Once the idea was in his mind, a surprising number of opportunities presented themselves. Passing through Vendôme one day, he talked to the son of his old headmaster about a trip to Rome he was planning.[46] He was going to dredge the Tiber for works of art that had lain buried there for centuries. Just the thing to impress one's old Latin teacher; but was he joking or was it really a good idea? Twenty-four years after Balzac's death, a government commission was set up to organize an archaeological exploration of the river-bed.[47] The important point in any case is that, for Balzac, finding treasure was a realistic proposition. So realistic that Auguste de Belloy was able to lure him away from his desk by telling him that his cousin's husband owned a wood in which there was said to be buried treasure. Balzac rushed to Poissy only to find that the land had been sold to a man who made his fortune in the grocery business.[48]

Strange to say, Balzac's treasure hunts are indicative of a new and more pragmatic approach – perhaps the result of becoming a property-owner? A story told by Gautier shows that when he set off on his expedition to Sardinia, he was already an experienced gold-digger, confident that research could do in reality what it had done in his novels. It was logical, therefore, that the reality should first take root in fiction, as Gautier explained. In *Facino Cane* in 1836, he had created a blind clarinettist who could 'see' gold through solid walls: 'Though blind', he tells the narrator, 'I always stop in front of jewellers' shops.'[49] Balzac would simply re-create his character. The blind man's psychic powers were supplied by geomancers and crystal-gazers. 'He claimed to have learned in this way the exact spot near the hill in Pointe-à-Pitre in Guadeloupe where Toussaint Louverture [leader of the black revolt in San Domingo] had had his booty buried by slaves who were shot immediately afterwards.'[50]

Balzac failed to obtain funding for the trip, and it all sounds suspiciously like one of his after-dinner stories. Yet his scrapbook contains a newspaper cutting on precisely that topic.[51] The writer tells of his failure to find the treasure, 'which was estimated in the colony at 30 million or more'. This particular plan is revealing in two respects. First, it shows that Balzac still imagined himself re-enacting the Napoleonic epic. He knew that Napoleon had tried to wrest Toussaint Louverture's 'secret' from him, and that even after the rebel general died of cold and hunger in a fortress in the Alps, stories of crates carried on mule-back up the hill in Guadeloupe under cover of darkness continued to surface in French ports.[52]

The second point of interest is the improvement Balzac made to Napoleon's method. Eveline had several friends and relatives who dabbled in the occult and it was thus that he met 'a Pole who looks for treasures by using telepathy'.[53] Perhaps with time this, too, will seem more prophetic than fantastic. The art of using ESP and a map to look for treasure has recently enjoyed a revival. An American scholar, former president of the Stratigraphic Oil Company, claims to have uncovered a prehistoric settlement in Arizona using just such a method. 'Archaeology today', he wrote in 1977, 'is in the throes of a revolution where ESP is replacing the spade as archaeology's primary tool.' 'The keys to a fabulous time machine are dangling in front of the archaeologist like a carrot before a mule.'[54] Balzac's sentiment exactly.

In the spring of 1838, the carrot took the form of the secret he had learned in the *lazaretto* at Genoa. A businessman called Guiseppe Pezzi had told him of ancient silver-mines in Sardinia that had been worked by the Romans. Unable to resist a good story, Balzac reasoned that with modern refining techniques there must still be great quantities of silver to be extracted from the rubble. A little research proved him right and though the samples promised by Pezzi never arrived, he decided to risk an expedition to that least civilized part of Europe. With its malarial swamps and bandit-infested hills, Sardinia was a dangerous island: a few years after Balzac's visit, an English traveller was advised to arrange ransom-money before heading into the interior.[55] Balzac's only obvious preparation was a kind of magic spell. With his superstition that anything printed black on white might become objectively true, he revealed in *La Maison Nucingen* at the end of 1837 that Eugène de Rastignac owed his fortune to 'silver-bearing lead-mines'. The words 'in Sardinia' were cautiously removed on the fourth proof.[56]

The account that follows – one of Balzac's best travelogues and in some ways like his whole life in miniature – is taken mostly from his long letter-diary to Eveline.

After five nights and four days on the coach, surviving on '10 *sous* of milk a day' and seeing Provence for the first time, he checked into a horrible hotel in Marseille. A banquet was held in his honour by local writers, and he found time to explore the antique shops, where he bought a snuffbox. Then he left for the port of Toulon. He was expecting his trip to last a week and planning a new career as a playwright if it failed. 'Now that I'm about to be there', he told his mother, 'I'm beginning to have a thousand doubts'. A steamboat was sailing for Corsica. After checking the price of tickets to Odessa – thinking of Eveline – he crossed the Mediterranean, 'suffering horribly and spending a lot of money'.

Cholera had broken out in Marseille six months before and he was quarantined in Ajaccio from 23 March to 4 April. There was nothing to do but eat, watch the sea and eat again. 'Boredom has struck me for the first time in my life, this being the first time I have experienced a wilderness.' George Sand had recently introduced him to the pleasures of smoking Latakia tobacco in a hookah[57] and he wished he had one with him. 'There are no *cabinets de lecture*, no prostitutes, no cheap theatres, no society, no newspapers, nor any of the impurities that betray the presence of civilization.' Children swirled in the streets like gnats; the women were xenophobic and 'the men spend all day strolling about smoking – incredible idleness ... much poverty and extreme ignorance of what is going on in the world.' 'I dressed like a pauper and I look like a lord.'

The letter from Ajaccio gives a valuable picture of Balzac coping with an unfamiliar mental state – the result of enforced idleness. Without the writing of novels to act as a brake, his mind raced on:

> I don't dare settle down to work, for I may have to leave at any minute. The situation is the exact opposite of my character, which is all resolution and activity. I went to see the house where Napoleon was born and it's a miserable shack. I was also able to rectify some errors. His father was a hugely wealthy landowner and not a bailiff as several mendacious biographers have claimed.

This was encouraging: Napoleon had had a far easier start in life than his literary successor.

Balzac's first reflections on a 'primitive' land were perhaps predictable – he was never more a Parisian (and less a Romantic) than when faced with unspoilt wilderness. Corsica was 'one of the most beautiful regions in the world' but it was wasted: 'the forests conceal enormous riches, as does the soil, about which nothing is known. It could support the finest marble, coal and mineral mines in the world but no one has studied the region because of the dangers.'

Even an unspoilt 'wilderness' had its consolations: the fact that no one knew who he was – until a law student recognized him and published an article in the local paper[58] ('Alas! What a bother! I can no longer do anything, good or bad, without publicity!'); a measly library in which he read three Samuel Richardson novels in as many days ('stupid and boring', except for *Clarissa Harlowe*, which he had read before); and a garrison of French soldiers. Thirty-four years later, one of the officers related an incident which Balzac modestly forgot to mention to Eveline. There was a side to his character, an unthinking generosity and courage that never shone with such clarity in the troubled air of Paris:

> What a stroke of good luck for the lieutenants of the Thirteenth when Balzac joined them at their table, conversing with them and entertaining them with his inexhaustible verve, his tales, so witty and so varied! . . . The first time I saw him was one morning at dawn when, impelled by his ardour and compassion, he ran on to the Place du Diamant to save an ass that was being attacked by more than twenty mastiffs. The poor distressed animal was fleeing before the abominable pack which seemed ready to devour it, and Balzac had thrown himself resolutely into the midst of all those hellhounds. Suddenly, the dogs, surprised at the arrival of reinforcements . . . turned against their victim's champion and I arrived just in time, sabre drawn and held aloft, to rescue the learned novelist in his turn. What a picture! It seems I looked quite forbidding, for Balzac, with his wicked sense of humour, laughed long and hard when he saw me and even examined me attentively. Our barking friends had fled and we congratulated each other on our victory. What a handsome head was Balzac's, covered with a cap of crimson velvet! What kindness and intelligence in his big, wide-open eyes, as serene as those of a child! How untidy and unpretentious he looked, the son and heir of a King's secretary who, when he so willed, regained all his dignity, his pretensions and his aristocratic airs![59]

The first danger had passed, but there were others to come. In the harbour, there was news of shipwrecks out at sea. Balzac decided not to wait and set sail with some coral fishermen bound for Africa. It was safer than travelling down through Corsica. Five days of 'execrable' fish soup, then another five days moored off Alghiero in a storm (quarantine again): 'I had to sleep on the deck and feed the fleas of which there are apparently a great many in Sardinia.' Balzac had arrived at the island of his dreams with no tools, no contacts, no mining permit and very little Italian. From the deck of the fishing-boat he peered at the shore: 'This is where Africa begins. I can see a ragged population, all naked and dark-skinned like Ethiopians.'

What happened next is not entirely clear. Relying, unfortunately, on local intelligence, he seems to have travelled on horseback into the mountains of Argentiera in the north-west; then, having gathered rock samples, returned to Alghiero. He was obviously in the grip of silver fever since he set off immediately on a journey into the interior which very few people (Sardinians included) had ever made. His account is important as a historical document, and also as proof that the stake in this particular venture was his life:

> I have just done all of Sardinia and have seen the sort of things you hear said about the Hurons and Polynesia. A whole uncultivated kingdom, real savages, no agriculture . . . goats everywhere nibbling the buds off and keeping all the vegetation at waist height. I who have not ridden for four years was on a horse for seventeen to eighteen hours at a stretch, without seeing any human habitation. I passed through virgin forests, bending over the saddle in fear of my life, because in order to cross them you have to follow streams that are covered with cradles of vines and branches which could put your eye out, smash your teeth and break your head. There are gigantic holm oaks, cork-trees, laurels, bracken 30 feet high. And nothing to eat.

Balzac's trek probably took him to Iglesias in the south-west and to the ancient mines of Domus Novas. Once back in Alghiero, he left again for Sassari where a coach service to Cagliari had been established two months before. By coach, he travelled down through the middle of the island by a new road which, as he reported a little later in *La Rabouilleuse*, took an enormous detour because the savages of Bonorva had shot one of the engineers through the head.[60] 'It's the same everywhere. In one district they make a horrible bread by turning the acorns of the holm oak into flour and mixing it with clay – a stone's throw from beautiful Italy! Men and women go naked with just a scrap of cloth, a holey rag to cover their genitals. . . . Everything lies fallow in the most fertile country in the world. And in the midst of that deep, incurable destitution, there are villages which have costumes of astonishing richness.'

Balzac finally reached Cagliari, from where he would sail for Italy on 17 April. Bad news was waiting. The man from Genoa who put the idea in his head in the first place had obtained a licence and formed a partnership with a company from Marseille. The mines were revived and to this day Iglesias is an important mining district. If Balzac had not been so impatient, things might have been very different. He would probably have made his fortune, lived in Italy, even given up writing. . . .

Strangely, he was not too upset – in part because he was already planning another expedition, in part because the object of the trip had lain mostly in the gamble itself. He thought almost with relief of the next challenge: writing plays. But as he wandered slowly homeward through Italy, something happened to his brain. Balzac without pen and paper, suffering from the heat, was a vague, timid creature, avoiding superficial contacts, taking refuge in a little room overlooking the gardens of Prince Porcia. In Milan, he entered his fortieth year, far from home, missing the rain of Paris, miserable under the pure blue sky of Italy – a rare glimpse of an un-Balzacian Balzac: 'If I stayed like this for two weeks, I'd be dead. I can't explain it. The bread I eat has no taste, the meat no nourishment and the water barely slakes my thirst. The air is dissolving me, and I look at the most beautiful women as if they were monsters.'

A letter arrived from Eveline's friend, Countess Thürheim, known to her friends as Loulou. She mentioned Eveline. 'I sat down on a café bench and stayed there for almost an hour, my eyes fixed on the Cathedral, fascinated by all that letter brought back to mind, and all the incidents of my visit to Switzerland passed before me in all their reality and with the whiteness of marble.' 'There, on 5 June at eleven o'clock, I lived for a year.' Shades of *La Peau de Chagrin* . . . It was time, before he dissolved completely, to return to 'that insulting city of Paris with its printing-works and twelve hours a day of deadening work'.

*

BALZAC RE-ENTERED it with a vengeance; but the life he resumed in the summer of 1838 was not exactly the same. His treasure-hunting period would last for about another two years and the events of that period can be seen as the surface activity of an increasingly desperate man. From time to time, he thought seriously of leaving France under an assumed name and starting afresh, like Vautrin dreaming of a new life as a plantation owner with 200 slaves.[61] One dream might serve to represent the others.

In July 1840, he warned Eveline of a new idea: 'I think I shall pack myself off to Brazil in a mad enterprise, which I have chosen precisely because it is mad.' No further details were given and the nature of Balzac's plan has remained unclear. However, two small facts may throw some light on it. First, in a story written that month, Balzac referred, in a peculiarly awkward image, to 'the veins of gambling, as tough as the gangue* in Brazil'.[62] Second, the painter Auguste Borget was about to return from a voyage round the world, during which he had kept in touch with Balzac and Zulma Carraud. When in South America, Borget had met the Bavarian artist, Johann Moritz Rugendas. Rugendas published an illustrated account of his Brazilian adventures. It was translated into French in 1835 and it may have been this that inspired Balzac with his 'mad' Brazilian enterprise.

The book contains some heartening information for would-be prospectors. With a mule and an African slave, 'one can travel in the interior for a whole year with only 500 piastres'. In many regions, especially the mountains of Vila Rica in Minas Gerais province, gold was plentiful; no attempt had been made to separate it from other minerals, and 'both techniques and legislation are in practically the same state as when these regions were first explored'. Even panning for gold in rivers was still a lucrative business.[63]

It is easy to picture Balzac reading of life as a rich slave-owner, gloating over the beautiful drawings of happy miners and Vila Rica itself (the modern Ouro Prêto), rising out of the rain-forest like the Lost City. Perhaps it was his attack of homesickness in Milan that kept him in France. More likely that than the letter he received from one of the chemists he had interviewed for *La Recherche de l'Absolu* in reply to an inquiry about gold-mines in Columbia: 'I strongly urge you to

* Ore-bearing rock.

abandon your idea. . . . There is a Spanish proverb which says that gold-miners and prospectors die mad and their children go to the workhouse.'[64]

The recurrence of this fantasy of buried treasure helps to explain Balzac's erratic behaviour – which would probably not have seemed so burlesque had he been successful. Hoping for gold acted as a substitute for religious faith, as it did with Grandet and Gobseck. The difference is that Balzac was able to turn it into something other than itself and never allowed the means to distract him from the end. The man who mounted expeditions to the end of the rainbow was about to try for the last time – in the words of one of his keenest readers – not just to *interpret* the world, but to *change* it.[65]

CHAPTER FOURTEEN

Barbarians

(1839–1842)

T HE OUTSTANDING paradox of the last ten years of Balzac's creative life is that the more he withdrew from public life, the more his own life was affected by it. Before, when things went wrong, there was always a hint of self-sabotage; now, mysterious coincidences began to link his activities with political events. History, seen through Balzac's life, bears an uncanny resemblance to Bad Luck.

What had happened since Louis-Philippe came to power in 1830? Everything and nothing. Nineteen coalitions had come and gone, Louis-Philippe had remained on the throne, and a generation had grown up to find every position of power already occupied. In *Z. Marcas* in 1840, Balzac seemed to predict the revolution that would sweep away the Bourgeois Monarch in February 1848: 'The youth of France will explode like the boiler of a steam-engine. Young people have no outlet; an avalanche of unrecognized abilities, of legitimate and anxious ambitions is piling up. . . . There are laws of fluctuation which govern generations and which the Roman Empire failed to take into account when the Barbarians arrived.'[1] Balzac was identifying again with people ten years younger than himself rather than with his contemporaries. Like them, he was always starting out afresh, in debt and celibate, and yet, like the elderly Z. Marcas – a political genius who refuses to serve the reigning 'Mediocracy' – he sensed that his political dreams would never come true. It was this uncomfortable blend of sympathy and lucidity that allowed him to foresee the February Revolution; and he knew already that it would be a personal disaster.

A year before Balzac made his prediction, another coalition collapsed. On 12 May 1839, the Liberal factions saw their chance and a violent insurrection occurred. It was brutally repressed and one of its leaders, Barbès, condemned to hard labour for life. Balzac was shocked by the pigheadedness of the Government and drafted a surprisingly inflammatory letter supposedly written by an educated peasant on a trip to Paris: 'Everything ends in gunshots and the gunshots end in executions. The person [Louis-Philippe] for whose benefit these things are done could stop them recurring.' The little-known 'Lettre de Jean Faitout', which was never published,[2] reveals an aspect of Balzac's relationship to events which hardly ever comes to the fore in his novels: a sense of social injustice inspired by the sight of poverty, degradation, and official violence. The same message recurs in an article 'Sur les Ouvriers', which was published: 'When a government unleashes its forces against the masses, one cannot say that the masses are in the wrong.' The Government had created a vast breeding-ground for the enemies of public order; it was like the last days of the Roman Empire, wrote Balzac, only this time intelligence was on the side of the Barbarians. In 1840, he recalled a visit to the Leads and the Wells of Venice. Compared to the slums of modern Paris, they were the height of luxury: 'There are 10,000 zinc-covered attic-rooms in Paris for which people pay one or two hundred francs a year, which are far worse and where many men of talent are forced to live. . . . What an outcry there would be if prisoners were treated in that way! Civilization is two-faced. It wants to be barbaric, but only in secret.'[3]

Balzac's position – a barbarian sympathizer with autocratic ideals – was actually quite straightforward (though the remedies he was to propose in the Preface of 1842 were, and are, highly contentious); but it was a position for which the politics of his time had no room. As a writer supplying a commodity whose inherent value was disregarded by those who controlled the market, he could see that both sides were snarled up in their own ideologies. Once politics – by way of the newspapers – began to infect his daily transactions, his professional life inevitably became a form of protest, a demonstration that political correctness – right or left – had only the most tenuous links with a sense of justice.

This all became ludicrously clear some time after he made friends with Armand Dutacq, editor of the left-wing paper, *Le Siècle*. With the Liberals, he found the same spirit of repression. The literary editor of the paper, Louis Desnoyers, wrote to him in December 1839 on the subject of his satirical sketch of the *notaire* – a species, said Balzac, whose success is directly dependent on its mediocrity: 'My opinion and that of Dutacq is that it would be dangerous to publish your piece on "Le Notaire" in *Le Siècle* because of the very large number of *notaires* who subscribe to the paper.' Balzac became all too familiar with this form of democratic censorship. Every page he submitted was scoured for naughty words:

> Those puritanical Liberals who produce *Le Siècle* ... have moral scruples and they go and demolish the Archbishop's Palace; it's so idiotic it's funny. They are afraid of the word *gorge* [bosom] and they do away with morality. They don't want to print the word *volupté* [sensual pleasure] and then they go and overthrow society.

This highly politicized atmosphere, in which Balzac moved further to what is conveniently termed the Right, whilst defending the basic rights of the proletariat, is reflected in a struggle for his political soul which goes on to this day in academic journals; but it gives the reader of his persuasive *obiter dicta* a chance to be profitably confused. A confusion which illuminates not so much Balzac's contradictions as the inadequacy of political terms as a tool for describing society. This is why the great *Scène de la Vie Politique* of this period, *Une Ténébreuse Affaire*, is not an exercise in ideological axe-grinding but the dramatic portrayal of a *situation* – 'thought coming up against an organizing force', intelligence against prudishness masquerading as political wisdom.

WHEN BALZAC returned from his Sardinian adventure, morals were an unaffordable luxury. What he needed was a short-cut. The shortest one he found forms a suitably embarrassing prelude to his career both as a dramatist and as a social campaigner.

Since the early 1830s, he had been jotting down Napoleon's sayings whenever he came across them in books or newspapers and had the brilliant idea of selling them all 'to a former hatter who is a bigwig in his *arrondissement*'. The hatter was a certain M. Gaudy, who 'wants to be awarded the Cross of the Légion d'Honneur and will get it when he dedicates the book to Louis-Philippe'.[4] The reason this was likely to work was that the Government was trying to boost its popularity by appealing to Bonapartist feeling. Balzac's *Maximes et*

Pensées de Napoléon, attributed to J.-L. Gaudy, Jr, did indeed have the desired effect – a medal for the hatter and 4000 francs for Balzac – although they seemed surprisingly absolutist, even for Napoleon. The reason was that Balzac had added several of his own. But if Napoleon never said that monarchism, like inequality, was a principle 'found in Nature', he should have, and the printed title of the book in Balzac's mind meant that he had. 'Why not order it?' he urged his favourite customer, Eveline. 'You would be buying one of the finest things of our time: the philosophy and soul of that great man, captured after much research by your humble serf.'⁵

Selling a book to the greater glory of a King he despised may seem flippant, but it was a good way to make money and offer the King advice at the same time. It also helps to elucidate Balzac's peculiar brand of political commitment. In the coming years, his plays, his campaigning for the Société des Gens de Lettres, his defence of Sébastien Peytel and the founding of another journal, the *Revue Parisienne*, would all be inspired by the same ambiguous desire to dominate the literary scene, pay off debts and see justice done.

That sense of right-minded convenience and reforming zeal that produced the hatter's maxims was equally apparent in Balzac's plays, but it was far less effective: they were to leave a trail of small disasters through the last ten years of his life and have even been elbowed out of French literary history in part because they were commercial failures. Biographically, they are just as interesting as the novels, and perhaps more so, since they show Balzac striking out into unexplored territory.

The first complete play to hurtle off his desk since *Cromwell* was *L'École des Ménages*, in which a married shopkeeper falls in love with his head shop-girl.⁶ The play was not performed until 1910, which is a shame since it might otherwise have been hailed as a landmark in the history of French theatre: a revival of Diderot's *drame bourgeois* and a foretaste of the Naturalist theatre of the late nineteenth century. As Baudelaire pointed out, Balzac was trying to inject some of the passion, humour and topicality of the popular Boulevard stage into the painted corpse of Romantic drama.⁷ Innovation and mass-consumption did not go well together. *L'École des Ménages* sat uncomfortably in a no man's land between classical tragedy and domestic farce. Balzac offered it to the newly founded Renaissance Theatre which had asked him for a play. They turned it down, wanting something safer, more traditional and less digressive.

Here, with the failure of his play, the real story of Balzac the dramatist begins; here, too, is another reason why his plays have been neglected. The performance always extended so far beyond the stage that the plays themselves are only a tiny fraction of his theatrical *œuvre*. To help him write *L'École des Ménages*, he recruited a starving poet called Charles Lassailly.[8] A familiar sight on the Boulevards, with his red and green trousers and gigantic nose, skinny and dishevelled, Lassailly was picked up by Gautier, transported to Balzac's new home, where he was given a room, fed on cutlets, sorrel and onions, and woken up every night before he went to sleep. Two of the sonnets attributed to Lucien de Rubempré in *Illusions Perdues* are by Lassailly,[9] but the only play that formed in his sleepy mind was an anti-monarchist allegory entitled *Les Taupes ou la Négation du Soleil*. In a desperate bid to finish the work, he agreed to be locked up in his room; but soon after, late one night, he opened the window and fled through the Parc de Saint-Cloud. He was already half-mad, and to judge by the neurotic aggression of his notes to Balzac, going insane was his last rational act: '*Mon cher Président*, I regret very much having received the reproaches you directed at me without my having offered the least explanation.' 'There is no point my eating your bread any longer and I am extremely sorry that my mental sterility has been of so little use on this occasion.' Like most writers who dealt with Balzac for any length of time, Lassailly had gained an unexpectedly clear view of his own shortcomings. In the lunatic asylum he found the company of ancient Greek philosophers and playwrights much less taxing than that of Balzac.

Subsequent events – and an unusual plumpness in Lassailly – suggest that Balzac really did try to help him. Just as he liked to present even his most idiosyncratic characters as social types, so he tended to view the minor personalities who flitted through his life as examples of a particular category of human being. His letters to the poet, after his ignominious escape, bring out his practical, paternal side, showing how stubborn and skilful he could be in minding other people's business; and he was soon to prove that he could make as much noise as Vigny about the policies and attitudes that produced the Chattertons and Lassaillys of the age.[10] Balzac's presidency of the

Société des Gens de Lettres, which he helped to form, showed him at his polemical best, campaigning for effective legislation against pirated editions and cut-throat contracts. In October 1839, he travelled to Rouen to put the Society's case in the prosecution of a journal which had been reprinting articles without paying for them. As he left the court and headed for the coach station, he was followed at a distance by a young man of seventeen who later had much to say about the uncomfortable position of artists in society. He was Gustave Flaubert, and this was one of literature's great non-meetings: he was too shy to introduce himself.[11]

In Balzac's eyes, the root of Lassailly's problem, apart from 'vanity' and sloth, was the Bourgeois Monarchy, and it was indignation at the Government's crass materialism that inspired his next play. *Vautrin* was the first Balzac drama to be performed, and probably meant an end to any hope of being elected to the Académie Française. The Vautrin character lacked the menacing subtlety of the Vautrin from *Le Père Goriot*; even so, the story of an intelligent criminal who infiltrates the highest orders of society, played with great plebeian gusto by Frédérick Lemaître, did not betray the moral fibre of an academician.

As with *L'École des Ménages*, the most dramatic part of the play was the drama that surrounded it. Assuming that anyone with the right bag of tricks could write a good play, he asked Victor Hugo to tell him what they were. He rented an attic room in the same building as his tailor and – luckily – friend, Buisson. It stood on the corner of the Rue Richelieu, close to the theatre, upstairs from the Café Frascati which had once been the famous casino.[12] There, Balzac invited his young friends to come and write the play for him. As usual, he was aiming at outright victory. The dream was a consortium that would consist, symbolically, of twelve literati, including an illustrator, Gavarni, and a publisher, Dutacq. Every stage in Paris, no matter how dingy or obscure, would be shared out among the twelve, who would then supply the theatrical needs of the entire city.[13] Gautier remembers turning up the day before the reading, when playwrights were supposed to read the whole play out in front of the director and cast. He asked what the subject was. Balzac was beginning to enjoy himself: 'If I tell you that, we'll never be finished!'[14]

The consortium never materialized, but it achieved its purpose: to make the humbler goal seem realistic. *Vautrin* stayed on target. Gautier produced another Bohemian who succeeded where Lassailly had failed: Laurent-Jan – crippled, sarcastic and very jolly, one of Balzac's most devoted friends in his last years. Complimentary tickets were issued. Even falling ill just as the text was about to be printed was not a problem. Balzac had a voucher inserted in the first edition, redeemable against a preface which the author promised to write as soon as he was out of bed. In short, when the curtain rose in a packed Porte-Saint-Martin Theatre on the evening of 14 March 1840, failure seemed so unlikely that Balzac had already sold his share of future profits for 5000 francs to a persistent creditor called Foullon.

In the past, Balzac had often allowed a germ of destruction to exist in his plans; but this time it looked like sheer misfortune.[15] Uncertain whether they were watching a comedy or a tragedy, the audience were reassured by Frédérick Lemaître, who played the last two acts for laughs – he had his own reputation to think of. In Act IV, he came on as a Mexican general with a Provençal accent (one of Vautrin's disguises) and a large toupee on his head. Some supposed this to be an impersonation of Louis-Philippe and the key to the whole play: so it was a political farce. . . . Not everyone noticed at the time; but the next day, *Vautrin* was banned – not, as it later turned out, by the Censor, Cavé (who had once written a satire against censorship), but by the Minister of the Interior, Rémusat – a man, said Balzac, 'who tries very hard to appear serious'.[16]

As so often, Balzac's mishaps became a magnifying-glass held up to the age. It was not a pleasant sight. In an unpublished section of his memoirs, Rémusat gloats about a visit from Victor Hugo, who came to appeal against the decision. Accompanied by Dumas and a silent, dignified Balzac, 'Hugo solemnly reproved me for attacking artistic freedom'. As the Minister smugly observes, they were wasting their time. The Government and the Opposition were all confirmed 'grocers' and proud of it;[17] and, as he does not observe, he had been in office for only two days and was trying to make himself popular. The ban was confirmed, Balzac was offered an indemnity, which he refused, and saw what would almost certainly have been a financial success smothered in the cradle. The worst of it was the loss of income; the ludicrous situation and the resulting publicity were, for the time being, a consolation.

The real reason for the banning of *Vautrin* has never been

established. The story of the toupee was blown up after the event, and it now seems likely that Balzac's master criminal fell prey to petty intrigue. The theatre-director, Harel, was about to go bankrupt, and if he could blame his downfall on the Censor, he might receive some compensation. There is also a suspicion that another bigwig thought he might have been insulted. The Censor's report likened Vautrin to the 'subversive' character, Robert Macaire – the ruthless con-man with an infectious sense of humour. A fair comparison, since the character had been created by Frédérick Lemaître. But then it went on in its inscrutable, meddlesome way to find 'aggravating circumstances' in 'the character of a Minister of Police, guilty of having abandoned his son who is taken in by a malefactor'.[18] This is a curious reading, since no such character appears in any version of the play. One is reminded here of Balzac's comment that the mania for identifying the models of his characters had taught him many domestic secrets which would otherwise have remained hidden.[19]

In the bureaucratic jungle, there was probably no such thing as a 'real reason' anyway; yet it seems that some subtle political sense had been at work after all. If anyone thought that Balzac was attacking Louis-Philippe, they were right. Not directly, of course; but it is interesting to note that Lemaître's entrance in the final act is preceded by this snide remark from one of the villains disguised as a bourgeois: 'We're only doing what everyone else does: getting rich!' In 1840, this would immediately have sounded a note of anti-Government protest. If the memory of the toupee was largely imagined, the impression was certainly real.

Vautrin should have been banned. As an example of Balzac's politics, it showed what a dangerous thing 'superior impartiality'[20] could be. By demonstrating that the bourgeoisie was its own aggressor, Balzac seemed to be attacking the foundations of the society he was defending – and a Government which had come to confuse its critics with its enemies.

ALTHOUGH THE Minister says nothing of it in connection with *Vautrin*, he may also have been thinking of another famous footprint left by Balzac on the Government's path: the Peytel Affair – one of the great *causes célèbres* of the nineteenth century, thanks mainly to

Balzac.[21] Trivially, it was just another interruption of the daily grind (Balzac calculated the resulting expenses and loss of income at 10,000 francs).[22] More usefully, it can be seen as a sign that his dramatic and political careers were closely entwined, dictated increasingly by distant aims that might never be achieved.

On 1 November 1838, at Belley near the border with Switzerland, the local doctor and magistrate were woken in the middle of the night by a young solicitor called Sébastien Peytel. Outside, his young wife lay in a carriage. She was dead. Peytel's story was this: he had been returning from Mâcon with a large sum of money when his servant stopped the coach on the Darde hill. The servant fired a shot which killed Mme Peytel. Peytel ran after him with his geologist's hammer and smashed his skull. In the light of day, the story seemed confused, and since Peytel was unpopular, nobody wanted to believe him. He was accused of murdering his wife and servant. On 30 August 1839 at Bourg assizes he was sentenced to death.

Balzac and Gavarni had known Peytel in the early 1830s when he wrote theatre reviews for *Le Voleur*. On hearing the verdict, they set off to defend their former colleague. Balzac was excited and optimistic. They arrived at Bourg on the night on 8–9 September 1839, interviewed Peytel in prison, then hired a carriage and drove to the scene of the crime. Back in Belley, Gavarni grew concerned that Balzac was jeopardizing Peytel's chances of an acquittal; he rushed around chatting to everyone he could find; he even buttonholed the Prefect on the main square and talked for some reason about the dangers of keeping young girls cooped up in boarding-schools.[23]

By 12 September he was back in Paris and gave up three more days to write the famous *Lettre sur le Procès de Peytel*. It was printed in three national newspapers at the end of the month. Thackeray found it long, dull and pompous (and wrote a tedious account of his own),[24] but it can reasonably be seen as one of Balzac's most gripping short stories. This time, a real life was at stake.

His ploy was to tell the truth and perhaps, it seems at first, too much of the truth. Here, for example, is his character sketch of the accused: 'quick-witted, hot-tempered, a man of great moral and physical strength; passionate, unable to control his impulses, he is proud, one might almost say vain, and at times, like most vain people, oversteps the bounds of truth (but in word alone); however, he is essentially good'. The decisive fact for Balzac was that Peytel's physiognomy was not that of a hypocrite – an echo of his belief that the occult sciences should be used in criminal investigation.[25]

Balzac's defence may seem to err on the side of honesty but it was actually quite cunning. This was the culmination of his sporadic legal career and he rose to the occasion, asking questions which went far beyond the case in hand. His idea was to show that the court had accepted only evidence against: the ugliness of Mme Peytel 'proved' that Peytel had married for money; Peytel had been a journalist and therefore must have 'studied crime in the theatres of Paris'. In slandering Peytel, the court was flouting the laws it enforced.

Next, Balzac recounted his visit to the scene of the crime. If Peytel had been a murderer he would surely have chosen a better spot: for example, a lonely stretch of road which he and Gavarni had discovered by a lake in the mountains, away from the customs patrols. Finally, a world recognizable as that of the *Scènes de la Vie Privée* was conjured up to save Peytel from the guillotine. This was the fruit of Balzac's impromptu street interviews in Belley and has the great interest of showing that, however exaggerated some of his provincial scenes may appear, that was what he actually saw: Peytel was the Lord Byron of Belley, the Parisian in the provinces, hated by usurers because he gave free legal aid to the poor, loathed by neighbours because his valet served dinner in white gloves and because one of the items in his little collection of antiques was a medieval chastity-belt. 'This belt wreaked havoc with public opinion.'

Balzac was unfortunately forced to conceal a vital piece of evidence – a detail provided by Peytel himself in a secret confession: his wife had been having an affair with the servant. Given that, everything falls into place: it was a *crime passionnel*. Peytel must have left the carriage for a moment and returned to find the lovers together. He fired a shot which hit his wife, then hammered the servant to death. Mme Peytel was six months pregnant. As she ran, she fell in a flooded field and drowned. Balzac was defending a man he knew to be a murderer, though he does hint in the *Lettre* that Peytel was a 'martyr to his honour'. In any case, the murder was not premeditated and he did not deserve to die.

Peytel's motive seems clear; but what of Balzac's? The attention given to his *Lettre* all over Europe led the usual band of nigglers to accuse him of self-advertisement. Anyone who reads the *Lettre* now is likely to reach a more ambiguous conclusion. First and foremost, it was a speech for the defence of his own profession and his honour as a writer, for the individual against the State, a condemnation of trial-by-newspaper (something which Balzac had to suffer every day), and – another autobiographical nuance – a plea not to judge a man on his 'youthful indiscretions' or his debts, or on a passion for collecting antiques. It was a plea, too, for proper forensic examinations. He was incensed at the stupid eradication of evidence – footprints, hairs and threads – and above all at the way justice could be incapacitated by mere habits of thought. For Balzac, the Peytel Affair was a chance to defend a principle, to see whether he could right some of the wrongs he denounced in his work, a real-life drama which might also end in a sort of redemption. Perhaps, too, in the back of his mind he was defending the honour of his own family, who, twenty years before, had buried their heads while Uncle Louis Balssa lost his for a crime he did not commit.

Justice had its way. The King was about to commute the sentence to hard labour when he received a letter informing him that an acquittal would have a detrimental effect on the *département* as a whole. This must have sounded like a reasonable argument since, on 28 October 1839, Peytel went to the guillotine.

Balzac was furious. He was in the middle of writing a pleasant Cinderella story called *Pierrette*; it was to be a gift for little Anna Hanska. After Peytel's death, bitterness twisted the plot and Balzac produced one of his cruellest tales.[26] The tragic end of the little orphan, enslaved, tortured and maimed by her foster-parents, is made to point to a depressing moral: 'Laws would be a fine thing for the rogues of society if God did not exist.' The blunt, polemical conclusion contrasts with the martyrdom allotted to other saintly victims in *La Comédie Humaine*. True, 'that admirable sentiment we call virtue' has a wonderful aesthetic appeal, but God himself turns up too late and seems little more than a social expedient or a convenient hypothesis.

It says much about the healing power of memory and the adaptability of Balzac's imagination that he later returned in fiction to the mountain road where the double murder took place. In an unfinished manuscript which dates from the last months of his creative life he re-created the idyllic scene on the road leading out of Belley –

the dainty villages, the Alpine pastures, the little lakes of melted snow – like a hope of recovering innocence, with just a hint of what had happened there ten years before: '"We shall talk of all that, dear nephew, when we reach the Darde hill. Sh!. . . Here's Martin the postboy!" he said, putting a finger to his lips. "You don't know what it's like in our part of the world; people's tongues are as busy as their ears."'[27]

A SIMILAR complaint was made of Balzac himself by the Minister for the Interior when a new journal called the *Revue Parisienne* arrived on his desk. Nothing seemed to stop the famous nuisance: the execution of Peytel, the banning of *Vautrin*, even the débâcle of the *Chronique de Paris* four years before. In July 1840, Balzac founded his second review. Though it had only three issues, the *Revue Parisienne* was the most important of his experiments in journalism: it carried his criticisms into a wider field and was his last sustained attempt to change the course of French history.

Balzac was never hesitant in borrowing good ideas. The main thing was to improve them so thoroughly that the original inventor looked like a bungling incompetent. An added advantage was that a market had already been created for the product. One of his first ideas for the stage, therefore, was to hijack Henri Monnier's well-known character, Joseph Prudhomme, the archetypal bourgeois, and then – artistically speaking – 'annihilate Monnier'.[28] Similarly, the idea for the *Revue Parisienne* came from Alphonse Karr, whose tiny pocket-sized review, *Les Guêpes*, had proved immensely popular. Armand Dutacq offered his administrative services and, in July 1840, Balzac launched a monthly review so compact that readers with less than perfect eyesight found it impossible to read.[29]

What they would have seen was a mini-panorama of French politics and politicians, prepared as an antidote to the regurgitated views of other papers. There was actually only *one* other newspaper in France, Balzac claimed, since all news was filtered through the Havas press agency. Havas himself owed his fortune to banking and so remained unscrupulously loyal to whatever government was in power. Consequence: 'that gigantic machine known as journalism is as simple as a roasting spit turned by a poodle'.[30]

The extremes of Balzac's politics were much as they had been in 1836; but a new impetus came from the workers' riots in Lyon and the insurrection in Paris. His attack on poor housing and industrial 'slavery' places the *Revue Parisienne* on the first wave of socialist writings. Proudhon's *Qu'est-ce que la Propriété?* was published in the same month as the issue of the *Revue Parisienne* that contains *Z. Marcas* and Balzac's article 'Sur les Ouvriers'. His diagnosis, however, placed him firmly on the other side of the barricades: the underlying problem was still the splitting up of big family fortunes, the honey-pots from which wealth should flow down through society. The workers, whom it was useless to blame, were 'the advance-guard of the Barbarians'; cannon-balls and prison-cells were ineffective, and only common justice and a powerful head of State would end the threat to civilization. Balzac's solution sounds very much like another prophecy: his call for a dictator would be answered by the counter-revolutionary measures leading up to the *coup d'état* of 1851.

Balzac himself is revealed in such a vivid light by these theoretical speculations because of his determined return to principles. One characteristic tenet, that makes the pages on literature an extension of the political editorials, is the very modern idea that critics, instead of simply airing their personal preferences, should explain exactly *how* a work of art was produced. The prize example was Stendhal's *La Chartreuse de Parme*. Balzac went through it like a museum guide who feels he shares some credit for the paintings, filling in Stendhal's suggestive lacunae with his own rich impasto – a brilliant example of criticism from the inside which delighted Stendhal, although he felt that Balzac had misunderstood the novel.[31]

The other principle was what might be called Balzac's foreign policy. Like the Government, he needed enemies. A novel by Latouche was taken to pieces in what was evidently intended to be the most irritating manner possible. Roger de Beauvoir, who had refused to take Balzac's side in the *Le Lys dans la Vallée* trial, was wrongly accused of usurping the nobiliary particle – an amazingly hypocritical assertion which almost involved Balzac in a duel. Best of all, in a review of *Port-Royal*, Sainte-Beuve was given a 10,000-word lesson in style, informed that the Duchesse d'Abrantès used to call him 'Sainte-Bévue',* then

---

* *Bévue* = 'blunder'.

ridiculed in a short story, *Un Prince de la Bohème*, in which Nathan spouts a stream of alembicated metaphors and opaque allusions, explaining to his bemused listeners: 'I am speaking Sainte-Beuve; it's a new French language.'[32]

What these smears and criticisms show is that Balzac's 'inspiration' often came from antagonism and a sometimes quite artificial irritation with rivals. Thus, the tender harmonies of *Le Lys dans la Vallée* had reportedly been an attempt to 'run Sainte-Beuve through with his pen'[33] by redoing his 'puritanical' novel, *Volupté* – which he actually admired.[34] (Sainte-Beuve concluded that Balzac successfully destroyed the novel on the 'there-goes-the-neighbourhood' principle.[35]) The excuse for these attacks was Sainte-Beuve's diatribe 'On Industrial Literature' in which he vilified Balzac for his grossly commercial approach to art. The article, followed by another attack six months later, appeared in the *Revue des Deux Mondes*. The *Revue* was directed by the one-eyed editor, François Buloz, and Buloz was the man who had sold the uncorrected proofs of *Le Lys dans la Vallée*. Balzac liked to see his enemies coagulate into cliques.

The strongest evidence of how fruitful a spirit of revenge could be came the following year. Balzac's *Mémoires de Deux Jeunes Mariées*, serialized in *La Presse*, was spurned by the same public that had just been mindlessly devouring Eugène Sue's interminable, rocambolesque novel, *Mathilde*. Balzac found it galling that Sue's rambling adventures were preferred to his own treatise on marital politics. He took *Mathilde*, borrowed the plot and wrote *La Fausse Maîtresse* which is naturally far better. Not content with that encroachment, he made the main character's apartment a copy of Sue's pretentious home in the Rue de la Pépinière – even giving it the same address – and presented it as a fine example of domestic architecture since the 1830 Revolution: pseudo-palaces squeezed into tiny spaces, crammed with baubles like a shop window – the image of a bored and confused society.[36]

When Dutacq withdrew his support from the *Revue Parisienne* in September 1840 (thus averting another financial disaster), Balzac's political ambitions virtually ended; but the original motives remained. The two short stories he contributed to his own review – *Z. Marcas* and *Un Prince de la Bohème* – both display a new impatience with the world they describe, and a certain difficulty of reaching a tidy conclusion: '"And the dénouement?" asked Lousteau. . . . "I don't believe in them," said Mme de La Baudraye. "You have to have the occasional elegant ending just to prove that art is as skilful as chance; but, my dear, when one reads a book a second time, one does so only for the details."[37]

The source of this deliberate flippancy was not just lack of time but a desire to grapple with contemporary events and an awareness that civilization itself was running out of time. Traces of this urgency can be found even in novels with little overt political content – particularly in the two stories of *La Comédie Humaine* which come closest to being *romans à clé*. First, *Béatrix*, based on Liszt's affair with Marie d'Agoult and containing an interestingly hermaphroditic George Sand character. 'This is top secret,' he told Eveline, who passed everything on to her brother with an ominous remark that *Béatrix* was 'so transparent as to be in very bad taste'.[38] Second, *Les Secrets de la Princesse de Cadignan*, based on an affair the Comtesse de Castellane had had with the Minister for Foreign Affairs, Count Molé:[39] 'It's about the pack of lies by which a thirty-seven-year-old woman . . . manages to pass herself off as a saint, a virtuous and modest young thing, in the eyes of her fourteenth lover.' One of Balzac's great themes: deceit in the service of genius.[40]

The real question is this: why, for once, did Balzac stick so closely to reality instead of conflating different models? Perhaps it was haste: for *Béatrix*, he copied whole sections of a book by Gautier on *Les Belles Femmes de Paris* – a strange thing to do in a *roman à clé*. Whether deliberately or not, he was also exploiting what has always been a marketable quality in a novel: thinly disguised revelations of what famous people got up to in private. Since almost everything he wrote now had its first run in the newspapers, there was a strong incentive to be sensational and up to date. This might explain the shrivelling up of the more esoteric *Études Philosophiques* (a group to which *Louis Lambert* and *Séraphîta* belong) and a mutation of the original plan which makes *La Comédie Humaine* top-heavy with *Études de Mœurs*. Sainte-Beuve sniggered too soon but nearly made a serious point when he claimed that Balzac was ending his life as he began, with dozens of trashy novels: posterity would see him as a gigantic whale, visible only by the hump in the middle.[41] The serious point is that as Balzac grew older, the gap between the time of writing and the date of the action narrowed.[42] His *romans à clé*, like his campaigns and

[329]

plays, are evidence of certain awkward questions: could modern life be interpreted as it happened, without the mists of historical hindsight? Were his diagnoses ever going to make a difference? Or, in *Béatrix* and *Le Cabinet des Antiques* (1839): what happens to young men from feudal oases in the provinces when they enter the modern world?

It is ironic – that is to say, highly significant – that it was in this period of wild-goose chases and campaigning, distractions and collaborations, temptations to abandon literature or to embark on a different kind of writing that Balzac found the immodest title for his *œuvre*. The words *La Comédie Humaine* first appear in a letter to an unknown publisher dating from January 1840.[43] Some say it was Auguste de Belloy's idea, others that it came from a group of poems by an unremembered poet. The English journalist, Henry Reeve, seems to have suggested that Balzac call his work *The Diabolical Comedy* as early as 1835.[44] But the expression crops up in other contexts[45] and what matters is the allusion to Dante's *Divine Comedy*. It was, so to speak, the last chance for an artist to make sense of a whole society in all its interrelated details, to find that inestimable treasure: a moral that fits everything. It might even be said that Balzac's growing pessimism at the state of modern society bears precisely on those aspects of fluidity and chaos that make such a global portrayal impossible.

FOR IF THE clouds were gathering over France in 1840, they were also piling up on Balzac's horizon. The storm first struck Les Jardies. Not much had gone right. Moving to Ville-d'Avray had put him beyond the reach of the National Guard of Paris, but in 1839 the Rural National Guard put him in prison. The house itself was still heading downhill. One day Balzac went out to inspect storm damage and tore the ligaments in his ankle.[46] His library at least was all in one place; but there were knocks at the door from creditors' agents. Everyone, including a dog (who has left no other trace), had to remain silent until they went away.[47] After that had happened a few times, Balzac moved all his furniture to the Viscontis' maisonette, and when a bailiff came to draw up an inventory he found nothing but a bed – an item not subject to distraint.

The dam collapsed at the end of 1840. Foullon, deprived of the profits from *Vautrin*, wanted his 5000 francs plus 2500 francs interest. Posters went up in Sèvres. M. de Balzac's vineyard was up for sale. The house on the mud-heap vanished into legend and Balzac rented a cunning little house in Passy on the western edge of Paris: 19 Rue Basse (now 47 Rue Raynouard). It was hidden between an upper and a lower road and had two entrances or, what was more to the point, exits. A new play was taking shape in Balzac's mind: 'It's about a man and the battles he has with his creditors, the tricks he uses to escape their clutches. I hope this time to have a success and at the same time to satisfy literary criteria.'[48] In view of the subject, it is interesting to note that *Mercadet* was to be a comedy.

In the meantime, disintegration was spreading to his romantic life, which had almost become a complete human comedy in itself; but it was a comedy made up of fragments and improvised episodes, with some good jokes but no clear message. Relations with Eveline were at their lowest ebb and in some respects never recovered. The correspondence was reduced to a trickle: four letters in 1839, six in 1840, five in 1841. And when Eveline fell silent in her turn, Balzac exploded in a rare display of anger:

> You really are being extremely petty! I see now that you are a creature of this earth! So! you stopped writing to me because my letters were infrequent. Well the reason is that I did not always have money for postage and I did not want you to know. Yes, that's how desperate things have been. . . . There were days when I proudly munched a bread-roll on the Boulevards. And I had terrible sufferings to endure: pride, dignity, hope, my future, everything has come under attack. . . . To think that after almost eight years you still do not know me! My God, forgive her, for she knows not what she does![49]

Forgiveness was useless in the circumstances. Balzac's stock of affection needed an outlet, but what woman would take everything he had to offer? He sifted through his letters, looking for signs of good breeding. One piece of fan mail had the right mix of sincerity and literary craft. He replied, and began a short affair with a woman called Hélène de Valette.[50]

The rich widow of a *notaire*, she had written to Balzac under her maiden name after reading *Béatrix* with its description of Guérande, which happened to be her home in Brittany. A letter to Eveline mentions a trip to Brittany in late spring 1841, presumably with Hélène.[51] They visited the scenes of *Béatrix*, as if Balzac were testing future critics of the geographical persuasion, two years *after* he wrote the novel. It was some time since he last fell in love, but he was still able to keep up a good fantasy. He rummaged through his wardrobe of past affairs: the trip to Brittany re-enacted a holiday with Mme de Berny in 1830; the name 'Marie', once used for the Duchesse d'Abrantès and the Marquise de Castries, was transferred to Hélène. The fantasy even survived a nasty letter from one of her ex-lovers, a novelist called Edmond Cador (which is not, as has previously been supposed, a pseudonym of Roger de Beauvoir):[52] Hélène, said Cador, was not the little Breton angel she pretended to be, but an experienced adulteress. Balzac asked her for an explanation. She panicked; but it seems he was genuinely interested, as a connoisseur, in the reasons and methods of her deception.

There was something sadly half-hearted about this affair. It was the last of those impromptu romances to which Balzac liked to give such a temporary–eternal quality. It ended undramatically in 1841 and Hélène re-emerged only after his death when she tried to blackmail Eveline by threatening to publish her correspondence with Balzac.

Other needs required less ingenuity and were easier to satisfy. Sarah Visconti was still the breath of fresh air she had always been and appears to have supplied Balzac with that unadulterated, adulterous fun that shocked Eveline in the *Contes Drolatiques*. A nice homage to their friendship was a little fable in the collective volume, *Scènes de la Vie Privée et Publique des Animaux*, entitled *Peines de Cœur d'une Chatte Anglaise*. It tells the story of a cat called Beauty from the town of Miaulbury in Catshire – a victim of repressive English mores. It was turned into a show in 1977 and went to Broadway,[53] but has never been seen, at least not publicly, for what it is: an allegory on several levels, social, juridical and sexual. The subject implicit in the title is what Balzac referred to in *Splendeurs et Misères des Courtisanes*, in a phrase equivalent in value to a whole page of social philosophy, as 'that part of her that was least like a Duchess'.[54]

There were, finally, several other 'pussy-cats' in his life who were meant to have an equally therapeutic effect. In fact, they show that Balzac, perhaps for the first time, was suffering from stress. For the first time, his behaviour seems chaotic, badly thought-out, almost as random as that of a normal person. Scraps of correspondence reveal a certain amount of casual promiscuity – a note from a girl called Jenny who worked as a waitress at the Café Frascati downstairs; and some transactions with Armand Dutacq involving 'Annette' and another 'Louise'.[55] Recourse to prostitutes was common enough to be relatively insignificant – but not with someone who had firm ideas about sex as a drain on creative energy. Here, the work appears far richer than his life. In *La Comédie Humaine*, shop-girls and waitresses earning money on the side have surnames and identities; in Balzac's life, they do not. These women were just distractions from the task of finding the global solution he hoped Eveline would provide. Only she could tie up all the loose ends of his life; but apparently she was not the great soul he wanted her to be. It was this longing to end the search that brought about the biggest single alteration in his emotional life – something far more important than his sporadic affairs with Hélène and Sarah.

It took the surprising form of a return to the family fortress: a rearguard action that prefigures the great conservative Preface to *La Comédie Humaine* in 1842, with its defence of the Family as the cornerstone of civilization.

In the midst of all his affairs, Balzac had been writing to his sister as if she too were a lover: 'One of the misfortunes of my life is our respective situation, which forces me to conceal the marks of a brotherly affection that knows no bounds and that grows stronger – and more difficult – with every day that passes. How you would have enjoyed sketching the outlines of my plays for me! But one must not think of what cannot be.'[56] The romantic tone may be attributable to a stylistic habit; but whenever Eveline showed a lack of devotion or confidence, it was to Laure that he turned. Sometimes she seemed as irritatingly prudent and prudish as their mother, but Balzac always associated her with the few idyllic moments of childhood: 'For her birthday we exchanged our tears! And the poor little thing was holding her watch in her hand. She had only twenty minutes – her husband is jealous of me.'[57] Eugène Surville had discovered that having Balzac as a brother-in-law was not easy, and his jealousy is an interesting comment on Balzac's relations with Laure.

Now that brother Henry was far away and doing badly, Balzac

also tried to rewrite his mother's role. Soon after moving to his new house in Passy, he took her in. It was his turn to look after her and he had much to be grateful for – in particular, money and secretarial help. First, however, Mme de Balzac's behaviour would have to be modified. Laure was asked to do the groundwork:

> If she wants to be happy, she will be, but make sure and tell her she must yield to happiness not frighten it away. She will have 100 francs a month for herself, a companion and a maid. . . . Her room is as elegant as I know how to make them. She has a Persian rug which I had in my own room at the Rue Cassini. Get her to agree not to object in any way to what I want her to wear. I should hate to see her badly dressed, and there will be no shortage of money for her clothes. I do not want her to be anything other than what she *must* be; otherwise, she would cause me a great deal of distress.[58]

There are echoes here of Mme de Balzac's nervous, dictatorial letters to her little boy. Balzac's roughness can best be explained by reference to the past: revenge for her coldness to him in childhood, or a desire to create the ideal family he never had. This may even be a rare example of embarrassment. Not surprisingly, he never managed to reverse the roles completely. Their cohabitation lasted barely a year and a half, each complaining that the other was the cause of all their woes. Mme de Balzac's parting letter makes it painfully clear what sort of atmosphere prevailed in the house at Passy: 'I shall not tell you of the grief that your coldness has caused me. No doubt you refuse to believe that I possess the sad advantage of having feelings. Rest assured that, if I thought you had wronged me, you are now forgiven. Your Mother, Widow Balzac.'[59]

The remarkable thing about this brief experiment in family life is not the outcome – mutual recriminations, emotional manipulation, Balzac consulting the doctor to see if his mother was mad, and dwelling on all the miseries of childhood – but the fact that he thought it might work. He even planned a trip with her to Switzerland.

Just over a year later, an advertising-board went up in front of what eventually became the seventeen-volume edition of *La Comédie Humaine* – the great Preface of 1842, with its comparison of human types to animal species; its theory that all creation proceeded from a single, primordial entity and diversified under the influence of environ-

Eveline Hanska in Vienna in 1835. Miniature by Daffinger, painted in the presence of Balzac: 'The last time I was calm enough to study you closely was at Daffinger's' (letter to Eveline, 3 June 1837). (Bulloz; Institut de France)

Count Wenceslas Hanski, Eveline's husband. Drawing by Kriehuber, 1835. (Musées de la Ville de Paris © SPADEM 1993.)

Balzac, by Benjamin Roubaud, *Le Charivari*, 12 October 1838. The caption – '*Balzac, nourri de gloire, est cependant bien gras. Par malheur ses succès ne lui ressemblent pas*' – contrasts the size of Balzac's stomach with the size of his literary success. The manuscript in the background is *La Vieille Fille*, the first serial novel in French literature. (Musées de la Ville de Paris © SPADEM 1993.)

Marie Du Fresnay, Balzac's presumed daughter, by Girouard–Lucquin. Marie's mother was the model for Eugénie Grandet. (Musées de la Ville de Paris © SPADEM 1993.)

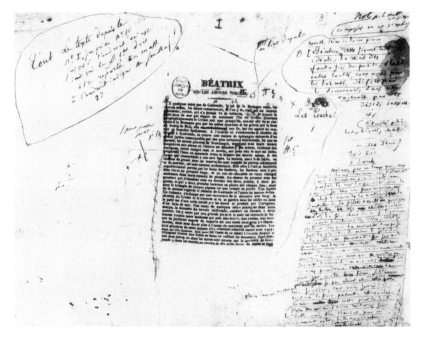

First page of the first proofs of *Béatrix*, showing the draft of the dedication to Sarah
Guidoboni-Visconti. The phrase inserted a few lines before the end is *'pleins d'amour
maternel'* – an allusion to Balzac's presumed son. The text circled on the left tells the
printer to move the entire opening section twenty-two pages into the novel. Balzac
later gave this set of proofs to Hélène de Valette. (Bibliothèque Municipale de Tours.
Ms. 1742.)

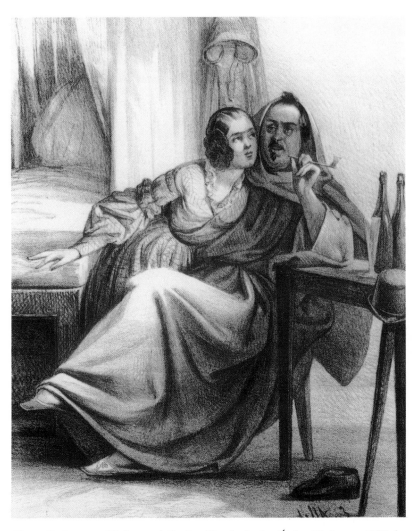

Above: Caricature of Balzac and Eveline Hanska in *Les Écoles*, 22 August 1839, by Edward Allet: Balzac-Séraphitus 'in his enforced solitude receiving the consolation of Santa Séraphita'.

Facing page: The Café Frascati (left), on the corner of the Rue Richelieu and the Boulevards. Balzac's Paris pied-à-terre in 1839 was an attic room above the café. Engraving by Bertrand from Balzac's 'Histoire et Physiologie des Boulevards de Paris' in *Le Diable à Paris* (1846).

The 'upside-down house' in Passy, Balzac's home from October 1840 to April 1847, now the Maison de Balzac. This photograph, by Monlien de Perthou, c.1896, shows the garden as it was in Balzac's time, with its grove of linden trees. (Musées de la Ville de Paris © SPADEM 1993.)

Daguerreotype of Balzac by an unknown photographer, May 1842. This print belonged to Balzac's housekeeper, Louise Breugniot. (Musées de la Ville de Paris © SPADEM 1993.)

'A sketch of her illustrious brother', 1843, inscribed by David d'Angers to Laure Surville. Balzac sent a copy to Eveline Hanska – though the copier had failed to recapture 'the sweetness, wit and genius of the model' (letter to Eveline, 2 March 1843). (Musées de la Ville de Paris © SPADEM 1993.)

'*Et vous, Honoré, en voulez-vous une tasse?*' Drawing by Grandville for a caricature entitled '*Thé Artistique Assaisonné de Grands Hommes*', 1845. The hostess is Delphine de Girardin. Franz Liszt is at the piano. (Musées de la Ville de Paris © SPADEM 1993.)

Above: 'Pantheon' of contemporary writers by Bertall, in *Le Diable à Paris* (1846). Ascending from the inkpot marked 'Ink for Serials' are: Hippolyte Rolle, Delphine de Girardin, Jules Janin, Gustave Planche, Théophile Gautier, Léon Gozlan, Alphonse Karr, George Sand, Frédéric Soulié, Balzac with his walking stick, Eugène Sue with the Wandering Jew (the title of one of his novels), Alexandre Dumas, Lamartine (the poet turned politician). At the top, from left to right: Victor Hugo, Chateaubriand and Béranger. Eugène Scribe stands to the left of Hippolyte Rolle. Directly below him, with top hat and arms folded, is Laurent-Jan.

Facing page: The 'little palace' in the Rue Fortunée (now the Rue Balzac), by Balzac's architect, Santi. The dome on the left is the Chapelle Saint-Nicolas, with a door leading into Eveline's bedroom. 'It's the only house like it anywhere in Paris' (letter to Eveline, 30 September 1846). (Roger-Viollet)

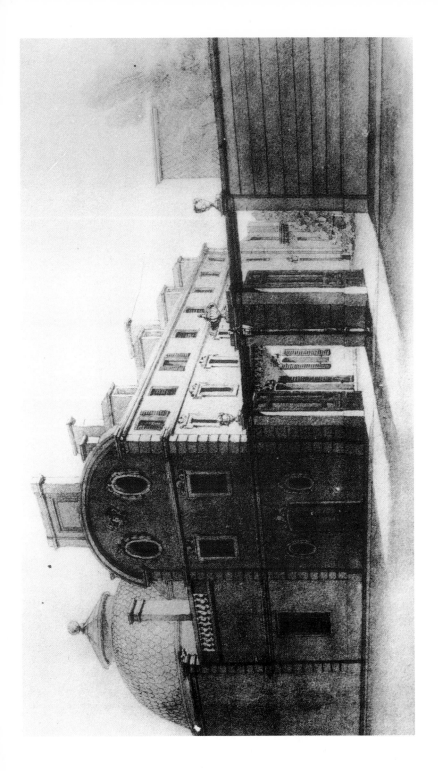

Wierzchownia, Eveline's home in the Ukraine, by Napoléon Orda. 'You didn't tell me that you had a river in front of your lawn, nor that you owned a Louvre' (letter to Eveline, 16 December 1840). (Musées de la Ville de Paris © SPADEM 1993.)

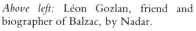

Above left: Léon Gozlan, friend and biographer of Balzac, by Nadar.

Above right: Henry Murger, author of *Scènes de la Vie de Bohème*, by Nadar. A visitor to the Rue Fortunée in 1850.

Left: Champfleury, literary disciple of Balzac and lover of his widow, by Nadar.

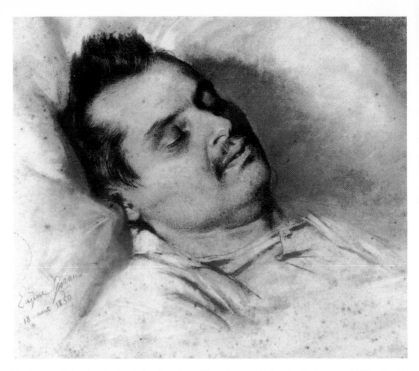

'Balzac on his Death-Bed', by Eugène Giraud, pastel dated 18 August 1850. Traditionally said to be Balzac an hour or so after death; but since Balzac died at 11.30 p.m. on 18 August, and since Giraud's visit preceded Victor Hugo's, the drawing was certainly completed while Balzac was still alive. (Besançon, Musée des Beaux-Arts et d'Archéologie; C. Choffet.)

ment; the destructive power of passion and the perfecting power of Society; the 'two eternal truths' that guided the author – Monarchy and Religion; his desire to depict 'the two or three thousand prominent figures of a period', to write the epic history that was missing for earlier civilizations. The Preface provides a splendid digest of Balzac's favourite ideas and is often used as a kind of certified crib-sheet. Here, readers were encouraged to think, is the key to the whole monument.

In fact, Balzac did not especially want to write it. When the socialist *Revue Indépendante*, edited by George Sand, published an unpleasant article on him, he thought he could persuade her to write the preface as a favour.[60] She was too busy, and Balzac admitted that 'simply reading all my works is quite an undertaking'.[61] (By now, *La Comédie Humaine* contained seventy-four novels and short stories, several titles being umbrellas for more than one work.) As a result, the Preface is both a summing-up and an expression of Balzac's views at a particular moment. Applied to all his work, it has a rather desiccating effect, and readers may wish to immunize themselves against its impressive generalities by reading some novels first. Balzac himself was aware of the danger and worried that the fictional world had already outgrown any clothes he might try to make it wear: it was true he had stood in a democratic election, but 'one should not infer from that the slightest contradiction between my actions and my philosophy'. And: 'if anyone tries to disprove me with my own arguments, it will be because they have misinterpreted an ironic remark or turned one of my own character's words against me.'

Apart from its interest as a personal manifesto – the most plausible attempt to marry science and art in the nineteenth century – the Preface is a masterpiece in its own right: Balzac's intellectual autobiography, the story of *La Comédie Humaine* from initial conception to the moment when the 'chimaera' became 'a reality, with its tyrannical commands that must be obeyed'. Like most autobiographies, it simplifies, seeks to eradicate contradictions and presents a happy image of its subject. Balzac wrote it in the same passionately organizing spirit that made him try to reorganize his mother and that kept the hope of a tidy married life alive. Some of his later novels are practically a scathing parody of the Preface with its assertion that 'the Family and not the Individual is the true social element;[62] but in the novels of the early 1840s, the Family always wins. The battle between order and chaos, intelligence and stupidity was about to begin, and Balzac was digging deep trenches: 'I have just re-read the Preface which opens *La Comédie Humaine*', he told Eveline, 'and those twenty-six pages have been harder to write than any novel, for their prominent position gives them a certain solemnity. There is something frightening about pronouncing those few words at the beginning of such a voluminous collection.' But the printed word had an objective force of its own. He went on, convinced again of his convictions, 'When you have read the Preface, you will never ask again whether I am catholic and what my opinions are. In this eclectic age of ours they are only too clear-cut.'[63]

CHAPTER FIFTEEN

The End of the Tunnel

(1842–1845)

THE PREFACE to *La Comédie Humaine* was also a private celebration of something that could not possibly be mentioned in print. By the time Balzac wrote it, an event had occurred that brought everything into focus, set a clear goal for the rest of his life and, ironically, ensured that *La Comédie Humaine* would never be completed. On 5 January 1842, a letter with a black seal arrived from Russia. He tore it open and read the news he had tried very hard not to hope for: Wenceslas Hanski had died on 10 November. The biggest hurdle to happiness had been removed. He snatched up his pen:

> Dearest darling, though this event brings within my grasp what I have ardently desired for almost ten years, I can, before you and before God, do myself the justice of saying that I have never had anything in my heart but complete submission and that, even in the cruellest moments, I have never sullied my heart with uncharitable wishes. One cannot prevent certain involuntary desires. . . . One cannot keep one's faith, one's heart, one's whole inner being, without hope. Those two motives which the Church turns into virtues have sustained me in my struggle; but I understand your regrets; they seem to me perfectly natural and sincere, especially after the protection that was not denied you.

Now, he went on, after this allusion to her long-suffering husband, he would be able to tell her everything he had had to keep silent (meaning that his declarations of love would become more detailed and more passionate); he would come to Russia as soon as his affairs were in order; he might even apply for Russian citizenship and defect to an autocratic regime. He could then launch a European magazine in St Petersburg. In the meantime, he would work non-stop and save Les Jardies, which had still not found a buyer. One obstacle had vanished and all the others would follow: Lamartine was keeping a rotten borough for him,[1] so he would finally be able to take his seat in Parliament and be worthy of his princess.

The letter of 5 January 1842 must be one of the most enthusiastic letters of condolence ever written. In the face of fresh hope all his misgivings flew away. His letters now became more regular and less reproachful, and the dominant theme of every letter was the same: marriage. Soon he would be forty-three and Eveline, as far as he knew, was in her mid-thirties, but they still had plenty of time to grow old and grey together. All his novels were to form one work, all his actions would have the same object, and all his dreams would be made to come true at the same time.

Two thousand miles away, Eveline was unable to appreciate the simplicity of the situation. When Balzac's letter arrived, Wenceslas had been dead for two months. She had already begun a new life and was discovering aspects of herself that marriage had concealed. Besides which, it was almost seven years since she had last seen Honoré and she was far from certain what role he should play in her future. As if to mark her new independence, a diary she kept for part of this period has survived. It was written, in French, for her daughter's enlightenment, and though most of the details still have to be deduced from Balzac's version, it allows us to step behind the mirror of his letters and to see her for a few months in her own right.[2]

Her first reaction was to postpone his visit. She had practical problems which she may have thought her French lover, with his debts and good ideas, would only exacerbate. Wenceslas Hanski's cousin, a bed-ridden millionaire–miser who wanted to leave his fortune to Anna Hanska, was trying to obtain an injunction that would prevent the estate from falling into the hands of that opportunist writer from France.[3] Even without a trial, she risked losing her estate: she was Polish, was not a member of the Orthodox Church, and her attachment to a foreigner was well known. In a moment of depression, she thought of entering a convent and even told 'Noré' that he was free now to do as he pleased – a phrase he called 'the most atrocious thing you could have done'.[4] It inspired the blatantly autobiographical novel, *Albert Savarus*, and the even more transparent story-within-a-story which the eponymous character is supposed to publish, thus, says the narrator, imitating 'some modern writers who make up for lack of imagination by writing about their own joys and sorrows or the mysterious events in their life'.[5] Like his character, Balzac saw the true purpose of his life's work eradicated, his political ambitions revealed in retrospect as a waste of time. He was also worried about his health. Stendhal died of a heart-attack in March 1842 and the novel is full of allusions to his work. It was an autobiography set in the future. He foresaw himself expiring 'like the messenger of Antiquity' who delivers his message and dies:[6] 'In seven years I shall be fifty. Will my life have been worth the trouble? I shall be a spent force.'[7]

Albert Savarus was a frantic plea to Eveline not to pull the magic carpet from under his feet and – perhaps another example of 'involuntary desires' – literary revenge on 'Aunt' Rosalie[8] who was doing all she could to stop her little Cousin Eveline moving to Paris. To Rosalie, Paris was still the city of blood-crazed revolutionaries who guillotined her mother in 1794. To Balzac, she was malice personified, the woman who relayed all the gossip she heard about him to Eveline. There is a character in *Albert Savarus* called Rosalie who, unlike the real Rosalie, succeeds in wrecking the hero's marriage plans. At the end of the novel, the fictional Rosalie happens to be on a steamboat on the Loire when it blows up: she loses her right arm, her left leg, her face is scarred, her health destroyed, and she spends the rest of her days in a nunnery.

All this was very distracting for someone who was still in mourning and determined to find her feet before re-entering what Balzac himself had called the prison of marriage. In September 1842, Eveline went to live in the capital, St Petersburg, where she was able to follow her court case and began to take an interest in life again. The opposite might easily have happened. St Petersburg society, she found, was a haven for pompous mediocrities; but her own observations are remarkably free of the back-biting that was endemic in her milieu. Her diary shows instead a delight in writing and a sharp sense of humour which sometimes contrasts strangely with her innocence – probably the result of inexperience rather than naivety. Widowhood brought new problems. She was courted by an old statesman, the Comte de Balk, once a lover of Mme de Staël. At first she failed to realize that she was encouraging him – 'I saw the eyes of that Icelandic volcano spewing out its fiery lava amidst its snow and ice' – and was then distressed at having 'infected' a man of his age with 'a sort of moral brain-fever'. It is interesting that at exactly the same time (March 1843) Balzac was describing Baron de Nucingen's terrible infatuation with the courtesan, Esther. Volcanoes are a common metaphor in *La Comédie Humaine*, but now he chose a more hopeful double-image which reminds us none the less of his secret worries. He, too, might end up as an old pet rather than a lover. . . . 'Compressed by the weight of affairs, stifled by continual calculations, by the endless preoccupations of the hunt for millions, adolescence and its sublime illusions reappear, shooting up and flowering like a prime cause or a forgotten seed whose effects, whose splendid blooms obey a chance event or a sun which suddenly shines late in the season.'⁹

It was thanks to a letter of introduction from Balzac that Eveline met the biggest challenge to her freedom: Franz Liszt. When Balzac foolishly boasted about his princess, Liszt decided to seduce her. He used his well-tried combination of romantic posturing, artificial anger at her 'prudishness' and, of course, breathtaking performances at the piano. Balzac sensed danger and warned her that Liszt was spoilt and brutish, 'as fatuous as an actor and as vicious as a public prosecutor – all he has is his fingers'.¹⁰ But Eveline fought her own battle. In recording her conversations with Liszt, she paints a memorable picture of someone who gradually disentangles self-delusion from what was beginning to look very much like love. She admitted to herself that her plan to become his *directeur de conscience* and thus to study 'an extraordinary personality' was a way of silencing her own conscience. Their last meeting, on 3 June 1843, gives striking evidence of her loyalty to Balzac and has therefore been ignored by critics who like to be upset by the thought of her knowing other men after Balzac's death. 'As for forgetting you', she told Liszt, 'it is difficult enough when one knows you and impossible when one loves you and is loved by you.' For someone who was lonely and had an almost religious respect for 'genius', this was a brave thing to do. She was just as capable as Balzac of keeping up a beautiful illusion, but, like Balzac – more than Balzac – she had learned to live with solitude, social as well as intellectual. She had a great desire to be in love but she was equally determined to retain control of her life, 'to banish the slightest trace of stormy emotions from my horizon, as calm and serene as an evening sky in autumn'. This was the sky in which Balzac's 'adolescence' and 'sublime illusions' were hoping to shine.

If Balzac had been able to read her diary he would have been extremely relieved to see her emerge from this difficult period still in love with him. She talks of his kindness, his nobility, his sweetness, his 'blazing intelligence' and his evergreen heart. It was not simply a case of seizing on the best available option. It was the act of someone who knew the value of happiness and, as she wrote with sad insight, the value 'of knowing what one is sacrificing and to what one is sacrificing it'. Balzac had been an excellent judge of her character, but for all his denials, he had also been the severest test of that character.

WHILE EVELINE'S life changed, Balzac's became more like itself than ever. In the period leading up to his romantic pilgrimage to St Petersburg in July 1843, he worked in a fever of anticipation, turning out some of his best and most hastily written stories – *Ursule Mirouët*, *Albert Savarus*, *Un Début dans la Vie*, the concluding part of *La Rabouilleuse*, *La Muse du Département* – and two works which he counted among his personal favourites: *Le Curé de Village* and *Honorine*. The former was intended to show how useful Christian repentance is to modern society – whatever its metaphysical value – just as *Le Médecin de Campagne* had demonstrated the civilizing effect of philanthropy.[11] It was partly a comment on what he saw as Eveline's unhealthy, emotional mysticism; he was slightly jealous of her God. In the latter, a husband secretly keeps his estranged wife in relative luxury by paying inflated prices for her artificial flowers – a fantasy which precisely fails to mirror Balzac's situation. In a similar vein, he began *L'Envers de l'Histoire Contemporaine*, its sensational title appealing to what a cynical author saw as the general public, while its subject (an undercover organization performing heroic acts of charity) was another attempt to win the Prix Montyon for virtuous fiction. Presumably, Balzac expected the judges not to have read the end of *Illusions Perdues* and the start of *Splendeurs et Misères des Courtisanes*, in which the increasingly sinister and more obviously homosexual Vautrin reappears, two fictional years after his arrest at the end of *Le Père Goriot*. In his new guise as a Spanish priest, the Abbé Herrera, the

[341]

character is physically different – shorter, fatter and much more like Balzac himself.[12] The arch-criminal whose roots can be traced to Balzac's early Gothic novels was being prepared for a scandalously happy end.

Apart from producing what might be called the longest sustained burst of good writing in the history of literature (if there were reliable equations for such things), he was also furiously revising his earlier novels for the complete edition of *La Comédie Humaine*, stitching together the melodramatic episodes that make up *La Femme de Trente Ans* and pointedly re-entitling the last part 'The Old Age of a Guilty Mother': everything was coming together in its proper moral order. Although his sentences sometimes disintegrate under the weight of revisions, *La Comédie Humaine* as a whole was becoming more coherent, and it may well be that working at speed was the only way to hold so many threads in his hand at one time.

Further assistance was provided by the usual discrepancy between product and motive: '*la grrrrrande Comédie Humaine*', as he had started to call it, and the less lofty aims of its author. He wanted, of course, to pay his debts – if only to convince Eveline of his financial competence – and to ensure that his publishers had enough material to keep them busy while he was away in Russia. Even then, he found himself plunging down side-tracks, writing jocular pieces for coffee-table books like *Le Diable à Paris*. Balzac's version of that light, allusive wit that was considered typically French (especially by the French) has survived quite well, and his tongue-in-cheek sketches of characters and city scenes are often republished under little-known titles for the eventual disappointment of the casual book-buyer. Balzac himself dismissed his humorous articles as helpings of 'that subtle silliness that appeals to the masses';[13] but combined with his naturalist's approach to human society, it produced such comic masterpieces as the *Monographie de la Presse Parisienne* in which he subdivides that shameful profession into its several species in a kind of journalistic *Voyage of the Beagle*.

Unlike Darwin, Balzac observed these species mostly in his brain. He was already a nocturnal creature and was now becoming subterranean too – literally as well as figuratively. From 1842 to 1845, there are few long letters to anyone but Eveline; each page, he told her, so she would have an exact measure of his love, represented '60 roubles'

(240 francs) of lost income. Most of the letters to other correspondents were the sort of message that would later have disappeared down the telephone-line. The two most frequently cited names are those of his closest business friends: first, Pierre-Jules Hetzel, a young publisher who remembered Balzac complimenting him, 'with a bizarre kind of naivety, on what he called my ruinous good faith'.[14] (Hetzel took the hint and sold some of Balzac's promissory notes to a third party, thus attaching himself to the growing band of Balzac's enemies.) Second, Balzac's solicitor, Gavault, who was 'like a mother' to him.[15] By this, he meant someone who was unthinkingly devoted and who, unlike most long-term benefactors, never lost respect for the beneficiary: 'After two years he still treats me with as much deference and admiration as ever! Isn't that the mark of a great soul?' The implied criticism of his unmaternal mother – who wanted the 21,000 francs her son still owed the family – was also a recognition that only people with a well-developed sense of self-sacrifice were able to put up with him: a typical mixture of ironic self-awareness and straightforward arrogance which explains why Balzac had such good friends for such short periods.

The model solicitor was one of the rare visitors to Balzac's little eighteenth-century house in the suburban village of Passy – now the Maison de Balzac. An unremarkable door opened on to a steep staircase leading down to an entrance that was invisible from the street. Nerval called it an upside-down house.[16] Balzac had rented the main section and western wing of the building, which has changed greatly since he lived there; but it still has the small rectangular garden overlooking what was soon to become the clinic of the alienist, Dr Blanche – where Nerval was treated – and what is now the Turkish Embassy; and it is still possible, when attending a meeting of the Friends of Balzac in the library two floors below street-level, to fantasize oneself into the opening pages of a Balzac mystery. From his letters to Eveline, we know that the study was south-facing; it had an oak ceiling, a red carpet, and walls covered in red velvet with vertical bands of black silk. In front of him was the miniature portrait of Eveline by Daffinger and, behind, a picture of the estate at Wierzchownia.

There, at a small wooden desk, the man who was still in hiding after so many years wrote long letters to Eveline and tried to sound completely honest. He confessed to his affairs with Henriette de Castries and Sarah Visconti; but both women, he claimed, were so vindictive that he was now 'more cruelly punished than you would have wished had you wanted revenge'.[17] All his idols were sacrificed. He even complained retrospectively of Mme de Berny's destructive jealousy. Whether or not he actually believed himself, it shows how desperate he was not to see Eveline slip away at the last. His affairs, he insisted, had been purely medicinal – refreshments for the athlete – and most of what she heard about him was preposterous: 'They think My Hugeness is capable of sending princesses into a swoon.' She should realize that, 'since 1833, Ev. has been the guiding principle and cause of all I have done', and that while his feet may have dangled in the mud, he was able to keep his 'heart, soul and immaculate love 1000 feet above'.[18]

It was perhaps because of this mystical ability that a peculiar situation developed in the house at Passy: for Balzac, it was a practical arrangement; for Eveline, a further test of her love.

When he rented the house, Balzac was careful to neglect the legal formalities: the lease was signed by a woman called Philiberte-Louise Breugnol and letters were to be addressed to the non-existent M. de Breugnol, or Brugnol. Louise Breugniot (her real name) was born in the mountains of the Massif Central in 1804 and kept house for Balzac for five years.[19] She had once done the same for his old enemy, Latouche; but Latouche abandoned her in 1839, perhaps after making her pregnant, and she took refuge with the poetess Marceline Desbordes-Valmore. On visits to Marceline, Balzac saw a beautiful, timid young woman, hardly the repulsive '*chouette*'* he talks about so convincingly to Eveline. Everyone else remembers her as an attractive blonde. She was fiercely defensive, trying to keep her dignity in difficult circumstances, and endowed with what Balzac and Marceline both saw as a canine sense of loyalty. After years of living in Paris, she still dressed like a country girl. Cousin Bette may be a partial mental image of her,[20] though the character's evil genius reflects the role she came to play in Balzac's life rather than her personality; and even then,

* Lit.: *owl*. Fig.: *old harpy* – by allusion to her fiancé, the sculptor Carle Elschoët, a model for Wenceslas Steinbock in *La Cousine Bette*.

he may have invented her 'crimes' in order to persuade Eveline that his feet were still clear of the mud.

The tragedy began when Mme de Balzac moved out, handing the keys to Louise Breugniot. On that occasion, she reported to Laure: 'That woman is the very spirit of probity and discretion. I have no qualms about leaving her in charge. She is fond of Honoré and looks after him well.'[21] So well that, despite having no education, she also took care of business. She learned to understand contracts, was as thrifty with Balzac's money as with her own, had a keen ear for what publishers and family members were saying behind her master's back, and was very nearly the perfect wife. Far too good to lose. . . . Day by day, Balzac created expectations he may even have intended to satisfy. In a letter written in 1857, Louise talks of the 'dreadful sadness' she felt when revisiting 'a house we nearly rented in Baden-Baden where we were to have ended our days together'.[22] There is no trace of such a retirement plan in Balzac's letters, but he did say something to Eveline of a cottage in the Pyrenees. Eveline was immediately suspicious. Wasn't that the sort of place a mountain girl might want to retire to? What exactly was the nature of their relations? Balzac leapt to his own defence: 'You mistook the servant for the mistress, which is very bad; but let's not talk of all that.' Louise may not have been a mistress, but she was certainly more than just a housekeeper, accountant and spy. When the letter with the black seal came and changed the future, they had been living together for over a year in the hideaway at Passy, and 'Mme de Brugnol' already belonged to Balzac's sentimental family.

IT IS EASY to sympathize with Eveline's efforts to discover the biographical truth about Honoré. Every aspect of himself he presented to the world was in some way extreme, and perhaps the best way to grasp him in all his rotundity is to view these simultaneous aspects separately, like the sequence of pictures in a kinetoscope. The difficulty is that the subterranean Balzac of the early to mid-1840s was someone who had succeeded in trimming his life of all the secondary motives and distractions that usually constitute half of normal existence. This is the frighteningly intense, almost bullish Balzac of the daguerreotype of 1842, which he admired for its 'truth' and 'precision'.[23] The general implication in Balzac's pose (which, despite its apparent rigidity, he would have held for less than a second) is that writing *La Comédie Humaine* called for the stamina of a sculptor and the self-abnegation of a hermit. The hand across the breast is faintly Napoleonic and apparently not, as has been suggested, a sign that Balzac had joined the Freemasons. An equally esoteric but more appropriate reading would be Gautier's assertion that Balzac believed in psychic waves which could make an impression on a photographic plate.[24] The daguerreotype is a study of a monomaniac, unable or unwilling to escape from his obsessions and habits,[25] struggling against time and illness, and looking to a future he carried within himself: the conqueror, the fantasizer, the disappointed child. It is also the Balzac who, in the early hours of a cold winter morning in 1844, described himself to Eveline in a love-letter only he could have written:

> This, in short, is the game I am playing. Four men will have led great lives: Napoleon, Cuvier, O'Connell,[26] and I want to be the fourth. The first one lived the life of Europe, with armies instead of blood! The second espoused the globe. The third made himself the incarnation of a people, and I – I shall have carried a whole society within my head. One might as well live like that as spend one's evenings saying, Spades, Trumps, Hearts! . . . or trying to work out why Mrs So-And-So did one thing or another. Yet something greater and happier than the Writer will have lived within me, and that is the Lover! My love is finer, greater and more complete than any of that! Without that fullness of heart I should never have accomplished one tenth of what I have done. I should never have had this ferocious courage. You should always tell yourself that in your moments of depression and you will see from the effect (my work) how great was the cause!

Taken out of context – as many things inevitably are in a biography – this may sound like arrogance masquerading as a compliment; but it would be more profitable to see it as an absence of false modesty and to compare it to the mental preparations of a runner before a race. The dominant tense in Balzac's self-portrait is the future perfect.

The same paring away of inessentials was apparent in his increasingly rare excursions into society. Most of his friends were really either acquaintances or accomplices: among the latter, Gautier and Nerval, who wrote or signed advertisements for Balzac's work disguised as book-reviews.[27] He was beginning to enjoy throwing his age about and it was mostly with young people of his own social background that he relaxed and became what it is tempting to call himself. Often, this meant laying on a large feast, sometimes with an unusual theme. On one occasion, the entire meal consisted of onions, which Balzac recommended as a purgative for mind and body: onion soup, onion purée, onion juice, onion fritters and onions with truffles. Two hours later, all his guests were sick.[28] Lamb-chops were also a favourite,[29] and virtually any deceptively simple dish that reminded him of those 'unsung geniuses' in the provinces (where 'monotony always turns the mind to cooking') 'who can render a simple plate of beans worthy of that nod with which Rossini acknowledges a piece that is perfectly performed'.[30] In any account of Balzac's life his stomach should be one of the heroes. Most of the time he was abnormally abstemious, but he could gorge himself like a camel at an oasis and drink – preferably Vouvray – without getting drunk: 'I am an expensive guest', he liked to say.[31] Feasting for Balzac was partly a spectator sport, until it came to the fruit course, when he would remove his cravat, undo his shirt and demolish a giant pyramid of pears or peaches,[32] homing in on 'those twisted, desiccated fruits with black patches that gourmets know from experience and under whose skins Nature enjoys placing exquisite tastes and odours'.[33] Pear was the dominant smell in his Passy retreat according to Nerval,[34] and at one point his pear reserves reached 1500.[35] The image of Balzac stockpiling fruit is a cheering contrast to the little boy in Tours ogling his classmates' *rillons* and *rillettes*; but eating was also a serious scientific interest. He wrote a short life of Brillat-Savarin for Michaud's *Biographie Universelle* and called for an international culinary language,[36] a kind of gourmet's periodic table that would allow the same dish to be created anywhere in the world – an idea later exploited to devastating effect by McDonald's. *La Comédie Humaine* itself is crammed with more dishes and drinks than most people consume in a lifetime: fifteen different types of fish, sixteen fruits (excluding all 'the rarest fruits from China' in *La Peau de Chagrin*), wines from thirteen different regions of France and nine other countries, etc., etc.[37] He might not have been too offended by Sainte-Beuve's remark that in 'the younger generation' Balzac was the favourite author of gluttons.[38]

It was a superficially different Balzac who put on his 'moral corsets'[39] to dine in town, where he met the writers and composers who were normally in circulation: Heinrich Heine, Astolphe de Custine (a potentially compromising relationship, since Custine had published an attack on Czarist Russia), Berlioz, Liszt and Chopin (whom Balzac hoped to recruit as a piano-teacher for Anna Hanska[40]), and Hans Christian Andersen, who sat with Balzac in the salon of the Comtesse de Bocarmé and described him, approvingly, as 'a little ball with square shoulders'.[41] However, if all the sightings of Balzac in the 1840s were put together, he would sound more socially active than he was: people simply remembered meeting him and a good Balzac story always helped to sell a volume of memoirs. One journalist claimed to have earned 800 francs (about £2400) in six months by writing 'the Balzac article' for his newspaper.[42] Balzac changed according to his setting. In the salons of Paris, people he considered his social equals or superiors found his behaviour disappointingly impeccable. A friend high up in the diplomatic service even offered him a job as a Government spy, perceiving that a *Comédie Humaine* with an official key would be extremely valuable to an embattled regime. But the wider the audience, and above all the less aristocratic, the more he loosened his 'corsets'.

The best example of Balzac in full flight was his most bumptious attempt to succeed as a playwright: *Les Ressources de Quinola*, originally entitled *L'École des Grands Hommes*.[43] The subject of the play was a strange one for the novelist of modern life.[44] It told the story of the man who invented a steamboat in the sixteenth century and deliberately sank it in Barcelona harbour in front of 200,000 spectators. The moral was that great minds are always vanquished by petty schemers and creditors, and Balzac made sure that the play itself would illustrate the moral by trying to do everything himself. He turned up for the reading at the Odéon with only four acts completed and improvised the fifth act in what was later felt by some to be the best performance of the play. Then, for several weeks, he directed rehearsals, corrected the text as they went along, dined with the actors and took the bus back to Passy every evening to catch up with his writing.[45] He also caught a bad cold.[46] In the meantime, he hired the entire theatre for the first three nights, sat behind the ticket-counter and sold the tickets in person at inflated prices, but only to members of the nobility and people with suitable references. He wanted an audience that would look like a scene from one of his Parisian novels. A handful of journalists were given insultingly bad seats; the head of the *claque* was told his services would not be required, and when Balzac changed his mind there was no time to rehearse the *claqueurs*, who did not know when to clap.

Shortly before the curtain went up on the evening of 19 March 1842, Balzac saw what he had done. The auditorium was three-quarters empty and had to be topped up with anyone who happened to be waiting for a seat. Since the Odéon was in the heart of the Latin Quarter, its regular customers were people who did not consider theatre-going to be a purely passive form of entertainment. The rest of the audience were annoyed at having paid so much for tickets and many of them later sued the management successfully. The result of Balzac's careful planning was that the players were drowned out by farmyard noises, pelted with missiles (including a cooked apple – evidence, surely, of premeditation), and though it struggled on for nineteen nights, *Quinola* sank like the famous steamboat. It was not performed again until 1863. After the curtain fell on the first night, Balzac went missing and was eventually found fast asleep in one of the boxes. Léon Gozlan records this as a sign of cheerful stoicism; physical and mental exhaustion seem more likely.

On the fourth night, when Balzac handed control of the theatre back to the management, the police cordoned off the *parterre*, expelled the most vociferous spectators and those who were left shouted words like 'Superb!' at inappropriate moments. By the standards of the time, it was not quite the disaster it might appear. Balzac himself was fairly pleased, though none the richer: '*Quinola*', he told Eveline, 'has been the object of a memorable battle, similar to the battle of *Hernani*. People came to boo it from beginning to end without wanting to hear any of it for seven consecutive nights.'[47] As most reviewers realized, the real subject of the play was 'Balzac Against His Contemporaries' and, in that respect, a modest success would have been a moral failure. This was the conclusion Balzac reached in a preface to the published edition. The 'treachery' of the critics, he wrote, was 'one of the best things that could have happened to the author: one gains experience and one loses false friends'.

None of this really confirms the conventional image of the lovable incompetent muddling his way through the most appalling scrapes. Aspects of the *Quinola* episode that recur elsewhere tend rather to suggest a healthy paranoia actively seeking its justification, and it seems that one of the principal causes of discord with Eveline was just such a suspicion on her part. Balzac had begun to indulge his fondness for testing intellectual tolerance with a new vigour, on as well as off the stage. George Sand was asked if she also wanted her servants to take her democratic precepts seriously.[48] He told the Catholic editor of the *Gazette de France*, the Abbé de Genoude, that he, too, believed in miracles 'for the excellent reason that he had performed some himself by the laying-on of hands, but had been unable as yet to resuscitate the dead'.[49] The writer and society hostess Virginie Ancelot reports with only mild amusement that Balzac deliberately embarrassed a politician 'of the highest merit' from Louisiana by explaining that only the pawnbroker stood between him and starvation, and that instead of praising him, people should give him money.[50] The politician, named only as M. G., can be identified as Charles ('Judge') Gayarré, which puts Balzac's rudeness into perspective. Gayarré was a mediocre historian who spent eight years 'convalescing' in France, then went home to become Secretary of State as a member of the Know Nothing Party, lost his job because of election fraud and wrote a political satire which the *Dictionary of American Biography* describes as 'remarkably mirthless'. An excellent choice of victim.

Whatever satisfaction Balzac derived from annoying people, he was following the advice he gave to Eveline. If gossips said he was a thief, she should 'tell them I'm a murderer' and explain that he escaped 'public retribution' only because of his 'immense charm'.[51] Perhaps there was an element of revenge for the days when he was only accidentally amusing and doted indiscriminately on the stars of high society. Perhaps, too, it was the result of hard work and illness. His old friend the ironmonger twice complained of his angry outbursts. Balzac put it down to the irritation caused by coffee, which normally was channelled on to paper;[52] but it was inevitable that someone who spent most of his time in his own company should treat other people as he treated himself – aggressively and, despite what everyone thought, with a pinch of salt. Even in *La Comédie Humaine*, Balzac's own characters poke fun at him – his obsession with middle-aged women, physiognomy, rational materialism, or the vital importance of Family, Property and Religion.[53] Almost every serious character has a silly counterpart. Gambara, the composer in search of the perfect symphony, lodges in the house of a restaurateur whose search for the perfect dish has led to his expulsion from Italy because his food is so disgusting: the Unknown Masterpiece reincarnated as spaghetti bolognese.

The other lesson to be drawn from Balzac's belligerence is that when he talked about himself he was also talking about an image which had acquired a life of its own. This is what distinguishes him from his bourgeois-hating colleagues in the younger generation. When he demanded a gargantuan fee for writing a piece on the Rue Richelieu (because obviously he would have to visit every shop in the street),[54] he was referring to his notorious passion for minutiae which made critics compare his descriptive passages to an auctioneer's catalogue.[55] 'Since we are accused of poaching on the preserves of portrait-painters, auctioneers and milliners,' says Bixiou in *La Maison Nucingen*, 'I shall not subject you to the description of the person in whom Godefroid recognized his mate.'[56] Balzac was now one of the most famous living people in Europe. His novels were available all over the world, from India to the United States, often in translation – far more translations, in fact, than are listed in library catalogues and bibliographies, the reason being that many of his novels were translated for newspapers and never appeared in book form. There were potted histories of his life and works. Complete strangers knew all about him. Friends told him of conversations they had overheard in buses and cafés about his private life and especially his debts.[57]

Balzac found some of this amusing, even flattering – a new type of dahlia that was named after him,[58] a whaling ship called *The Balzac*,[59] the ceremonial ox in the Mardi Gras Carnival christened 'Goriot'[60] – but most of it was embarrassing and intrusive. In Russia, a reproduction Balzac bust was on sale; in one region, ladies prided themselves on knowing all his characters in chronological order; and there was a man in the Ukraine who went to church every Sunday and, like Antoine Doisnel in François Truffaut's *Les Quatre Cents Coups*, lit candles to his hero.[61] Balzac never confused these phenomena with intelligent recognition of his genius. They seemed rather to be the opposite. In some respects, his public image had changed very little since the days of *La Peau de Chagrin*; but it was projected now on to a much larger screen. A scene from *La Muse du Département* was cited in Parliament as proof that novelists were becoming too immoral for the good of the nation. The journalist, Étienne Lousteau, sits in a carriage with Dinah Piédefer, the 'Muse' of the title. The significant detail is that Dinah's dress is made of organdie, 'the only material that cannot be smoothed out again once it has been crumpled'. Lousteau sees his rival approach on a horse and crumples the dress to make it look as though Dinah has succumbed. . . .[62] 'The *députés*', wrote Balzac, 'thought that I was alluding to the most atrocious obscenity and to what in such a short space of time would have been impossible!'[63] It was a ludicrous misunderstanding but a nice addition to the long history of governments engaging in textual analysis. It shows, too, that Balzac was right to be suspicious of fame, because the fantasies of the reader easily became realities for the writer. The debate about what Dinah actually had done to her foreshadows the law of 1850 which effectively banned serial novels because they were 'demoralizing' the working classes.

Balzac certainly contributed to his own legend. Unlike many of his contemporaries, however, most of his efforts at self-advertisement were supposed to draw attention to his work, not to his personality. As early as 1835, when he wrote a chapter of *Séraphîta* at the printer's in a matter of hours,[64] he had learned to exploit emergencies by doing in public what he normally did in private (sometimes known as 'showing off'). In 1844, he did something similar with *Les Paysans*: 'When the workers saw me writing 6000 lines in ten days, they were really horrified. The typesetters are actually reading the book – something which hardly ever happens – and there's a general murmur of admiration, which is all the more gratifying since the novel is an attack on democracy and the people.'[65]

Some of this was sheer braggadocio – anything Dumas and Sue could do, he could do better; and it was not quite as miraculous as it seemed. As with the last act of *Quinola*, the stories had already fermented in his brain and his pen or mouth simply acted as syphons. Strange to say, these exhibitions also had a practical side. When he set off for the printer's with his camp-bed and manuscripts, he was looking for a technology to suit his technique. In June 1843, just before leaving for Russia, he went to live in the printing-works at Lagny to the north-east of Paris. For nineteen hours a day he took the pages hot off the presses, made corrections, handed them back, then wrote the next part of the novel while the corrected pages were reprinted. Twenty workers were kept busy for a month and two novels were completed: part three of *Illusions Perdues* and part one of *Splendeurs et Misères des Courtisanes*.[66]

This is probably the first recorded instance of a novelist using a word-processor, with human beings and a hydraulic press instead of microchips and a laser-printer. One of the humans worked so hard that he began to spit blood.[67] Even then, it was far too slow: a steam-powered press, he told Eveline, would have been much faster, but it was too expensive.

After his exhausting stint at Lagny, Balzac finally felt able to leave Paris. His worst creditor, Foullon, had been paid off, yet another play – *Paméla Giraud* – had been left for a playwright called Jaime to lick into shape (it was a flop at the Gaîté Theatre while Balzac was away), and a jeweller delivered the three wedding-rings Balzac had ordered: they were made to fit one of Eveline's gloves inflated with air. He was to sail from Dunkirk on a ship called *The Devonshire*. The captain was a friend of Gozlan, and Balzac would be given the best cabin. He felt 'like a bride'[68] or, as he later said when apologizing to Eveline for his infantile behaviour, like a dog about to see its master after a long absence.[69] On 19 July 1843, he left for the Channel coast, and two days later, as the *Corsaire* reported, to the chagrin of 'thousands of inconsolable widows', set sail for Russia and a marriage 'so romantic that anything the most fertile of our novelists has ever dreamt up pales in comparison'. The announcement was premature: marriage remained a dream for another six years.

THE ST PETERSBURG Balzac discovered in 1843 after a nine-day crossing was a shining, modern city, very new and very cold. St Isaac's Cathedral was still under construction. The granite quays, deserted avenues and the mansions with their wrought-iron gates were unwelcoming and so were most of the people he met. Outside the circles in which Eveline moved, Honoré de Balzac was a hero. Since the early

[353]

1830s, he had been famous in Russia and most of his novels and short stories had appeared in translation.[70] Pushkin had predicted that Balzac would be France's greatest novelist.[71] On 22 July, the young Dostoevsky, who had already read most of Balzac's work, returned to St Petersburg and found the papers full of news about his visit.[72] His young contemporaries gave the novelist a standing ovation at the Mikhailovsky Theatre. Higher up in society, the atmosphere was very different. Relations with France were strained. After Custine's *La Russie en 1839*, any French writer was bound to be treated with suspicion. With her trial, her hostile relations and gossiping friends, Eveline would have to be careful. Balzac was watched closely by the authorities and was very discreet. The Minister of Police, Count Orloff, later reported to the Czar that Balzac behaved 'like a perfect gentleman', 'visited the curiosities of our capital and returned promptly to Paris'.[73]

At midday on 29 July, the perfect gentleman turned up at the door of Mme Hanska's town-house in the Grande Millione and found her, for the first time without her husband, 'as beautiful and as young' as when he last saw her in Vienna – or so he wrote in her album. He, on the other hand, looked much older and he knew it. In Paris, he had been suffering from nervous fevers and trembling; references to his 'inflamed complexion' suggest high blood-pressure. During his stay, they were granted permission to attend a review of the Imperial Guard so that Balzac could see the Czar. The result was sunstroke, which brought on more agonizing attacks of arachnoiditis. He slept badly because of fleas in his hotel room, and the visit as a whole was a melancholy prelude to married life. They planned a secret visit to Paris and consoled each other for the chilly, inquisitive reception Balzac was given. He almost didn't care; it gave him time 'to penetrate that heart that is full of unassailable riches and sincere affection, to study, involuntarily, that noble, angelic character'.[74] They walked along the banks of the Neva, Balzac read from his novels[75] (in particular *Une Fille d'Eve*, in which, by experiencing 'the miseries of passion', a young woman learns to appreciate 'the delights of a happy household'[76]); and there were long games of chess during which he concentrated on Eveline's face more than on the board. She was happy to be with 'the star I have chosen for my destiny' (she wrote in her diary): 'a star which falls from the heavens. . . . May it fall on my heart, not to be extinguished, but to mingle its eternal light with more ephemeral flames so as to ensure its lasting life.' Sometimes the star shone a little too brightly: 'I am working at my character,' he told her four months later, 'so you won't hurt yourself on its sharp edges. I am trying not to have any more outbursts.'[77] She still doubted his financial expertise.

Apart from Balzac's letters, only one detailed glimpse of the famous couple in St Petersburg has survived, and it seems to be quite representative. They were seen by Bolesław Markiewicz, who became a popular writer of 'reactionary' novels in which patriotic heroes fight single-handed against Polish intrigue and nihilism.[78] That might explain his unkind remarks about Eveline who 'never stopped talking', but he should have been welcoming to Balzac, whose picture he had pinned to his wall when he was a student. He almost failed to recognize him:

> Our group was taking tea in an elegant drawing-room full of flowers and plants when there appeared a woman of about forty years. She was well-built not to say rather fat, with a broad face and a somewhat inelegant gait. Behind her was a man who was also quite short and tubby, with long hair like that of a *moujik*, in the fashion of the previous decade. . . . That, I thought, is Balzac, the author of *Eugénie Grandet* and *Le Père Goriot*, that large man with a vulgar, somnolent face who looks like an army major in need of a haircut!
> . . . The ladies kept asking him questions. He answered them tersely, in short sentences, and finally fell silent altogether, looking even more sombre and lethargic than when he arrived. . . . After an hour and a half or two hours, he began to cast pleading glances in Hanska's direction. She answered his silent supplications and rose from the table.[79]

Balzac's haircut is a touching detail: how often had he told Eveline that he was her humble *moujik*? But his lethargy is a sign of the illnesses that were to poison the last years of his life. When he left her in St Petersburg in early October, he was still exhausted and in pain. Eveline gave him some smoked tongue and a handkerchief to tie round his neck, and he set off, already tired and depressed, across the rough plains of Livonia.

The same impression of age and illness emerges from the diary of a young Russian sculptor called Ramazanov who, with another young sculptor, happened to be in the coach with Balzac on the long journey back to Western Europe. (Sea-sickness as much as curiosity recommended the land route.) The sculptor's diary[80] is one of those very rare documents that bother to record seemingly trivial incidents. As a result, Balzac is brought to life so vividly that it is as well to remember that this was him at his lowest ebb. He had just been in tears at leaving Eveline.

Balzac's endless supply of opinions made him an excellent travelling companion. He complained incessantly of the food in the roadside restaurants – stale bread, salty butter, rotten meat and no milk – and looked forward to stopping in Valka (Latvia) for a nice dinner in a pâtisserie, but there was nothing to be had: 'It was funny to see Balzac,' wrote the sculptor, 'wrapped up in his pelisse, wearing gigantic fur-lined boots and a fur hat, his hands in a woman's muff, tramping through the mud and growling, "What kind of town is this!"' At Gulbene they found a restaurant and were served by 'an extremely ugly, hunchbacked old woman'. 'Balzac was surprised I did not make a sketch of her; but where's the pleasure in blotting one's sketch-book with nasty faces when there are so many pretty ones to draw?': an example, not just of two ages meeting, but also of two aesthetics. Balzac was still too modern for some tastes.

After passing through Riga, they crossed the frontier, which appeared to be guarded by nothing but two chickens (a source of great amusement to Balzac), and then all through Prussia it rained. Balzac likened it to the thin gruel they were forced to eat. At Tilsitt (now Sovetsk) they changed their clothes: a chance for Balzac to show off his torso which the sculptor admitted would make an excellent model for Bacchus. He then persuaded the postmaster to leave at the crack of dawn by going to see his daughters who said they would die if they didn't get to meet the great novelist. On 14 October, they reached Berlin. Balzac toured the city with the sculptor, accusing him of walking too fast and comparing everything unfavourably to France and favourably to St Petersburg. Passers-by stopped to look, either because they recognized him or because of 'his extremely voluminous coat, large stomach, strawberry-coloured neck-scarf and a peculiar way of walking like a duck'. Balzac gave the sculptors a farewell dinner – soup, venison, macaroni *au gratin, mayonnaise de poisson*, half a bottle of Madeira, a bottle of Château Margaux and a little dessert – and stayed in Berlin for excursions to Leipzig and Dresden. He dined at the French Embassy with the Duchesse de Dino, who found him 'clumsy and common',[81] saw Humboldt again, and visited Wilhelm Tieck at his home in the company of an old countess, 'a mummy with a green eye-shade whom I took to be a domestic divinity'.[82]

All in all, it was a wretched journey and a sign of things to come: energy running low, fluctuating moods, constant illness and a feeling that simply existing no longer came easily – *'une difficulté d'être'*.[83] For the first time, the petty inconveniences of life were affecting him. He was bored, homesick, more than a little xenophobic and exasperated at the inefficiency of modern transport: 'The German railways are an excuse for eating and drinking. They keep stopping, the passengers get out, eat, drink and get back in again, so that the stage-coach in France is just as fast as their railway.'[84]

So far, Balzac's journey home is easy to follow; but then, all of a sudden, his trace on the map of Europe disappears. On 21 October, he was in Dresden; on 3 November, back in Paris. The official story was that he sailed up the Rhine from Mainz to Cologne, suffering horribly from arachnoiditis, and then travelled back through Belgium.[85] But this is the only possible time at which he and Louise Breugniot could have seen the house she later revisited in Baden-Baden. Louise must have crossed France to meet him and they would have sailed, not north, but south, eventually returning to France after a week together. From home, Balzac reported to Eveline that several months away from his desk had 'rejuvenated' his brain.[86] Maybe his versatile housekeeper should take some of the credit.

Balzac's life after his return to Paris has already been described. It was a year 'devoid of happiness and full of work',[87] the only changes being for the worse. Dr Nacquart prescribed leeches for his arachnoiditis, opium (externally applied) for his neuralgia and – unrealistically – rest in bed for his bronchitis: 'Alone with a head full of tasks I mustn't think of!. . . I ended up devouring twelve books a day!'[88] Other sufferings included colds and toothache, a nasty attack of jaundice and, after working on proofs for twelve hours, another unspecified *coup de sang* in February 1844. After the attack, he found himself coughing blood. 'That's probably done me good', he decided, and then took the proofs to the printer's, visited Saint-Germain-des-Prés, where, unusually for him, he said a prayer for Eveline, walked down to the river, bought the *Mémoires* of the Duc de Lauzun on the *quai* and read them in the bus on the way home to Passy. The moral to be drawn from the confessions of the great lover, Eveline heard, was that 'one can only be happy by loving a single woman'.[89]

In addition to all his illnesses, there were some peculiarly unpleasant interruptions. Anna Hanska's old governess turned up – a 'silly goose'[90] who thought she wanted to be locked up in a nunnery for the rest of her life but seemed more interested in French pâtisseries, thus confirming Balzac's warnings about the ravages of virginity. And then the landlord filled the empty apartments at Passy with a colony of launderers who brought with them the greatest enemy known to writers: noisy children. Balzac guessed that their racket would cost him 30,000 francs a year; but there was no time to move and no money to buy a house in Paris. He finished a story based on an idea from Eveline: a young girl, Modeste Mignon, writes a fan-letter to the famous poet, Canalis, and accidentally falls in love with his secretary. He set the story in Le Havre, where he had to go and collect his trunk, and deemed it a masterpiece. Then he began the novel, *Les Paysans*, which Marx cites in *Das Kapital* as an exact analysis of how a country's economy can be suffocated by usurers. Balzac's life had served him well; and he hoped to be able to gather some valuable information in the near future on the estate at Wierzchownia.

The end of the tunnel was still in sight, but would it be night or day on the other side? Eveline had finally won her legal battle and Balzac was organizing her clandestine trip to Paris. Since the Czar would not allow her to visit France, they would have to use his passport: Eveline would be his sister and Anna his niece, and he would go and meet them in Dresden. He wrote from Passy on 24 April 1845, remembering the days they had spent together almost twelve years before, planning the future that still seemed to be retreating like a mirage: 'Will Anna recognize her old friend from Geneva in a white-haired old gentleman whom urchins call big fatty [*gros patapouf*] when he passes in the street? This seems to me a cause for some anxiety.'

CHAPTER SIXTEEN

Revolution

(1845–1848)

PHYSICAL 'DECADENCE', as Balzac called it, was really a very small and unavoidable problem. His body was preparing for retirement and the life of love and leisure he had promised and denied himself for so long. Like Crevel's majestic waistline in *La Cousine Bette*, corpulence was the mark of a successful, self-made man, a man who weighed heavily in the scales of history, and as Balzac's slimming tips remind us (long walks before breakfast, washing in cold water and no *café au lait*), Eveline was equal to him in that respect. True, he had had heart problems, but he did not associate illness with obesity. The main source of anxiety was a question Balzac never asked directly in his letters but which casts a bigger shadow than his waistline over his remaining years: why was the wedding postponed until he was almost dead? The imaginative answer is that Balzac was fulfilling the prophecy he had often made: death would be waiting for him at the finishing-line. The other answer, which may be just a more detailed version of the first, is that Eveline had the prudence Balzac had been looking for in a wife ever since he placed himself under the tutelage of Mme de Berny.

There were, of course, his debts, to which we shall bid farewell at this point before Eveline begins to pay them off. Balzac had been insolvent now for two decades, often short of pocket-money but rarely of credit. For him, this was a point in his favour; he looked forward to hearing her cry of admiration when she perused his accounts.[1] Perhaps it was a reasonable expectation. If she could have read the biography of Balzac's money published in 1938 by René Bouvier and Édouard Maynial, she would have seen his various financial disasters rippling on for years like the after-shocks of earthquakes, though she may well have been impressed by the fact that he did in the end achieve a kind of mobile stability. It was a pity Balzac was never able to share the whole story with her. Since the mid-1830s, paying for everything by writing novels had been out of the question, so that when he boasted of having beaten off poverty with his pen, he was hardly doing justice to his ingenuity or to the truth. At the end of 1845, his debts were at their lowest for ten years (145,521 francs – about £450,000 today), thanks mainly to a series of minor crimes which he viewed in the light of certain practical observations, for example that we owe our borrowed money to our creditors' greed:[2] a simulated sale of Les Jardies, promissory notes signed by friends who owed him nothing, loans secured under other names, and a pretence of poverty so that creditors would accept a percentage of their due and count themselves lucky. This explains why visitors to the palatial residence he moved into in 1847 were asked to believe that he was simply acting as the caretaker: 'I'm poorer than ever!' he told Gautier, with a humble, smarmy air. 'None of this belongs to me. I furnished this house for a friend who is due to return.'[3] The house in the Rue Fortunée (now the Rue Balzac), in a quiet area off the Champs-Élysées, was the last heroic manifestation of Balzac's financial psychology. By filling the house with expensive 'bargains' – works of art and antique furniture – he was creating the ideal environment for his future wife and at the same time supplying her with several reasons not to marry him: by the end of 1847, when the last debts resulting from the *Chronique de Paris* had finally been eradicated, his total debt had climbed to a new height of 217,248 francs. The ensuing arguments with Eveline are echoed in Balzac's play about the over-ambitious speculator, Mercadet: 'I admire the fertility of your conceptions', concedes the debtor's wife, 'but it pains me to have to hear the quips and cranks with which you try to fool yourself.'[4] The fact that Eveline began to pay off his debts, fund their holidays and generally take over as business manager may be the best objective proof we have of her love for him: there is certainly no sign that she ever allowed herself to be convinced that his debts were really 'investments'.

If debts were not the deterrent they might have been, Eveline had other reasons to postpone the wedding. Running the estate at Wierzchownia was impossible at a distance, especially since her stewards were dishonest, and it was by no means a foregone conclusion that it would continue to provide a regular income. Nor was it certain she would be allowed to keep it if she married a foreigner. Her daughter's marriage therefore became an urgent priority: the estate could be handed over to Anna, who would pay her mother an allowance. With this in mind, she agreed to receive Balzac in Dresden, so he could give his expert opinion of Anna's fiancé, Georges Mniszech, a polite and affable young man with a large estate in the western Ukraine (debt-ridden but creditworthy) and a passion for collecting insects. In 1845, Georges was twenty-two, immature enough to make a good companion for the seventeen-year-old Anna. At the end of April, Balzac travelled to Dresden, shortly after being made a *chevalier* of the Légion d'Honneur, an honour which he seems to have greeted with silence, perhaps because he had his eye on bigger prizes. His happy energy swept away the miseries of Dresden, where Eveline had been ostracized for refusing to be drawn on the subject of her lover. The four of them got on famously and adopted the names of characters from a popular farce, *Les Saltimbanques*. Eveline was Atala and Balzac, as head clown, was Bilboquet. It was like being a child again. He kept them all entertained and was treated with affection and sometimes, inevitably, condescension: Bilboquet either didn't notice or didn't care.

New names for a new life. The closer he came to marriage with Eveline, the more he talked about how cruel his mother had been to him in childhood and – perhaps another reason for postponing the wedding – the more Eveline wondered whether she could live up to his enormous expectations. Balzac urged her again and again not to worry. All the agonizing waiting, he thought, would soon be over. His *louploup* (a punning reference to the wolves of Wierzchownia) was more perfect than ever and the past was not a sign of things to come. He could still write and still make money: 'Just when I think I've become a cretin, my faculties return with greater brilliance than before. Fear and grief are the hands of the cook that shine the pots and pans, and the rough sand they use and their scrubbing make us think we are ill.'[5] The only problem now was that 'serious people have begun to realize that I am more a historian than a novelist. They have stopped complaining, which is rather alarming: I need them snapping at my heels for another ten years.'[6]

The comfortable conviction that his works would be counted among the 'Classics'[7] was apparently not an obstacle to creativity, and yet, reading *La Comédie Humaine* in chronological order, we now reach the more distant corners of the museum, with some works still in packing crates, others deservedly obscure and, seemingly out of place, two or three masterpieces. The period of unfinished novels had begun – *Les Petits Bourgeois*, *Le Député d'Arcis*, *Les Paysans* – each one a giant study intended to fill a gap in *La Comédie Humaine*; but unfinished novels are hardly something new in Balzac's life and it would be wrong to talk of a decline in creative energy without mentioning all the distractions that occupied his time: travelling, house-hunting and collecting furniture for the new home. The biggest single obstacle can be measured quite precisely: the letters to Eveline, which, from 1845 until his death, account for over two-fifths of his total output. Whenever they were apart, he was too impatient to work. It was the first sign that his two great passions – Eveline and *La Comédie Humaine* – might be incompatible. But when she and Anna came on their secret visit to Paris in July 1845, he suddenly began to write again. The 'triple martyrdom' of 'heart, head and business'[8] temporarily came to an end, and so should the idea that marriage would necessarily have meant the end of his career as a writer.

Eveline and her daughter stayed in a rented apartment close to the house in Passy. They spent a fortune on clothes and jewellery, went to the theatre and did not meet Balzac's family. When Eveline called to see her 'husband–lover', she found him hard at work on a topic so depressing that it shows how happy and secure he was feeling. *Petites Misères de la Vie Conjugale* reveals what happens when the 'high-tide of the honeymoon' goes out for good.[9] Balzac's analysis of a relationship degenerating into mutual envy and emotional manipulation takes the form of a series of vignettes reminiscent of Daumier cartoons (especially a wretched outing to the country with ungrateful child and gloating mother-in-law) and is notable for its lack of practical solutions. This, the old Romantic was saying, is what modern marriage, treated as 'a good business deal', really is: a counter-image of the marriage he predicted for himself. Just in case Eveline should wonder, when he revised *Physiologie du Mariage* for the sixteenth volume of *La Comédie Humaine* in 1846, he added a short concluding sentence: 'If ever I marry . . . you may be certain that I shall offer my admiring contemporaries the spectacle of a model household.'[10]

Eveline was able to put this to the test when they went at the end of July to Touraine, visiting some of the Loire châteaux – Blois,

Amboise, Chambord[11] – and then on an antique-collecting holiday through Holland and Belgium. They parted company in Brussels in late August; Balzac went back to Paris, spent most of his time looking for a house, then set off again to be with her in Baden-Baden where he stayed for a week. For most of 1845 and 1846, Eveline was close enough to exert a strong gravitational pull and from one summer to the next Balzac became a full-time tourist and a part-time writer: the only major work from this period is the third part of *Splendeurs et Misères des Courtisanes* which appeared in July 1846. Having returned to Passy at five in the morning on 5 October 1845, he set off yet again on the 23rd to meet Eveline, Anna and Georges at Chalon-sur-Saône. They spent two weeks together, sailing from Toulon to Naples where he left them to winter in Italy. (Eveline was not quite as frugal as her advice to Balzac might suggest.) He then sailed up the coast in a storm with nothing to drink but champagne, saw the yellow flood of the Tiber and the Arno far out at sea and visited Pisa in the pouring rain. At Marseille, he joined the writer and poet, Joseph Méry, gave him a lesson in the art of bargaining with antique-dealers, bought 1500 francs' worth of porcelain and jewellery and was back home on 17 November. In his mind, Paris had changed. Familiar sights now reminded him of Eveline: 'It is extremely difficult to write. . . . We must be reunited. Since Dresden I have done nothing. . . . My heart is as worn out as my brain, indifferent to anything that is not a part of itself, and there is a fortune to be earned.' He went shopping for Georges and Anna, planned a bedroom for the house he had yet to find, and visited the Conciergerie prison where Lucien de Rubempré hangs himself at the end of the third part of *Splendeurs et Misères des Courtisanes*.

During this emotional exile in his own city, Balzac attended a hashish-taking session in the Hôtel Lauzun organized by the alienist Joseph Moreau. This is an important interlude because it offers a glimpse of Balzac's intellectual activity in a period dominated by monotonous emotions. Baudelaire was present at the soirée in the magnificent seventeenth-century mansion overlooking the Seine on the Île Saint-Louis. In *Les Paradis Artificiels* he reports that Balzac merely sniffed at the green jelly and handed it back: 'He found the idea of thinking in spite of himself deeply shocking.' 'It is indeed hard to imagine the theoretician of *will-power*, that spiritual twin of Louis

Lambert, agreeing to part with even the smallest speck of that precious *substance*.'[12] Balzac, however, had also parted with some of that other precious substance and afterwards complained to the Doctor that, though he took the dose of hashish, he 'did not get [his] money's worth', the reason being that he had exercised his '*organs* of thought' from an early age and was immune to madness. The fact that 'not experiencing all the phenomena' included hearing 'celestial voices', 'descending Lauzun's staircase for twenty years' and 'seeing the gilt and paintings of the salon in incredible splendour' says something about his normal state of mind. His interest in the drug was both personal (for euthanasia if Eveline decided not to marry him) and scientific. He wondered if it would be possible one day to discover the physical causes of madness or even to reconstruct the brain of a cretin by creating 'a thinking apparatus' – 'a wonderful experiment I have been thinking of for the last twenty years . . . If we can put a mind back together again, we shall know how they fall apart.'[13]

Balzac's psychiatric speculations in his letter to Dr Moreau (which are simultaneously far behind and far ahead of his time) show the enormous quantity of ideas he crammed into the tiny spaces he left himself for literary work in these years, and it is interesting to see him return in a rare moment of leisure to the preoccupations of his youth. His inspiringly cranky treatises on fashion, stimulants and human motion might have been joined by many others, and it is all too easy to find uses for his mind or to plan sequels to his actual career. Unlike some of his readers, Balzac never once considered his love for Eveline a sacrifice of something else. Four months after leaving Italy, he made the same journey in reverse to meet his lover in Rome, where he had a brief audience with the Pope in April 1846, apparently treating it as part of the tourist trail: he kissed the 'hierarchical slipper' and had a rosary blessed for his mother.[14] That spring, they crossed the Alps and visited Solothurn, Geneva, Berne and Basel, then Heidelberg where Balzac left her. On 28 May, he was back in Passy in a state of 'enormous nervous excitement', took a four-hour bath, slept for twenty hours and six days later took the train to Tours.

This little visit to his native region marks a turning point in Balzac's frantic life in 1845–6. For a long week he stayed in Saché. His aim was to inspect the Château de Moncontour which can still be seen overlooking the Loire on the road from Tours to Vouvray. Another dream with a long history: Balzac had described it sixteen years before with its turrets and terraces, its shining roofs, its 'cloak of ivy' and its wine-cellars dug out of the rock.[15] The idea was to use it as a country home, since Eveline had misgivings about leading a prominent social life in Paris; but the result of the visit was quite unexpected. Despite impressive calculations of profits to be gleaned from the vineyards and gardens of Moncontour, Eveline refused to put up the money. Saché, on the other hand, where so many of his novels had been conceived, brought some dormant seeds to life. He returned to Paris with his head 'full of ideas'[16] and began work on the two stories that form the melodramatic *finale* of his creative life: *Le Cousin Pons* and *La Cousine Bette*.

The writing of these two novels – known jointly as *Les Parents Pauvres* (*The Poor Relations*) – is a more remarkable achievement than it first appears. All the travelling and feverish anticipation had taken a heavy toll and the Balzac who sat down again at his desk was a different person – a phoenix, perhaps, but one that was half-consumed by the flames. From 1845, as his letters grow in number, the topics they cover decrease. Obsessions flooded into the space no longer filled by writing: the search for a house (which may explain why *La Cousine Bette* is so much a novel of interiors), the railway shares he bought with Eveline's money and whose value dropped disastrously year by year, the battle to bring his debts down to an acceptable level, the sluggishness of his mind and, above all, the agony of waiting and his determination that Eveline should retain the right impression of him. There is such a full-blooded, lumbering frenzy in Balzac's daily chronicle of hope and despair that one wonders what creature he might have been without the escape-valve of literature: something like the restless, homicidal monster in the early *Centenaire*. The impression of a man devoured by his own appetites may have something to do with the fact that he wrote letters as a kind of therapy, pausing to think even less than he did when speaking (or so he said); and yet it is a curiously self-conscious sort of violence. Even a stream of consciousness flowed from his pen as a coherent story and it still seems prudent to assume that Balzac the protagonist and Balzac the narrator are not the same. Tales of his 'manic' behaviour were designed as urgent appeals to end his suffering. On the morning of 5 January 1846, a letter had come from Eveline in which she complained that her sister Aline, then in Paris, had heard Balzac gossiping about their affair:

I was devastated. I closed the letter and put it in my side-pocket. At first, I was to be seen in tears, then I was overcome by a great sadness which had the following physical effects. Yesterday, two inches of snow fell on the streets of Paris. I was wearing short boots and cotton socks as in summer. I had myself dropped off on the Rue de Rivoli and I walked and walked, trudging through the slush all the way across Paris amidst an enormous crowd which I did not see, through traffic to which I paid no heed, my face contorted with horror like a madman – and people were looking at me! . . . I walked from the Rue de Rivoli to the area behind the Hôtel de Ville, through the most crowded streets, without noticing the people, the carriages or the cold – nothing. If anyone had asked me what time of day it was or what the weather or the season were or what city I was in, I should have been unable to reply. I was senseless with grief. Sensibility is the blood of the soul and mine was gushing out through my wound. . . . This involuntary injustice of yours destroyed me; I felt a club beating on my head at every step.[17]

Balzac's account of what was actually a short walk to collect another order from the jeweller, Froment-Meurice, has the same proud detachment and interest in the effects of extreme passion as in his novels. He was a blind man with a keen eye for the telling detail, still capable of crafting a good story and especially of making his reader hope for a happy ending.

There were also more regular manifestations of what Balzac himself called his monomania. On his walks through Paris and on holidays with Eveline, he combed the antique-shops and spent enormous sums on furniture and paintings which he then attributed to famous craftsmen and artists, usually erroneously. Many of these objects turn up in the collection of Cousin Pons, whose judgment is as reliable as Balzac's is not. He acquired a chest of drawers and a writing desk which the dealer assured him had belonged to Marie de Medici and Henri IV; he then persuaded Léon Gozlan to publish an article on the two pieces in the *Musée des Familles* so that he could sell them for £3000 to Sir Robert Peel or some other English notable.[18]

Art meant magic money. Auguste Lepoitevin noted his former protégé's new line of business with a mixture of envy and amusement:
'M. de Balzac no longer wishes to be a novelist full of skill, tediousness
and perceptive remarks; he has decided to become a furniture salesman.' 'Naive people assume that when he goes to Germany or Italy he
does so in order to study customs and characters; but he's no fool.
The only reason he tours those countries is to buy and sell old
canvasses and antique chests. . . . He is cured of all those literary
illusions that make one hope to find fame and fortune at the end of an
octavo volume.'[19]

Balzac might have agreed with some of this; he said much the
same to Eveline whenever she refused to pay for one of his 'follies' – a
'priceless' painting, a Chinese vase, or a chess-set in ebony and ivory
with jewel-encrusted pieces and insects etched in the white squares –
another present which he spent five hours trying to knock down from
4000 to 1500 francs: 'It seems a folly to you because you haven't seen
it.'[20] Eveline herself was a fluent shopper, especially in Paris, and she
may have infected Balzac with the virus; but his ability to create
temptations for himself and to see a masterpiece in every old frame
was worrying. Was it a profitable hobby, as he claimed, or a dangerous
addiction? And is it a significant coincidence that one of the dealers on
his list of creditors is a man called Mage whose address is that of the
curiosity-shop in *La Peau de Chagrin*? Balzac's letters offer a selection
of answers. According to some, he was lining a nest for Eveline: 'a
perfectly natural impulse that one finds in all animals'[21] (except, as she
might have pointed out when Balzac went on to record his expenses,
that only human beings spend 100,000 francs in three years on
furniture and ornaments). According to others, he collected antiques
because he couldn't help it: 'Never become a collector', he warned
Méry after taking him round the antique-shops of Marseille. 'You
would be selling yourself to a demon as jealous and demanding as the
demon of gambling.'[22] Wheedling on the one hand, an artistic pose
on the other. There can be little doubt that Balzac suffered from
collector's fever, but its precise nature is difficult to define. In some
ways, it was a new form of literary creation: his *trouvailles* in the street
became material possessions instead of characters and stories. Some of
the pleasure lay in what was normally an illusion of outwitting the
dealer, some in seeing a masterpiece restored. His portrait of the old

man who cleaned a painting he had picked up in Rome is like a page from *Le Cousin Pons*, 'a scene worthy of the *Études Philosophiques*': the dealer, Menghetti, had '*smoked* the painting in order to hide some scratches ... When we removed Menghetti's *smoke*, we found the grime of the church candles, and when that was removed there reappeared the most extraordinary masterpiece, the paint as fresh as if it had been painted yesterday.'23 (This rediscovered masterpiece is one of the paintings that is stolen from the collection of Cousin Pons in the novel. The real painting has also disappeared.24) Balzac's joy at finding a work by Sebastiano del Piombo or Albrecht Dürer produced what may be the best definition of his 'mania': it was a 'consolation' for his 'immense labours', he told the restorer. A consolation, because beautiful objects, as Cousin Pons finds out, are the only lovers that never grow old, the only relations that never betray. The atmosphere of claustrophobia, paranoia, fear of loneliness and death that surrounds the old collector is more and more a part of Balzac's world. Collecting was both a symptom and a cure: 'No depression or spleen can survive the application to the soul of that poultice known as a mania. Let all those no longer able to drink from what has always been called "the cup of joy" take to collecting something (people have even been known to collect posters!) and they will find the solid gold of happiness minted into small change. A mania is pleasure transmuted into an idea. And yet old Pons should not be envied . . .'25 Like Balzac, he had a 'vice' that was incompatible with his passion: in Pons's case, it was food, in Balzac's, Eveline.

Le Cousin Pons bears the traces of another form of obsession that coincides with Balzac's collecting period: a growing tendency to rely on superstition as a source of information. Balzac had cultivated his gullibility as a type of psychological defence and his only doubts now concerned interpretation. When his clothes caught fire on a candle, he asked Eveline if fire was 'a good sign'.26 When a piece of his tooth fell out, he noted that the same tooth had disintegrated in St Petersburg at the same time of day and for the same reason (eating lettuce, which does rather emphasize the coincidence): 'What does this mean?' he wondered. 'Has something happened to you? I beg you, please, a letter!'27 He consulted palmists and cartomancers, one of whom – a certain Balthazar – impressed him with an approximate description of Eveline and a prediction of imminent happiness: he would suffer an apparently fatal illness at the age of fifty but would then recover to live for another thirty years.[28] When he heard that the sorcerer had been sent to jail for performing illegal abortions as a side-line, he concluded that 'one can be a great cartomancer and a rogue at the same time'.[29]

Being superstitious was not just a logical consequence of his scientific principles. Ever since debts and a distant lover had placed much of his life under remote control, he had good reason to consider superstition as a necessary, even a rational mode of thought. He was also unusually well equipped to believe in the supernatural. Proustian moments, conjured up at will, had become everyday events. A flower, a word or a picture projected three-dimensional images of Eveline into the room: she moved, she spoke, she wound her watch; the scent of her writing-paper was 'a boat loaded with memories that carries me far away'.[30] References to these exhausting hallucinations become noticeably more frequent as Balzac grows older and they may even be symptoms of a neurological disorder. For him, they were an important point of contact with Eveline's mysticism and proof that faith could live happily with rational materialism. This is the cheering message of *Ursule Mirouët* in which an atheist doctor is converted to Christianity – in a very unchristian fashion – by an amazing demonstration of 'Jesus's favourite science',[31] animal magnetism, here in the form of telepathy. Balzac's own superstitious habits – wiping pens on a scrap of Eveline's silk dress,[32] noting every sighting of iron in the street[33] or using a 'magic' seal with an Arabic inscription[34] – resemble religious practices, and his ability to seize on what would now be considered a psychological phenomenon and treat it as a transcendental truth is one of the great charms of his work. Unlike many of his Romantic contemporaries, he had always been able to revel in scientific speculation without collapsing into spiritual crisis. In this, he seems closer to Jung than to the Middle Ages: some of his remarks on a significant 'simultaneity of ideas and feelings'[35] prefigure the concept of synchronicity.

The difference now was that superstition, like collecting, had become a fixed idea that masked unpleasant realities, a comforting distraction rather than a basis for scientific investigation. Superstition, he once said, was 'the most indestructible form that human thought can take',[36] and it was as much the power of the idea itself as the putative reality that mattered. His aims were far humbler than before, happiness was more important than knowledge. He no longer talked of acquiring omniscience, but simply of completing *La Comédie Humaine*; and instead of the future, he had begun to dwell on the past, transformed and synthesized by memory. 'The older I become', he told Eveline, 'the more respect I have for the past'[37] – and, he might have added, the more I fear the future. Redeeming past experience was a powerful motive for finishing the great work and marrying Eveline, and superstition was one means of uniting past, present and future. If only everything could be gathered together, the unity of creation and individual destiny would appear. One night, he spent three hours looking for a letter he had written to her, 'for every expression of the soul that falls into the abyss of oblivion seems to me irreparable'.[38]

AFTER HIS restorative week at Saché in June 1846, Balzac's manias took on the milder appearance of an illness that would soon be cured by marriage. In June he began a short story called *Le Parasite* that eventually expanded into *Le Cousin Pons*; and then in July, *La Cousine Bette*. *Les Parents Pauvres* was supposed to pay off Hetzel and his mother and show the exponents of that 'bastard genre',[39] the serial novel, that popular fiction did not have to be sensationalist trivia. Balzac's sarcastic cliffhangers, discordant variations on the 'happy families' theme and titillating chapter titles ('Pretty Women on the Path of Libertines', 'An Artist, Young and Polish – What Else Could He Do?', etc.) make *La Cousine Bette* his most effective harnessing of market forces to serious literature. It was his first comprehensive success for several years and the first novel written entirely *ex nihilo* since 1843. Intent on destroying the opposition, he was surprised to find himself writing 'a great masterpiece, outstanding among my finest works'.[40]

Perhaps not so surprising after all. Just as 'the cork that blocks the cerebral torrent'[41] popped out, a third name began to figure in his marriage plans: Eveline had become pregnant at the hotel in Solothurn. The child, he was certain, would be a boy and he would be christened Victor-Honoré. 'We shall live in complete tranquillity, raising to our greater glory and happiness Victor-Honoré whose name alone stirs my heart and makes me write page upon page.'[42] 'Never have I had so much courage, for never have I had so much to save.'[43] Balzac had been a father before, at least once; but this would be the first child to bear his name and much of his excitement came from the assumption that Eveline would now be forced to marry him as soon as possible. Fired by the news, he worked for the rest of 1846 on *Les Parents Pauvres* and tried to make his new confidence rub off on Eveline: 'Do not be appalled by my purchases. I talk about them, but between the hatching of the plan and the money leaving my purse, there is a great deal of reflection. . . . Depend on my enormous stock of common sense. Once you begin to share my life, you will see so much evidence of it that you will no longer mistake the fantasies that come out in speech for realities.'[44] Why, one might think, did he not say this long before? There are several other such confessional phrases that hint at a revision of his old procedures in preparation for a less hectic way of life: 'I no longer wish to deceive myself by thinking that I can do the impossible.'[45] The wish itself was self-deception.

Despite assurances that he could 'magnetize' her for a safe journey from Leipzig to Paris ('because of my labours and my chastity, my magnetic powers are now at their peak'[46]), Eveline remained in Germany. Balzac visited her once in September, returning via Metz,[47] where he hoped a friend would find him an illiterate mayor who could marry them without the usual formalities.[48] Still Eveline demurred. With despair and depression looming once again, he had to be content with the marriage of Georges and Anna, celebrated in Wiesbaden in October 1846: 'One of the richest heiresses of the Russian Empire, Mlle la Comtesse Anna de Hanska', said *Le Messager*, has married 'the representative of the old and illustrious house of Vandaline, the Count Georges Mniszech. M. de Balzac was one of the witnesses.'[49] Balzac was also the author of the announcement, which one of Eveline's two older sisters, Aline, found in poor taste.[50] Recounting her visit to Passy, he claimed that Aline was 'provincial' and 'pretentious' and that she thought the same of him. He was, according to her, bragging, letting his enemies know how important he was about to become: Count Mniszech was the 'grand-nephew of the last King of Poland, a direct descendant of the father of the famous and unfortunate Marina Mniszech, whose biography was written by the Duchesse d'Abrantès'.

Honoré de Balzac would belong to a family of kings. The Duchesse de Castries, 'who wishes me nothing but bumps and boils',[51] would be furious.

The idea that, in Balzac's mind, the embryonic Victor-Honoré was an incentive to marry is apparently confirmed by the fact that, after a brief storm, his Indian summer survived the dreadful news that came on 1 December. Eveline had had a miscarriage. 'Victor-Honoré' would have been a girl. Worse than that, she was in too delicate a state to cope with a visit from Balzac. Over the New Year, he was back in the slough of 'mental apathy', too gloomy even to enjoy rummaging through the antique-shops – 'the surest sign of despondency'.[52] Victor-Honoré had to be urgently replaced with another catalyst. Balzac found it first in the political climate. Everything would have to be settled before the continent was torn apart by revolutions. Polish patriots were being tortured in Siberia, 'populations are being harried by idiotic little monarchs, England is battling with Ireland, which will either destroy it or gain its independence, the whole of Italy wants to shake off the Austrian yoke, and Germany wants its freedom. Believe me, we are on the brink of political catastrophes.'[53] Balzac had temporarily forgotten his own predictions of a revolution in France, or was pretending to have forgotten them.

The other inducement he had to offer his bride was the 'little palace' he was now furnishing in the Rue Fortunée with the same erotic frenzy with which Baron Hulot and Crevel pour all their money into a love-nest for the irresistible Valérie Marneffe (the comparison is Balzac's).[54] The house had been built before the Revolution by the financier Nicolas Beaujon. Balzac agreed on a price of 50,000 francs, which was eventually paid by Eveline in 1850. Thirty-two years later she resold it for 500,000 francs to one of the Rothschilds. On the outside, it looked 'like a barracks',[55] on the inside, once restored, it would be a monument of 'gigantic oriental and Babylonian propor-tions', a museum dedicated to his love – 'just as Catholics have beautiful churches'.[56] On one side there was a narrow garden adjoining the house of 'a painter of execrable seascapes' called Gudin,[57] and on the other, something that should appeal to Eveline: a door that led directly from the bedroom into the Chapelle Saint-Nicolas. The original, profane purpose of the house was revealed in the existence of a secret apartment that 'a woman might inhabit *without the servants knowing*.[58] 'All that remains to complete the miracle is for me to find buried gold in the cellar.'[59]

Balzac now set about completing the miracle himself. Even before 1847, the total cost of furnishing 'Beaujon's folly' was 100,000 francs. When all the crates and chests had arrived from all over Europe there would be approximately ten clocks, twelve candelabra, thirty-six vases (mostly Sèvres or Chinese), 1500 francs' worth of mirrors ('absolutely necessary'), 3000 kilograms of brass and gilded bronze, a salon in white and gold, a green salon on the first floor (Eveline's favourite colour) with everything in marquetry and malachite, a study, a library and a gallery containing twenty-six old masters (according to Balzac's attributions) and a mahogany chair that could be raised or lowered to the desired height. The inventory covers forty-seven pages. Each room was planned in Balzacian detail. In the WC (estimated cost: 1680 francs) the knob on the chain would be in green Bohemian glass; there would also be two Chinese flower-vases, a Japanese bowl, a porcelain and mahogany bidet, an oak toilet-seat with green velvet and gold studs, two engravings of Girodet's *Seated Nymph* and a chamber-pot 'having belonged to Mme de Pompadour'.[60] The 23,000 francs from *Les Parents Pauvres* were 'swallowed like a strawberry' and 'the 25,000 francs from *Les Paysans* will vanish in a puff of smoke',[61] but hopefully the little army of builders and decorators wouldn't realize: 'Everything is behind schedule, and the workers have a kind of animal instinct – they can smell the lack of money and then they become as wicked and malicious as monkeys; they won't give me a minute's peace.'[62] The plan was to make them work quickly: first, because haste suggested an ability to pay;[63] second, because the house would be finished and the debtor was always in a stronger position than the creditor, or so Balzac had always tried to believe. This, he explained, after another alarming computation of costs, was how 'women who inspire passions' should be treated: 'You are my whim, my passion, my vice ... my mistress, my comrade, my *louploup*, my brother, my conscience, my happiness and my wife, and you must also be the object of my follies ... for you are all my hope and all my life. If only you knew how carefully I am arranging everything!' 'And when you see it, you will say, "What, Noré, is that all it cost?"'[64]

Whether out of curiosity, love or panic, Eveline wrote in January 1847 to say she was coming to Paris, and Balzac experienced another exhausting reversal of emotions. His letters grew more intimate and invigorating than ever and are especially revealing because they imply that after all there was an element of play-acting in the reproaches and recriminations that he usually treated as near catastrophes:

> This will be the first time we shall have been together on our own with nobody else. There will be no one to restrain us and we shall both be able to behave as wickedly as we like. You will be beaten and I will be scolded – like never before. Be sure and be in good health! . . . We shall go on a trip to Mainz: I have to pay 26 francs to Schwab [an antique-dealer] . . . You must behave yourself! I shall devour you with caresses. And, my darling Line, I shall allow you to smoke for a whole day. Ah! *louploup*! three days from now![65]

On 4 February 1847, he rushed from Paris to collect Eveline in Frankfurt. By 15 February, she was installed in a 'charming' apartment close to the Champs-Élysées in the Rue Neuve-de-Berry. During her stay, Balzac exchanged the tribe of launderers in Passy for the horde of carpenters and plasterers in the Rue Fortunée. As before, Eveline acted as a stimulant and was able to witness his last heroic display as a novelist. The nest had been approved; *La Cousine Bette* had been hailed as a masterpiece, even by his enemies; and now the peacock showed its feathers. That April, three newspapers were running Balzac novels simultaneously – an achievement not even Dumas or Sue could match (and, as Balzac liked to point out, Dumas had a 'factory' of novelists working for him): *Le Cousin Pons* was in *Le Constitutionnel*, the unfinished *Le Député d'Arcis* in *L'Union Monarchique*, and *La Dernière Incarnation de Vautrin* in *La Presse*. He would never again enjoy such a public triumph, and *La Comédie Humaine* itself was never finished, and perhaps never could have been, but it is nice to know that Balzac savoured his success to the full, including the success he would continue to have after his death. The 1847 foreword to the collection of Paris scenes entitled *Les Comédiens Sans le Savoir* is his last published statement on his work. Written by him, signed by his publisher, the text is so uninhibited and happy that it can fairly be considered as an objective appraisal of his place in world literature – Balzac's own conclusion to his biography.

Of those few living writers, he wrote, who can reasonably expect to live beyond their century, 'there is one who, perhaps more than any other, can justify the colossal reputation he enjoys' – a man who, from an early age, '"sustained a mad struggle", as he somewhere declares, "fighting poverty with my pen!"' (The reader is referred at this point to *Illusions Perdues*.) With his 'magical style' and 'miracles of imagination', M. de Balzac 'probed deeper than any other writer the thousand recesses of the human heart' and became 'infatuated with a glorious idea whose greatness never once intimidated his genius'. 'Never has any human brain produced anything so vast, well-ordered and complete as *La Comédie Humaine*', with its men and women moving about in the frame of the novel as they do 'in the official frame of real life'. Though he forced himself into 'the skimpy columns of the newspaper serial' ('it being in his nature always to seek out unknown paths'), 'M. de Balzac managed to find for this new brand of literature a vigour that recalled the most active period of his literary youth'. 'Men like M. de Balzac achieve real greatness only after their death'; and so, one day, he will stand alongside his only equal – Molière, who, 'were he alive today, would be writing *La Comédie Humaine*'.[66]

Balzac mentions Molière more often than any other writer, and the comment that he usually makes about him is that he was able to see both sides of every situation.[67] In the foreword to *Les Comédiens Sans le Savoir*, Balzac was looking only at one side of his own situation: the long ascent and the summit he almost reached.

IN EARLY MAY 1847, Eveline left Paris to reimpose order on Wierzchownia so that, as she put it, Balzac would not be marrying a pauper. He accompanied her as far as Frankfurt and set off again immediately for Paris; but the city was now a cemetery. 'My house is a coffin. I see my *loup* at every hour of the day. Everything here reminds me of something heartbreaking. I am literally dying of an indefinable illness' – an illness which he then defined as 'the absence of happiness briefly glimpsed'.[68] He was drained of ideas, dwelling on vivid memories of their trips together, 'loving like a woman but with the energy of a man', still 'too young' not to be dangerously love-sick, yet too old to 'wind up' his brain again. Like the woman in the fairy-tale, he had wished for a palace but always seemed to end up back in his garret: 'When the salon is completed it will cost 63,000 francs and the dining-room 36,000. It's terrifying. I shall concoct some gargantuan novels and successful plays, and eat crusts of bread smeared with garlic like the Jews.'[69] The railway shares bought with Eveline's money were now 300 francs below their purchase price. Novels with huge, ambitious subjects – *Les Paysans*, *Les Petits Bourgeois*, *Le Député d'Arcis*[70] – were left unwritten, and the cost of the palace continued to rise. 'All the paper I cut and arranged for manuscripts goes off loaded with correspondence.'[71] Each tiny paragraph in Balzac's letters represents an interruption from the workers he would soon have to pay. He had problems with his servants, who had promised his neighbour a secret viewing of the house while the master was out. After a relatively untroubled year, he was constantly ill or injured – agonizing stomach pains, aching legs and a whole series of twisted ankles. He was worried, quite rightly, about his heart. Outside the palace in the Rue Fortunée, events were taking an ominous turn: 'You can't imagine how much ground *communism* has gained – a doctrine that consists in overturning everything, *sharing everything*, even produce and commodities, among all men considered as brothers.'[72] Worst of all, he was afraid that Eveline now despised him for bickering about money. He was a broken man living in a crumbling world, but a man who had, as usual, a theory to explain it all: 'The dose of happiness exceeded my soul's capacity . . . my ideal was realized, my dream of happiness came true, and now everything has come to a halt and I feel nothing. . . . Nothing stirs me, everything obsesses me, the smallest action – filing papers, supervising work – intimidates me. . . . I had dozens of subjects and now everything has gone; ruination will come, but I am oblivious to it. I shall try to go and see a new play tonight.'[73]

Balzac's solitary life, the destruction of Eveline's letters and his habit of putting on his 'Balzac costume' in society make it hard to corroborate any impression of hidden motives in his correspondence. Nevertheless, there is a clear sense that in all his physical and emotional suffering he was twisting the knife in the wound in order to speed a happy conclusion. On Saturday, 14 August 1847, he took the train to L'Isle-Adam and saw again the valley and forests where he had stayed thirty years before with his father's friend, Villers-La Faye: 'It was like a dream. . . . I walked without stopping for seven hours like a soldier on a march. . . . I saw everything without being moved, without the emotion I was expecting to feel. Ah! if only my Line had been with me, I could have said, "There beneath that tree I dreamed of glory;

here I thought of a woman who might love me; there I bemoaned a mother's tyranny", etc. – everything would have meant something!"[74] Balzac had won his two trophies – love and glory – but had done nothing to undermine his mother's 'tyranny'. He still owed her 4000 francs, which she desperately needed, in part to pay for Laurence's two boys. Compared to his other debts, 4000 francs was a pittance: his tailor, for instance, received 8830 francs from him in June 1847. The only immediate action he took on his mother's behalf was to stipulate in his will, which he drew up that June, that Eveline should pay her the modest sum of 3000 francs a year after his death. Everything else (including his debts) was to go to Eveline, with mementos for Georges and Anna, his sister, brother and nieces, his presumed daughter, Marie Du Fresnay, the solicitor Gavault, Alexandre de Berny, Dr Nacquart, Zulma Carraud and Justin Glandaz, an old school-friend whom he appointed executor. For himself, he requested the cheapest form of burial.[75]

Balzac's will again raises the suspicion that his love for Eveline was measured against hostility to his mother, and the same arithmetic might account for his peculiar treatment of his housekeeper, Louise Breugniot. The final, largely self-inflicted unpleasantness before Balzac left for Wierzchownia was their separation. The bare facts, stripped of Balzac's embroidery, are that he tried to help her find a job: Baron Rothschild was asked to make 'a pretty woman' happy by recommending her for a licence to sell stamped paper.[76] He also gave her some furniture and some of the 10,000 francs he owed her. When she married a widower the following year, the ceremony was attended by Balzac's mother, brother-in-law, the ironmonger Dablin, and Balzac's friend, Laurent-Jan.[77] It was practically a family affair. Eveline, on the other hand, heard a horrific story that seems to concern a different person altogether: the 'infamous' Mme de Brugnol had stolen several letters from Eveline (the number varies) and was blackmailing her former employer. She wanted 30,000 francs and a written apology for the way she had been treated. Balzac's rage at her 'betrayal' has no definite basis in reality and seems to have been a convincing hysterical performance put on for the benefit of his jealous fiancée. Whether or not Louise Breugniot actually resorted to blackmail, Balzac's righteous horror at her evil deeds (reflected, of course, in her 'hideous' face), the contradictions in the details he gave to Eveline, and his decision not to prosecute all point to a furious burning of bridges. The only lasting trace of the incident is the incineration of all the letters he had received from Eveline: 'the saddest day of my life . . . in a single hour I relived fifteen years. I threw them into the fire one by one, looking at the dates! I salvaged a few flowers, a few scraps of dress and some sashes; but my grief I shall keep for myself – nothing could express it.'[78] Balzac was then on the point of leaving for Russia: it was useless to stay any longer in his 'mausoleum' where work had become impossible. He was disappointed with himself, his frustrations and fears directed against the world, grimly intensifying his loneliness as he watched the letters shrivel up in the flames.

The tone of pathos in Balzac's chronicle is a sure sign that something was about to change. When he left Paris on the evening of 5 September 1847, he was in a very different mood, as if purified of the past. The head clown's tragic mask was turned towards a France that was about to be overrun by revolutionaries, and 'Bilboquet' looked to the future with the happy, distracted face of comedy.

He marked the occasion with his finest piece of travel-writing. Written for the *Journal des Débats* and entitled *Lettre sur Kiev*, this long, unpublished article contains almost nothing on Kiev and everything on his journey to Wierzchownia. Its most remarkable feature is its hero: for the first time in a text intended for publication, Balzac was indulging in direct autobiography. All his other self-portraits had been rapid sketches or 'confessions' attributed to characters. Now it was as if he no longer felt the need to incarnate himself in fictional creatures. Vautrin was head of the Sûreté, Lucien de Rubempré was dead, and Balzac was happy to be himself, at one with the lover who was setting off for what the jailed magician had told him would be the second part of his life.

ON 5 SEPTEMBER, Balzac turned up 'heroically' at the station with a small trunk, an overnight bag, 'not an atom of paper except for a passport', and a basket containing coffee essence, sugar, stuffed tongue, cuttle-bone (for polishing teeth), and a little bottle of aniseed encased in wicker. He had equipped himself with two indispensable words: '*Milk* in German, *liko* in Polish' (*sic* for *Milch* and *mleko*). The journey was to take eight days, despite several tense moments caused by uncompleted sections of railway which threw him on the mercy of local transport. The slightest delay and he would miss all his connections, which in any case seemed to him over-optimistic: 'There is nothing as deceitful as a railway timetable.' Impatience saved him: 'I am incapable of waiting. It is an incorrigible fault in my nature. When travelling, I cannot understand people who want to dawdle, especially when they are on their way to visit friends . . . I arrived ten days before the letter in which I announced my arrival.'

At seven o'clock the next morning, he found he had to cross Brussels to catch the train for Cologne. Eating breakfast, 'I noticed in the glances of one of my fellow detainees, who was also eating breakfast, that form of close attention that is bestowed on those unfortunate trained monkeys known as European celebrities, among whom, rightly or wrongly, I am counted. But for all my reputed knowledge of the human heart, I had no idea whether the stranger was friend or foe.' Luck was on his side. Standing on the platform was the family of the Russian *chargé d'affaires*, Kisseleff: thanks to them, he was able to overcome the 'administrative stupidity' that deposited everyone's luggage in a giant heap at Cologne station. 'With sadness in my heart, I bade a cheery farewell to my protectors, for I was about to enter the desert that faces any traveller who is entirely ignorant of foreign languages.'

Similar inconveniences awaited him at every step: queues in which Englishmen were always first, the four categories of German stagecoach – the 'fastest' being the *Extrapost* which was so fast that it had to change horses at every stage and was soon overtaken by the *Schnellpost* – and, at Breslau, the loading of his luggage into the wrong train. Seeing his trunk about to set off for Vienna, Balzac caused 'a one-man riot' by crying out 'in the voice I intend to use one day for quieting stormy debates in the Chamber': 'My petulance was mistaken for drunkenness – a notion to which, I must confess, my highly-coloured complexion gives an appearance of truth.' In France, such ineptitude would cause 'a revolution'; in Breslau, people simply 'stuffed their pipes, began to smoke and smiled at the futility of the whole operation'. It was hard to decide which was worse.

With the help of a physician from the Austrian Embassy who was taking despatches to Metternich (another significant stroke of luck), Balzac reached the devastated region of Galicia, where 60,000 peasants had died of starvation – an indirect result, he said, of the fashionable utopias put about by Polish refugees 'who know nothing of their own country'. Here, the original documentary aim of the *Lettre* finally becomes apparent. 'Let men die and long live principles!' 'On every road there were starving spectres, chased away with whips as they flung themselves at the coaches.' For Balzac, the solution was to replace Austrian domination with Russian feudalism – the first sign of the anachronistic, wishful politics of his last years (though in this he was in agreement with most Galician peasants). Anything that happened in Europe now was a possible impediment to his marriage.

By the time he reached the Russian frontier at Radziwiłłow, it no longer felt like Europe. He was 'succumbing to fear of the unknown, losing my imperturbable impatience which, in my case, is a form of *sang chaud* – far superior to *sang froid*'. A customs official refused to allow him across the border because he had run out of printed forms (an incident which produced an admiring comment from Balzac on that 'blind obedience' so painfully lacking in France); but he was rescued by an important official called Hackel who invited him in for a meal, thus earning himself a complete edition of *La Comédie Humaine*. General Hackel placed him in a *kibitka* with a complementary cushion and he set off for Dubno, travelling through the night. The *kibitka* was a covered sledge with no suspension, pulled by a horse at the speed of a locomotive through dark pine forests; here and there, tree trunks lay across the road. Balzac looked at the stars and listened to the sleigh-bell. 'To reach the Ukraine was not just my desire but a need, for it meant being able to rest and I felt I had strength left only for another twenty-four hours.' From Dubno to Annapol, there were uninterrupted fields of wheat, and 'every 50 versts, either on the roadside or on the horizon, I saw one of those rare and splendid dwellings surrounded by parks, with their copper roofs shimmering in the distance'. At Berdichev, with its rickety houses all 'dancing the polka', the main road came to an end and the black soil of the Ukraine began. He was engulfed in a crowd of Jews who all showed a disturbing interest in his gold watch-chain. Balzac's anti-semitism is not unusual for the time and survived his friendship with Baron Rothschild and Léon Gozlan. The Jews of Berdichev are typified in the *Lettre* as exotic creatures with an instinctive appreciation of gold and precious stones. Those lacking the instinct, he affirms, are considered geniuses and brought up to become rabbis. Miraculously, he found a French tailor who organized a *bouda* that would take him the 40 miles to Wierzchownia, across the 'steppes': 'It was the desert, the kingdom of wheat, the prairies of Fenimore Cooper and their silence.' 'The sight filled me with dismay and I fell into a deep sleep. At half-past five, I was woken by the cry of the Hebrew greeting the Promised Land. I saw a Louvre or a Greek temple, gilded by the setting sun, overlooking a valley. It was the third valley I had seen since crossing the border!'

Balzac's *Lettre* ends here, at the palace he used to gaze at on his study wall. He had arrived in the middle of a cholera epidemic and at the end of autumn, and would be forced to stay through the winter. There, at last, on his 'desert island' in a sea of wheat he enjoyed a quiet family life with Eveline, Anna and Georges, talking, reading, writing very little and sampling 162 different recipes for flour.[79] 'This is a strange country', he told his sister. 'For all its magnificence, they lack our most basic comforts. Wierzchownia is the only estate in the region that has an oil-lamp and a hospital. There are 10-foot mirrors but no wall-hangings.'[80] The possibilities for making money were endless. . . . This was supposed to be good news for Laure: her husband's engineering projects continued to fail, and her two daughters had nothing but debts for dowries. Since 1840, she had been trying to supplement their income by writing stories.

In his second letter (November 1847), Balzac described his new setting: 'At the moment I have a delightful little apartment consisting of a salon, a study and a bedroom. The study is in pink stucco with a fireplace, superb carpets and convenient furniture. The windows all have clear glass so I can see the countryside in all directions. You can imagine what this Louvre is like when I tell you they have five or six apartments like this one to give to visitors.'[81]

In the four and a half months he spent at Wierzchownia, Balzac put most of his energy into being happy. Apart from the unfinished *Lettre sur Kiev*, he wrote only two fragments and the second part of *L'Envers de l'Histoire Contemporaine*. One of the fragments, *La Femme Auteur*, was perhaps intended as a cautionary tale for sister Laure. The other includes a list of thirty-four characters, none of whom had previously appeared in *La Comédie Humaine*. The fictional world was still trying to expand and renew itself; but the completed work, *L'Initié*, sounds in parts like the lamentations of an old man, deploring the disappearance of faith, devotion and discipline. It was his last novel. Scenes from his life are scattered throughout it like involuntary memories: his legal studies, his tracking of passers-by in the streets of Paris, the restaurant in the Rue de Tournon, his pamphlet on primogeniture, battles with publishers, and the deserted quartier near the Observatoire where he wrote *Le Dernier Chouan* and where, in *L'Initié*, the invalid Vanda (the daughter of a Polish woman) lives in what she thinks is luxury – in reality, an illusion created by her father, who, by scrimping and saving and selling all his books, has filled one room of their hovel with treasures. In Paris, to cheer him up, Laurent-Jan had bought him a translation of Dickens's *The Cricket on the Hearth*. Balzac deemed it a 'flawless masterpiece' and was impressed by the fact that Dickens, then only twenty-six, had received '40,000 francs' for it.[82] Writing *L'Initié*, he may have remembered Dickens's cosy domestic story, in which Caleb Plummer surrounds his blind daughter with pleasant fantasies. Both tales point to the same moral, intentional or not: love, illusions and money are the key to earthly happiness.

As BALZAC slowed down and adapted to life as a feudal lord, events at home were speeding up. France was still in the early stages of industrialization. The resulting unemployment and hunger were creating pressure for democratic reform, particularly in Paris and Lyon, unable to cope with the great migration from the provinces that had begun in the days of Balzac's father. Elsewhere in Europe, François Guizot's government pursued its politics of appeasement, actively tolerating the sort of repression Balzac had witnessed in Galicia; but France in the meantime had become a haven for revolutionaries from Poland, Austria and Italy. Reformist groups had reorganized, and the workers of Paris, some of whom were hard at work on Balzac's new home, were preparing to reconquer the republic that had been won and lost in 1830.

From his pink-walled study in the Ukraine, surrounded by wheatfields, Balzac saw things differently. For him, peasants, not the urban proletariat, were the revolutionary threat. With one foot firmly planted in the *ancien régime*, he had portrayed the species in *Les Paysans* as an economic termite – a view with which Proudhon agreed[83] – sly, greedy, idle, sullen, promiscuous and stupid, seething with negative energy, sitting unprofitably on little parcels of land they had stolen from the great estates that should now be restored to their former integrity. At Wierzchownia, he noticed a satisfying contrast in the Russian breed: they at least did not own property. They set off for work, smiling and singing songs, living proof that a benevolent dictator was the next best thing to God. Presumably, Balzac wrote to one of the Russian Ministers on whose goodwill he depended, those jolly bands of serfs were not put on just for his benefit, 'in the same way that the Crimea was populated for Catherine the Great by Potemkin'.[84] True, they stole from their masters, 'purged' themselves with corrosive vodka and sometimes had to be whipped, but they were happy, secure and drunk under the wing of a revered Emperor. For Balzac, the only obstacle to Russia realizing its potential as a world power was its landowners who, like the late M. Hanski, lacked initiative and expertise; but he would have been horrified by the remedy that began to take effect seventy years later. As a Soviet Balzac scholar reported in 1937 with a certain pious pleasure, Mme Hanska's estate 'has now been transformed into a Special School of Agronomy where the descendants of the Hanskis' serfs can acquire the knowledge they need in order to exercise their profession'.[85] (It still is.) Some of Balzac's remarks remind one of Zulma Carraud's complaints that he was insensitive to the plight of the poor; but his contradictions arise in part from the difficulty of finding a suitable perspective. Writing *L'Initié* in the Ukraine, he gave a detailed account of what it meant to be poor in Paris, whilst viewing conditions on his doorstep on a highly abstract level. Why, anyway, should he put his happiness at risk when the Censor would be reading all his letters? He was clearly delighted to have pleasant things to report, and in Balzac's case it was certainly true, as he never tired of saying, that Russia was now the safest place in Europe.

At the end of January 1848, Balzac left 'very sadly' for France. He was forced to make a payment on his railway shares and was worried about the house in the Rue Fortunée: his mother had been told to call for him once a week so that the servants would expect him any minute. He arrived on 15 February in poor health. He was hoping to sell *L'Initié* to a newspaper and launch the second part of his career: another *Comédie Humaine*, but this time on the stage.

It was then that everything went wrong – for Balzac and for the reigning bourgeoisie. On 22 February, a political banquet organized by two left-wing newspapers turned into a demonstration against the Government. The National Guard were called out, but on the 23rd they took the side of the marchers. That evening, on the Boulevard des Capucines, the army fired on the insurgents; barricades went up, Paris fell to the mob, and on 24 February, Louis-Philippe abdicated. Two days later, a provisional government declared the Republic at the Hôtel de Ville.

The February Revolution was witnessed by two quite distinct Balzacs. One was a bourgeois businessman, fretting about his property and profits. On the 23rd, 'seeing that there were strange goings-on, I changed my clothes and went out. The whole of our *faubourg* was barricaded, the streets abandoned to the rabble and they were smashing those beautiful lanterns and building barricades. The patience of the troops was sublime!'[86] When the Government collapsed, he wrote again to Eveline: 'As far as we're concerned, here are the results. – Anarchy. They've changed the style of the newspapers, which means there will be no more serial novels and no more money to be earned from writing. The book trade will vanish.' Work had stopped in the Rue Fortunée, people were invoking that 'fateful trinity', *Liberté*, *Égalité*, *Fraternité*, and calling each other '*tu*'; there were all the signs of class warfare. Amazingly, Balzac compared himself to the despised Bourgeois Monarch; he was 'as humiliated in [his] hopes as Louis-Philippe'.[87] The only ray of hope, he told his adoptive family in the Ukraine, was that France would need to import a lot of wheat that year.[88]

Yet on 24 February, in the midst of the barbarian horde that ransacked the Tuileries Palace and brought to an end the regime whose history occupies a large part of *La Comédie Humaine*, a short, fat figure was seen by several people inspecting the devastation and commotion around him 'with piercing eyes'.[89] It was Honoré de Balzac hunting for historical souvenirs. He snatched up a sheet of paper that turned out to be the last history lesson given to the Comte de Paris. He also picked up something else: a shred of velvet from the throne.[90] It was a relic of the society he had spent the last nineteen years describing and, as it were, bringing to life. While the July Monarchy fell apart at his feet, the defender of Throne and Altar was still collecting data.

CHAPTER SEVENTEEN

Home

(1848–1850)

BALZAC'S PROGNOSIS of an agrarian revolution was entirely wrong, which is interesting since the largest gap in his panorama of French society is the urban proletariat, to which he seemed oblivious or indifferent. This is Balzac's clearest surface difference with Dickens, who was admittedly describing a more heavily and more cruelly industrialized society. The working classes and, by extension, the poor and destitute, appear only in glimpses or abstractions, as in the magnificent introduction to *La Fille aux Yeux d'Or* – one of the most memorable summaries of nineteenth-century urban economic conditions. Characters are seen rising out of or sliding down into the social limbo, but almost never while they are actually in it. The gap is all the more noticeable since Balzac's own half-peasant family was not as firmly entrenched in the bourgeoisie as it liked to think. In 1836, one of Laurence's children had (to use Balzac's image[1]) floated up from the mud at the bottom of society, uneducated, unclothed, unfed. His brother-in-law Surville was in constant danger of being thrown into debtors' prison, and Balzac himself had spent most of his adult life teetering between extremes of wealth and poverty.

Seen biographically, this apparent blind-spot contains a valuable lesson: the encyclopedic *Comédie Humaine* does not after all include samples of all its author's experience. Many times he had walked through the city at night, quite fearlessly, down the sort of streets one is afterwards surprised to find on a map. It was a habit imposed on him to some extent by the law that prohibited the arrest of debtors between sunset and sunrise.[2] Balzac roamed the city like a peaceable vampire with an almanac in his pocket; but whatever horrors he saw, he chose not to describe them. In his later years, in *Splendeurs et Misères des Courtisanes* and in *Les Parents Pauvres*, he made some effort to portray the lowest orders: Baron Hulot, the splendidly degenerate representative of the old Empire, is driven deeper and deeper down through the layers of the Parisian Hades by his craving for sex and eternal youth, and as he sinks, affords an insight into the various stages of poverty and degradation. He ends as a scrivener writing letters for the illiterate – as if Balzac were acknowledging the parts of society he had not been able or willing to record. But it is perhaps his last completed novel, *L'Initié*, with its self-effacing philanthropists seeking out the deserving poor, that provides a literary explanation. Balzac's honest view of poverty shows a world where moral categories break down, where human beings make little impact on their environment and where tedium stifles the exercise of the will, without which no Balzacian character can survive. The urban poor *are* present in his work, but they are not given a voice – something that might be interpreted either as a serious omission or as a fine example of historical realism; though it might also be thought typical of the *parvenu* that the poor people whose story he tells in *L'Initié* happen to be fallen aristocrats.

THROUGHOUT the Revolution, Balzac gave the impression of a man who had been caught unawares. The rise to prominence in the new Government of an elegiac poet, Lamartine, seemed to him to sum up the whole farcical situation, though he did try to use his connection in high places to obtain a contract for his brother-in-law the engineer: 'I believe I may be of some use to you', wrote literature's most famous living monarchist, 'by recommending my brother-in-law, a great worker who was persecuted for his republican opinions by the Restoration and by the last administration.'[3] It is true that even in one of his last works, *Les Comédiens Sans le Savoir*, Balzac was still attributing a certain moral superiority to a character on the left wing;[4] but it should also be said that, six days before writing to Lamartine, he was boasting to Eveline that the state of anarchy had made everyone realize how right he was to be an absolutist: 'Even my brother-in-law has come round to my way of thinking. . . .'[5]

With a poet in power, any popular figure was likely to have greatness thrust upon him. There was a rumour that Balzac had rushed back from the Ukraine in order to take a seat in the new Parliament. Five days into the Republic he wrote to Georges and Anna with news of February's 'Shakespearean' street drama: 'I went everywhere, except to the Hôtel de Ville, where I was afraid of being *requisitioned* for the Republic. There was one horribly laughable incident that I shall relate to you alone: in the Rue de Richelieu I was recognized and there was a shout of *"Vive M. de Balzac!"* which restored the legs of my youth to me and I was able to make my getaway down a side-street.'[6]

The popular perception of Balzac's politics was mercifully uninformed (Marx and Engels might have called it far-sighted), but there was a fine line between being construed a hero or a traitor, and when the revolutionary Club de la Fraternité Universelle invited him to stand for election and 'to come and have *my political sentiments appreciated* at its first meeting', he sent an open letter to the newspapers explaining his position:[7] he had already declared his willingness to support 'the empire that must be founded' at a time, he added with imperceptible sarcasm, 'when France must call on all its strength and intelligence'. However, the job of founding a regime that would last more than a few months (another pointed remark) demanded a stronger and more courageous man than himself. Balzac's letter was a model of diplomacy and ambiguity. He even managed to turn it into a free advertisement by referring to the plays he was hoping to write. These, too, would be a contribution to the Republic: by going about his business as usual he would be 'giving work to the printing trade, to the theatrical and publishing worlds and to the press. Those industries and enterprises nourish a score of other trades which are all in the doldrums at present. Reviving those trades is a mission in itself!' The irony not mentioned by Balzac is that popular support for his political career came only with the advent of a regime whose ideals were directly opposed to his own.

Balzac's real, undiluted sentiments emerge in all their down-to-earth extremism in letters to Eveline and in an unpublished 'Lettre sur le Travail',[8] in which he details various forms of republican stupidity: electing uneducated people on principle, reserving the word *travailleur* for anyone who has calluses on their hands, calling for equal hours and pay without regard to economic consequences. Balzac would have been delighted by the fall of the Soviet empire. The world had long since slipped out of the crude embrace of convictions and principles: 'Capital agrees with everything I say, but without saying so, for Capital has no voice.' The Revolution was simply frightening it away, turning 'men of intelligence' into beggars and exiles. With their mixture of horror and hilarity, Balzac's letters are one of the best (and least used) first-hand accounts of the February Revolution – with or without their legitimist conclusions. 'Yesterday, I had to light up the house (36 sous' worth of lanterns!) for a tree of liberty they were planting on the Place Beaujon. . . . No, really!'[9] 'Two days ago, [21 April], Laurent-Jan did something magnificent: he stopped a column of a thousand workers who were roaming the boulevards and said to the leaders, who were singing the *Marseillaise*, "My friends, what's that you're singing? There is no *impure blood*, there are no more *tyrants*, and we have no *furrows* any more.* So, you see! . . ." They stood there like idiots. Gozlan said, "They've managed to create a republic without republicans".'[10] 'It's like the end of the world. Debtors aren't paying, creditors aren't suing, governments aren't governing, the troops are disarmed, magistrates aren't prosecuting, the legs are leading the head!' It was like 1793 all over again, but with clowns instead of heroes.[11] The only signs of public protest from Balzac were suitably comic: his reluctance to allow *Vautrin* to be revived as a political satire (because people would realize there was nothing political about it after all),[12] and, more subtly, turning up at a 'Writers' General Assembly' held at the Institut wearing Cossack trousers and 'aristocratic' yellow gloves.[13] All in all, he remained remarkably cheerful and was able, in mid-catastrophe, to report to Eveline that the Republic was doomed, share-prices had shot up and he was rich beyond their wildest dreams. 'Did you not notice', he went on merrily, 'that it's *the First of April*?'

By symbolic coincidence, it was Lamartine who was told of Balzac's private agenda when he met him in the avenues between the Chambre des Députés and the Invalides: '"What are you doing?" I asked him. "I am awaiting," Balzac replied, "the happiness of earthly angels. I love and am loved by the most enchanting mystery-woman on earth. She is young, unattached, and has an independent fortune whose income can only be counted in millions. . . . You see in me the happiest of men."'[14] His good-luck story harks back to 1821 when he told Laure of an unlikely plan to emulate Lamartine by wooing a

---

* Cf. *La Marseillaise*, vv. 3–4 and refrain: '*Contre nous de la tyrannie / L'étendard sanglant est levé.*' '*Marchons, marchons! / Qu'un sang impur abreuve nos sillons!*'

wealthy foreign lady with his Romantic verse. But he also had a practical reason for buttonholing the poet: the new republican leader was to provide him with a passport. Lamartine was happy to oblige. Unfortunately, with revolution spreading to other parts of Europe, Russia had closed its borders and Balzac anxiously awaited permission to enter the Empire.

In the meantime, he set to work on producing a repertoire of comedies and dramas to rival that of Molière. He would complete it at Wierzchownia and have the plays performed in Paris. It was the perfect job for semi-retirement: plays, unlike novels, says one of his characters, can be worked on sporadically and require very little polishing; good dialogue simply occurs to one or does not – there is no point racking one's brains trying to find it.[15] With this approach, it is no great wonder that only two plays were completed. One was *La Marâtre*, a 'bourgeois tragedy' in which a mother and a stepdaughter are in love with the same man. The heroine has opium dropped in her cup of tea, commits suicide by taking arsenic, and there is a pesky child called Napoleon who helps with the exposition by asking awkward questions. Balzac's goal was to transplant the domestic dramas of his novels into the theatre; but his unspoken aim was to appeal to a mass audience, and in succeeding, he almost disappears behind a mask of theatrical sophistication. The second play sounds more like Balzac himself and has been described as 'the best comic work of its time to appear on the French stage'.[16] *Mercadet* had existed in some form since 1840 and it resonates with all his debtor's experience and all the nervous anticipation of the last eight years. The mainspring of the plot is that Mercadet is hoping for the return of an associate who absconded with 150,000 francs to make his fortune in the East. The associate's name is Godeau and he never appears on stage. Balzac's *Mercadet* is a nineteenth-century *Waiting for Godot* in which money takes the place of metaphysics.

History had the last laugh. Balzac's suspicion that the Revolution was his personal enemy was confirmed by the fate of both plays. *La Marâtre* was premiered on 25 May 1848 at the Théâtre Historique and, at last, Balzac knew the thrill of a successful first night; but because of civil unrest the auditorium was half-empty. After only six performances, the director closed the theatre, left for England with the actors, and although *La Marâtre* was resurrected in July, the initial momentum was lost. Instead of the 25,000 he predicted, it produced only a few hundred francs. *Mercadet* was even more unlucky. Balzac propelled it through the reading stage by giving one of his single-handed improvised renditions, using a different voice for each character, performing all the actions and shedding most of his clothes in the process.[17] Another dream of adolescence came true. It was accepted by the Théâtre de la République – the new, politically correct name for the Comédie Française; but it was delayed until after Balzac's departure for Russia, and Laurent-Jan, acting as his agent, was unable to prevent rival playwrights from having their plays put on instead. Only two copies of *Mercadet* were printed, which makes it the rarest of Balzac first editions.[18] It was performed almost exactly a year after his death and, as dramatic irony demands, was a huge success.

In June 1848, the counter-revolution occurred when Balzac had said it would three months before.[19] The provisional government had failed to ease the hunger and unemployment that swept it into power, and after six days of street-fighting a workers' revolt was savagely repressed by those civilized bourgeois Balzac had always known would be forced by their own policies to act as barbarians. Thousands were shot, imprisoned or deported, the army gained control and in the elections the following December, Louis Napoleon Bonaparte, nephew of the Emperor, became President. After the *coup d'état* of December 1851 and the plebiscite the following year, he was confirmed as Emperor Napoleon III, owing much of his support to the Napoleonic legend Balzac's novels had helped to keep alive. The deposed king, Louis-Philippe, remained in exile in Surrey and died eight days after Balzac on 26 August 1850.

During the June Days, as in the 1830 Revolution, Balzac was far from the theatre of events, 'breathing lungfuls of [his] native air': he had left for Saché on 3 June, thus evading his National Guard duty once again and, perhaps, avoiding a violent death at the hands of 'anarchists'. In the Indre Valley, 'whose beauty outlives every revolution',[20] he fought his own civil war. The ancient forests with their 'dowager' trees, the birds and flowery fields, the syrupy-sweet delights of twenty-five-year-old Vouvray, 'the valley described in *Le Lys*' and the exemplary peasants of Touraine at first had the same effect on him as spa-waters on Eveline:

Misery seems 1000 miles away. There is no Mme Hancha [*sic*] to keep happy by staying busy, and so instead of attacking *Les Petits Bourgeois* I give in to idleness like a horse recovering from a race. I am physically contented, which means I can abandon myself wonderfully to heartache, and I stroll about thinking of us instead of the comedies and plays I came here to write. The slightest thing reminds a man of his wife when he loves her. You can't imagine how the pigeons of Saché prevent me from working; there are as many here as at Wierzchownia. . . . They come flocking on to a roof in front of my window and set me *Wierzchowni-ing*.[21]

But as the rain settled in and news of massacres came from Paris, Balzac felt the final onset of his illness – or illnesses. Climbing just a few stairs or writing a letter exhausted him; his heart was weak, palpitating at the slightest exertion; the coffee sent for from Paris had no effect; and now his eyesight was failing.

On 4 July 1848, he left Saché for the last time, spent a night at Azay-le-Rideau and reached the Rue Fortunée on the evening of 6 July. After attending the funeral of Chateaubriand, he dined at his sister's house and went home in a carriage. He was too tired to walk and there were soldiers on street corners shouting, 'Who goes there?': 'The deaf and the absent-minded are being shot.'[22] His time was spent preparing for a departure that might still be months away. His mother would manage the house and train the servants, and – not coincidentally – she was now receiving a small monthly allowance from Honoré. Laurent-Jan would take care of literary business and was authorized to make any changes to his plays that directors might demand. Everything was ready; there was nothing to do but wait; impatience was eating him alive and his writing ground to a halt.

Finally, on 20 August, a letter came from Count Orloff, Minister of Police. Balzac literally jumped for joy and 'almost compromised the existence of the furniture': the barrier at Radziwiłłow had been raised – 'for me, it is the gate of Paradise!'[23] It was a huge relief. He was one of very few Frenchmen allowed into Russia in the period following the February Revolution, and the apostil attached to Count Orloff's petition by the Czar himself shows how fortunate he was: 'Yes, yes, but under strict surveillance.'[24] Balzac made some last-minute preparations, ordering two years' worth of clothes from the tailor who had recently written off part of his debt. A servant called François Munch would be left in charge when Mme de Balzac was away. For once, he was pleased with his domestic help: 'The Alsatian is a solid fellow – not very bright, but very honest. He will undoubtedly make an excellent coachman later on. I shall keep a close eye on him.'[25]

On 20 September, he left for Russia, expecting to be away for a few months. The journey seems to have been less of a record-breaking attempt than the previous one. His only complaint was that he caught a bad cold – this, too, an indirect result of anarchy, which was now infecting Germany: 'To avoid the cigar-smoke of the Prussian generals who were in first class with me, I kept the window open.'[26] After crossing the border, he convalesced with Georges Mniszech's brother on their estate in Wiśniowiec and from there he wrote to Eveline, asking for horses to be arranged. These are the last words in Balzac's longest novel – a correspondence spanning sixteen years, almost one-quarter the length of *La Comédie Humaine*: 'Personally, I would rather have locomotives than horses. / How happy I was once sitting in the railway carriage! / Just three days now!'[27]

He was to spend the next year and a half at Wierzchownia. Atala and Bilboquet would never again be apart.

WHEN BALZAC left Paris in the autumn of 1848, he left his own past behind and confirmed that one great passion (Eveline) had vanquished the other (*La Comédie Humaine*). Emotionally and intellectually, he now belonged to the old order and his political solutions sound more and more like a hopeless desire to re-create the past, or the past as it survived in Russia. 'I belong to that opposition that is known as Life',[28] he told Laure in 1849 during his last stay at Wierzchownia; but Life was in the past and in the future was Death, represented, not by a leering skull but by a young fogey like Victorin Hulot, son of Baron Hulot in *La Cousine Bette* – a character who is the ideal opposite of the novelist who created him, someone who was brought up under the July Monarchy that came to power in 1830 and reaped the rewards of its petty materialism in 1848.

Victorin was the very model of the young man manufactured by the 1830 Revolution: a mind wrapped up in politics, full of respect for his own aspirations but keeping them in check behind a solemn mask, very envious of established reputations, uttering grandiloquent phrases instead of those incisive *mots* that are the pearls of French conversation, yet perfectly proper and correct, mistaking haughtiness for dignity. People like him are walking coffins that contain a Frenchman of older times. Occasionally the Frenchman stirs and kicks out against his English envelope; but ambition restrains him and he consents to be stifled. These coffins always go draped in black cloth.[29]

Balzac was still the conscientious though disapproving 'secretary' of French society, and it is to this depressing personage that he gives the last word at the end of *La Cousine Bette*. Like Victorin's father, Baron Hulot, Balzac had remained tragically young; but in his scorn for the blandness of the new generation and belligerent nostalgia for the age of Napoleonic heroes, there is a terrible envy of youth; perhaps, too, a sense of divine injustice.

The new type of Frenchman also had a setting worthy of him. Paris was changing for the worse. Balzac had always been enthusiastic about asphalt, gas-lighting, well-stocked shops and efficient urban transport, but like most admirers of modernity he eventually found himself praising the things that were destroying his own past. Several years before Baron Haussmann began his programme of modernization 'the speculator's hammer' was becoming over-active. Yellow plaster tenements were springing up, ceilings were being lowered, gardens obliterated, the wall of private life demolished. Picturesque trades were becoming extinct, and even the 'unspeakable horrors' of prostitution that had fascinated the adolescent Balzac in the arcades of the Palais-Royal were being brought under official control, numbered, sanitized and, as it were, tarted up. The arts were swamped by petty bourgeois tastes and mass-produced goods, and the period's lasting contribution to archaeology would be 'an ignoble rubbish-heap of pasteboard, plasterwork and coloured drawings'.[30] Balzac's comments on sections of the Musée d'Orsay can be imagined.

The continuous line that linked the modern city with the Middle Ages was being severed. The opening paragraph of *Les Petits Bourgeois* – dedicated to Eveline but never completed – shows that Balzac's reactionary views were not simply the result of nostalgia, fear and discomfort, but a realization that the world of endless interconnections he had recorded and created in his work was also slipping away: 'The description of the Saint-Jean Turnstile in the opening pages of the SCENE OF PRIVATE LIFE entitled *Une Double Famille* seemed, at the time, unnecessarily tedious; and yet that authentic remnant of old Paris exists now only in those printed words. The construction of the present Hôtel de Ville swept away a whole *quartier* . . . Alas! the old Paris is disappearing at a frightening speed.'[31] It is interesting that the architectural oddity whose loss Balzac deplored had already been swept away when he described it the first time in 1830. He was mourning the loss of his own past in the Marais, where he first learned to unravel the mysteries of Paris. Yet with the sense of alienation there is also a faint note of triumph: the more impoverished the modern world became, the more the value of *La Comédie Humaine* would increase.

Balzac had already said his farewell to Paris and to an important part of the Human Comedy in the penultimate section of *Splendeurs et Misères des Courtisanes*. Lucien de Rubempré stands in his cell at the Conciergerie writing a suicide note to the criminal who first appeared in the Pension Vauquer as Vautrin. As he looks out over the Palais de Justice, that 'living, generating force'[32] known as Thought takes over from his conscious mind:

> Lucien saw the Palais in all its original beauty. The colonnade was slender, young and fresh. The abode of Saint Louis reappeared as it once had been; he marvelled at its Babylonian proportions, its Oriental arabesques. He accepted this sublime vision as a poetic farewell to civilized creation. As he made arrangements for his death, he wondered how such a marvel could exist unknown in the centre of Paris. Lucien was two separate people; the poet strolling about in the Middle Ages under the arcades and turrets of Saint Louis, and a Lucien who was preparing his suicide.[33]

There were also two Balzacs: one who stood in the present, sending down the bucket to that reservoir of energy, the Middle Ages, and the other whose life had been a long suicide. Balzac brilliantly places the hallucination in what for him had always been the home of the creative mind – the prison-cell, where he first saw at once the wonderful vision and the enormous cost of the vision.

*

BALZAC ARRIVED at Wierzchownia on 2 October 1848. From there, he wrote to the publisher, Hippolyte Souverain, saying that he would be trapped by snow and ice for the winter. 'No part of the world can compare with the one in which I now live for tranquillity.' 'I shall return with many works completed.'[34] He probably set about correcting the seventeenth volume of *La Comédie Humaine*, containing *Les Parents Pauvres*; but though all the other partially corrected volumes have survived (the so-called *Furne corrigé* which, perhaps unfortunately, provides the basis of most modern editions[35]), this one has not; nor did any of his other plans come to fruition. Life, at first, was too pleasant. Mme Hanska's valet saw a man who had every reason to be happy: 'I remember that every night at about two o'clock when he had finished writing in the room upstairs, the Countess would instruct me to take him a scalding hot cup of coffee.' 'I always found them sitting by the fireside, and they talked and talked until morning . . . Whatever could they find to talk about for so long?'[36]

Balzac was well liked by the servants: 'You could see', wrote the valet, inadvertently adding a useful footnote to the history of Balzac's politics, 'that he was very intelligent – far more intelligent even than those French tutors our neighbours send for from abroad to educate our children, for only a very wise man is so considerate towards poor people and servants.' When writing to Laure and her two daughters, Balzac was slightly less appreciative. They were to send him their recipes for onion purée and tomato sauce because the beef and mutton were old and stringy and 'we need all the tricks and frills of Parisian cuisine'. 'We console ourselves with excellent tea and delicious milk products, for the vegetables are abominable: the carrots smell of rape and the turnips smell of nothing. On the other hand, there's no end to the groats they produce – from millet, buckwheat, oats, barley, etc. Soon, they will be making them from tree-bark.'[37] For a life-long gourmet who once said there was nothing worse than a misunderstood stomach,[38] this was a sign of true devotion.

Anna and her husband Georges, after spending their way across Europe, had already settled in at Wierzchownia, where life was cheap. Balzac was treated as 'the old man of the family', surrounded by the 'respect and affection' of his little tribe.[39] By the servants and peasants, he was treated as a king: 'The domestic who serves me here was recently married', he told Laure, 'and he and his wife came to pay their respects to their masters. The woman and the man actually lie down flat on their stomachs, hit the floor three times with their heads and kiss your feet' – a real kiss, he specified, not the sort one gives to the Pope. 'Only in the East do they know how to prostrate themselves. Only there does the word *power* really mean something. One should either rule as the Emperor of Russia does or not bother at all. A man arrived from Wiśniowiec bringing various things and wished his masters *a happy reign*.'[40]

The idea of Honoré I ruling an ancient kingdom with peasants spreadeagled at his feet is especially agreeable since it occurs in a letter to Laure: the bulk of his correspondence begins and ends with his sister, which should remind us that, for all the appearance of a 'tragic destiny', most of the dreams they had shared for him in childhood had come true. After thirty years of wishing, he was still a bachelor, but for much of his life he had been in love with women who loved him or allowed him to live in a constant ecstasy of soon-to-be-requited love. France had fallen to the forces he denounced in his work, but in the Ukraine he enjoyed a privilege few of his contemporaries were to know: first-hand experience of his political ideals in action.

Back home, his own servants were hard at work – the Alsatian butler, the Italian cook, Zanella, and, of course, his mother. The first important task on her long list was to complete the formalities of her son's application to the Académie Française. Not a promising start. In January 1849 he received only four votes, including those of Hugo and Lamartine, and thus remained in the company of Molière and all the other great writers who were never Academicians. Most of the other jobs had to do with the house and the payment of his debts; for that matter, even the Académie, in Balzac's mind, would have meant a fee for working on its official Dictionary (which might then have cast a wider net than it did). Yet the apparent, practical aim of these letters home was not their only object. The avalanche of details concerning furniture and money covers up a more interesting and complicated plan: Balzac had created exactly the sort of unstable situation that, in his novels, would normally signal impending and spectacular disaster. His fortune, both financial and emotional, was now a hostage to his mother, and he was entirely to blame.

The honeymoon period was short: Honoré's 'enchanted castle' afforded his mother 'a comfort befitting [her] age and rank;'[41] but doing a physically demanding full-time job at the age of seventy-one for an employer who took her to task in schoolmasterly letters proved to be a nightmare. She was tormented by her son's creditors, worried about stains and breakages, and unable to sleep when the only other person in the house was the old Alsatian: 'If that fellow should be seized with a passion and enter my chamber, what would become of me?'[42] (A sharp assessment of his character, as Balzac was to discover.)

Not surprisingly, she struggled to implement his deceptions and ruses: 'Lead them to believe', he instructed her before sending her to the bank, 'that the 20,000 francs will *probably* be paid back in July.'[43] She was to remember only to use her maiden name (unknown to most of his creditors) and to refer to the money he still owed Sarah Visconti as 'the Gossart account' – in case Eveline heard of it. Chocolate-boxes were to be wrapped in something other than newspaper (because all printed matter was stopped at the border); and she should always pay full postage on letters and packets. 'They have to pay for those which arrive and they are too tactful to mention it to me. I am still just a guest here – magnificently and royally treated – but still a guest who must not abuse their hospitality.'[44]

Either Balzac wanted his mother to see how hard his daily life had been, or he simply had – or pretended to have – absurdly high expectations of her. The inevitable crisis that came in March was his last, possibly unconscious attempt to cauterize the wound that had been festering since childhood. For the last time, he looked into the inner 'emptiness' for which he blamed his mother and which he had tried to fill with grand ambitions, 2000 characters and at least eight lovers. It was not enough. Europe's greatest novelist, fiancé of Countess Hanska, friend of duchesses and diplomats, was still Mme de Balzac's little disappointment.

On 22 January 1849, he told her in what was plainly an inflammatory phrase that his friends at Wierzchownia thought it ludicrous that she should accuse him of not writing to his nieces as often as he should. Mme de Balzac rose to the bait and retaliated in a letter that ranged from the pitiful to the imperious and with a curious mixture of '*tu*' and '*vous*': 'I, like you, my son, am sensitive to shades of feeling. You completely misunderstood what I said and your comments were uncalled-for.'

Balzac then took the cue he had provided himself with and entered into a great fury. Every letter that arrived at Wierzchownia was read out in the salon, and already too many details about his debt-ridden family had emerged. Now his mother's 'fit of independence' had put at risk the glorious dénouement he had been planning since 1833. An unhappy ending was still possible: for years, Mme Hanska had been victimized by her own litigious family and was naturally wary of taking on another.[45] 'Here', he explained to Laure in a long and anxious letter, 'she is wealthy, loved, respected, spends no money and is reluctant to leave for a place where she sees nothing but turmoil, debts, expenses and new faces. Her children are very worried for her.'[46]

In reacting to his mother's 'cold and haughty letter', Balzac revealed more about himself than perhaps he meant to. According to him, the reason the letter was potentially so disastrous was that for the three people with whom he was living, he was the object of unfailing admiration, 'and those three dear people *never forgive* those who offend them in their feelings for me' (the offence being his mother's treatment of him as 'a little boy'). The image he projects of a desperately ambitious, snobbish family is strongly reminiscent of the *Scènes de la Vie de Province*: they should realize, he wrote, that 'marriages are like cream – the slightest thing, a change in the air or a smell can make it turn . . . good marriages call for infinite care'.[47] But was the object of his anger their embarrassing indiscretions or Mme de Balzac's refusal to stop behaving like a mother? 'Your letters remind me of those staring, angry looks with which you used to terrify your children when they were fifteen and which, now that I'm fifty, completely miss their mark.'[48] The key to these confused and violent letters is the fact that Eveline appears in them as the mother of her loving children. In effect, Balzac was setting one mother up against the other, with himself as the prize: 'In Mme Hanska, I have and shall always have the best and most devoted friend . . . but her children do not want to jeopardize the future of a mother whom they *absolutely adore*, and they are quite right.'[49]

The last sentence amounts to an astonishing admission and leads one to the paradoxical conclusion that engineering his marriage was perhaps the only thing he did *not* do out of love for Eveline. The marriage was certainly strongly associated in his mind with passionate feelings towards his mother; and as he said himself, he was still in many ways a young man, loving and hating in equal proportions, balancing one relationship against the other.

Balzac's motives must in the end remain obscure – passionate love and social aspirations were always difficult to disentangle – but they should not be allowed to eclipse the ghastly reality that accounts for his jitteriness and Eveline's hesitancy. A disturbing picture of the alternative to Wierzchownia was taking shape: a frenetic family of Parisian bourgeois with huge pretensions and debts to match, who all appeared to suffer from the same stubborn exuberance as Uncle Honoré. There was a brother-in-law whose brilliant engineering ideas had recently taken him to debtors' prison and were now about to send him to the gold-rush in California. (Balzac urged him to think of something more practical – like an undiscovered gold-mine.[50]) There was an old family friend, Mme Delannoy, who had been forced to sell her personal mementos because Honoré had borrowed all her savings (Eveline was horrified and managed to find the money); and there were other tragi-comic figures, memorably evoked in the diary of Laure's elder daughter, Sophie.[51] One of her uncles was swimming in luxury and money – though no doubt 'that beautiful, noble Countess Hanska' will 'think him beneath her'; but the other uncle was far away in Mauritius, separated from the family not just by an ocean but by 'an abyss of ingratitude and poverty'. Then there was Montzaigle, the disgraced widower of Laurence, now in his sixties, still the would-be man of fashion, thrilled with his 'mechanical umbrella' and ridiculously given to blushing. The grandmother was always sick and had perfected an unignorable cough, while the mother of the family trembled for everyone else. A play based on *La Cousine Bette* was on at the theatre and they had been given free tickets; but 'Mama has decided we shan't go because it is too immoral'. Finally, there were regular visits from a 'Bohemian' writer in charge of Uncle Honoré's affairs, 'very amusing and irresistibly witty, but dirty both morally and physically'. 'He likened *Mercadet* to a steak that must be accompanied by virtuous potatoes, by which he means the supporting roles.' Laurent-Jan was now forty, and his roguishness was well past its prime. As Balzac observed in a letter to Laure, he was too old to be a rebel: 'If only he could see that his behaviour is a sign of bourgeois *envy* . . . he would change his ways for ever.'[52] Laurent-Jan, in other words, was just the sort of person who would fit in nicely with the Balzac tribe, satisfying at the same time their sense of fun and their need to feel respectable.

With that instinctive ability to surround himself with ironies, Balzac had been defending an institution that was once again his most dangerous enemy. There was, however, a certain logic in the paradox, which he revealed to his mother with an ambiguity that might almost be thought affectionate. The society he had drawn from himself had been adhering all along to its own peculiar set of family values: 'You and God are well aware that you have not exactly smothered me with caresses or kindness since I came into this world, and you were right to do so, for had you loved me as you loved Henri, I should probably have ended up where he is; and, in that sense, you have been a good mother to me.'[53]

Eveline now found herself caught between the Devil (in the form of the Balzacs) and the deep blue sea (represented by wheat-fields). Reasons for postponing the wedding were becoming clearer and more numerous all the time. The harvest of 1849, already half-flattened by a hailstorm, was ruined by a weed that had 'the same effect as locusts'.[54] In a six-week period, there were four disastrous fires; lightning destroyed a mill outside his window. As the wheat-fields and the sheep-pens burned, Balzac saw the money that would have paid for the palace going up in flames. Throughout the region hundreds of homeless peasants were demanding housing. A whole new town would have to be built. Chernobyl, Eveline told her daughter in what now seems a chilling omen, 'is nothing but a plain; of more than a thousand houses not a single one remains'.[55] And now, just when the magic pen was most needed, her lover was too ill to write.

After July 1849, when it was confirmed that marriage would mean losing the estate, Balzac seems to have abandoned all hope of returning to Paris as a married man; but the date of his return was put back again and again. His mother was given reassuring explanations. In October, the snow was too thin for sledging, and then the winter was too mild; but in February 1850, his departure was postponed again. First, 'Galicia is full of gangs of armed bandits foraging in broad daylight';[56] second, the thaw was not yet over. He now expected to leave in April. But the real reason – and it was this that finally precipitated his marriage – was that Balzac had started on the rapid descent to death.

*

THE LAST YEAR and a half of Balzac's life is a story in which the causes are obscure, the effects all too obvious and where his body unfortunately steals the show. The author of *La Comédie Humaine* had an encyclopedic decline: bronchitis, a type of 'cephalic fever', gastric fever, ophthalmia, peritonitis, erysipelas. For most of the doctors who treated him, the central problem was cardiac hypertrophy – his big heart was swollen. The cause of this has been variously identified as overwork, hypertension, atherosclerosis, even syphilis, which is possible but unprovable.[57] The diagnosis of Dr Nacquart, who had known him as a patient since 1815, is probably the most reliable in its scrupulous vagueness: 'An old heart complaint, frequently aggravated by working through the night and by the use or rather the abuse of coffee, to which he had recourse in order to counteract man's natural propensity to sleep, had just taken a new and fatal turn.'[58] The only diagnosis that might account for all the symptoms would be one based on Balzac's theory that human beings have a finite store of vital fluid which decreases with every action and desire – a view to which Dr Nacquart himself subscribed: like Raphaël de Valentin, he was suffering from premature old age.

For someone of Balzac's vitality, the symptoms were catastrophic: difficulty in breathing, problems with circulation, loss of appetite and general exhaustion. As usual, Laure was given the full details. In June 1849, he had 'a terrible attack', vomiting and hallucinating as if he had taken hashish: 'My head weighed millions of kilos and for nine hours I was unable to move it; and then when I tried to move it, I experienced dizzying pains which I could describe only by comparing my head to the dome of St Peter's and the pain to sounds echoing about in the space under the dome.'[59] After twelve days in bed, he decided – with an interesting choice of image – that the 'riot' that pitted his 'excellent temperament' against his illness had reached a happy conclusion. Sickness was proletarian and the body it attacked aristocratic. Another crisis came in October, this time a fever that lasted thirty-four days, with the first ominous signs of dropsy (oedema). In January 1850, he was in bed again for ten days; 'but the ladies had the adorable kindness to keep me company without being repelled by my spitting, which was just like vomiting with seasickness'.[60] Despite this disheartening relapse, and in line with his belief that travelling was good for his health, he and Eveline braved the cold winds and packs of horse-devouring wolves to attend the annual contracts fair in Kiev at the end of the month. He languished in a hotel bed for twenty days with 'the most atrocious cold I have had in my life'.[61] Even describing exhaustion, his energy was apparent, and it is hard not to reach the conclusion that his desperate desire to recover contributed to his death: 'With every wish I shall diminish, just as thy days shall be decreased. . . .'

It is unfortunately far easier to assess the treatment Balzac received than it is to determine the principal cause of death. The doctor at Wierzchownia was a medical dinosaur called Knothe. 'Like many geniuses', wrote Balzac in a mood of furious optimism, 'he has little affection for the art in which he excels and practises it only with reluctance.'[62] Dr Knothe's inscrutable use of folk remedies and lack of professional zeal make him the all-too-real equivalent of Balzac's brilliant Dr Moses Halpersohn in *L'Initié*. For Balzac, the secret powders, raw cabbage and lemon juice on an empty stomach prescribed for his heart were in some way connected with the ancient mysteries of the East and therefore preferable to the more conventional approach of Knothe's son – a preference no doubt influenced by the latter's diagnosis of rapid and irreversible decline.[63] Some idea of Knothe's methods can be gleaned from a letter to Laure in November 1849 which, incidentally, is the only place where Balzac's unusual sympathy for animals seems to desert him. The following was a cure for gout:

> Once every two days [Mme Hanska] dips her feet in a freshly opened piglet, for the entrails must still be quivering when the feet go in. I do not need to tell you how fervently the little pig cries out, not realizing how honoured it should feel. . . . With piglets, pills galore and infernal potions, marvellous results have been obtained; but the best treatment would be a different climate, lots of exercise and the waters of Baden-Baden every year.[64]

Balzac had often alerted his readers to the disappearance of medieval homeopathic remedies and the arrogant empiricism of modern medicine;[65] but, as he said, his novels were 'speculative',[66] and it is touching to see him revert to a more mundane and reliable solution when Eveline's health was at stake.

Whether or not they knew or admitted to each other that he was dying, it was now that Eveline agreed to marry him and the biographer is sent clumping into the already muddy waters of motivation. The single important fact – that Eveline married him five months before he died – has sometimes been taken out of context, interpreted with a dose of misogyny and chauvinism, and made to signify that she was acting out of cynical self-interest. Even with the worst will in the world, this is quite patently improbable. By abandoning the estate to Anna – a decision Balzac rightly calls 'a heroic resolution'[67] – she was increasing the likelihood of losing everything to her first husband's relations or to the Czar. The only material benefit was the chance to live in Paris, and this was no longer the attractive prospect it might have seemed before the Revolution and before she knew much about the Balzacs. If Honoré died, she would be alone in the Rue Fortunée with debts, strange servants and a mother-in-law who promised to be peculiarly intrusive. And how many other skeletons in the cupboard might there not be? Furthermore, her husband was already considered a national treasure. For someone who valued privacy and had suffered from the sort of attention now associated with tabloid newspapers, this was hardly an incentive. When they travelled to Berdichev for a quiet ceremony in the parish church of St Barbara's on the morning of 14 March 1850, it was surely an act of compassion on her part. Honoré's last wish would be granted before he died, even if it meant an uncertain future for herself. Whether or not she was pleased with herself for taking the decision is another matter. For him, as he told Zulma Carraud, it was 'the happy dénouement of that great and noble romance that has lasted sixteen years'.[68]

Immediately after the ceremony, they returned to Wierzchownia, arriving at half-past ten in the evening. Eveline spent their wedding-night in bed with rheumatism and arthritis. Balzac was exhausted, his eyes growing dim ('a terrible state for a newly-wed man to be in'), and vowing to work as he had done in 1840–1: 'Thus we can be certain that, by 1852, our little household will at least be comfortably off.'[69] The target was still retreating.

With the roads still muddy, M. and Mme Honoré de Balzac left on 24 April 1850 for what would now be home. From the Hôtel de Russie in Brody (Austrian Galicia), Eveline wrote to her daughter with worrying news: 'I am not at all happy about his health. His fits of breathlessness are becoming more and more frequent; he is in a state of extreme weakness, he has no appetite and is sweating profusely, which weakens him even more. At Radziwiłłow they found him so changed that they barely recognized him.' Even as she wrote, the dying man burst in, having argued their luggage past the customs-men: 'He has completed all his business with admirable energy and we shall be able to leave today. I see now how poorly I understood that adorable creature. I have known him for seventeen years and every day I notice a quality I did not know he had. If only he still had his health!'[70]

By 9 May, they were in Dresden, quarrelling as usual about 'bargains', each scolding the other and spending far too much money. Balzac rejoiced in the petty tribulations of conjugal life and wrote his last letters home. His mother was to fill all the vases with fresh flowers, and Laure was to make sure that she was out of the house when they returned: 'Her dignity would be compromised if she helped us with our unpacking.'[71] The Alsatian servant would be left to guard the house. Eveline added a polite message for 'the mother to whom I owe my excellent and most perfect husband', thanking her for looking after their house, regretting that it had made her ill and hoping her son would soon recover under 'the enlightened care of his excellent friend, Dr Nacquart'.[72]

Balzac and his bride arrived back in Paris late at night on 20 (or perhaps 21) May 1850. It was his fifty-first birthday. The journey had almost killed him. After two days without food or sleep, he could neither walk nor see and continually lost consciousness; but before he could enter 'paradise', there was one more catastrophe to be endured.

The story is told, appropriately enough, by two bills: one from a locksmith, the other from a lunatic asylum.[73] When the carriage drew up outside the house, all the lights were blazing but no one answered the bell. A locksmith was sent for, the gates were opened, and they forced their way in to find the servant sitting there still defending the house against intruders: he had gone completely mad. Living in the physical manifestation of Balzac's mind, waiting for its owner to return at any minute had been too much. He was led off to the asylum and Balzac, who had hoped to impress his princess rather differently, was put to bed. The next day, Alfred de Vigny was visiting the painter who lived next door. Gudin took him to a window at the side of the house and pointed out 'in the neighbouring courtyard a travelling carriage covered in dust which he said had just turned up unexpectedly: Balzac had arrived with a Muscovite woman. I had always believed the Russian woman to be a fantasy and was amazed to learn she was real.'[74]

AT FIRST, Balzac seemed to recover and even went out on various errands, mostly to do with the customs-office: treasures were still arriving at the Rue Fortunée. But from the beginning of June, he was confined to his bedroom next to the Chapelle Saint-Nicolas and had to dictate all his business letters to Eveline. The last sentence in his own hand is a *post-scriptum* on a letter to Gautier, who was leaving for Italy: 'I can neither read nor write.' That was on 20 June. By mid-July, he was almost too weak even to dictate.

Several doctors were called in by Nacquart. The patient's body had begun to swell up alarmingly. He was bled, purged, given diuretics, sedated, ordered to eat only cold food in small portions, wear spectacles and not to talk; but, as Laure knew from experience, 'boredom will do him more harm than a few words'.[75] Early in July, peritonitis was diagnosed and a hundred leeches were placed on his stomach. He developed albuminuria – a symptom of kidney disease – and suffered the indignity of bedsores and mouth-ulcers. All this time, he remained cheerful and courageous, making excruciating puns, joking about death, and worrying more about his sick brother-in-law than about himself. He was even talking of the stories that were forming in his head: there were still large gaps in *La Comédie Humaine* and time was running out.

Some of his fears at least were unfounded. As far as he could tell, Eveline and his sister liked one another; the nieces called her 'the Adorable One'; and Madame Mère had done everyone a favour by going to stay with a friend and 'ridding you all of a poor old invalid'. Laurent-Jan kept everyone amused and irritated Eveline.

Meanwhile, the outside world had heard of Balzac's condition. On 3 July, the President sent for news and it was reported in the papers next day that Balzac was on the verge of a recovery.[76] Victor Hugo twice came to see his fellow literary giant. History converged on the Rue Fortunée: Balzac was dying and Hugo would soon be in exile. He arrived at the gloomy-looking house in the deserted avenue, the last gate on the right coming from the Champs-Élysées. A servant's face appeared at a small grille, then disappeared; the gate was opened on to a narrow garden. Tarmacked paths led through the flower-beds to the front door. As the visitor entered the salon, the colossal marble bust of Balzac by David d'Angers caught the eye.[77] 'You will be stupefied', he had written at the time to Eveline, 'when you see the Olympian head David has managed to extract from my fat bulldog face.'[78] The model himself was down a corridor, up a red-carpeted staircase cluttered with vases, statues, paintings and chests, then along another corridor. The bedroom door was open and Balzac was propped up in bed on a pile of pillows and red damask cushions, with a system of belts and pulleys for moving him in bed.

He was already much larger either than life or art. Blisters the size of heads were regularly lanced; a rubber mat was placed on the carpet; bowlfuls of water flowed out of him. Balzac's sense of humour had always stood up well to pain, and now, with his vital fluids draining away, he joked with Hugo about his dramatic decomposition and enormous size. A condition well worth observing. He was still delighted about marrying into the aristocracy and amazed that Hugo had given up his peerage so serenely. He chided him for what he called his demagogy; then he showed off his private entrance into the Chapel – from the throne of Wierzchownia to the altar of the Rue Fortunée. Finally, he tottered with his guest as far as the landing and called out to Eveline, 'Make sure and show Hugo all my paintings.' By candle-light, Hugo saw a fantastic array of old masters, including a Holbein and a Porbus, the painter Balzac had brought back to life in *Le Chef-d'Oeuvre Inconnu*.[79] He was still in good spirits, expecting to make a recovery. The doctors had given him six weeks to live.

Here, the last mystery of Balzac's life – a very sad and sordid story – must be mentioned and, if not laid to rest, at least shown to be a very insubstantial ghost.[80] In 1907, the writer Octave Mirbeau wrote a book about a motorcar tour through Belgium; it included a story he had heard from the painter Jean Gigoux, who is known to have been Eveline's lover after Balzac's death. The same story was told to Auguste Rodin while he was working on Balzac's statue: as Balzac lay on his death-bed, Eveline, furious with him for dying and sickened by his repulsive decline, was 'consoling' herself in the next room in bed with Gigoux. At Anna's request, the chapter was excised from the published work, but it became known and has been given credence by some serious scholars. Gigoux's account is memorable for its puerile boasting and Mirbeau's version for his impatience with doting Balzac fans; yet they do appear to explain some of the comments of people who watched him die. His sister talks of some 'final afflictions' he had to endure,[81] and both Zulma Carraud and Laurent Duhamel, son of Balzac's niece, Valentine, claimed much later that Honoré and Eveline had 'completely fallen out' by the time he died. The facts, then, which might provide the basis of some more qualified (and, as it happens, less depressing) speculations, are as follows.

First, at the time of Balzac's death, Gigoux was having an affair with his fellow painter's wife next door, and, as we know, Gudin's windows looked on to Balzac's house. Gigoux does not appear to have met Eveline until 1851, when he painted Anna's portrait, but his ego was certainly large enough to bridge the gap between two different periods. Second, Eveline's relations with Honoré had always been enlivened by disputes, and a seventeen-year-old relationship seen in action for the first time by members of one family would inevitably attract a variety of interpretations. Eveline was not a heavenly angel from a pre-Balzacian novel, nor did she have the inhuman consistency expected of people caught up in a sequence of events that will eventually be seen as a story with a moral. She was alone in a foreign country, caring for a husband who was dying a horrible death, and it was for this that she had sacrificed her wealth and peace of mind. Balzac's family watched her closely and wondered if she loved him enough. Laure wrote to her mother in July 1850: 'M. Nacquart is asking for a man to look after him. My sister-in-law is a riddle to me. Is she aware of the danger or not?. . . If she is then she's heroic. She complains about her head and her legs, my brother says she is sleeping very well; he seems to want someone to look after him. . . .'[82]

The only solid evidence of any 'final afflictions' can be found in a letter written by Eveline herself in June 1851 to her first lover after Balzac, Champfleury. A young writer called Henry Murger – the author of *La Vie de Bohème* – had called at the house. Eveline told Honoré it was a name that would go far: 'He answered with his angelic smile: "Don't go falling in love with a name." "Oh," I replied, "If you could see the man himself – how thin and puny he is! . . ." "So he introduced himself, did he?" "Oh," said I, "I was guessing, or rather I think it was him – at least, I suppose . . ." "It's all right," he said, half-laughing, half-sulking, "but once I'm better, you won't be seeing any more of those young men you guess or suppose. . . ." (imitating my stupidity).'[83] Perhaps it was a shame that Balzac retained his powers of observation to the end; perhaps it was unfortunate too that he had been such a model of infidelity; but the fact that Eveline later had as little as possible to do with the Balzacs shows that she tried hard to keep him happy in his last weeks: as far as he was aware, they all got on together. When Balzac's mother died in 1854, her solicitor wrote to suggest that Eveline might wish to 'defend her memory' (i.e. pay her debts). In refusing, she gave a vivid description of her last weeks with the dying man:

> For four months, I was not the wife, but the *nurse* of M. de Balzac. By caring for my husband in his incurable illness, I ruined my health as I destroyed my personal fortune by accepting the legacy of debts and difficulties he bequeathed me. If I did any more, I should compromise the future of my children, who are entirely foreign to the Balzac family, as I myself have become by the death of my husband, who ended in such a grievous and tragic fashion a union of four and a half months.[84]

Ironically, the only person involved in the story who can be judged on evidence is Gigoux himself; and if his story has a moral, it would be Balzac's axiom that 'Great men are like rocks in the ocean – only oysters [i.e. "dimwits"] can stick to them.'[85]

IT IS ON 5 August 1850 that Balzac slips away from us into the silence before death, with a letter so full of his spirit that it might almost have been planned as his last. Good news had come. His business adviser, Fessart, informed him that the venerable debt left over from Les Jardies (25,000 francs) had finally been settled – best of all, the creditor had died and Balzac had been able to redeem his own debt at the auction for 50 francs. A real bargain! Eveline sat by the bed and took dictation:

> When I received your letter I knew already of your success, but, believe it or not, I was less affected by the success itself than by the evident delight it caused you. . . . Success we may have in business, but in sickness my sufferings have redoubled. Since I had the pleasure

of seeing you, the Devil has relieved me of sleep, taste and movement
... I have nurses who enable me to perform the actions that are
indispensable for life itself when one is only nominally attached to it.
My wife is beginning to find the task beyond her strength, and I am
in pain from an abscess on my right leg. . . . This, I think, must be
the price exacted by heaven for the great happiness of my marriage.[86]

In the thirteen days that remained, Balzac had brief spells of
delirium and was astonished at the behaviour of his mind when he
came round. Perhaps it was during one of these moments of aberration
that he called for Horace Bianchon, the great physician of *La Comédie
Humaine*, saying that only he could save him.[87] The anecdote dates
from long after Balzac's death and was supposed to be another sign of
his innocent belief in his own creations – proof that he had still not
lost his grip on illusion; but it sounds like Balzac in his normal state
of mind, and if he did call for Bianchon, it was surely a humorous
recognition that nothing now could save him.

By 17 August, gangrene had set in and the doctors gave him up.
No more incisions could be made to relieve the swelling. Balzac spent
a difficult last night. He was in great pain, worried about the fate of
his unfinished novels and anxious for Eveline: 'My wife is more
intelligent than I', he had told Hugo, 'but who will support her in her
solitude? I have accustomed her to so much love.'[88] By morning, he
was silent and could see nothing. The priest of Saint-Philippe-du-
Roule, who officiated in the chapel next door, was summoned and
Balzac received the last sacraments; he gave some sign that he
understood. An hour later, he squeezed his sister's hand, and then the
agony began.

That evening, after dinner, Hugo arrived, having heard the news.
Balzac's mother was in the death-chamber with a servant and the
nurse. (Eveline must have retired for a moment – a fact that was later
seized upon by Mirbeau.) 'His face was purple, almost black, leaning
to the right, unshaven, his grey hair cut short; his eye was open and
staring. I saw him in profile and, seen thus, he looked like Napoleon.
. . . An unbearable stench rose from the bed. I lifted the blanket and
took Balzac's hand. It was covered with sweat. I pressed it, but he did
not return the pressure.'[89]

Shortly after Hugo left the house, Balzac's suffering ended. The long wait was over. It was half-past eleven on 18 August 1850. He was fifty-one years old.

A cast was taken of the famous hand that wrote a hundred stories and the moulder sent the bill to 'M. Balsaque'.[90] His face had been sketched by an artist who captured the signs of suffering and exhaustion, and also a faint smile – perhaps the remnant of a dream, or artistic embellishment, or just pure chance. The death was declared by Laurent-Jan and Balzac's brother-in-law, and the body was prepared for burial. It was carried through into the Chapelle Saint-Nicolas to which, it will be remembered, Balzac owned the right of access – or rather his wife did when she finished paying for the home of her husband's dreams just over a month later.

Balzac lay in state for two days, next door to the monument of one of his two great passions – a mausoleum on the outside, a treasure-house within, it was demolished thirty-two years later by one of the Rothschilds. Nothing now remains of it. But the other monument, that was also so near to completion, was teeming with life – and something more than life. Having taken and stored up all the vital energy of its creator, *La Comédie Humaine* was just beginning to exert its powerful and imperceptible influence on reality.

CHAPTER EIGHTEEN

The Human Comedy

(Epilogue)

ON WEDNESDAY, 21 August 1850, the streets in the fashionable area of the Faubourg du Roule were filled with traffic and a large crowd of people, to the considerable annoyance of Achille Fould, Minister of Finance.[1] It was a dull, overcast morning; the Minister was on his way to an important meeting; and no Minister should ever be held up in the course of his duties – not even by a funeral procession.

Achille Fould had been the first name of weight from the world of high finance to lend support to the new President, and as a result the weekly soirées of his elder brother Bénédict had become a focus of political life where affairs of state could be discussed on a full stomach and in the company of that handful of people who make up the élite of Parisian society. After dinner that evening, Achille found himself standing next to the famous 'Prince of Critics', Jules Janin, who some said was the model for a cynical character in Balzac's *Un Grand Homme de Province à Paris*. At the time, Janin had been less than pleased with the compliment, and when he reviewed the novel in the *Revue de Paris*, he dismissed it as a slanderous attack on his 'noble and cherished profession' – by which he meant journalism: Balzac was a vulgar man obsessed with sex, money and the seamy side of life, and self-respecting people should have nothing to do with him. But that was eleven years before.[2]

'Ah!' said the Minister. 'You're a journalist and a writer, M. Janin. You'll be able to tell me about that funeral I saw with such a large crowd behind it. I am told it was a writer of novels, a man of letters like yourself. . . .'

'That, Monsieur', replied Janin, to the astonishment of those who heard him, 'was quite simply one of the greatest men, one of the most penetrating geniuses and most brilliant minds of our time'; and he went on, in terms that were soon to become a commonplace of Balzac criticism, 'You should read all those wonderful books, Monsieur, and have your political colleagues read them too – your administrators, your financiers, your industrialists, your agronomists, your engineers, your magistrates, in fact, everyone – and you will be amazed, one and all, at the prodigious quantity of lessons that each of you in your separate spheres will find there.'[3]

Death had drawn the final veil from Balzac's work and revealed it, to some, as a deeply immoral and dangerous depiction of unnaturally vicious people, to others, as a monumental social history, the most ambitious, most thoroughly useful piece of literature since Molière. As Victor Hugo had shown so provocatively that morning in his funeral oration at Père Lachaise, Balzac had rebounded from the gates of death into the public domain. Now he belonged to his readers: 'Unbeknownst to himself, whether he wills it or not, with or without his consent, the author of this enormous, extraordinary work belongs to the powerful race of revolutionary writers,' said Hugo.[4] Standing at the graveside, Eveline must have winced at this travesty of her husband's legitimist intentions. But Balzac had always known that his novels, like children, would eventually go their own way: 'Even the most profound author does not always understand – one might even say never understands – the different meanings of his work, nor its true scope, nor the harm or the good it may do.'[5]

Balzac's funeral had brought together almost every writer in Paris, along with a large contingent of the public that we still see through his eyes. There were also some anonymous workers who had admired him and suffered for him more than any critic: typesetters.[6] The pall-bearers were Victor Hugo, Alexandre Dumas, a representative of the Société des Gens de Lettres and, for the Government, Jules Baroche, Minister of the Interior, who had just voted in a law effectively banning serial-novels. The chief mourners were Balzac's brother-in-law and Laurent-Jan. Technically, it was a third-class funeral;[7] in reality, it was a day of national mourning, and to many of the young writers who thought of Balzac as their master, the setting of a sun, the Romantic age cut short.

'When we reached the grave', wrote Hugo, 'which was high up at the top of the hill, there was an immense crowd; the path was steep and narrow, and as they climbed, the horses were scarcely able to pull the hearse, which rolled down backwards.' A few moments later, as he claimed Balzac for the revolutionary cause, Hugo stood on the spot where Rastignac stands as Père Goriot is buried and where he sheds the last tears of his childhood.

> The coffin was lowered into the grave. . . . The priest said the last prayer and I spoke a few words.
>
> While I spoke, the sun fell lower in the sky. In the distance I saw the whole of Paris in the resplendent mists of the sunset. Almost at my feet, the soil was slipping away into the grave, and I was interrupted by the dull thud of the earth as it dropped on to the coffin.[8]

THAT WAS the end of one story – and the beginning of another. Balzac had left behind him, not just an enormous *œuvre* that had already begun to achieve international recognition, but also one of those tense domestic situations he so liked to describe.

Balzac's widow and mother lived together for a time in polite discomfort in the Rue Balzac. There were awkward dinners and games of whist with the Survilles. Eveline and her sister, Caroline, found them common and boring and they said so out loud, in Polish. After a few months, Mme de Balzac went off to live with a friend. She died in 1854. Laure continued to try to support her family with her writing, her best work being the affectionate life of her brother published in 1858. It included some of the letters Balzac had sent to her from his garret in the Rue Lesdiguières. They proved that he had indeed worked his way up from humble origins – social, financial and, as she hinted quite strongly, intellectual.

The rich heiress of young Honoré's dreams proved to be worthy of his memory and equal to his debts. She decided to find another genius in need of a 'conscience' and, like Balzac before her, combined literary expediency with the satisfaction of more personal needs.

Her first helper was the founder of the movement called 'Realism', which claimed Balzac as its prophet: a thirty-year-old writer of short stories called Champfleury. In 1848, Champfleury had called to see Balzac at the Rue Fortunée when he was warned by the novelist that if he continued to write such skimpy little tales his brain would shrivel up.[9] Eveline gave him a chance to act on the master's advice. As keeper and part-originator of the flame, she felt entitled to warm her hands at it and even to add some extra fuel. Champfleury was seduced (his migraine cured by her 'magnetic' hands) and persuaded to finish the uncompleted *Le Député d'Arcis*: 'Since literature has been turned into a manufacturing industry and works of art into saleable commodities,' she told him, 'let us follow the trend. M. de Balzac's creditors, if not the public, will thank us for it.'[10]

Regrettably, Champfleury suffered from scruples, as well as from something remarkably similar to the symptoms experienced by Balzac's 'secretaries', Sandeau and Lassailly. Overworked, and intimidated by the sexual power of a woman he called 'a female Balzac', he retired in May 1851 to a clinic in Neuilly, recommending as his replacement a writer Balzac had known in the early 1830s, Charles Rabou. Under Eveline's direction, Rabou took what she gave him of *Le Député d'Arcis* and *Les Petits Bourgeois* and added 'conclusions' that were many times longer than the fragments left by Balzac. She assured her go-between with the publishers that Balzac had designated Rabou for the task before he died, which was convenient but not true.[11] The novels were published in 1854. There was no mention of the posthumous extension of *Les Petits Bourgeois*, and it is not as easy as one might hope to detect the point at which Balzac's wine turns into Rabou's water. It was Eveline, too, who supervised the 1853 edition of Balzac's works, which now included his plays, the *Contes Drolatiques* and the works written too late to be inserted in *La Comédie Humaine*. She also presided over the twenty-four-volume Lévy edition of 1869–76, to which various essays, articles and one volume of letters were added. It was this edition that was used for several English translations of *The Human Comedy* that marked the centenary of Balzac's birth.

Like many editions of the time, the text of the letters is highly unreliable; yet Eveline has been criticized much more severely for her sexual than for her textual infidelity. Instead of wishing that the dream-woman had died with the dreamer, one might as well be pleased by the late evidence that Balzac's appetites must have been satisfied in his lifetime. In fact, there is something agreeably symbolic in her devour-ing of Balzac's literary successors. In the aftermath of *La Comédie Humaine*, their little stories are like the chattering and coughing in the audience when the orchestra falls silent – and they knew it. Balzac had helped himself to such a large slice of reality that it seemed to some there was little left. It was a feeling best expressed by another young writer who came to the door in the Rue Balzac hoping to obtain some unpublished Balzac manuscripts.[12] Baudelaire's tribute in an essay of 1859 is the finest depiction of the Balzac who made himself at home in the minds and works of Dostoevsky, Flaubert, Zola, Proust, Henry James and practically every novelist who came after him:

> Balzac was able to turn that vulgar genre into something admirable – always curious and often sublime – because he threw his whole being into it. I have often been amazed that Balzac's great glory was his reputation as an observer, for it always seemed to me that his principal merit lay in his being a visionary, and an impassioned visionary. All his characters are gifted with that ardour of life that animated himself. All his fictions are as deeply coloured as dreams. From the highest peaks of the aristocracy to the lowest depths of the people, all the actors of his *Comedy* are more greedy for life, more active and cunning in the struggle, more patient in misfortune, more gluttonous in the gratification of desire, more angelic in devotion than they appear in the comedy of the real world. In Balzac, even the door-keepers have genius. All his minds are weapons loaded to the muzzle with will. Just like Balzac himself.[13]

THE LAST LIVING inhabitant of an authentically Balzacian reality remained in the palace he had chosen for her. She was joined there by Anna and Georges, who left Wierzchownia in the hands of Dr Knothe. The quiet avenue and the high wall surrounding the house gave it an air of mystery, like a strange abandoned factory with the dome of a chapel rising beside it. Balzac's bedroom and library were left as they were and closed off. The rest was a museum shrouded in gloom, and as its occupants grew old and decrepit, too fat to leave the house, the façade fell into disrepair, crumbling on to the pavement outside. The last descriptions of Eveline show her sitting in the salon on a gilded armchair covered in crimson silk or on a chaise-longue, reading books, still the *grande dame*, imposing and charming, with a 'haughty yet sensuous expression' under the magnetic gaze of Balzac's marble bust.[14] She and her daughter Anna gradually converted what was left of their fortune into clothes and jewellery from the best shops in Paris. Eugénie Grandet becomes a miser like her father; Balzac continued to spend money from beyond the grave. His son-in-law Georges died insane in 1881 and though his insect collection paid some of the bills, they were forced to sell the house in January 1882. Eveline retained the right to live there until she died. Three months later, on 11 April 1882, she passed away at the age of seventy-six (by Balzac's reckoning). Anna retired to a convent in the Rue de Vaugirard, where she died without children in 1915.

At Eveline's death, the chaos that Balzac had held at bay broke in. The auction of his paintings, furniture and books was a hasty, undignified affair. Creditors invaded the palace and his letters and unfinished manuscripts were scattered throughout the neighbourhood. The collector, Viscount Spoelberch de Lovenjoul, arrived almost too late. Letters to the Russian princess were rescued from a cobbler's across the road, and fragments of novels and studies were salvaged from a grocer's shop where they were about to be turned into paper bags. Thanks to Lovenjoul, the great romance of Balzac's life survived the death of its protagonists. The material empire had dissolved, but Balzac's true legacy fell into safe hands.

Eveline was placed in the same grave as Honoré, and there was one more story in the cemetery where Lucien de Rubempré and Père Goriot were buried, where Rastignac challenged Paris to a duel and where Balzac used to walk about in the days of the Rue Lesdiguières: 'I rarely venture out, but when my mind has begun to ramble, I go and cheer myself up at Père Lachaise!. . . and while I wander about in search of the dead, all I see are the living.'

Even today, Balzac's grave is one of the busiest parts of the cemetery, haunted by all the characters he conceived but never had time to pull into full existence. (Those he did create can be seen among the living.) As he showed at the end of *La Cousine Bette*, Thought survives the Thinker. . . . Just when the tragedy seems to be over, the characters punished or rewarded – not necessarily according to their just deserts – and everything returns to normal, Adeline Hulot notices a light under her husband's door. Hulot is whispering to the new kitchen maid, Agathe, 'the sort of knowing girl that comes up to Paris from the provinces every day': 'My wife has not long to live and if you like, you could be a Baroness.' Three days later, Adeline dies of grief and – 'something that must be very rare – tears were seen to fall from the eyes of a dead woman'.

As for Hulot, that most Balzacian of characters, a figure of fun, an embodiment of will-power, lust and the spirit of indomitable life – he, too, should die for the story to be complete; but before Balzac can bring himself to end his life – sensing perhaps that his own was almost at an end – the character marches out through the back door of the novel and is likely to turn up in the most unexpected places:

Baron Hulot left Paris three days after his wife's funeral. Eleven months later, Victorin learned indirectly of his father's marriage with Mlle Agathe Piquetard, solemnized at Isigny on 1 February 1846.

'Parents can oppose the marriage of their children, but children can do nothing to prevent the follies of their parents in their second childhood,' said Maître Hulot to Maître Popinot, who was speaking to him of this marriage.

APPENDICES

Balzac after 1850

Immediately after his death, Balzac became the focus of three debates that lie at the heart of the political, cultural and social life of the late nineteenth century.[1] Was he, as Hugo had decreed at Père Lachaise, an unwitting revolutionary, or, as Balzac himself would have us believe, a defender of Throne and Altar? Related to this argument – which effectively made the point that almost every shade of opinion can eventually be found somewhere in *La Comédie Humaine* – was the question of Balzac's 'Realism'. Did the self-proclaimed historian of private life make it all up? Was that wonderful spectacle really nineteenth-century France or an image of Balzac's brain? In 1858, an important study by Hippolyte Taine confirmed Balzac's view of himself as a literary 'Naturalist' *and* a visionary – 'the largest store of documents we have on human nature'.[2] This was the Balzac of the Realists, claimed by Zola as the father of the Naturalist novel, the experimental scientist who funnelled the phantasmagoria of Romanticism into the test-tube of the modern novel.[3]

The third debate forming Balzac's rite of passage into posterity was one he had tried to settle in his own lifetime by drawing up a list of all his female characters, dividing them, half-seriously, into virtuous and vicious, and showing that the former outweighed the latter.[4] No one believed him or understood the irony. His novels were associated with those familiar *fin-de-siècle* worries: the death of literature and the degeneration of the species. Young men were said to have been coaxed into lives of unscrupulous fortune-hunting by Balzac's most 'Balzacian' characters: 'What consciences have been crushed under the feet of that giant! How many have *sunk*, waving above the slime-heap in which they were about to perish a page snatched from some volume of *La Comédie Humaine!*'[5] Balzac was in tune with an age he never knew. Emphasis fell on his theory that will-power is the force behind all human activity. This is the Nietzschean Balzac embodied in Rodin's statue – the image of an image – which has probably been as influential as any critical study.

When the *Correspondance* was published in 1876, the revelation of the 'real' Balzac brought a surge of interest. For the first quarter-century after his death, he was less popular with the reading public than Eugène Sue, Dumas and George Sand; now, sales of his novels increased, far exceeding those of his former rivals. *La Comédie Humaine* became a classic, partly reflecting a more modern view of the novel, and when the *Lettres à l'Étrangère* (Eveline) began to appear in 1894, Balzac acquired the halo of a Romantic hero. But there was still something wrong. From his earliest years, he seemed to have cared more about personal glory than artistic excellence, and *La Comédie Humaine* itself was a very unseemly sort of classic: an ocean of cynicism and sordid detail with tiny islands of respectability like *Eugénie Grandet*. The general feeling – not only in France – was that Balzac must indeed be counted as one of the great writers, perhaps the world's greatest novelist, but that, ideally, it would have been someone else.

The full scope and interest of *La Comédie Humaine* was revealed more slowly, not by ideological wrangling but by Balzac's massive, paternal influence on other writers – especially on those who were also subjected to censorship and tended to apply aesthetic rather than moral criteria: Baudelaire, who came to see Balzac as an ideal version of himself;[6] Dostoevsky, who translated *Eugénie Grandet* at the age of twenty-two;[7] and Gustave Flaubert, whose *L'Éducation Sentimentale* is in some respects a Balzac novel run backwards. To Flaubert, as to Henry James, Balzac was an ambiguous father figure, exasperating, admirable and curiously reminiscent of Bernard-François Balzac as seen by his son: 'What a man he would have been had he known how to write!' wrote Flaubert. 'But that was the only thing he lacked. After all, an artist would never have accomplished so much nor had such breadth.'[8]

In English-speaking countries, Balzac's novels were handled with surgical gloves. (Elizabeth Barrett Browning's enthusiastic comments about his 'Dutch hand' and 'Italian soul' are exceptional.[9]) He was lumped together with all those other 'revolting' French novelists – Dumas, Sue and Hugo.[10] Charlotte Brontë told Mrs Gaskell that Balzac's novels 'leave such a bad taste in my mouth'. George Eliot called *Goriot* 'a hateful book'[11] – which might serve as the basis of an interesting study of contrasting notions of 'Realism'. Balzac's moral degeneracy was compounded by his chaotic style (French writers were proverbially supposed to be 'clear'), his insatiable appetite for brute fact, his melodramatic imagination and his unhealthy fascination with the paranormal – which is precisely what later attracted W. B. Yeats. To judge by comments heard during the writing of this book, Balzac has never entirely shaken off his aura of depravity, though this is more commonly construed now as a point in his favour.

Between the end of the century and the Second World War, the English Balzac evolved into a curious hybrid. 'An inarticulate Shakespeare';[12] a realist who conferred reality on what was patently untrue;[13] an untalented genius;[14] a 'coarse, large germinating spirit';[15] 'a gigantic dwarf'.[16] A crescendo of more sympathetic voices began in the 1880s: Swinburne, Oscar Wilde, and Henry James whose essays on Balzac are perhaps the finest ever written by one novelist about another. Their comments prepared the way for a spate of translations, culminating in the magnificent 'Caxton' edition of *The Human Comedy* which marked the centenary of Balzac's birth in 1899.[17]

Since then, Balzac has infiltrated almost every domain of literature and criticism. The early debates about his work have borne fruit, partly because of a less nationalistic attitude to individual creation or the need to apply more subtle lenses to a period long since passed from living memory, and also, it must be said, because of the decreasing importance attached by literary critics to biographical data. The long-term effect of the debate about Balzac's politics has been to free his work from his own distracting obsessions. Ever since Karl Marx praised him in *Das Kapital* for his 'profound grasp of real conditions',[18] historians and sociologists have used Balzac's work as an unorganized encyclopedia (though attempts have been made to categorize Balzac's data: there are studies listing every colour of eye and hair, every taste and smell, every dish, every illness, garment, building, street, insect and even 'thought' in *La Comédie Humaine*). The most influential voice of what is loosely termed 'Marxist' criticism has been that of Walter Benjamin, who saw Balzac as the first hero of modern life, the Mohican of the Big City or the private detective, living and expressing the struggle of an old world of ideas in a new world of commodities, laying the ironic foundations of a Modernist aesthetic, focusing all the major currents of Romantic and pre-Romantic thought and projecting them into our century.

Balzac's influence has proved sufficiently vast, inscrutable and nourishing for his novels to have escaped the moral fundamentalism brought to bear in recent years by those who practise literary criticism in the hope of acquiring some literary sensibility. The original moral debate has taken more rewarding forms. Psychoanalytical and feminist critics have found his 'androgynous' genius a valuable source of information on creative neuroses and the condition of women in the nineteenth century. From a different perspective, Camille Paglia identifies Balzac as a central figure in our still 'pagan' Western civilization, the author of 'the century's first completely Decadent work' (*Sarrasine*).[19] The paradox – which never struck Balzac as a dilemma – that the biggest distortions produce the most convincing illusions has made *La Comédie Humaine* a testing-ground for theories of meaning.[20] His language, once castigated for its obscurity or presented as the typical vehicle of Realism, is studied for its anarchic, semiotic tendencies. The 'medieval' Balzac of the *Contes Drolatiques* turns out to have been a Postmodernist *avant la lettre* . . .

Now, as the second centenary of Balzac's birth approaches, the Caxton edition, along with its American predecessor (Philadelphia, 1895–1900), is still the only complete *Human Comedy* in English. The Chinese Government-sponsored translation – the second in the series after Shakespeare – has recently been completed, underscoring once again Balzac's posthumous debt to Karl Marx. Hundreds of editions, translations and critical studies are published every year. But while all Balzac's major novels have been available since the end of last century and reprinted many times, English readers who want to explore the rest of *La Comédie Humaine* still have to rely on chance encounters in secondhand bookshops.

Unknown masterpieces are waiting to be rediscovered.

La Comédie Humaine

Balzac's history and critique of Society was never completed. The Catalogue of *La Comédie Humaine* which he drew up in 1845 listed fifty-two titles of 'works that have yet to be written'. Remnants of some of these projects can be found in volume XII of the Pléiade edition. The table below (following the same order as this edition) shows Balzac's epic in its fullest state. It includes some unfinished works (indicated by a *) which are too voluminous to be counted as mere fragments. The biggest gaps occur in the *Scènes de la Vie Politique* (eight titles planned) and the *Scènes de la Vie Militaire* (twenty-three titles). The *Études Philosophiques*, 'in which the ravages of thought are depicted', and the *Études Analytiques*, which were supposed to provide a complete explanation of the principles behind every form of human behaviour, were greatly outweighed in the end by the *Études de Mœurs*.

The dates following each title are the dates of composition. These can be used as an alternative order of reading, though it should be remembered that final versions may be quite different from the original drafts. A third possible order – by time of action – is given by W. H. Royce in *Balzac As He Should Be Read*.

Avant-propos (1842)

Études de Mœurs

SCÈNES DE LA VIE PRIVÉE

La Maison du Chat-Qui-Pelote (1829)
Le Bal de Sceaux (1829)
Mémoires de Deux Jeunes Mariées (1838–41)
La Bourse (1832)
Modeste Mignon (1844)
Un Début dans la Vie (1841–2)

Albert Savarus (1842)
La Vendetta (1830)
Une Double Famille (1830)
La Paix du Ménage (1829)
Madame Firmiani (1832)
Étude de Femme (1830)
La Fausse Maîtresse (1841)
Une Fille d'Eve (1838–9)
Le Message (1832)
La Grenadière (1832)
La Femme Abandonnée (1832)
Honorine (1842)
Béatrix (1838–45)
Gobseck (1830)
La Femme de Trente Ans (1829–34)
Le Père Goriot (1834–5)
Le Colonel Chabert (1832)
La Messe de l'Athée (1836)
L'Interdiction (1836)
Le Contrat de Mariage (1835)
Autre Étude de Femme (1832–9)

SCÈNES DE LA VIE DE PROVINCE

Ursule Mirouët (1840–1)
Eugénie Grandet (1833)

Les Célibataires
Pierrette (1839–40)
Le Curé de Tours (1832)
La Rabouilleuse (1840–2)

Les Parisiens en Province
L'Illustre Gaudissart (1833)
La Muse du Département (1843)

Les Rivalités
La Vieille Fille (1836)
Le Cabinet des Antiques (1836–8)

SCÈNES DE LA VIE POLITIQUE

Un Épisode Sous la Terreur (1829)
Une Ténébreuse Affaire (1838–40)
Le Député d'Arcis (1839–47)*
Z. Marcas (1840)

SCÈNES DE LA VIE MILITAIRE

Les Chouans ou la Bretagne en 1799 (1828–9)
Une Passion dans le Désert (1830)

SCÈNES DE LA VIE DE CAMPAGNE

Les Paysans (1838–45)*
Le Médecin de Campagne (1832–3)
Le Curé de Village (1838–9)
Le Lys dans la Vallée (1834–5)

Études Philosophiques

La Peau de Chagrin (1830–1)
Jésus-Christ en Flandre (1830–1)
Melmoth Réconcilié (1834–5)
Le Chef-d'Oeuvre Inconnu (1831; 1837)
Gambara (1837)
Massimilla Doni (1837)
La Recherche de l'Absolu (1834)
L'Enfant Maudit (1831–6)
Adieu (1830)
Les Marana (1832–3)
Le Réquisitionnaire (1831)
El Verdugo (1829)
Un Drame au Bord de la Mer (1834)
Maître Cornélius (1831)
L'Auberge Rouge (1831)

Sur Catherine de Médicis
Introduction (1841)
Le Martyr Calviniste (1837–41)

La Confidence des Ruggieri (1836–7)
Les Deux Rêves (1830)

L'Élixir de Longue Vie (1830)
Les Proscrits (1831)
Louis Lambert (1832)
Séraphîta (1833–5)

Études Analytiques

Physiologie du Mariage (1826–9)
Petites Misères de la Vie Conjugale (1830–45)

Pathologie de la Vie Sociale
Traité de la Vie Élégante (1830)
Théorie de la Démarche (1833)
Traité des Excitants Modernes (1839)

APPENDIX III

Money

Multiplying francs by three provides a rough equivalent of 1994 prices in pounds sterling: though the price of certain commodities varied enormously, overall inflation was negligible for most of Balzac's lifetime. The *relative* cost of things was quite different, however, and so the real or psychological value of sums can be gauged only by making specific comparisons. All prices are for Paris.

Francs

0.15	Breakfast (bread-roll and milk)
0.20	Bottle of table wine
0.35	Short bus-ride
1.10	Dinner for one in cheap restaurant
1.60	Short cab-ride
1.00–5.00	Seat at Odéon Theatre
2.00–4.00	One pair cheap trousers
4.00–5.00	One month's subscription to a *cabinet de lecture*
5.00–15.00	One month's rent, garret room
15.00	Copy of first edition of *Le Père Goriot* (2 vols)
50.00	Dinner for one in expensive restaurant
55.00–70.00	Monthly wages of Balzac's servants (lodging included)
100.00+	One pair trousers from good tailor
1000.00+	Annual rent, two-bedroom ground-floor apartment
2000–2700	Salary of deputy chief clerk in Government office
3000	Balzac hopes to survive on this *per annum*, 1828–30
4000–5000	Salary of chief clerk in Government office
52,000	Purchase price of large, three-storey house in middle-class area

Sources: CH, V, 271, 292, 294; VII, 621; VIII, 23; XII, 67, 721; *Corr.*, V, 27, 377; *LH*, I, 395; J.-Cl. Caron, *Générations Romantiques. Les Étudiants de Paris et le Quartier Latin* (A. Colin, 1991), pp. 135, 144, 148; Baudelaire (1973), I, lxxi.

NOTES

Works listed in the Bibliography are referred to by author only, or in the case of more than one work by the same author, by author and date. The following abbreviations have been used (for full references, see the Bibliography):

CH: *La Comédie Humaine*, ed. Castex, 12 vols.
Corr.: *Correspondance*, ed. Pierrot, 5 vols.
LH: *Lettres à Madame Hanska*, ed. Pierrot, 2 vols.
OC: *Oeuvres Complètes*, ed. Bardèche, 28 vols.
OD: *Oeuvres Diverses*, vol. I, ed. Castex.

INTRODUCTION

1. James (1878), 117.
2. *Corr.*, III, 337.

PART ONE

CHAPTER ONE
PROVINCIAL LIFE
(1799–1814)

1. *Anatomie des Corps Enseignants*, *CH*, XII, 842. On the theories of Bernard-François: Surville (1858), 9.
2. James (1884), 18.
3. *L'Apostrophe*, *OD*, 148–9.
4. *Corr.*, I, 461.
5. *Sténie*, *OD*, 722–5; *Le Curé de Tours*, *CH*, IV, 214, and *L'Illustre Gaudissart*, IV, 576.
6. *Z. Marcas*, *CH*, VIII, 836.
7. On Bernard-François's early career: Audebrand, ch. 3; Bouteron (1954), 25–32; Felkay (1990); Havard de la Montagne (1987).
8. Audebrand, ch. 3.
9. Gautier (1858), 92.
10. Surville (1858), 12.
11. Hennion.
12. *LH*, II, 146.
13. Brua.
14. *Entre Savants*, *CH*, XII, 541.

15. *LH*, I, 607.
16. Audebrand, ch. 3.
17. *LH*, II, 146.
18. Besson.
19. *LH*, I, 309; *Anatomie des Corps Enseignants*, *CH*, XII, 843.
20. *L'Apostrophe*, *OD*, 147.
21. *CH*, IV, 858.
22. Dutacq; Métadier (1968). Strictly speaking, it was a different street. Number 25 Rue de l'Armée d'Italie, where Balzac was born, was number 39 Rue Nationale, when it disappeared. The Balzacs' new home was at 29 Rue d'Indre-et-Loire, now 53 Rue Nationale.
23. *CH*, IX, 971–2.
24. *La Recherche de l'Absolu*, *CH*, X, 736.
25. Weelen (1950 and 1951). The building is now the Hôtel du Théâtre (not to be confused with the unrelated Hôtel Balzac a few doors away).
26. *Le Lys dans la Vallée*, *CH*, IX, 973.
27. Weelen (1950 and 1951).
28. On Vendôme and its teachers: Bertault, ch. 2; Guyon (1947), chs 2 and 3; Vannier.
29. Préteseille.
30. Mareschal-Duplessis, letter to A. Baschet, 20 July 1855, in Spoelberch de Lovenjoul (1888), 401–2.
31. For a recipe: *Larousse Gastronomique*, 802 and 1160.
32. Prospectus quoted by Bonhoure, 308.
33. Martin-Demézil.
34. Mareschal-Duplessis (see n. 30).
35. *Louis Lambert*, *CH*, XI, 607.
36. De Maistre, 206–8.
37. Champfleury (1878), 16–17.
38. *Louis Lambert*, *CH*, XI, 603.
39. *Physiologie du Mariage*, *CH*, XI, 967.
40. *Louis Lambert*, *CH*, XI, 593.
41. Fargeaud and Pierrot, 31–2.
42. Part of *La Femme de Trente Ans*. On fictional traces of Henry: Citron (1986), ch. 6.
43. See n. 28.
44. Pupil quoted by Bonhoure. See also Fargeaud (1968), 116, quoting H. Derouin, *Le Collège de Vendôme de 1813 à 1818* (1893).
45. Adrien Brun in *L'Indicateur* (Bordeaux), quoted by Bardèche, 22. Brun may have been reminded of the treatise by Raphaël de Valentin's *Théorie de la Volonté* in *La Peau de Chagrin* (*CH*, X, 138). Laure also claims that

the *Traité* (like 'everything' in *Louis Lambert*) was real: Surville (1858), 20.

46. Letter from J. Fontémoing, 9 August 1831, *Corr.*, I, 555; Mareschal's letter in Spoelberch de Lovenjoul (1888), 401–2; *Louis Lambert*, *CH*, XI, 603.

47. Baudelaire (1975–6), II, 441.

48. Letter from Adrien Brun, 14 April 1831, *Corr.*, I, 509.

49. The word is used by Balzac in *Louis Lambert*, *CH*, XI, 637; cf. XI, 1531 (variant *c*) and, below, p. 201.

50. Surville (1858), 21. Laure may have been remembering *La Rabouilleuse*: 'Public education will never solve the difficult problem of developing mind and body simultaneously' (*CH*, IV, 288). The title of *La Rabouilleuse* (originally, *Les Deux Frères*) is explained by Balzac half-way through the novel. Flore Brazier, the title character, earns her keep by chasing crayfish upstream with a tree-branch into a fisherman's net – an operation which, according to Balzac, was known in the Berry as *rabouiller* (*CH*, IV, 386–7).

51. *L'Enfant Maudit*, *CH*, X, 934; also, *ibid.*, 905 and 940; *La Recherche de l'Absolu*, X, 798; *Louis Lambert*, XI, 605.

52. *CH*, IX, 584–6. Tissot's *Traité* quoted by Le Yaouanc (1959), 208–10. Surville (1858), 21–4.

53. *Splendeurs et Misères des Courtisanes*, *CH*, VI, 753.

54. *Anatomie des Corps Enseignants*, *CH*, XII, 842.

55. Fargeaud (1961).

56. *CH*, V, 193.

57. *La Vieille Fille*, *CH*, IV, 935; *Traité des Excitants Modernes*, XII, 305.

58. Citron (1967), 339–42. On Henry: Fargeaud and Pierrot.

59. Gédéon (1966); Le Yaouanc (1962 and 1964); Surville (1858).

60. *Le Cousin Pons*, *CH*, VII, 519.

61. *Sur Catherine de Médicis*, *CH*, XI, 373.

62. *Une Double Famille*, *CH*, II, 18.

63. *Splendeurs et Misères des Courtisanes*, *CH*, VI, 673.

64. *La Femme de Trente Ans*, *CH*, II, 1040; *La Rabouilleuse*, IV, 296.

65. *Le Lys dans la Vallée*, *CH*, IX, 979.

66. *CH*, XI, 967.

67. *La Grande Bretèche*, part of *Autre Étude de Femme*, *CH*, III, 720.

68. Mozet (1979); Fargeaud and Pierrot, 31; *CH*, IX, 979–80.

69. See n. 67.

70. *Le Lys dans la Vallée*, *CH*, IX, 981.

71. *Corr.*, V, 595.

72. *LH*, II, 146.

73. *Le Lys dans la Vallée, CH*, IX, 989.

74. Ibid., 992.

75. *Béatrix, CH*, II, 735.

76. *Les Paysans, CH*, IX, 326.

77. Quoted in Castex (1950), xlviii.

78. *CH*, XI, 1566.

79. *La Femme de Trente Ans, CH*, II, 1053 and 1612; 'Croquis', *La Caricature*, 25 November 1830: *CH*, XII, 1064. See also *LH*, II, 602.

80. *Le Lys dans la Vallée, CH*, IX, 982–5.

81. Balzac later purchased the Duc d'Angoulême's tea-service: *LH*, II, 1033; Baschet, 231.

82. Guyon (1947), 21, quoting Cournot, *Souvenirs; Corr.*, I, 16–17.

83. B.-F. Balzac (1809); Gédéon (1986).

84. *Corr.*, II, 710.

85. Gozlan (1946), 72.

CHAPTER TWO
PARISIAN LIFE
(1815–1819)

1. Surville (1858), 25.

2. *LH*, I, 122.

3. Ibid., 618.

4. Mark 11: 24.

5. *Illusions Perdues, CH*, V, 269.

6. *LH*, I, 307 and 524.

7. Surville (1858), 26.

8. *Sur Catherine de Médicis, CH*, XI, 210.

9. On Mlle de Rougemont: Surville (1858), 30. On Beaumarchais: *Sur Catherine de Médicis, CH*, XI, 445 and *Théorie de la Démarche*, XII, 291.

10. *Quelques Souvenirs, ou Notes Fidèles sur mon Service au Temple* (1814): Le Yaouanc (1962); Prioult (1965); *Le Lys dans la Vallée, CH*, IX, 978–9.

11. *Le Lys dans la Vallée, CH*, IX, 1686, variant *a* (first proof).

12. *La Rabouilleuse, CH*, IV, 271; also *Mémoires de Deux Jeunes Mariées*, I, 242–3.

13. *OD*, 1103–4.

14. Review of *La Chine et les Chinois* by Auguste Borget, *La Législature*, October 1842: *OC*, XXVIII, 456.

15. *CH*, III, 447–8.

16. Michelet, 204.

17. *Illusions Perdues*, *CH*, V, 142.
18. *CH*, V, 357, 360–1.
19. *Le Véritable Conducteur Parisien* (1828), quoted by R. Chollet in *CH*, V, 1271.
20. *Le Lys dans la Vallée*, *CH*, IX, 978; cf. Mme Balzac's letter to Honoré, p. 41.
21. *LH*, I, 691.
22. *La Chine et les Chinois*, *OC*, XXVIII, 470.
23. Letter to Mme Hugo: Gédéon (1966).
24. *Anatomie des Corps Enseignants*, *CH*, XII, 844; also *Splendeurs et Misères des Courtisanes*, VI, 789, and *Louis Lambert*, XI, 649.
25. Surville (1858), 28.
26. Fargeaud (1965); Surville (1858), 106.
27. Described in *Le Colonel Chabert*, *CH*, III, 312–17; Surville (1858), 31.
28. *Un Début dans la Vie*, *CH*, I, 843.
29. *Le Colonel Chabert*, *CH*, III, 373.
30. *CH*, XI, 904.
31. 'Le Notaire' in *Les Français Peints par Eux-Mêmes* (1840), *OC*, XXVIII.
32. Ibid.
33. *Code des Gens Honnêtes; ou l'Art de ne pas être Dupe des Fripons*.
34. *Un Épisode sous la Terreur*, *CH*, VIII, 433.
35. Guillonnet-Merville appears under the name Derville in Scribe's 'comédie-vaudeville', *L'Intérieur de l'Étude* – an apologia for business dinners – as he does in Balzac's novels.
36. Mirecourt (1854), 18.
37. É[douard] M[onnais], 'Honoré de Balzac', *Revue et Gazette Musicale*, 1 September 1850: Citron (1977).
38. J. de Pétigny, *La France Centrale* (Blois), 4 March 1855, in Spoelberch de Lovenjoul (1888), 377–81.
39. É. Monnais: Citron (1977).
40. See n. 34.
41. *LH*, I, 560; *Corr.*, IV, 549.
42. *Corr.*, I, 266.
43. *La Chine et les Chinois*, *OC*, XXVIII, 456.
44. Surville (1858), 32–3.
45. On this period in the University: Sainte-Beuve (1852).
46. *Louis Lambert*, *CH*, XI, 649.
47. *La Peau de Chagrin*, *CH*, X, 75.
48. *OD*, 554.
49. Ibid., 1097–9.

50. *CH*, X, 133.
51. *OD*, 535.
52. *LH*, I, 437–8.
53. *Corr.*, I, 20 and 22; Surville (1858), 45.
54. *Physiologie du Mariage*, *CH*, XI, 952–5.
55. 'Avant-propos', *CH*, I, 11.
56. Lestang.
57. *Les Marana*, *CH*, X, 1073.
58. Lichtlé.
59. Surville (1858), 36.
60. 3 December 1819, in Ducourneau and Pierrot, *Les Études Balzaciennes*, 348–9.

CHAPTER THREE
DREAMS
(1819–1820)

1. E.g. Lawton, plate 5.
2. *La Peau de Chagrin*, *CH*, X, 137–8.
3. Ibid., 135–6.
4. Ibid., 133.
5. Pétigny, in Spoelberch de Lovenjoul (1888); Auguste Fessart, marginalia in a copy of Laure's biography: Spoelberch de Lovenjoul (1903), 127.
6. *CH*, X, 1203.
7. Gozlan (1862), 214.
8. *CH*, X, 134.
9. On Dablin: Fargeaud (1964).
10. *Corr.*, I, 40.
11. *OD*, 517.
12. *LH*, I, 634.
13. *OD*, 573–4.
14. *Corr.*, I, 30.
15. *La Peau de Chagrin*, *CH*, X, 137.
16. *CH*, X, 495.
17. *Corr.*, I, 31.
18. Ibid., 36.
19. Ibid.
20. *LH*, I, 648; also *Modeste Mignon*, *CH*, I, 509–10.
21. *Corr.*, I, 66.
22. *OD*, 1669.
23. Ibid., 1683–4.

24. *Corr.*, I, 42.
25. On Eugène Surville: Meininger (1963).
26. Surville (1858), 64. Andrieux later became Perpetual Secretary of the Académie Française.
27. Ibid., 12.
28. 16 August 1820: *Corr.*, I, 84–5.
29. *Corr.*, I, 159.
30. Audebrand, ch. 3.
31. *CH*, I, 496.
32. *La Muse du Département*, *CH*, IV, 713–14.
33. Maigron, 51–9.
34. *OD*, 589.
35. *Corr.*, I, 52.
36. *OD*, 698; on the etymology: 1511.
37. *LH*, II, 451.
38. *OD*, 703.
39. *Sténie*, *OD*, 723–4.
40. James (1878), 75.
41. *Facino Cane*, *CH*, VI, 1019–20.
42. *Physiologie du Mariage*, *CH*, XI, 930.
43. *Les Petits Bourgeois*, *CH*, VIII, 180.
44. *Une Ténébreuse Affaire*, *CH*, VIII, 579.
45. *Pensées, Sujets, Fragmens*, *OC*, XXVIII, 661. Balzac's scrapbook, which he called his 'larder', dates from about 1830; it disappeared after the 1950 Balzac Exhibition at the Bibliothèque Nationale. On transcriptions and editions, see *CH*, XII, 839–40.
46. See Balzac's 'Histoire et Physiologie des Boulevards de Paris', in *Le Diable à Paris*, II, 103–4.
47. Young, 103.
48. See n. 46.
49. *Corr.*, I, 62.
50. Ibid., 38.
51. Peter Brooks observes that both monuments are 'Napoleonic markers' (Brooks, 173).

CHAPTER FOUR
GUTTER POETRY
(1821–1822)

1. *LH*, I, 398.
2. Sandeau.
3. Letter to Mme Aupick, 30 August 1851: Baudelaire (1973), I, 177.

4. *Illusions Perdues*, *CH*, V, 379.
5. *Corr.*, I, 95.
6. *Le Réquisitionnaire*, *CH*, X, 1109.
7. Surville (1858), 182–3.
8. *CH*, VIII, 768.
9. *Corr.*, I, 168–9.
10. Ibid., 113.
11. Fargeaud (1961) and Havard de la Montagne (1964).
12. Ducourneau (1962), 29.
13. *La Femme de Trente Ans*, *CH*, II, 1114.
14. *LH*, I, 607.
15. *Corr.*, I, 101.
16. *LH*, I, 811.
17. *Corr.*, I, 101.
18. Ibid., 102.
19. Vitu, 16–22.
20. *CH*, V, 294.
21. Lacroix, 10 May 1882.
22. *Corr.*, I, 103.
23. Jules Viard, *Le Figaro*, 24 September 1854: Vitu, 17.
24. Audebrand, ch. 3.
25. 'Lettre sur Sainte-Beuve', *Revue Parisienne*, 20 August 1840.
26. Laure, notes for a second edition of her biography of Balzac (which never appeared): Barbéris (1965; 1985), 9.
27. *Corr.*, I, 41–2.
28. Ibid., 133.
29. Charles Weiss, *Journal*, 26 September 1833, in Smethurst, 396.
30. Barbéris (1965; 1985), 175.
31. *Corr.*, I, 133.
32. Her letter and Laure's reply in Pierrot (1959), 251–8.
33. *Petites Misères de la Vie Conjugale*, *CH*, XII, 107; Champfleury (1861), 81.
34. See p. 280.

34. See p. 280.

CHAPTER FIVE
DIVINE INTERCOURSE
(1822–1824)

1. *OD*, 906.
2. Adèle Hugo, in Arrigon (1927), 48–9.
3. *LH*, I, 511.

4. Ruxton, 57–74.
5. Ibid., 57–60; Meininger (1969).
6. Balzac to Laure, October 1821: *Corr.*, I, 115.
7. Meininger (1969), 226.
8. Letter from Alexandre de Berny, 27 July 1836: *Corr.*, III, 118.
9. (?) March 1822: *Corr.*, I, 139. The letters to Mme de Berny date from March–October 1822: *Corr.*, I, 143–209.
10. *CH*, VII, 494.
11. *LH*, II, 1054.
12. *Pensées, Sujets, Fragmens*, *OC*, XXVIII, 662.
13. *LH*, I, 398–9; *Corr.*, I, 717–18.
14. *OC*, XXVIII, 661–2.
15. Letter to Laure, 12 October 1822: *Corr.*, I, 209.
16. Letter to Laure, 29 August 1824: Ducourneau and Pierrot, *Les Études Balzaciennes*, 453–4.
17. 1 November 1822: *Corr.*, I, 210.
18. On Pollet and publication of *Le Vicaire des Ardennes*: Barbéris (1965; 1985).
19. Meininger (1968).
20. 28 July 1822: *Corr.*, I, 192.
21. Letter to Édouard Soulier, July 1821: Delacroix, I, 129.
22. Pichois (1965), II, 44.
23. *CH*, V, 477–8.
24. Bruce Tolley (1963) shows that the author was not, as previously supposed, Balzac's father.
25. Guyon (1947), 732–5.
26. *The Bride of Lammermoor*.
27. Genesis 27:29.
28. To appear in vol. II of *OD*. In the meantime, see Chollet (1991) and Leroy, especially 78–82. Leroy points to anti-Jesuitical views in Balzac's novels before and after the *Histoire*. For a detailed summary of contemporary polemic on the *droit d'aînesse* and the Jesuits: Nerval, ed. J. Guillaume and C. Pichois, I, 1459–62.
29. Cf. *Théorie de la Démarche* (1833): 'Nothing wears us out so much as convictions. You can have opinions, if you keep them to yourself instead of trying to defend them. But convictions! My God! What a waste of energy!' (*CH*, XII, 294).
30. *Corr.*, I, 228 and 242.
31. *D'ung Paoure qui avoit Nom le Vieulx-par-chemins*, *OD*, 419.
32. *Le Nègre*, in *OD*. Report from the reading committee: *OD*, 1687.
33. *Corr.*, V, 674.

34. First version of the country doctor's 'Confession': *CH*, IX, 1423.
35. *LH*, I, 679.
36. Ibid., 794.

CHAPTER SIX
THE PRICE OF FREE ENTERPRISE
(1824–1828)

1. Sandeau, 95.
2. *Traité des Excitants Modernes*, *CH*, XII, 303.
3. *LH*, II, 597.
4. Ernest Prarond: Robb (1988), 43.
5. Baudelaire (1975–6), II, 8; Robb (1988), 115–49.
6. Gautier (1858), 76; Baschet, 140.
7. Barbéris (1963), 13.
8. Or, in *LH*, I, 663: 'Genius must never be in fashion.'
9. *Illusions Perdues*, *CH*, V, 462.
10. Barbéris (1963). The postface was never used.
11. Guyon (1947), 724; Tolley (1961).
12. Gautier (1858), 84–5; Gozlan (1946), 143–8; Second, 35 and 47–8.
13. *LH*, II, 777.
14. Memoirs of Étienne Arago, recorded by Jules Claretie: Arrigon (1924), 184–5. Laure also mentions her brother's suicidal 'temptations': Surville (1858), 93.
15. *CH*, VII, 496.
16. *LH*, I, 596.
17. Ibid., II, 153.
18. *Illusions Perdues*, *CH*, V, 269.
19. *LH*, I, 345.
20. 'Voyage de Paris à Java' (1832), *OC*, XXVII, 194.
21. *LH*, I, 346.
22. One of the poems resurfaces as an ode recited by Lucien de Rubempré in *Illusions Perdues*: *CH*, V, 203–4.
23. *LH*, II, 852.
24. *Les Employés*, *CH*, VII, 885.
25. *Melmoth Réconcilié*, *CH*, X, 358.
26. *Le Père Goriot*, *CH*, III, 164. Balzac attributes the idea to Rousseau, though it probably came from Chateaubriand's *Le Génie du Christianisme* (P. Ronaï, quoted by R. Fortassier, *CH*, III, 1280). Dostoevsky, 84.
27. Ducourneau and Pierrot; Bardèche, 120–1; Tolley (1962, 1963, 1964).
28. Armstrong.

29. L. F. J. de Bausset, *Mémoires Anecdotiques sur L'Intérieur du Palais* (1827). See Tolley (1962) and Chollet (1983), 22.
30. Lacroix, 157–8 and 177; Chollet (1983), 96; Goulard.
31. Prioult (1936), 347–54.
32. Ducourneau and Pierrot, *AB 1960*, 195–202.
33. *CH*, XI, 176.
34. Letter to Duchesse d'Abrantès, 19 July 1825: Pierrot (1972), 348–9.
35. MS published in Guise (1985).
36. *LH*, I, 626; also I, 324. On Balzac's 'infallible' system: Mirecourt (1854), 61, and Werdet (1859), 293.
37. *La Rabouilleuse*, *CH*, IV, 325.
38. *Le Père Goriot*, *CH*, III, 171; *La Peau de Chagrin*, X, 194.
39. Pichois (1956).
40. *Corr.*, I, 259.
41. On Balzac the printer: Hanotaux and Vicaire. The list of books printed by Balzac is completed in Tolley (1959).
42. Hanotaux and Vicaire, 345 and 349–51.
43. *CH*, XII, 721–2.
44. *LH*, I, 387.
45. *Les Petits Bourgeois*, *CH*, VIII, 61; *Le Médecin de Campagne*, IX, 400.
46. 'De la mode en littérature', *La Mode*, 29 May 1830; *OC*, XXVI, 273.
47. Letter to Laure, 9 June 1826; in Arrigon (1924) and Ducourneau and Pierrot, *AB 1960*, 200, n. 1.
48. Chantemesse; *Dictionnaire de Biographie Française*; Larousse; and some unreliable stories in Léger. Léger's book is a digest of the memoirs of a dishonest Versailles magistrate called Victor Lambinet. After being ostracized by local society, he consoled himself by inventing prurient anecdotes about it. Lambinet's lasting contribution to Balzac studies is himself: an example of the all-seeing, all-imagining gossip who plays such an important role in the *Scènes de la Vie de Province*. The original MS is described in Lagny (1974).
49. Larousse; Junot appears in Gros's painting, 'Le Combat de Nazareth'.
50. See Rousseau; but Balzac's collaboration is confirmed by a letter from the Duchess, August 1830: *Corr.*, I, 560.
51. Jasinski.
52. Abrantès, II, 89, n. 1. On Balzac's attraction to her: Ancelot, 95–6.
53. *CH*, XI, 935.
54. *Valentine et Valentin*, *CH*, XII, 355; Hanotaux and Vicaire.
55. *CH*, XII, 355–7.
56. The *Dictionnaire* is by G. L. Brismontier: Tolley (1959), 216–17.
57. Gozlan (1946), 107.

58. *CH*, V, 137–8, and R. Chollet's note, 1151.
59. Hillairet, II, 652; Vandam, I, 288.
60. Vigny, letter dated 15 September 1850.
61. Review of *Richelieu* by George James (a protégé of Walter Scott), in *Feuilleton des Journaux Politiques*, 14 April 1830; *OC*, XXVI, 624; Chollet (1983), 137–40.
62. Delécluze, 284.
63. *Traité de la Vie Élégante*, *CH*, XII, 257.
64. *LH*, I, 455.
65. *CH*, II, 1128; see Picon, 81.
66. *Physiologie du Mariage*, *CH*, XI, 1197.
67. Arrigon (1924), 227.
68. Corbin, 207–33.
69. *CH*, III, 690.
70. *L'Illustre Gaudissart*, *CH*, IV, 586.
71. *Illusions Perdues*, *CH*, V, 268.
72. Ségu, 16.
73. *Illusions Perdues*, *CH*, V, 270. On Balzac's watches: Meyer-Petit.
74. *LH*, I, 432.
75. *Le Cousin Pons*, *CH*, VII, 678, and A. Lorant's note, 1462.
76. *Une Fille d'Eve*, *CH*, II, 352, and *La Recherche de l'Absolu*, X, 789.
77. Chollet (1983), 536.
78. *LH*, I, 52.
79. Ibid., 922.
80. Ibid., 391.
81. *Le Diable à Paris*, II, 350.
82. *LH*, I, 474 and 625; II, 4.
83. In her biography (1858) and in a letter to Baronne de Pommereul dated 10 December 1833: Surville (1932), 103.
84. *CH*, X, 201, and P. Citron's note, 1310.
85. *Corr.*, I, 336.
86. *La Peau de Chagrin*, *CH*, X, 199–200.
87. Werdet (1859), 331.

PART TWO

CHAPTER SEVEN
THE LAST OF THE CHOUANS
(1828–1830)

1. Pontavice de Heussey.
2. *Corr.*, I, 344.

3. Sainte-Beuve (1834); Mozet (1980)

4. Fargeaud (1968) and in *CH*, X, 650.

5. *CH*, VIII, 946–7 (quoted from the first edition).

6. Ibid., 936.

7. *LH*, I, 122.

8. *Corr.*, I, 461.

9. James (1905), 75.

10. Pommereul's wife and nephew, quoted in Pontavice de Heussey. See also Aubrée.

11. Lemer, 130–2.

12. *Corr.*, I, 349.

13. *CH*, *Les Chouans*, VIII, 916.

14. On Balzac's admiration for his political opponents: Engels (letter to Margaret Harkness, April 1888), 92; Lukács. Also Sand (1971), II, 157–8 and 204; and Chapter 8, n. 64.

15. Preface (1845), *CH*, VIII, 903.

16. Sainte-Beuve (1851), 368–90.

17. Auger, 368; Monnier, II, 101; Ségu, 34.

18. *CH*, III, 53.

19. Sand (1971), 155.

20. Werdet (1859), 325ff.

21. *LH*, I, 34 and 42–3.

22. Watripon.

23. *Corr.*, I, 397–8. Review in *Mercure de France du XIXe siècle*, 27 June 1829.

24. This aspect of Balzac first received critical attention in 1913 (Taube). Recent studies by Citron (1967 and 1986).

25. Yeats, 446.

26. *Petites Misères de la Vie Conjugale*, *CH*, XII, 102.

27. An expurgated edition of Duckett's *Dictionnaire de la Conversation et de la Lecture*, to which Balzac contributed.

28. On the history of the word: G. Robb, *La Poésie de Baudelaire et la Poésie Française, 1838–1852* (Aubier, 1993), ch. 9.

29. *Illusions Perdues*, *CH*, V, 145–6.

30. *CH*, V, 147.

31. Wilde, 16.

32. Goncourt (1989), II, 639–40. The piece of after-dinner gossip lovingly preserved by the Goncourts which has Balzac and Mme de Berny chasing each other on all fours in the nude (Balzac playing the part of dog and hunter) almost certainly originates in Balzac's frequent allusions to Otway's *Venice Preserved*. In *La Rabouilleuse*, Flore's relations with her master are described by allusion to Aquilina, who indulges Antonio in a

similar fashion, with a whip (*CH*, IV, 403). In *Physiologie du Mariage*, the scene is said to be symbolic of certain types of relationship (*CH*, XI, 1071).

33. Balzac uses the word '*femme*' in this sense in *Physiologie du Mariage*: *CH*, XI, 910, and A. Michel's note, 1771.

34. *Corr.*, II, 207; also I, 681.

35. *Illusions Perdues*, *CH*, V, 479.

36. *CH*, III, 222. In *Le Curé de Village*, there are similar suggestions about Rastignac's youngest brother, Gabriel, future Bishop of Limoges (*CH*, IX, 701–5).

37. *CH*, VIII, 1224–5.

38. *Le Diable à Paris*, II, 343.

39. Audebrand, ch. 3; Surville (1858), 8.

40. *LH*, I, 607 and 902.

41. Ibid., 246.

42. *La Paix du Ménage* is dated 'La Bouleaunière, juillet 1829'.

43. *Pensées, Sujets, Fragmens*, *OC*, XXVIII, 661; *L'Élixir de Longue Vie*, *CH*, XI, 476.

44. *L'Élixir de Longue Vie*, *CH*, XI, 484.

45. *CH*, X, 321 and 323; later incorporated into *Jesus-Christ en Flandre*.

46. See P. Citron's introduction: *CH*, X, 1129.

47. Note by R. Guise in *CH*, XI, 1426.

48. *CH*, XI, 1190–4.

49. *LH*, I, 28.

50. Ibid.

51. *La Femme Vertueuse* (= *Une Double Famille*), *CH*, II, 19.

52. *Les Proscrits*, *CH*, X, 547.

53. Spoelberch de Lovenjoul (1888), 403.

54. Gozlan (1946), 101.

55. Lamartine, 15.

56. Lacroix, 181 and 186.

57. Reviews of *Physiologie du Mariage* in Barbéris (1967), 62–5; summary in *CH*, XI, 1747.

58. Letter from J.-A.-T. Vautor Desrozeaux, 27 April 1833: Le Yaouanc (1968), 34.

59. Sand (1964–91), I, 825 (7 March 1831).

60. *CH*, XI, 903; on this subject, see A. Michel.

61. Mirecourt (1854), 44.

62. *Corr.*, I, 559.

63. Fontaney, 30 (7 September 1831).

64. *CH*, IX, 929–30. Balzac's Gallic origins also stressed in *Sténie* (*OD*, 726) and *LH*, I, 92.

65. 'Des artistes', *La Silhouette*, 25 February, 11 March and 22 April 1830.
66. See also Goncourt (1925), 104–5, Lacroix, 181 and Surville (1858), 198–9.
67. On Balzac's journalism in this period: Chollet (1983).
68. *CH*, XII, 218–19.
69. See for example *Le Curé de Village*, *CH*, IX, 814.
70. 'Avant-propos', *CH*, I, 11.
71. *LH*, II, 735.
72. Ibid., I, 456.
73. *Le Cousin Pons*, *CH*, VII, 566.
74. *CH*, XII, 266–71.

CHAPTER EIGHT
ABSOLUTE POWER
(1830–1832)

1. Letter to Zulma Carraud, 14 April 1830: *Corr.*, I, 452–3.
2. *La Peau de Chagrin*: the title (*'chagrin'*) is ambiguous.
3. *CH*, X, 197.
4. *Les Écoles*, 22 August 1839: see illustrations and *Corr.*, III, 687–8 and 693–4.
5. The editors apologized, but the artist published a sarcastic apology of his own – 'Very Humble Honourable Amends to a Very Irreverend Father' – calling Balzac *'le succulent Séraphitus'* and observing that 'No genius is entirely sane' (Allet).
6. 'Le Répertoire des contrefaçons belges de Balzac', in Van der Perre.
7. Vol. IX, ch. 4.
8. *CH*, X, 1189 (introduction by Philarète Chasles to Balzac's *Romans et Contes Philosophiques*); also Félix Davin's introduction to the *Études Philosophiques*: *CH*, X, 1213.
9. 'Voyage de Paris à Java': *OC*, XXVII, 191. The same idea is applied, by implication, to music in *Les Chouans* (CH, VIII, 912).
10. *CH*, X, 111, 104 and 237.
11. Ibid., 85.
12. Ibid., 86–7.
13. Goncourt (1989), I, 639–40 (30 March 1875).
14. Bourget, 194.
15. *LH*, I, 155.
16. *Le Curé de Tours*, *CH*, IV, 202; also *Théorie de la Démarche*, XII, 300.
17. Guyon (1974).
18. *LH*, I, 172.
19. *CH*, X, 102.

20. 11 August 1831: Spoelberch de Lovenjoul (1888), 167–8.
21. 14 August 1831. This and other reviews in Barbéris (1968). There are also several supposedly ludicrous quotations in the *Revue Théâtrale, Journal Littéraire, non Romantique*; later, *L'Anti-Romantique*. (First known occurrence of the adjective '*Balzachien*' on 8 September 1833.)
22. Letter to Victor Pavie (18 September 1831) in Sainte-Beuve (1935), I, 263.
23. Letter to Chancellor von Muller, 17 November 1831, in Albrecht, 79–80, and Lukács, 98. According to Goethe's diary, he read the novel on 10 and 11 October 1831.
24. *CH*, X, 167 (the friend is Rastignac).
25. Simonnin and Nézel.
26. 'Le Bol de Punch', in Gautier (1833).
27. Protogenes' food was indeed *lupins* and not *lapins* (rabbits). See Michaud. Protogenes, who is said to have spent seven years on one painting, is a possible source for *Le Chef-d'Oeuvre Inconnu*.
28. Gautier (1858), 67.
29. Arrigon (1927), 111–12.
30. Anonymous review in the *Sténographe des Chambres*, 4 August 1831: Tolley (1965), 322–4.
31. *LH*, I, 24.
32. Amédée Pichot, in Spoelberch de Lovenjoul (1903), 27–8.
33. See Maury. Olympe was the model for Judith in Horace Vernet's painting, 'Judith et Holophernes'.
34. *LH*, I, 25.
35. Ménière, 214.
36. Arrigon (1927), 184–5; Lucas, 125.
37. Frédéric Soulié in 1834: Arrigon (1927), 185.
38. *LH*, I, 195.
39. *CH*, X, 225–6.
40. *OC*, XXVII, 198–9, and *CH*, XII, 312. See also *LH*, I, 32.
41. 'Des mots à la mode', *La Mode*, 22 May 1830, and 'Des salons littéraires et des mots élogieux', *La Mode*, 20 November 1830. Balzac's view matches a description of Nodier's salon in Ancelot, 124–6.
42. *CH*, X, 145.
43. Werdet (1859), 359.
44. See *Corr.*, I, 588.
45. Ibid., 653.
46. *OD*, 335.
47. *CH*, X, 1349 (variant *c*).
48. Paul Lacroix, in *L'Abeille Impériale*, 1856: Balzac (1950–3), xiii, 11.

49. *LH*, I, 205.
50. *Droll Stories*, trans. Alec Brown (London: Elek, 1959).
51. Prologue of the *Troisième Dixain*.
52. *Corr.*, I, 499.
53. Swinburne, IV, 306 (letter to Theodore Watts, 8 October 1882).
54. *OD*, 518.
55. *CH*, XII, 650.
56. *Revue Parisienne*, 25 July 1840: *OC*, XXVIII, 96–7.
57. *CH*, XII, 653.
58. Letter ix (20 December 1830).
59. *Corr.*, II, 34; Arrigon (1927), 197–8; Célestin, 125.
60. *LH*, I, 122.
61. Bodin (1969), 305.
62. *CH*, XII, 271.
63. 'Des artistes. II', *La Silhouette*, 11 March 1830.
64. Engels, 92; see also his letter to Laura Lafargue, 13 December 1883 (314), and cf. the more even-handed remarks of George Sand on Balzac's impartiality (letter to Eveline de Balzac, 24 November 1853): Sand (1964–91), XII, 169. It is likely that Engels knew Sand's introduction to the 1853 Houssiaux edition of Balzac's works and found in it the famous idea that Balzac's noblest characters 'always turned out to be republicans or socialists'. See also Pagès (1866), who quotes Hugo's speech and goes on to say that Balzac 'proposes twenty reforms which are the obvious negation of the political system he claims to embrace'. Balzac himself points to some 'socialist ideas' in *Vautrin* (*Corr.*, IV, 158).
65. Lacroix. For chronological tables of Balzac's actual output, see Vachon.
66. *Corr.*, I, 732.
67. *LH*, I, 433.
68. Gilot, 18. Balzac gives only the street-name. Picasso presumably identified the house by the spiral staircase mentioned at the beginning of the story.
69. Bernard, 44. *Le Chef-d'Oeuvre Inconnu* was also one of Marx's favourite stories (letter to Engels, 25 February 1867: Engels and Marx, 314–15).

CHAPTER NINE
MADNESS
(1832)

1. Preface (1835), *Le Lys dans la Vallée*, *CH*, IX, 915–16; *Corr.*, III, 131; *LH*, I, 668; see also *Albert Savarus*, I, 938 and *Un Prince de la Bohème*, VII, 807.
2. J. Pommier, quoted by M. Lichtlé, *CH*, XI, 569.

3. *CH*, XI, 1531 (variant *c*).

4. The passage was removed. The reason for the narrator's disappearance is given later in the story as 'a fever' (*CH*, XI, 637).

5. *Corr.*, II, 82.

6. Bouvier, 126.

7. *Corr.*, II, 66–7.

8. Ibid., 30.

9. Ibid., 53.

10. Ibid., 66.

11. Ibid., 61.

12. *CH*, V, 791–2.

13. *Corr.*, II, 289–91 and 297–300; see also *LH*, I, 38–9.

14. Henry Murger and his 'Water-Drinkers', mentioned by Baudelaire, and by Champfleury in 1845: Robb (1988), 52–3.

15. *Corr.*, II, 45.

16. *Le Lys dans la Vallée*, *CH*, IX, 989.

17. Description in *LH*, I, 402.

18. *LH*, I, 36.

19. *Corr.*, II, 48. Saché's other tourist attraction today is the studio of the artist, Alexander Calder.

20. Gozlan (1946), 28.

21. *CH*, III, 1089.

22. *OC*, XXVII, 189.

23. Lesser, 7.

24. *LH*, II, 19 and 477.

25. Le Yaouanc (1959), 335–94.

26. Yeats, 438. *Louis Lambert* had a similar effect on Flaubert, who recognized himself in the character and some of his writing in the text: letter to Louise Colet, 27 December 1852 (Flaubert, II, 218–19). See also Bruneau, 119–22.

27. Train, 143–4. Mr Train informs me that the anecdote was found in an Italian evening newspaper; its origin is unknown. The doctor was probably Moreau de Tours.

28. *Aventures Administratives d'une Idée Heureuse*, *CH*, XII, 769.

29. Laughton, I, 38–9: letters of Henry Reeve to his wife (28 January 1835) and E. H. Handley (2 February 1835).

30. Gozlan (1946), 31–4. According to Desnoiresterres (132–3) it was the ring of Mohammed's cousin and son-in-law, Ali.

31. Léger, 211–12. The reference to nihilists is an anachronism.

32. Hammer-Purgstall was the author of the Arabic (not Sanskrit) inscription in the 1838 edition of *La Peau de Chagrin*.

33. *LH*, I, 705–6.
34. Ibid., II, 97.
35. *OC*, XXVII, 130, and *CH*, III, 1491.
36. Sand (1971), II, 157.
37. *Corr.*, II, 89.
38. Ibid., III, 126.
39. J. Lecomte, 59–60; Sainte-Beuve (1834); Werdet (1859), 139–40.
40. Wedmore, 82.
41. *OC*, XVI, 534.
42. *Théorie de la Démarche*, *CH*, XII, 265.
43. Baschet, 182; Gozlan (1946), 52.
44. *LH*, II, 35.
45. *Corr.*, I, 559 and 684.
46. Ibid., II, 453.
47. Second, 7.
48. *Corr.*, II, 65–6. Balzac's story is confirmed by Second.
49. *LH*, II, 8.
50. Ibid., I, 33; *Corr.*, II, 230 and 233. The note itself (also mentioned by Zulma Carraud) was probably printed separately and inserted in the issue. It has yet to be rediscovered.
51. *CH*, X, 1066.
52. Letter to Delacroix, 23(?) September 1840: Sand (1964–91), V, 145. See also *Petites Misères de la Vie Conjugale*, *CH*, XII, 133. In a piece written for the *Revue Parisienne*, Balzac attributes this idea to 'a highly intelligent woman' (*OC*, XXVIII, 182), which suggests that the piece *is* by Balzac and not by Louis de Cardonne (cf. M. Bouteron, in Balzac (1912–40), XL, 725).
53. *Corr.*, II, 116–17.
54. Citron (1986), 160.
55. *Corr.*, II, 21.
56. *Le Colonel Chabert*, *CH*, III, 350.
57. *La Duchesse de Langeais*, *CH*, V, 1012–13.
58. Letters from the Marquise de Castries to Sainte-Beuve in Antoine.
59. Chasles, 303.
60. *La Femme de Trente Ans*, *CH*, II, 1125.
61. *Corr.*, II, 36–7.
62. *CH*, X, 143.
63. Fray-Fournier.
64. *Corr.*, II, 108.
65. *CH*, IX, 705–6.
66. Arrigon (1927), 228–9.

67. *CH*, X, 262–3 and 268.

68. Ibid., 269–70 and 1341–2.

69. Ibid., 152.

70. Ibid., 131.

71. *LH*, I, 25.

72. *Corr.*, II, 215–16.

73. *OD*, 305.

74. Supposedly a warning issued to tourists at Westminster inspecting the axe that decapitated Charles I (*CH*, V, 989).

75. *La Duchesse de Langeais*, *CH*, V, 987, *Louis Lambert*, XI, 642, *Séraphîta*, XI, 792 and *Physiologie du Mariage*, XI, 949.

76. *CH*, IX, 1430.

77. *Le Père Goriot*, *CH*, III, 116; *Pierrette*, IV, 119.

78. *OC*, XXVIII, 661.

79. *CH*, X, 158, and P. Citron's note, 1290.

80. *OC*, XXVIII, 665.

81. *LH*, I, 157.

82. Spoelberch de Lovenjoul (1903), 73–6.

83. Quoted in the diary of his wife, Mélanie, 20 May 1835: *Corr.*, II, 678.

84. The anecdote appears in various forms, notably in Sainte-Beuve (1864), 109–10. Cf. Balzac's letter to Sandeau, 30 July 1835, which suggests a friendly attempt to distract him rather than self-centredness (*Corr.*, II, 709).

CHAPTER TEN
THE IDEAL WOMAN
(1832–1834)

1. Auger, 368.

2. 'Avant-propos', *CH*, I, 10.

3. *LH*, II, 503.

4. *OC*, XXVIII, 687.

5. *LH*, I, 11.

6. On Eveline: Spoelberch de Lovenjoul (1896); Korwin-Piotrowska (1938); R. Pierrot's note in *LH*, I, 54.

7. Views of Wenceslas vary. According to one of the two main accounts, he was a whip-happy, medieval tyrant; the other says he was kind, gentle and patient, 'managing as best he could his enormous estate' (this was also Balzac's view). The first account appeared in the Soviet Union in 1937; the other was published in Paris in 1933 by a Polish aristocrat. Both views are probably correct. (Grossman, 126; Korwin-Piotrowska (1933), 73–5.)

8. Korwin-Piotrowska (1933), 70.
9. A few notes have also survived: *LH*, I, 13 (n. 3) and II, 681.
10. Letter to François Buloz, 30 July 1860: Sand (1964–91), XVI, 32.
11. See Citron (1968).
12. *LH*, I, 25.
13. *OD*, 1077.
14. 3 April 1833: Pierrot (1972).
15. *LH*, I, 31.
16. *Corr.*, II, 457.
17. *LH*, I, 494.
18. This explains the allusion in *Théorie de la Démarche* (*CH*, XII, 265).
19. *Le Journal des Dames et des Modes*, 20 April 1833 (Kleinert).
20. *Corr.*, II, 253.
21. *CH*, IX, 419.
22. *LH*, I, 532.
23. *CH*, IX, 1432; see also Guyon (1951).
24. Werdet (1859), 183–4, and (1879), 40.
25. Bouteron (1933), 934; Woollen.
26. Prefatory note, not used in the final version: *CH*, IX, 1432.
27. Mirecourt (1854), 59–60.
28. Loménie.
29. *LH*, I, 38; Daniel 4: 33.
30. *CH*, IX, 434.
31. Unpublished foreword to Laure's collection of tales, *Le Compagnon du Foyer* (1854): Lorant (1960), 177–9.
32. 16 May 1866: Sand (1964–91), 883.
33. The Gosselin affair: *Corr.*, II, 138, 238, 241, 385, 431 and 511–12.
34. Nerval, II, 1233 (eyewitness account); Monselet (n.d.), ch. 1 (based on the account of one of the playwrights, Jaime).
35. Desnoiresterres, 106–10; Monselet (n.d.), 5.
36. Gozlan (1946), 126.
37. *Albert Savarus*, *CH*, I, 913.
38. Bernard 'has painted actual manners, without those monstrous and terrible exaggerations in which late French writers [Balzac or Dumas] have indulged' (Thackeray, 85). Henry James calls Bernard 'a second-rate genius': Balzac '"started" him, as the phrase is. It is true that he started him left foot foremost' by recommending that he 'try his hand at historical novels' (James (1878), 187–8).
39. *LH*, I, 105, 679 and 818.
40. 10 December 1833: *LH*, I, 107. The Warsaw library containing Eveline's letters to her brother Henri was destroyed in 1944.

41. Louvet de Couvray's *Les Amours du Chevalier de Faublas* (1787–9).
42. *Corr.*, II, 389–94.
43. Charles Weiss, 2 October 1833: Smethurst, 396–7.
44. *LH*, I, 439.
45. *CH*, III, 1198.
46. *LH*, I, 278.
47. Ibid., 166.

CHAPTER ELEVEN

FAMILY PLANNING

(1834–1836)

1. *Corr.*, II, 390.
2. Ibid., V, 228; see also *Le Cousin Pons*, *CH*, VII, 1405, variant *c*.
3. Chancerel and Pierrot.
4. *LH*, II, 771 and 822.
5. For example, Ferragus: *CH*, V, 876.
6. Ibid., III, 148–9.
7. Ibid., 1075–6.
8. *Corr.*, II, 391.
9. 1 July 1834: Liszt, I, 97.
10. *La Rabouilleuse*, *CH*, IV, 363.
11. Ibid., 364; Guignard, 32–6.
12. *Mémoires de Deux Jeunes Mariées*, *CH*, I, 351.
13. See Fargeaud and Pierrot, 52; Citron, 'Sur deux zones obscures' (1967); H. Gauthier, in *CH*, III, 512–13.
14. *Le Contrat de Mariage*, *CH*, III, 650 and 652–3.
15. *Corr.*, II, 644; *LH*, I, 146, 182 and 187.
16. *César Birotteau*, *CH*, VI, 290.
17. *Théorie de la Démarche*, *CH*, XII, 282.
18. *LH*, I, 210.
19. Ibid., 194.
20. Surville (1858), 95–6.
21. *La Prisonnière*: Proust (1988), III, 666–7.
22. Apart from the 437-page index in *CH*, XII (based on the index by F. Lotte, revised by P. Citron and A.-M. Meininger), the best summary is Pugh (1974); see also Balzac's own remarks in the 1839 preface to *Une Fille d'Eve* (*CH*, II, 264–6, with a sample biographical sketch of Rastignac).
23. Canfield, 19; Castex (1960), 461–73.
24. In Royce (1946), 12.
25. Lotte (1961).

26. *CH*, I, 128 and III, 537 (Paul); III, 60 (Rastignac); III, 542 (Mme Évangélista); V, 145 (Lucien). For a thorough analysis, see Abraham.

27. See n. 21.

28. Clément de Ris, 315; address in *Ferragus*, *CH*, V, 818.

29. Stephen, 304.

30. *Le Père Goriot*, *CH*, III, 161.

31. *CH*, IX, 454 and X, 988. Gondrin appears in a list of characters to be reused in the unwritten *Scènes de la Vie Militaire* (*OC*, XXVIII, 703).

32. Pugh (1964), 228.

33. Letter to Hippolyte Castille, *La Semaine*, 11 October 1846: *OC*, XXVIII, 491. R. Fortassier, however, sees Vidocq in the character, Bibi-Lupin, the head of the Sûreté who arrests Vautrin (*CH*, III, 15).

34. Bouteron (1954), 119–36; Bowring, 144–6. On Vidocq: Stead, and the edition of Vidocq's memoirs by J. Savant.

35. *Traité des Excitants Modernes*, *CH*, XII, 323–4.

36. *CH*, III, 61.

37. Ibid., 54.

38. *Traité de la Vie Élégante*, ibid., XII, 238.

39. 'Polichinelle'.

40. On Sandeau: Silver.

41. *LH*, I, 199. Concerning the mysterious reference to George Sand as 'Zulma' in this letter: 'Zulma' is the name of the succubus in one of the *Contes Drolatiques*.

42. *LH*, I, 298.

43. Surville (1858), 97–8.

44. *LH*, I, 281.

45. Lotte (1963).

46. *LH*, I, 206.

47. *Corr.*, II, 632.

48. *LH*, I, 145.

49. *Corr.*, II, 689.

50. Ibid., III, 191.

51. Ibid., IV, 137 and 196.

52. Ibid., II, 722.

53. *Le Père Goriot*, *CH*, III, 144. Another example in the description of Lucien de Rubempré (p. 155, above), and in Baudelaire's early sonnet, 'Il est de chastes mots que nous profanons tous . . .' Ryszard Engelking tells me that Daniel Darc's *Petit Bréviaire du Parisien* (1883) defines '*Ange*' as 'Neither man nor woman; the *Auvergnat* of Heaven', and that '*Auvergnate*', in Alfred Delvau's *Dictionnaire Érotique Moderne*, is defined as a member of 'the third sex'.

54. *Corr.*, IV, 65 and 92.
55. *LH*, I, 257. 'Anchises' is the name of La Palférine's groom in *Un Prince de la Bohème* (*CH*, VII, 815).
56. *CH*, VI, 344–5 and variant *e*.
57. *Lettres à la Présidente* (i.e. Apollonie Sabatier), 19 October 1850: Citron (1986), 87.
58. Pichois (1956).
59. *La Maison Nucingen*, *CH*, VI, 344.
60. Davin's complaints reported in the obituary by É. Monnais: Citron (1977).
61. *CH*, I, 1160, 1159 and 1172.
62. Ancelot, 98.
63. *LH*, I, 241.
64. Ibid., 195. Oscar Wilde had a replica made of Balzac's walking-stick (Sherard, 26).
65. Girardin.
66. *LH*, I, 241.
67. *CH*, I, 767.
68. *Corr.*, II, 623.
69. Ibid., 629.
70. *LH*, I, 226.
71. Ibid., 194.
72. *Le Curé de Tours*, *CH*, IV, 244.
73. Lukács, 61–2; *Le Lys dans la Vallée*, *CH*, IX, 1084ff.
74. *Le Père Goriot*, *CH*, III, 140.
75. F. Davin, introduction to *Études de Mœurs au XIXᵉ siècle*, *CH*, I, 1147. (On Davin's introduction, see p. 261.)
76. *LH*, I, 461–2.
77. Werdet (1879), 98.
78. *CH*, V, 1088. *Le Journal des Dames et des Modes*, 10 July 1836 and 20 November 1837 (Kleinert).
79. Sainte-Beuve, 'M. de Balzac' (1850), II, 349.
80. *La Fille aux Yeux d'Or* (third part of *Histoire des Treize*) is dedicated to Eugène Delacroix. The dedication follows the 'postface' to *Ne Touchez Pas la Hache* – 'Don't Touch that Axe, Eugene' is the title of an early improvisation by Pink Floyd.
81. *La Fille aux Yeux d'Or*, *CH*, V, 1099.
82. Werdet (1879), 67ff.
83. *LH*, I, 143.
84. Gautier (1858), 78–9.
85. *Corr.*, II, 655 and 659.

86. *CH*, X, 459.
87. *Corr.*, II, 641 and 646.
88. Ibid., III, 71.
89. Gautier (1858), 78.
90. *LH*, I, 387.
91. Bouteron (1954), 147–62.
92. Count O'Donnell, letter to Baron de Frénilly, 12 June 1835: Dédéyan (1981), 243–4.
93. On Sarah: Adamson and Pierrot; Arrigon (1932); Lagny (1974 and 1979); Léger.
94. *La Fausse Maîtresse*, *CH*, II, 198; also *La Muse du Département*, IV, 672.
95. Ducourneau (1962), 155.
96. Léger, 186–7.
97. See illustrations.
98. See Meininger (1963), 65.
99. E.g. *Béatrix*, *CH*, II, 681; *L'Interdiction*, III, 469; *Le Curé de Village*, IX, 692; *Les Marana*, X, 1045.

CHAPTER TWELVE
ILLUSIONS LOST AND FOUND
(1836–1837)

1. Bouvier, 191.
2. *LH*, I, 335.
3. Comtesse de Bassanville, *Les Salons d'Autrefois* (1863): Blanchard, 25.
4. Arrigon (1932), 148.
5. E.g. *LH*, I, 23.
6. Ibid., 186.
7. Ibid., 416.
8. Ibid., 339.
9. *Gambara*, *CH*, X, 495–6.
10. *LH*, I, 311.
11. Arrigon (1932), 95 and 183.
12. *Figaro*, 15 December 1837: Spoelberch de Lovenjoul (1888), 359–61.
13. *CH*, IX, 932.
14. 31 July 1837: Guise (1984).
15. *LH*, I, 894.
16. Ibid., 306.
17. Werdet (1859), 206.
18. Letter to Louise, 8 March (?) 1836: *Corr.*, III, 40.
19. *LH*, I, 313.

20. Gozlan (1946), 140.
21. *LH*, I, 342. See the chapter on Werdet in Felkay (1987), and, for the following account, Werdet (1859), 122, 169, 171, 178 and 180.
22. Karr, 286–8.
23. *LH*, I, 291–2.
24. Ibid., 347.
25. Quoted by Felkay (1987), 219.
26. Sophie Koslowska, letter of June 1836: Adamson and Pierrot, 115–16.
27. On Balzac in Turin: Prior.
28. On Caroline Marbouty: Serval, and her own works, published under the name Claire Brunne.
29. *Corr.*, III, 171.
30. Brunne (1842), preface.
31. Serval, 9.
32. Ibid., 13.
33. Marquis Félix de Saint-Thomas: *Corr.*, III, 172.
34. *Corr.*, III, 147.
35. Cesare (1986–91).
36. Antonio Lissoni, *Difesa dell'onore delle armi italiane oltraggiato dal signor di Balzac*.
37. *CH*, X, 573.
38. Ibid., 567.
39. *Louis Lambert*, *CH*, XI, 648.
40. On Balzac and the *roman feuilleton*: Guise (1964).
41. *CH*, VII, 891.
42. *LH*, I, 391.
43. The science of character or the study of types.
44. 24 October and 5 November 1836: Castex (1957), xxxiv–v. Cf. for instance the section on the Chevalier de Valois's face, only half of which turns red during digestion. The fact that this is the *left* half, 'according to some physicians', indicates a *'ladie's man'* (*sic*). Balzac refuses to accept responsibility for 'these scientific assertions' (phrase added on the fourth proof): *CH*, IV, 812–13 and 1480.
45. Sainte-Beuve (1834).
46. *Corr.*, III, 189.
47. *CH*, III, 38.
48. On Balzac in Milan: Cesare (1975); Gigli; Guise (1962); Milner.
49. *LH*, I, 370.
50. *Alessandro Manzoni, reminiscenze* (1882): Gigli, 52–5.
51. Gigli, 60–1.
52. *Corr.*, III, 265.

53. Balzac perhaps meant SS. Giovanni e Paolo (cf. *Corr.*, V, 270).

54. The Palazzo Contarini-Fasan was not built until the fifteenth century.

55. *LH*, I, 464.

56. *La Femme Supérieure* became *Les Employés*, *La Haute Banque* became *La Maison Nucingen*, and *Les Artistes* was never written.

57. Hillairet, I, 511 and Supplément, 57.

58. *Corr.*, III, 325–7; more details in Viennet, 206–7.

59. *LH*, I, 390.

60. Ibid., 170.

61. Ibid., 408.

62. Ibid., 404.

63. Les Jardies, now in Ville-d'Avray, was part of Sèvres before the Revolution.

64. *LH*, I, 406.

65. Ibid., 296.

66. *Le Journal des Dames et des Modes*, 20 March 1837 (Kleinert).

67. *La Presse*, 6 December 1836.

68. Balzac's comments on the portrait: *LH*, I, 296, 347, 387, 399, 416 and 438.

69. Ibid., 382, and *Modeste Mignon*, *CH*, I, 518 ('especially true in literature').

70. *LH*, I, 347.

71. Ibid., 388, 389 and 393.

72. *Une Fille d'Eve*, *CH*, II, 310.

73. Ibid., 317; *Béatrix*, II, 715; *Le Curé de Village*, IX, 652.

74. *Le Lys dans la Vallée*, *CH*, IX, 996–7.

75. Letters to Louise in *Corr.*, III.

76. Quoted by R. Pierrot, ibid., 829–31.

77. *Sardanapale* was performed in 1844, attributed to Lefèvre alone. Its author, Théaulon, is not mentioned. The play was reviewed by Nerval, who said that Lefèvre was too '*honnête*' for such an immoral subject . . . (Nerval, I, 801).

78. In 1972, a historian called Jean Savant published *Louise la Mystérieuse ou l'Essentiel de la Vie de Balzac*. She was, he claimed, none other than Balzac's housekeeper, Philiberte-Jeanne-*Louise* Breugniot, known as Mme de Brugnol (see below, p. 344). The book contains some valuable research on Mme de Brugnol, but in 'identifying' Louise, the author purports to clear up almost every enigma associated with Balzac's life, so that even the edible pieces of nut are contaminated by his sledgehammer. A mainstay of Savant's theory is that critics have conspired to cover up the truth – in this case, that Balzac had sex with his housekeeper, which

has long been accepted as probable. Thierry Bodin and René Guise have shown conclusively that most of Savant's conjectures are either unsubstantiated or wrong (*AB 1974*, 353–68 and 368–77). To give a flavour of his method: Mme de Brugnol's handwriting is quite different from that of the letter from Louise. Explanation: Mme de Brugnol must have suffered an injury to the wrist in 1836. (As a housekeeper, she would have been prone to such injuries.)

79. Monselet (n.d.), 8.

80. Sources on Atala other than those cited below: *Biographie des Acteurs*; *Dictionnaire de Biographie Française*; Larousse; Mirecourt (1855).

81. Most published sources state that Atala was born in Évreux in 1817. Her birth and death certificates show that she was born in Orléans on 4 December 1819 and died in Villeurbanne near Lyon on 29 March 1894.

82. Arago, 104.

83. *Journal des Comédiens*, 22 April 1830: Descotes, 308.

84. Ronteix, 176–7.

85. Adèle Hugo, 584–7.

86. Two possibilities: 1. Aguado, Marquis de Las Marismas (see above, p. 182). 2. Lezay-Marnésia, who wrote a play in 1837 and whose memoirs show that he was familiar with the theatrical world; but there are no other hints of liberalism, political or moral (Lezay-Marnésia, 268–73).

87. Hervey, 196.

88. L.-H. Lecomte, I, 279 and 303–4; Baldick, 153.

89. Lyonnet. Visit mentioned in Stirling, I, 247.

90. Schopp, 368. Atala is a minor character in Dumas's *Histoire de mes Bêtes*, in which it emerges that one of his collaborators in 1847 was Louis Lefèvre.

91. *CH*, VII, 439–40.

92. See R. Chollet's introduction to *Illusions Perdues*: *CH*, V, 78.

93. *LH*, I, 160.

94. *Corr.*, III, 26 and 30.

PART THREE

CHAPTER THIRTEEN
BURIED TREASURE
(1838)

1. Gozlan (1946), 20–2; Karr, 307.

2. Gozlan (1946), 21.

3. Letter to Zulma Carraud: *Corr.*, III, 419.

4. Eyma and Lucy, 218; Gozlan (1946), 63.

5. Lemaître, 239. On Balzac's 'secret' irrigation system: *Corr.*, IV, 777.

6. Gautier (1858), 87; also Karr, 309.

7. *Pierre Grassou*, *CH*, VI, 1095.

8. *LH*, I, 459.

9. *Petites Misères de la Vie Conjugale*, *CH*, XII, 75. Balzac also 'described' his house in *Mémoires de Deux Jeunes Mariées*: *CH*, I, 364–6.

10. Gozlan (1946), 25.

11. Ibid., 24; Second, 42.

12. Letter from Marquis Damaso Pareto, 5 August 1838: *Corr.*, III, 418.

13. Nerval, in *La Presse*, 7 October 1850: Nerval, II, 1209.

14. Later changed to *Qui terre a guerre a*.

15. In *Le Père Goriot*. See illustrations.

16. *LH*, I, 319.

17. Ibid., 432.

18. Ibid., 388.

19. Ibid., 308.

20. Ibid., 439.

21. *CH*, VI, 127.

22. Gozlan (1946), 53–5.

23. *CH*, IX, 1056–7, and introduction by J.-H. Donnard: *CH*, IX, 908.

24. The letter in *Corr.*, II, 648–9 should be dated 5 March 1834 (see *CH*, XI, 1607).

25. *Séraphita*, *CH*, XI, 739 and 764.

26. *CH*, III, 1195, variant *h*.

27. Ibid., X, 628; Cabanès, 198 (on Gay-Lussac).

28. Stephen, 322.

29. *CH*, X, 700.

30. Ibid., 631–2 and Fargeaud (1968), 581–2.

31. *CH*, X, 779–80.

32. The editor was Maurice Schlésinger, the model for Jacques Arnoux in Flaubert's *L'Éducation Sentimentale*.

33. *LH*, I, 419.

34. Gozlan (1946), 167–8.

35. Part V, book 2, ch. 1.

36. H. Monnier, in Werdet (1859), 344–5; Gautier (1858), 87.

37. Delord, 26.

38. *Les Français Peints par Eux-Mêmes* (1840), translated the same year. See *Pictures of the French*, p. 9, for a definition of the '*esprit épicier*' from the *London Review*: 'something obsolete, vulgar, and awkward, tinged with the ridiculous'. Balzac's sketch of the Grocer appears to have been reprinted by the editors of an undiscovered work called *La Grammaire des Épiciers* (reviewed in *Les Écoles*, 3 October 1839, 375).

39. *LH*, I, 655. Other related schemes: centralizing the production of *pains d'épice* (including regional varieties) in a Paris suburb (Léger, 88), and advising a young writer to name his journal *The Grocer's Monitor* – which, so named, made 20,000 francs in its first year (Lemer, 127–8).

40. *LH*, I, 459.

41. *Corr.*, IV, 157–8.

42. See p. 366.

43. *Corr.*, V, 247–8.

44. Letter to Maurice Dudevant, 15 September 1840: Sand (1964–91), V, 129.

45. *Corr.*, V, 547.

46. Mareschal-Duplessis, in Spoelberch de Lovenjoul (1888), 402 (possibly during a trip to Saché in August 1837).

47. 'Tibre', in Larousse.

48. *Corr.*, III, 448.

49. *CH*, VI, 1027.

50. Gautier (1858), 68.

51. *OC*, XXVIII, 680. Balzac alludes to Toussaint Louverture's silence in *Z. Marcas* (1840): *CH*, VIII, 840–1.

52. Nemours, especially 118–24 and 241–9.

53. *LH*, I, 367.

54. Goodman, 14–15. For a general survey: Williams.

55. Tyndale, I, 87.

56. *CH*, VI, 387 and 1304, variant *e*.

57. *LH*, I, 443; *Corr.*, III, 379.

58. Étienne Conti, future *député* and secretary to Napoleon III.

59. Jouenne d'Esgrigny-d'Herville, 437–8.

60. *CH*, IV, 361.

61. *Le Père Goriot*, *CH*, III, 141.

62. *Z. Marcas*, *CH*, VIII, 839.

63. Rugendas, I, 26–7 and 35; plates 21 and 22.

64. *Corr.*, IV, 148.

65. Karl Marx, *Theses on Feuerbach* (1845): Marx (1975), 423.

CHAPTER FOURTEEN
BARBARIANS
(1839–1842)

1. *CH*, VIII, 847.

2. Barbéris, *AB 1965*, 264–7.

3. Fragment written for the *Revue Parisienne*: *OC*, XXVIII, 185. See also *Le*

Catéchisme Social: 'Modern industry does not feed its slaves', etc. (Guyon (1933), 126).

4. See Donnard.

5. *LH*, I, 465.

6. Nerval, in *La Presse*, 7 October 1850: Nerval, II, 1210–11. Generally: Milatchitch.

7. Robb (1988), 262–6.

8. On Lassailly: Beauvoir; Desnoiresterres, 141–3; Gozlan (1946), 40–1; Kaye; Monselet (1866), 50; Nerval (see n. 6); Werdet (1859), 352–3.

9. On Balzac's corrections to Lassailly's work: Bodin (1989).

10. On Balzac's poor opinion of Vigny's *Chatterton* – the apotheosis of a parasite and a plagiarist: Bertaut (quoting Auguste Barbier), 37–40.

11. Raitt, 84.

12. Buisson was a tenant, not the owner: Felkay (1972), 376, n. 7. On Frascati's, see Balzac's 'Histoire et Physiologie des Boulevards de Paris', in *Le Diable à Paris*, II, 97. Lucien de Rubempré gambles there in *Illusions Perdues*: *CH*, V, 550.

13. Second, 47–8. List of theatres in *Corr.*, II, 573.

14. Gautier (1858), 14.

15. On the *Vautrin* affair: Guise (1966), 191–216.

16. *Revue Parisienne*, 25 July 1840: *OC*, XXVIII, 167.

17. Rémusat, III, 310 and 347. The part on *Vautrin* published in full by R. Pierrot in *Corr.*, IV, 845–6.

18. *OC*, XXIII, 7–8.

19. Letter to George Sand, 18 January 1840: *Corr.*, IV, 19.

20. George Sand, letter to Eveline de Balzac, 24 November 1853: Sand (1964–91), XII, 169.

21. Perrod.

22. *LH*, I, 502.

23. Goncourt (1989), I, 46 (1852).

24. Thackeray, 212.

25. Liszt, II, 143 (letter dated May 1841).

26. On *Pierrette* and the trial: J.-L. Tritter's introduction (*CH*, IV, 7–9).

27. *Un Caractère de Femme*, *CH*, XII, 464.

28. *LH*, I, 409.

29. 'Aux abonnés de la *Revue Parisienne*', 25 September 1840: *OC*, XXVIII, 247.

30. *OC*, XXVIII, 197.

31. Stendhal, 383–405. The contents of Stendhal's letter can be deduced from the three surviving drafts.

32. *CH*, VII, 809. In *Le Corsaire-Satan*, Balzac is reported saying that he

escaped unwanted attention from fans in Germany by travelling under the name 'Sainte-Beuve'. (Anon.)

33. Jules Sandeau, quoted by Sainte-Beuve in *Portraits Contemporains*, II, 357.

34. *LH*, I, 186.

35. Sainte-Beuve (1926), 109.

36. *CH*, II, 188 (introduction by R. Guise) and 200–3; also *LH*, I, 551.

37. *Un Prince de la Bohème*, *CH*, VII, 838.

38. Regard, xiii.

39. Meininger (1962).

40. One of Balzac's favourite anecdotes concerns Sixtus V, who pretended to be terminally ill so that even his enemies would elect him Pope. They did, and he recovered. See Balzac's 'Lettre sur Paris', 29 November 1830, and the Index in *CH*, XII.

41. Sainte-Beuve (1840) and (1973), 165.

42. Abraham, 273–5.

43. *Corr.*, IV, 33–7, and R. Pierrot's note.

44. Baldensperger; Laughton, I, 40.

45. For example in J.-B. Gresset's *La Chartreuse* (1735): 'Loin de l'humaine comédie ... Nous réaliserons enfin / Cette petite république' (vv. 644–8).

46. *LH*, I, 484.

47. Gozlan (1946), 118.

48. *LH*, I, 510.

49. Ibid., 502.

50. Regard, 395ff.

51. Balzac's trip is confirmed by a Nantes newspaper, *Le Breton*, 24 April 1841: Ducourneau and Pierrot, *AB 1973*, 393.

52. Samuel-Loumeau Cador (1816–73), alias Edmond: short-story writer, political economist and contributor to *La Presse* and the *Revue de Paris* (*Dictionnaire de Biographie Française*); also G. Lubin, in *AB 1968*, 403–9.

53. Fortassier (1985), introduction.

54. *CH*, VI, 877.

55. *Corr.*, IV, 152 and 222.

56. Ibid., III, 444.

57. *LH*, I, 339; also 471.

58. *Corr.*, IV, 217.

59. Ibid., 298.

60. *Corr.*, IV, 444–7; *LH*, I, 574–5. The article was a review of *Quinola* (see below, p. 348).

61. *LH*, I, 575.

62. *CH*, I, 13; see Prendergast, 99.
63. *LH*, I, 594.

CHAPTER FIFTEEN
THE END OF THE TUNNEL
(1842–1845)

1. Probably Mâcon: see *LH*, II, 248.
2. Diary published by A. Lorant (1962).
3. Letter from Anna Hanska: Korwin-Piotrowska (1933), 300–1.
4. *LH*, I, 557 and 587.
5. *CH*, I, 938.
6. Ibid., 976–7.
7. *LH*, I, 655.
8. Rosalie Rzewuska, who lived in Vienna, was actually an older cousin of Eveline.
9. *Splendeurs et Misères des Courtisanes*, *CH*, VI, 576–7.
10. *LH*, I, 869.
11. Ibid., 510.
12. *CH*, VI, 430 and P. Citron's note, 1318.
13. *LH*, I, 917.
14. Letter to Armand Dutacq, quoted by R. Pierrot: *Corr.*, III, 830.
15. *LH*, I, 556.
16. *La Presse*, 28 October 1850: Nerval, II, 1234.
17. *LH*, I, 561–2.
18. Ibid., 800.
19. On Louise Breugniot: Lorant (1967), I, 78–97; Savant (but see Ch. 12, n. 78).
20. See, however, A.-M. Meininger's introduction to *La Cousine Bette*: *CH*, VII, 29–30.
21. Lorant (1967), I, 81.
22. Letter to Auguste Fessart, in Lorant (1967), I, 97–9.
23. *LH*, I, 580.
24. *Le Courrier Balzacien*, new series, no. 45, p. 27; Maison de Balzac, 19.
25. See description by Curtius, 451.
26. On Cuvier, see above, p. 48. Daniel O'Connell (1775–1847), 'the Liberator': agitator for reform in Ireland.
27. As revealed by Baudelaire in 'Comment on paie ses dettes quand on a du génie'.
28. Baschet, 151.
29. Werdet (1859), 282.

30. *La Rabouilleuse*, *CH*, IV, 400.

31. *Traité des Excitants Modernes*, *CH*, XII, 311.

32. Gozlan (1946), 26.

33. *Les Paysans*, *CH*, IX, 212.

34. *La Presse*, 28 October 1850: Nerval, II, 1234.

35. *LH*, II, 20.

36. *Petites Misères de la Vie Conjugale*, *CH*, XII, 148.

37. Lotte (1962); see also Courtine.

38. Sainte-Beuve (1876), 135.

39. *LH*, I, 641.

40. *Corr.*, V, 30.

41. Quoted by R. Pierrot: *Corr.*, IV, 803.

42. Champfleury (10 April 1848).

43. Milatchitch; for reviews of *Quinola*: 125–34.

44. See Baudelaire's comment at the end of his 1846 *Salon*: Baudelaire (1975–6), II, 496.

45. Ibid., II, 268.

46. Letter to Comtesse Merlin, February or March 1842: *Le Courrier Balzacien*, new series, no. 9, p. 20.

47. *LH*, I, 566.

48. Ibid., 791.

49. Nettement, 269–70.

50. Ancelot, 99–100.

51. *LH*, II, 18.

52. *Corr.*, III, 586.

53. E.g. *Autre Étude de Femme*, *CH*, III, 698 (on 'individualism'); *La Muse du Département*, IV, 705 (women of thirty); Ch. 12, n. 44, above (physiognomy); and most of *La Recherche de l'Absolu*.

54. Second, 33–4; Vandam, 48. The piece referred to is the unwritten 'Voyage de découverte exécuté dans la rue Richelieu' (see *LH*, I, 639 and *CH*, VII, 1123–4). Balzac's works actually contain over a dozen descriptions of different properties in the Rue Richelieu (Raser).

55. For example Mesuré, 18–19.

56. *CH*, VI, 349.

57. *Corr.*, IV, 90–1.

58. *LH*, I, 487.

59. Ibid., II, 106.

60. Ibid., 21.

61. *Corr.*, V, 264.

62. *CH*, IV, 726–7.

63. *LH*, I, 667.

64. Ch. 5: 'Les Adieux'. See Werdet (1859), 167–8, and H. Gauthier, in *CH*, XI, 1611.
65. *LH*, I, 917.
66. For a list of what Balzac produced at Lagny: Pommier (1957), 237.
67. *LH*, I, 694 and 696.
68. Ibid., 704.
69. Ibid., 896.
70. See studies by M. Lichtlé and V. Miltchina in Meyer-Petit *et al.*, 52–88.
71. Quoted in the memoirs of A. O. Smirnova, and by Véra Biron in Meyer-Petit *et al.*, 99.
72. V. Biron, ibid., 102–3.
73. Bérard, 359.
74. *LH*, I, 763.
75. Korwin-Piotrowska (1933), 361.
76. *CH*, II, 261.
77. *LH*, I, 763.
78. Mirsky, 282.
79. Grossman, 77–80.
80. Ibid., 83–111; extracts translated from the original by Anne Klimoff in Meyer-Petit *et al.*, 146–50.
81. *Chronique de 1831 à 1862* (1909), in *LH*, I, 717, n. 6.
82. *LH*, I, 718.
83. Ibid., 722, alluding to Fontenelle.
84. Ibid., 721.
85. Ibid., 723 and n. 1.
86. Ibid., 754.
87. Ibid., 884.
88. Ibid., 923.
89. Ibid., 817.
90. Ibid., 865.

CHAPTER SIXTEEN
REVOLUTION
(1845–1848)

1. *LH*, II, 960.
2. *Mercadet*, Act I, Scene 6.
3. Gautier (1858), 121.
4. *Mercadet*, Act I, Scene 6.
5. *LH*, II, 29.
6. Ibid., 34.

7. Ibid., 67.

8. Ibid., 15.

9. *CH*, XII, 58.

10. Ibid., XI, 1205.

11. Eveline de Balzac, letter to Champfleury, 27 April 1851: Mme de Balzac, 16.

12. Baudelaire (1975–6), I, 438–9; Robb (1988), 65–6 (Gautier's account). Balzac's own account in *LH*, II, 134, 153 and 166.

13. December 1845: *Corr.*, V, 69–72.

14. *Corr.*, V, 109.

15. *La Femme de Trente Ans*, *CH*, II, 1085.

16. *LH*, II, 215.

17. Ibid., 149.

18. Ibid., I, 826, 922 and II, 830.

19. Lepoitevin Saint-Alme.

20. *LH*, II, 697.

21. Ibid., 662.

22. *Corr.*, V, 93.

23. *LH*, II, 266.

24. *CH*, VII, 684.

25. Ibid., 491.

26. *LH*, II, 371.

27. Ibid., I, 940.

28. *Corr.*, V, 793.

29. *LH*, I, 665.

30. Ibid., 782 and 634.

31. *CH*, III, 822; also *Louis Lambert*, XI, 640.

32. *LH*, I, 645 and II, 861.

33. Ibid., I, 672 and II, 523.

34. Bouteron (1954), 181–7: 'Bedouck ou le talisman de Balzac'.

35. *LH*, II, 269.

36. *Le Médecin de Campagne*, *CH*, IX, 404.

37. *LH*, I, 512.

38. Ibid., 470.

39. Ibid., II, 213.

40. Ibid., 260–1.

41. Ibid., 455.

42. Ibid., 255.

43. Ibid., 232.

44. Ibid., 253–4.

45. Ibid., 111.

46. Ibid., 421.
47. *Le Charivari*, 19 September 1846: *Le Courrier Balzacien*, no. 16 (November 1983).
48. *LH*, II, 230.
49. Quoted by R. Pierrot in *LH*, II, 374.
50. *LH*, II, 407.
51. Ibid., 454.
52. Ibid., 455.
53. Ibid., 478.
54. Ibid., 442.
55. Ibid., 399.
56. Ibid., 99.
57. Ibid., 544.
58. Ibid., 365.
59. Ibid., 361.
60. Ibid., 370, 465, 469, and 'Inventaire de la Rue Fortunée': 1019–51.
61. Ibid., 414.
62. Ibid., 472.
63. Ibid., 409.
64. Ibid., 530.
65. Ibid., 539–40.
66. *CH*, VII, 1709–14.
67. The writers most often cited by Balzac are Molière (204 times), Walter Scott and Voltaire (142), Hugo (136), Byron and Rousseau (135), Rabelais (111): Delattre.
68. *LH*, II, 617–18.
69. Ibid., 591.
70. On *Le Député d'Arcis*: Muret, I, 62–5.
71. *LH*, II, 658.
72. Ibid., 657.
73. Ibid., 664.
74. Ibid., 670.
75. *Corr.*, V, 229. See Ch. 18, n. 7.
76. Letter written before 6 November 1846: R. Pierrot, *AB 1991*, 48–9.
77. *LH*, II, 760.
78. Ibid., 681.
79. *Corr.*, V, 252.
80. Ibid., 247.
81. Ibid., 265.
82. *LH*, II, 618. Cf. Dickens, 615: publisher's account ending June 1846 shows £294 6s 5d.

83. Proudhon, 294.
84. Letter to Count Ouvaroff, October 1847: *Corr.*, V, 255.
85. Grossman, 115.
86. *LH*, II, 713.
87. Ibid., 722.
88. Ibid., 754.
89. Jubinal; Champfleury (10 April 1848), in Baschet, 230–1 and Champfleury (1861), 77; Gozlan (1946), 171.
90. *LH*, II, 718.

CHAPTER SEVENTEEN
HOME
(1848–1850)

1. *Les Petits Bourgeois*, *CH*, VIII, 83.
2. Edmond Got, *Journal* (30 May 1847): Blanchard, 75; Gozlan (1946), 30; Vandam, 45; Werdet (1859), 287. On Balzac's connections with literary Bohemia: Robb (1987).
3. 29 February 1848: *Corr.*, V, 283; see also Second, 35.
4. *CH*, VII, 1200, and A.-M. Meininger's note.
5. *LH*, II, 717.
6. Ibid., 727.
7. *Corr.*, V, 294–5; reprinted in *Notre Histoire* (1848), 259.
8. *OC*, XXVIII; see also Barbéris (*AB 1965*) on Balzac's projected article on 'Communism'.
9. *LH*, II, 782.
10. Ibid., 811.
11. Ibid., 845.
12. Champfleury (1861), 79; see, however, Ch. 8, n. 64.
13. Champfleury (19 May 1848); also Lemer, 165. On this and a later meeting (25 July): Banville, *Mes Souvenirs*, in Robb (1988), 75–6.
14. Lamartine, 94.
15. *Mémoires de Deux Jeunes Mariées*, *CH*, I, 382.
16. Milatchitch, 300.
17. Edmond Got, reported by Jules Claretie, *L'Opinion Nationale*, 26 October 1868: *LH*, II, 974.
18. One of the copies was rediscovered by Spoelberch de Lovenjoul (*OC*, XXIV, 135–7).
19. *LH*, II, 741 and 745.
20. Ibid., 862.
21. Ibid.

22. Ibid., 895.
23. Ibid., 985.
24. *Corr.*, V, 325.
25. *LH*, II, 579.
26. Ibid., 1010.
27. Ibid., 1011.
28. *Corr.*, V, 556.
29. *CH*, VII, 97.
30. 'Ce qui disparaît de Paris', *Le Diable à Paris*, I, 18.
31. *CH*, VIII, 21–2.
32. Ibid., VI, 791.
33. Ibid., 794.
34. *Corr.*, V, 418.
35. Balzac's corrections are incomplete and inconsistent. Editions published during his lifetime and under his supervision may be thought to provide a more reliable text.
36. Tomasz Hubernarczak, recorded by Eveline's nephew, Adam Rzewuski, in *Le Messager Polonais*, 19 May 1928: Korwin-Piotrowska (1933), 137 and 456.
37. *Corr.*, V, 561.
38. *Le Cousin Pons, CH*, VII, 531.
39. *Corr.*, V, 524.
40. Ibid., 630.
41. Ibid., 415.
42. Ibid., 644.
43. Ibid., 458.
44. Ibid., 460.
45. Ibid., 510–12.
46. Ibid., 520.
47. Ibid., 521.
48. Ibid., 510.
49. Ibid., 522.
50. Ibid., 547.
51. January–April 1849, in Lorant (1964).
52. *Corr.*, V, 670.
53. Ibid., 512.
54. Ibid., 629.
55. *LH*, II, 1074.
56. *Corr.*, V, 723.
57. On Balzac's final illnesses: Le Yaouanc (1966); Lorant (1961); Métadier (1964).

58. 'Notes sur les derniers moments de M. de Balzac': Baschet, 157–60.

59. *Corr.*, V, 584–5.

60. Ibid., 697.

61. Ibid., 723.

62. Ibid., 665.

63. Ibid., 584.

64. Ibid., 664–5.

65. See especially *L'Initié*: *CH*, VIII, 376.

66. *Corr.*, V, 70.

67. Ibid., 735.

68. Ibid., 743.

69. Ibid., 741.

70. *LH*, II, 1075–7.

71. *Corr.*, V, 758.

72. *Ibid.*, 764.

73. Spoelberch de Lovenjoul (1896), 102–5.

74. Vigny: letter to Vicomtesse du Plessis, 15 September 1850.

75. Family letters on Balzac's last months in Lorant (1961).

76. *Le Siècle*, 4 July 1850: Lorant (1961), 80.

77. Hippolyte Hostein, in Spoelberch de Lovenjoul (1888), 394.

78. 3 December 1843: *LH*, I, 734.

79. Hugo (1887). The 'Holbein' must have been either the 'St Peter' or the 'Alchemist' purchased in Basel (*LH*, II, 204). No Porbus appears in the Inventory or anywhere else.

80. Mirbeau; see also Bardèche, 604–5; Descaves; Lorant (1961); Pommier (1965, p. 673, and 1966).

81. Surville (1858), 209.

82. There is a more precise echo of what seems to be Laure's opinion in Flaubert's correspondence – but twenty-seven years after the event and third-hand: 'What a lamentable life! And do you know how he ended? He told Mme de Surville, who passed it on to Mme Cornu: "I am dying of grief" – the grief his wife was causing him!' (Letter to Edma Roger des Genettes, 3 [August] [1877], Club de l'Honnête Homme, XV, 586; to appear in vol. V of Jean Bruneau's edition.)

83. Letter to Champfleury, 8–9 June 1851: Mme de Balzac, 53.

84. Letter to Me Delapalme: Lorant (1961), 90.

85. *LH*, I, 433.

86. *Corr.*, V, 795–6.

87. Claretie, 182; *Intermédiaire des Chercheurs*, LVI (1907), 740: Jarry, 54.

88. Fortunée Hamelin, letter to Comtesse Kisseleff, quoting Hugo: Spoelberch de Lovenjoul (1888), 406.

89. Hugo (1887).
90. Spoelberch de Lovenjoul (1896), 108.

CHAPTER EIGHTEEN
THE HUMAN COMEDY
(EPILOGUE)

1. Desnoiresterres, 145.
2. Janin (1839).
3. Lemer, 1–3.
4. Hugo (1985).
5. *Petites Misères de la Vie Conjugale*, CH, XII, 102.
6. *La Silhouette*: Maurois, 598.
7. There were in fact nine classes of funeral, plus the *'service ordinaire'* which Balzac had requested for himself (Balard).
8. Hugo (1887).
9. Champfleury (1861), 80.
10. Letter to Champfleury, 26 July 1851: Spoelberch de Lovenjoul (1901), 307; Mme de Balzac, 128. Champfleury described his 'seduction' in a novel, *L'Avocat Trouble-Ménage* (Dentu, 1870). See also his verbal account in Dufay.
11. CH, VIII, 1247 and 1594.
12. Baudelaire (1973), I, 177; Robb (1988), 82.
13. Baudelaire (1975–6), II, 120.
14. Jarry, 61–4, quoting Countess Kleinmichel and Stanislas Rzewuski (nephew of Eveline).

APPENDIX I
BALZAC AFTER 1850

1. On Balzac's posthumous reputation in France (1850–1900): Bellos.
2. Taine, 94.
3. In *Le Roman Expérimental* (1880), Zola takes Balzac's scientific analogies as seriously as possible and chooses the example least likely to prove his point (Baron Hulot in *La Cousine Bette*). Cf. the conversation recorded by a professor at Moscow University who visited Balzac on 1 June 1839. Balzac interrupted himself: 'Oh! that was a falsehood! That won't do at all. If I were a historian, I might be excused, but in a novelist it's unforgivable.' Stepan Petrovitch Chevyriov, translated by A. Klimoff in Meyer-Petit *et al.*, 168–73. See 172.
4. In the 1835 preface to *Le Père Goriot*: CH, III, 43–4.

5. Jules Vallès, *Les Réfractaires* (1866), in Bellos, 117.

6. Robb (1988), 352–7.

7. Dormoy, 433; V. Biron in Meyer-Petit *et al*.

8. Flaubert, II, 209 (letter to Louise Colet, 16 December 1852).

9. Browning, VIII, 316 (letter to Mary Russell Mitford, 20 May 1844).

10. Anonymous article in *Fraser's Magazine*, February 1843: Adamson (1986), 272.

11. Quoted in Adamson (1986), 274.

12. Stevenson, II, 146 (October 1883).

13. Saintsbury, 510–12.

14. Baring, 64.

15. Strachey, 225.

16. D. H. Lawrence, in Aldous Huxley, *Vulgarity in Literature* (1930): Dédéyan (1983), 307.

17. This was the second English edition of *The Human Comedy*, published in 53 volumes from 1895 to 1911; it included the *Contes Drolatiques* and Christophe and Cerfbeer's 'Repertory of the *Comédie Humaine*'; the illustrations were taken from the Philadelphia edition (1895–1900).

18. Marx (1991), III, 130.

19. Paglia, 389–407.

20. See especially Roland Barthes's *S/Z* (1970), trans. R. Miller, introduction by R. Howard (London: Cape, 1975), with the text of *Sarrasine*.

SELECT
BIBLIOGRAPHY

WORKS CITED

(Unless otherwise indicated, the place of publication is Paris)

AB = L'Année Balzacienne

Abraham, Pierre. *Créatures chez Balzac*. 4th ed. Gallimard, 1931.

Abrantès, Duchesse d'. *Souvenirs d'une Ambassade et d'un Séjour en Espagne et en [sic] Portugal, de 1808 à 1811*. Ollivier, 1837.

Adamson, Donald, and Roger Pierrot. 'Quelques lueurs sur *La Contessa*'. *AB 1963*, 107–21.

Adamson, D. '*Le Père Goriot* devant la critique anglaise'. *AB 1986*, 261–79.

Adamson, D. 'La Réception de *La Comédie Humaine* en Grande-Bretagne au XXe siècle'. *AB 1992*, 391–420.

Albrecht, Roland. 'Jalons pour l'étude de la fortune de Balzac en Allemagne'. *AB 1970*, 77–102.

Allet, Edward. 'Très humble amende honorable à un très irrévérend père'. *Les Écoles*, 5 September 1839.

Ancelot, Virginie. *Les Salons de Paris: Foyers Éteints*. Tardieu, 1858.

Anon. Article on Balzac in Germany. *Le Corsaire-Satan*, 28 July 1845.

Antoine, Gérald. 'Lettres inédites de la Marquise de Castries à Sainte-Beuve'. *Revue d'Histoire Littéraire de la France*, October–December 1954, 423–51.

Arago, Jacques. *Physiologie des Foyers et des Coulisses de tous les Théâtres de Paris*. Chez les marchands de nouveautés, 1841.

Armstrong, Anthony. 'Balzac et *Marie Stuart*'. *AB 1991*, 432–40.

Arrigon, Louis-Jules. *Les Débuts Littéraires d'Honoré de Balzac*. Perrin, 1924.

Arrigon, L.-J. *Les Années Romantiques de Balzac*. Perrin, 1927.

Arrigon, L.-J. *Balzac et la 'Contessa'*. Éditions des Portiques [1932].

Aubrée, Étienne. *Balzac à Fougères ('Les Chouans')*. Perrin, 1939.

Audebrand, Philibert. *Mémoires d'un Passant*. Calmann-Lévy, 1893.

Auger, Hippolyte. *Mémoires*. Ed. P. Cottin. Aux Bureaux de la *Revue Rétrospective*, 1891.

Balard, ancien ordonnateur des convois de la Ville de Paris. *Guide des Familles*. Chez l'auteur, 1858.

Baldensperger, Fernand. 'Une suggestion anglaise pour le titre de la *Comédie Humaine* de Balzac'. *Revue de Littérature Comparée*, October–December 1921, 638–9.

Baldick, Robert. *The Life and Times of Frédérick Lemaître*. Hamish Hamilton, 1959.

Balzac, Bernard-François. *Mémoire sur les moyens de prévenir les vols et les assassinats, et de ramener les hommes qui les commettent aux travaux de la Société, et sur les moyens de simplifier l'Ordre judiciaire*. Tours: Mame, April 1807.

Balzac, B.-F. *Mémoire sur le scandaleux désordre causé par les jeunes filles trompées et abandonnées dans un absolu dénuement; et sur les moyens d'utiliser une portion de population perdue pour l'État, et très funeste à l'ordre social*. Tours: Mame, April 1808.

Balzac, B.-F. *Mémoire sur deux grandes obligations à remplir par les Français*. Tours: Mame, 1809.

Balzac, B.-F. *Histoire de la Rage, et moyen d'en préserver, comme autrefois, les hommes*. Tours: Mame, 1810.

Balzac, B.-F. *Histoire de la Rage, avec le moyen d'en préserver, comme autrefois, les hommes, et de faire cesser plusieurs autres maux par une taxe sur la population canine; suivie d'Observations sur l'Économie politique et particulière touchant les Subsistances*. Tours: Mame, 1814.

Balzac, B.-F. *Opuscule sur la statue équestre que les Français doivent faire ériger pour perpétuer la mémoire de Henri IV et de leur amour envers sa dynastie, avec des recherches sur les anciens monuments de ce genre*. Tours: Mame, 1814.

Balzac, Honoré de. *La Comédie Humaine*. 12 vols. Gen. ed. Pierre-Georges Castex. Gallimard, Pléiade, 1976–81. Editors of individual works: Pierre Barbéris, Suzanne Bérard, Patrick Berthier, Thierry Bodin, Nicole Cazauran, Roland Chollet, Pierre Citron, Jean-Hervé Donnard, Madeleine Fargeaud, Rose Fortassier, Lucienne Frappier-Mazur, Bernard Gagnebin, Henri Gauthier, Jeannine Guichardet, René Guise, Moïse Le Yaouanc, Michel Lichtlé, André Lorant, Anne-Marie Meininger, Arlette Michel, Nicole Mozet, Roger Pierrot, Maurice Regard, Guy Sagnes, Colin Smethurst and Jean-Louis Tritter.

Balzac, Honoré de. *Oeuvres Diverses*. Vol. I. Gen. ed. Pierre-Georges Castex. Gallimard, Pléiade, 1990. With the collaboration of Roland Chollet, René Guise and Nicole Mozet.

Balzac, Honoré de. *Oeuvres Complètes*. 40 vols. Ed. Marcel Bouteron and Henri Longnon. Conard, 1912–40.

Balzac, Honoré de. *L'Oeuvre de Balzac*. 16 vols. Ed. Albert Béguin and Jean-A. Ducourneau. Formes et Reflets, 1950–3.

Balzac, Honoré de. *Oeuvres Complètes*. 28 vols. Gen. ed. Maurice Bardèche. Société des Études Balzaciennes, Club de l'Honnête Homme, 1955–63.

Balzac, Honoré de. *Oeuvres Complètes Illustrées*. 30 vols. Gen. ed. J.-A. Ducourneau. Les Bibliophiles de l'Originale, 1965–76. (Reproduces Balzac's annotated copy of the Furne-Hetzel edition of *La Comédie Humaine*.)

Balzac, Honoré de. *Correspondance*. 5 vols. Ed. Roger Pierrot. Garnier, 1960–9. (For letters published, re-dated or revised since 1969, see *AB 1991*, 29 and 51, and *Le Courrier Balzacien*, 47 (1992), 32–42.)

Balzac, Honoré de. *Lettres à Madame Hanska*. 2 vols. Ed. R. Pierrot. Laffont, 1990. (Replaces the four-volume Delta edition, 1967–71.)

Balzac, Mme Honoré de (Eveline Hanska). *Lettres Inédites à Champfleury (1851–1854)*. Ed. L. Uffenbeck and E. Fudakowska. Champion-Slatkine, 1989.

Balzac, Laure de. See Surville.

Barbéris, Pierre. 'Les Adieux du bachelier Horace de Saint-Aubin'. *AB 1963*, 7–30.

Barbéris, P. *Aux Sources de Balzac: les Romans de Jeunesse*. 1965; Geneva: Slatkine, 1985.

Barbéris, P. 'Trois moments de la politique balzacienne'. *AB 1965*, 253–90.

Barbéris, P. 'L'accueil de la critique aux premières grandes oeuvres de Balzac'. *AB 1967*, 51–72 and *AB 1968*, 165–95.

Bardèche, Maurice. *Balzac*. Julliard, 1980.

Baring, Maurice. *French Literature*. London: Benn, 1927.

Baschet, Armand. *Honoré de Balzac, Essai sur l'Homme et sur l'Oeuvre; avec Notes Historiques par Champfleury*. Giraud et Dagneau, 1852; Geneva: Slatkine, 1973.

Baudelaire, Charles. *Correspondance*. Ed. Claude Pichois and Jean Ziegler. Gallimard, Pléiade, 1973.

Baudelaire, Charles. *Oeuvres Complètes*. Ed. C. Pichois. Gallimard, Pléiade, 1975–6.

Beauvoir, Roger de. *Profils et Charges à la Plume: Les Soupeurs de Mon Temps*. Faure, 1868.

Bellos, David. *Balzac Criticism in France, 1850–1900*. Oxford: Clarendon Press, 1976.

Benjamin, Walter. *Charles Baudelaire: A Lyric Poet in the Era of High Capitalism*. Trans. H. Zohn. London: NLB, 1973.

Bérard, Suzanne. 'Le Dernier voyage de Balzac en Russie'. *Revue de Littérature Comparée*, April–June 1950, 348–62.

Bernard, Émile. *Souvenirs sur Paul Cézanne*. A la Rénovation Esthétique [1921].

Bertault, Abbé Philippe. *Balzac et la Religion*. Boivin, 1942; Geneva: Slatkine, 1980.

Bertaut, Jules. *Balzac Anecdotique*. Sansot, 1908.

Besson, Lucette. 'Les Parents nourriciers de Balzac'. *AB 1988*, 27–44.

Biographie des Acteurs de Paris. Chez les éditeurs, 1837.

Blanchard, Marc. *Témoignages et Jugements sur Balzac*. Champion, 1931.

Bodin, Thierry. 'Balzac et Zulma Carraud'. *AB 1969*, 303–6.

Bodin, T. Review of Savant, *Louise la Mystérieuse*. *AB 1974*, 368–77.

Bodin, T. 'Au ras des Pâquerettes'. *AB 1989*, 77–90.

Bonhoure, Gaston. *Le Collège et le Lycée de Vendôme*. Picard, 1912.

Bourget, Paul. 'Une des énigmes de Balzac'. *Pages de Critique et de Doctrine*. Vol. I. Plon-Nourrit, 1910.

Bouteron, Marcel. 'Balzac et le prix Montyon'. *Revue des Deux Mondes*, 15 December 1933, 926–34.

Bouteron, M. *Études Balzaciennes*. Jouve, 1954.

Bouvier, René, and Édouard Maynial. *Les Comptes Dramatiques de Balzac*. Sorlot, 1938.

Bowring, Sir John. *Autobiographical Recollections*. Ed. L. B. Bowring. London: King, 1877.

Brooks, Peter. *Reading for the Plot: Design and Intention in Narrative*. Oxford: Clarendon Press, 1984.

Browning, Elizabeth Barrett and Robert. *The Brownings' Correspondence*. Ed. P. Kelley and S. Lewis. Winfield, Kansas: Wedgestone Press, 1984–91.

Brua, Edmond. 'La mère de Balzac a-t-elle réellement allaité son premier-né?' *AB 1966*, 360–5.

Bruneau, Jean. *Les Débuts Littéraires de Gustave Flaubert, 1831–1845*. Armand Colin, 1962.

Brunne, Claire (Caroline Marbouty). *Ange de Spola (études de femmes)*. Magen, 1842.

Cabanès, Dr Auguste. *Balzac Ignoré*. 2nd ed. Albin Michel [1911].

Canfield, A. G. 'Les Personnages reparaissants dans *La Comédie Humaine*'. *Revue d'Histoire Littéraire de la France*, January–March and April–June 1934, 15–31 and 198–214.

Castex, Pierre-Georges, ed. *Falthurne*. Corti, 1950.

Castex, P.-G., ed. *La Vieille Fille*. Garnier, 1957.

Castex, P.-G., ed. *Le Père Goriot*. Garnier, 1960.

Célestin, Nicole. 'Balzac et la chronique tourangelle'. *AB 1965*, 121–9.

Cesare, Raffaele de. *Balzac e Manzoni, cronaca di un incontro*. Lecce: Milella, 1975.

Cesare, R. de. 'Sur le Comte Guidoboni-Visconti'. *AB 1982*, 107–28.

Cesare, R. de. *La Prima fortuna di Balzac in Italia* (1830–50), *Aevum, Rassegna di scienze storiche, linguistiche e filologiche*. Milan, 1986–91.

Champfleury. 'Notes du Citoyen Champfleury sur les choses, les hommes et les animaux, depuis la Révolution'. *Le Corsaire*, 10 April 1848.

[Champfleury]. Anon. 'Assemblée générale des littérateurs'. *Le Corsaire*, 19 May 1848.

Champfleury. *Gazette de Champfleury*. Blanchard, 1856.

Champfleury. *Grandes Figures d'Hier et d'Aujourd'hui*. Poulet-Malassis et De Broise, 1861; Geneva: Slatkine, 1968.

Champfleury. *Balzac au Collège*. Patay, 1878.

Chancerel, André, and Roger Pierrot. 'La Véritable Eugénie Grandet: Maria du Fresnay'. *Revue des Sciences Humaines*, October–December 1955, 437–58.

Chantemesse, Robert. *Le Roman Inconnu de la Duchesse d'Abrantès*. Plon, 1927.

Chasles, Philarète. *Oeuvres. Mémoires*. 2nd ed. Vol. I. Charpentier, 1876.

Chollet, Roland. *Balzac Journaliste: Le Tournant de 1830*. Klincksieck, 1983.

Chollet, R. 'Autour de la publication de l'*Histoire Impartiale des Jésuites*'. *AB 1991*, 91–109.

Citron, Pierre. 'Sur deux zones obscures de la psychologie de Balzac'. *AB 1967*, 3–27.

Citron, P. 'Le Testament de la mère de Balzac'. *AB 1967*, 339–42.

Citron, P. 'Le Rêve asiatique de Balzac'. *AB 1968*, 303–36.

Citron, P. 'Un article sur la mort de Balzac'. *AB 1977*, 179–92.

Citron, P. *Dans Balzac*. Seuil, 1986.

Claretie, Jules. *La Vie à Paris. 1882*. 2nd ed. Havard, n.d.

Clément de Ris, Louis. *Portraits à la Plume*. Didier, 1853.

Corbin, Alain. *Le Miasme et la Jonquille*. Flammarion, 1986.

Courtine, Robert. *Balzac à Table*. Laffont, 1976.

Curtius, Ernst Robert. *Balzac*. Bonn: Friedrich Cohen, 1923.

Dédéyan, Charles. 'Balzac et Astolphe de Custine à Vienne'. *AB 1981*, 237–44.

Dédéyan, C. 'Aldous Huxley et Balzac'. *AB 1983*, 303–12.

Delacroix, Eugène. *Correspondance Générale*. Ed. A. Joubin. Plon, 1935–8.

Delattre, Geneviève. *Les Opinions Littéraires de Balzac*. PUF, 1961.

Delécluze, Étienne-Jean. *Souvenirs de Soixante Années*. Lévy, 1862.

[Delord, Taxile]. *Les Petits Paris: Paris-Bohème, par les Auteurs des Mémoires de Bilboquet*. Taride, 1854.

De Maistre, Joseph. *Cinq Lettres sur l'Éducation Publique en Russie* (June–July 1810). In *Considérations sur la France*. Roger et Chernoviz, 1910.

Descaves, Pierre. *Les Cent-Jours de Mr de Balzac*. Calmann-Lévy, 1950.

Descotes, Maurice. *Le Drame Romantique et ses Grands Créateurs*. PUF, n.d.

Desnoiresterres, Gustave. *M. de Balzac*. Permain, 1851.

Le Diable à Paris. Paris et les Parisiens. Hetzel, 1845–6.

Dickens, Charles. *The Letters of Charles Dickens*. Vol. IV. Ed. K. Tillotson. Oxford: Clarendon Press, 1977.

Dictionnaire de Biographie Française, 1933–.

Donnard, Jean-Hervé. 'À propos d'une supercherie littéraire'. *AB 1963*, 123–42.

Dormoy, Nadine. 'Balzac dans la critique russe'. *AB 1992*, 421–37.

Dostoevsky, Fyodor. *Crime and Punishment*. Trans. D. Magarshack. Penguin, 1975.

Duckett, William, ed. *Dictionnaire de Conversation à l'Usage des Dames et des Jeunes Personnes, ou Complément Nécessaire de Toute Bonne Éducation*. Langlois et Leclercq, 1841.

Ducourneau, Jean-A., and Roger Pierrot. 'Calendrier de la vie de Balzac'. *Les Études Balzaciennes*, nos 2, 5–6, 8–9 and 10; *AB 1960–6*, 68–74, 76, 77 and 79.

Ducourneau, J.-A. *Album Balzac*. Gallimard, Pléiade, 1962.

Dufay, Pierre. 'Champfleury et Mme Hanska'. *Mercure de France*, 1 April 1908.

Dumas, Alexandre. *Histoire de mes Bêtes*. 1868; Calmann-Lévy, n.d.

Dutacq, Jean. 'La Maison de famille'. *Le Courrier Balzacien*, 4–5 (May 1949), 61–8.

Engels, Friedrich, and Karl Marx. *On Literature*. Moscow: Progress Publishers, 1976.

Eyma, Xavier and Lucy, A. de. *Écrivains et Artistes Vivants, Français et Étrangers: Biographies avec Portraits*. Librairie Universelle, 1840.

Fargeaud, Madeleine. 'Laurence la mal aimée'. *AB 1961*, 3–27.

Fargeaud, M., and R. Pierrot. 'Henry le trop aimé'. *AB 1961*, 29–66.

Fargeaud, M. 'Le premier ami de Balzac: Dablin'. *AB 1964*, 3–24.

Fargeaud, M. 'Madame Balzac, son mysticisme et ses enfants'. *AB 1965*, 3–33.

Fargeaud, M. *Balzac et 'La Recherche de l'Absolu'*. Hachette, 1968.

Felkay, Nicole. 'Le Tailleur Buisson et les *Études de Mœurs*'. *AB 1972*, 375–80.

Felkay, N. *Balzac et ses Éditeurs, 1822–1837: Essai sur la Librairie Romantique*. Promodis, 1987.

Felkay, N. 'Le Paris révolutionnaire de Bernard-François Balzac'. *AB 1990*, 51–9.

Flaubert, Gustave. *Correspondance*. Ed. Jean Bruneau. Gallimard, Pléiade, 1973–.

Fontaney, Antoine. *Journal Intime*. Ed. R. Jasinski. Les Presses Françaises, 1925.

Fortassier, Rose, ed. *Peines de Cœur d'une Chatte Anglaise*. Flammarion, GF, 1985.

Fray-Fournier, A. *Balzac à Limoges*. Limoges: Ducourtieux, 1898.

Gautier, Théophile. *Les Jeunes France, Romans Goguenards*. 1833; Ed. R. Jasinski. Flammarion, 1974.

Gautier, T. 'Honoré de Balzac', *L'Artiste* and *Le Moniteur Universel*, March–May 1858. In *Honoré de Balzac par Théophile Gautier*. Ed. Cl.-M. Senninger. Nizet, 1980.

Gédéon, Léon. 'Balzac au Lycée Charlemagne'. *AB 1966*, 368.

Gédéon, L. 'La Pyramide du Louvre'. *Le Courrier Balzacien*, new series, 24 (1986), 17–18.

Gigli, Giuseppe. *Balzac in Italia*. Milan: Treves, 1920.

Gilot, Françoise, and C. Lake. *Life with Picasso*. 1964; Virago, 1990.

Girardin, Delphine de. *La Canne de M. de Balzac*. 1836; Éditions du Bateau Ivre, 1946.

Goncourt, Edmond and Jules de. *Gavarni, l'Homme et l'Oeuvre*. Fasquelle, 1925.

Goncourt, E. and J. de. *Journal: Mémoires de la Vie Littéraire*. Ed. R. Ricatte. Laffont, 1989.

Goodman, Jeffrey. *Psychic Archaeology*. 1977; Panther, 1979.

Goulard, Roger. 'Balzac et les *Mémoires de Sanson*'. *Mercure de France*, 1 November 1950, 461–9.

Gozlan, Léon. *Balzac en Pantoufles*. Horizons de France, 1946. Compiled from *Balzac en Pantoufles* (1856) and the following.

Gozlan, L. *Balzac Chez Lui: Souvenirs des Jardies*. Lévy, 1862.

Gozlan, L. *Balzac Intime. Balzac en Pantoufles. Balzac Chez Lui*. Librairie Illustrée [1886].

Grossman, Leonid. *Balzac en Russie*. 1937; Zeluck, 1946.

Guignard, Romain. *Balzac et Issoudun*. Gaignault, 1949.

Guise, René. 'Balzac et l'Italie'. *AB 1962*, 245–75.

Guise, R. 'Balzac et le roman feuilleton'. *AB 1964*, 283–338.

Guise, R. 'Un grand homme du roman à la scène'. *AB 1966*, 171–216.

Guise, R. Review of Savant, *Louise la Mystérieuse*. *AB 1974*, 353–68.

Guise, R. 'Balzac et *Le Charivari* en 1837'. *AB 1984*, 133–54.

Guise, R., ed. *L'Excommunié*. *AB 1985*, 31–101.

Guise, R., ed. *Le Sorcier* [=*Le Centenaire*]. Corti, 1990.

Guyon, Bernard, ed. *Le Catéchisme Social*. La Renaissance du Livre, 1933.

Guyon, B. *La Pensée Politique et Sociale de Balzac*. Armand Colin, 1947; 1967.

Guyon, B. *La Création Littéraire chez Balzac. La Genèse du 'Médecin de Campagne'*. 2nd ed. Armand Colin, 1951.

Guyon, B. 'Une lettre inédite de Balzac à Gosselin'. *AB 1974*, 305–10.

Hanotaux, Gabriel, and Georges Vicaire, *La Jeunesse de Balzac: Balzac Imprimeur, 1825–1828*, 1903; Ferroud, 1921.

Hanska, Eveline. See Mme Honoré de Balzac.

Havard de la Montagne, Philippe. 'Un beau-frère de Balzac: A.-D. Michaut de Saint-Pierre de Montzaigle'. *AB 1964*, 39–66.

Havard de la Montagne, P. 'Rétif de la Bretonne a-t-il connu le père de Balzac?' *Études Rétiviennes*, December 1987, 105–11.

Hennion, Horace. 'Louis-Daniel Balzac'. *Le Courrier Balzacien*, 8–9 (November 1950), 159–60.

Hervey, Charles. *The Theatres of Paris*. Paris: Galignani; London: Mitchell, 1846.

Hillairet, Jacques. *Dictionnaire Historique des Rues de Paris*. 6th ed. Éditions de Minuit, 1976.

Hugo, Adèle. *Victor Hugo Raconté par un Témoin de sa Vie* (1863): Original version in *Victor Hugo Raconté par Adèle Hugo*. Ed. S. and J. Gaudon *et al*. Plon, 1985.

Hugo, Victor. 'Discours prononcé aux funérailles de M. Honoré de Balzac'. *Actes et Paroles. I. Avant l'Exil, 1841–1851*. Ed. J.-Cl. Fizaine. Laffont, 1985.

Hugo, V. 'La Mort de Balzac'. *Choses Vues*. Hetzel and Quantin, 1887, 285–91.

Hunt, Herbert J. *Honoré de Balzac*. University of London, 1957.

James, Henry. *French Poets and Novelists*. London: Macmillan, 1878.

James, H. *A Little Tour in France*. 1884; New York: Weidenfeld & Nicolson, 1987.

James, H. *The Question of Our Speech. The Lesson of Balzac. Two Lectures*. Boston: Houghton, Mifflin, 1905.

James, H. *Notes on Novelists, with Some Other Notes*. London: Dent, 1914.

Janin, Jules. Review of *Un Grand Homme de Province à Paris. Revue de Paris*, 15 July 1839, 145–78.

Jarry, Paul. *Le Dernier Logis de Balzac*. Kra, 1924.

Jasinski, René. 'La Duchesse d'Abrantès plagiaire'. In *A travers le XIXe siècle*. Minard, 1975.

Jouenne d'Esgrigny-d'Herville. *Souvenirs de Garnison, ou 40 Ans de Vie Militaire*. Dumaine, 1872.

Jubinal, Achille. 'Chronique des lettres et des arts'. *Le Voleur Littéraire et Artistique*, 10 March 1848.

Karr, Alphonse. *Le Livre de Bord*. Vol. II. Calmann-Lévy, 1879.

Kaye, Eldon. *Charles Lassailly (1806–1843)*. Droz, Minard, 1962.

Kleinert, Annemarie. 'Balzac et la presse de son temps . . . le *Journal des Dames et des Modes*'. *AB 1988*, 367–93.

Korwin-Piotrowska, Sophie de. *Balzac et le Monde Slave: Mme Hanska et l'Oeuvre Balzacienne*. Champion, 1933.

Korwin-Piotrowska, S. de. *L'Étrangère. Eveline Hanska de Balzac*. Armand Colin, 1938.

Lacroix, Paul. 'Simple histoire de mes relations littéraires avec Honoré de Balzac'. *Le Livre. Bibliographie rétrospective*, 10 May, 10 June and 10 September 1882.

Lagny, Jean. 'Victor Lambinet et Balzac'. *AB 1974*, 291–304.

Lagny, J. 'Sur les Guidoboni-Visconti'. *AB 1979*, 97–111.

Lamartine, Alphonse de. *Balzac et ses Oeuvres*. Lévy, Librairie Nouvelle, 1866.

Lambinet, Victor. See Léger.

Larousse, Pierre. *Grand Dictionnaire Universel du XIXe Siècle*. 1866–79.

Larousse Gastronomique. Ed. R. Courtine. London: Hamlyn, 1988.

Latouche, H. de. *Olivier*. Ed. H. d'Alméras. Société des Médecins Bibliophiles, 1924.

Laughton, John Knox. *Memoirs of the Life and Correspondence of Henry Reeve*. London, New York and Bombay: Longmans, Green and Co., 1898.

Laurencin, Michel. *La Vie Quotidienne en Touraine au Temps de Balzac*. Hachette, 1980.

Lawton, Frederick. *Balzac*. London: Grant Richards, 1910.

Lecomte, Jules. 'Les Écrivains du foyer de l'Opéra'. *Les Lettres de Van Engelgom*. Ed. H. d'Alméras. Bossard, 1925.

Lecomte, L.-Henry. *Un Comédien au XIXe siècle: Frédérick Lemaître*. Chez l'auteur, 1888.

Léger, Charles, ed. *Balzac Mis à Nu et les Dessous de la Société Romantique d'après les Mémoires Inédits d'un Contemporain* [Victor Lambinet]. Gaillandre, 1928.

Lemaître, Frédérick. *Souvenirs de Frédérick Lemaître, publiés par son fils*. Ollendorff, 1880.

Lemer, Julien. *Balzac: sa Vie, son Oeuvre*. Sauvaître, 1892.

[Lepoitevin Saint-Alme, Auguste]. 'Luis de Padilla'. 'Génies excentriques'. *Le Corsaire-Satan*, 30 September 1845.

Leroy, Michel. 'Balzac et les Jésuites'. *AB 1991*, 71–89.

Lesser, Ruth. *Linguistic Investigations of Aphasia*. Arnold, 1978.

Lestang, Henri de. *L'Affaire Balssa*. Guitard, 1934.

Le Yaouanc, Moïse. *Nosographie de l'Humanité Balzacienne*. Maloine, 1959.

Le Yaouanc, M. 'Balzac au Lycée Charlemagne'. *AB 1962*, 69–92.

Le Yaouanc, M. 'Précisions sur Ganser et Beuzelin'. *AB 1964*, 25–38.

Le Yaouanc, M. Review of Métadier, *Balzac au Petit Matin*. *AB 1966*, 442–4.

Le Yaouanc, M. 'Satellites des Balzac'. *AB 1968*, 25–45.

Lezay-Marnésia, Albert, Comte de. *Mes Souvenirs*. Blois: Lecesne, 1854.

Lichtlé, Michel. 'Balzac à l'École du droit'. *AB 1982*, 131–50.

Liszt, Franz. *Correspondance de Liszt et de la Comtesse d'Agoult, 1840–1864*. Ed. D. Ollivier. Grasset, 1933–4.

[Loménie, Louis de]. *Galerie des Contemporains Illustres, par un Homme de Rien*. Brussels: Hen, 1841.

Lorant, André. 'Histoire de Lélio'. *AB 1960*, 177–83.

Lorant, A. 'La Maison infortunée. Lettres inédites sur la dernière maladie de Balzac et sur les sentiments de sa veuve'. *AB 1961*, 73–94.

Lorant, A., ed. 'Journal de Mme Hanska'. *AB 1962*, 3–34.

Lorant, A., ed. 'Le Journal de Mlle Sophie Surville'. *AB 1964*, 83–108.

Lorant, A. *Les Parents Pauvres d'Honoré de Balzac*. Droz, 1967.

Lotte, Fernand. 'Le "Retour des personnages" dans *La Comédie Humaine*'. *AB 1961*, 227–81.

Lotte, F. 'Balzac et la table dans *La Comédie Humaine*'. *AB 1962*, 119–79.

Lotte, F. *Armorial de la Comédie Humaine*. Garnier, 1963.

Lucas, Hippolyte. *Portraits et Souvenirs Littéraires*. Plon-Nourrit [1890].

Lukács, Georg. *Balzac und der Französische Realismus*. Berlin: Aufbau Verlag, 1952.

Lyonnet, Henry. *Dictionnaire des Comédiens Français*. Geneva: Bibliothèque de la Revue Universelle Internationale, n.d.

Maigron, Louis. *Le Roman Historique à l'Époque Romantique*. Champion, 1912.

Maison de Balzac. *Nadar. Caricatures et Photographies*. Paris-Musées, 1990.

Marbouty, Caroline. See Brunne.

Martin-Demézil, Jean. 'Balzac à Vendôme'. In *Balzac et la Touraine*. Tours: Gibert-Clarey, 1949.

Marx, Karl. *Early Writings*. New York: Vintage, 1975.

Marx, K. *Capital*. Trans. D. Fernbach. Vol. III. Penguin, 1991.

Maurois. André. *Prométhée ou la Vie de Balzac*. Hachette, 1965.

Maury, Chantal. 'Balzac, Olympe Pélissier, et les courtisanes de *La Comédie Humaine*'. *AB 1975*, 199–215.

Meininger, Anne-Marie. '"Une princesse parisienne" ou les Secrets de la Comtesse de Castellane'. *AB 1962*, 283–330.

Meininger, A.-M. '*La Femme abandonnée*, *L'Auberge rouge* et la Duchesse d'Abrantès'. *AB 1963*, 65–81.

Meininger, A.-M. 'Eugène Surville, "modèle reparaissant"'. *AB 1963*, 195–250.

Meininger, A.-M. 'Théodore. Quelques scènes de la vie privée'. *AB 1964*, 67–81.

Meininger, A.-M. 'La Saisie du *Vicaire des Ardennes*'. *AB 1968*, 149–61.

Meininger, A.-M. 'André Campi'. *AB 1969*, 135–45.

Meininger, A.-M. '*Les Petits Bourgeois*: Genèse et abandon'. *AB 1969*, 211–30.

Ménière, Dr Prosper. *Mémoires Anecdotiques sur les Salons du Second Empire*. Ed. E. Ménière. Plon-Nourrit, 1903.

[Mesuré, Fortuné]. *Le Rivarol de 1842, Dictionnaire Satirique des Célébrités Contemporaines, par Fortunatus*. Au Bureau du *Feuilleton Mensuel*, 1842.

Métadier, Paul. *Balzac au Petit Matin*. La Palatine, 1964.

Métadier, P. 'La Maison des Balzac à Tours'. *Balzac à Saché*, 11 (1968), 10–15.

Meyer-Petit, Judith. 'La Montre de Balzac'. *Le Courrier Balzacien*, new series, 44 (1991), 12–15.

Meyer-Petit, J. *et al. Balzac dans l'Empire Russe. De la Russie à l'Ukraine*. Paris-Musées / Éditions des Cendres, 1993.

Michaud, Louis. *Biographie Universelle Ancienne et Moderne*, new edition, 1843–.

Michel, Arlette. *Le Mariage chez Honoré de Balzac: Amour et Féminisme*. Les Belles Lettres, 1978.

Michelet, Jules. *Écrits de Jeunesse*. Ed. P. Viallaneix. 3rd ed. Gallimard, 1959.

Milatchitch, D. Z. *Le Théâtre de Honoré de Balzac*. Hachette, 1930.

Milner, Max. 'Deux témoignages italiens sur Balzac'. *AB 1960*, 191–4.

Mirbeau, Octave. *La 628-E8* (1907). In *La Mort de Balzac*. Ed. P. Michel and J.-F. Nivet. Tusson, Charente: Du Lérot, 1989.

Mirecourt, Eugène de. *Les Contemporains. Balzac*. Roret, 1854.

Mirecourt, E. de. *Les Contemporains. Frédérick Lemaître*. Havard, 1855.

Mirsky, D. S. *A History of Russian Literature*. Routledge & Kegan Paul, 1968.

Monnier, Henri. *Mémoires de Monsieur Joseph Prudhomme*. Librairie Nouvelle, 1857.

Monselet, Charles. *Mes Souvenirs Littéraires*. Librairie Illustrée, n.d.

Monselet, C. *Portraits après Décès*. Faure, 1866.

Mozet, Nicole. 'Texte et Biographie: à propos de la mère de Balzac'. *AB 1979*, 209–10.

Mozet, N. 'Biographie et description'. *AB 1980*, 295–7.

Muret, Théodore. *A Travers Champs: Souvenirs et Propos Divers*. Garnier, 1858.

Nacquart, Dr Jean-Baptiste. 'Notes sur les derniers moments de M. de Balzac'. In Baschet, *Honoré de Balzac*, 157–60.

Nemours, Col. A. *Histoire de la Captivité et de la Mort de Toussaint-Louverture*. Berger-Levrault, 1929.

Nerval, Gérard de. *Oeuvres Complètes*. Ed. J. Guillaume and C. Pichois. Gallimard, Pléiade, 1984, 1989.

Nettement, Alfred. *Histoire de la Littérature Française sous le Gouvernement de Juillet*, 2nd ed. Vol. II. Lecoffre, 1859.

Pagès, Alphonse. *Balzac Moraliste: Pensées de Balzac Extraites de la Comédie Humaine*. Lévy, 1866.

Paglia, Camille. *Sexual Personae. Art and Decadence from Nefertiti to Emily Dickinson*. 1990; London: Penguin, 1992.

Perrod, Pierre Antoine. *L'Affaire Peytel*. Hachette, 1958.

Pichois, Claude. 'Les Vrais "Mémoires" de Philarète Chasles'. *Revue des Sciences Humaines*, January–February 1956, 71–97.

Pichois, C. *Philarète Chasles et la Vie Littéraire au Temps du Romantisme*. Corti, 1965.

Picon, Gaëtan. *Balzac*. Seuil, Écrivains de Toujours, 1956.

Pictures of the French. A Series of Literary and Graphic Delineations of French Character. By Jules Janin, Balzac, Cormenin, and Other Celebrated French Authors. London: Wm S. Orr and Co., 1840. (Translation of *Les Français peints par eux-mêmes*.)

Pierrot, Roger. 'Balzac vu par les siens en 1822'. *Les Études Balzaciennes*, 7 (April 1959), 249–58.

Pierrot, R., ed. 'Quinze lettres de Balzac'. *AB 1972*, 347–62.

'Polichinelle'. 'La Famille maigre'. *Gazette des Femmes*, 2 December 1843.

Pommier, Jean. *L'Invention et l'Écriture dans 'La Torpille'*. Droz, Minard, 1957.

Pommier, J. 'Balzac 1965. Le *Prométhée* d'André Maurois'. *Revue d'Histoire Littéraire de la France*, October–December 1965, 657–82.

Pommier, J. 'Eve de Balzac, sa fille, son amant'. *AB 1966*, 245–85.

Pontavice de Heussey, R. du. 'Balzac en Bretagne'. *Le Livre: Bibliographie rétrospective*, 10 September 1885.

Prendergast, Christopher. *Balzac: Fiction and Melodrama*. London: Arnold, 1978.

Préteseille, Abbé Bernard. 'Le Compte de chaise de Madame Balzac'. *Le Courrier Balzacien*, 4–5 (May 1949), 78–82.

Prior, Henry. 'Balzac à Turin'. *Revue de Paris*, 15 January 1924,

Prioult, Albert. *Balzac avant la Comédie Humaine*. Courville, 1936.

Prioult, A. 'Balzac et Lepître'. *AB 1965*, 317–22.

Proudhon, P.-J. *Carnets*. Ed. P. Haubtmann. Vol. II. Rivière, 1961.

Proust, Marcel. *A la Recherche du Temps Perdu*. Ed. J.-Y. Tadié. Vol. III. Gallimard, Pléiade, 1988.

Proust, M. *Contre Sainte-Beuve*. Ed. P. Clarac and Y. Sandre. Gallimard, Pléiade, 1971.

Pugh, Anthony. 'Personnages reparaissants avant *Le Père Goriot*'. *AB 1964*, 215–37.

Pugh, A. *Balzac's Recurring Characters*. University of Toronto Press, 1974; London: Duckworth, 1975.

Raitt, Alan. 'Balzac et Flaubert: une rencontre peu connue'. *AB 1988*, 81–5.

Raser, George. *Guide to Balzac's Paris: An Analytical Subject Index*. Choisy-le-Roi: Imprimerie de France, 1964.

Regard, Maurice, ed. *Béatrix*. Garnier, 1962.

Rémusat, Charles de. *Mémoires de ma Vie*. Ed. C. H. Pouthas. Plon, 1960.

Robb, Graham. 'Un modèle possible de La Palférine'. *AB 1987*, 399–404.

Robb, G. *Baudelaire Lecteur de Balzac*. Corti, 1988.

[Ronteix, Eugène]. Léonard de Géréon. *La Rampe et les Coulisses, esquisses biographiques des directeurs, acteurs et actrices de tous les théâtres*. Chez tous les marchands de nouveautés, 1832.

Rousseau, Hervé. 'Quelques précisions sur la Duchesse d'Abrantès et Balzac'. *AB 1968*, 47–58.

Royce, William Hobart. *A Balzac Bibliography*. Chicago University Press, 1930.

Royce, W. H. *Balzac As He Should Be Read*. New York: Giraldi, 1946.

Rugendas, Maurice (Johann Moritz). *Voyage Pittoresque dans le Brésil*. Trans. M. de Golbéry. Paris and Mulhouse: Engelman, 1835.

Ruxton, Geneviève. *La Dilecta de Balzac. Balzac et Mme de Berny, 1820–1836*. Plon, 1909.

Sainte-Beuve, Charles-Augustin. *Cahiers*. Lemerre, 1876.

Sainte-Beuve, C.-A. *Cahiers. I. Le Cahier Vert (1834–1847)*. Ed. R. Molho. Gallimard, 1973.

Sainte-Beuve, C.-A. *Correspondance Générale*. Ed. J. Bonnerot. Stock, 1935–.

Sainte-Beuve, C.-A. *Mes Poisons*. Ed. V. Giraud. Plon, 1926.

Sainte-Beuve, C.-A. Review of *La Recherche de l'Absolu*. *Revue des Deux Mondes*, 15 November 1834. In *Portraits Contemporains*. Vol. II. Lévy, 1870.

Sainte-Beuve, C.-A. 'De la littérature industrielle'. *Revue des Deux Mondes*, 1 September 1839. In *Portraits Contemporains*.

Sainte-Beuve, C.-A. 'Dix ans après en littérature'. *Revue des Deux Mondes*, 1 March 1840. In *Portraits Contemporains*.

Sainte-Beuve, C.-A. 'M. de Balzac'. *Le Constitutionnel*, 2 September 1850. In *Causeries du Lundi*. Vol. II. Garnier, 1852.

Sainte-Beuve, C.-A. 'M. de Latouche'. *Le Constitutionnel*, 17 March 1851. In *Causeries du Lundi*. Vol. III. Garnier, 1852.

Sainte-Beuve, C.-A. 'De la retraite de MM. Villemain et Cousin'. *Le*

Constitutionnel, 24 May 1852. In *Causeries du Lundi*. Vol. VI. Garnier, 1853.

Sainte-Beuve, C.-A. Review of Hippolyte Taine, *Histoire de la Littérature Anglaise*. *Le Constitutionnel*, 6 June 1864. In *Nouveaux Lundis*. Vol. VIII.

Saintsbury, George. *A Short History of French Literature*. 6th ed. Oxford: Clarendon Press, 1901.

Sand, George. *Correspondance*. Ed. G. Lubin. Garnier, 1964–91.

Sand, G. *Histoire de ma Vie*. In *Oeuvres Autobiographiques*. Ed. G. Lubin. Vol. II. Gallimard, Pléiade, 1971.

Sandars, Mary F. *Honoré de Balzac: His Life and Writings*. 1904; Port Washington, N.Y. and London: Kennikat, 1970.

[Sandeau, Jules]. *Vie et Malheurs de Horace de Saint-Aubin*. In Balzac, *La Dernière Fée*. 1836; Pressédition, 1948.

Savant, Jean. *Louise la Mystérieuse ou l'Essentiel de la Vie de Balzac*. Cahiers de l'Académie d'Histoire, 1972.

Schopp, Claude. *Alexandre Dumas. Le Génie de sa Vie*. Mazarine, 1985.

Scribe, Eugène. *L'Intérieur de l'Étude ou le Procureur et l'Avoué*. Barba, 1821.

Séché, Alphonse, and Jules Bertaut. *La Vie Anecdotique et Pittoresque des Grands Écrivains. Balzac*. Michaud [1910].

Second, Albéric. *Le Tiroir aux Souvenirs*. Dentu, 1886.

Ségu, Frédéric. *Un Maître de Balzac Méconnu: H. de Latouche*. Les Belles Lettres, 1928.

Serval, Maurice. *Une Amie de Balzac: Mme Marbouty*. Émile-Paul, 1925.

Sherard, Robert. *Oscar Wilde. The Story of an Unhappy Friendship*. London: The Hermes Press, 1902.

Silver, Mabel. *Jules Sandeau, l'Homme et la Vie*. Boivin, n.d.

Simonnin, [Antoine] and Théodore N[ézel]. *La Peau de Chagrin, ou le Roman en Action: Extravagance Romantique, Comédie-Vaudeville en Trois Actes*. Quoy, 1832.

Smethurst, Colin. 'Balzac et le *Journal* de Charles Weiss'. *AB 1968*, 395–8.

Spoelberch de Lovenjoul, Charles de. *Un Dernier Chapitre de l'Histoire des Oeuvres de Balzac*. Dentu, 1880.

Spoelberch de Lovenjoul, C. de. *Histoire des Oeuvres de H. de Balzac*. 3rd ed. Calmann-Lévy, 1888.

Spoelberch de Lovenjoul, C. de. *Un Roman d'Amour*. Calmann-Lévy, 1896.

Spoelberch de Lovenjoul, C. de. *La Genèse d'un Roman de Balzac. 'Les Paysans'*. Ollendorff, 1901.

Spoelberch de Lovenjoul, C. de. *Une Page Perdue de H. de Balzac*. Ollendorff, 1903.

Stead, John. *Vidocq. A Biography*. Non-Fiction Book Club, 1953.

Stendhal. *Correspondance*. Ed. H. Martineau and V. Del Litto. Vol. III. Gallimard, Pléiade, 1968.

Stephen, Sir Leslie. *Hours in a Library*. Smith, Elder, 1874.

Stevenson, Robert Louis. *The Letters of Robert Louis Stevenson*. Ed. Sidney Colvin. London: Heinemann, 1923.

Stirling, Edward. *Old Drury Lane: Fifty Years' Recollections of Author, Actor, and Manager*. London: Chatto & Windus, 1881.

Strachey, Lytton. *Landmarks in French Literature*. 1912; Oxford University Press, 1943.

Surville, Laure. *Balzac, sa Vie et ses Oeuvres d'après sa Correspondance*. Librairie Nouvelle; Jaccottet, Bourdilliat et Cie, 1858.

Surville, L. *Lettres à une Amie de Province*. Ed. A. Chancerel and J.-N. Faure-Biguet. Plon, 1932.

Swinburne, Algernon Charles. *The Swinburne Letters*. Ed. C. Y. Lang. Vol. IV. Yale University Press, 1960.

Taine, Hippolyte. 'Balzac'. *Journal des Débats*, February and March 1858. In *Nouveaux Essais de Critique et d'Histoire*. Hachette, 1865.

Taube, Otto von. 'Balzac homosexuel'. *Jahrbuch für sexuelle Zwischenstufen*, 1913, 174–90.

Thackeray, William Makepeace. *The Paris Sketch Book*, 1840; New York: Lovell, n.d.

Tolley, Bruce. 'Balzac the Printer'. *French Studies*, July 1959, 214–25.

Tolley, B. 'The "Cénacle" of Balzac's *Illusions Perdues*'. *French Studies*, October 1961, 324–37.

Tolley, B. 'Un ouvrage inconnu de Balzac'. *AB 1962*, 35–49.

Tolley, B. 'Les Oeuvres diverses de Balzac (1824–1831)'. *AB 1963*, 31–64.

Tolley, B. 'Balzac et les romans de Viellerglé'. *AB 1964*, 111–37.

Tolley, B. 'Horace Raisson juge de *La Peau de Chagrin*'. *AB 1965*, 322–4.

Train, John. *Remarkabilia*. London: Allen & Unwin, 1984.

Tyndale, John Warre. *The Island of Sardinia*. London: Bentley, 1849.

Vachon, Stéphane. *Les Travaux et les Jours d'Honoré de Balzac: Chronologie de la Création Balzacienne*. Presses Universitaires de Vincennes, CNRS, Université de Montréal, 1992.

[Vandam, Albert]. *An Englishman in Paris (Notes and Recollections)*, 2nd ed. London: Chapman & Hall, 1892.

Van der Perre, Paul. *Les Préfaçons Belges. Bibliographie des Véritables Originales d'Honoré de Balzac Publiées en Belgique*. Brussels, Chez l'auteur, 1940.

Vannier, Daniel. *En Marge de 'Louis Lambert': Balzac au Collège de Vendôme*. Beaugency, 1949.

Vidocq, François. *Les Vrais Mémoires de Vidocq*. Ed. J. Savant. Éditions Corrêa, 1950.

Viennet, Guillaume. *Journal*. Ed. Duc de la Force. Amiot, Dumont, 1955.

Vigny, Alfred de. 'Lettres inédites d'Alfred de Vigny'. *Revue des Deux Mondes*, 1 January 1897.

[Vitu, Auguste?]. *Le Corsaire-Satan en Silhouette*. Ed. G. Robb. Publications du Centre W. T. Bandy d'Études Baudelairiennes, 1985.

Watripon, Antonio. Article on H. de Latouche. *Béranger*, 15 November 1857, 4–5.

Wedmore, Sir Frederick. *Life of Honoré de Balzac*. London: Walter Scott, 1890.

Weelen, Jean-Edmond. 'Balzac et la pension Le Guay'. *Revue des Sciences Humaines*, January–June 1950, 94–103.

Weelen, J.-E. 'Comment Balzac apprit à lire'. *Balzac à Saché*, 29 April 1951, 31–4.

Weiss, Charles, *Journal 1823–1833*. Ed. S. Lepin. Annales Littéraires de l'Université de Besançon, 1981.

Werdet, Edmond. *Portrait Intime de Balzac: sa Vie, son Humeur et son Caractère*. Dentu, 1859.

Werdet. E. *Souvenirs de la Vie Littéraire: Portraits Intimes*. Dentu, 1879.

Wilde, Oscar. 'The Decay of Lying'. *Intentions* (1891). London: Methuen, 1913.

Williams, Stephen. *Fantastic Archaeology: The Wild Side of North American Prehistory*. University of Pennsylvania, 1991.

Woollen, Geoff. 'Balzac et le prix Montyon'. *AB 1983*, 179–200.

Yeats, W. B. *'Louis Lambert'*. In *Essays and Introductions*. London: Macmillan, 1961.

Young, Arthur. *Travels in France During the Years 1787, 1788, 1789*. London: George Bell & Sons, 1892 [*sic* for 1792].

Zola, Émile. *Le Roman Expérimental* (1880). Ed. A. Guedj. Flammarion, GF, 1971.

INDEX OF CHARACTERS

INDEX OF WORKS